Ultimate React Design Patterns for High Performance

Build Clean, Scalable and Enterprise-Ready React Applications with Advanced Patterns and Performance Techniques

Nabendu Biswas

www.orangeava.com

First Published: October 2025

Published By: Orange Education Pvt Ltd, AVA®

Address: 9, Daryaganj, Delhi, 110002, India

275 New North Road Islington Suite 1314 London,

N1 7AA, United Kingdom

ISBN (PBK): 978-93-49888-14-2

ISBN (E-BOOK): 978-93-49888-92-0

Scan the QR code to explore our entire catalogue

www.orangeava.com

Dedicated To

My Wife, Shikha

And

My Son, Hriday

About the Author

Nabendu Biswas is a seasoned **Full Stack JavaScript Developer** and **Senior Software Engineer** with over **21 years of IT experience** across global investment banks, product companies, and startups. Over the last decade, he has developed expertise in the **React ecosystem**, delivering scalable, high-performance web applications across domains such as **finance, retail, AI, and education technology**.

Nabendu's career includes senior roles such as **Architect, Team Lead, and Associate Architect**, where he successfully led UI teams, drove micro-frontend architectures, and guided complex enterprise-scale applications. His most recent assignments include working as a **Senior Full Stack Developer** on critical projects for Iris idea, where he modernized large-scale React and Node.js codebases, optimized performance, and eliminated security vulnerabilities.

He is also a **published author of 8 books on JavaScript, React, and frontend development, including the popular title *Full-Stack Web Development with* MERN.** Through these works, he has helped thousands of developers transition from beginner to advanced levels.

Beyond authoring books, Nabendu has also worked as a **corporate trainer and mentor**, training more than **1000 students** and **50+ corporate teams in JavaScript, React, and MERN stack**. His engaging teaching style extends to his **YouTube channel and tech blog**, where he shares knowledge about React, modern web technologies, and career growth in software development.

A passionate innovator, Nabendu has also **explored Generative AI**, creating chatbots and 3D avatars with lip-sync capabilities, using React Fiber and LLaMA. His curiosity and constant drive for learning keep him at the cutting edge of frontend technologies, including **TypeScript, GraphQL, serverless architecture (AWS/Azure), and performance optimization**.

When he is not coding or writing, Nabendu enjoys spending time with his family, his two dogs, and reading about AI/ML, space, and emerging technologies.

About the Technical Reviewers

Gaurav Patel is a Senior Software Engineer with over eight years of experience developing and maintaining projects of varying complexity to enhance efficiency and capabilities. He has strong expertise in web technologies and frameworks, including JavaScript, AngularJS (2–6), ReactJS, Redux, jQuery, NodeJS, ExpressJS, and Spring Boot. Gaurav has extensive experience in building Ajax-driven web applications, implementing Web Services, and creating responsive UIs. His technical proficiency also spans MySQL, NoSQL, HTML5, CSS3, Docker, Kubernetes, GitLab, .NET, Python, AWS, and CI/CD pipelines. Known for his quick learning and effective communication skills, Gaurav thrives in environments that encourage continuous learning and growth.

Sunil S is a seasoned Frontend Developer with nine years of experience designing and building user-centric, high-performance web applications. Currently, a Senior Frontend Developer at Reltio, he specializes in ReactJS, NextJS, Material UI, TypeScript, and JavaScript. Sunil also has backend experience with NodeJS and Express, enabling him to deliver seamless end-to-end solutions. His professional interests include micro-frontend architecture, modular and scalable application design, and performance optimization. Recognized for his problem-solving ability and collaborative approach, Sunil emphasizes writing clean, maintainable codes, and applies strong testing practices using Jest, React Testing Library, and Playwright.

Anjani Kumar Varma is an Associate at Cognizant Technology Solutions with four years of experience developing scalable, React-based applications for a leading retail client. Skilled in React, Redux, Jest, React Testing Library, and Module Federation, he focuses on performance optimization through lazy loading, tree shaking, and memory leak prevention. As part of Cognizant's core governance team, Anjani has implemented initiatives such as pre-commit hooks for optional chaining, automated removal of console logs in production, and improved Webpack configurations. He actively conducts knowledge-sharing sessions on unit testing, and has implemented Adobe tagging as well as Quantum Metrics, enabling advanced analytics and behavioral insights. Anjani has also contributed to resolving memory leaks, addressing security vulnerabilities, and enhancing performance through the transition to CommonJS packages. His work has directly improved application reliability and user experience for millions of retail customers.

Acknowledgments

There are a few people I want to thank for the continued and ongoing support during the writing of this book. First and foremost, I would like to thank my wife for continuously encouraging me to write the book. I could have never completed this project without her support.

I am also grateful to the courses, and the companies that supported me throughout the learning process of web development. I thank them for all the hidden inspiration and support they provided.

My gratitude also goes to the editorial team at Orange Education Pvt Ltd for their unwavering support and patience, and for granting me ample time to successfully complete and publish this book.

Preface

This book, *Ultimate React Design Patterns for High Performance*, is written for React developers who already know the fundamentals, and want to level up to become senior frontend developers. In today's software industry, writing functional React applications is not enough – to succeed in large-scale, enterprise environments, you need to understand design patterns, architecture, and performance optimization.

The goal of this book is to bridge that gap. It will guide you step by step from intermediate knowledge of React toward mastering advanced design patterns, scalable architectures, and performance techniques that set apart a professional React engineer.

The book is organized into multiple chapters, each addressing a specific advanced concept in React:

- **Chapters 1–3** introduce design patterns, layout components, and container components to help you structure clean and reusable UI code.
- **Chapters 4–6** cover controlled/uncontrolled components, Higher-Order Components (HOCs), custom hooks, and functional programming patterns – essential techniques for building robust, reusable, and scalable components.
- **Chapters 7–8** dive into advanced concepts and hooks, including portals, error boundaries, and clean coding practices that enable scalable project architecture.
- **Chapters 9–12** deal with API integration, React Query, state management patterns, and performance optimization, ensuring that your apps remain responsive under real-world load.
- **Chapters 13–17** focus on **Design Systems** building UI components in Figma, encapsulating styles, spacing patterns, complex styles, and finishing with a full design system project.

- **Chapters 18–21** conclude with **Advanced TypeScript techniques**, teaching you to strongly type hooks, reducers, generics, and component patterns – a must-have skill in enterprise projects.

Thus, by the end of this book, you will not only be confident in applying React design patterns and performance optimizations, but also in architecting scalable and clean codebases that can withstand enterprise demands. This is the skillset expected from a senior frontend developer, and this book is designed to get you there!

I hope this book inspires you to build better, cleaner, and more scalable React applications.

Get a Free eBook

We hope you are enjoying your recently purchased book! Your feedback is incredibly valuable to us, and to all other readers looking for great books.

If you found this book helpful or enjoyable, we would truly appreciate it, if you could take a moment to leave a short review with a 5 star rating on Amazon. It helps us grow, and lets other readers discover our books.

As a thank you, we would love to send you a free digital copy of this book, and a **30%** discount code on your next cart value on our official websites:

www.orangeava.com

www.orangeava.in (For Indian Subcontinent)

☑ **Here's how:**

Leave a review for the book on Amazon.

Take a screenshot of your review, and send an email to **info@orangeava.com** (it can be just the confirmation screen).

Once, we receive your screenshot, we will send you the digital file, within 24 hours.

Thank you so much for your support – it means a lot to us!

Downloading the code bundles and colored images

Please follow the links or scan the QR codes to download the ***Code Bundles and Images*** of the book:

https://github.com/ava-orange-education/Ultimate-React-Design-Patterns-for-High-Performance

The code bundles and images of the book are also hosted on ***https://rebrand.ly/0d0d2f***

In case there's an update to the code, it will be updated on the existing GitHub repository.

Errata

We take immense pride in our work at **Orange Education Pvt Ltd,** and follow best practices to ensure the accuracy of our content to provide an indulging reading experience to our subscribers. Our readers are our mirrors, and we use their inputs to reflect and improve upon human errors, if any, that may have occurred during the publishing processes involved. To let us maintain the quality and help us reach out to any readers who might be having difficulties due to any unforeseen errors, please write to us at :

errata@orangeava.com

Your support, suggestions, and feedback are highly appreciated.

DID YOU KNOW

Did you know that Orange Education Pvt Ltd offers eBook versions of every book published, with PDF and ePub files available? You can upgrade to the eBook version at **www.orangeava.com** and as a print book customer, you are entitled to a discount on the eBook copy. Get in touch with us at: **info@orangeava.com** for more details.

At **www.orangeava.com**, you can also read a collection of free technical articles, sign up for a range of free newsletters, and receive exclusive discounts and offers on Print Books and eBooks.

PIRACY

If you come across any illegal copies of our works in any form on the internet, we would be grateful if you would provide us with the location address or website name. Please contact us at **info@orangeava.com** with a link to the material.

ARE YOU INTERESTED IN AUTHORING WITH US?

If there is a topic that you have expertise in, and you are interested in either writing or contributing to a book, please write to us at **business@orangeava.com**. We are on a journey to help developers and tech professionals to gain insights on the present technological advancements and innovations happening across the globe and build a community that believes Knowledge is best acquired by sharing and learning with others. Please reach out to us to learn what our audience demands and how you can be part of this educational reform. We also welcome ideas from tech experts and help them build learning and development content for their domains.

REVIEWS

Please leave a review. Once you have read and used this book, why not leave a review on the site that you purchased it from? Potential readers can then see and use your unbiased opinion to make purchase decisions. We at Orange Education would love to know what you think about our products, and our authors can learn from your feedback. Thank you!

For more information about Orange Education, please visit **www.orangeava.com**.

Table of Contents

CHAPTER 1
Introduction to Design Patterns

Introduction

This chapter gives a brief introduction to design patterns, and covers the requirements to start with the installation of NodeJS and NPM (Node Package Manager) on a Windows system, These software are primarily required for ReactJS coding.

Besides this, we will also learn to install Visual Studio Code, also popularly known as VS Code. This is a light-weight code editor which is helpful in coding in ReactJS. All these three requirements are completely free to install on Windows, Mac and Linux.

Structure

In this chapter, we are going to discuss the following topics:

- Introduction to Design Patterns
- Requirements

Introduction to Design Patterns

Design patterns are an advanced concept in ReactJS which means designing the code in an efficient way. These advanced concepts allow us to write an effective code, by using patterns such as controlled and uncontrolled components.

We will also learn other advanced concepts like memoization which optimizes the performance of React. The readers will be able to develop enterprise level React systems for reusability. We will use React Hooks, Context API, HOCs, Custom hooks and React functional programming to build reliable apps that scale.

By understanding these design patterns, developers can develop scalable, maintainable and optimized React applications.

Requirements

Since this book is about advanced React concepts, the Basic understanding of React and JavaScript is required. You should have Node and NPM installed on your machine because React requires both to create applications, and install dependencies. Besides this, Visual Studio code should also be installed on your machine. Next, we will learn to install these on Windows. The setup for Mac and Linux is quite similar, and can be done easily.

Node and NPM Installation Windows

First, we need to go to the official NodeJS download url which is https://nodejs.org/en/download. Afterwards. click on **Download Node.js vXX.XX.X** button. During the time of writing the book, it was v20.12.2.

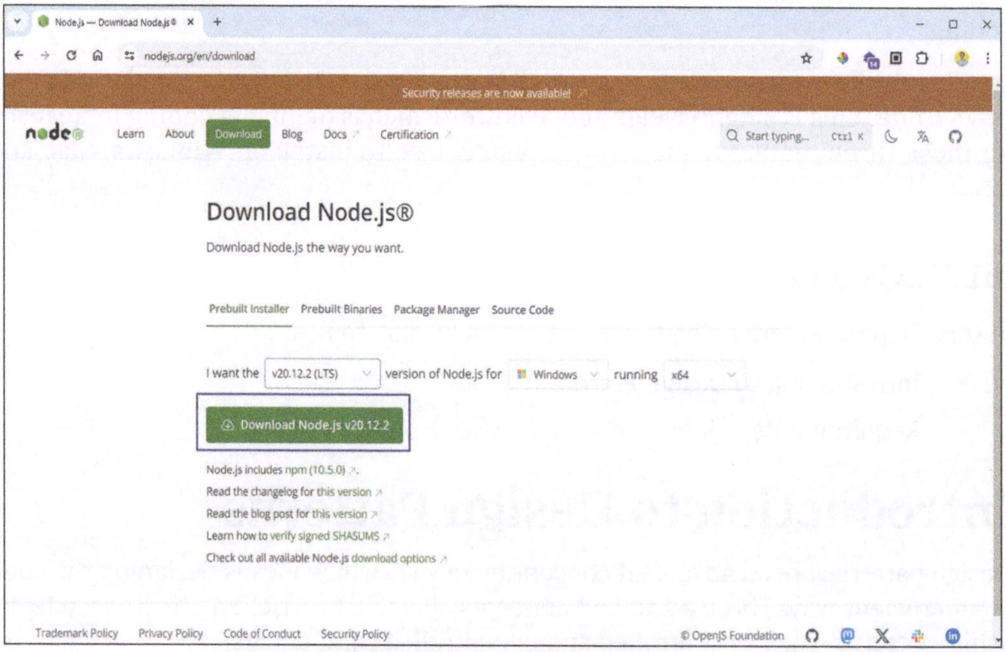

Figure 1.1: *Node Install Link*

Next, on the top side of the browser, we will see the '`msi file`' being downloaded. Click on the '`Open`' icon to run the file directly.

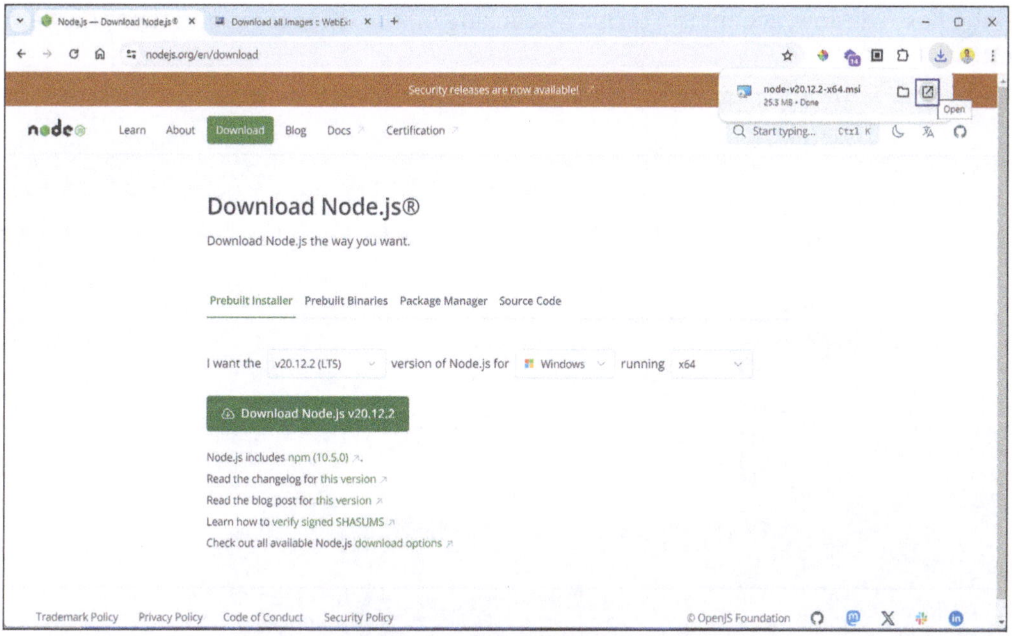

Figure 1.2: Node Downloaded

A pop-up will come that will start the '**`Node.js Setup Wizard`**'. Here, click on the **`Next`** button.

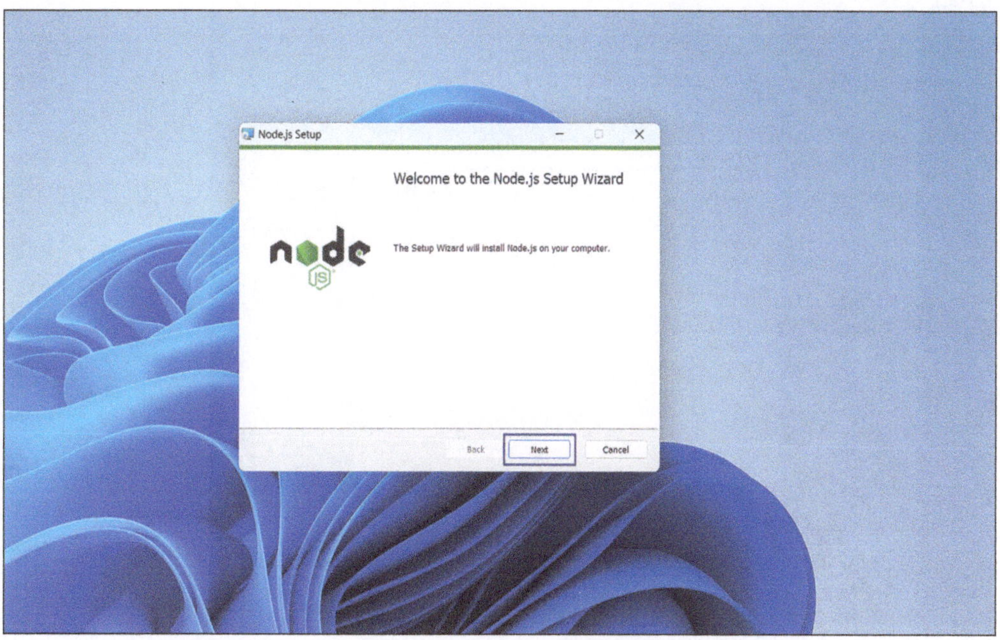

Figure 1.3: Node Setup Wizard

In the next window, accept the terms by clicking on the '`checkbox`', and then the '`Next`' button.

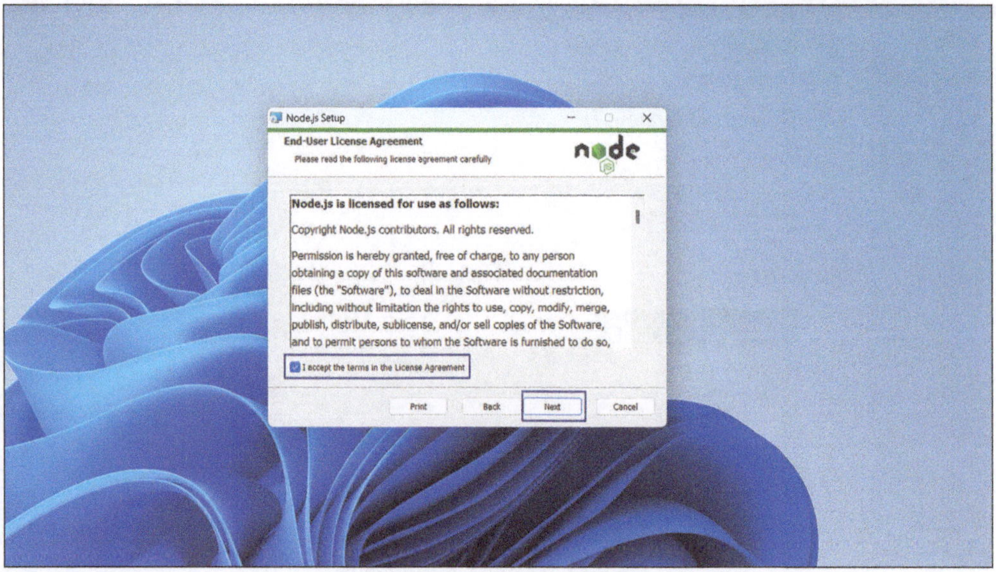

Figure 1.4: *Node License Agreement*

Next, it will show the default directory to install NodeJS. Here, then click on the '`Next`' button.

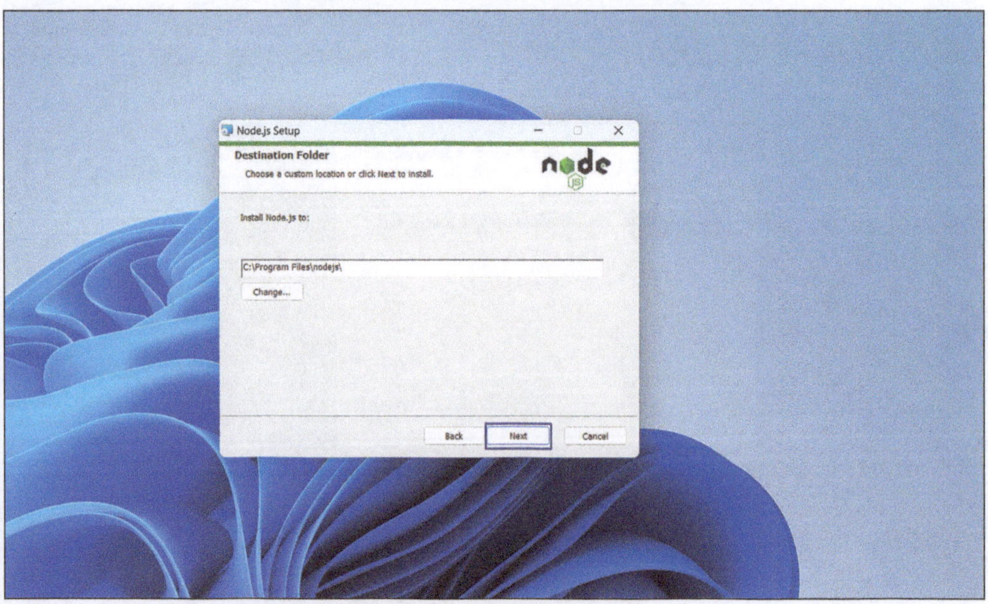

Figure 1.5: *Node Default Path*

In the next screen also, click on the '**Next**' button.

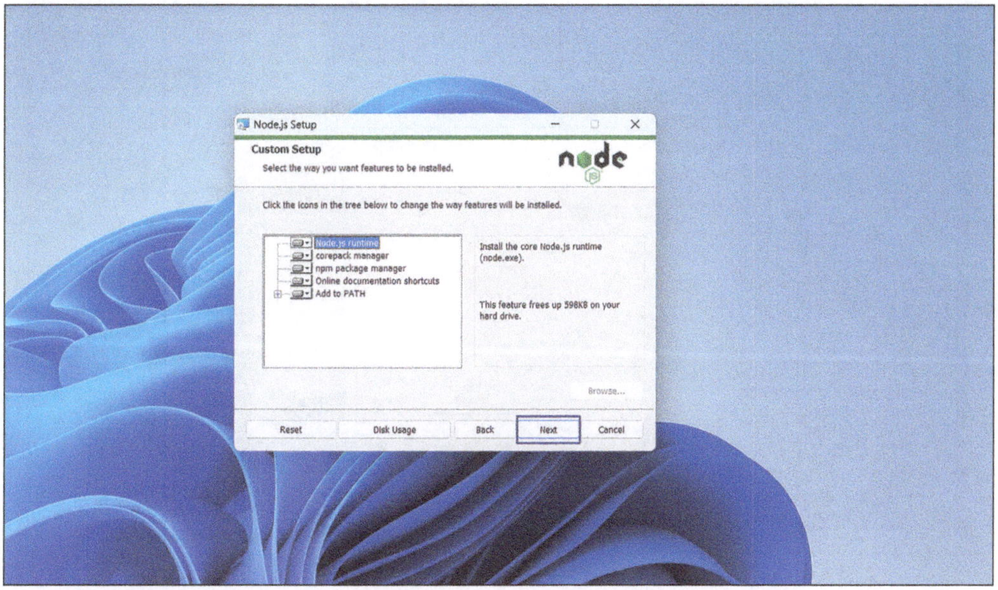

Figure 1.6: *Node Features*

Now, the wizard will install all the necessary tools. Here, select the '**checkbox**' and then click on the '**Next**' button.

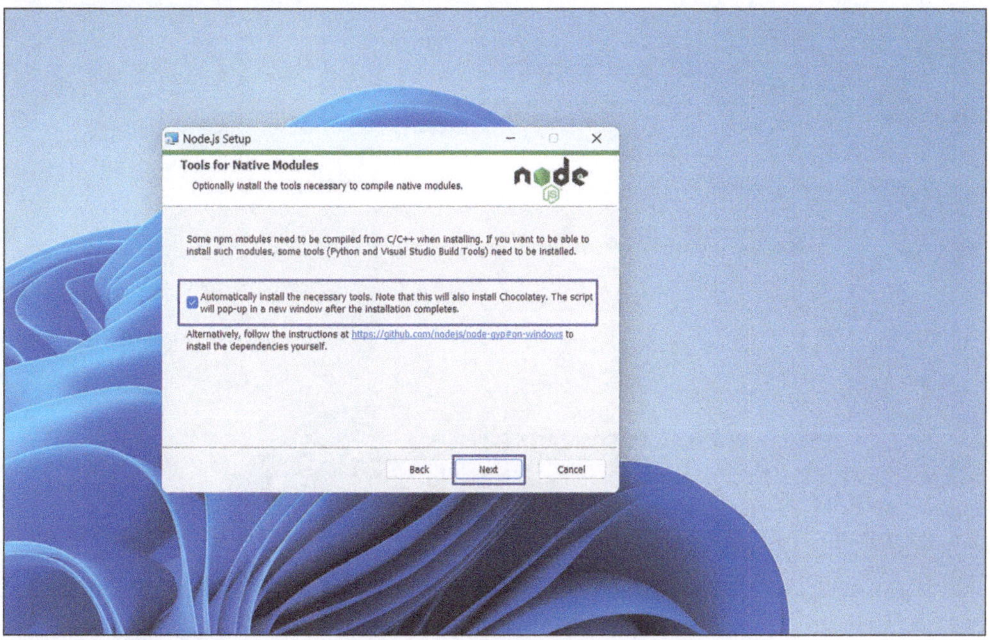

Figure 1.7: *Node Necessary Tools*

Finally, we will get the '**`Install`**' button. Click it, and install NodeJS.

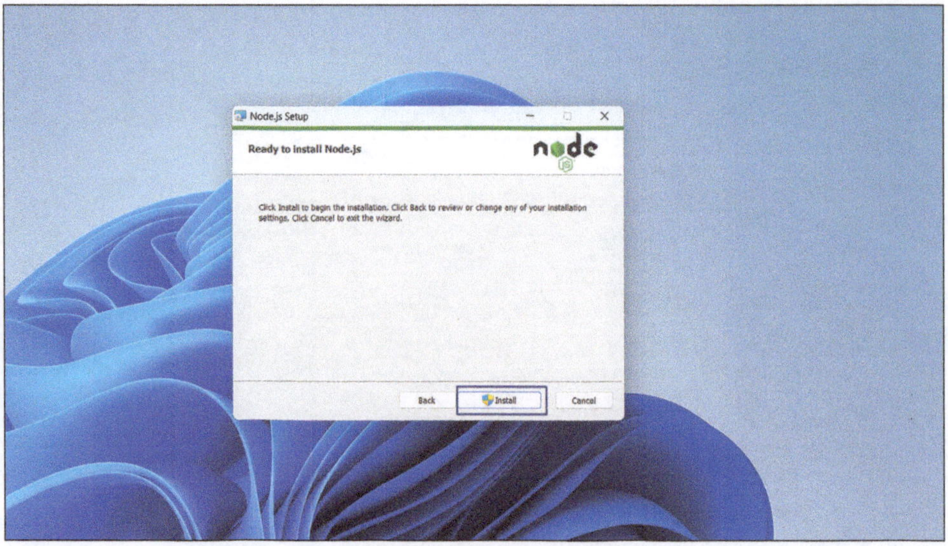

Figure 1.8: *Node Install*

It will take around 1 minute to install '**`NodeJS`**', and the progress bar will show the status.

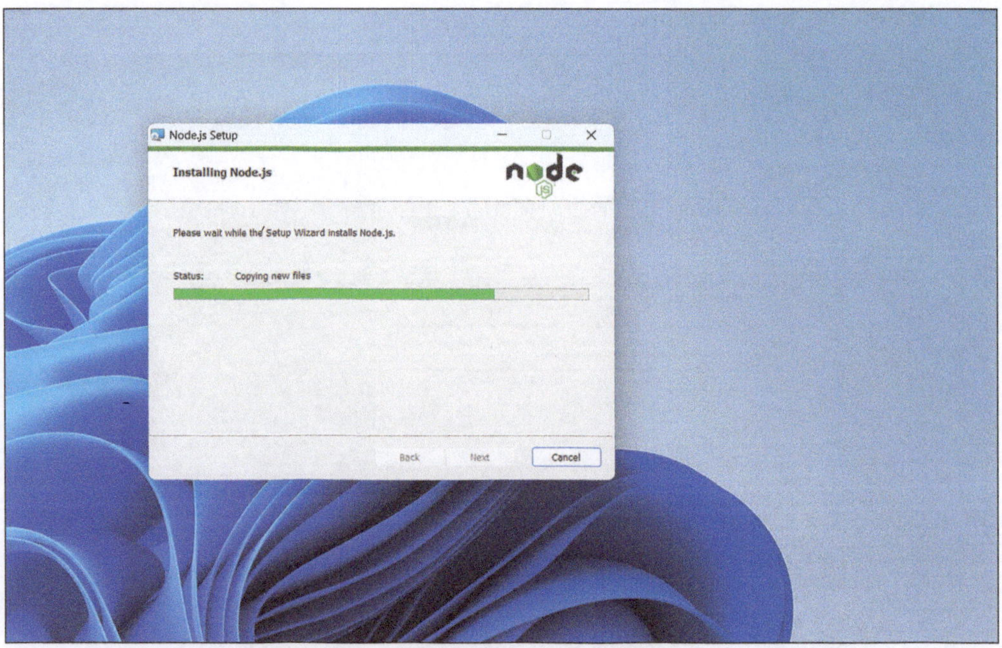

Figure 1.9: *Node Install Progress*

Once the installation is complete, click on the '**`Finish`**' button.

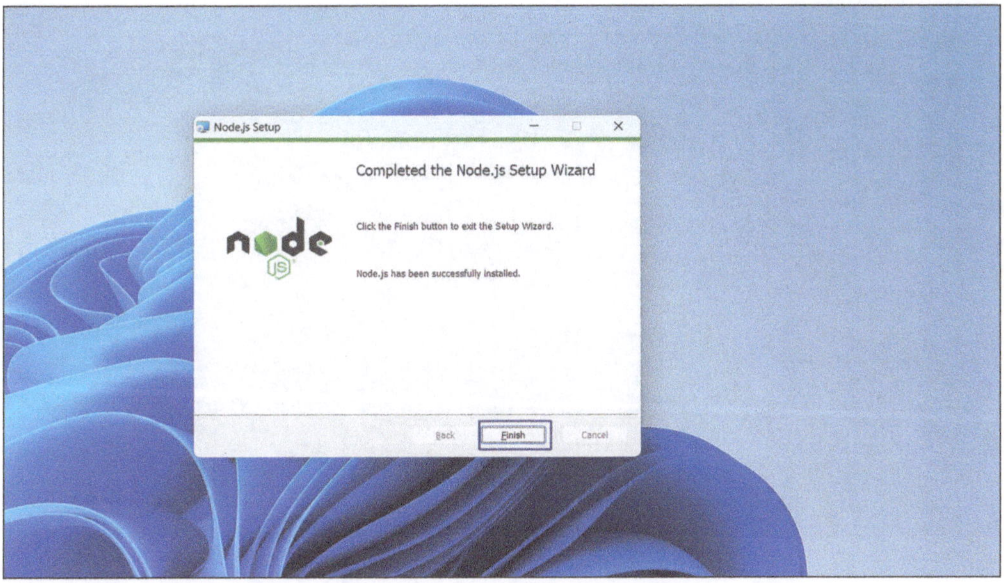

Figure 1.10: *Node Install Finish*

Now, the setup for additional tools will start. It will open the command line, where we need to click on any button.

Figure 1.11: *Node Additional Tools*

Now, open any terminal and run the command node '-v'. It will give the '**Node**' version installed which is 20.12.2 in our case.

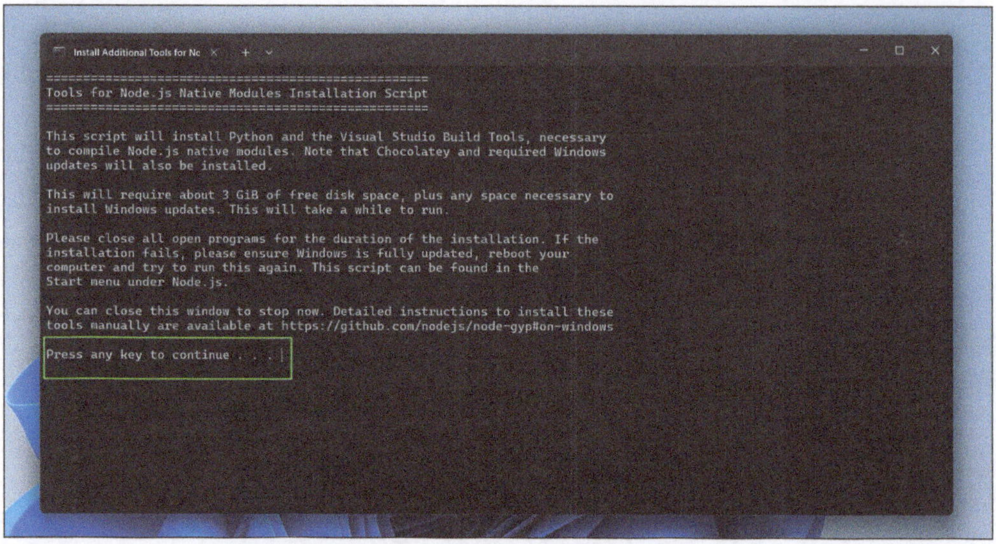

Figure 1.12: Node Version

Now, in the terminal, run the command **`npm -v`**. It will give the NPM version installed which is 9.5.0 in our case. NPM stands for Node Package Manager that is automatically installed with Node installation:

Figure 1.13: NPM Version

VS Code Installation Windows

To download Visual Studio Code or VS Code, first go to **`https://code.visualstudio.com/`**, and click on the **`download`** button. This site automatically detects your operating system.

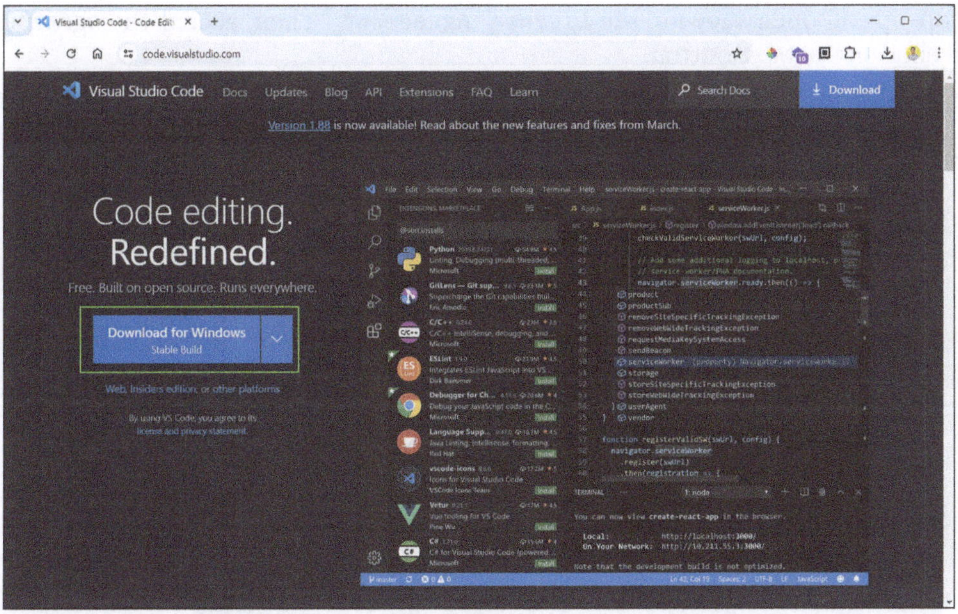

Figure 1.14: VS Code

Download the Link

Afterwards, on the top side of the browser, we will see the VS Code file being downloaded. Click on the **`Open`** icon to run the file directly.

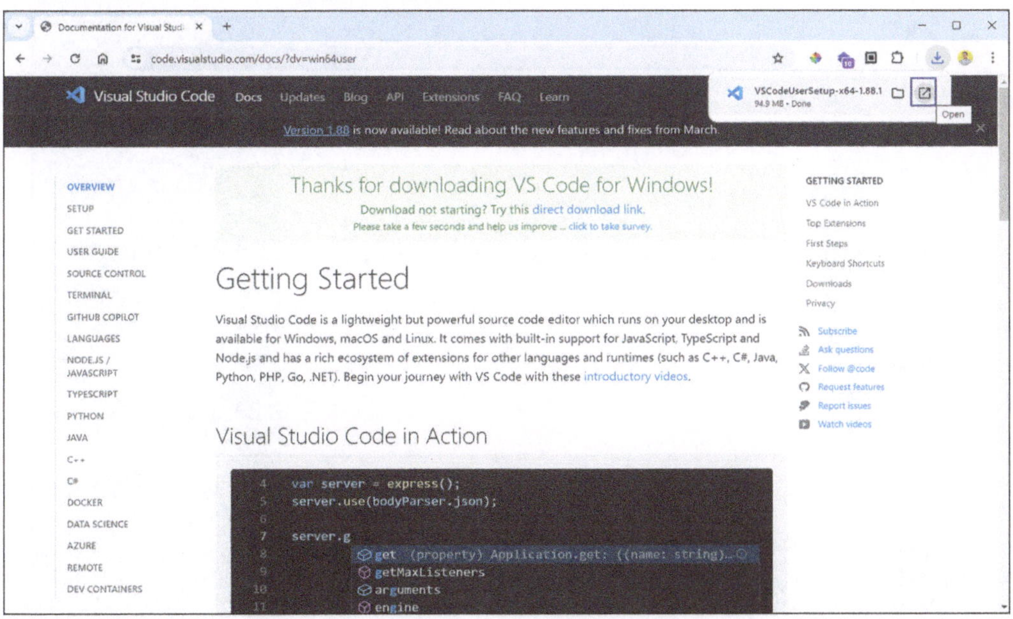

Figure 1.15: VS Code Downloaded

A pop-up will open showing the **`License Agreement`**. Then, accept the agreement, and click on the **`Next`** button.

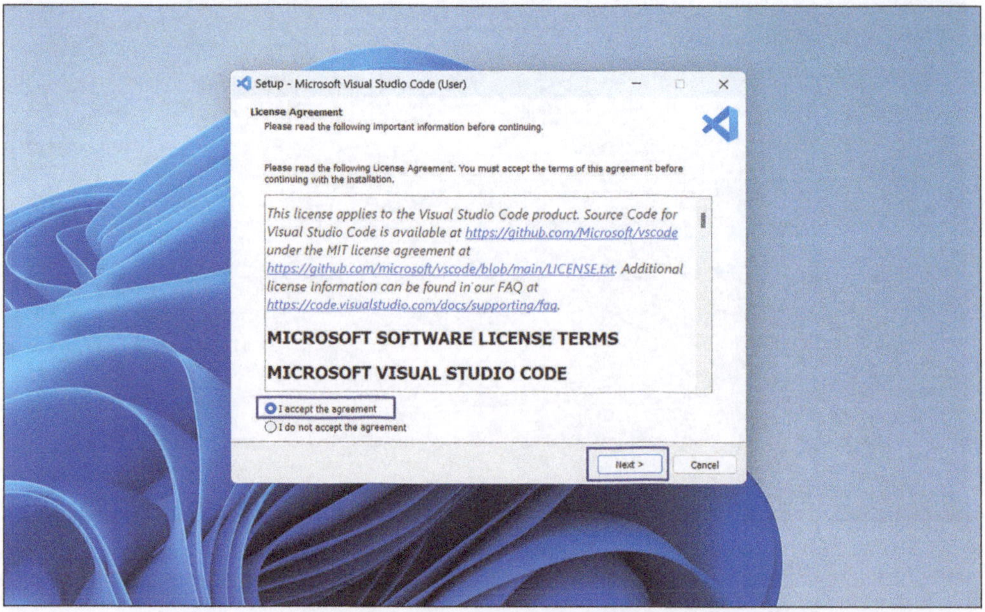

Figure 1.16: VS Code License Agreement

The next window will show the path on which VS Code will be downloaded. Here, just click on the **`Next`** button.

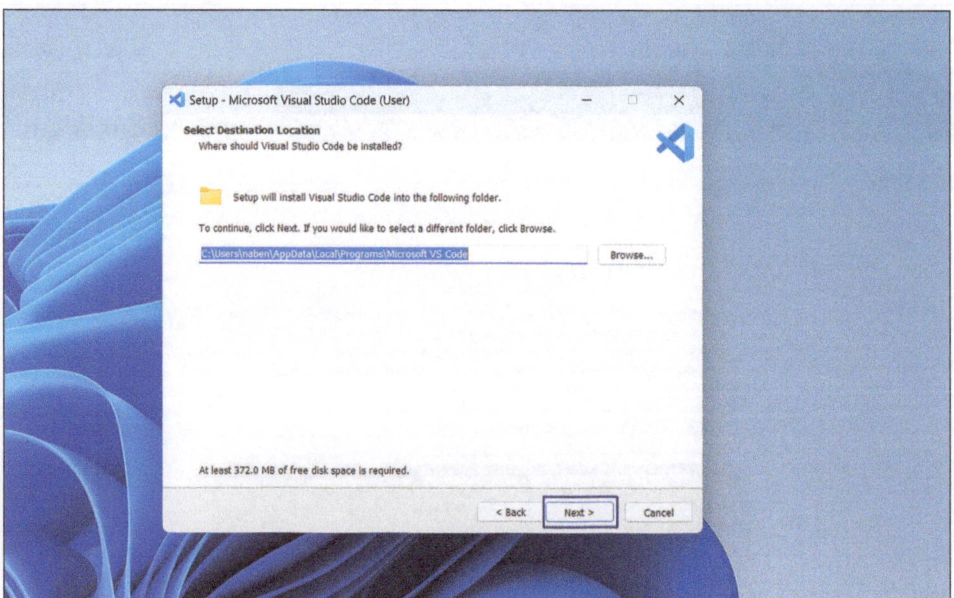

Figure 1.17: VS Code Install Location

In the next pop-up, just click on the **Next** button.

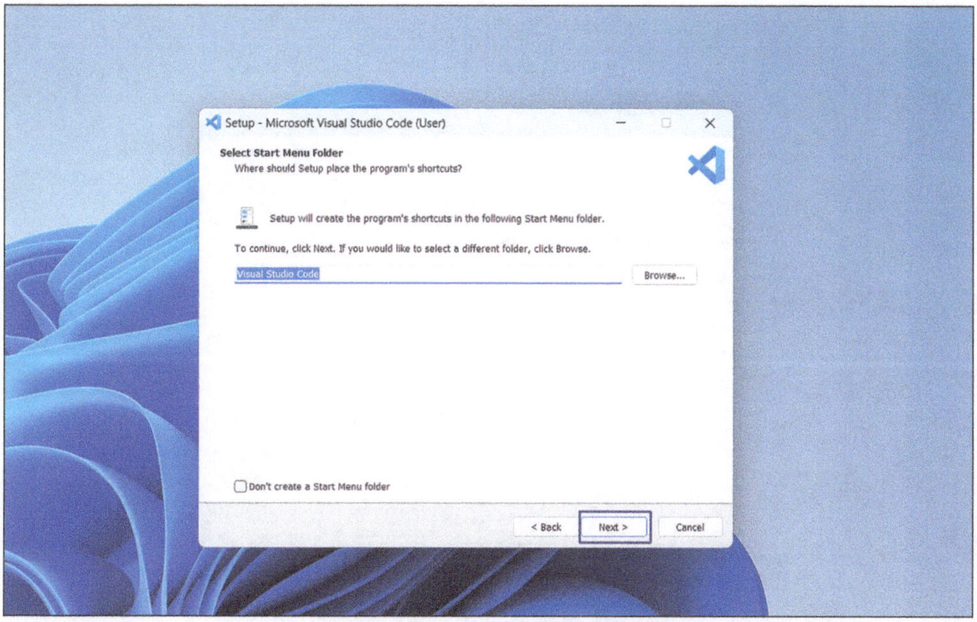

Figure 1.18: *VS Code Shortcut*

In the next pop-up, select all of the check boxes for a better experience. Then click on the **Next** button.

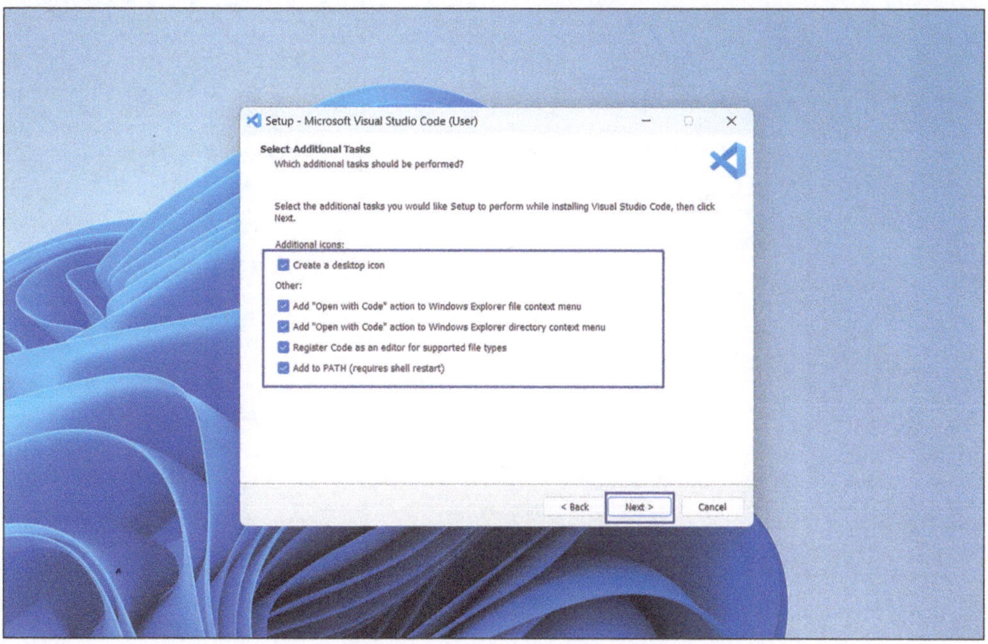

Figure 1.19: *VS Code Options*

Finally, click on the **`Install`** button.

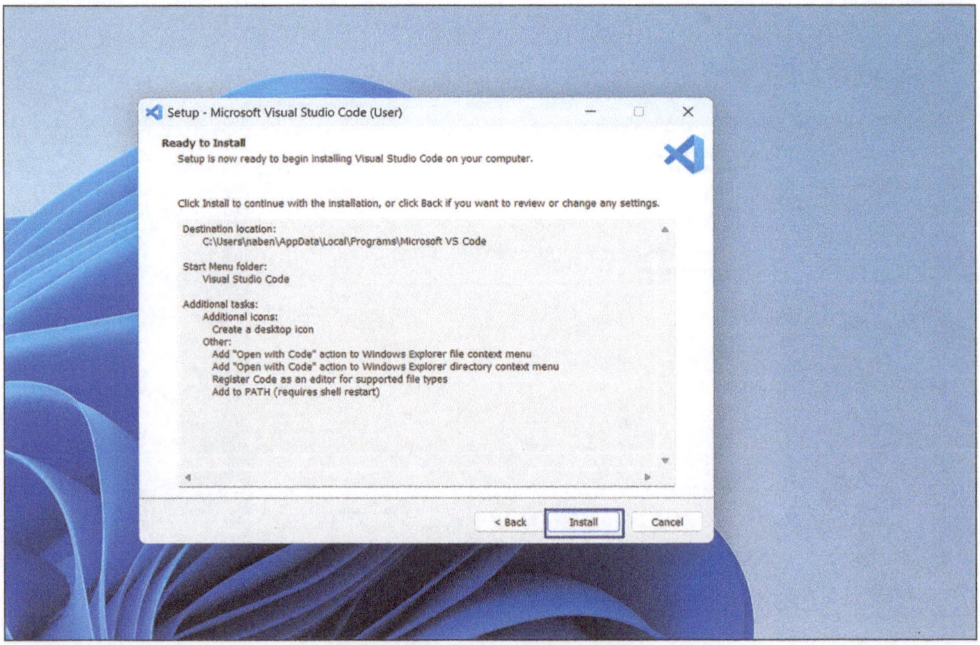

Figure 1.20: *VS Code Install*

It will take around two (2) minutes to install the **VS Code**.

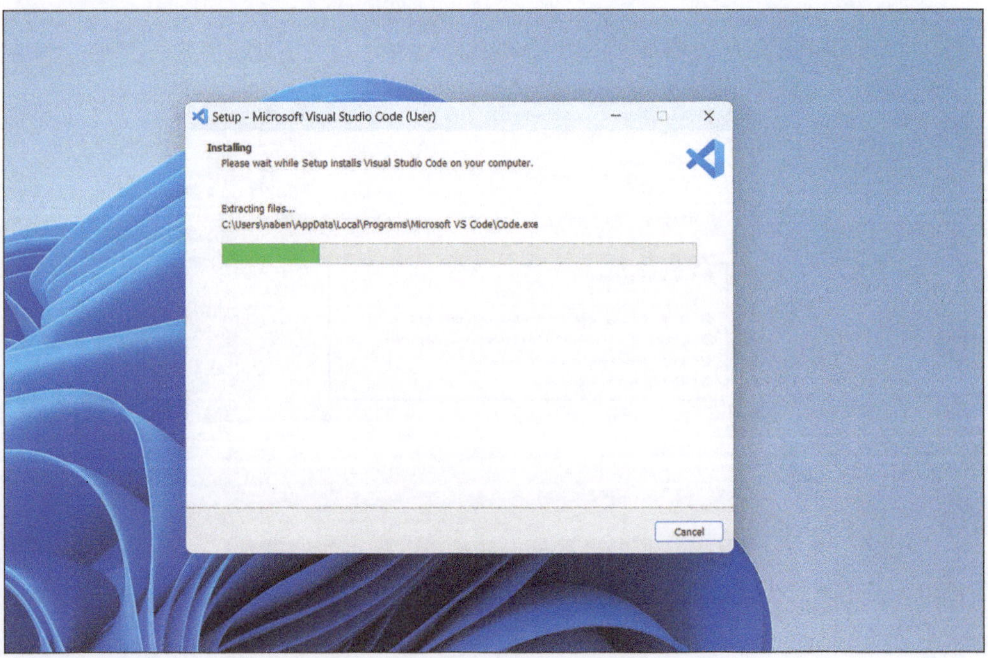

Figure 1.21: *VS Code Install Progress*

Once the installation is complete, click on the **`Finish`** button. Keep the default checked option of Launching VS Code.

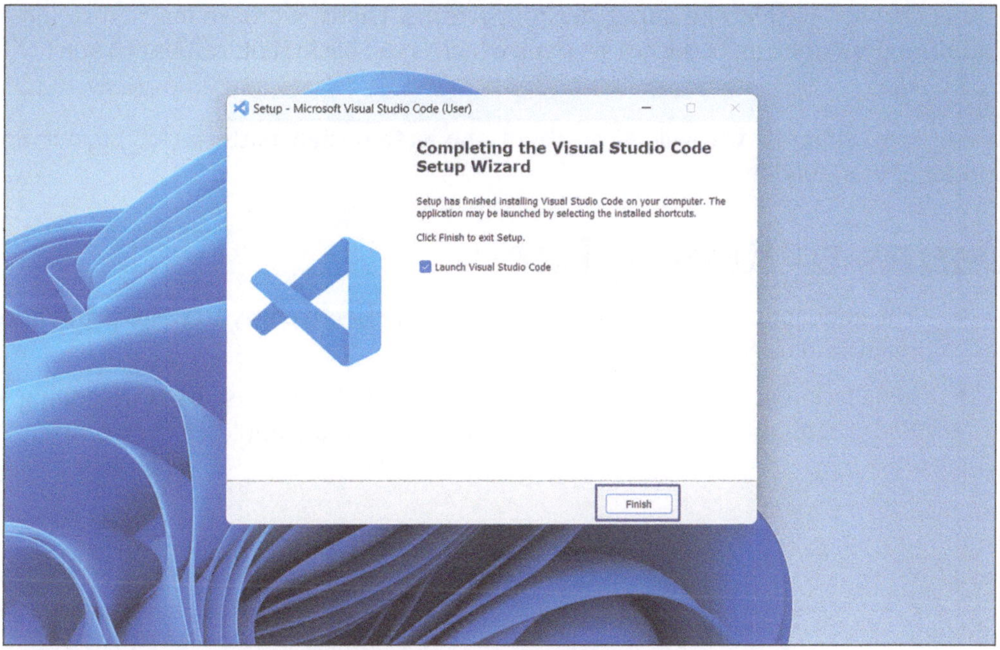

Figure 1.22: *VS Code Install Complete*

Next, the VS code will open, and we will see the version information.

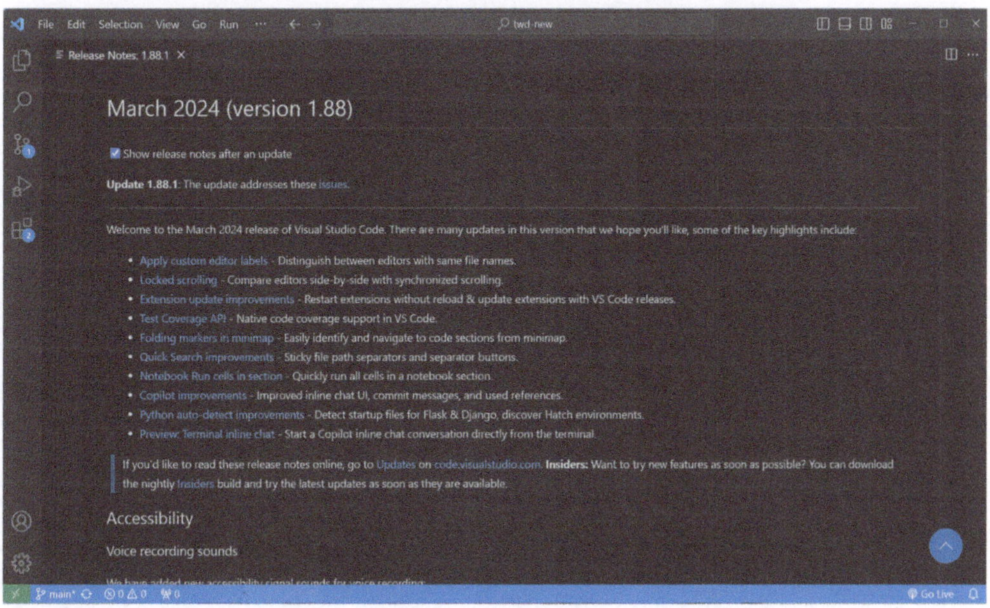

Figure 1.23: VS Code

Conclusion

In this chapter, we learned about design patterns. Lastly, we have learned to install NodeJS and VS Code on windows systems which is the basic requirement to start with the book.

In the next chapter, we will learn about the first design patterns of Layout and Container components.

Points to Remember

- The concept of Design Patterns which is an effective way to write production ready and highly optimized React Code.
- Installation of NodeJS, NPM and VS Code that are must to start coding in ReactJS. All these three can be easily installed, and completely free to use.

CHAPTER 2

Layout Components

Introduction

In this chapter, we will start with Design Patterns. We will first learn in detail about design patterns. Afterwards, we shall learn about the three types of Layout Components. The first Layout Component will be **Screen Splitter** which is known as **Split Screen Pattern** also. In this, we pass the components as props, generally more than one. The second Layout Component is the Lists, in which we deal with the List in the most professional way. Lastly, we will learn about Modals, where we are going to create the most effective modal, without using any external library.

Structure

In this chapter, we will discuss the following topics:

- Design Patterns Details
- Layout Components
  - Screen Splitter
  - Lists
  - Modals

Design Patterns Details

In this book, we will be exploring various React Design patterns that address the common challenges encountered during application development, using React. Let us first know what design patterns are, and their impact.

Design patterns can be defined as effective solutions to common application development challenges. Not all solutions are effective. Some approaches lead to decreased performance, and reduce maintainability, commonly referred to as Anti-patterns.

Design patterns, on the other hand are the most optimal and effective solutions to those challenges. The design patterns which we will be learning in this book differs from the Object Oriented Programming. This is because React has moved away from Class-based Components to Functional Components.

These patterns address challenges encountered in React development. We will check how to create reusable layouts for organising components, including Split Screens and Modals. We will also learn to reuse complex logic among components, instead of duplicating codes.

We will also learn to share codes for tasks such as fetching data from API. Another thing that we will learn is working with forms in React. We will also incorporate concepts of functional programming in our React application. We will learn how live and recursive functional programming concepts can be integrated into React.

Layout Components

In this chapter, we will first look into the important concept of Layout components. These are specialised components that focus on organising all the components, within a web page. In this chapter, we will explore these three layout components.

- **Split Screens:** Multiple components are arranged in different sections of the page.
- **Lists:** Displaying data in List format.
- **Modals:** Contents displayed on top of the actual page.

We will understand the fundamental concepts behind layout components, and ways to create them effectively. For example, when we develop a component for the side navigation bar such as below, we generally include the HTML structures and styles within the component itself.

We have created a simple React app where the **`App.js`** is calling a **`Navbar component`**, and passing a style and children prop.

```
import './App.css';
import Navbar from "./components/Navbar";
function App() {
  const navbarStyle = {
    backgroundColor: 'blue',
    color: 'white',
    padding: '10px'
  }
  return (
    <Navbar style={navbarStyle}>
      <h1>This is a Navbar</h1>
    </Navbar>
```

```
    );
}
export default App;
```

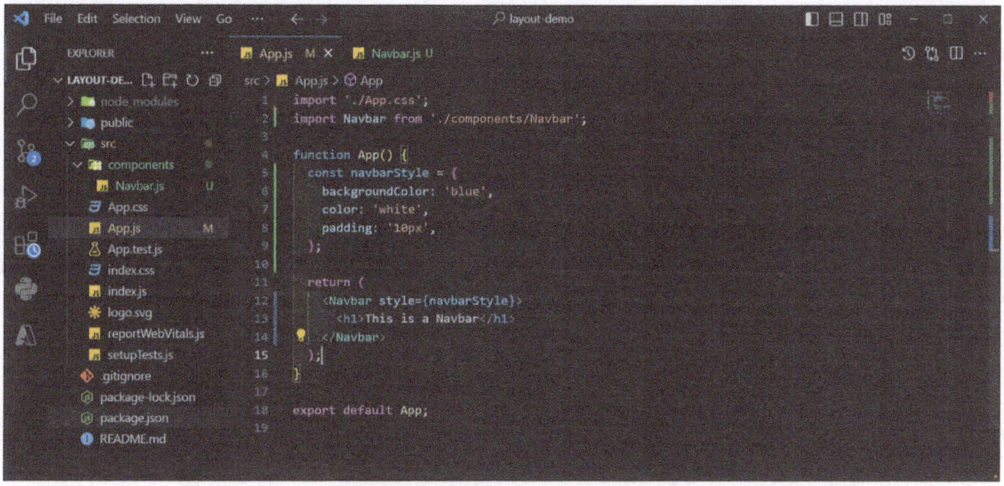

Figure 2.1: *Starting with App.js*

In the **`Navbar.js`** file, we are taking those two props, and displaying them:

```
const Navbar = ({ style, children }) => {
    return (
        <nav style={style}>
            {children}
        </nav>
    )
}
export default Navbar
```

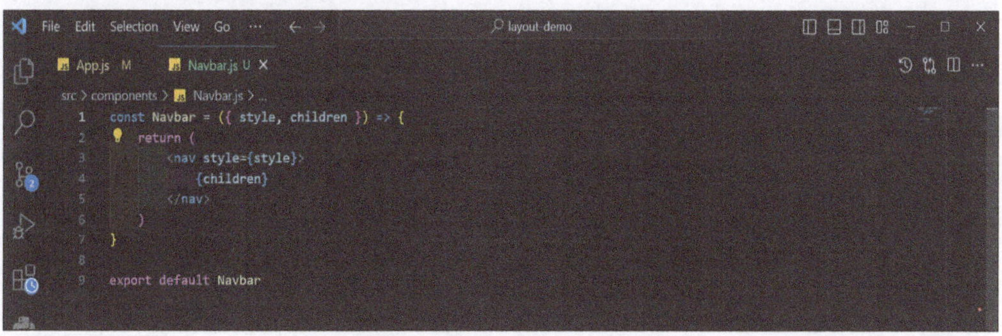

Figure 2.2: *Navbar Component*

Our app running on http://localhost:3000/ is displaying the **`Navbar`** properly.

Figure 2.3: *Localhost Showing Navbar*

With the Layout component, we adopt a different approach. We separate the actual layout styles into dedicated components, and only insert the specific component. Our **`App.js`** now contains two components: **`LayoutComponent`** and **`SideNavBar`**.

```
import './App.css';
import LayoutComponent from "./components/LayoutComponent";
import SideNavBar from "./components/SideNavBar";
function App() {
  const navbarStyle = {
    backgroundColor: 'blue',
    color: 'white',
    padding: '10px'
  }
  return (
    <LayoutComponent style={navbarStyle}>
      <SideNavBar />
    </LayoutComponent>
  );
}
export default App;
```

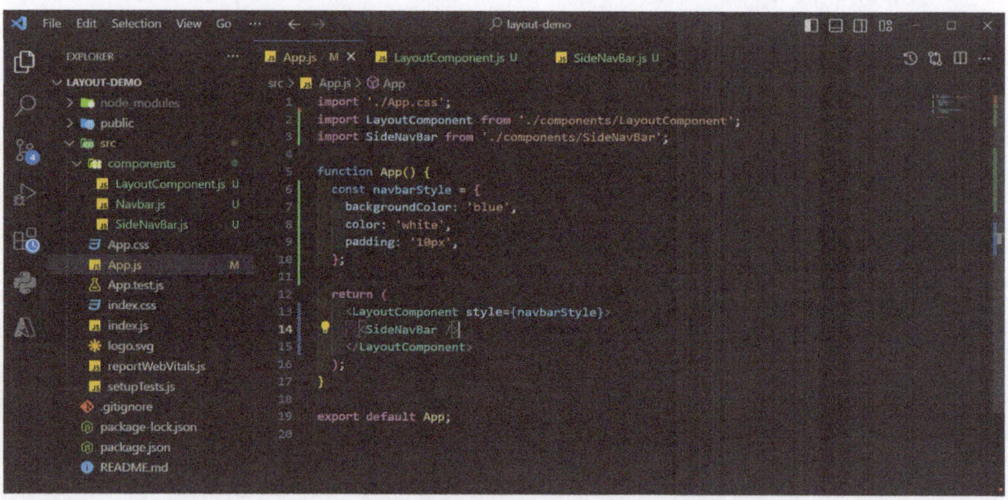

Figure 2.4: *Restructuring App.js with Layout Design Pattern*

The **LayoutComponent** file is similar to the **Navbar.js** file we created earlier. It contains the props of style and children, and shows the following code.

```
const LayoutComponent = ({ style, children }) => {
    return (
        <nav style={style}>
            {children}
        </nav>
    )
}
export default LayoutComponent
```

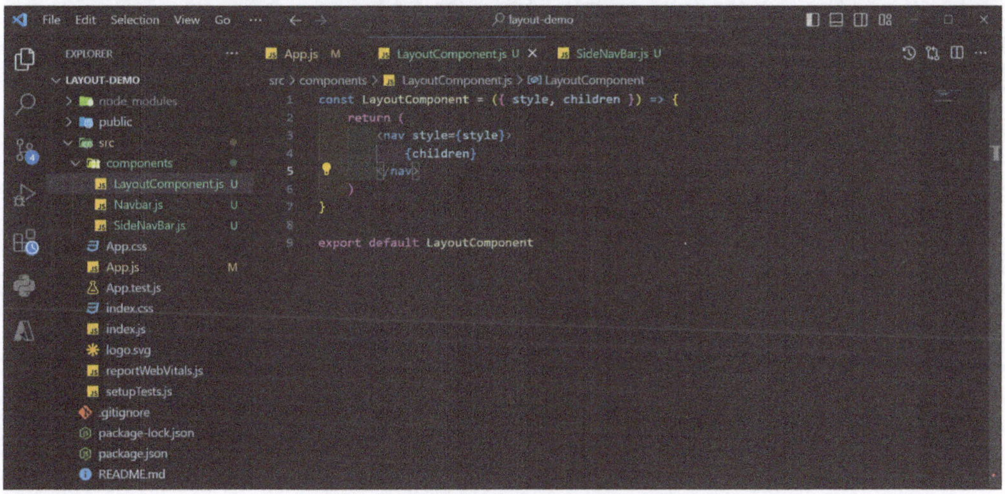

Figure 2.5: *The LayoutComponent*

The **SideNavBar.js** component will contain our **h1** code.

```
const SideNavBar = () => {
    return (
        <h1>This is a Navbar</h1>
    )
}
export default SideNavBar
```

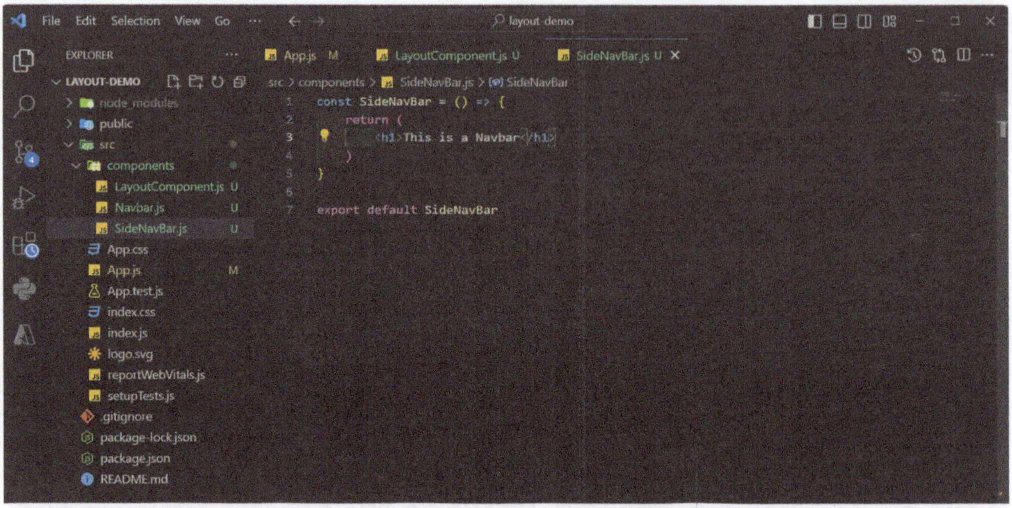

Figure 2.6: *The SideNavBar.js File*

Our app running on http://localhost:3000/ is displaying the Navbar, as in the earlier case.

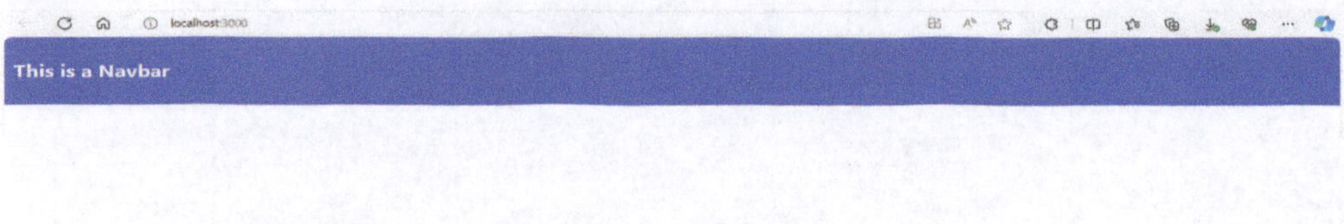

Figure 2.7: *Localhost with Layout Component*

This separation allows us to decouple the component logic from its specified placement on the page, giving us greater flexibility for future use.

Screen Splitter

Now, we will start with the first Layout Component which is known as **`Split Screen Pattern`**. We have first added the famous **`CSS-in-JS`** library of styled-components that will help us style our React code.

Next, we shall create a new file, **`SplitScreen.js`** inside the components folder. Here, we have first imported the styled from styled-components. Next, we have made a **`Container`** and **`Panel`** style for flex effect. Our **`SplitScreen`** component is taking two props - Left and Right.

```
import styled from "styled-components"
const Container = styled.div`
    display: flex;
`
```

```
const Panel = styled.div`
    flex: 1;
`
const SplitScreen = ({ Left, Right }) => {
    return (
        <div>SplitScreen</div>
    )
}
export default SplitScreen
```

***Figure 2.8:** Creating SplitScreen.js and Installing Styled-Components*

We have updated the return statement in the **`SplitScreen.js`** file. Here, we have added the **`Container`** styled component first, and inside it two **`Panel`** components: The **`Left`** and the **`Right`** components, which we are being received as props.

```
<Container>
    <Panel>
        <Left />
    </Panel>
    <Panel>
        <Right />
    </Panel>
</Container>
```

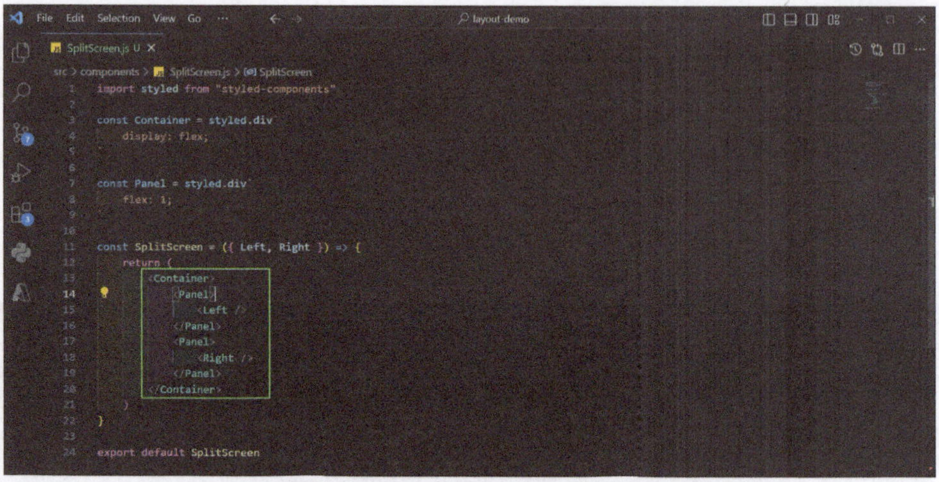

Figure 2.9: *Adding Styled-Components in SplitScreen.js*

Next, we will update the **`App.js`** file, to call the **`SplitScreen`** component. We are passing two props, left and right here. Both of these are calling components that we have created here only.

The **`LeftComp`** has an **`h2`** with a background of yellow, and the **`RightComp`** has an **`h2`** with a background of orange.

```
import SplitScreen from "./components/SplitScreen";
const LeftComp = () => <h2 style={{ background: 'yellow' }}>Left
Component</h2>
const RightComp = () => <h2 style={{ background: 'orange'
}}>Right Component</h2>
function App() {
  return (
    <SplitScreen Left={LeftComp} Right={RightComp} />
  );
}
export default App;
```

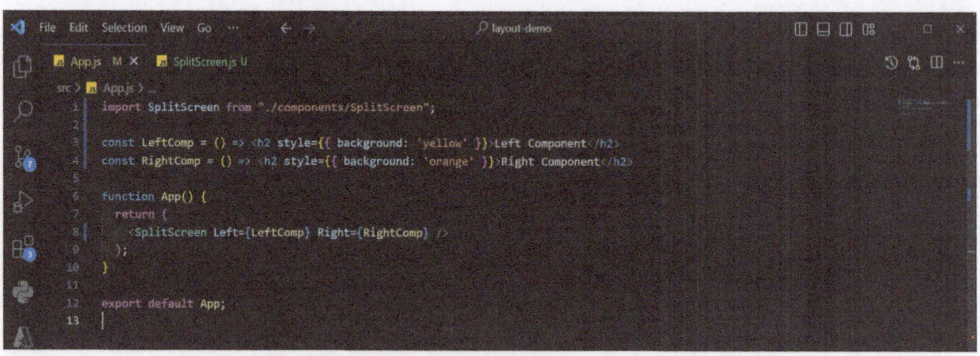

Figure 2.10: *Calling SplitScreen from App.js*

Back to our app running on http://localhost:3000/, we will see the **Left** Component and the **Right** Component with correct background colour. Each is taking half of the screen width due to **flex: 1**.

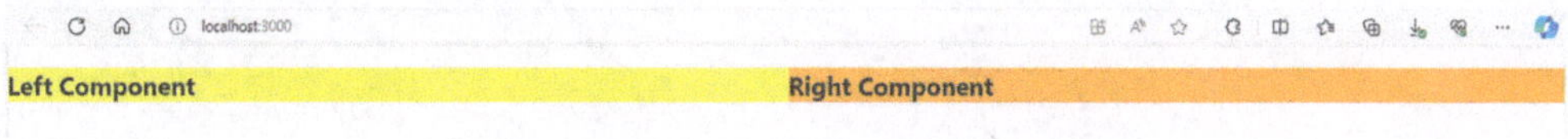

Figure 2.11: *SplitScreen on Localhost*

Screen Splitter Enhancements

We will make slight modifications in the Split Screen Pattern to make it more usable. Here, we will update our components so that the **Left** Component occupies less size than the **Right** Component.

So, in the **SplitScreen.js** file, we are getting two new props of **leftWidth** and **rightWidth** which have default parameters also of 1.

Afterwards, we will add a prop of flex in the Panel styled component. This is a feature of the styled components where we can pass props like this. We have updated the flex on the Panel styled component to take the prop of flex.

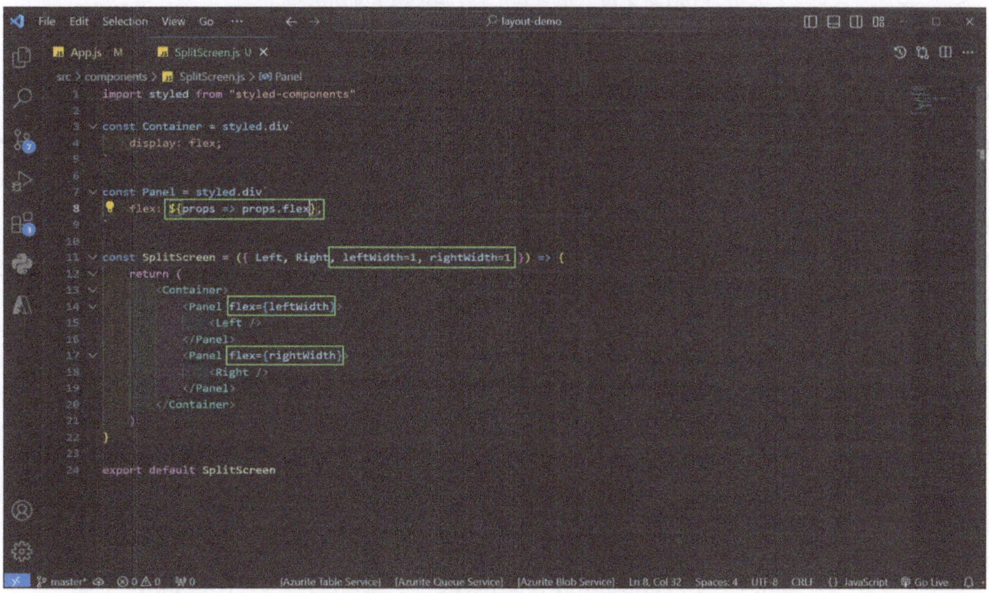

Figure 2.12: *Adding Data in SplitScreen.js*

Now, in the **App.js** file, we will pass the props of **leftWidth** and **rightWidth**. Notice that the **rightWidth** is 3.

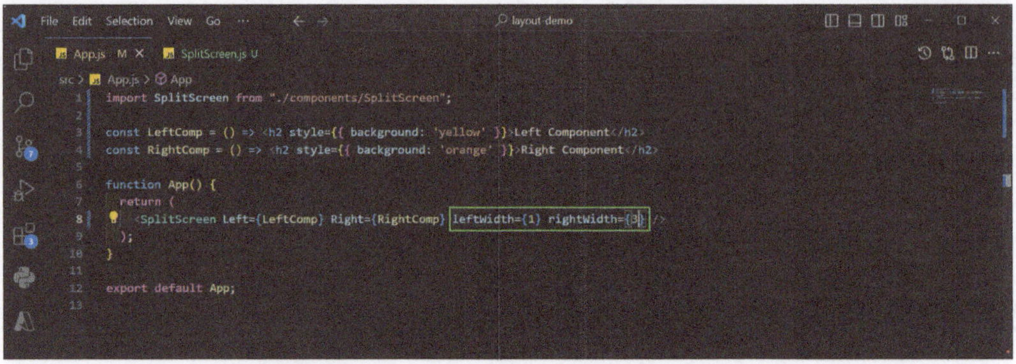

Figure 2.13: *Sending New Props from App.js*

Back to our app running on http://localhost:3000/, we will see that the **`Left Component`** is one-third of the **`Right Component`**. This is due to flex: 3 on the right component, and **`flex:1`** on the left component.

Figure 2.14: *Updated Screen in Localhost*

Lists

Next, we shall look into the List and the List items as a Layout component. We will look into the most professional React component design pattern for dealing with these kinds of components.

We have first created a new **`data`** folder inside the **`src`** folder. Inside it, we have created two files - **`authors.js`** and **`books.js`**.

The **`authors.js`** contains an **author's** array of objects. For each author, we have the **`name`**, **`age`**, **`country`**, and **`books`**.

```
export const authors = [
    {
        name: "Nabendu Biswas",
        age: 42,
        country: "India",
        books: ["TypeScript Basics", "Practical GraphQL"]
    },
    {
        name: "Ami Ganatra",
        age: 36,
```

```
            country: "India",
            books: ["Ramayana Unravelled", "Mahabharata Unravelled"]
        },
        {
            name: "Chetan Bhagat",
            age: 45,
            country: "India",
            books: ["400 Days", "Five point someone"]
        }
    ]
```

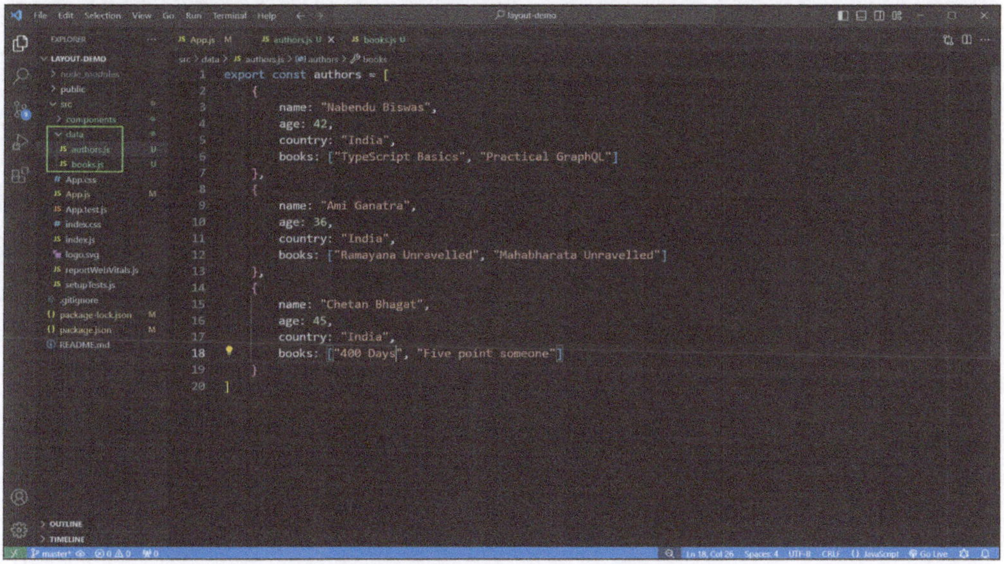

Figure 2.15: *Adding Data in authors.js File*

The **books.js** contains a **books** array of objects. For each author, we have the **name**, **pages**, **title**, and **price**.

```
    export const books = [
        {
            name: "TypeScript Basics",
            pages: 300,
            title: "Nabendu Biswas",
            price: 3500
        },
        {
            name: "Ramayana Unravelled",
            pages: 380,
            title: "Ami Ganatra",
            price: 380
        },
        {
```

```
            name: "400 Days",
            pages: 356,
            title: "Chetan Bhagat",
            price: 206
        }
    ]
```

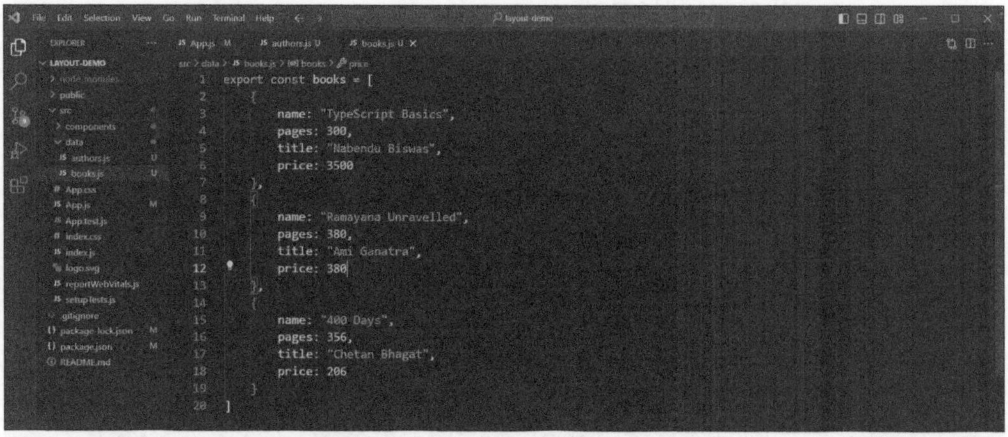

Figure 2.16: *Adding Data in books.js File*

Next, we will create the components to show the lists. So, inside the **`components`** folder, create two folders: **`Authors`** and **`books`**. Both of these folders contain **`LargeListItems.js`** and **`SmallListItems.js`** files.

The following is the content of the **`SmallListItems.js`** file which will show small details from the **`author.js`** file. Here, we are just getting the author as prop, and then restructuring the name and age from it. After that, we are showing them inside a paragraph tag.

```
const SmallAuthorListItems = ({ author }) => {
  const {name, age} = author;
  return (
    <p>Name: {name}, Age: {age}</p>
  )
}

export default SmallAuthorListItems
```

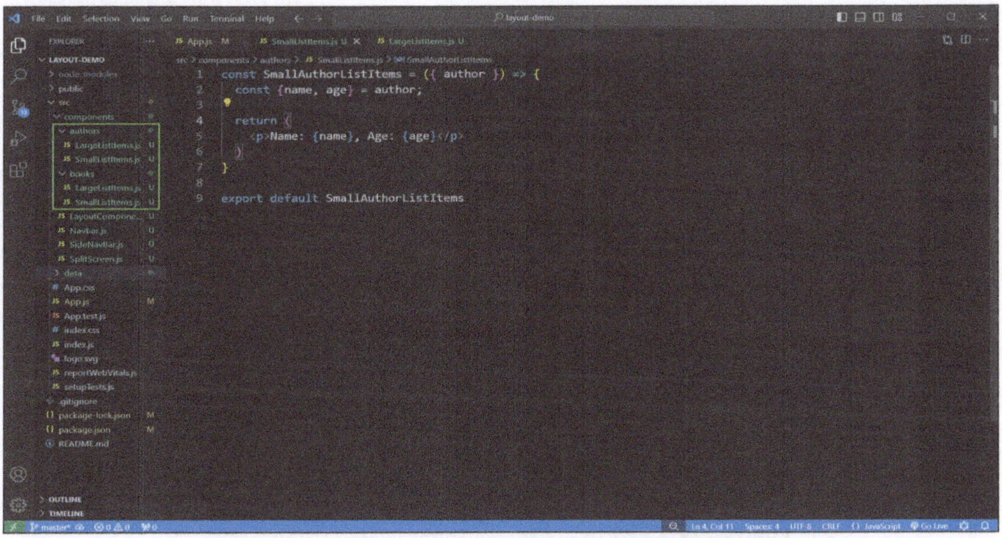

Figure 2.17: *Creating SmallListItems.js File for Authors*

Next the **LargeListItems.js** file will show large details from the author.js file. Here, we are again getting the author as prop, and then restructuring the **name**, **age**, **country** and **books** from it. After showing the name, age and country, **since the books is an array, we are looping through it, using a map and showing it.**

```
const LargeAuthorListItems = ({ author }) => {
    const {name, age, country, books} = author;
    return (
      <>
        <h2>{name}</h2>
        <p>Age: {age}</p>
        <p>Country: {country}</p>
        <h3>Books</h3>
        <ul>
            {books.map(book => <li key={book}>{book}</li>)}
        </ul>
      </>
    )
  }
  export default LargeAuthorListItems
```

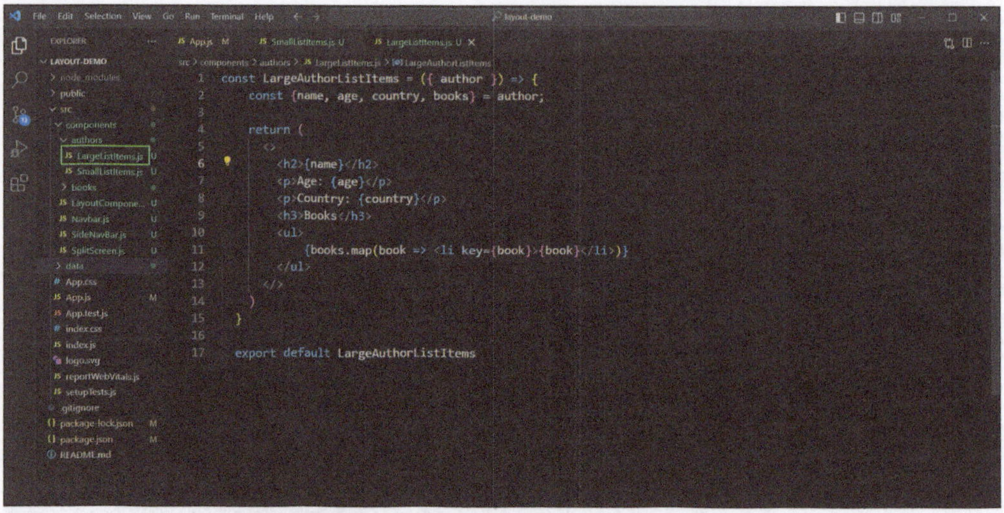

***Figure 2.18**: Creating LargeListItems.js File for Authors*

Now, we will have a single component showing both Small List and Large List. So, create a **`lists`** folder inside the **`components`** folder. Inside it create a **`RegularList.js`** file. This component is taking three props - **`items`**, **`sourceName`** and **`ItemComponent`**.

We are first looping through items, using map and then calling the **`ItemComponent`** with a key and **`sourceName`** as an item.

```
const RegularList = ({ items, sourceName, ItemComponent }) => {
  return (
    <>
        {items.map((item, i) => <ItemComponent key={i} {...{
[sourceName]: item }} />)}
    </>
  )
}
export default RegularList
```

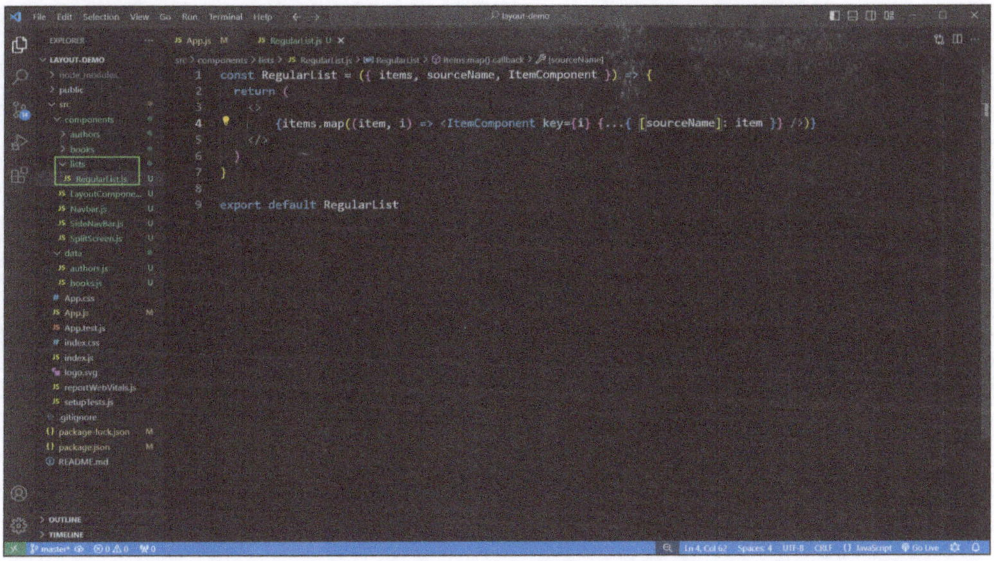

Figure 2.19: *Creating RegularList.js File*

Finally, in the **App.js** file, we will call the **RegularList** component two times. Here, we are passing the items props from the author's component. We are keeping the **sourceName** as author, and the **ItemComponent** as **SmallAuthorListItems** or **LargeAuthorListItems**.

```
import LargeAuthorListItems from "./components/authors/LargeList
Items";
import SmallAuthorListItems from "./components/authors/SmallList
Items";
import RegularList from "./components/lists/RegularList";
import { authors } from "./data/authors";
function App() {
  return (
    <>
      <RegularList items={authors} sourceName={"author"} Item
Component={SmallAuthorListItems} />
      <RegularList items={authors} sourceName={"author"} Item
Component={LargeAuthorListItems} />
    </>
  );
}
export default App;
```

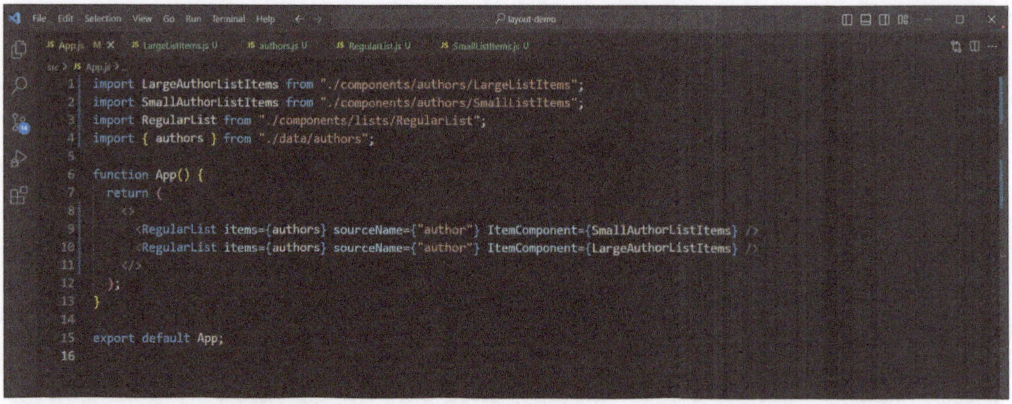

Figure 2.20: *App.js File Calling RegularList Component*

Finally, our app running on http://localhost:3000/ will show both the author's small details and large details.

Figure 2.21: *Localhost Showing Both Small and Large Lists*

We are now going to implement the Small and the Large List items for the books. For this in the earlier created **`SmallListItems.js`** file for the books, add the following content.

Here, again we are getting the book prop and restructuring it to get the **`name`** and **`price`**. After that we are displaying the **`name`** and **`price`** in the **`return`** statement.

```
const SmallBookListItems = ({ book }) => {
  const { name, price } = book;
  return (
    <p>Name: {name}, Price: ₹ {price}</p>
```

```
    )
}

export default SmallBookListItems
```

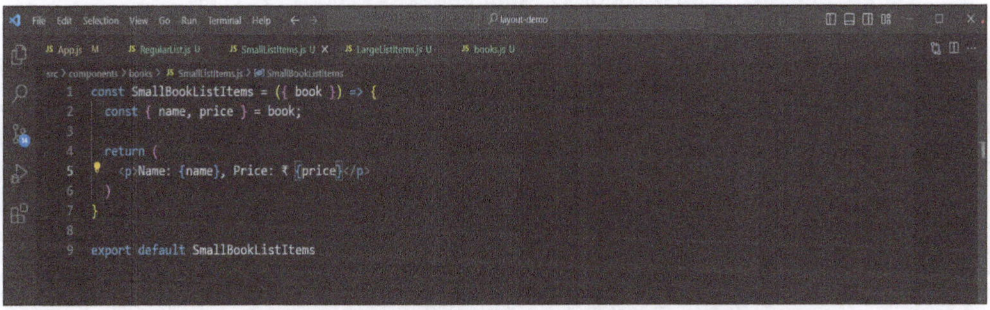

Figure 2.22: *Creating SmallListItems.js File for Books*

Next, we will update the **`LargeListItems.js`** file for the books, and add the following content.

Here, again we are getting the book prop and restructuring it to get the **`name`**, **`price`**, **`title`**, and **`number of pages`**. After that, we are displaying the **`name`**, **`price`**, **`title`**, and **`pages`** in the **`return`** statement.

```
const LargeBookListItems = ({ book }) => {
    const { name, price, title, pages } = book
    return (
        <>
            <h2>{name}</h2>
            <p>₹ {price}</p>
            <h3>Title</h3>
            <p>{title}</p>
            <p>Number of pages: {pages}</p>
        </>
    )
}
export default LargeBookListItems
```

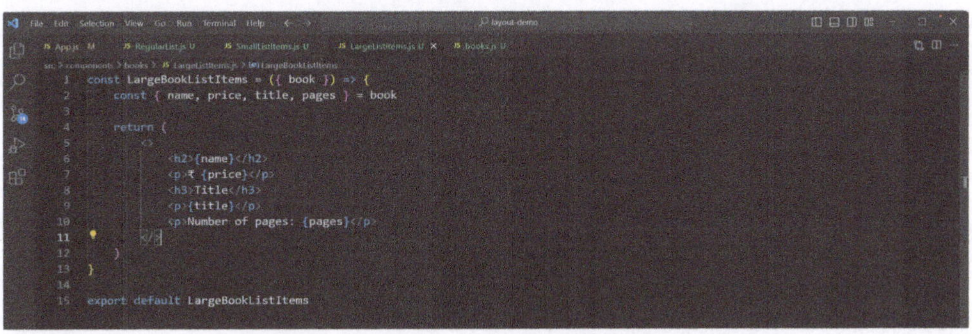

Figure 2.23: *Creating LargeListItems.js File for Books*

Finally, we are adding these components to the **App.js** file as earlier.

```
<RegularList items={books} sourceName={"book"} Item
Component={SmallBookListItems} />
<RegularList items={books} sourceName={"book"} Item
Component={LargeBookListItems} />
```

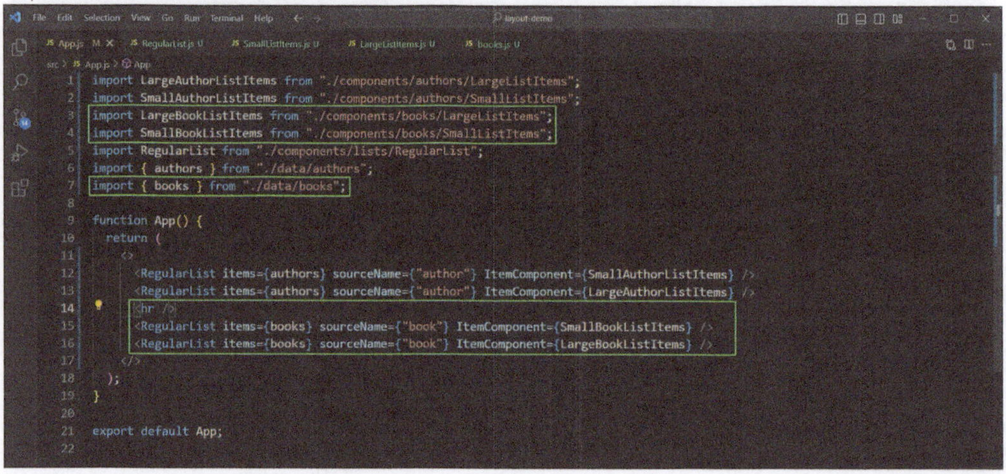

Figure 2.24: *Calling RegularList for Books from App.js*

Finally, our app running on http://localhost:3000/ will show both the small and large details of the books.

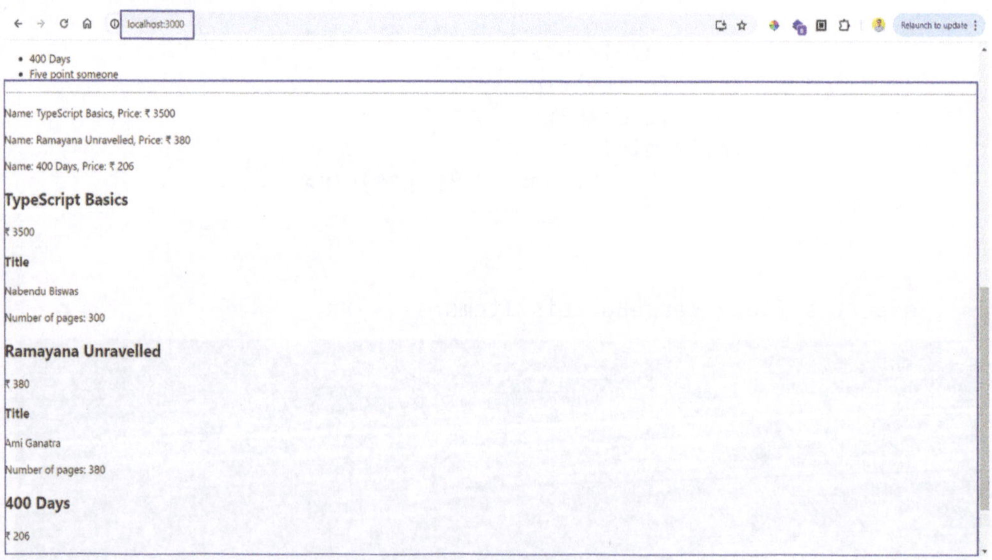

Figure 2.25: *Localhost Showing Books*

Modals

The last type of the layout component that we are going to talk about are called Modals. The modals are very popular and common in every project. So, in this section, we are going to focus on how exactly we are going to implement the related design patterns.

We can use a lot of external libraries to create a Modal in ReactJS, but we will create a modal using a simple design pattern. First create a **`Modal.js`** file inside the **`components`** folder.

Here, first we are importing **`useState`** and styled components. Next, we have created an empty styled component of **`ModalBackground`** and **`ModalContent`** which we are going to update soon.

Inside the component of **`Modal`**, we are first taking a prop of children. Next, we have a show state. Inside the **`return`** statement, we have a button called **`Show Modal`** that will set the show to true.

Now, when the show is true, we will show the **`ModalBackground`** which contains the **`ModalContent`**. The **`ModalContent`** further contains a button to **`Hide Modal`** and the children props.

We are also setting the show to false, when we click anywhere in the background, or at the **`Hide Modal`** button. We also need to set the **`stopPropagation`** on the **`ModalContent`**, or else event propagation will cause issues.

```
import { useState } from "react";
import styled from "styled-components";
const ModalBackground = styled.div``;
const ModalContent = styled.div``;
const Modal = ({ children }) => {
    const [show, setShow] = useState(false);
    return (
        <>
            <button onClick={() => setShow(true)}>Show Modal</button>
            {show && (
                <ModalBackground onClick={() => setShow(false)}>
                    <ModalContent onClick={e => e.stopPropagation()}>
                        <button onClick={() => setShow(false)}>Hide
Modal</button>
                        {children}
                    </ModalContent>
                </ModalBackground>
            )}
        </>
    )
}
```

```
export default Modal
```

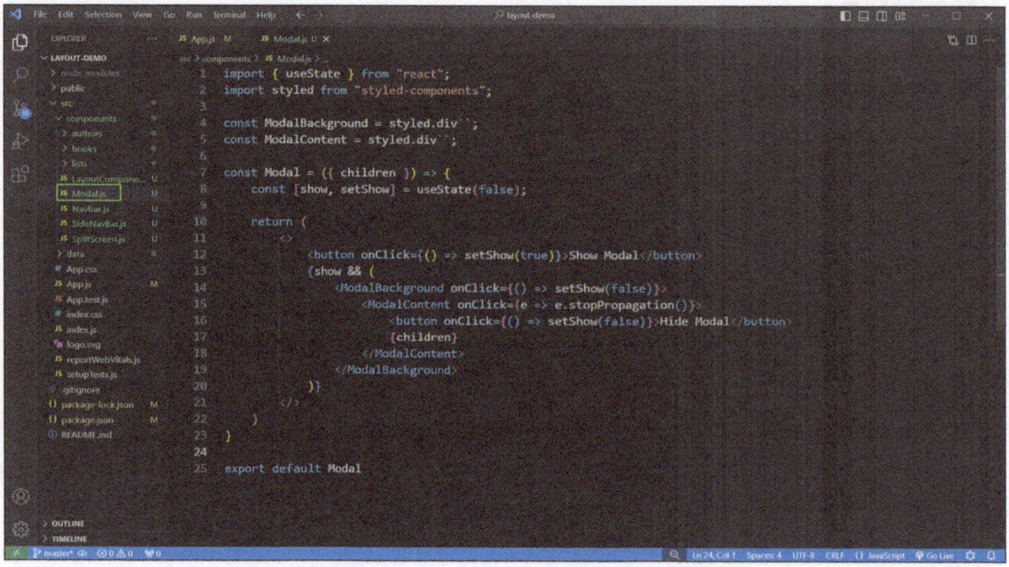

Figure 2.26: *Creating Modal.js File*

Next, we will add styles in **ModalBackground** and **ModalContent**. These are simple styles with a dark background, and a lighter content area.

```
const ModalBackground = styled.div`
    position: absolute;
    left: 0;
    top: 0;
    overflow: auto;
    background: #00000070;
    width: 100%;
    height: 100%;
`;
const ModalContent = styled.div`
    margin: 12% auto;
    padding: 24px;
    background: wheat;
    width: 50%;
`;
```

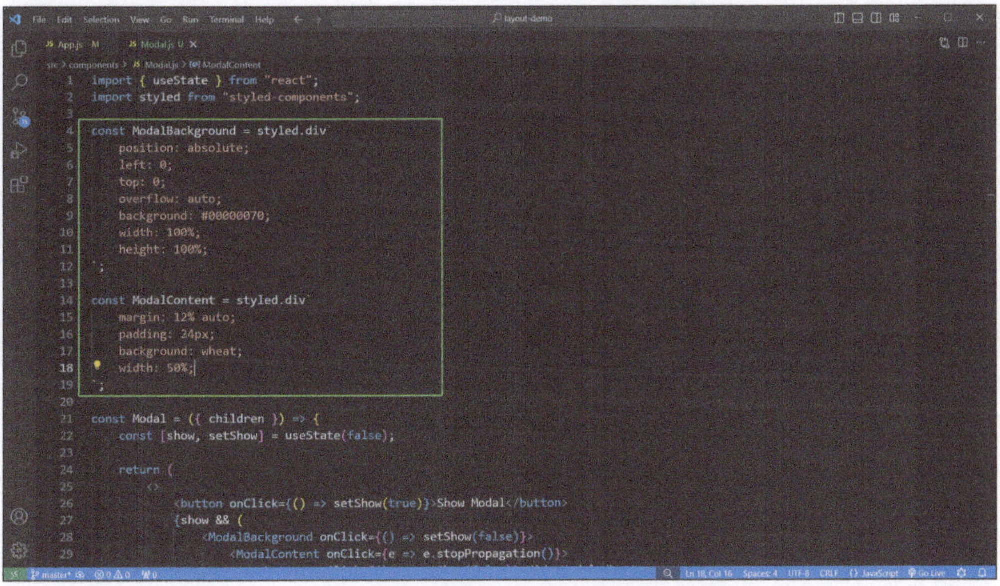

Figure 2.27: *Adding Styles in Modal.js File*

Now, in the **`App.js`** file, we will show that the **`Modal`** component will pass **`LargeBookListItems`** as children prop.

```
import Modal from "./components/Modal";
import LargeBookListItems from "./components/books/LargeListItems";
import { books } from "./data/books";
function App() {
  return (
    <>
      <Modal>
        <LargeBookListItems book={books[0]} />
      </Modal>
    </>
  );
}
export default App;
```

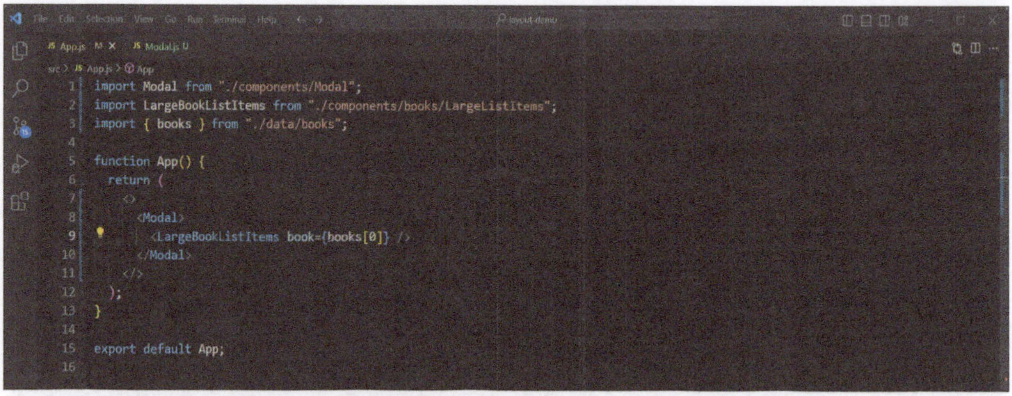

***Figure 2.28:** Calling Modal Component from App.js*

Finally, our app running on http://localhost:3000/ will show a **`Show Modal`** button. We need to click on this button to show the **`Modal`**.

***Figure 2.29:** Localhost Showing Show Modal Button*

The **`Modal`** is being shown now. Clicking on the **`Hide Modal`** button, or anywhere outside (the black part) will close the **`Modal`**.

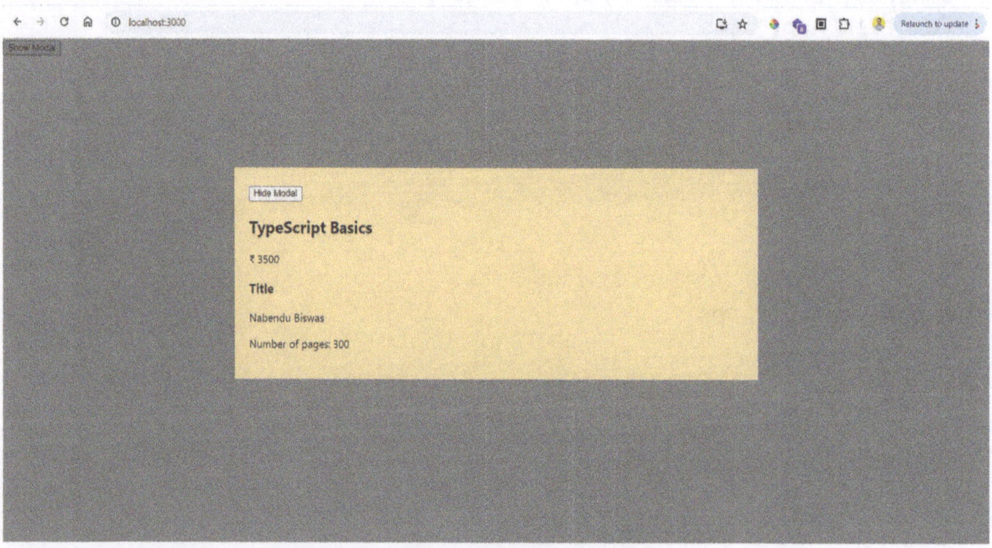

***Figure 2.30:** Modal Being Displayed*

Conclusion

This chapter provided a comprehensive exploration of design patterns, followed by a deep dive into the three fundamental types of Layout components. Through hands-on ReactJS coding exercises, we solidified our understanding of each component. We began by examining the Screen Splitter component, followed by a thorough exploration of List components. Finally, the chapter culminated in the creation of simple Modals, using well-established design patterns.

In the next chapter, we will learn about **Container Components**. They are responsible for handling data loading and data management of child components.

Points to Remember

- Creating Screen Splitter design, where we pass more than one component as props.
- Creating Lists components, using the perfect design pattern.
- Creating Modals, without using external libraries and easy design patterns.

CHAPTER 3
Container Components

Introduction

In this chapter, we will be exploring an important React design pattern known as **Container Components**. Container components are React components responsible for handling data loading and data management on behalf of their child components.

First, we will look into the container component overview. It is the reason behind using container components. After that, we will do a Server Setup, where we will build a simple NodeJS app, which we will use in this chapter. Next, we will create a Loader component that will be getting data from the server created earlier.

Next, we will get the data for the user, and then the resource. After that we will learn about the Data Source component, where we will do the API call from the parent component. Lastly, we will convert everything to the Render props pattern, which is much easier than the Children pattern, used earlier.

Structure

In this chapter, we are going to discuss the following things.

- Why Container Components
- Server Setup
- Loader Component
- DataSource Component
- Render Props Pattern

Container Components Overview

To check the need for container components, let us now check a child component, which loads its own data, and displays it independently.

We have created a new react app, and then created a component **`WithoutContainer`** in it. This is a simple component which is doing API calls to JSON placeholder endpoints, and showing the returned posts.

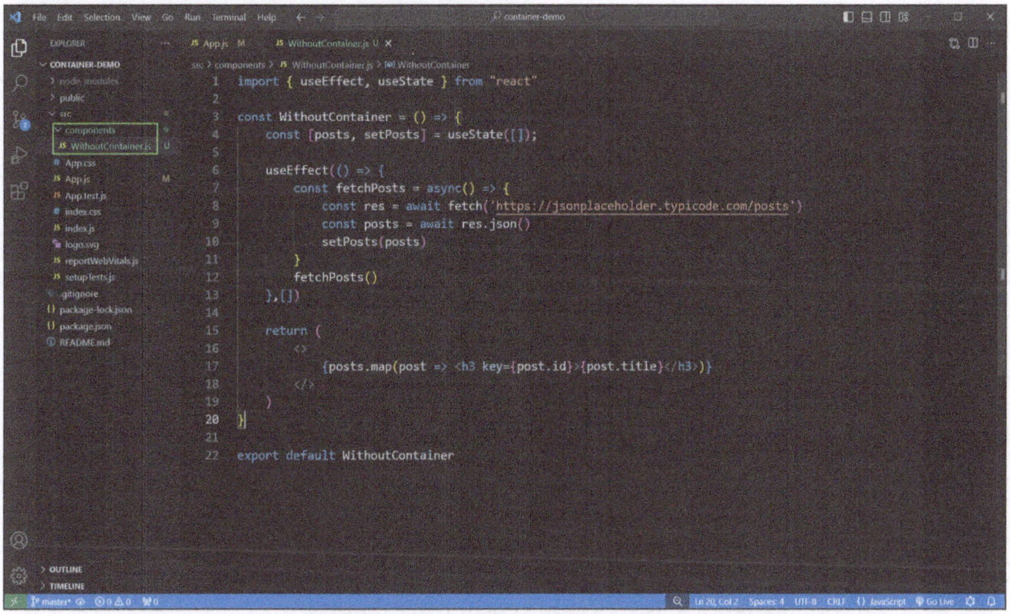

Figure 3.1: *Creating WithoutContainer.js File*

Next, we will show this component from the **`App.js`** file.

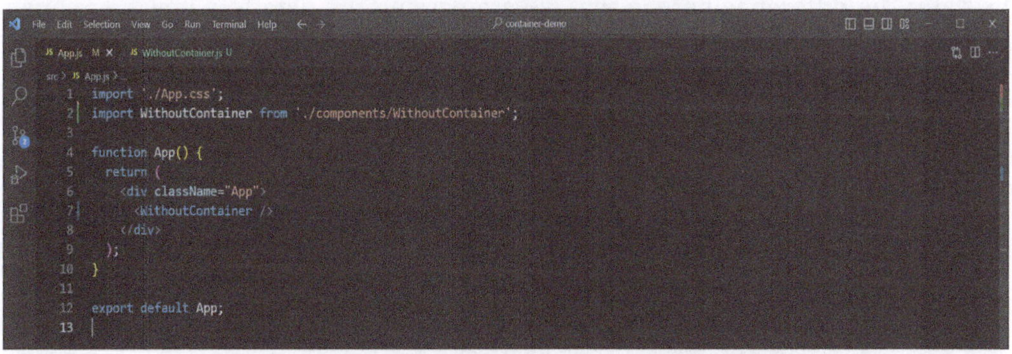

Figure 3.2: *Adding WithoutContainer in App.js File*

The title of all posts will be shown in http://localhost:3000/.

Figure 3.3: *Localhost Showing Post Data*

This method is ok for smaller projects, but a problem comes when multiple child components need to share the same logic for data loading. This is where **`Container Components`** come into play.

The container handles the data retrieval process, and automatically passes it down to the child component. We will rewrite our earlier logic now.

We have created a new file **`WithContainer.js`**, and here as demonstrated earlier, we are calling the API endpoint inside **`useEffect`**, and setting it to post, when we get the data. The difference here is that we are passing the data to a new component called **`ChildComponent`**.

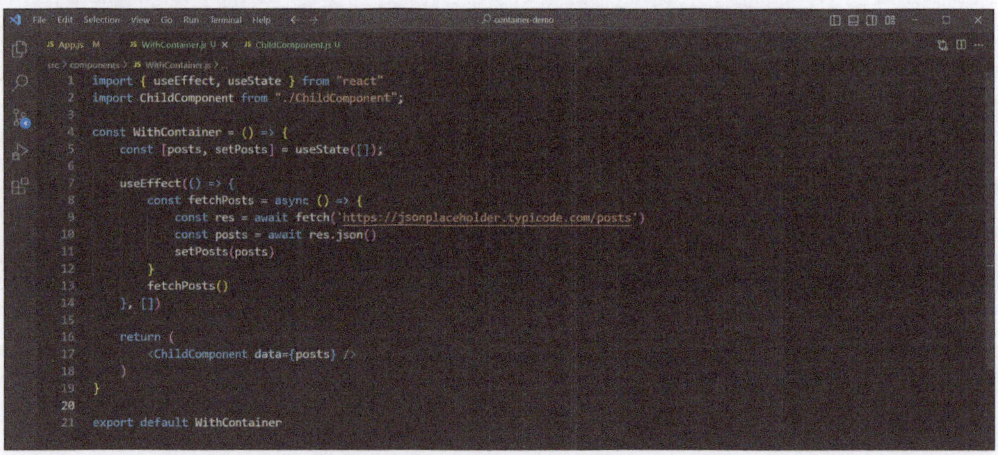

Figure 3.4: *WithContainer.js File*

Next, the **`ChildComponent`** will get the data as props. We are looping through it using a map, and showing the title.

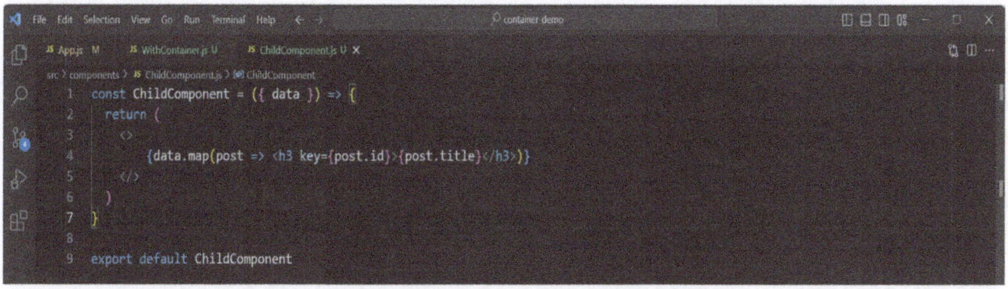

Figure 3.5: ChildComponent.js File

Now, in the **App.js** file, we have changed the code to show the **WithContainer** component.

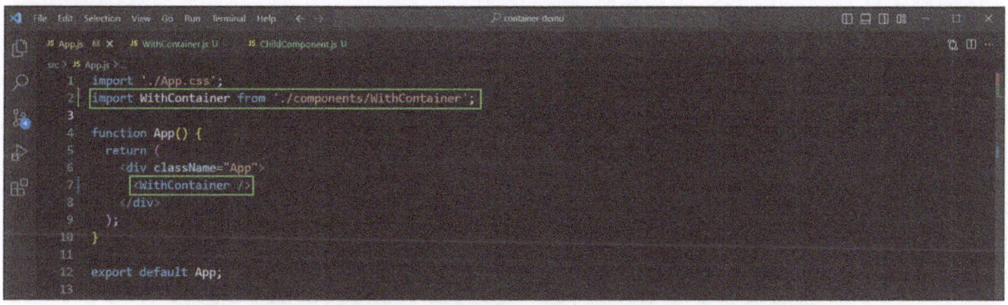

Figure 3.6: Calling WithContainer from App.js File

The title of all posts will be shown as earlier in http://localhost:3000/

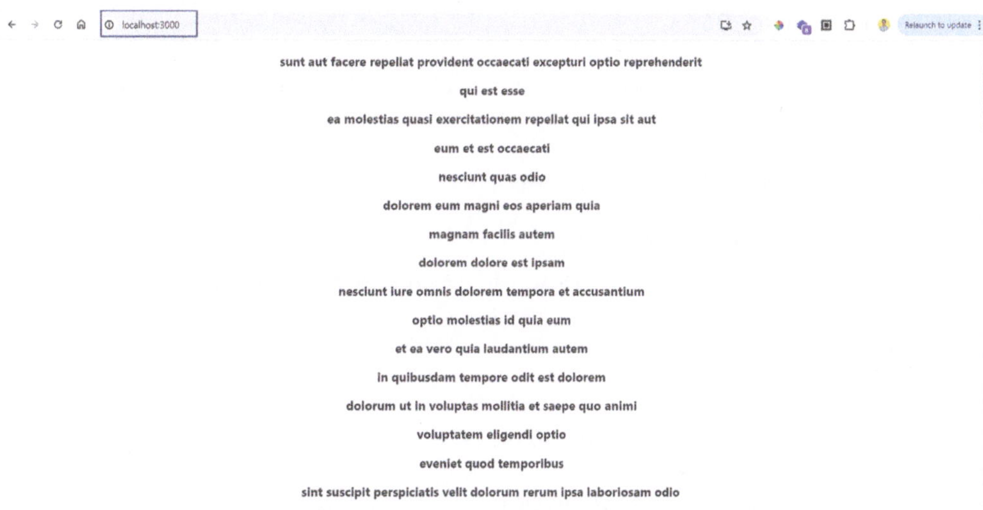

Figure 3.7: Localhost Showing Posts

So, the **Container** component follows a principle, where the **child** components are unaware of the management of their data.

Server Setup

We are going to create a simple NodeJS server now, which we are going to use next in the chapter. So, first create a **server.js** file in the main folder. Here, after importing express, we are using it. Next, we have a **currentUser** object, users and books array of objects. We have three simple **GET** requests, and a **POST** request next.

```
const express = require("express");
const app = express();
app.use(express.json());
let currentUser = {
  name: "Nabendu Biswas",
  age: 42,
  country: "India",
  books: ["TypeScript Basics", "Practical GraphQL"]
};

let users = [
    {
        name: "Nabendu Biswas",
        age: 42,
        country: "India",
        books: ["TypeScript Basics", "Practical GraphQL"]
    },
    {
        name: "Ami Ganatra",
        age: 36,
        country: "India",
        books: ["Ramayana Unravelled", "Mahabharata Unravelled"]
    },
    {
        name: "Chetan Bhagat",
        age: 45,
        country: "India",
        books: ["400 Days", "Five point someone"]
    }
];
let books = [
    {
        name: "TypeScript Basics",
        pages: 300,
        title: "Nabendu Biswas",
        price: 3500
    },
    {
        name: "Ramayana Unravelled",
```

```
            pages: 380,
            title: "Ami Ganatra",
            price: 380
        },
        {
            name: "400 Days",
            pages: 356,
            title: "Chetan Bhagat",
            price: 206
        }
];
app.get("/current-user", (req, res) => res.json(currentUser));
app.get("/users/:id", (req, res) => {
  const { id } = req.params;
  console.log(id);
  res.json(users.find((user) => user.id === id));
});
app.get("/users", (req, res) => res.json(users));

app.post("/users/:id", (req, res) => {
  const { id } = req.params;
  const { user: editedUser } = req.body;
  users = users.map((user) => (user.id === id ? editedUser :
user));
  res.json(users.find((user) => user.id === id));
});
```

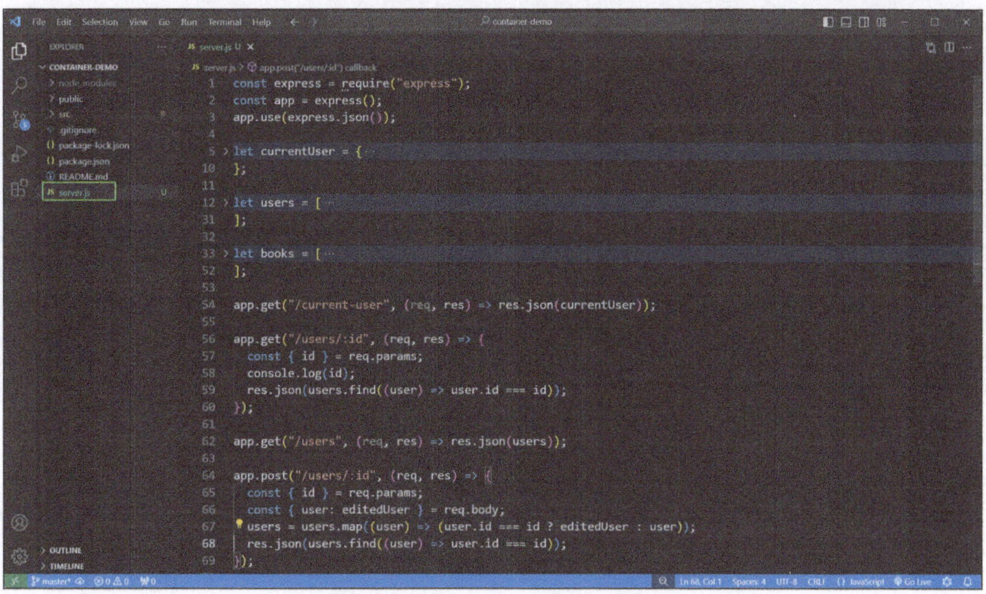

Figure 3.8: *Creating server.js File*

Now, we will have two more **`GET`** requests, and the app listening on **`port 9090`**.

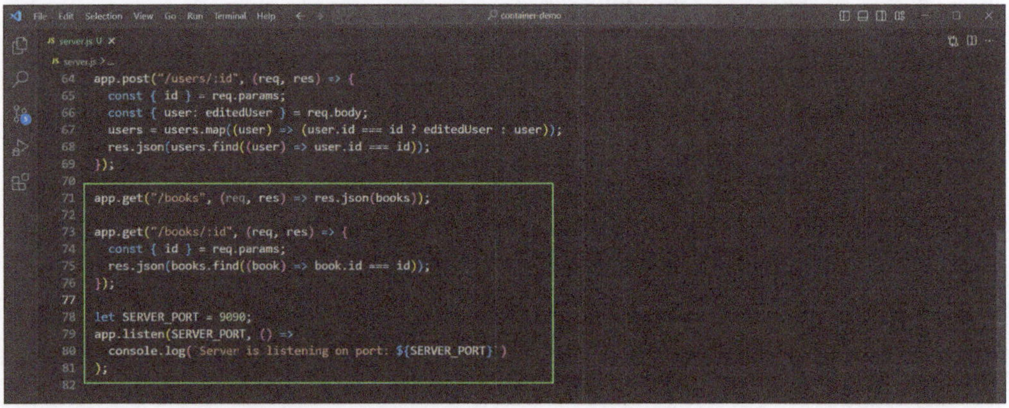

Figure 3.9: *Adding More Routes in server.js File*

Since, we are having the client and server at the same place, so in the **`package.json`** file, we will add the proxy. Then, we will also add the express in dependencies. Next, we will do **`npm i`** to install the new package of express.

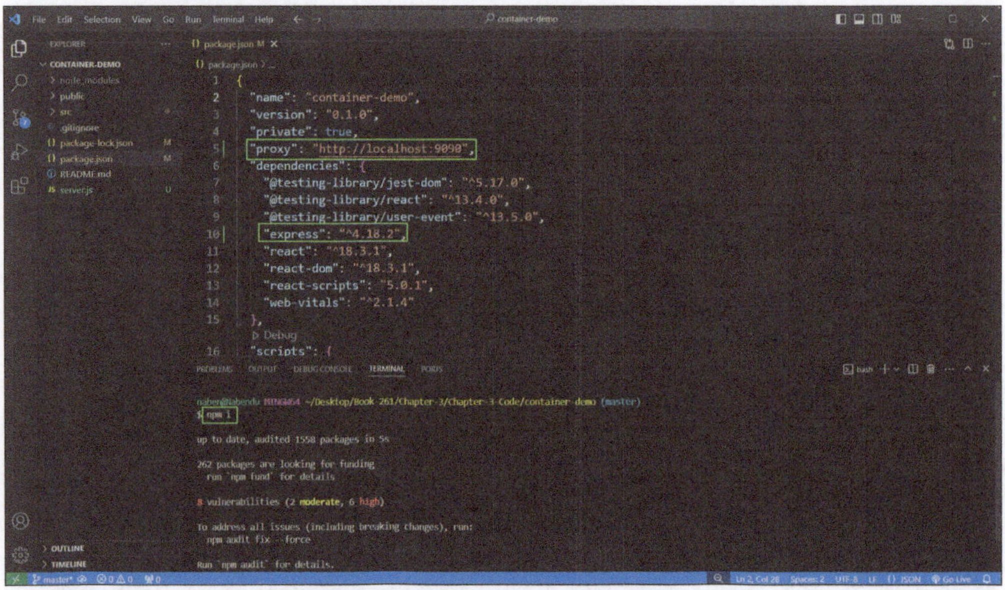

Figure 3.10: *Adding Proxy and Express*

Now, create a **`BookInfo.js`** file in the **`components`** folder. Here, we are taking the book props, and restructuring it to **`name`**, **`price`**, **`title`** and **`pages`** as well as showing them in the **`return`** statement.

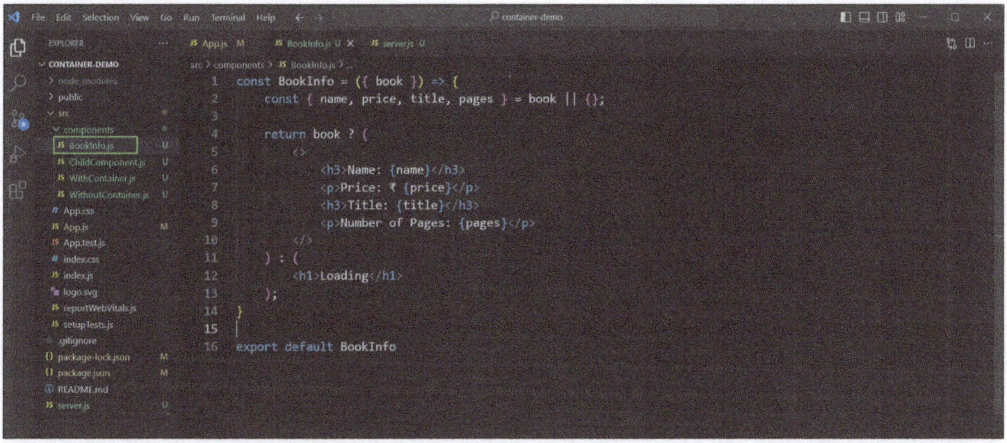

Figure 3.11: *Creating BookInfo.js File*

Next, we will create a **`UserInfo.js`** file in the **`components`** folder. Here, we are taking the user props, and restructuring it to name, age, country and books, as well as showing them in the **`return`** statement.

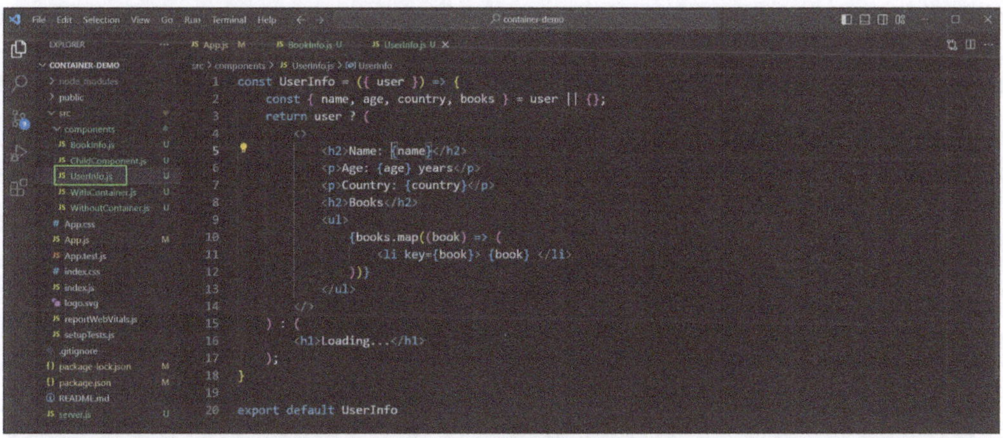

Figure 3.12: *Creating UserInfo.js File*

Now, to start the server, we have opened the in-built terminal in VS Code. Next, run the command, **`node server.js`** in it.

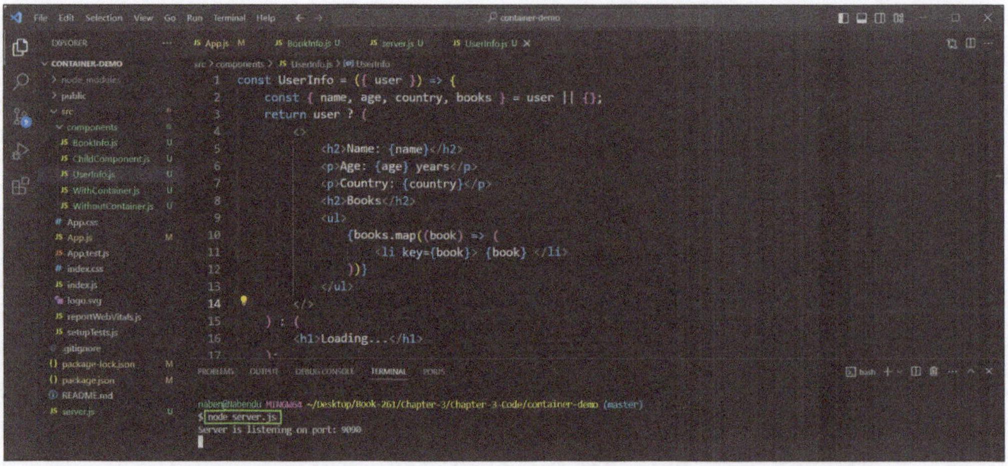

Figure 3.13: *Running the Server with node server.js Command*

Loader Component

We will be having a container component for loading the current user data. This is called a Loader Component. For this, we will create a **`CurrentUserLoader.js`** file inside the **`components`** folder. We have also installed **axios** from the in-build terminal.

Here, first we have imported axios and the hooks. Then, we have created a new state of user. Inside the **`useEffect`**, we are calling the GET endpoint of **`/current-user`** from the **`server.js`**. Once we get the data, we are adding it to the user state.

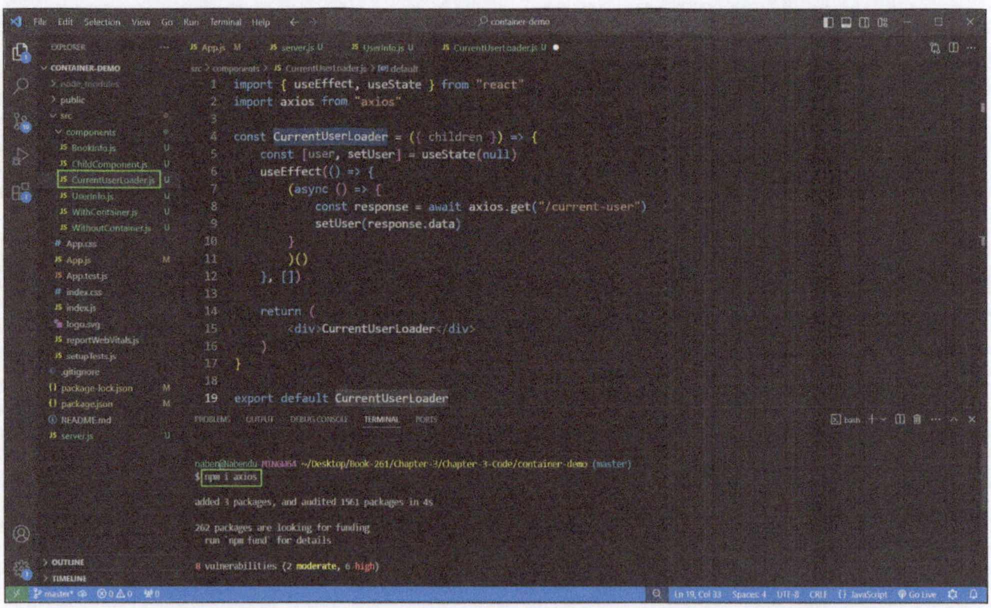

Figure 3.14: *Creating CurrentUserLoader.js and Adding Axios*

Now, in the **`App.js`** file, we will first import the **`CurrentUserLoader`** and **`UserInfo`** components. Inside the return, we are calling the **`UserInfo`** from inside the **`CurrentUserLoader`** as children.

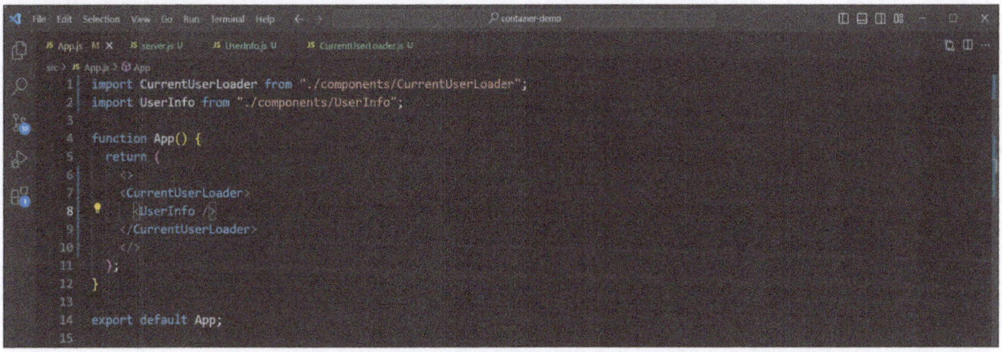

Figure 3.15: *Calling CurrentUserLoader from App.js File*

Back in the **`CurrentUserLoader.js`** file, we are first importing **`Children`**, **`isValidElement`** and **`cloneElement`** from react. Next, we are using the **`Children`** API to map through the children props. Here, we are first validating each child through **`isValidElement()`**. Next, we are cloning the child to the user, using **`cloneElement()`**.

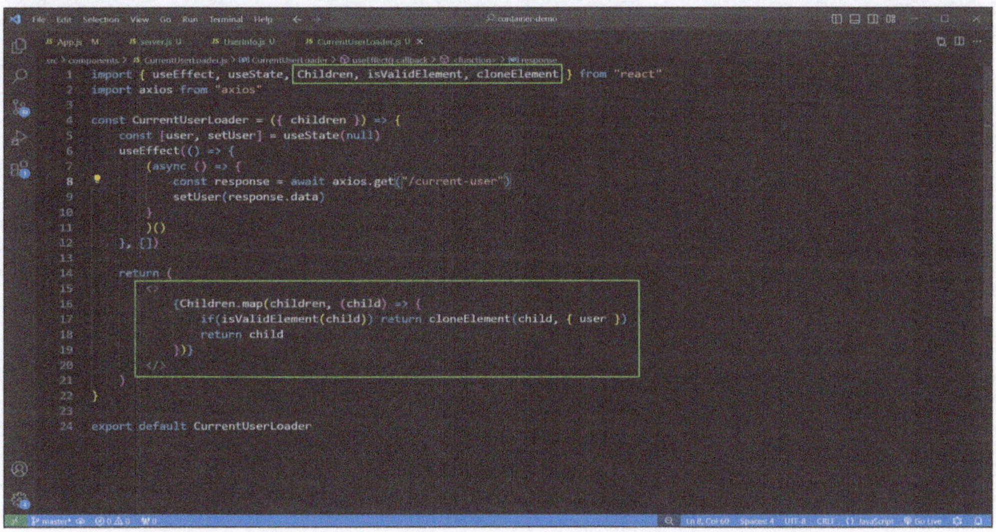

Figure 3.16: *Adding Children and cloneElement in CurrentUserLoader.js File*

Now, in http://localhost:3000/, we will see our Current User Data.

***Figure 3.17:** Getting the Current User Data in Localhost*

User Data Loader

We have seen the code to get the current user. Now, we will write the code to fetch the data of a user based on ID. So, we will create another file **`UserLoader.js`** inside the **`components`** folder.

It is completely similar to **`CurrentUserLoader.js`** file, but here, we are getting the **`userId`** also as props. Using the **`userId`**, we are hitting a new **`GET`** endpoint to get the details of a particular user.

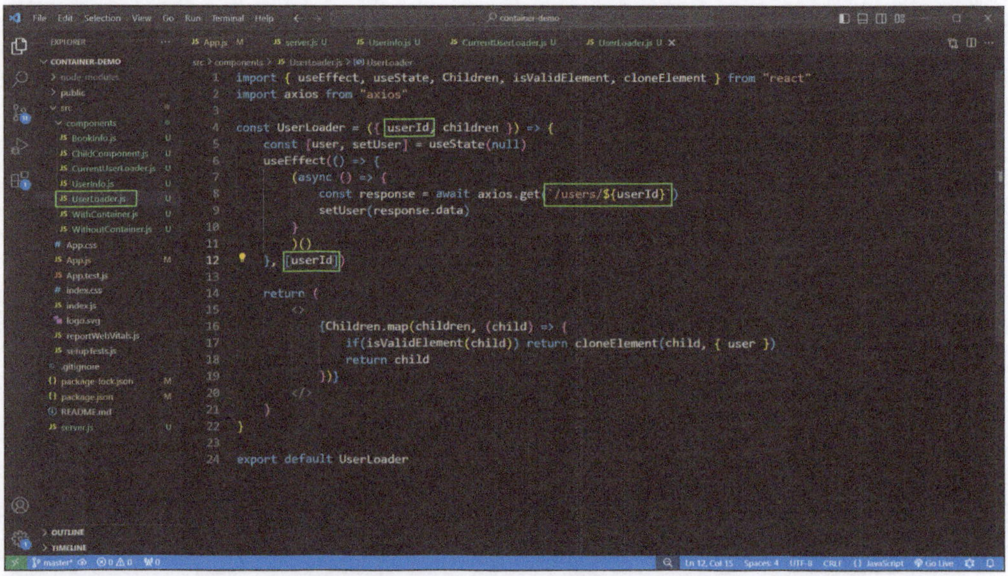

***Figure 3.18:** Creating UserLoader.js File*

We made one mistake earlier, and that was not to include the ids for all users in the **`server.js`** file. Now, we have added the same, and also restarted the backend server by running the **`node server.js`** file again.

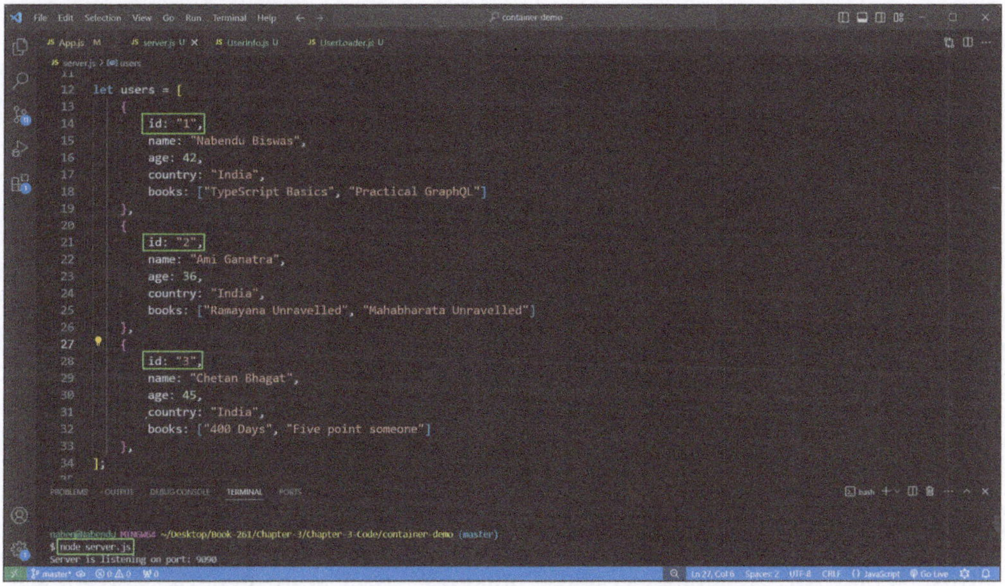

Figure 3.19: *Adding Ids for Users in server.js File*

Now, back in the **`App.js`** file, we will call the **`UserLoader`** component, and pass the **`userId`** in it. We are passing the **`UserInfo`** component as Children props.

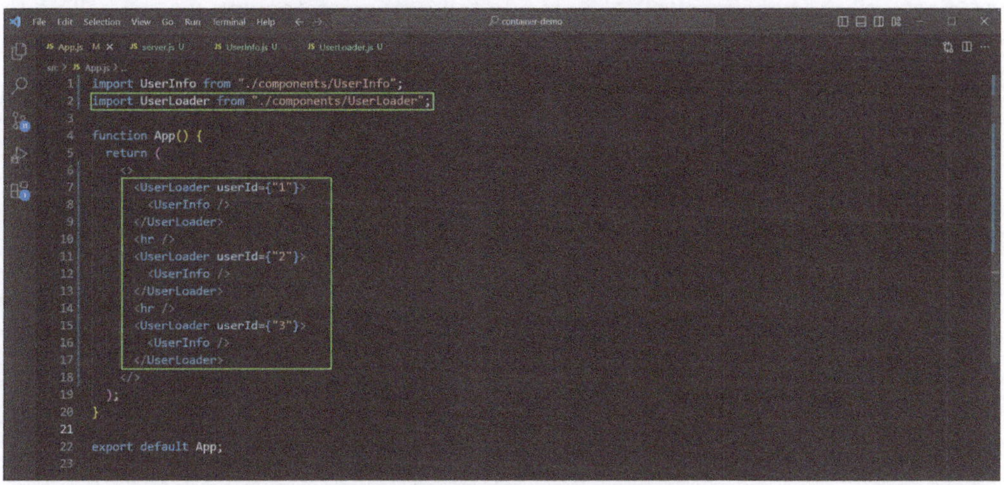

Figure 3.20: *Calling UserLoader from server.js File*

Now, in http://localhost:3000/, we will see the three User Data.

Figure 3.21: *Localhost Showing User Data*

Resource Data Loader

In this section, we are going to make our code even more generic, and create a component for fetching user data or book data. For doing this, we will create a new file called **`ResourceLoader.js`** inside the **`components`** folder.

This component will get two props called **`resourceUrl`** and **`resourceName`**, and in the **`useEffect`** call the **`resourceUrl`**. Also, inside the **`return`** statement, we are calling the **`resourceName`**.

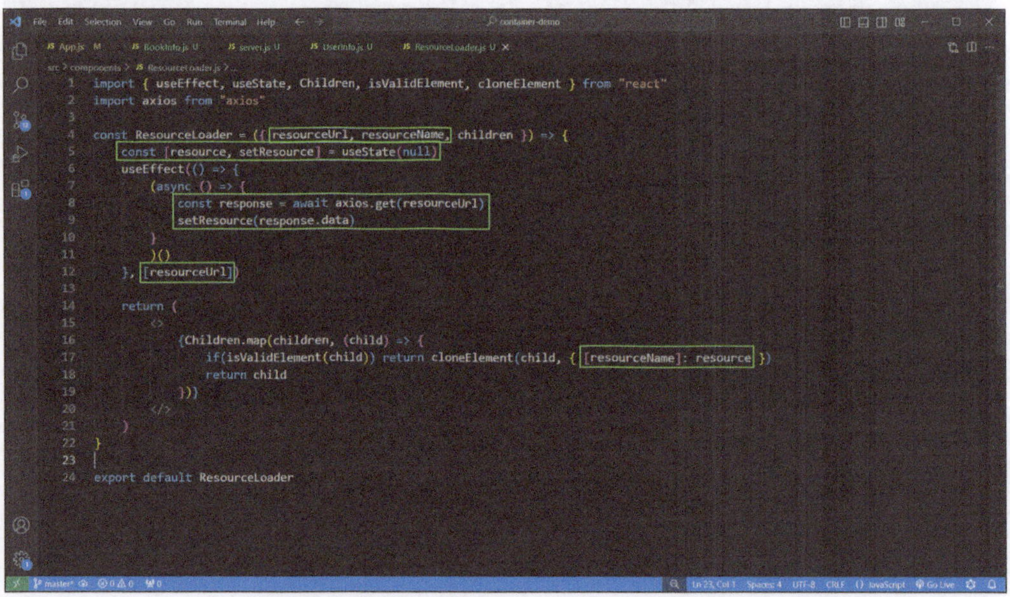

Figure 3.22: *Creating ResourceLoader.js File*

Again, we have made one mistake earlier, and not included the ids of all books in the

server.js file. So, we have added the same, and also restarted the backend server by running the **node server.js** file again.

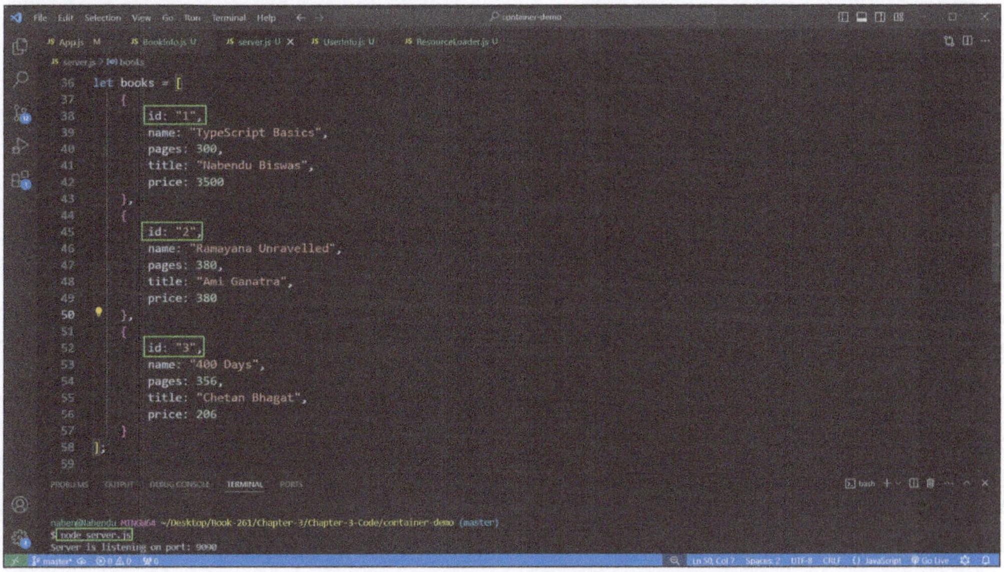

***Figure 3.23:** Adding Ids of Books in server.js File*

Now, in the **App.js** file, we will call the **ResourceLoader** component. Here, we are passing the **resourceUrl** and **resourceName** props so that we are able to call both the **UserInfo** and **BookInfo** components as Children props.

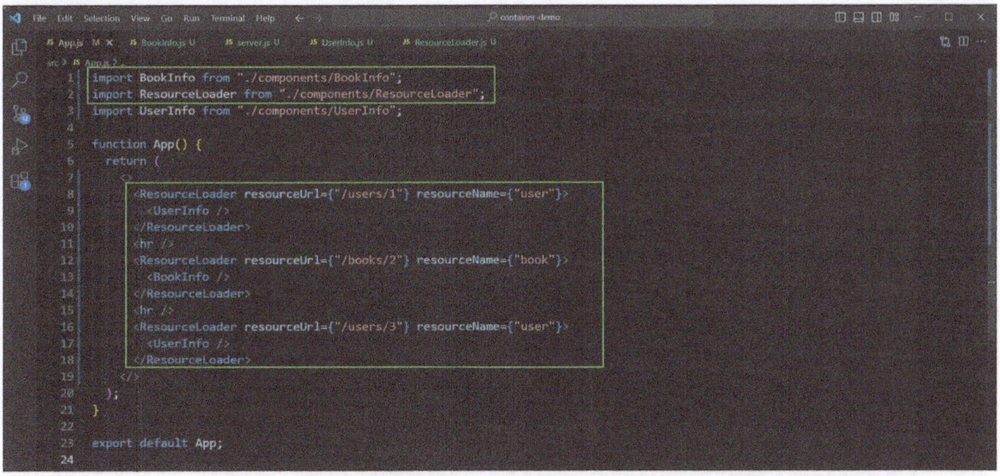

***Figure 3.24:** Calling ResourceLoader from App.js File*

Now, in http://localhost:3000/, we are able to get both the Book and the User Data.

Figure 3.25: *Localhost Showing Book and User Data*

DataSource Component

We will make the components made in the previous section even more generic. We will create a new container component that is not even aware of the axios call. So, we will create a file, **`DataSource.js`** inside the **`components`** folder.

It is almost similar to the **`ResourceLoader.js`** file, except that we are getting a **`getData()`** instead of the **`resourceUrl`**. Hence, we are updating the **`useEffect`** accordingly.

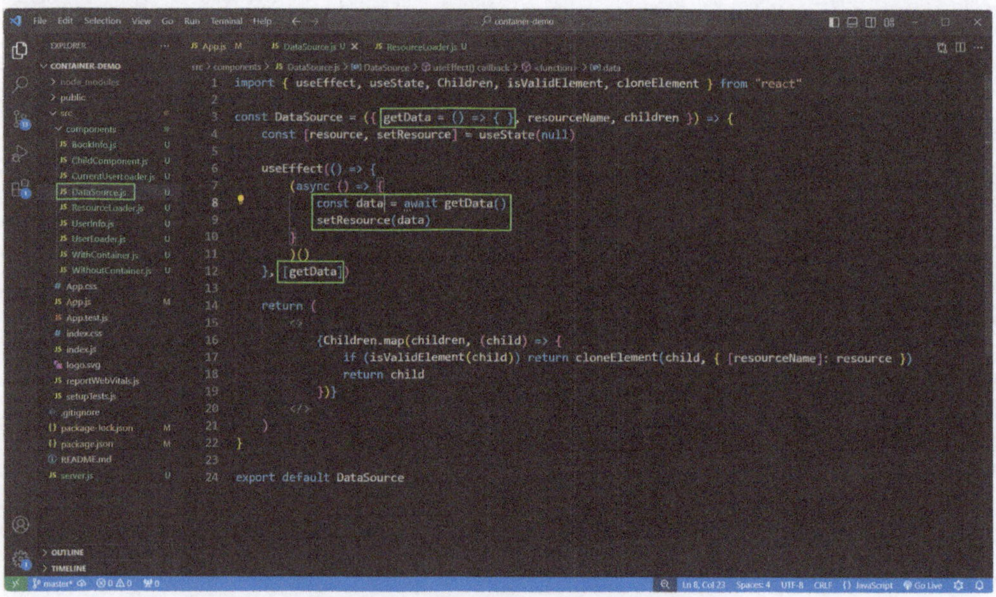

Figure 3.26: *Creating DataSource.js File*

Back in the **App.js** file, we are importing axios, **DataSource** and **UserInfo** first. After that, we have a **getDataFromServer** function which gets an **url** parameter, and does a '**get call**' through axios, as well as returns the received data.

Inside the **return** statement, we are calling the **DataSource** component, and passing the props of **getData** and **resourceName**. Here, we are passing **UserInfo** as children props.

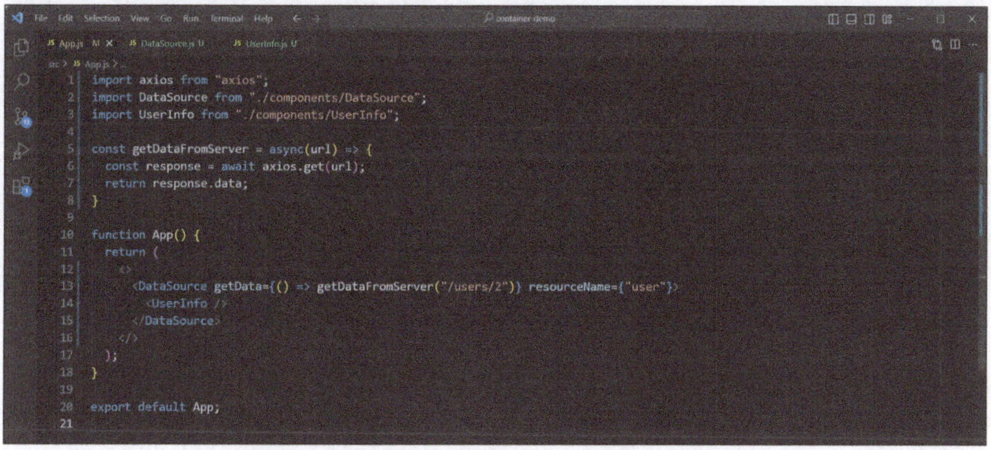

Figure 3.27: *Calling DataSource from App.js File*

Now, in http://localhost:3000/, we are getting the User Data of the second user.

Figure 3.28: *Localhost Showing User Data of the Second User*

Render Props Pattern

In the previous components such as **DataSource** or **ResourceLoader**, we have used the clone element, which is quite a good approach. But we have an alternative way to render props.

So, create a new file, **DataSourceRender.js** inside the **components** folder. It is similar to our **DataSource.js** file, but here we are passing the render props. Also, with the render prop, we will return the resource.

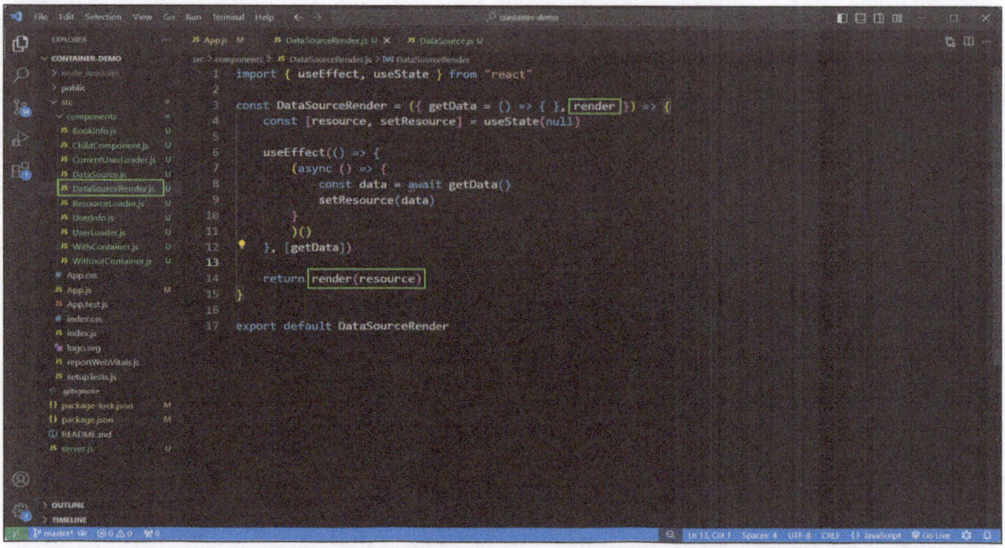

Figure 3.29: *Creating DataSourceRender File*

Back in the **`App.js`** file, we are calling the **`DataSourceRender`** component. Here, we are first passing the **`getData`** props, as earlier. But we are also passing the render props, where in the resource, we are calling the **`UserInfo`** component, and passing the resource for the user.

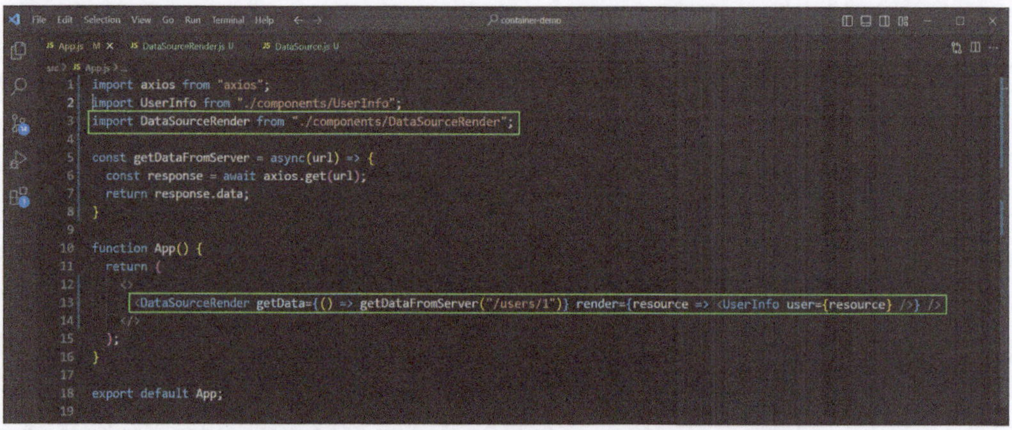

Figure 3.30: *Calling DataSourceRender from App.js File*

Now, in http://localhost:3000/, we are getting the User Data of the first user.

Figure 3.31: *Localhost Showing User Data of the First User*

Conclusion

In this chapter, we have learnt first, why to use container components. After that, we build a simple NodeJS server which is used in this chapter. Next, we have learnt about loader components. Here, we have learnt about the user data loader and resource data loader.

Then, we learnt about the **`DataSource component`**, and lastly, we have converted a major part of the code, using the Render Props pattern.

In the next chapter, we will learn about controlled and uncontrolled components which is a common way in React for creating forms.

Points to Remember

- We should know where to **`useContainer`** Components.
- Creating **`Loader`** Components and **`DataSource`** Components by getting json data from API.
- Using the **`Render props`** pattern to simplify the complex **`Children`** pattern.

CHAPTER 4
Controlled and Uncontrolled Components

Introduction

In this chapter, we will be exploring Controlled and Uncontrolled components.

These patterns are common in React, and hence, it is essential to understand their differences and use cases. We will learn about both of them in detail in the upcoming sections.

Structure

In this chapter, we are going to discuss the following topics:

- Uncontrolled Components
- Controlled Components
- Controlled Modals
- Uncontrolled Flows
- Controlled Flows

Uncontrolled Components

React uncontrolled components are those where the component itself manages its own internal state, and the data within the component is typically accessed, only when specific events happen.

We have created a new React project called **`ctrl-unctrl-demo`** for this chapter. Here, we will create a file called **`UncontrolledForm.js`** inside the **`components`** folder. It contains a simple form with a name and age input fields. We are using **createRef** to have references to these input fields.

We also have a button of type **submit**, which will run a function called **submitHandler**. Here, we have the usual React code to prevent default. After that, we are console logging the name and age with the **current.value**.

```
import { createRef } from "react"
const UncontrolledForm = () => {
    const nameRef = createRef()
    const ageRef = createRef()
    const submitHandler = e => {
        e.preventDefault()
        console.log(nameRef.current.value)
        console.log(ageRef.current.value)
    }
    return (
        <form onSubmit={submitHandler}>
            <input type="text" placeholder="Enter Name" ref={nameRef}
/>
            <input type="text" placeholder="Enter Age" ref={ageRef}
/>
            <button type="submit">Submit</button>
        </form>
    )
}
export default UncontrolledForm
```

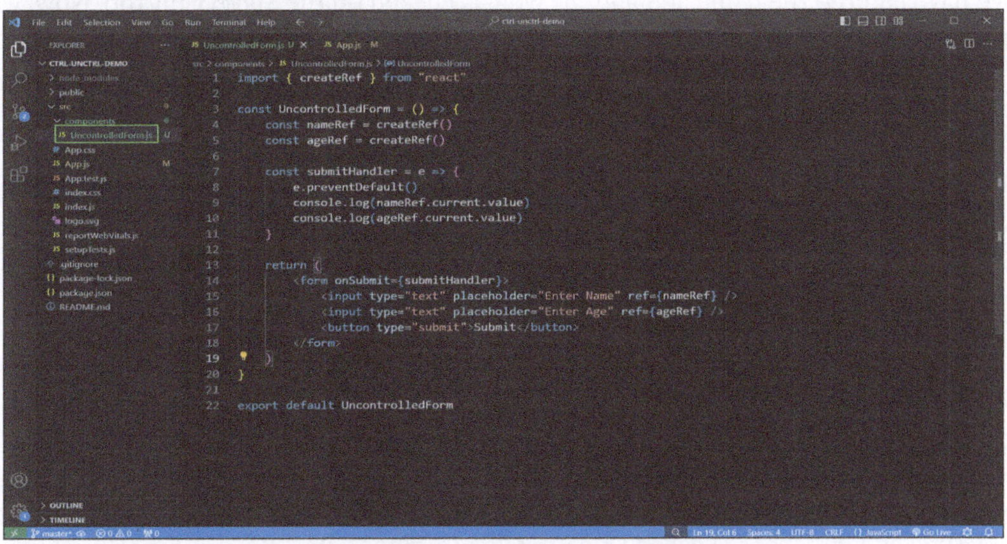

Figure 4.1: *Creating UncontrolledForm.js File*

From the **App.js** file, we are calling the **UncontrolledForm** component.

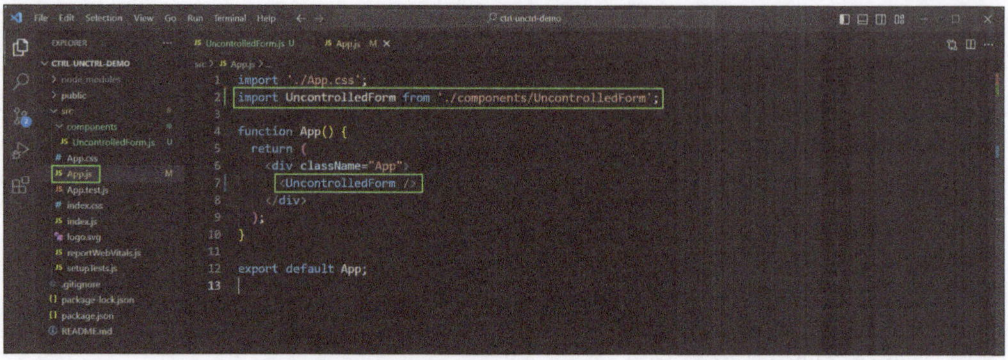

Figure 4.2: *UncontrolledForm from App.js File*

As with **`React`** projects, we will run it with **`npm start,`** and in http://localhost:3000/, we will see the form with the placeholder texts.

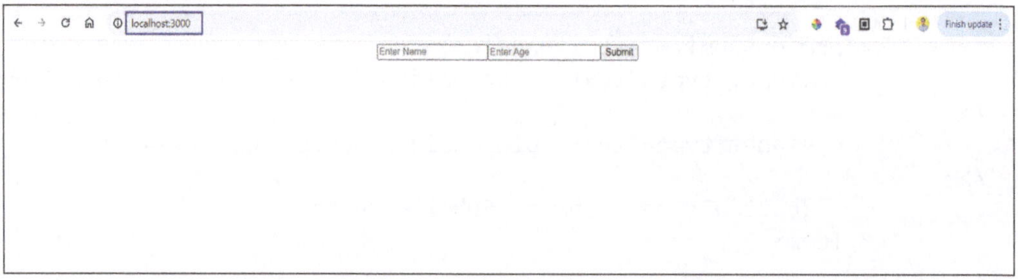

Figure 4.3: *Localhost Showing UncontrolledForm*

We have entered the name and age, as well as clicked on the **`Submit`** button. Now, we are seeing the entered name and age in the console.

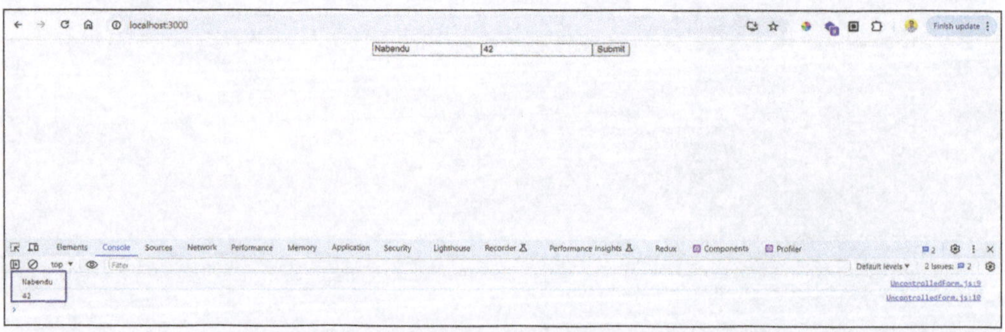

Figure 4.4: *Entered Name and Age Showing in Console*

In this uncontrolled component, the form is not accessible from outside components and parent components, so we have used the **`createRef`** to access the form. Hence, this type of component is called Uncontrolled Components.

Controlled Components

The Controlled Components are those components in which we use a state to manage the fields. Whenever the state is changed, the value gets changed, and we can control them.

Thus, create a new file called **ControlledForm.js** inside the **components** folder. Here, we have a name and age state variables. Inside the form, the value is equal to name and age for the input field.

We have **onChange** handlers in both. So, when the user types on any of them, it will re-render the component, and we will have better control on it. Here, we also have a **Submit** button, which on clicking will show the entered name and age.

```
import { useState } from "react"
const ControlledForm = () => {
    const [name, setName] = useState('')
    const [age, setAge] = useState('')
    const submitHandler = e => {
        e.preventDefault()
        console.log(name)
        console.log(age)
    }
    return (
        <form onSubmit={submitHandler}>
            <input type="text" placeholder="Enter Name" value={name}
onChange={e => setName(e.target.value)} />
            <input type="text" placeholder="Enter Age" value={age}
onChange={e => setAge(e.target.value)} />
            <button type="submit">Submit</button>
        </form>
    )
}
export default ControlledForm
```

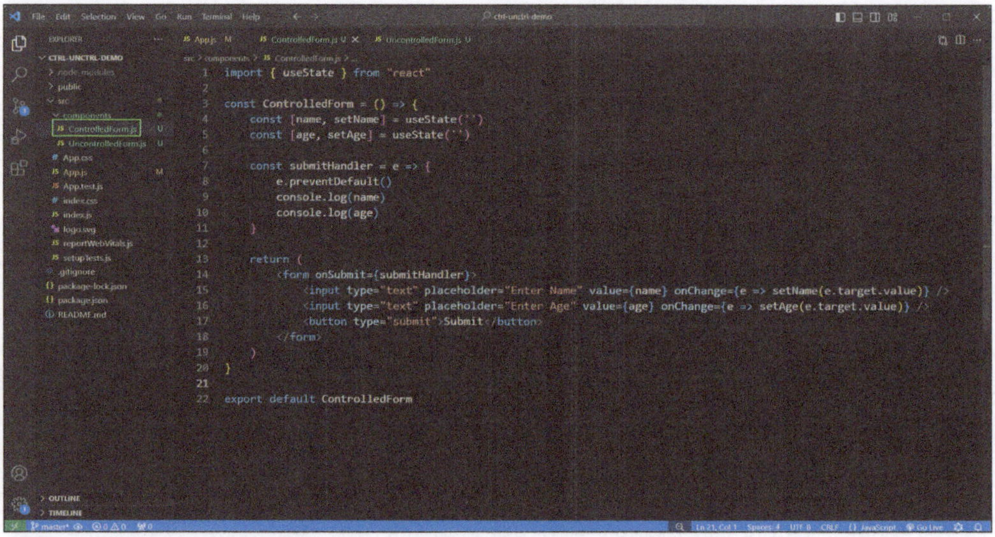

Figure 4.5: *Creating ControlledForm.js File*

Next, we will add this **`ControlledForm`** component in the **`App.js`** file.

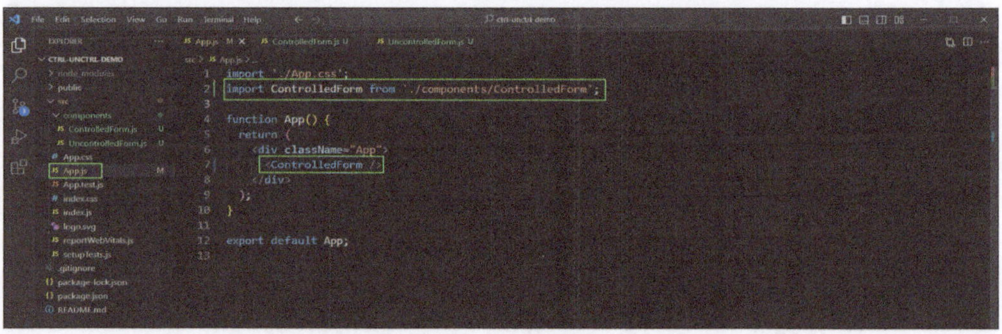

Figure 4.6: *ControlledForm from App.js File*

Now in http://localhost:3000/, we will see the form. On entering the value, and clicking on the **`Submit`** button, we can see the same in the console.

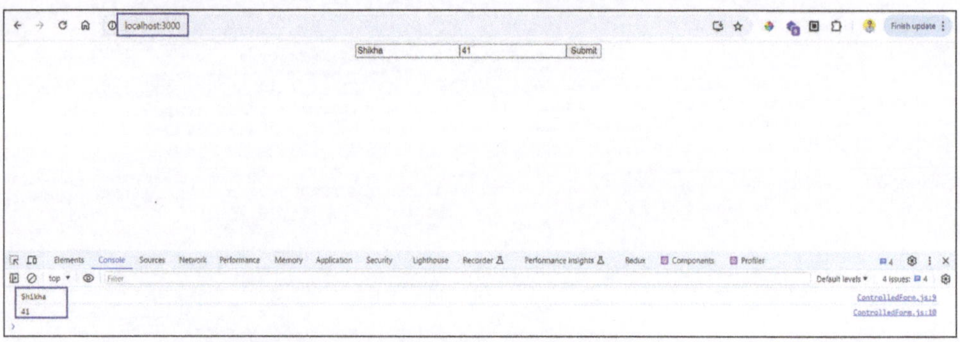

Figure 4.7: *Entered Name and Age Showing in Console*

Now, this seems like the earlier Uncontrolled form only. Hence, what is the benefit? As told earlier, we have better control on the form elements. To show the same, we have created a new state called **error**. After that in a **useEffect** with dependent of age, which means it will run on initial render, and on age change. Here, we are checking if the age is less than 9. It is, then gives an error message, or else an empty screen.

Inside the return statement, we are showing the error, if it is available.

```
const [error, setError] = useState('')
useEffect(() => {
   Number(age) < 9 ? setError('Age cannot be empty or less than 9')
: setError('')
}, [age])
```

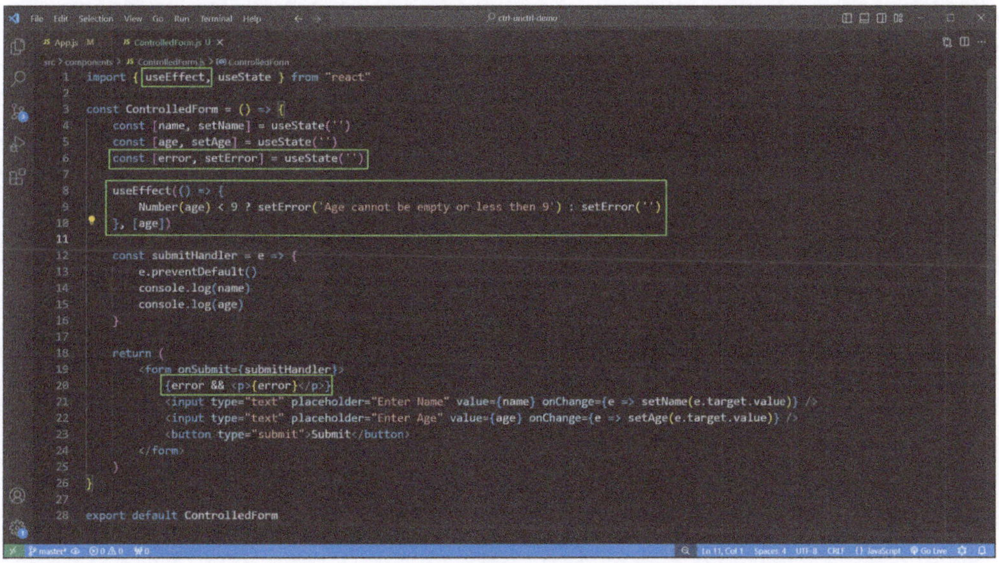

Figure 4.8: *ControlledForm Changes*

Back in http://localhost:3000/, we will see the error, as we have not entered anything in age.

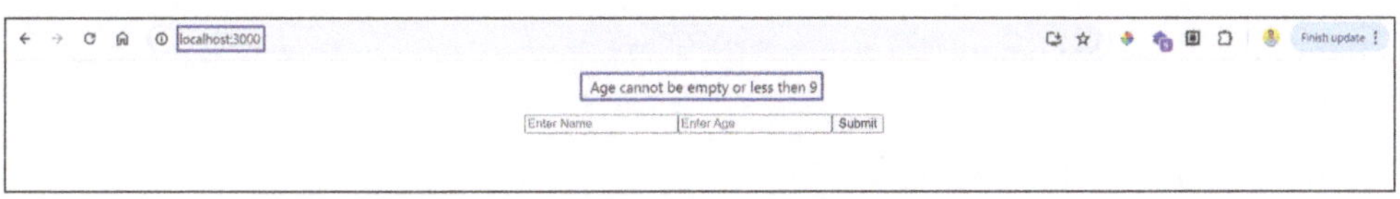

Figure 4.9: *Localhost Error on No Age*

Now, we have entered the age 8, which is less than 9 and so, we are still getting the error.

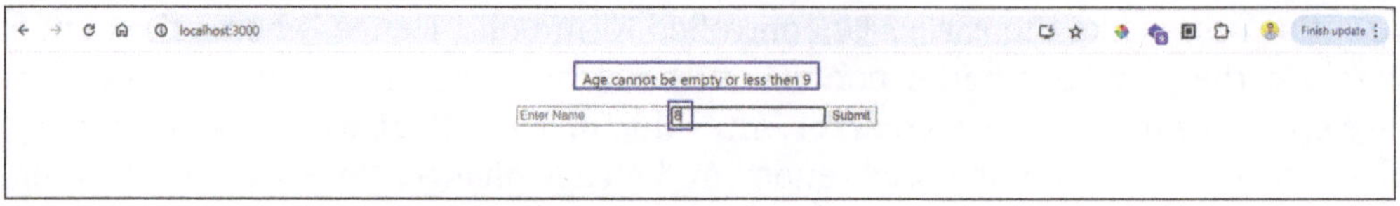

Figure 4.10: *Localhost Error on Age Less Than 9*

But if we enter 9, then the error is gone.

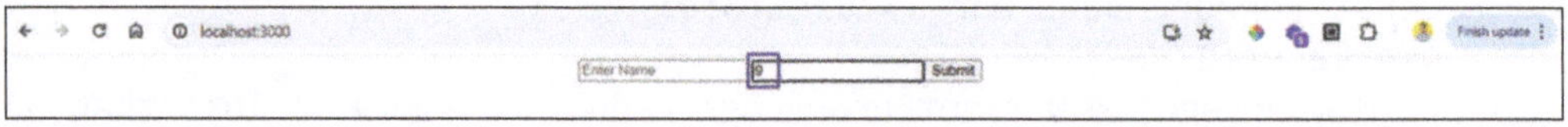

Figure 4.11: *Localhost Success on Age of 9*

Controlled Modals

One of the salient features of Controlled Components is that they can be controlled from the parent component also. Now, we have added the **`Modal.js`** file in our components folder. It is the same modal that we had created in *Chapter 2, Layout Components*.

```
import { useState } from "react";
import styled from "styled-components";
const ModalBackground = styled.div`
    position: absolute;
    left: 0;
    top: 0;
    overflow: auto;
    background: #00000070;
    width: 100%;
    height: 100%;
`;
const ModalContent = styled.div`
    margin: 12% auto;
    padding: 24px;
    background: wheat;
    width: 50%;
`;

const Modal = ({ children }) => {
    const [show, setShow] = useState(false);
    return (
        <>
            <button onClick={() => setShow(true)}>Show Modal</button>
            {show && (
                <ModalBackground onClick={() => setShow(false)}>
                    <ModalContent onClick={e => e.stopPropagation()}>
```

```
                        <button onClick={() => setShow(false)}>Hide
Modal</button>
                        {children}
                    </ModalContent>
                </ModalBackground>
            )}
        </>
    )
}
export default Modal
```

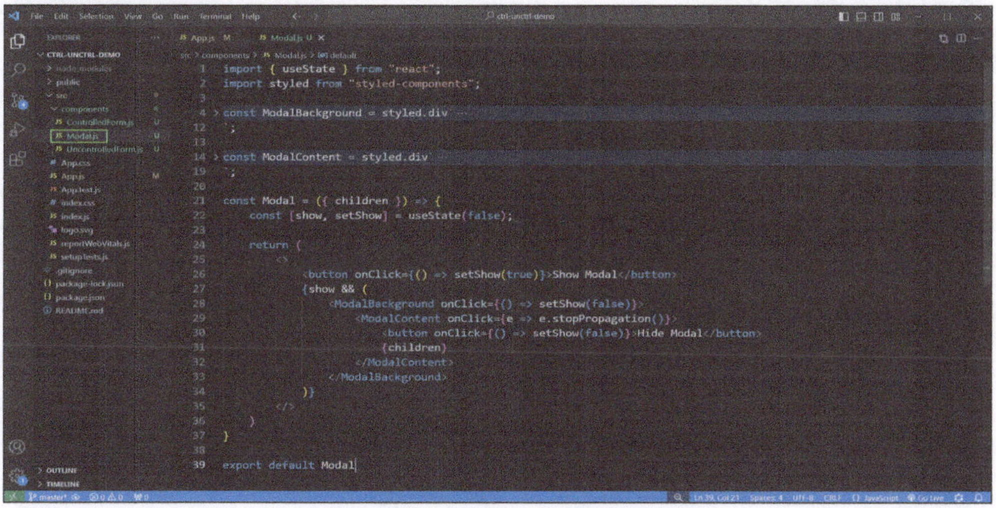

Figure 4.12: *Creating Modal.js File*

Now, we will be calling it from the **`App.js`** file.

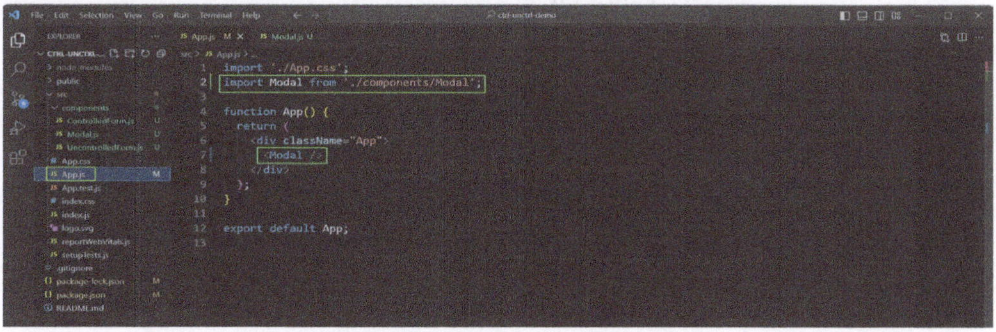

Figure 4.13: *Modal from App.js File*

Next, in http://localhost:3000/, we have the modal shown on clicking the **Show Modal** button.

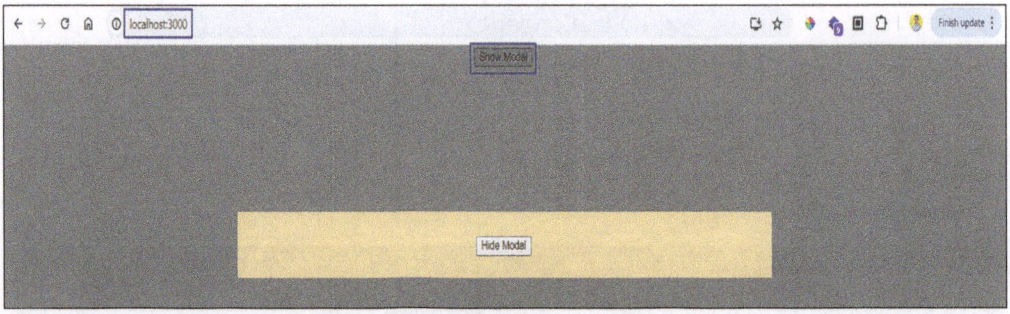

Figure 4.14: *Localhost Showing Modal*

Now, this is an uncontrolled modal, because we cannot control it from the **App.js** file. So, we will create a new **ControlledModal.js** file in the components folder. It is similar to the Modal Component in styling, but we are getting two new props of show and **onClose**.

The show props are showing the Modal, and the **onClose** will close the modal.

```
const ControlledModal = ({ show, onClose, children }) => {
    return (
        <>
            {show && (
                <ModalBackground onClick={onClose}>
                    <ModalContent onClick={e => e.stopPropagation()}>
                        <button onClick={onClose}>Hide Modal</button>
                        {children}
                    </ModalContent>
                </ModalBackground>
            )}
        </>
    )
}
```

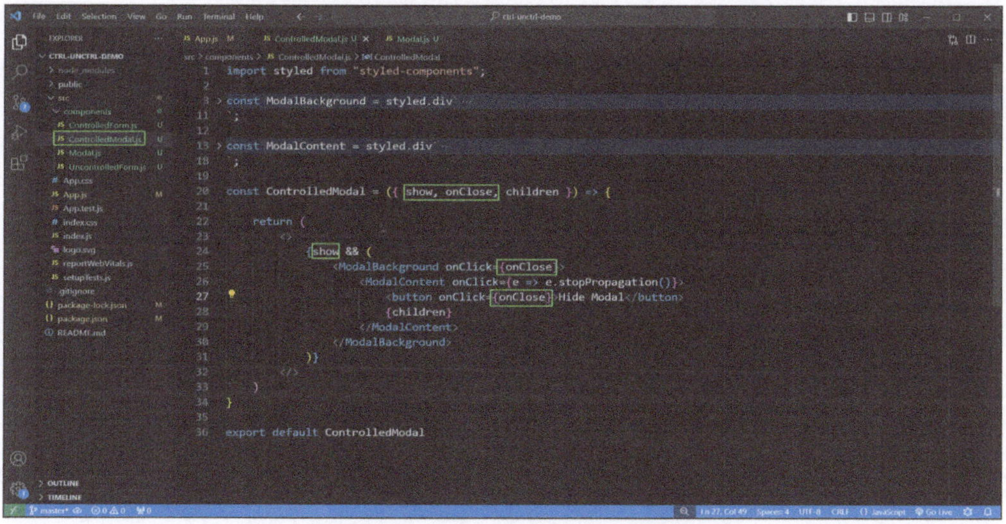

Figure 4.15: *Creating ControlledModal.js File*

Now, in **App.js**, we will first import the **ControlledModal** and also the **useState** hook. Next, we have a show state variable, and inside the **return** statement, we will be passing the show and **onClose** as props.

We also have a button to display the modal here. In the button, we are using the show in showing the different text of **Hide Modal** and **Display Modal**.

```
function App() {
  const [show, setShow] = useState(false)
  return (
    <div className="App">
      <ControlledModal show={show} onClose={() => setShow(false)}>
        <h3>This is a Controlled Modal</h3>
      </ControlledModal>
      <button onClick={() => setShow(!show)}>{show ? 'Hide Modal'
: 'Display Modal'}</button>
    </div>
  );
}
```

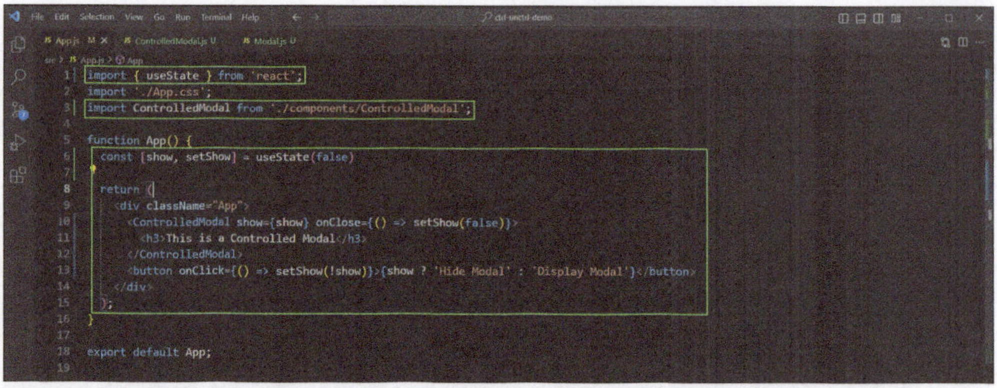

Figure 4.16: *ControlledModal from App.js File*

Back in http://localhost:3000/, we will see the **`Display Modal`** in the button, because the state show is false.

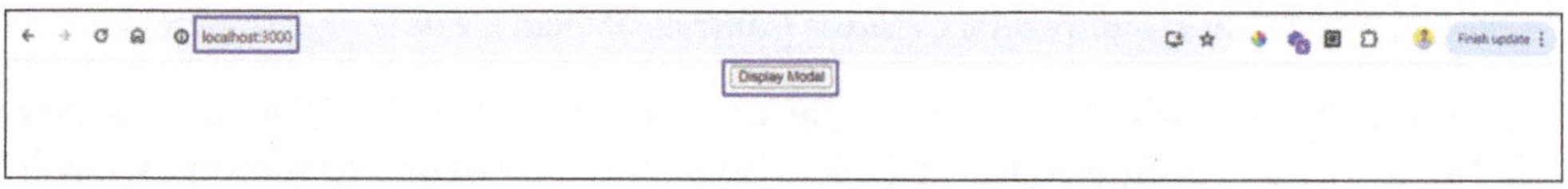

Figure 4.17: *Localhost Showing Display Modal Button*

Now, when we clicked on the button, it displayed the **`Hide Modal text,`** and also the modal was shown properly.

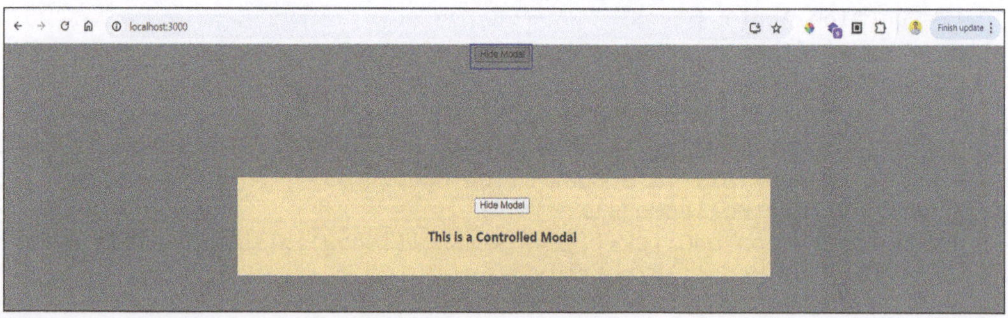

Figure 4.18: *Clicking on Button Showing Modal*

Uncontrolled Flows

In this part, we will learn about **`Uncontrolled Flows`**, and more specific onboarding flows. There are applications where we fill a form, which is going to have several steps that happen when we click a button. Additionally, each step will ask you for specific information such as name, age, and so on. Each step will have a **`Next`** and **`Previous`** button.

Each step is going to grab some data from the client till you reach the last step of that flow. We need to save the data till it reaches the last flow. For this, we will create a new file called **UncontrolledFlow.js** inside the **components** folder. Here, we are taking the children prop first. After that, we have a state called **currentStepIdx**.

We have a function called **nextStep** which will increase the **currentStepIdx** by 1. Then we have a **currentChild** variable that we are getting by using the Children, and converting to an array. Inside the array, we are passing the **currentStepIdx**.

Next, in an **if** statement, we are checking if the **currentChild** is a valid element, and returning the **currentChild** as well as the **nextStep**, or else, we are just returning the **currentChild**.

```
import { Children, cloneElement, isValidElement, useState } from "react"
const UncontrolledFlow = ({ children }) => {
    const [currentStepIdx, setCurrentStepIdx] = useState(0)
    const nextStep = () => setCurrentStepIdx(currentStepIdx + 1)
    const currentChild = Children.toArray(children)[currentStepIdx]
    if(isValidElement(currentChild)) return cloneElement(currentChild, { nextStep })
    return currentChild;
}
export default UncontrolledFlow
```

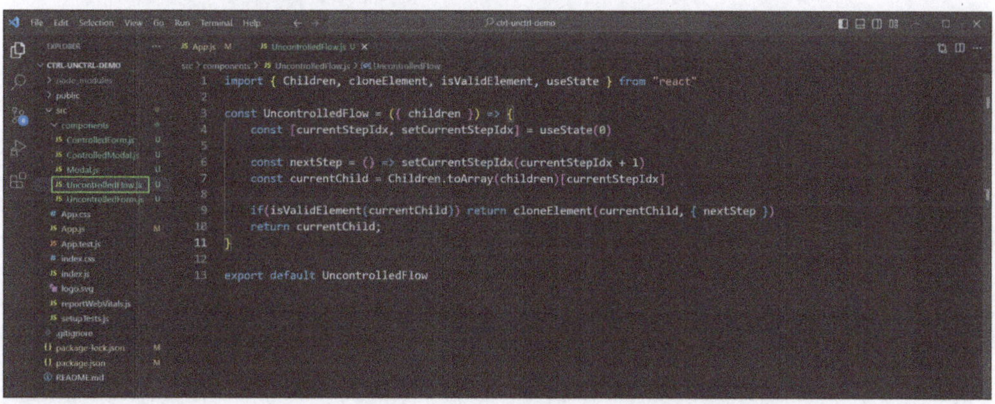

Figure 4.19: *Creating UncontrolledFlow.js File*

Now, in the **App.js** file, we are first importing the **UncontrolledFlow**. After that, we have three functions called **FirstStep**, **SecondStep**, and **ThirdStep** which are taking the **nextStep** as props. They are having a simple **h1**, and a button which on clicking will call the **nextStep**.

```
import './App.css';
import UncontrolledFlow from './components/UncontrolledFlow';
const FirstStep = ({ nextStep }) => {
  return (
```

```
    <>
      <h1>Step No. 1</h1>
      <button onClick={nextStep}>Next</button>
    </>
  )
}

const SecondStep = ({ nextStep }) => {
  return (
    <>
      <h1>Step No. 2</h1>
      <button onClick={nextStep}>Next</button>
    </>
  )
}
const ThirdStep = ({ nextStep }) => {
  return (
    <>
      <h1>Step No. 3</h1>
      <button onClick={nextStep}>Next</button>
    </>
  )
}
```

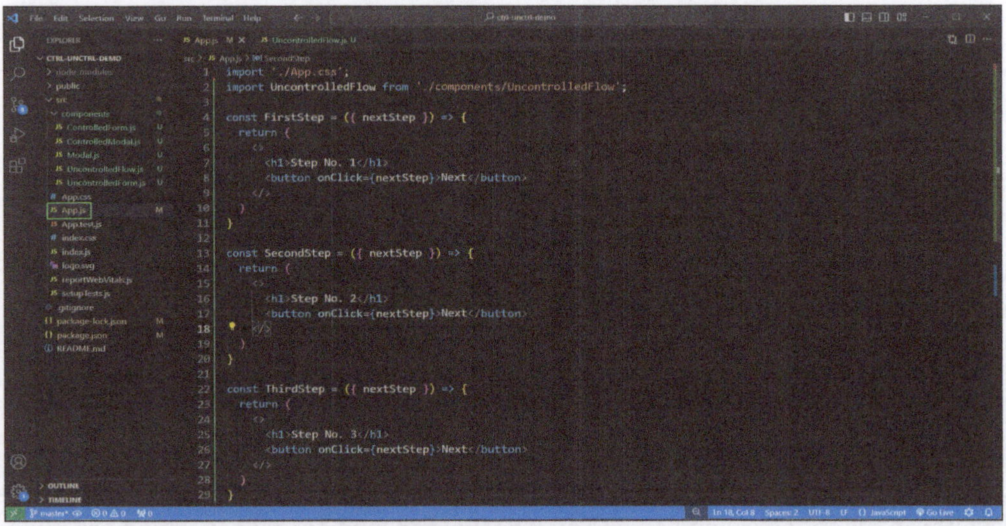

***Figure 4.20:** Steps in App.js File*

In the **return** statement, we will call the **UncontrolledFlow**, and inside it will pass the **FirstChild**, **SecondChild**, and **ThirdChild** as children props.

```
function App() {
  return (
```

```
        <div className="App">
          <UncontrolledFlow>
            <FirstStep />
            <SecondStep />
            <ThirdStep />
          </UncontrolledFlow>
        </div>
      );
    }
    export default App;
```

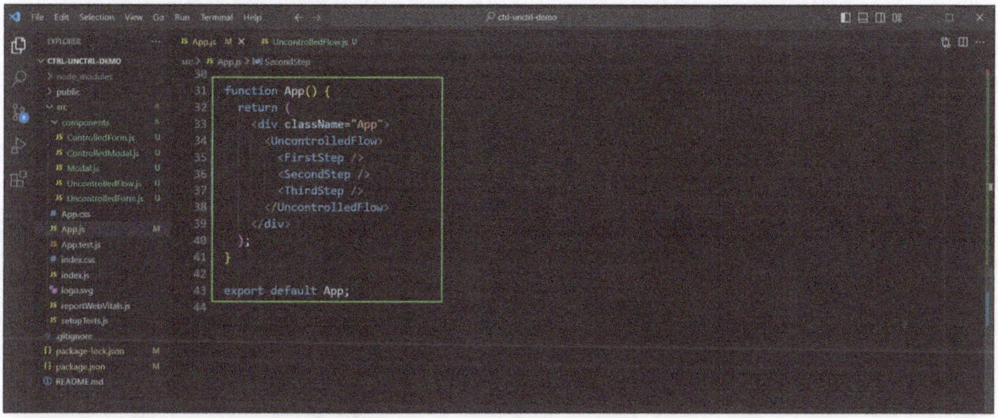

Figure 4.21: *UncontrolledFlow from App.js File*

Now, in http://localhost:3000/, we will first find the **`Step No. 1`** text, and a **`Next`** button from the **`FirstStep`** component. Then click on the **`Next`** button.

Figure 4.22: *Localhost Showing Step 1*

We are been shown the **`Step No. 2`** text, and the **`Next`** button in http://localhost:3000/

Figure 4.23: *Localhost Showing Step 2*

Collecting Data

The uncontrolled flow which we created in the previous section, will be changed to a controlled flow in the next section. The uncontrolled flow just goes to the next step, but does not collect any data. In this part, we are going to collect the data, and use it.

Now, in the **UncontrolledFlow.js file**, we will add one more props called **onDone**. Also, we have created a state variable called **data** which is an object. In the **nextStep** function, we are passing **dataStep** parameters. Inside it, we are first incrementing the current index.

After that in **newData**, we add data with **dataStep** using object restructuring. Next, we will show an alert with the **newData**. After that in an if statement, we are checking that **nextStepIndex** is less than the length of all items. And if it is, then we are updating the current index. Else, if it is the last index, we are calling the prop **onDone,** and passing **newData** in it. Finally, we are setting the data to the **newData**.

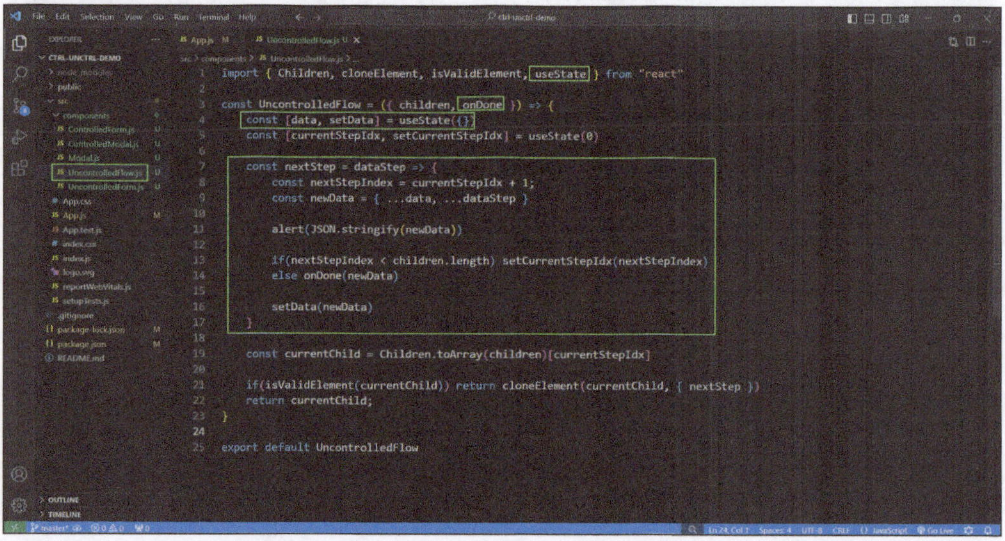

Figure 4.24: *Updating UncontrolledFlow.js File*

Now, in the **App.js** file, we will be updating all the steps. Here, in the **onClick**, we are also passing the **dataStep**, which is an object.

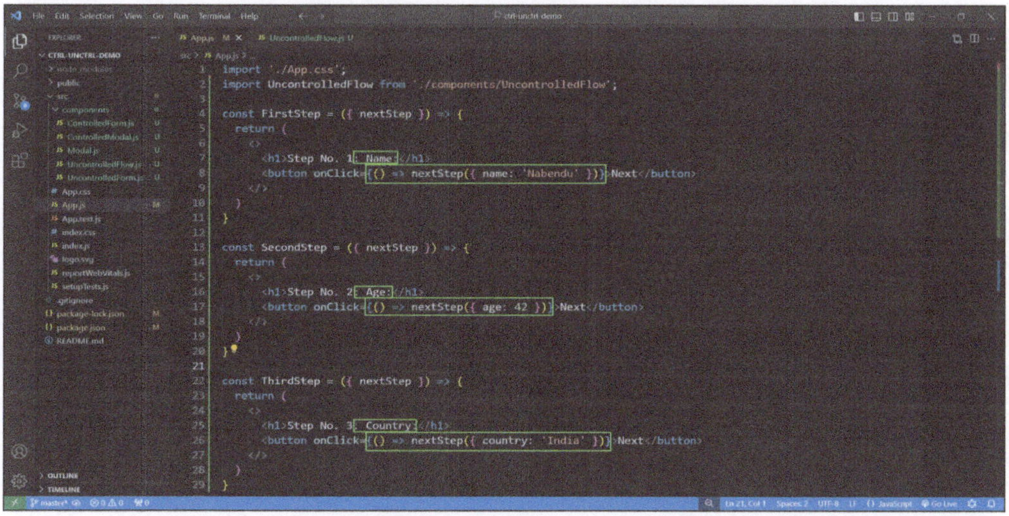

Figure 4.25: *Updating Steps in App.js File*

Next, in the **`UncontrolledFlow`**, we are passing the **`onDone`** props which will take the data, and show an alert.

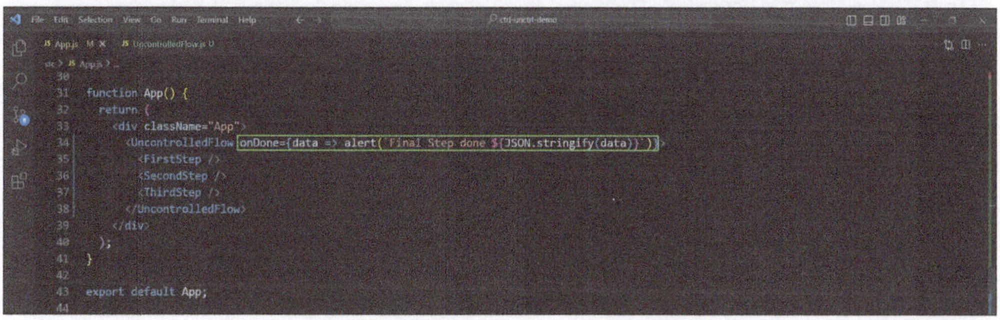

Figure 4.26: *Adding Props in App.js File*

Now, in http://localhost:3000/, click on the **`Next`** button, and we will see the alert with the name object.

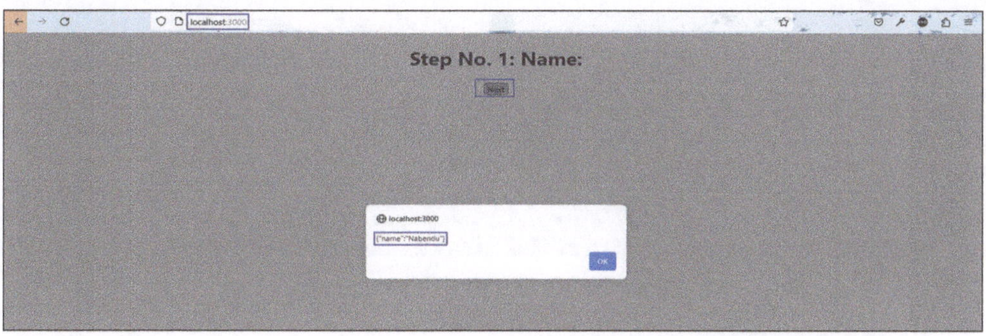

Figure 4.27: *Localhost Name*

On the next click, we will see the alert with the object containing the name and age.

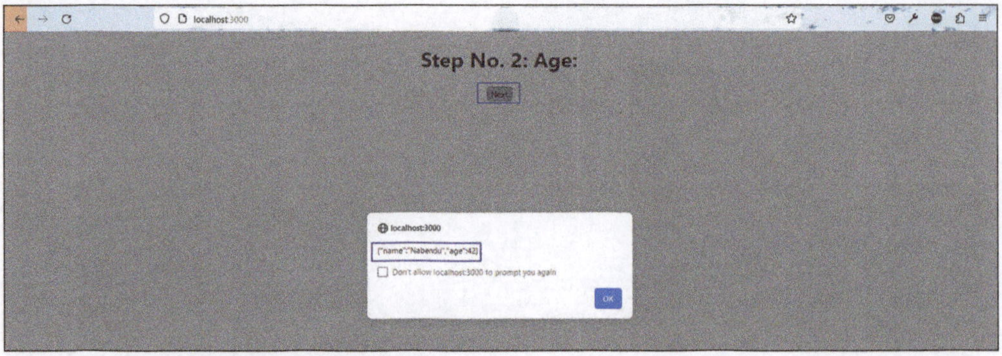

Figure 4.28: *Localhost Name and Age*

On the next click, we will see the alert with the object containing name, age, and country.

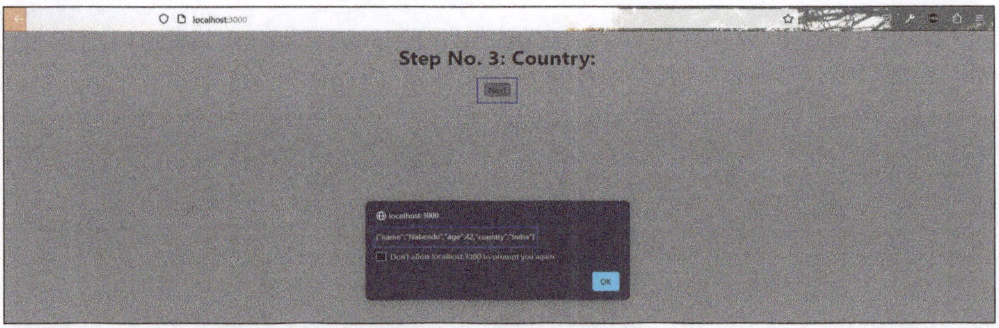

Figure 4.29: *Localhost Name, Age and Country*

Finally, on the last click, we will see the message of the **`Final Step done`** with the complete object.

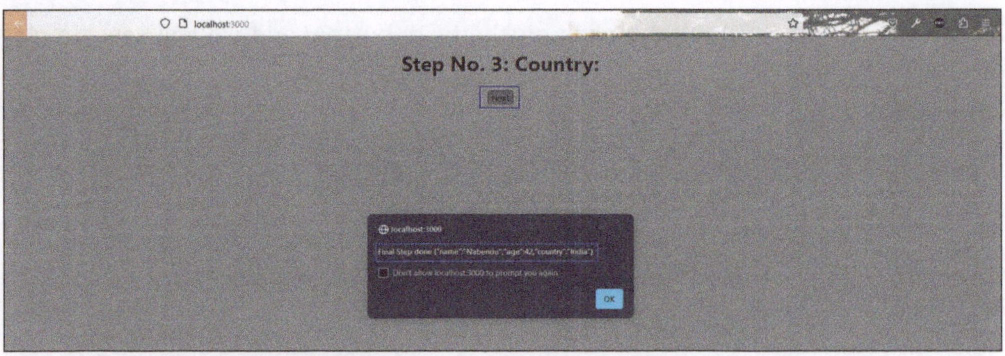

Figure 4.30: *Localhost Final Step*

Controlled Flows

In this section, we will convert our uncontrolled flow into controlled flow. So, first create a new file called **ControlledFlow.js**, and inside it put the following content. This file has far less content than the **UncontrolledFlow.js** file, because we will move the controlling part to the parent component of **App.js**.

Here, we have a **nextStep** function which is taking an argument, and passing it to the **onNext callback** function. Also, we are getting the **currentIndex** as props, and using it in **currentChild**. All the state logic is not here, and has been moved to **App.js** file, which we will check next.

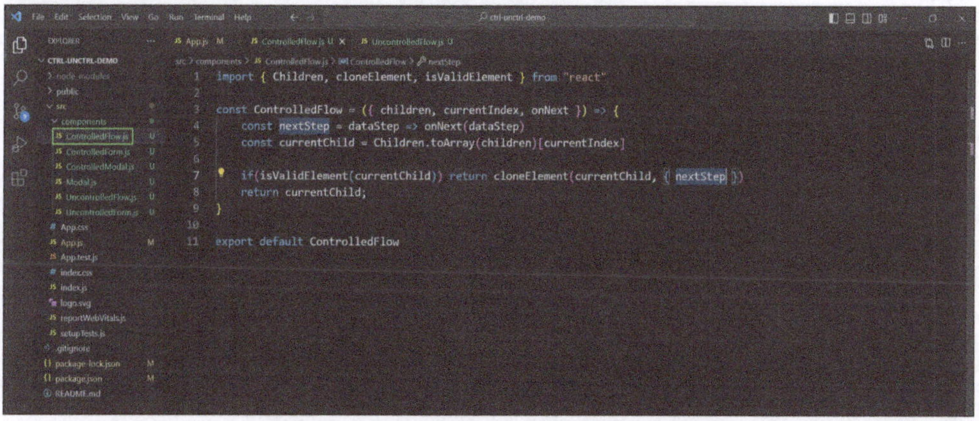

Figure 4.31: *Creating ControlledFlow.js File*

Now, in the **App.js** file, we have the data and the **currentStepIdx** state. We also have the **nextStep** function which is updating the data and **currentStepIdx**. Inside the **return** statement, we are calling the new **ControlledFLow** component, and passing the **currentIndex** as well as the **onNext** index props.

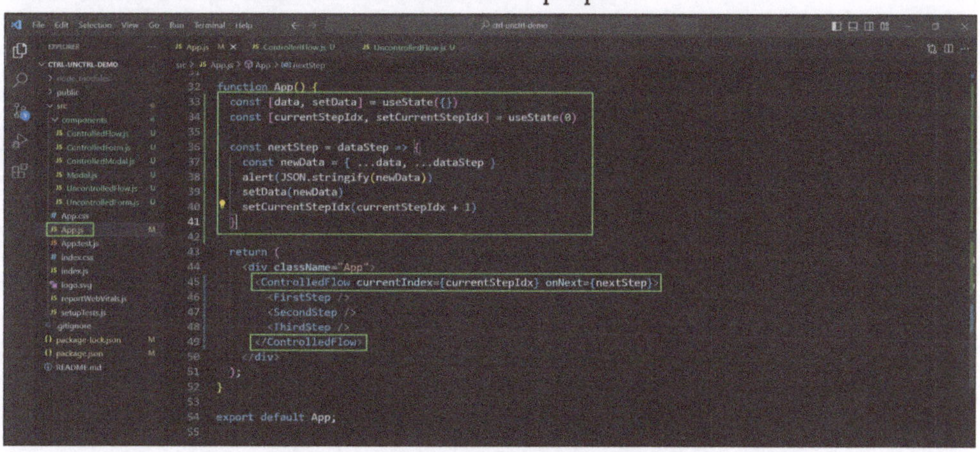

Figure 4.32: *ControlledFlow in App.js File*

Back in http://localhost:3000/, the app is working as earlier, and clicking on the **`Next`** button will open an alert with the object.

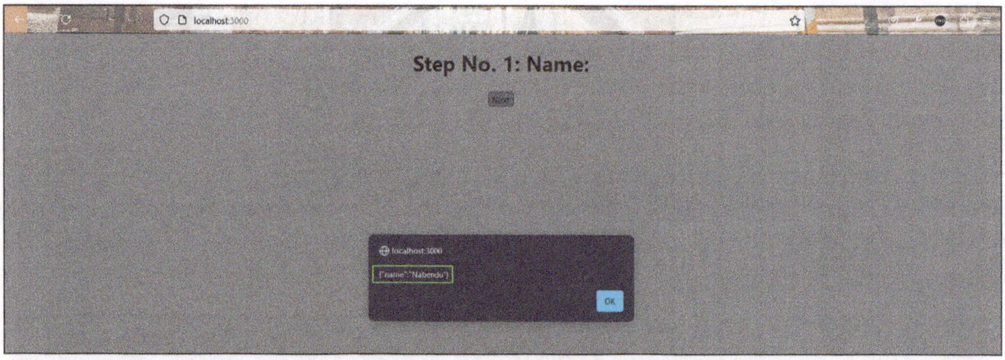

Figure 4.33: *Localhost Showing Name*

Clicking on the last **`Next`** button, will show the complete object.

Figure 4.34: *Localhost Showing Name, Age and Country*

Now, the controlled flow works similar to the uncontrolled flow, except that the main logic is now in the **`Parent`** Component. However, there is not much difference from the uncontrolled flow, only that we can control the steps from the parent file.

So, in the **`App.js`** file, we have first changed the age in **`SecondStep`**. The **`ThirdStep`** is also changed to have a different statement. The earlier **`ThirdStep`** has now been made the **`FourthStep`**.

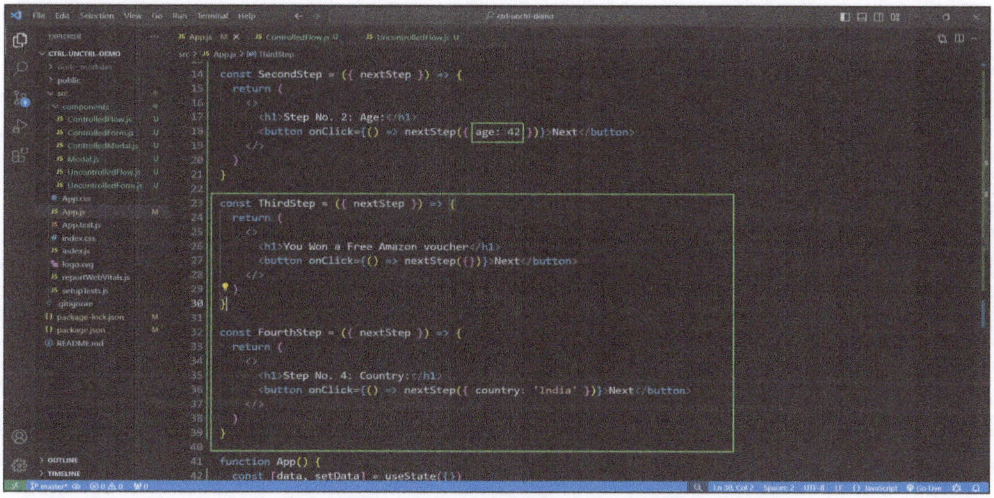

Figure 4.35: *Creating FourthStep in App.js File*

Now, inside the **`return`** statement, we are showing the **`ThirdStep`** component, only if the age is greater than 45. This age, we will get from the **`SecondStep`**.

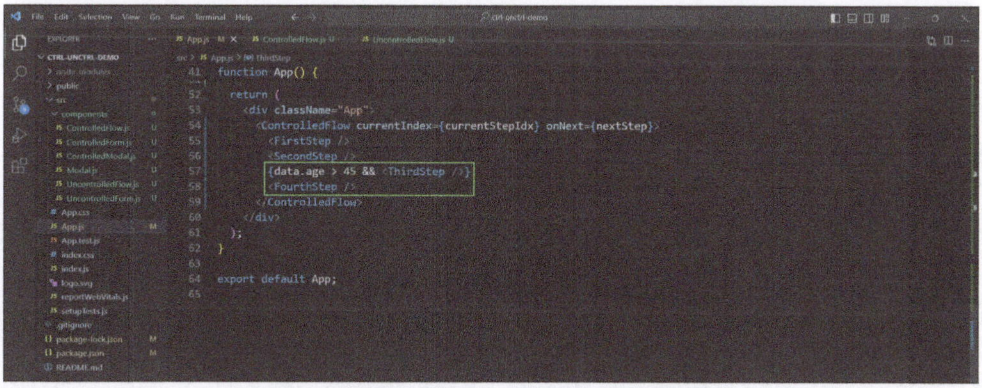

Figure 4.36: *Conditional ThirdStep in App.js File*

Back in http://localhost:3000/, when we click on **`Step No. 2`**, we will get the user name and age.

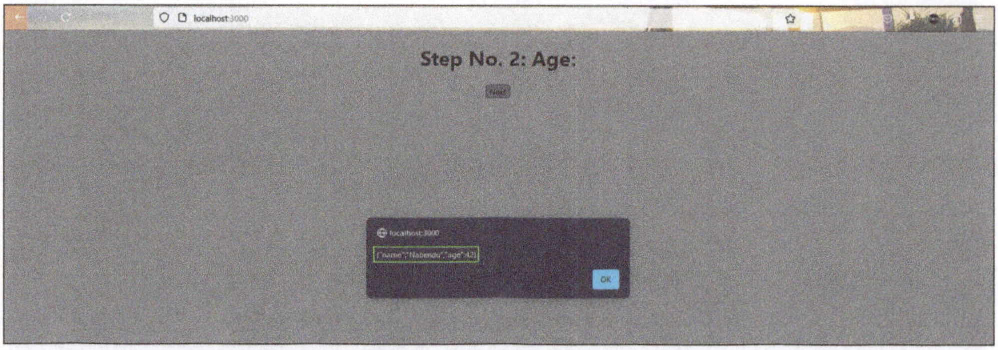

Figure 4.37: *Localhost Showing Name and Age*

Clicking on **`OK`** in the alert, we will skip **`Step No. 3`**, and to go to **`Step No. 4`**. This happens because the age is less than 45.

Figure 4.38: *Localhost Skipping Step No. 3*

Back in **`App.js`**, we will make the age as 46 in the **`SecondStep`**.

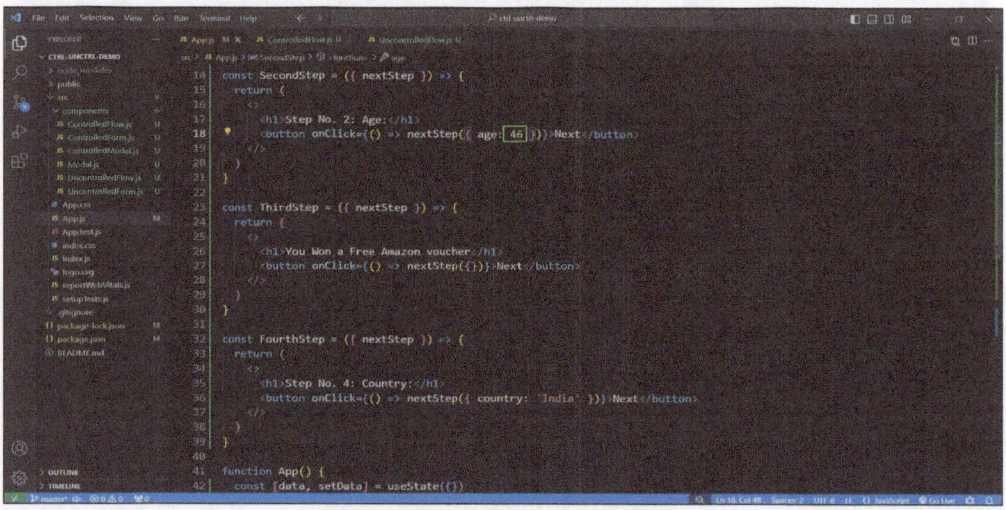

Figure 4.39: *Changing Age in App.js*

Back in http://localhost:3000/, when we click on **`Step No. 2`**, we will get the user name and age.

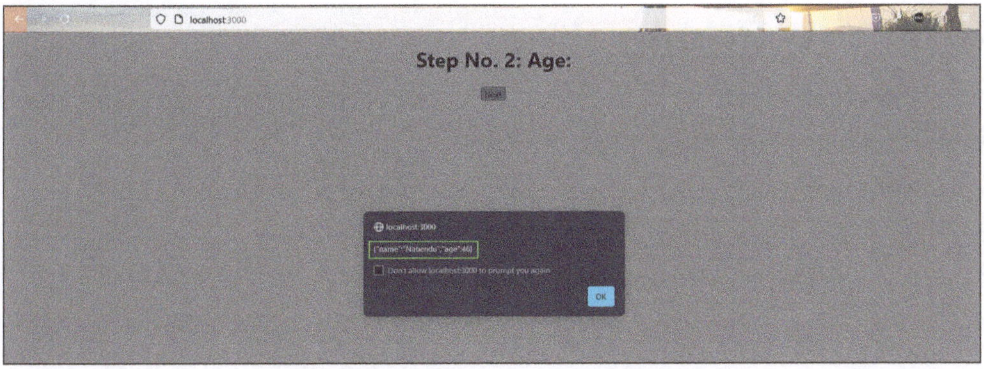

Figure 4.40: *Localhost Showing Name and Age*

Clicking on **`OK`** in the alert, we will show **`Step No. 3`** because the age is greater than 45.

Figure 4.41: *Localhost Showing Step 3*

Conclusion

In this chapter, we have learnt first about uncontrolled components in which the component itself manages its internal state. It is generally done by using common features of Refs in React, which are used in form. Next, we have learnt about Controlled components, where we have used the state in a form to manage it. Next, we have learnt to create a Controlled Modal, where we have used the modal created in the previous chapter.

After this, we have created the Uncontrolled Flow. The flow is basically a feature in which we can go to different steps from a component. Lastly, we created the Controlled Flow, where we have moved the main code of the flow to the parent component. In this way, we were able to manage it better.

In the next chapter, we will learn about two commonly used design patterns of Higher Order Components and Custom Hooks.

Points to Remember

- Different ways to write form, using Uncontrolled and Controlled Components.
- Creating a Controlled Modal.
- Different ways to create flows, using Uncontrolled and Controlled Patterns.

CHAPTER 5
Higher Order Components and Custom Hooks

Introduction

In this chapter, we will be exploring Higher Order Components (HOCs) and Custom Hooks. Both of these are commonly used React patterns, and we will see how to optimise them using React patterns.

We will cover two different topics in this chapter, the first of which is HOCs. HOCs are basically functions which return a component after enhancing it. Then we will learn about custom hooks that help us to create hooks like **`useState`** and **`useEffect`**. We can use them for common functionalities.

Structure

In this chapter, we are going to discuss the following topics:

- Introduction to HOC
- Checking Props with HOC
- Data Loading with HOC
- Updating Data and Building Forms
- Enhancing HOC Patterns
- Introduction to HOC
- Fetching a User with Custom Hooks
- Fetching a Resource with Custom Hook

Introduction to HOC

In this chapter, we will learn about Higher Order Components (HOCs). HOCs are components that instead of directly returning JSX, returns another component.

Most of the people reading this book are aware that React components simply return JSX which represents the DOM elements to be rendered in their place. But with HOCs, we introduce an additional layer, instead of directly returning JSX. In fact, HOCs return another component that in-turn returns JSX.

Higher Order Components (HOCs) essentially function as return components. They are like component factories that generate new components, when they are called. But why do we want to create HOCs?

Firstly, HOCs enable us to share behavior among multiple components. Additionally, HOCs allow us to add extra functionality to the existing components.

Checking Props with HOCs

In this part, we will create an HOC, and pass props in it. For this, we will be using the code from *Chapter* 3, *Container Components*. Here, we have only the **`server.js`** and **`UserInfo.js`** from the earlier chapter.

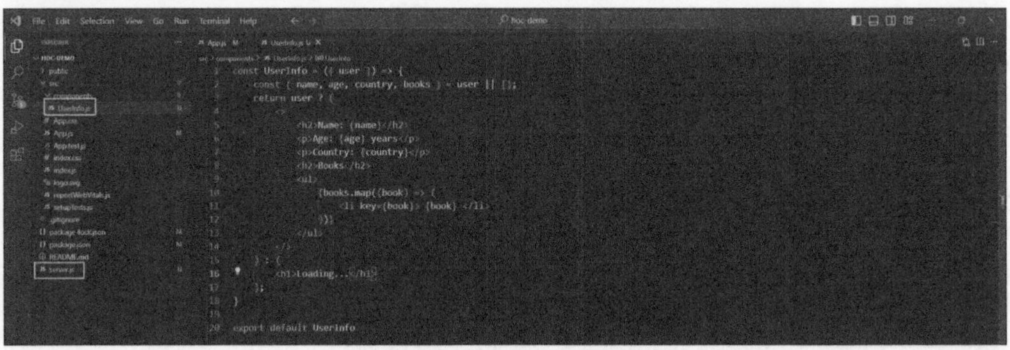

Figure 5.1: *Creating the Project*

In the **`App.js`**, we have removed all the codes.

Figure 5.2: *App.js File*

Next, inside the **`components`** folder, we will create a **`logProps.js`** file. It is an HOC which takes a component, and then inside the component, takes the props and returns it.

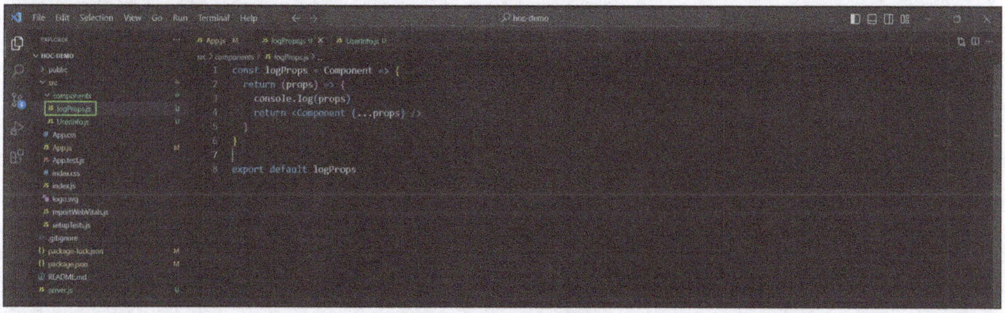

Figure 5.3: *LogProps.js File*

Now, in the **`App.js`** file, we will first import the **`logProps`** and the **`UserInfo`** file. Thus, we have created an **`UserInfoWrapper`** constant. It takes the **`logProps`** component, and passes the **`UserInfo`**.

Then inside the **`return`** statement, we pass the **`UserInfoWrapper`** and the example props of test and **`numTest`**. We also run the **`npm i`** command in the terminal to install all packages from the **`package.json`** file.

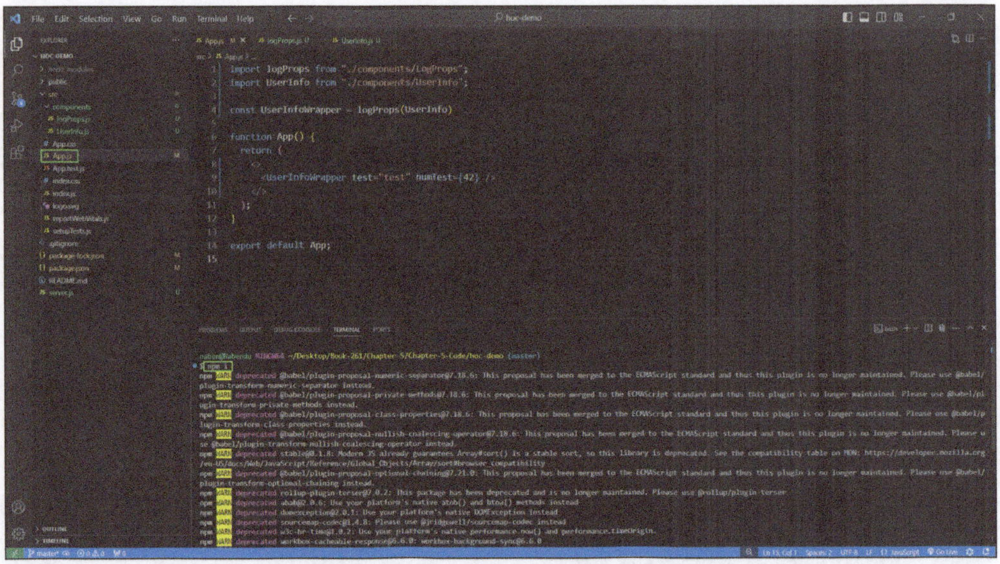

Figure 5.4: *Updating App.js and npm Install*

Now, we will run the server with **`node server.js`** from a terminal, and the react component with **`npm start`**.

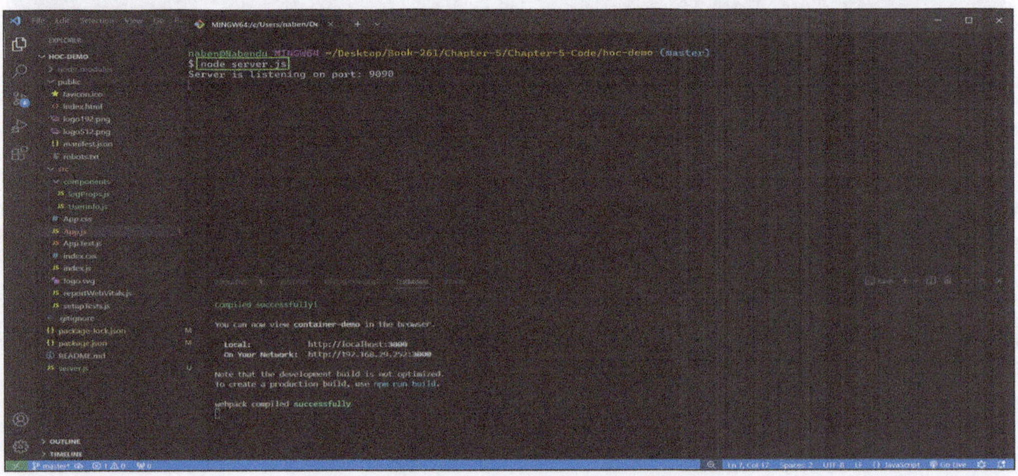

Figure 5.5: *Running Frontend and Backend*

Next, going to http://localhost:3000/, we will show the **`props in the console`** from the **`logProps.js`** file.

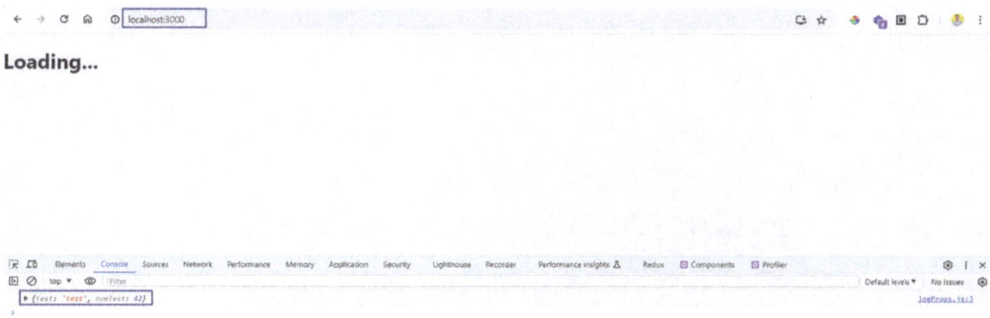

Figure 5.6: *Localhost Console Showing Object*

Data Loading with HOC

In the previous section, we have created the HOC, but were only showing props in the console. Now, in this section, we will show the real data. So, create a new file, **`includeUser.js`**, and put the following code in it.

In this HOC, we are passing a Component and a **`Prop`** called **`UserId`**. Inside the **`return`** statement, we have a state called user and a **`useEffect`**, which is getting the data from **`/users/userId`** endpoint.

Once we get the data from the single user, and set it in the user, we are returning the component with user prop.

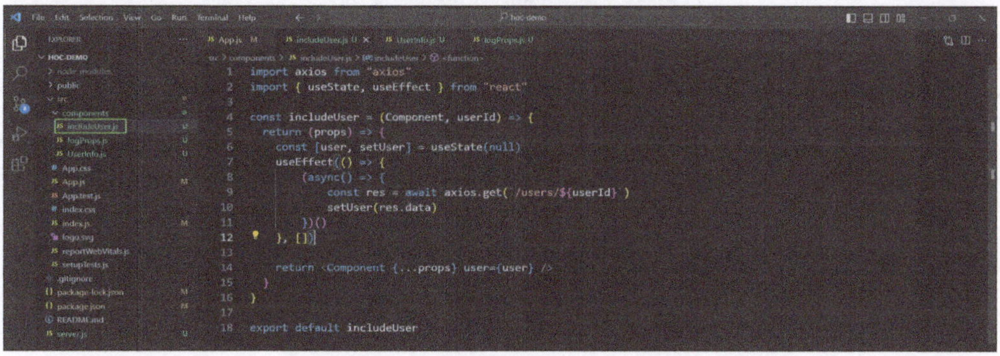

Figure 5.7: *Creating includeUser HOC*

Back in the **`App.js`** file, we will create a new **`UserInfoLoaderWrapper`** in which we will call the **`includeUser`** component. In it, we will pass the **`UserInfo`** and a **`userId`** of 3.

Next, we are calling this **`UserInfoLoaderWrapper`** from the **`return statement`**.

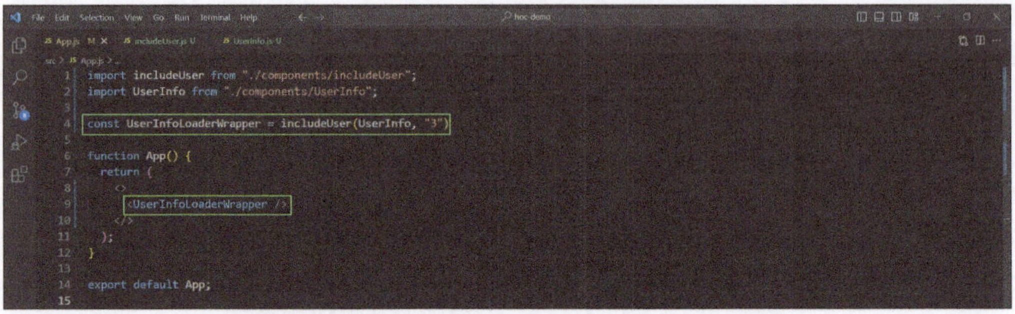

***Figure 5.8:** Calling UserInfoLoaderWrapper from App.js*

Back in http://localhost:3000/, we will see the data for the user with id 3. To get the data, make sure that the backend is running.

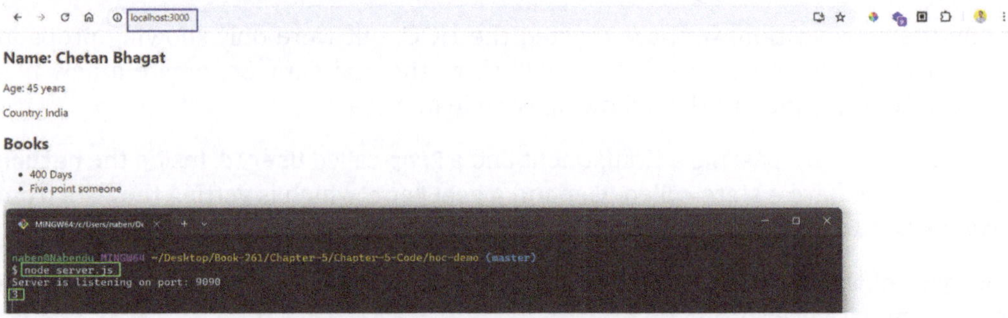

***Figure 5.9:** Localhost Showing User*

Updating Data and Building Forms

In this part, we will enhance our HOC created in the previous part. We are going to have an HOC which does both **GET** and **POST** requests. For the **POST** request, we will have a form.

For this, we will first create a new file, **updateUser.js** in the **components** folder. It is a HOC which is taking **Component** and **UserId** as props. After this, we are returning the props as earlier HOCs, and creating two state variables of **initialUser** and user inside it.

Next, we have a **useEffect** in which we are doing a **GET** api call to get a user with a specific id. We are also setting the received user to **initialUser** and user. Thereafter, we have an **onChangeUser** function that updates the user with the passed updates.

Then, we have an **async** function called **onPostUser** which is doing a **POST** call to update a specific user. We are also setting the **received user** to **initialUser** and the **user**. Thus, we have an **onResetUser** to set the user to the **initialUser**.

Lastly, we are returning the component with the props of the user, **`onChangeUser`**, **`onPostUser`** and **`onResetUser`**.

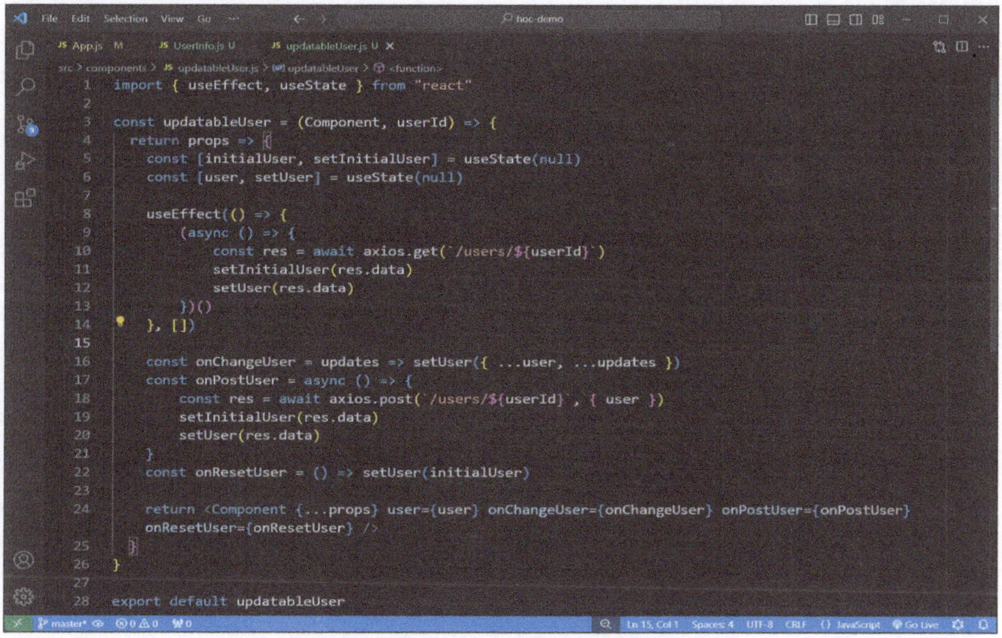

***Figure 5.10:** Creating updateUser HOC*

Now, we will create a component called **`UserInfoForm`**. Here, in the HOC **`updatableUser`**, we shall pass the props of the user, **`onChangeUser`**, **`onPostUser`**, and the **`onResetUser`**. Next, we are extracting the name and age from the user.

If the user is there, we are returning the name and age input boxes, as well as the two buttons for **`Reset`** and **`Save`**. If the user is not there, we will return a loading text. We will also pass the **`userId`** of 3.

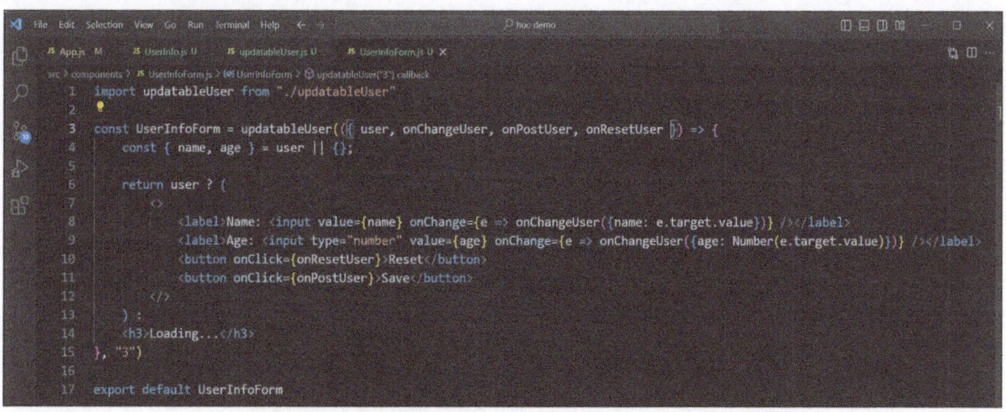

***Figure 5.11:** Creating UserInfoForm Component*

Now, in the **`App.js`** file, we will import the **`UserInfoForm`** component. Also, make sure that the frontend starts with **`npm start`**, and the backend with **`node server.js`** commands.

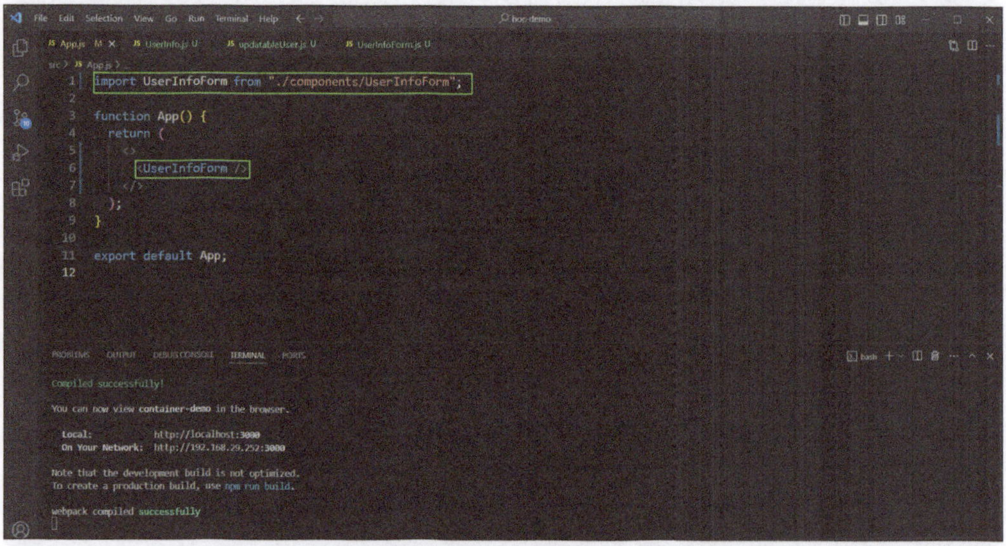

Figure 5.12: *Calling UserInfoForm from App.js*

Next, in http://localhost:3000/, we will see the **`user`** with the **`userId`** of 3. Also, try to change something, and hit the reset button, it will again become the same content.

Figure 5.13: *Localhost Changed Content*

We have changed the content, and hit the **`save`** button. This content will be retained, even if we hit the **`refresh`** in the browser.

Figure 5.14: *Localhost Saved Contents*

Enhancing HOC Pattern

In this part, we are going to enhance the HOC component created in the previous part. So, create a new file called **`updateResource.js`** inside the **`components`** folder. Here, we are first importing the axios, and then the **`useState`** and **`useEffect` hooks**. We have a **`toCapital`** function that makes the first letter as capital, and we will use this function later.

Next, in the **`updateResource`** component, we shall pass the props of the component, **`resourceUrl`** and **`resourceName`**. In the **`return`** statement of props, we have an **`initialResource`** and resource state, first.

Later, in the **`useEffect`**, we call the **`resourceUrl`** with axios, setting the result to **`initialResource`** and resource. Next, we have an **`onChange`** function that takes the updates of props, and sets the resource to resource and updates combined, into a restructured data.

Next, we have an **`onPost`** function which does a POST api call to **`resourceUrl`**. It will pass the **`resourceName`** containing the resource data. After that, we set the initial resource and the updated resource as the response. Lastly, we have an **`onReset`** function which sets the resource as **`initialResource`**.

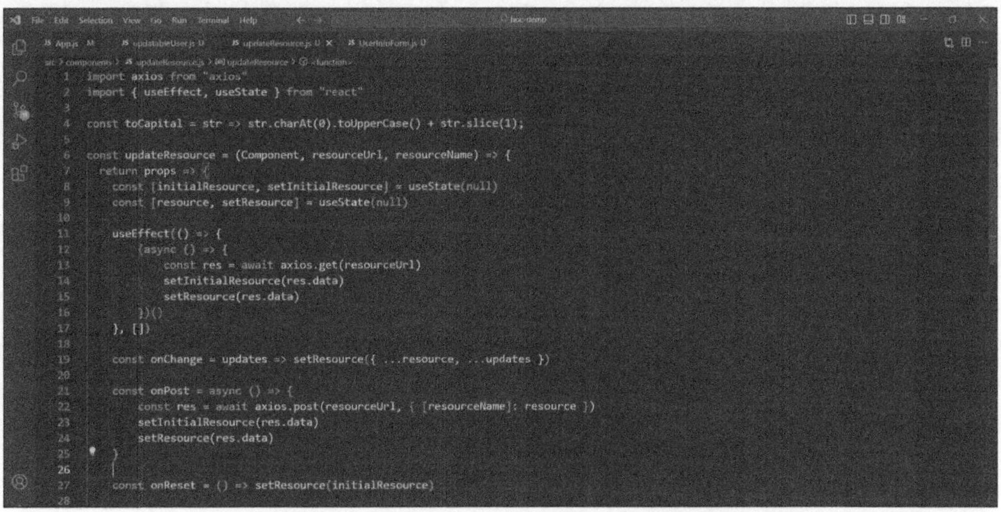

Figure 5.15: *Creating updateResource Component*

We have some more codes left in the **`updateResource.js`** file. Here, we have **`resourceProps`** which is an object. It is first taking **`resourceName`**, and then making it equal to the resource. Next, **`onChange`**, **`onPost`** and **`onReset`** keys are taken. With the help of **`toCapital`**, the first letter of **`resourceName`** will be made capital. If a user is passed, then we will get an **`onChangeUser`**, **`onPostUser`** and **`onResetUser`** as keys.

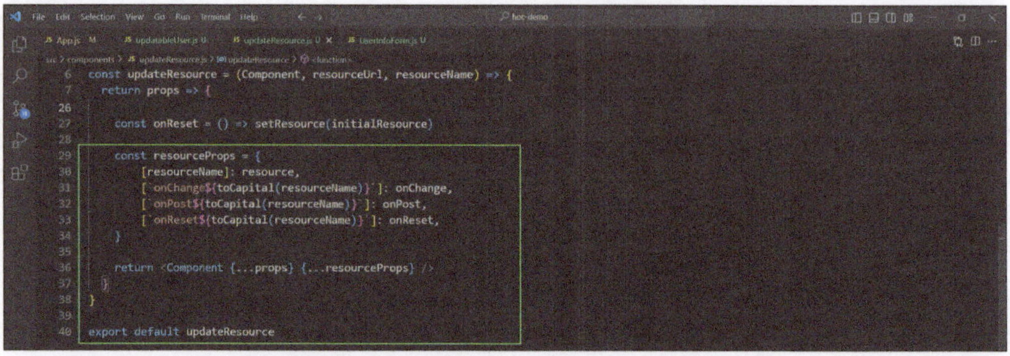

Figure 5.16: *Completing updateResource Component*

Now, in the **`UserInfoForm.js`** file, we will import the **`updateResource`** first. Next, we have changed the parameters as **`/users/2`** and user.

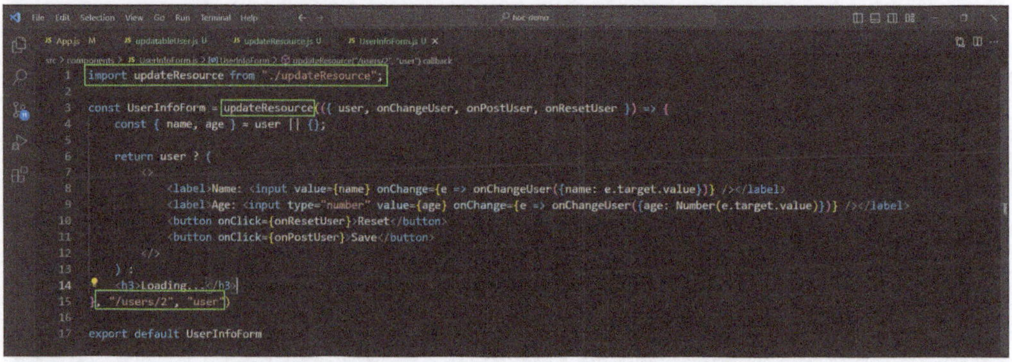

Figure 5.17: *Calling updateResource from UserInfoForm*

Next, go to http://localhost:3000/, but make sure both the frontend and backend are running. Here, change anything, and hit reset, and it will be changed to the earlier data. Also, change the **`Name`** or **`Age`**, and hit **`Save`**. This will save the data.

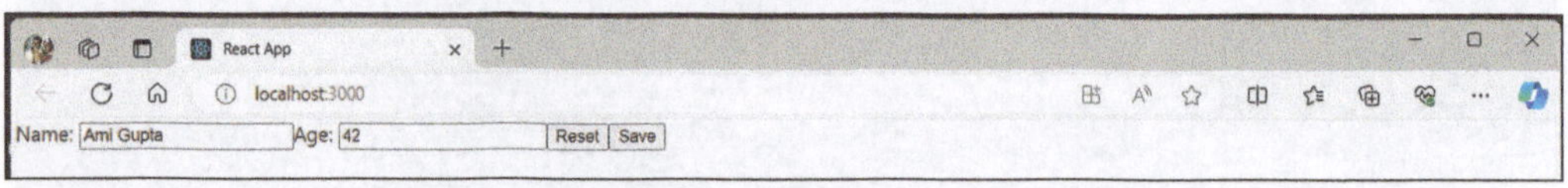

Figure 5.18: *Localhost with Reset and Save*

Introduction to Hooks

In this part, we will learn about custom hooks which are a very powerful design pattern. Custom hooks allow us to combine the existing React hooks such as **`useState`** and **`useEffect`**, and create reusable hooks tailored to specific functionalities.

This allows us to abstract complex behavior into reusable units. Custom hooks should begin with the **`use`** keyword like **`useState`** and **`useEffect`** hooks.

Fetching a User with Custom Hooks

For the hooks, we will create a new **hooks-demo react project**. In the **`package.json` file**, we will add a proxy for our NodeJS code, also adding the dependencies of axios and express.

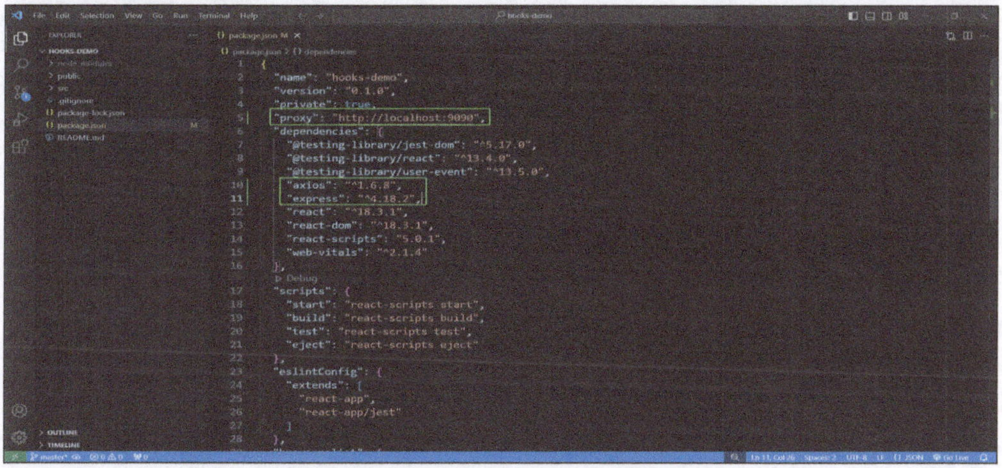

***Figure 5.19:** Creating HOC-DEMO Project*

Now, we will add the **`server.js`** file and **`UserInfo.js`** file from *Chapter 3, Container Components*.

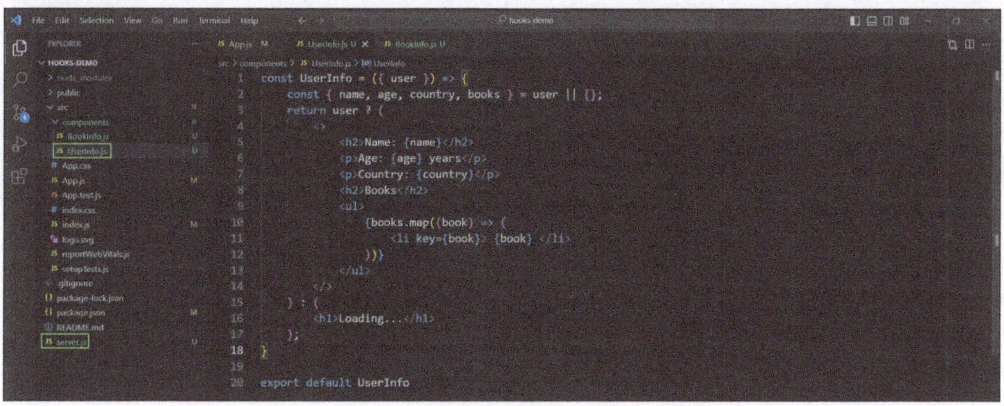

***Figure 5.20:** UserInfo and Server File*

Also, add the **BookInfo.js** file from *Chapter* 3.

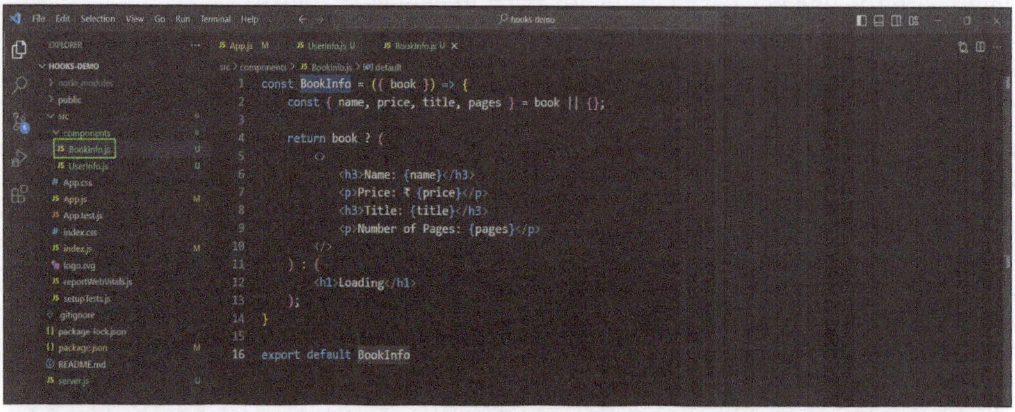

***Figure 5.21:** BookInfo File*

Now, we will create our first custom hook of **useCurrentUser**. Here, we are first importing the **useEffect** and **useState**. After this, we are importing the axios.

Inside the hook, we have a user state. Next, we are doing an API call inside the **useEffect** hook to **/current-user**. The response is stored in the user state. Lastly, we are returning the user.

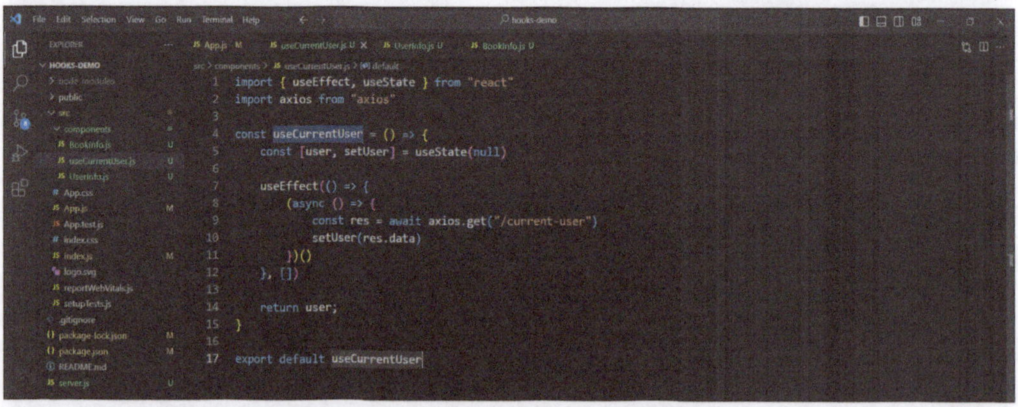

***Figure 5.22:** useCurrentUser Custom Hook*

Next, in the **UserInfo.js** file, we will import the **useCurrentUser**. Afterwards, we will call it, and store the user.

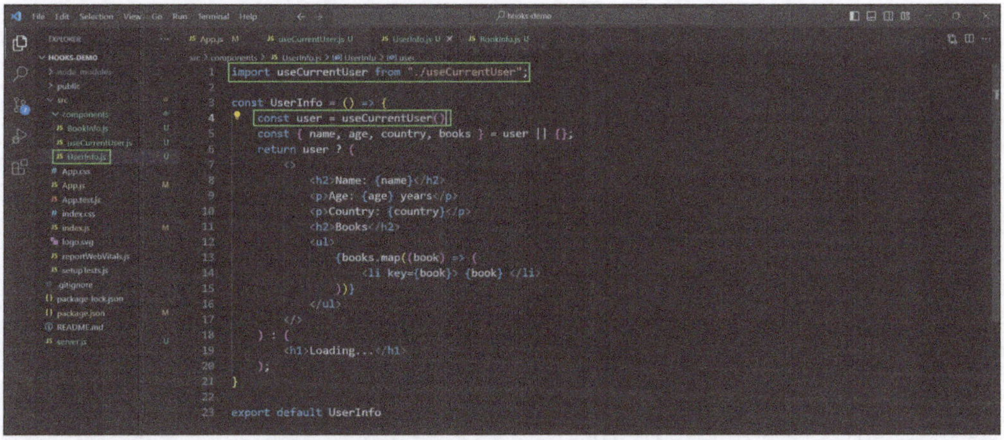

Figure 5.23: *UserInfo Calling useCurrentUser*

In the **App.js** file, we will import and use the **UserInfo** component. Since it is a new project, we shall also add all the dependencies by running the **npm i** command from the terminal.

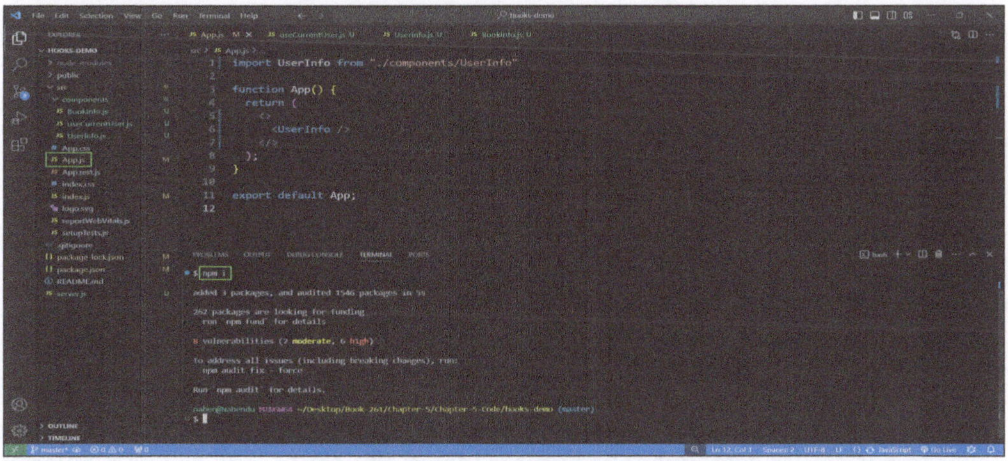

Figure 5.24: *App.js Calling UserInfo*

Next, open a terminal, and run the command **node server.js** to run the **NodeJS code**. Also, run the **npm start** command to run the **React code**.

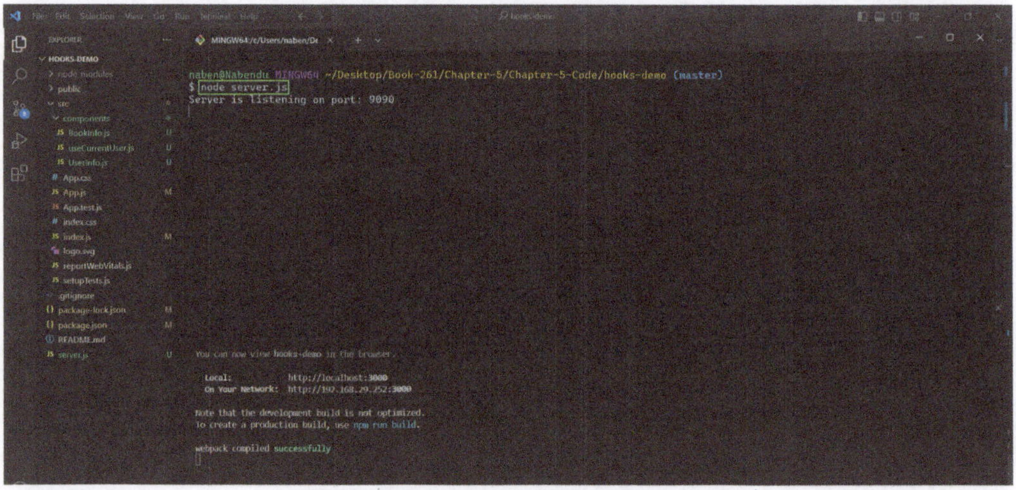

Figure 5.25: *Backend and Frontend Running*

Now, go to http://localhost:3000/, and here we will get the current user from **`server.js`** file.

Figure 5.26: *Localhost Showing the Current User*

Then, we will create another custom hook called **`useUser.js`**. This custom hook is similar to our earlier custom hook, but it is taking an **`userId`**, and calling a different API endpoint to get that specific user.

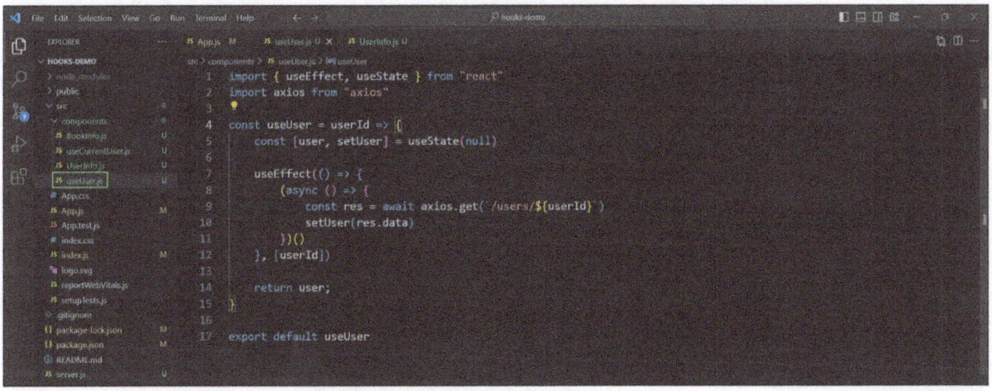

***Figure 5.27:** useUser Custom Hook*

Next, in the **`UserInfo.js`** file, we will make some changes. Here, we will get the props for **`userId`**, and we will call the **`useUser`** hook with the **`userId`**.

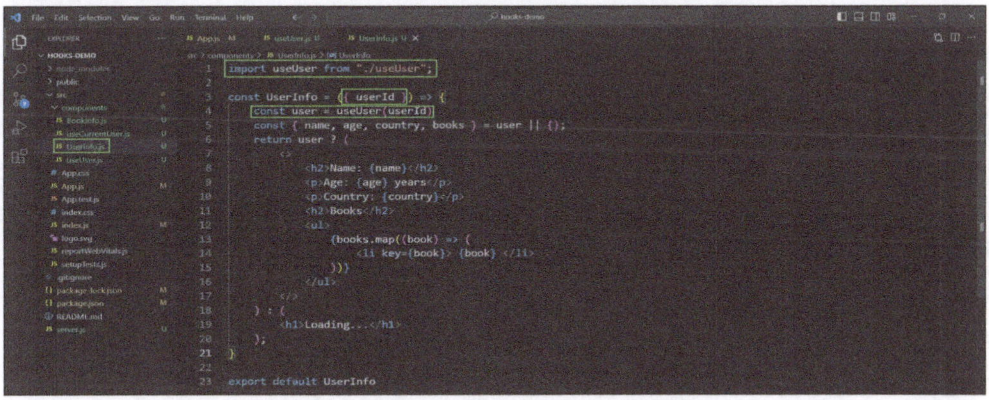

***Figure 5.28:** useUser in UserInfo.js File*

Now, in the **`App.js`** file, we will call the **`UserInfo`** component with different props and **`userId`**.

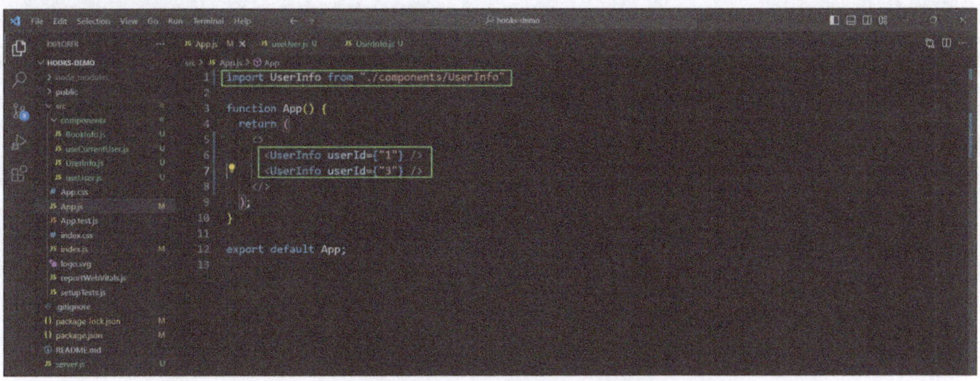

***Figure 5.29:** UserInfo in App.js*

Next, go to http://localhost:3000/, and here, we will get the two users.

Figure 5.30: *Localhost Showing All Resources*

Fetching a Resource with Custom Hooks

We will make a hook which is more generic, and will fetch both the hook and the user. Now, create a new custom hook called **`useResource.js`**. It is similar to the **`useUser`** custom hook, but we will be getting a **`resourceUrl`** in props.

In the **`useEffect`** through axios, we will hit the **`resourceUrl`** through GET api. The **`useEffect`** also has a dependency on **`resourceUrl`**.

Finally, we will be returning the resource.

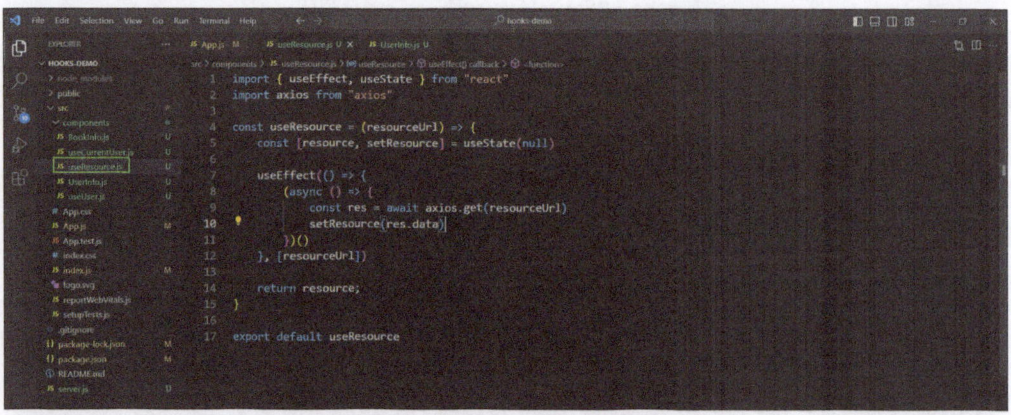

Figure 5.31: *useResource Component*

Now, in the **UserInfo.js** file, we will import the **useResource** custom hook, and use it. In the **useResource**, we will pass the **/users** with **userId** as props.

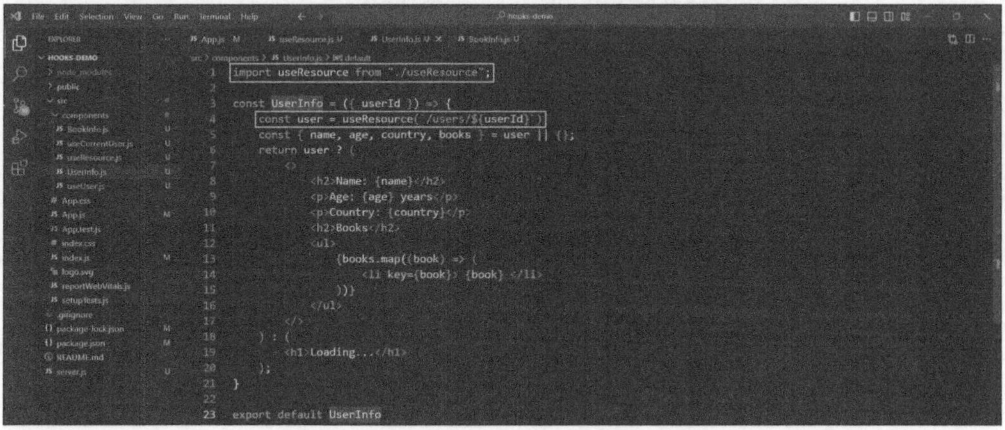

Figure 5.32: *useResource in UserInfo.js*

Next, we will also change the **BookInfo.js** file. Here, we are getting the **bookId** as props, and again using the **useResource** component as well as passing the **/books** with **bookId**.

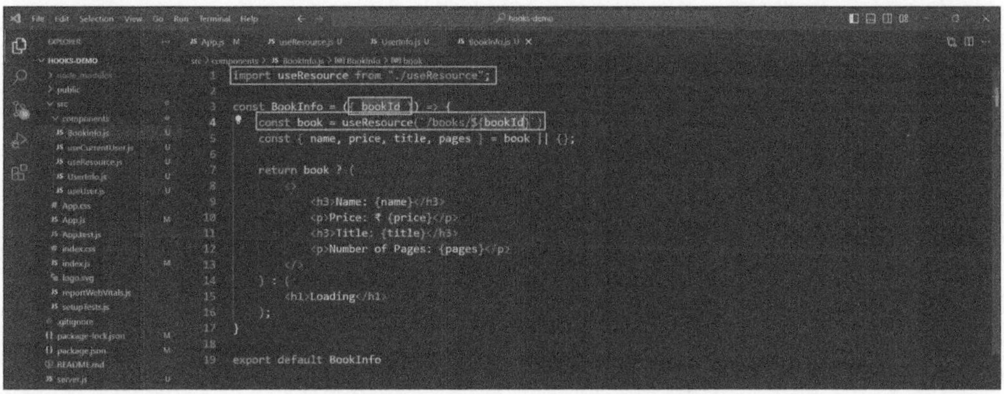

Figure 5.33: *useResource in BookInfo.js*

Now, in the **App.js** file, we will use both **BookInfo** and **UserInfo** components, and pass the **userId** as well as **bookId**, respectively.

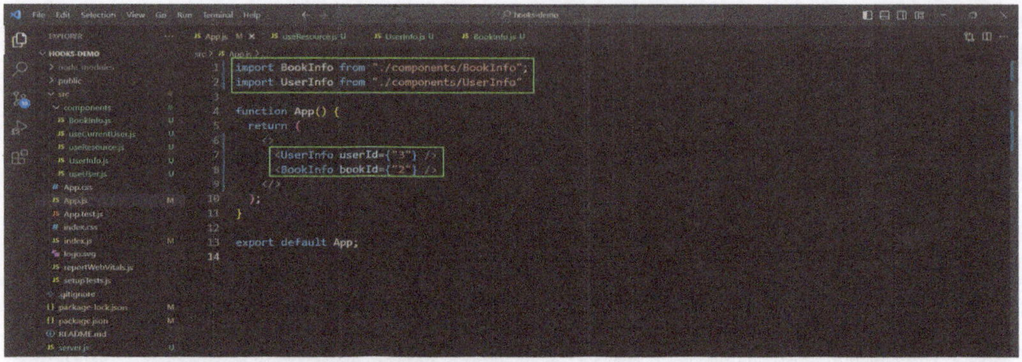

Figure 5.34: *BookInfo and UserInfo in App.js*

Now, go to http://localhost:3000/, and here, we will get from both the user and book components.

Figure 5.35: *Localhost Showing Both Resources*

Conclusion

In this chapter, we have first learnt about the HOC pattern. They return another component instead of returning JSX. Here, we first learnt about checking props with HOC. Then we performed data loading with HOC.

We built a form with HOC, and also learnt to enhance it. After that we moved to hooks. Here, we have first fetched a user with a custom hook.

Lastly, we have updated this hook to fetch any resource. In the next chapter, we will learn about **functional programming**.

Points to Remember

- Checking props, updating data, and building forms with HOC.
- Enhanced HOC pattern to use HOC in an effective way.
- Creating a custom hook to fetch user data.
- Fetching different kinds of data with a custom hook.

Chapter 6
Functional Programming and More Patterns

Introduction

In this chapter, we will explore how Functional Programming principles influence React's modern design and how they can help us write cleaner, more predictable, and reusable code. Functional programming focuses on using pure functions, immutability, and composition rather than relying on shared states or side effects. These principles not only make our React components easier to maintain but also improve performance and testability.

We will begin by understanding the concept of functional programming in React and how it has gradually replaced class-based components. You will learn how React leverages these ideas through Hooks, Higher-Order Components (HOCs), and Compositions. Moving forward, we will explore several advanced patterns – including Recursive Components, Partial Components, Compound Components, and the Observer Pattern. Each of these patterns demonstrates how functional programming concepts can be practically applied to solve real-world UI problems efficiently.

By the end of this chapter, you will be able to write components that are modular, reusable, and easier to scale. You will also gain insight into how these patterns work together to make React a powerful framework for building complex applications while keeping the code functional, elegant, and maintainable.

Structure

In this chapter, we are going to discuss the following topics:

- Introduction to Functional Programming
- Recursive Components

- Compositions
- Partial Components
- Compound Components
- Observer Pattern

Introduction to Functional Programming

Functional programming is an approach to organise code that emphasises minimising mutation, and state change. It utilises pure functions independent of external data, and treats functions as first class citizens.

Let us discuss the applications of functional programming in React. One of the applications is Controlled components which we have learnt in *Chapter 4, Controlled and Uncontrolled Components*. React has also moved away from Class components to Functional components in 2020, with React 16.8. They offer a straightforward way to define the components.

The HOCs discussed in *Chapter 5, Higher Order Components and Custom Hooks* are yet another example of Functional Programming in React. We will see three additional design patterns to see the influence of functional programming. They are Recursive Components, Compositions and Partial Components.

Recursive Components

The recursive pattern is a component that calls itself from inside. We have first created a new react project called **`functional-demo`**. Here, in the App.js, the boiler-plate code is removed, and a nested object is stored in a constant called **`nestedObj`**.

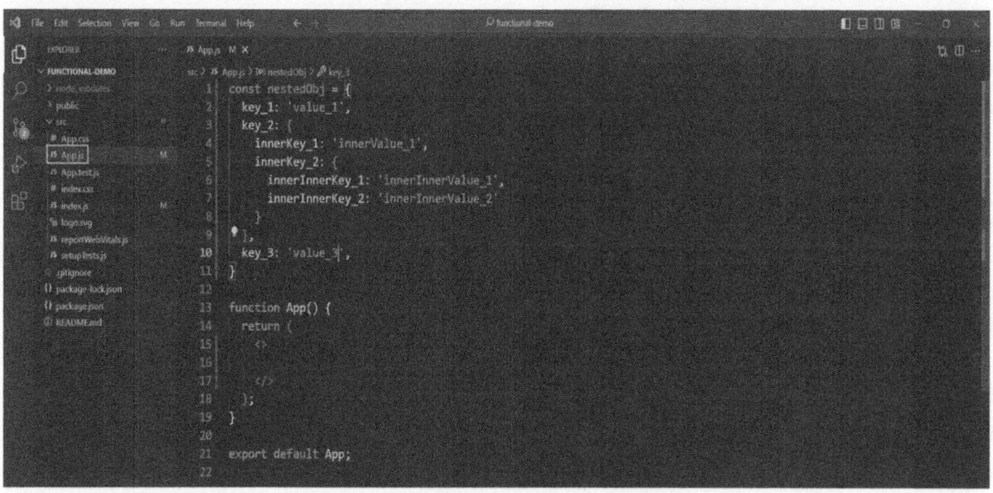

Figure 6.1: Nested Object in App.js

Next, we have created a **components** folder, and inside it a **RecursiveComponent.js** file. Here, we first have a function called **isObject** which takes the data, and checks whether it is an object with the **typeof operator**. Also, we are checking if it is not null, because the **typeof null** is also an object in JavaScript.

Inside the **RecursiveComponent**, we are getting data props. Here, we are first checking if the data is not an object, then returning a li with the data. Then we have created a pair variable which is using **Object.entries** to return an array containing the key and value of the object.

Now, inside the return statement, we are mapping through the pairs and in an **li** showing the key, but calling the **RecursiveComponent** again with the value. Now, again when the component runs, and finds that the value is not an object, then it returns it, or it will go into the return statement again. In this way, if the object is nested, it will go till the last.

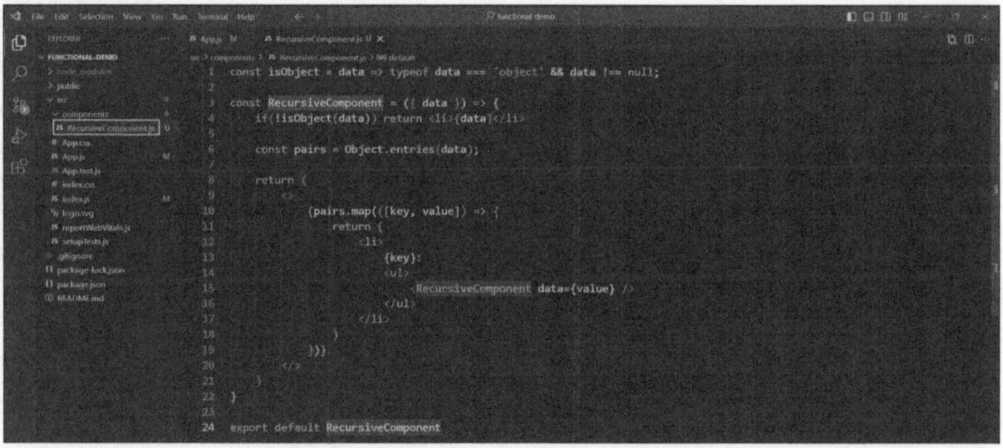

Figure 6.2: *Creating Recursive Component*

Next, we will add the **RecursiveComponent** in the **App.js** file, and pass the **nestedObj** as data.

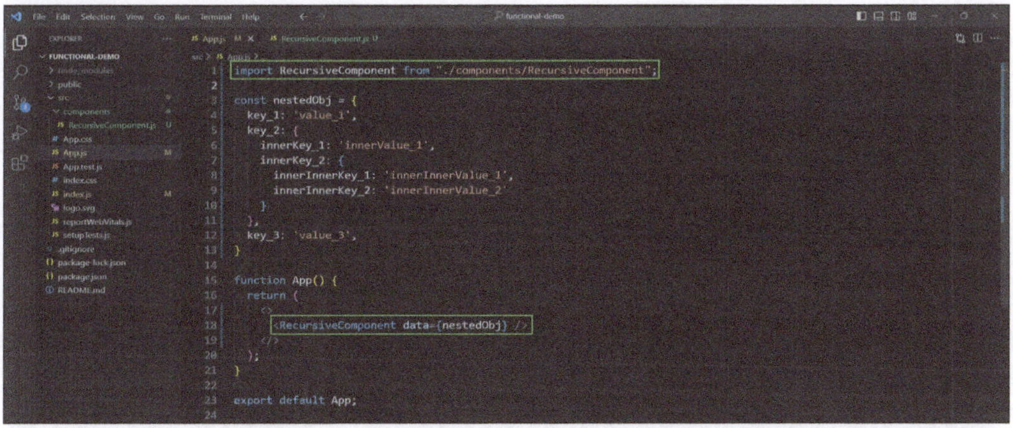

Figure 6.3: *Calling Recursive Component from App.js*

Now, in http://localhost:3000/, we will get the perfect structure of the nested object.

Figure 6.4: *Nested Object in Localhost*

Compositions

The next functional pattern which we will look into is the Compositions. Composition component is the inheritance pattern in the programming world. But here, it has slight differences, and we will look into it through code.

We will create a new file called **`Composition.js`** inside the **`components`** folder. Inside it, we have a main component called **`Button`**. It is taking **`size`**, **`color`**, **`text`** and **`paddingSize`** as props. After this, it is using them to create a customizable button.

This is achieved by using **`size`**, **`color`** and **`paddingSize`** in the style, and text for the button text. Also, notice that if the size is passed as small, we are making the **`fontSize`** as 12px, or else, it is 32px.

Next, we have a **`RedButton`** and **`GreenButton`** component which are passing different props to the Button component. Also, in both the components, we have **`{...props}`** which means that they can take props from the component from where they are called.

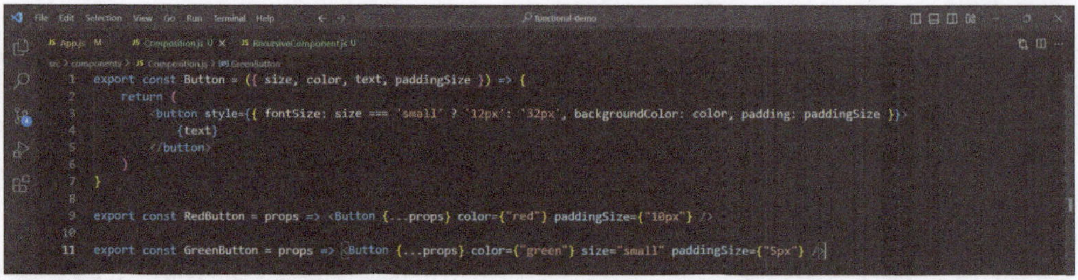

Figure 6.5: *Creating Composition.js File*

Back in the **`App.js`** file, we will import the **`RedButton`** and **`GreenButton`** components, and pass the text props.

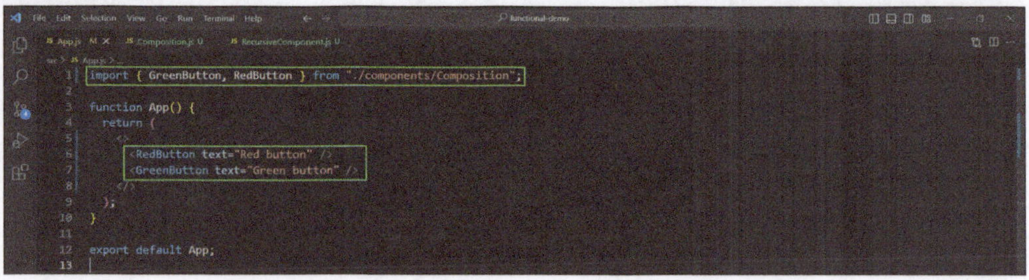

Figure 6.6: *Calling Composition Components from App.js*

Now, in http://localhost:3000/, we see both the **`RedButton`** and **`GreenButton`**.

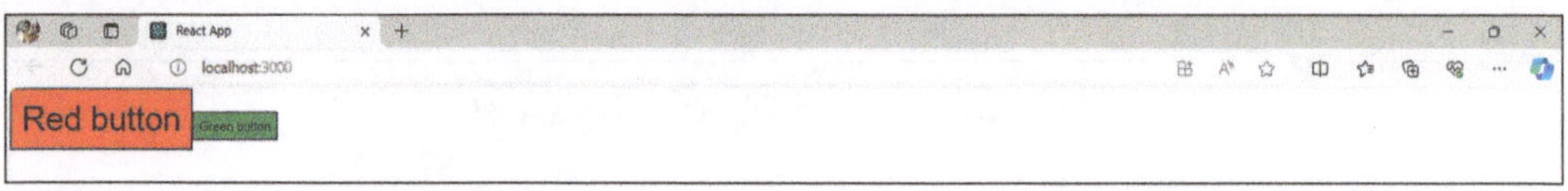

Figure 6.7: *Localhost Showing Composition Components*

Partial Components

Next, we will learn about using composition patterns for creating inheritance. After this, we will look into another pattern called the Partial Pattern. This is actually the next step of the **`Composition Pattern`** which simply allows us to use a part of the component, rather than all of it.

And for achieving this, we are going to use the higher order component pattern for creating a **`Partial`** component. So, we will create a new file called **`PartialComponent.js`** inside the **`components`** folder.

Here, we have a HOC called **`PartialComponent`** which is taking a **`Component`** and **`partialProps`** as props. It is then returning the **`Component`** with **`partialProps`** and **`props`**. After this, we have the **`Button`** component which is similar to what we have created in Composition.js file.

Next, we have a **RedButton** that is called the **HOC PartialComponent**. It is passing the Button component and the props of color as well as the **paddingSize**. Lastly, we have the **SmallRedButton** which is again calling the **PartialComponent**, but it is passing the **RedButton** as a component, and size of small as props.

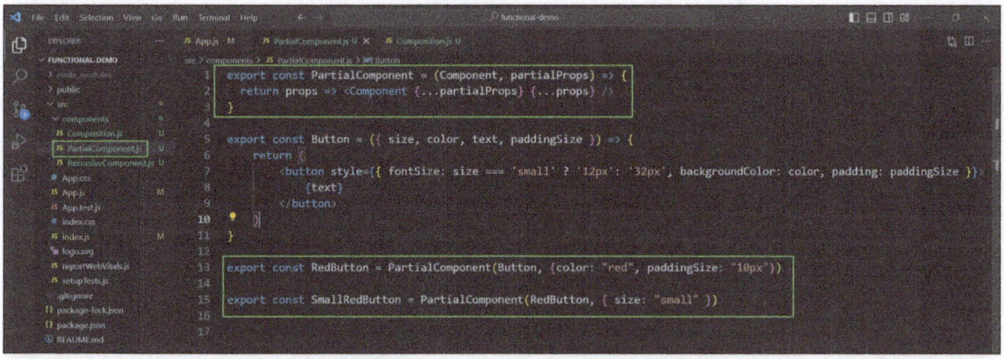

Figure 6.8: *Creating Partial Component*

Now, in the **App.js** file, we are calling the **RedButton** and **SmallRedButton** with text props.

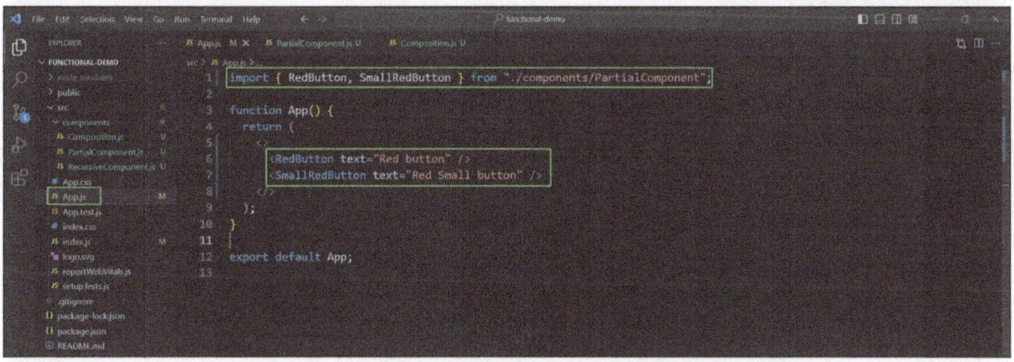

Figure 6.9: *Calling Partial Component from App.js*

Next, in http://localhost:3000/, we see both the **RedButton** and **SmallRedButton**.

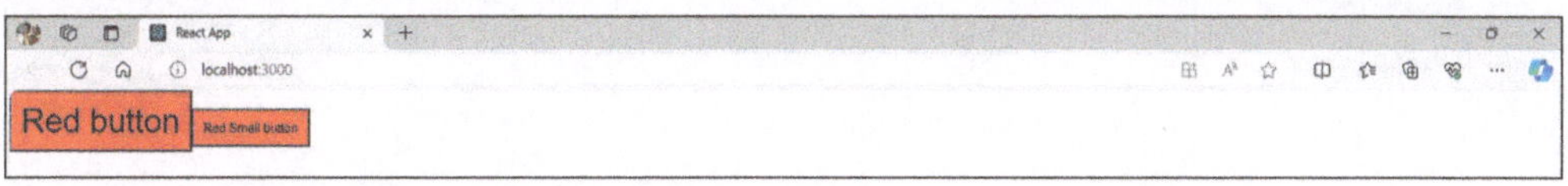

Figure 6.10: *Localhost Showing Partial Component*

Compound Components

Building components in React can get complex very fast, especially when we have a component that has sub-components. This is going to be displayed or rendered, based on some props that were passed to them. In this case, you may enter a hell of nested props, and other components.

Let us take an example here. For this part, we have created a new React project called **`patterns-demo`**. Here, in the **`App.js`** file, we are calling a Card component. In this component, we are passing three props - header, footer, and children. The header and footer props have styles also in it.

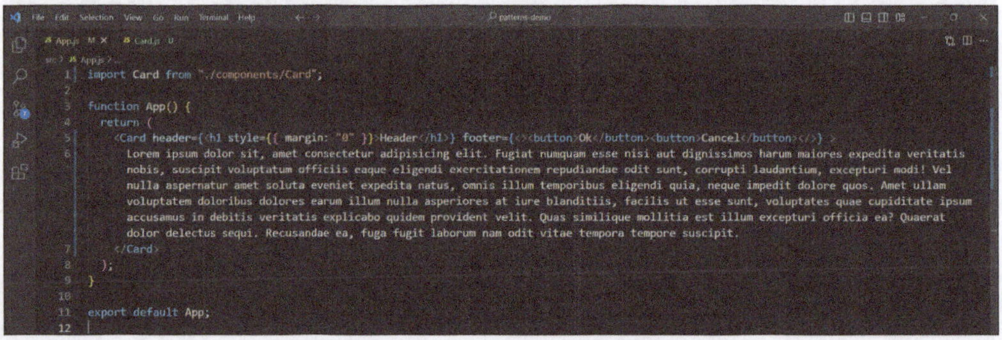

Figure 6.11: *App.js Calling Card Component*

Next, in the **`Card.js`** file, we are taking the header, footer and children props. Now, if the header props are available, we are showing it with some styles. The same is with footer props, and we are showing the children props directly with styles.

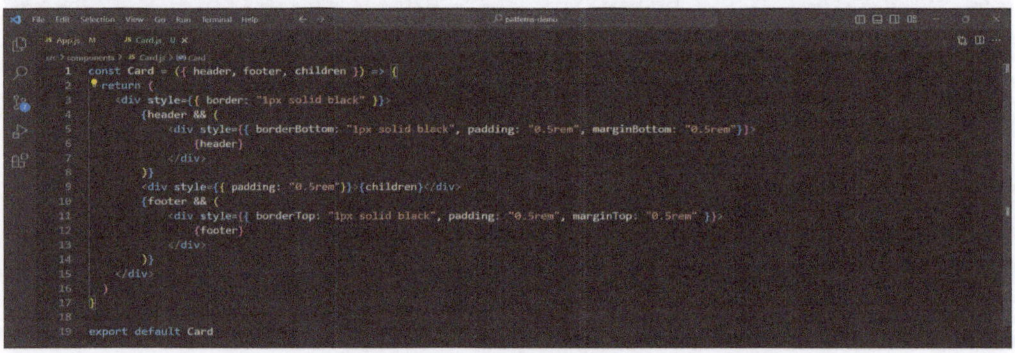

Figure 6.12: *Card Component*

Now, in http://localhost:3000/, we see all three props displaying the component.

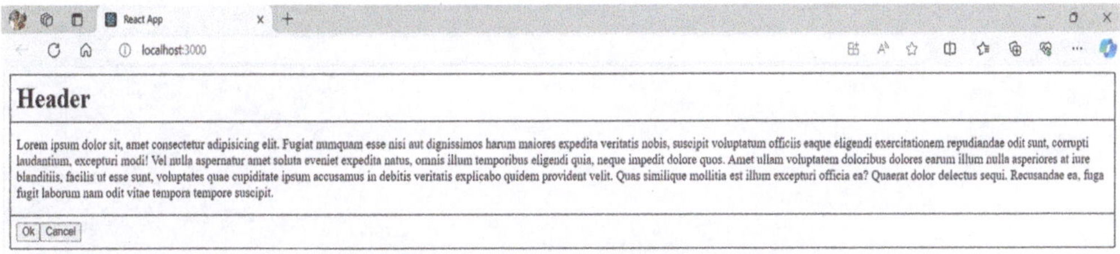

Figure 6.13: *Localhost Showing Card Component*

There is nothing wrong in this example, but due to complexity, and a lot of statements in both **`App.js`** and **`Card.js`**, it is hard to read. So, to fix this problem, we will use the **`Compound Components`**.

The idea of `Compound` Components is breaking down a component into several sub components, and composing those sub-components together to achieve a greater component.

So, we will create a new **`Header`** and **`Footer`** components, and move our earlier code of Header and Footer there. These components are expecting a children prop, so while calling Header and Footer, we will pass them as children props.

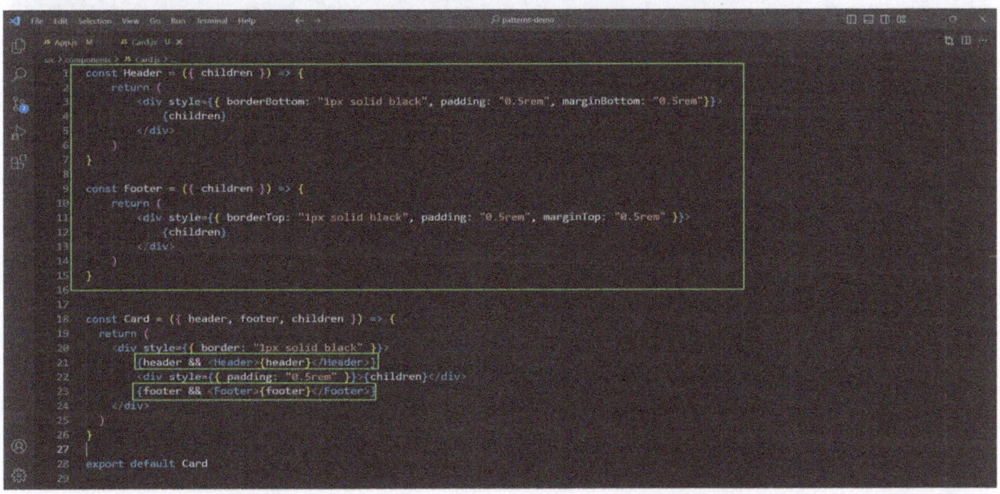

Figure 6.14: *Creating Header and Footer Components*

We had made it simpler, but yet not achieved the **`Compound component pattern`**. To achieve that, we will first create a Body component, containing the body part. Also, we are going to attract the Header, Footer and Body to the instance of the whole component.

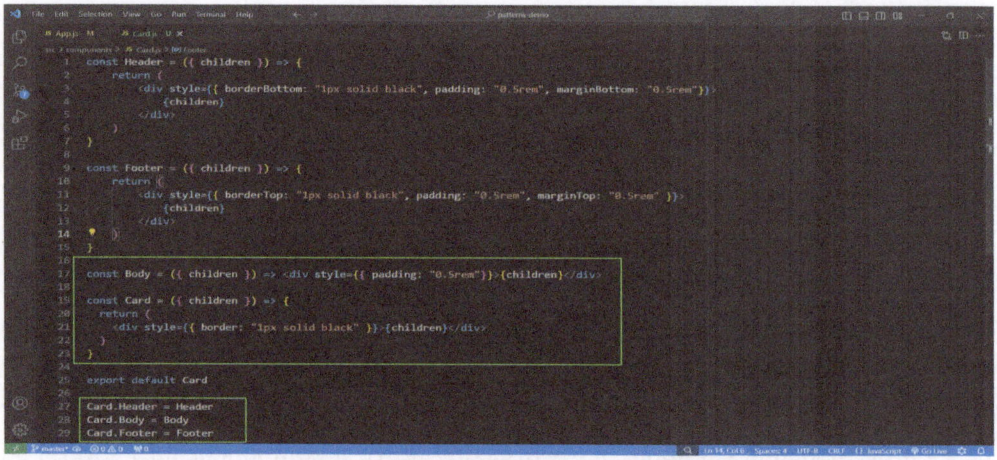

Figure 6.15: *Creating Body Component*

Now, back in the **App.js file**, we will call the **Card.Header**, **Card.Body** and **Card.Footer**, and pass the props as children.

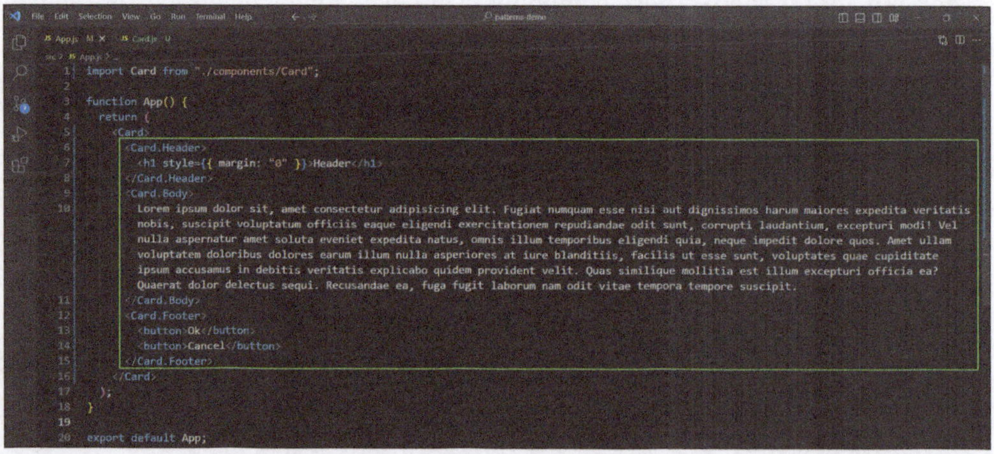

Figure 6.16: *Calling Compound Component*

Back in http://localhost:3000/, everything is as earlier, but we have made the code simpler with the **Compound Component**.

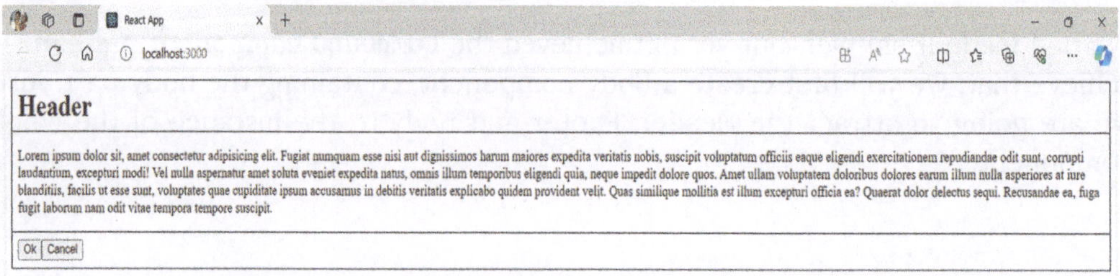

Figure 6.17: *Localhost Showing Compound Component*

Observer Pattern

Next, we will look into the **Observer pattern**. Whenever two components want to communicate in React, they usually communicate through their parent component. But, if we want the two components to communicate, without including the parent component in the process, there are several ways like Context API and Redux.

But in this part, we will use a different pattern called the **Observer patterns**, to achieve the same. For this, we will need to emit an event from a component, and receive it in another component. We can achieve it by writing the whole code, but we will use a third party library called **mitt** for this.

We have also created a new react project called **observer-demo** for this part. Here, we have cleared the App.js, and installed mitt through integrated terminal, using **npm i mitt**.

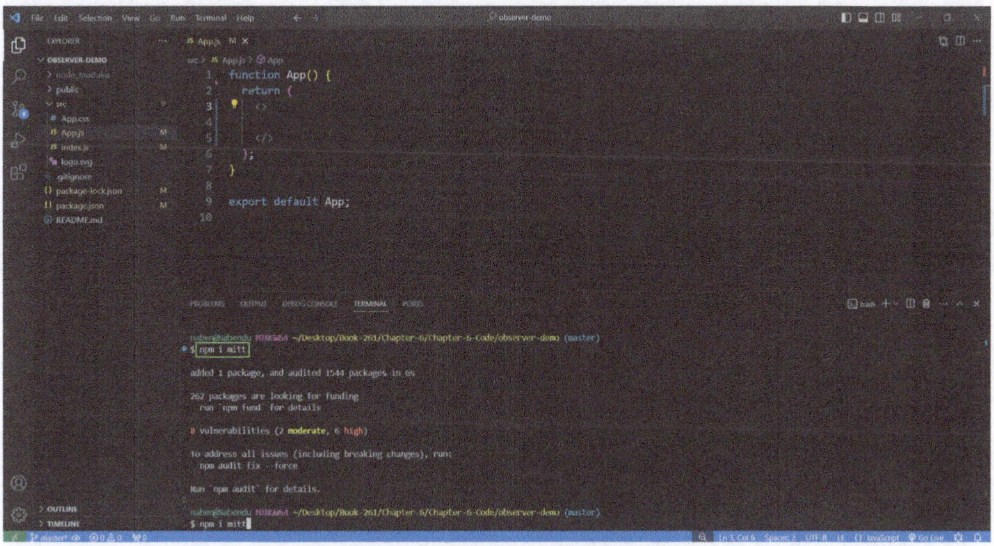

Figure 6.18: *Installing mitt Package*

Now, create a **Buttons.js file** inside a **components** folder. Here, we have two buttons for increment and decrement, which are calling for appropriate functions.

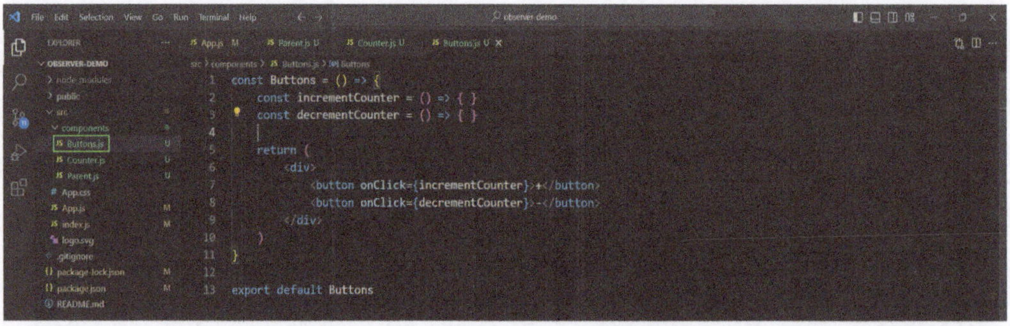

***Figure 6.19:** Creating Buttons.js Component*

Next, create a **`Counter.js` file** inside a **`components` folder**. Here, we have a state variable of count which has been shown inside the **`return` statement**.

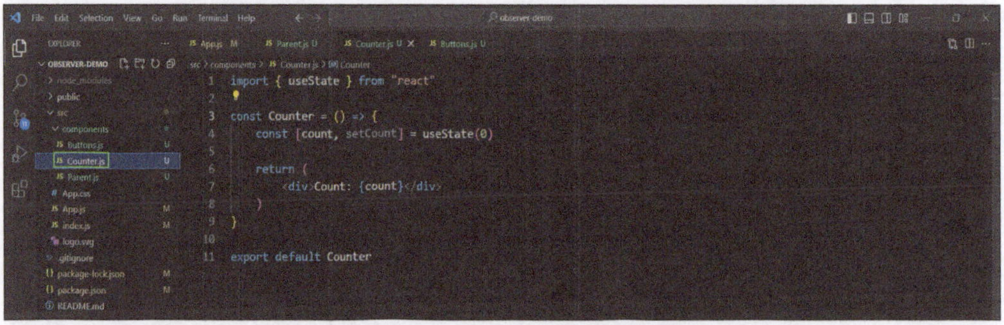

***Figure 6.20:** Creating Counter.js Component*

Now, create a **`Parent.js` file** inside a **`components`** folder. Here, we are calling both the **`Buttons`** and **`Counter`** components.

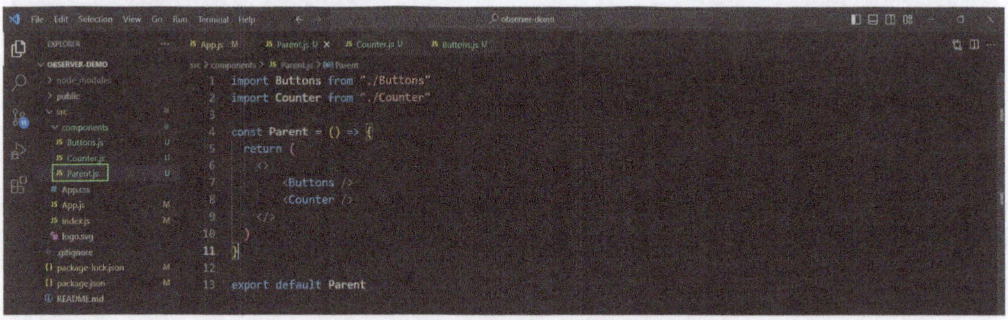

***Figure 6.21:** Creating Parent.js Component*

In the **`App.js`** file, we will call the **`Parent` component**. Here, we have also created an **emitter**, using **`mitt`**.

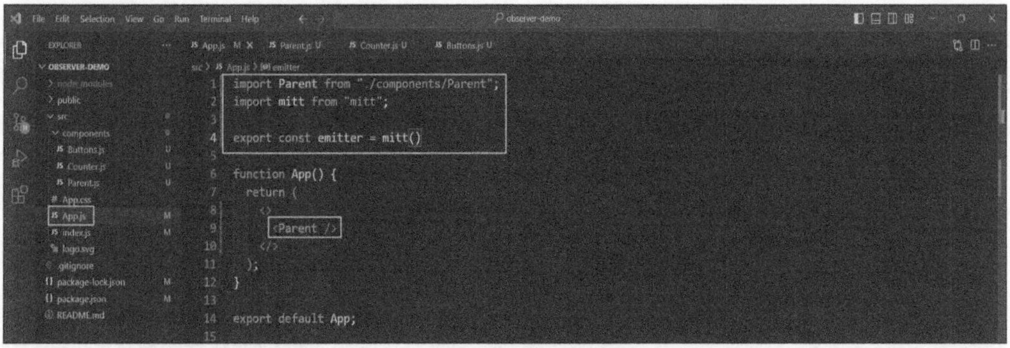

Figure 6.22: *Adding mitt and Calling Parent Component from App.js*

Now, back in the **`Buttons.js`** file, we will first import the emitter from **`App.js`**. Next, we shall use the **`emitter`** to emit the increment string, when the user clicks on the increment button.

We also emit a decrement string, when the user clicks on the decrement button.

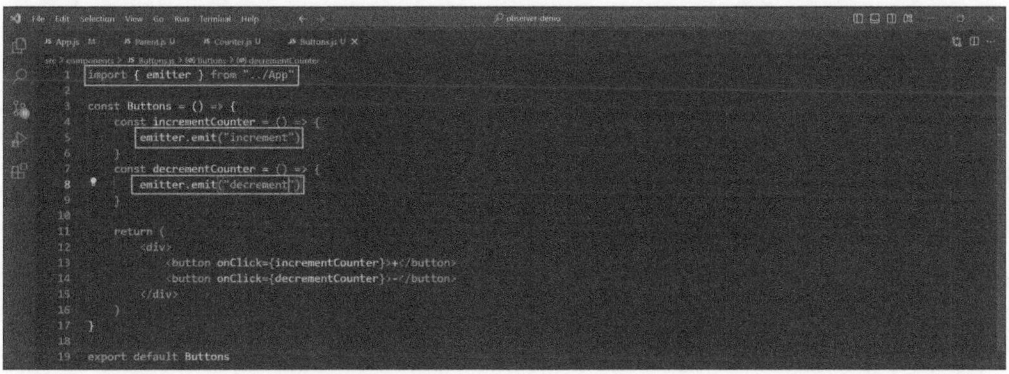

Figure 6.23: *Emitting from Buttons.js*

Now, back in the **`Counter.js`** file, we will import the emitter first. After that inside an **`useEffect`** hook, we have an **`onIncrement`** and **`onDecrement` function**, which increase and decrease the count respectively.

Next, we are using **`emitter.on()`** to catch the increment or decrement string. After receiving any of them, we will call the **`onIncrement`** or **`onDecrement`** function. We are also clearing both emitters, when the component is unmounted, using the **return pattern** of **`useEffect`** hook.

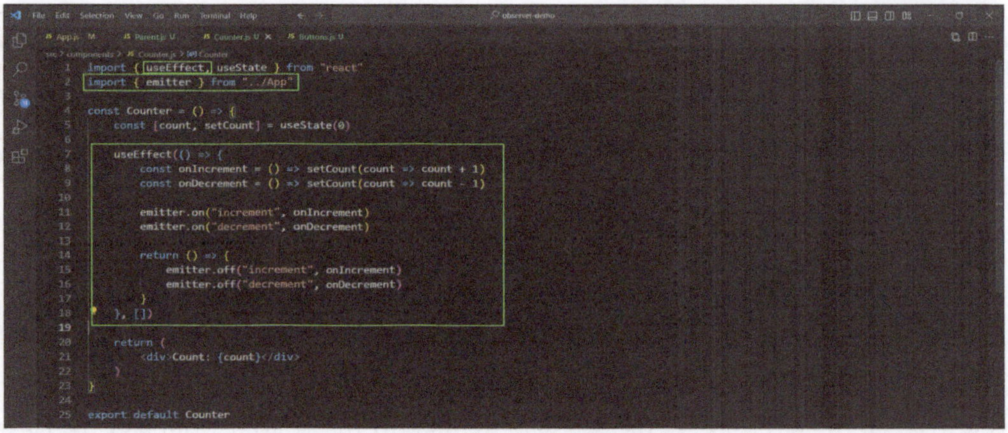

Figure 6.24: *Receiving Emits in Counter.js*

Now in http://localhost:3000/, the increment and decrement are working fine.

Figure 6.25: *Counter Working in Localhost*

Conclusion

In this chapter, we have first learnt about Functional Programming, which is the way to do modern programming in React. In functional programming, we have first learnt to use recursive functions in which the component calls itself. After that, we have learnt about compositions that are inheritance patterns.

Lastly, we have learnt about partial components in functional programming which is the next step in compositions.

Next we have learnt about two additional patterns of Compound Components and Observer Patterns. In the Compound Component, we have broken down a large component into sub-components. And in the Observer Component, we have used an emitter to emit data directly between sibling components.

In the next chapter, we will learn about **advanced components** and **hooks**.

Points to Remember

- Using a recursive pattern to write an efficient code.
- Using inheritance with compositions.
- Partial components to enhance compositions.
- Breaking larger components into sub-components, using compound components.
- Passing data between sibling components using observers.

CHAPTER 7
Advanced Concepts and Hooks

Introduction

In this chapter, we will be learning about the Advanced Concepts like React Portals, Forwarding Refs and others. After this, we will learn about some hooks such as **`useLayoutEffect`**, **`useCallback`** and many others.

Structure

In this chapter, we are going to discuss the following topics:

- React Portals
- Error Boundaries
- Keys
- **`useLayoutEffect`** and **`useId`**
- **`useDeferredValue`**
- **`useTransition`**

React Portals

Firstly, we are going to talk about React portals, and how they can help us. For this, we have created a small component. Here, in the **`App.js` file**, we have a button called Show Message, and clicking on it will open an Alert component. Clicking back on the Alert component will close the component.

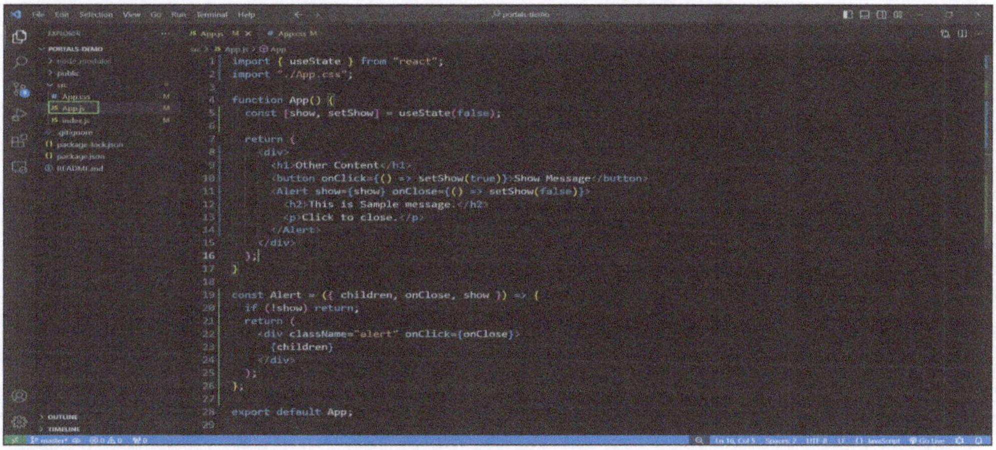

Figure 7.1: *Alert in App.js*

We also have a simple style in **`App.css`** for the same.

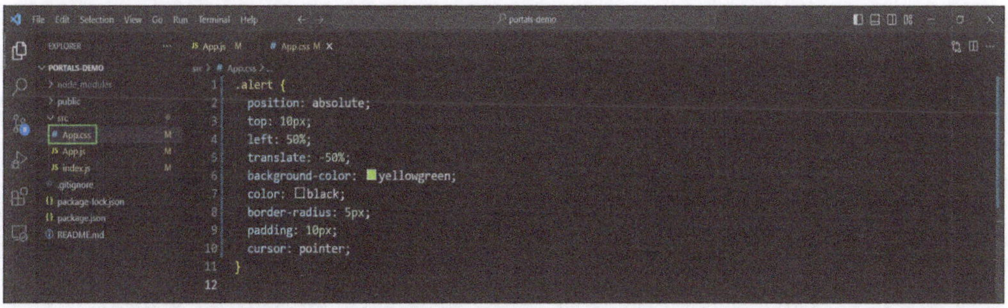

Figure 7.2: *Styles in App.css*

Now, in http://localhost:3000/, we can click on the **`Show Message`** button, and it will show the **`Modal`**. Click back on the **`Modal`** to close it.

Figure 7.3: *Localhost Showing an App Component*

Now, whenever we have elements in the **`React`** component, they are going to be painted into the DOM, the way you see them in actual components. If we inspect it, we will get the whole code inside the div with the id of root.

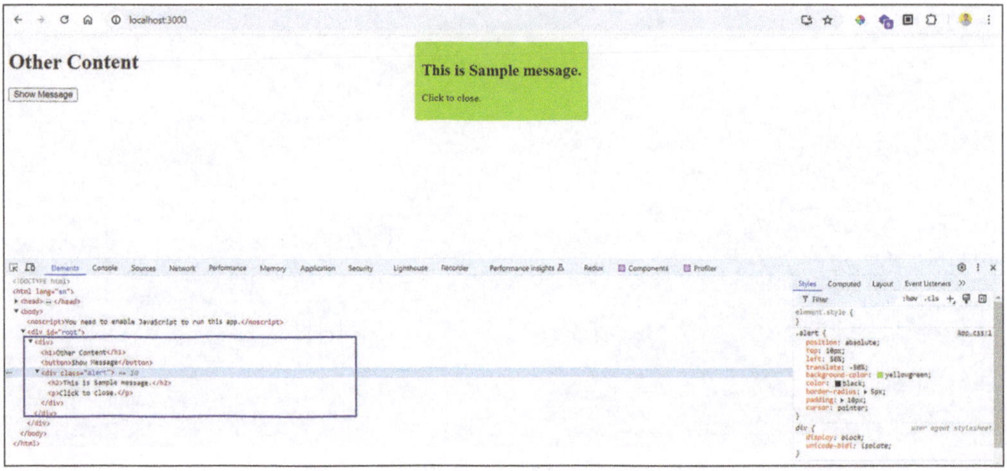

Figure 7.4: *DOM for an App Component*

Sometimes, we want to place our elements such as the **`Alert` component** in some other elements. So, let us break the program by adding some style in our primary **`div`** in the **`App.js` file**.

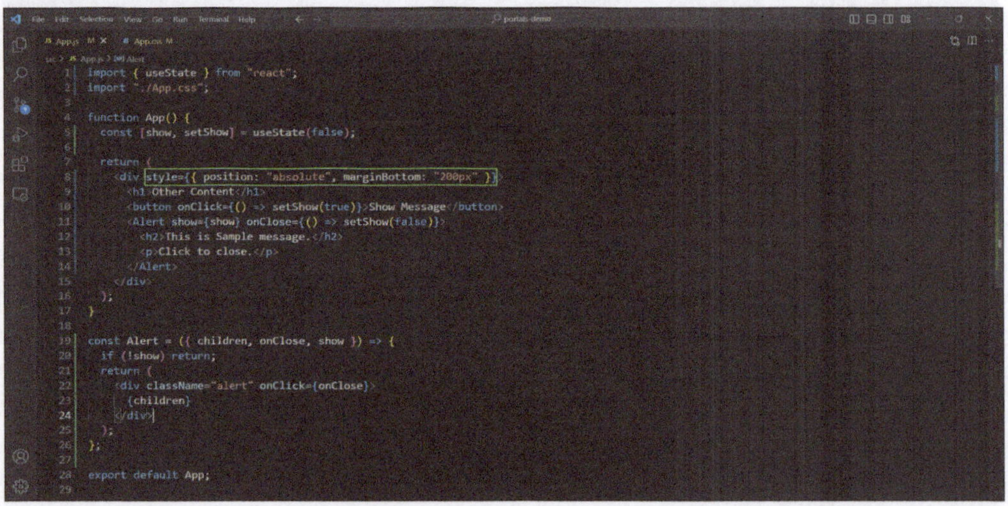

Figure 7.5: *Styles in the Main Div*

We added this style to the main **`div`**, but it broke the **`Alert`** component, and it is not in the proper place.

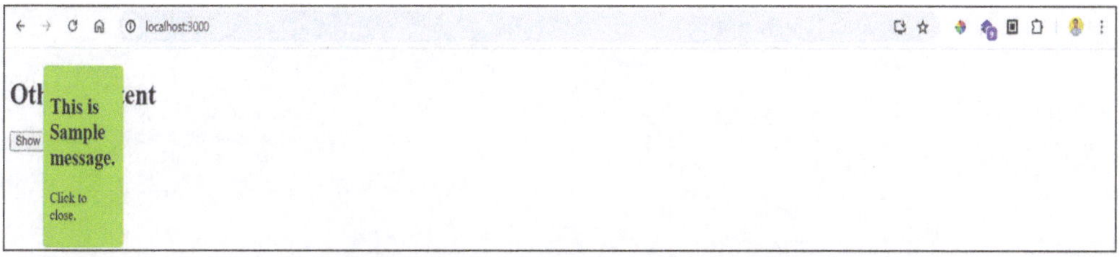

Figure 7.6: *Alert Component Broken in Localhost*

So, we want to keep the place of the alert here only, but we wanted it to be printed in the actual DOM somewhere else. We want it to be attached to another div, rather than the current **`div`**.

Hence, to do this, we need portals. For this, we will create a new div with the id **`of alert-holder`** in the **`index.html`** **file**.

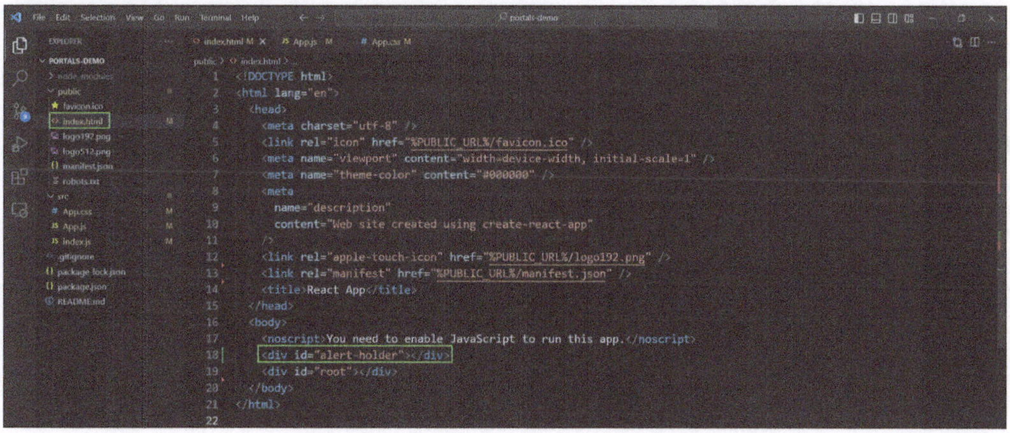

Figure 7.7: *Creating a New Div in index.html*

Back in the **`App.js`** **file**, we will first import **`createPortal`** from react-dom. Now, in the Alert component, the return will call the **`createPortal`**. Inside this, we will be passing the earlier div as the first parameter, and in the second parameter will be selecting the div alert-holder with **`document.querySelector`**.

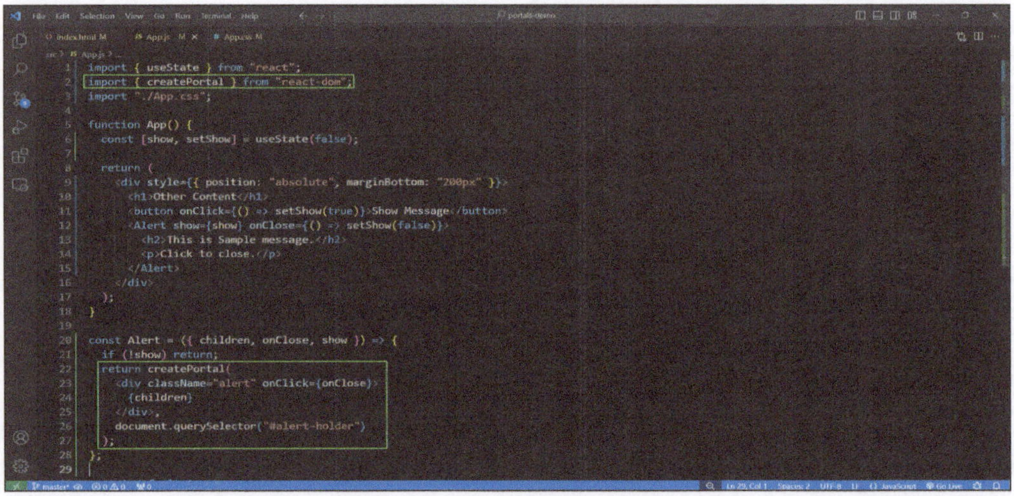

Figure 7.8: *createPortal in App.js*

Now, in http://localhost:3000/, we can click on the **Show Message** button, and it will show the Modal at the right place. Also, in the **Inspect of Elements**, we will see the **div** with id alert-holder containing the Alert component. The div with the id of root is shown in *Figure 7.9*.

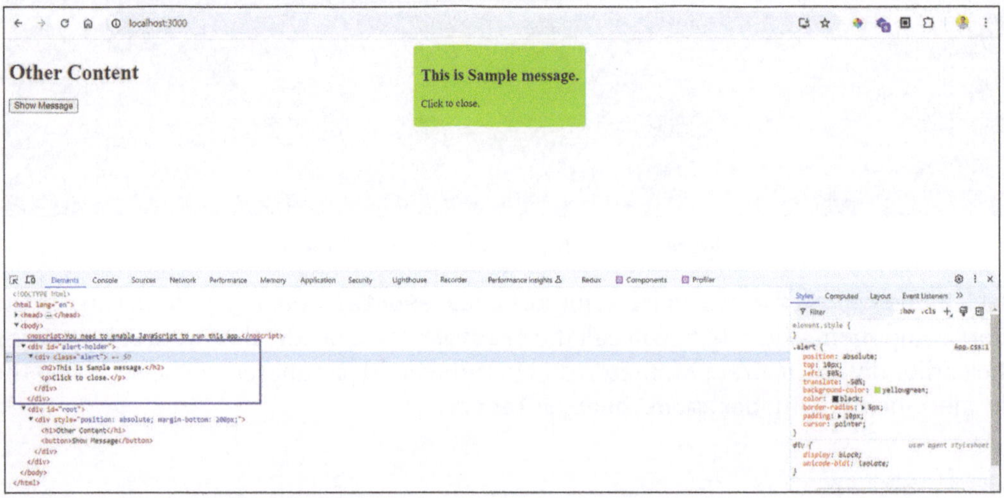

Figure 7.9: *Localhost Showing Modal Correctly*

Error Boundaries

However, there is one thing which we can get in all React projects, and that is an error. For checking errors, we have created a new React project. Here, in the **App.js**, we have an h1 called as a **Child Component**.

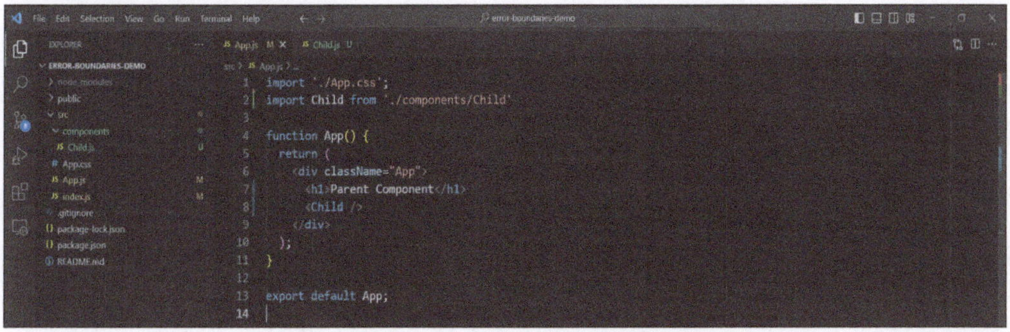

Figure 7.10: *App.js Rendering Child Component*

The **`Child.js` file** contains a simple **`h1`**.

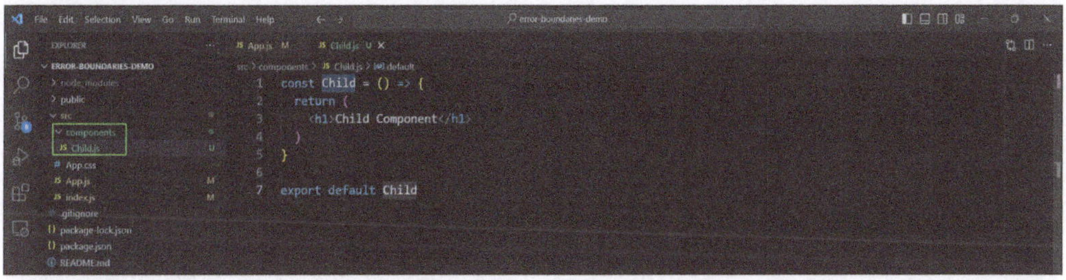

Figure 7.11: *A Simple Child Component*

When we run the project in localhost, we get the content from both **`App.js`** and **`Child.js`.**

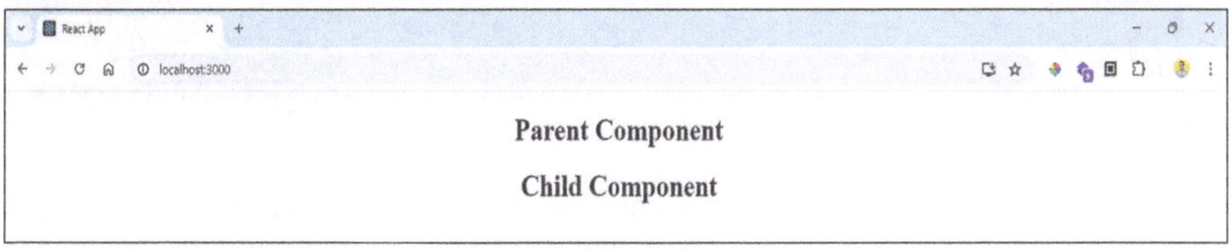

Figure 7.12: *Localhost Showing Parent and Child Components*

In real projects, the error will be thrown automatically, when there are some errors. But in this project, we will throw errors from the Child component, using the new Error function.

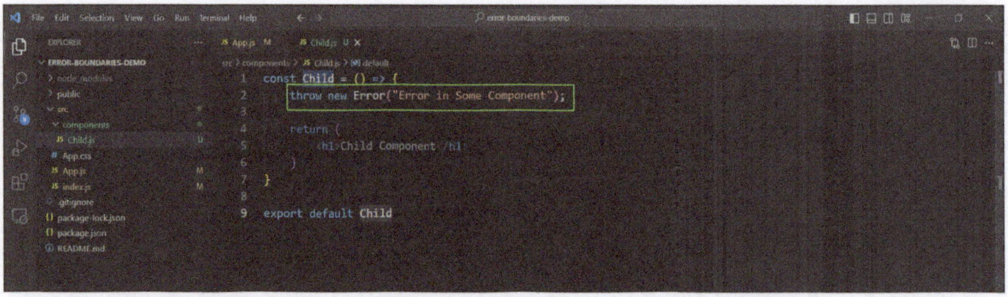

Figure 7.13: *Throwing Error from Child Component*

Back in http://localhost:3000/, we will get the normal error.

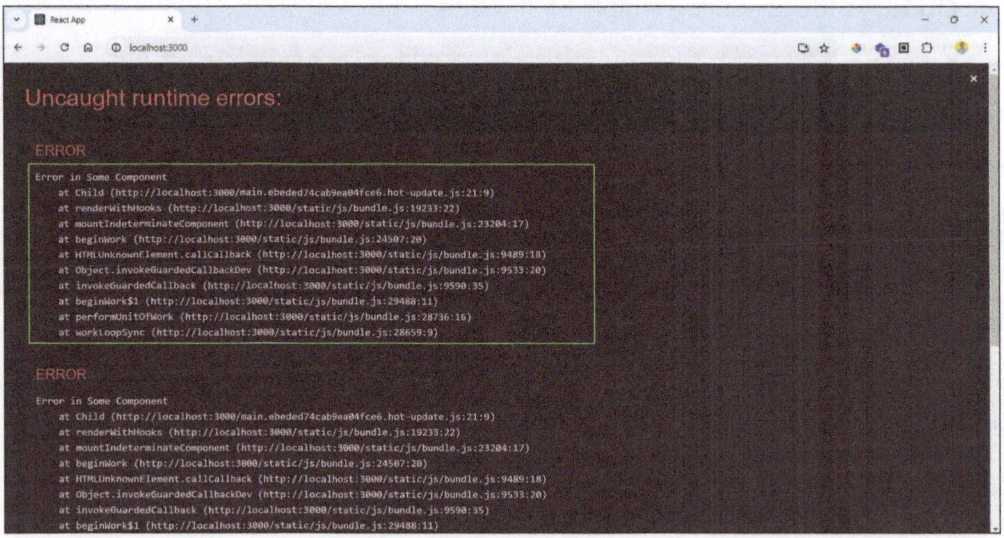

Figure 7.14: *Normal Error in Localhost*

Next, getting a normal error is a bad user experience. And here, Error boundaries come into play. So, create a new file called **`ErrorBoundary.js`** in the **`Components`** folder. Here, the **`ErrorBoundary`** is needed to be a class based component. We have a state called **`hasError`** in the constructor.

Then, we have a lifecycle method of **`getDerivedStateFromError()`**, which will make the **`hasError`** state to be true. Inside the **`render ()`**, we are first checking in an **`if`** statement. This means, if the **`hasError`** is there, it will return the fallback. If that is not the case, then will return the children.

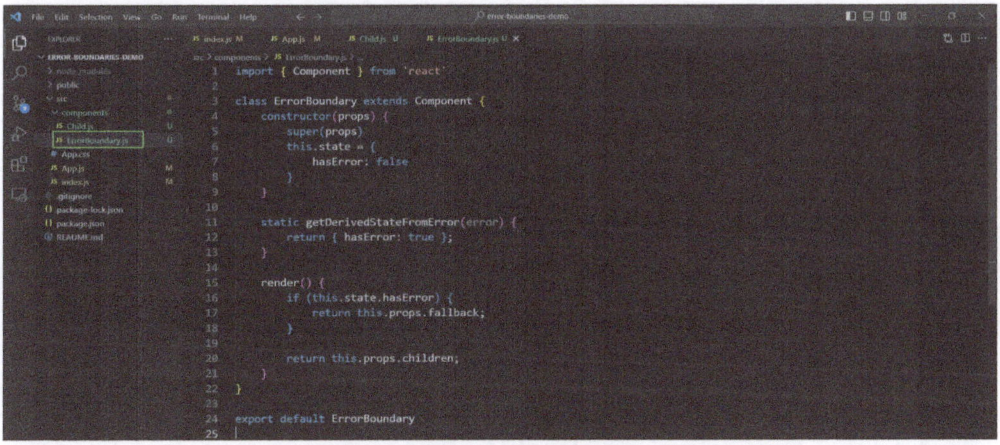

Figure 7.15: *Creating ErrorBoundary Component*

Now, this **`ErrorBoundary` component** can be used anywhere to get the error. We will first wrap it in the **`index.js`** file and the **`App`** component. In the **`ErrorBoundary`**, we will also send the fallback props.

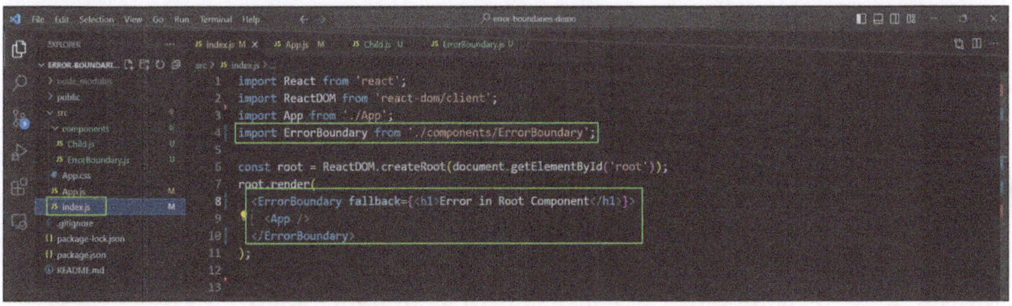

Figure 7.16: *Adding ErrorBoundary in index.js*

Since, our **`Child Component`** is already throwing an error, the **`ErrorBoundary`** will catch it, and show the message from the fallback.

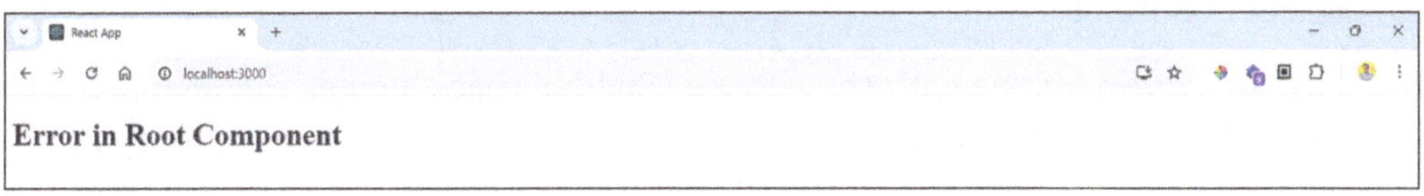

Figure 7.17: *Localhost Showing Meaningful Error*

We can wrap the **`ErrorBoundary`** with other components also. For instance, we are wrapping the **`Child component`** with it.

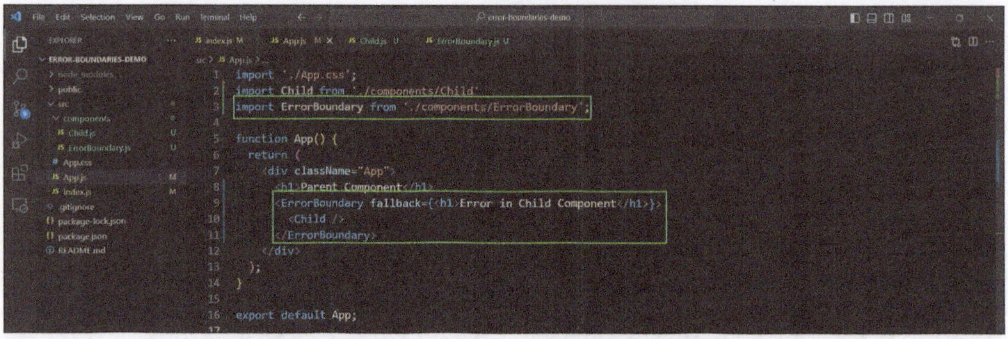

Figure 7.18: *Adding ErrorBoundary in App.js*

Back in http://localhost:3000/, we will get the Parent Component message shown and will get the error message for the **`Child Component`**. So, in the **`ErrorBoundary`** Component, we should wrap at various places to track the correct error.

Figure 7.19: *Localhost Showing Error from App.js*

Keys

In this part, we are going to learn about the keys and state preservation in React. However, they can sometimes be a little bit tricky to understand.

We have created a new project, and in the **`App.js`** file, firstly, we have a state of **`changeShirts`** which is initially false. Now, depending on the **`changeShirts`** value, we are showing a heading with Shirt Count or Shoes Count. We are also calling a Counter Component in both of them.

After this, we have a button with the name of Switch that changes the **`changeShirts`** and in-turn, the h1 with the **`Counter`** Component.

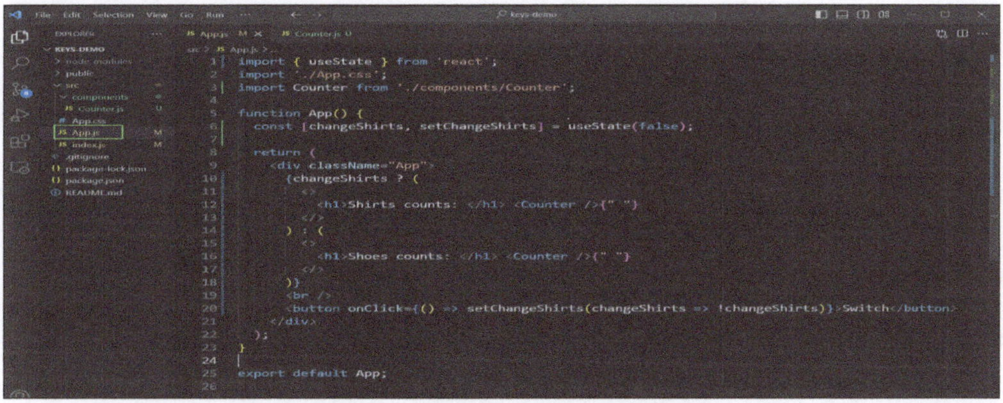

Figure 7.20: *App.js for Keys Demo*

Now, in a **`components`** folder, create a **`Counter.js`** file. It has a count state which can be incremented or decremented using buttons.

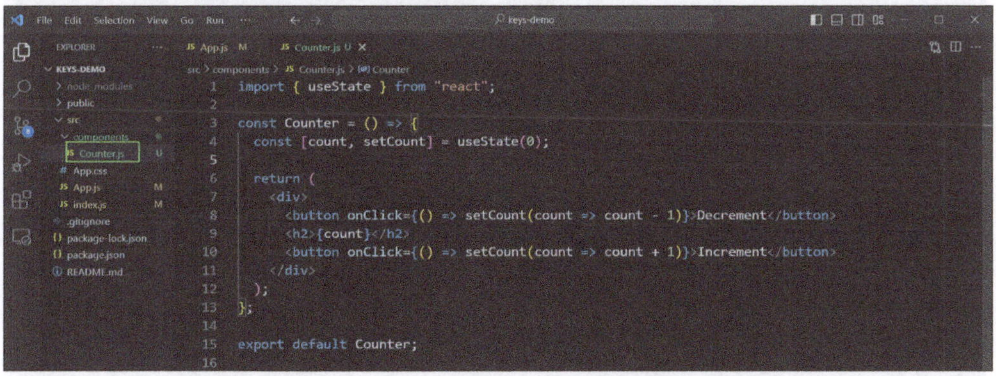

Figure 7.21: *Counter.js with Increment and Decrement*

Next, running the project in http://localhost:3000/ will show the Shoes count first which can be incremented or decremented by clicking the appropriate button.

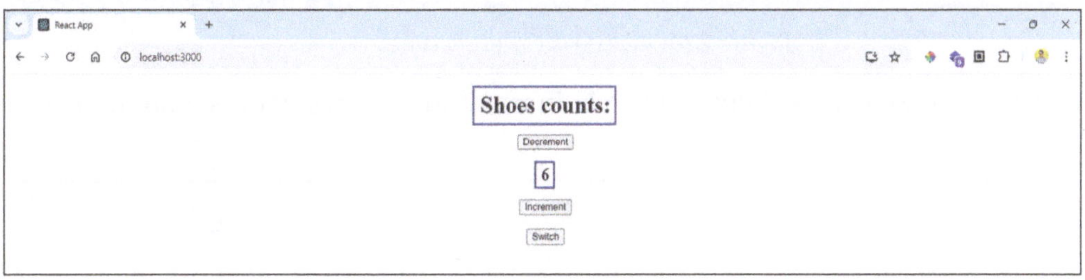

Figure 7.22: *Localhost with Increment, Decrement and Switch*

Now, click on the **`Switch`** button, and it will change to Shirts counts. But the problem is that still the old count has been shown in the following illustration.

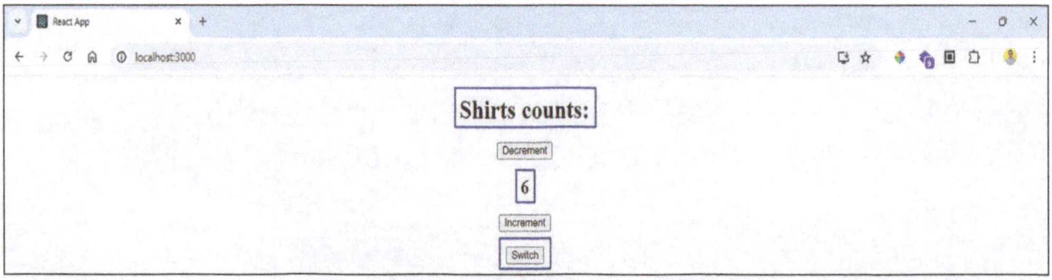

Figure 7.23: *Localhost with Switch Action*

One simple way to fix this issue is to create different parents for each counter. So, whenever a React looks at the parent for both the states, it is going to find out that they are at different locations in the tree. Hence, we will update the App.js to have a div for Shirts count, and a section for Shoes count.

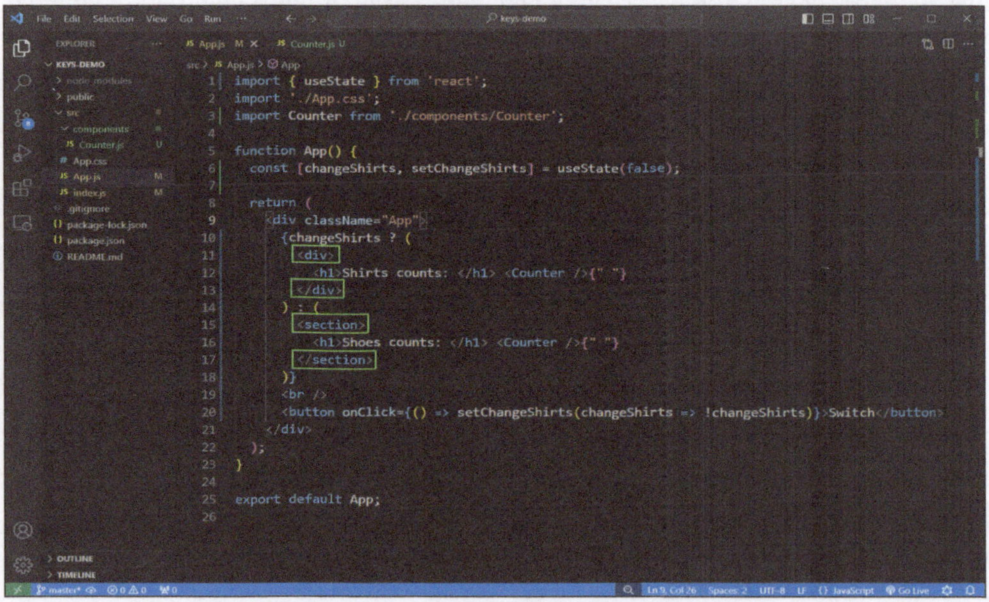

Figure 7.24: *Adding div and section to App.js*

Now, in http://localhost:3000/, we will first get into Shoes counts, and increase its value.

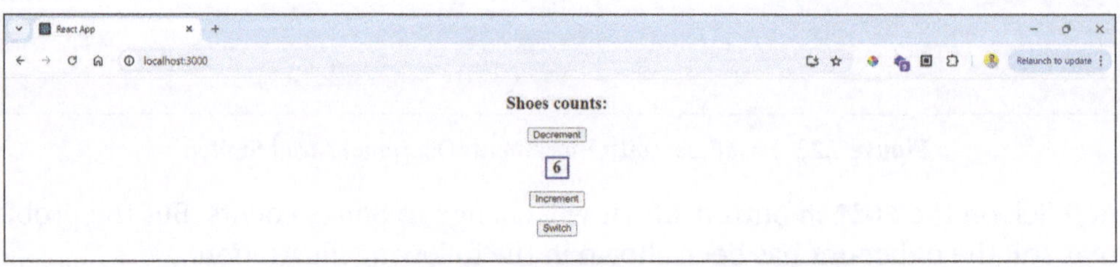

Figure 7.25: *Localhost Showing Shoes Counts*

Next, click on the **Switch** button, and we will see the count being set to 0 again.

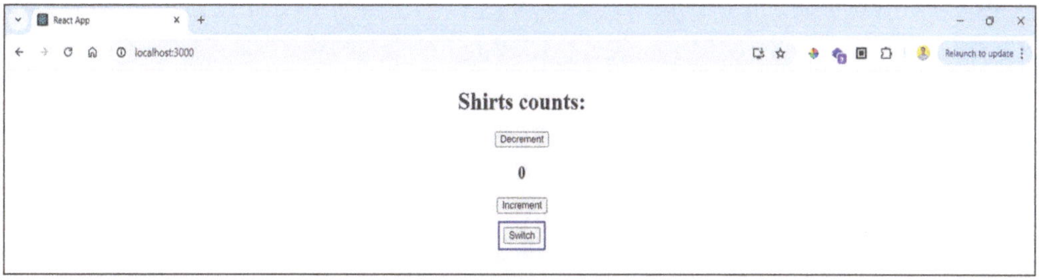

***Figure 7.26**: Localhost Showing Shirts Counts*

Most of the time, we do not want to change the style of a component such as having div and section in this case. We can use a better way of using keys. So, by using a key, you can determine a component to be unique from other specific components that are actually the same.

Again, we will update the **App.js** to have different keys for both the **Counter** components.

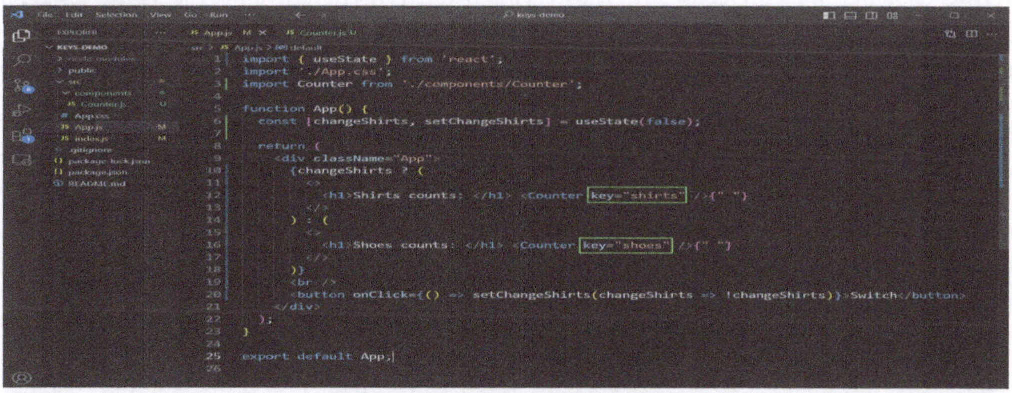

***Figure 7.27:** Adding Key in App.js*

Now, in http://localhost:3000/ we will first get into Shoes counts again, and decrease its value.

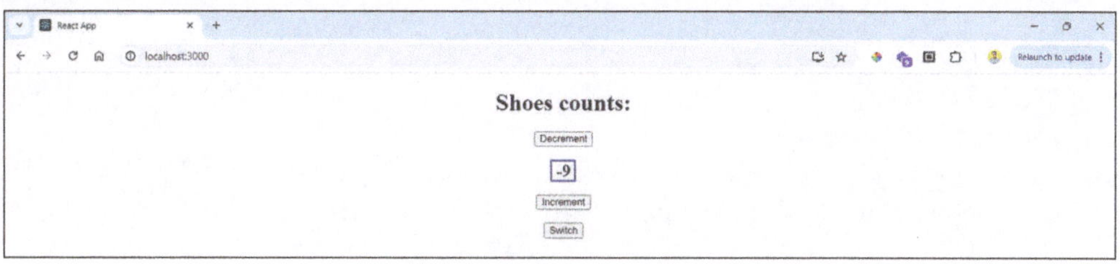

***Figure 7.28:** Localhost Showing Shoes Counts*

Next, click on the **Switch** button, and we will see the count being set to 0 for Shirts count.

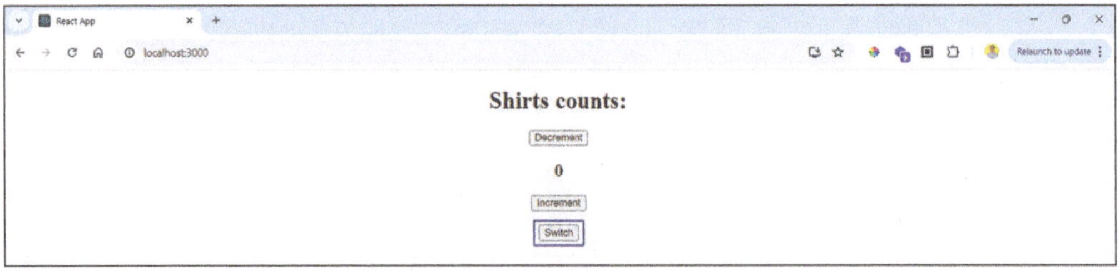

Figure 7.29: *Localhost Showing Shirts Counts*

useLayoutEffect and useId

In this part, we are going to learn about advanced hooks called **useLayoutEffect** and **useId**. First, let us start with the **useLayoutEffect** hook. For this, we have created a new project, and updated the **App.js** as illustrated in the following figure.

In this, we will check an issue which can appear with the useEffect hook. Here, we have a show state that is changed, when we click on a button. It will show a text that has some static style in the tooltip and a changed style which depends on the top.

The top is actually calculated through the **useEffect**. Here, during the initial render, the top will be set to 0, because the **buttonRef.current** is null. But when we click on the button, then the show will be changed, and hence, the **useEffect** will run again. It will get the bottom of the button, and set the top to bottom + 30.

We are also using performance to make our app run slow, when we click the button.

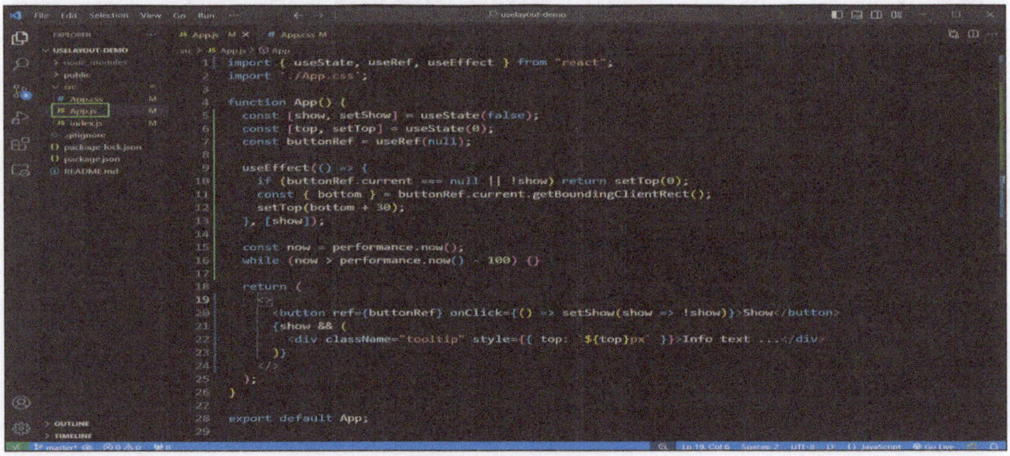

Figure 7.30: *App.js for useLayout Demo*

In the **App.css,** we will remove all styles, and put the style for tooltip only.

Figure 7.31: *App.css for Styling*

Now, in http://localhost:3000/, we will first see the Show button, but the **useEffect** has also run and set the top to 0.

Figure 7.32: *Show Button in Localhost*

Now, when we click on the **Show** button, we will see the real issue. The "**Info**" text will start from top, and then come to its current position. This happens when we click on the Show button, as the show state changes, and the **useEffect** will run again.

But the problem with **useEffect** running with dependency is that it renders the whole component first which will have the top as 0 for Info text. After that the bottom will be calculated, and the top will be changed to bottom + 30. So, we will see the Info text moving from top to bottom. We are also able to see it perfectly because of slowing down the app with performance.

Figure 7.33: *Show Button Showing Info Text*

Thus, to solve the issue of rendering the app first, and then the code in **useEffect**, we will change it to **useLayoutEffect**. Now, this hook works a bit differently than **useEffect**. It will first run the complete code written inside it, and then the code in the return part.

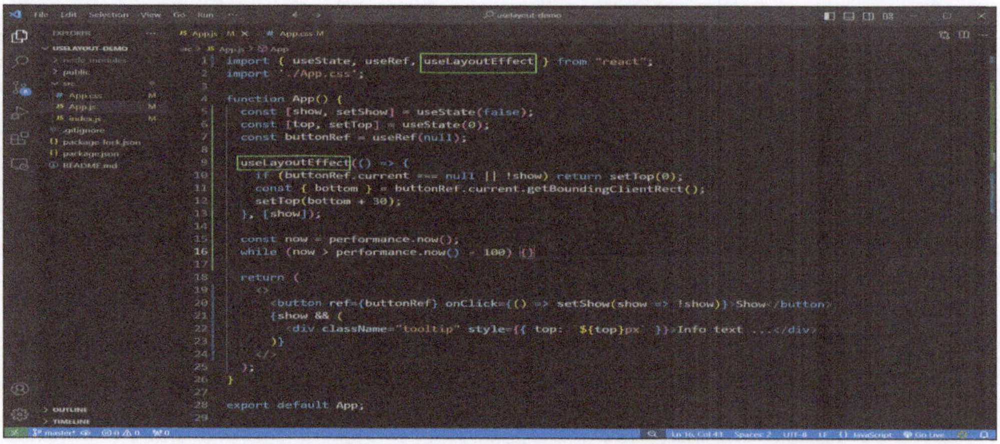

Figure 7.34: *useLayoutEffect to Solve the Issue*

Now, in http://localhost:3000/, again click on the **`Show`** button and the Info text will not show an animation from top to bottom. It will directly appear at the bottom.

Figure 7.35: *Info text Issue Solved in Localhost*

Next, we will learn about the useId hook, and for this we have created another project. The **`App.js`** contains a call to Form Component two times, and a lorem text in-between them.

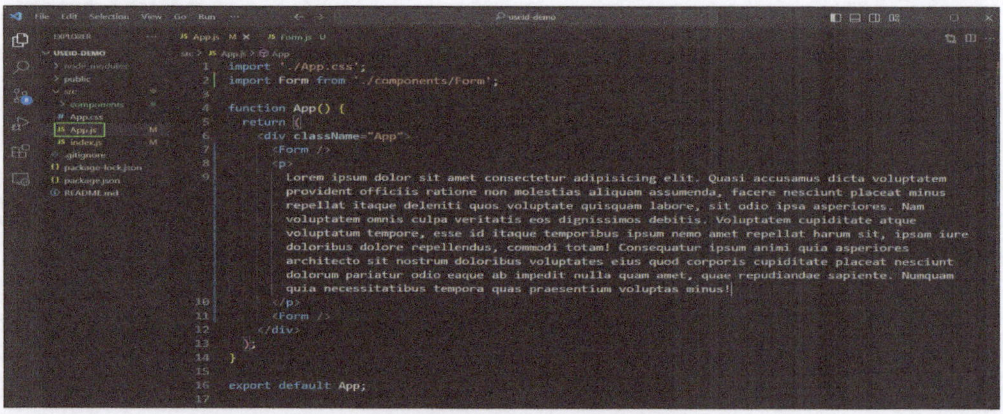

Figure 7.36: *App.js for useId Demo*

In fact, we have created a **`Form.js`** file inside a **`Components`** folder. It simply has a label and input for Email. We have to give a unique form (**`htmlFor`** in React) with the same id in HTML that we have given as an email.

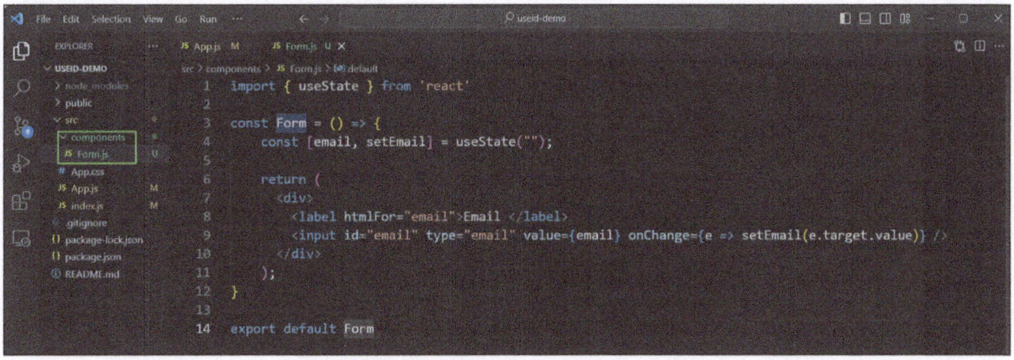

Figure 7.37: *Simple Form Component*

Next, in http://localhost:3000/, we will see the for and id for both the forms as the same. However, it is not a good thing in both React and HTML.

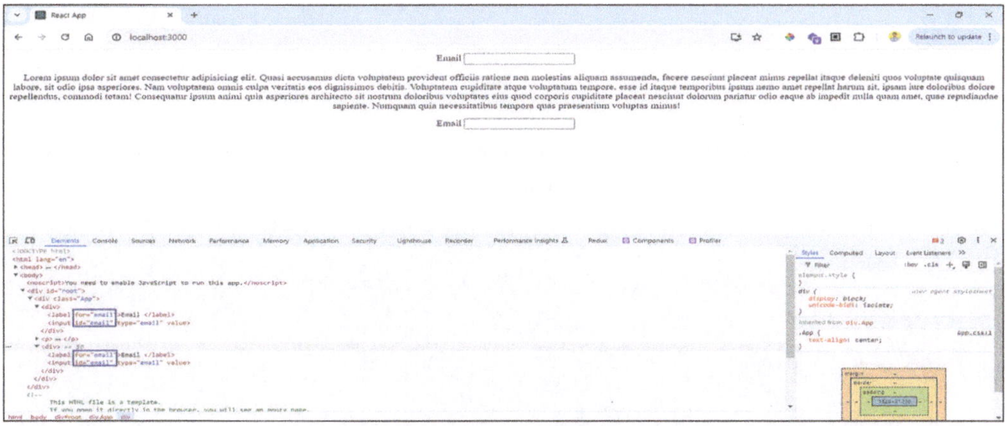

Figure 7.38: *Localhost Showing Same Ids*

To fix this issue, most people use **`Math.random()`** to generate random ids.

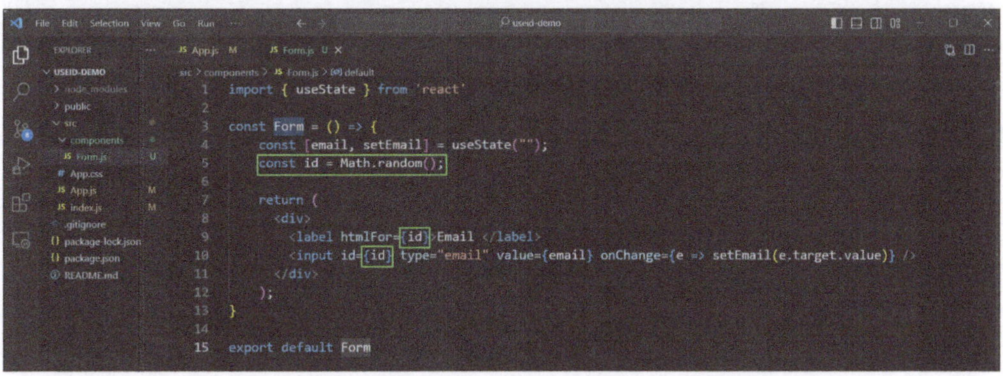

Figure 7.39: *Using Math.random for ID*

Back, in http://localhost:3000/, we will see random ids for both Forms. But type anything in email, it will keep on changing. It means every time we will get a different random id which cannot be stored on the server side.

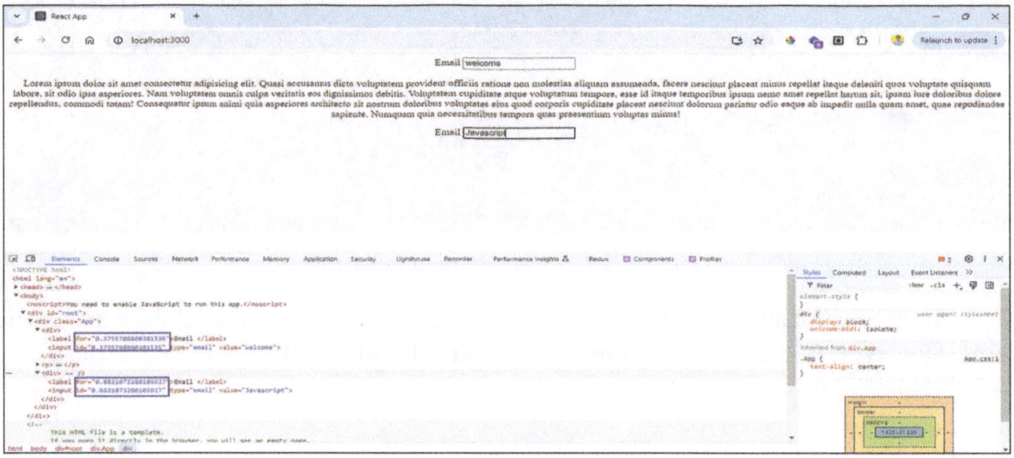

Figure 7.40: *Getting Random Ids in Localhost*

For this, we will use the React hook of **useId** to generate a random id that does not change. So, we are adding the same in the **Form.js** file.

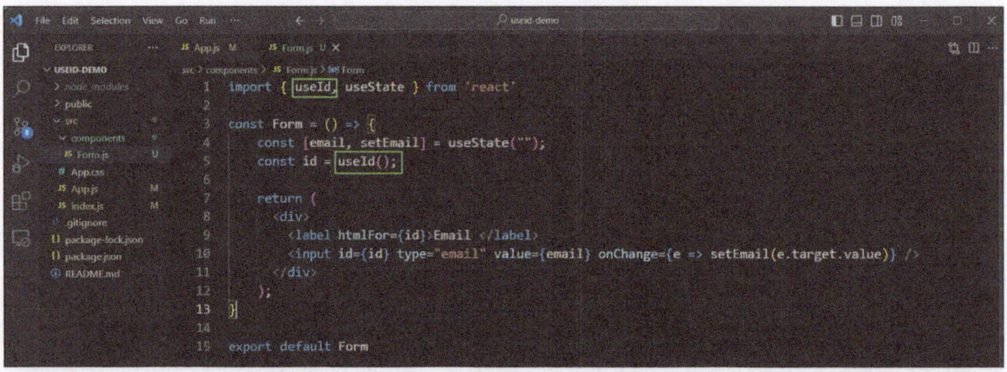

Figure 7.41: *Using useId for Random Ids*

Back, in http://localhost:3000/, we will see random ids which do not change even when we type something in input.

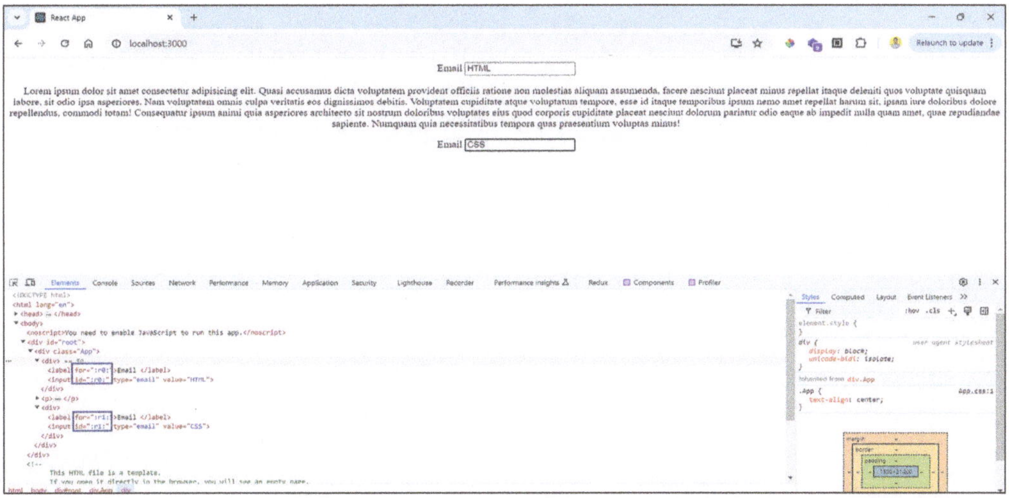

Figure 7.42: *Localhost Showing Random Ids*

Now, if we have more input fields, then we can use the **useId** again. But a better way is to use it a single time only. Add email suffix in id for email, and age suffix in id for age.

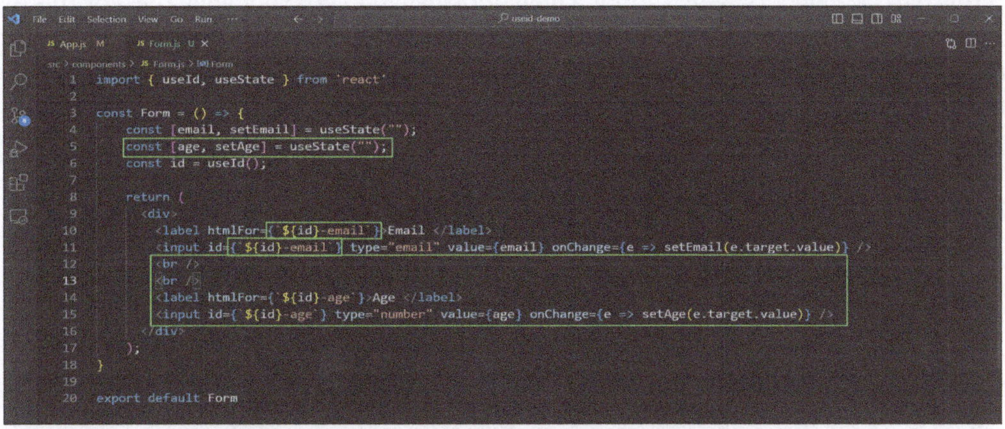

Figure 7.43: *Adding Random Ids for Email and Age*

Back, in http://localhost:3000/, we will see a random id with the correct suffix.

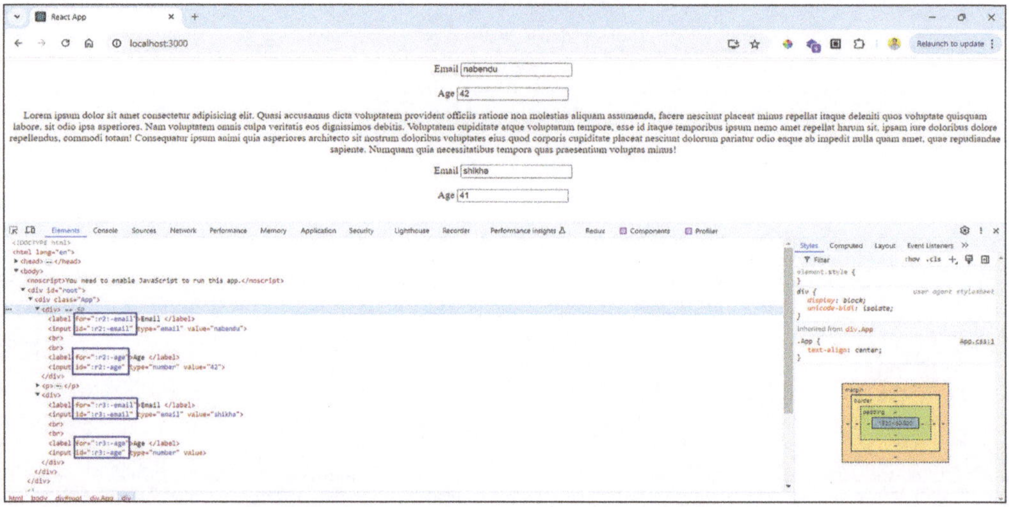

Figure 7.44: A Localhost Showing Random Ids

useDeferredValue

In this part, we will first learn about a new hook called **useDeferredValue**. For this, we have created a new project, and in the **App.js,** have the following code. Here, we have an input which changes a state called **keyword**. Later, this passes into a state to a new component called **SlowComponent**.

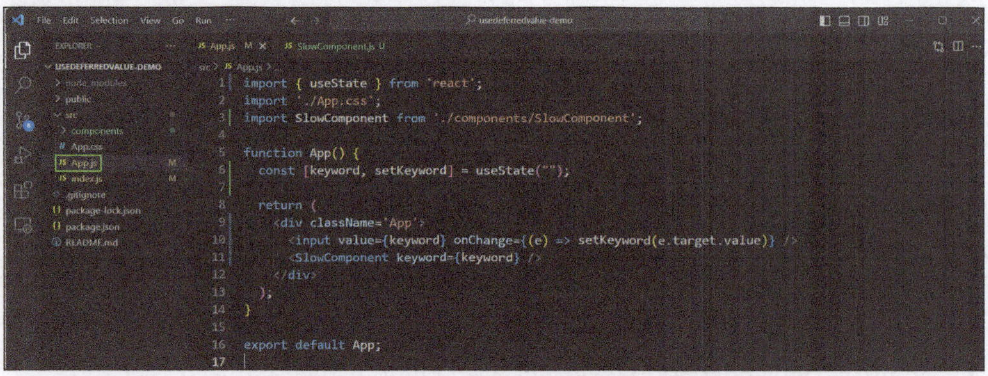

Figure 7.45: App.js for useDeferredValue Demo

Next, we have a **SlowComponent.js** file inside a **components** folder. It is taking the keyword and showing it. But, we have also introduced slowness in it, using performance.

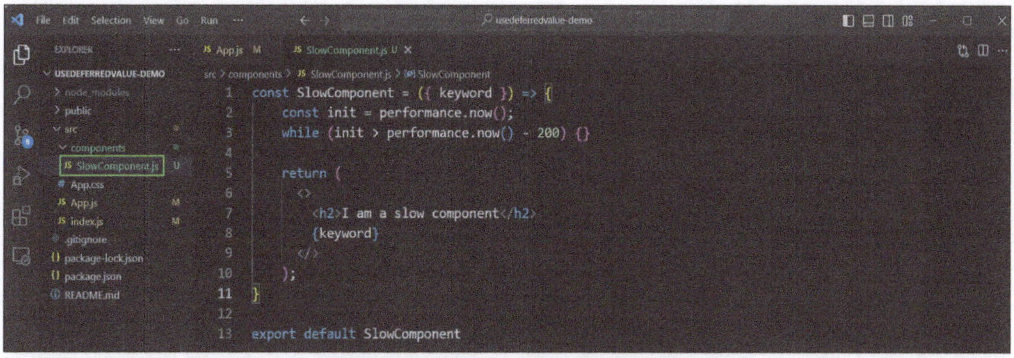

Figure 7.46: *SlowComponent.js File*

Now, in http://localhost:3000/, we will type something in the input, and we will see the output after a delay.

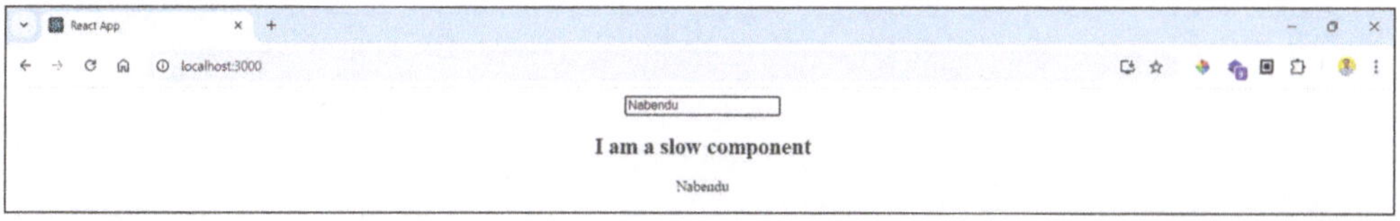

Figure 7.47: *Localhost Showing SlowComponent*

First, we will try to solve this issue with **`React`** memo. So, in the **`SlowComponent.js`** file, we will use memo.

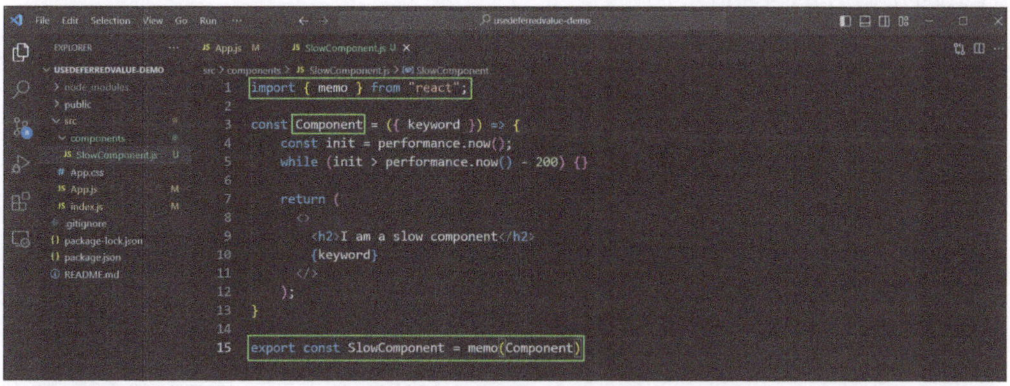

Figure 7.48: *Using Memo in SlowComponent*

But the import of **`SlowComponent`** will be different in **`App.js`** now.

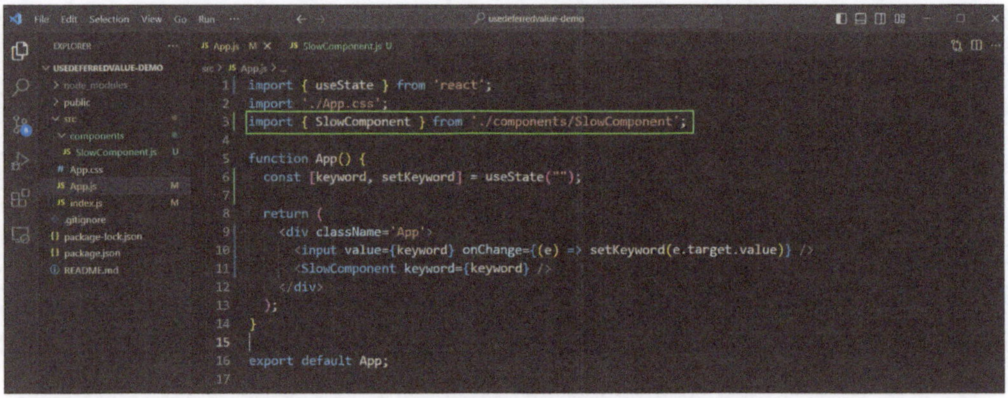

Figure 7.49: *Updating SlowComponent in App.js*

But in http://localhost:3000/, we will still see the slowness when we type something.

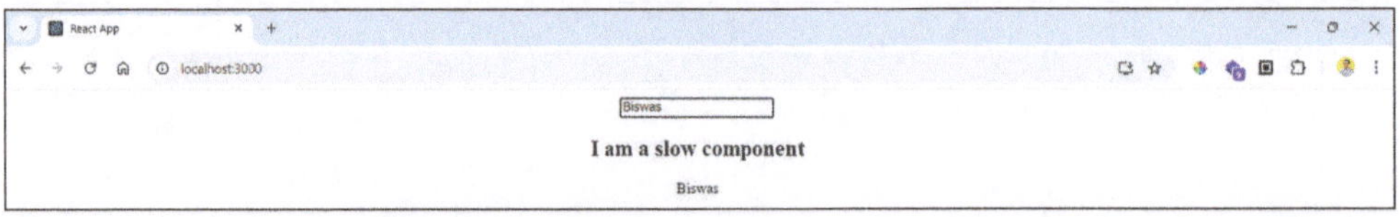

Figure 7.50: *Localhost Still Showing Slowness*

The react memo is required here, but in combination with another hook called **`useDeferredValue`**. For this, when the user is going to type in the input, we are going to pass a deferred version of it.

For this in the **`App.js`** file, we will use the **`useDeferredValue`** hook, and pass the keyword to it. Now, in the **`SlowComponent,`** we will pass the **`deferredKeyword`**.

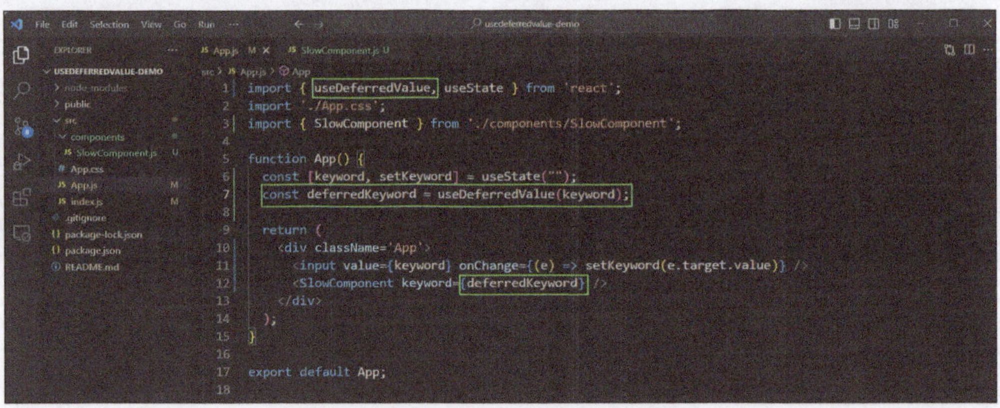

Figure 7.51: *useDeferredValue in App.js*

But, in http://localhost:3000/, when we type anything fast, it will show at once, which is the user experience that we want.

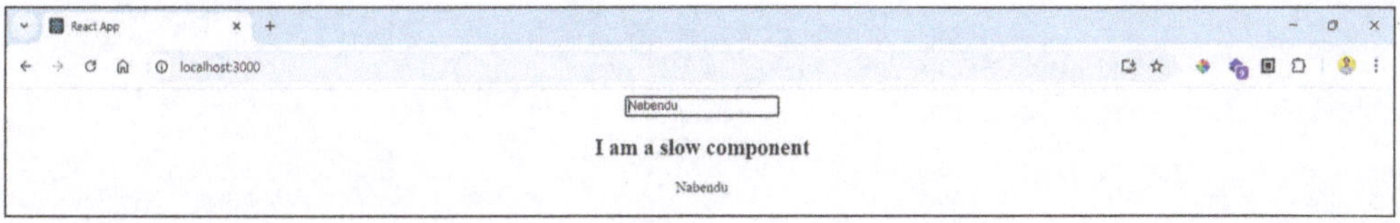

Figure 7.52: *No Slowness in Localhost*

useTransition

In this part, we will use a similar hook to **`useDeferredValue`**, but it is used in a different scenario. For this, we will look into our new app. We have created a new app with the **`create-react-app`** command, and then installed **`styled-component`** in it for styling.

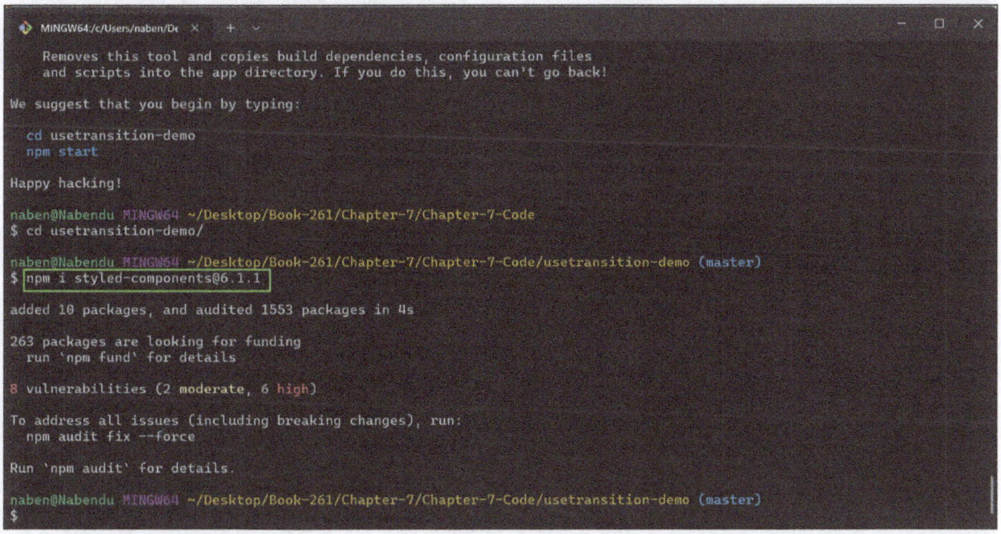

Figure 7.53: *New Project with Styled-components*

For the styling, create a components folder and a file **`StyledComponents.js`** inside it. Here, we have styles called **`StyledButton`** and **`ReviewsContainer`**.

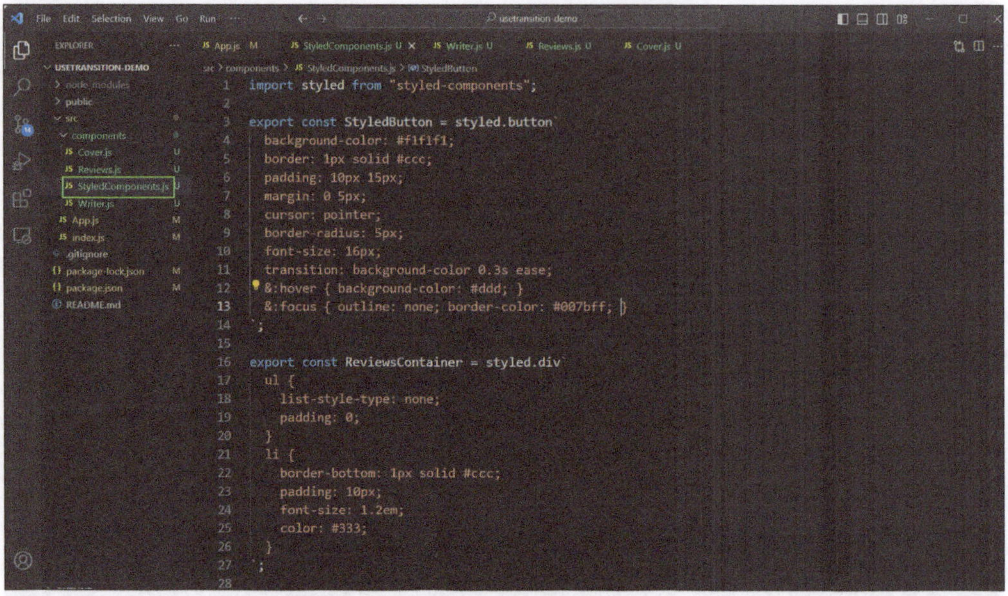

Figure 7.54: *Styles in StyledComponents.js*

We will add some more styles for **`WriterContainer`**, **`CoverContainer`**, and **Emoji** in the file **`StyledComponents.js`**.

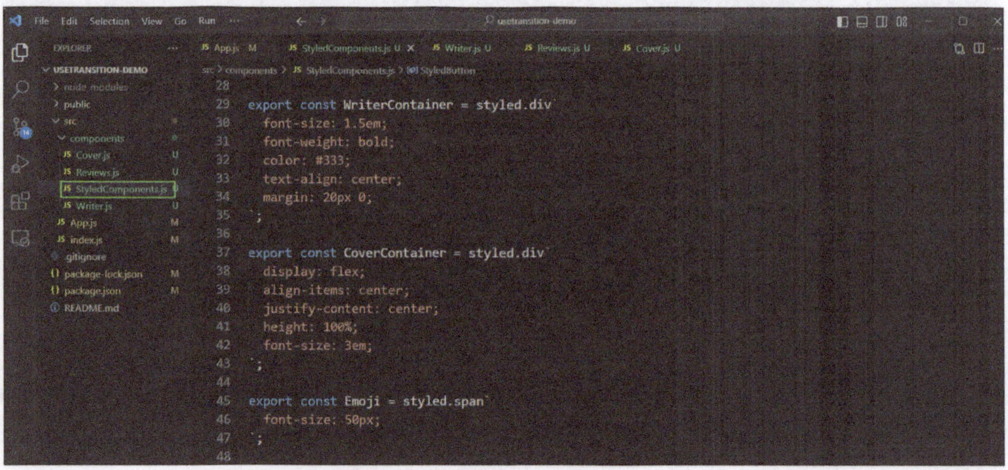

Figure 7.55: *More Styles in StyledComponents.js*

Now, create a component called **`Writer.js`**, which has a simple text, and uses the styled component.

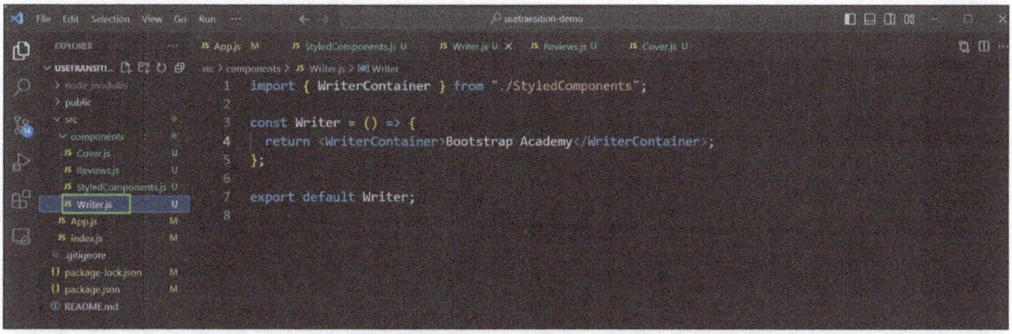

Figure 7.56: *Writer.js File*

Next, create the **`Reviews.js`** component which will show 300 review texts. It also has performance used to introduce delays.

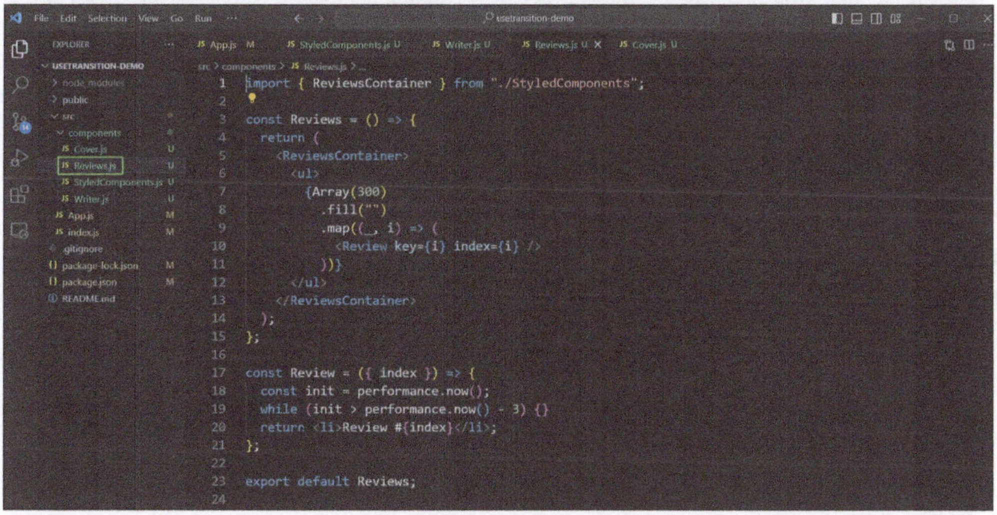

Figure 7.57: *Reviews.js File*

The last component is **`Cover.js`** that shows a simple Emoji.

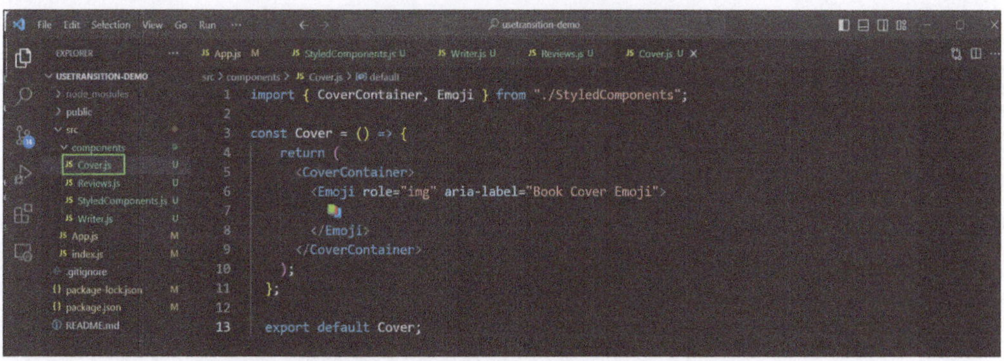

Figure 7.58: *Cover.js File*

Now, in the **App.js** file, we will have three buttons. Clicking on each of them will show the **Cover**, **Reviews** or **Writer** component, because of the change in state.

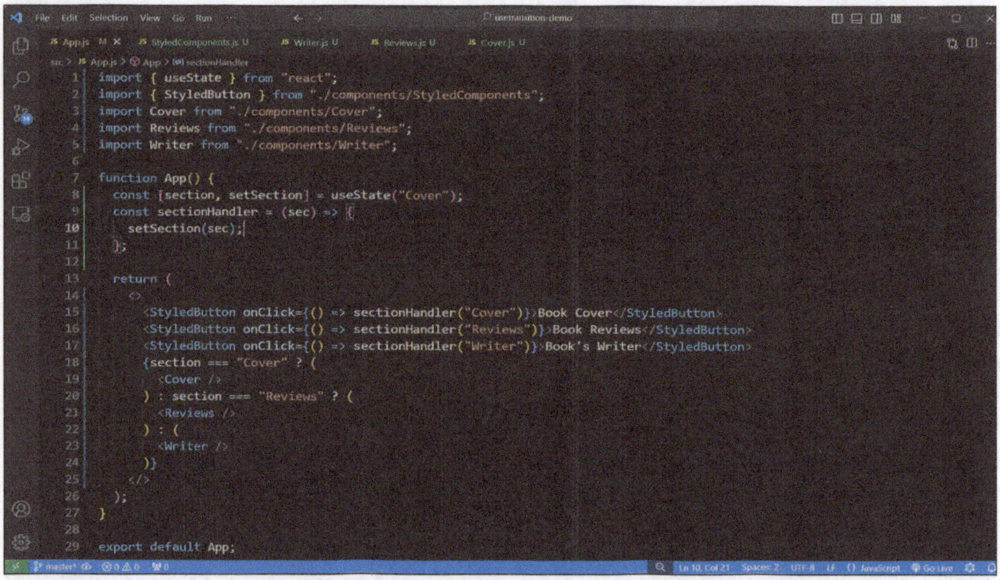

Figure 7.59: *App.js Showing All Components*

In http://localhost:3000/ by default, the **Cover** component will be shown which shows the emoji.

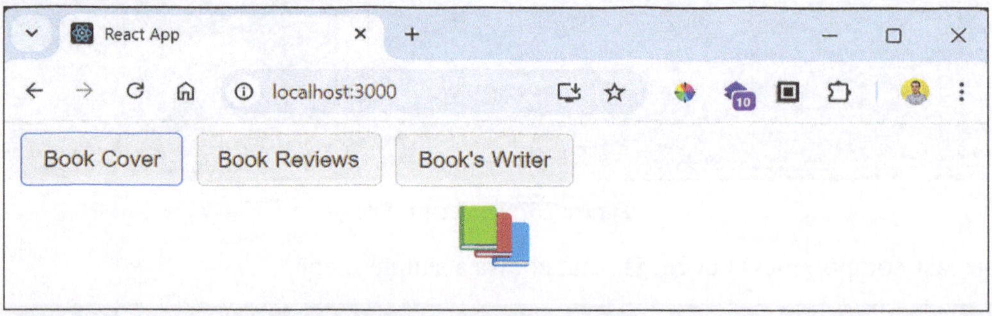

Figure 7.60: *Localhost Showing Book Cover*

Clicking on the **Book's Writer** button will show the simple text.

Figure 7.61: *Localhost Showing Book's Writer*

Clicking on the **`Book Reviews`** will show the 300 reviews with a bit of delay, because of the addition of performance in the code.

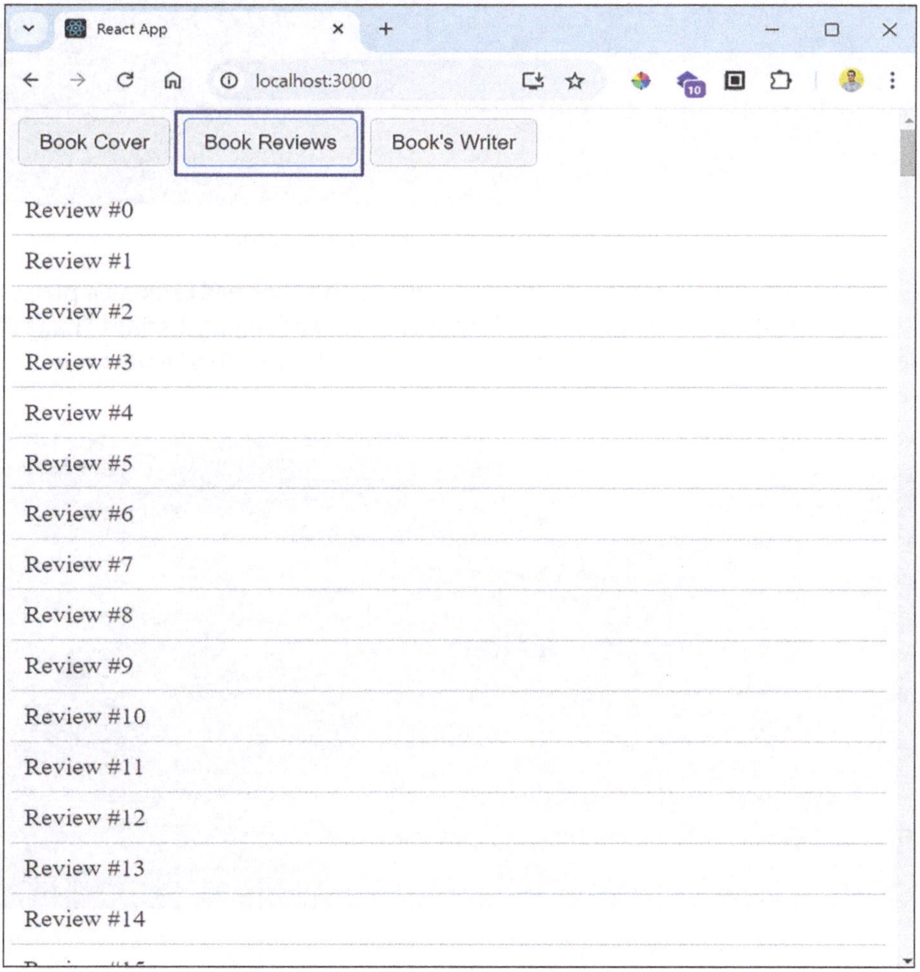

Figure 7.62: *Localhost Showing Book Reviews*

There is a problem in the system. When you click on **Book Reviews**, the system freezes, because it takes some time. To solve this issue, we have to use a new react hook called **useTransition** in the **App.js file**. We are also calling a **Button** component here that we are going to create next.

Figure 7.63: *Adding useTransition in App.js*

Next, we have created the **Button component** which takes **onClick** as a prop. After that, we have the **useTransition** hook that has **isPending** and **startTransition**. Inside the return statement, we have updated the **StyledButton** to use **startTransition** for the **onClick**.

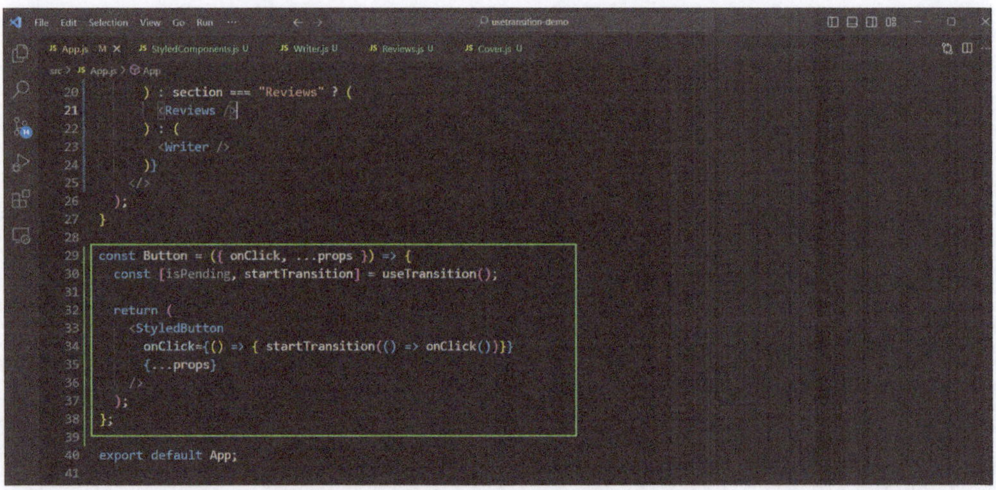

Figure 7.64: *Using useTransition in App.js*

Now, in http://localhost:3000/, click on **Book Reviews**, and then quickly on Book's

Writer. It will work perfectly with no delays, and the screen will not freeze due to slowness of Book Reviews.

Figure 7.65: *Localhost Working Perfectly*

Conclusion

In this chapter, we have first learnt about React Portals which lets you render some child in different parts of a DOM. After this, we have learnt about Error Boundaries that are a way to catch errors, and show meaningful statements.

Next, we learnt about keys which are a way to preserve the state in React. After this, we learnt about **`useLayoutEffect`** that lets us solve the issue of rendering with **`useEffect`** hook.

Next, we learnt about the **`useId`** hook which allows us to effectively generate random keys. We also learnt about the **`useDeferredValue`** hook which is helpful when we search something in input fast, and want all to be used at once.

Lastly, we learnt about the **`useTransition`** hook that allows us for a smooth transition, in case when some section takes time to load, and we click on other sections.

In the next chapter, we will learn Element props first, and then optimizing context API. After this, we will learn to use less **`useEffect`**. Then we will learn about General Architecture, and finally about Route and Encapsulating components.

Points to Remember

- Using portals to render children in different parts which is required sometimes.
- Using error boundaries to show meaningful errors.
- Using keys to preserve the state in React.
- Using **`useLayoutEffect`**, instead of **`useEffect`**, to change the rendering sequence.
- Using **`useId`** to create random keys.
- Using **`useDeferredValue`** and **`useTransition`** to solve concurrency issues.

CHAPTER 8

Clean Code Tips and Scalable Architecture

Introduction

In this chapter, we will first learn about Clean Code tips in React. Here, we will learn to first use Element prop, and then Optimizing Context API. After that, we will learn about using less **`useEffect`** hook. Next, we will learn about scalable architecture. Here, we shall learn about General Architecture, Route Components, and Encapsulating Components.

Structure

In this chapter, we are going to discuss in detail about the following topics.

- Using **`Element`** Prop
- Optimizing Context API
- General Architecture
- Route Components
- Encapsulating Components

Using Element Prop

First, we are going to see the use case of Element prop. We have created a new project in which in this **`App.js` file**, we are using a Button component to pass different size props. We also have an anchor tag that will cause issues later.

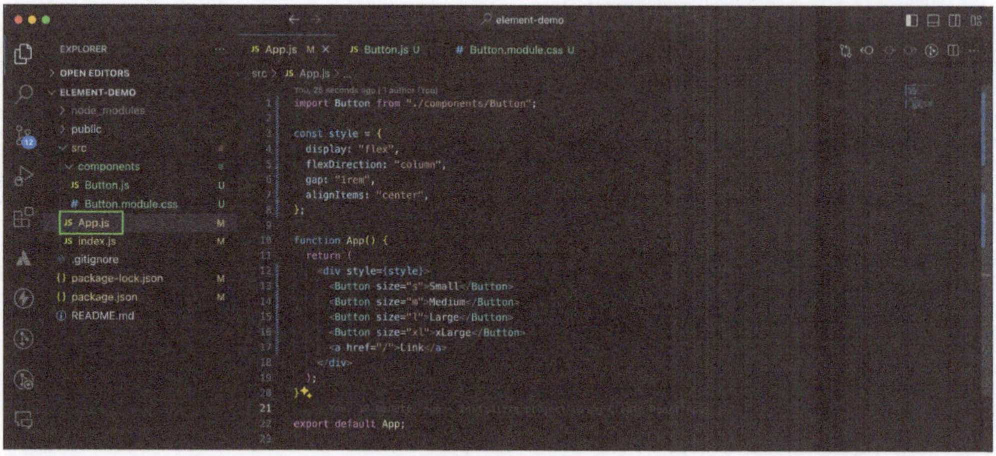

Figure 8.1: *App.js File*

Now, in a **`Button.js` file**, in the **`components`** folder, we have the following code. Here, we are simply taking the props, and showing a button. We are also showing styles from the **`Button.module.css` file**.

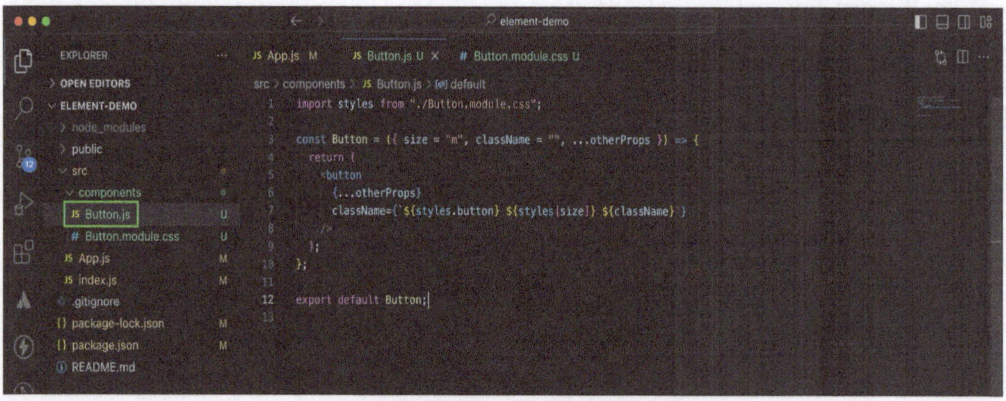

Figure 8.2: *Button.js File*

The **`Button.module.css`** file contains the following styles.

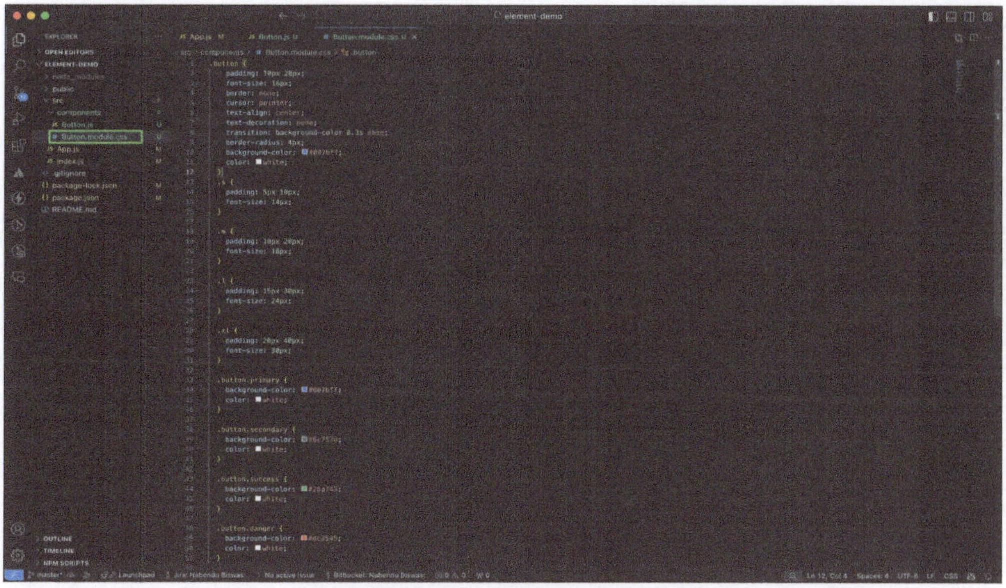

Figure 8.3: *Button.module.css File*

Now, in http://localhost:3000/, we can see the odd anchor tag, showing a different style.

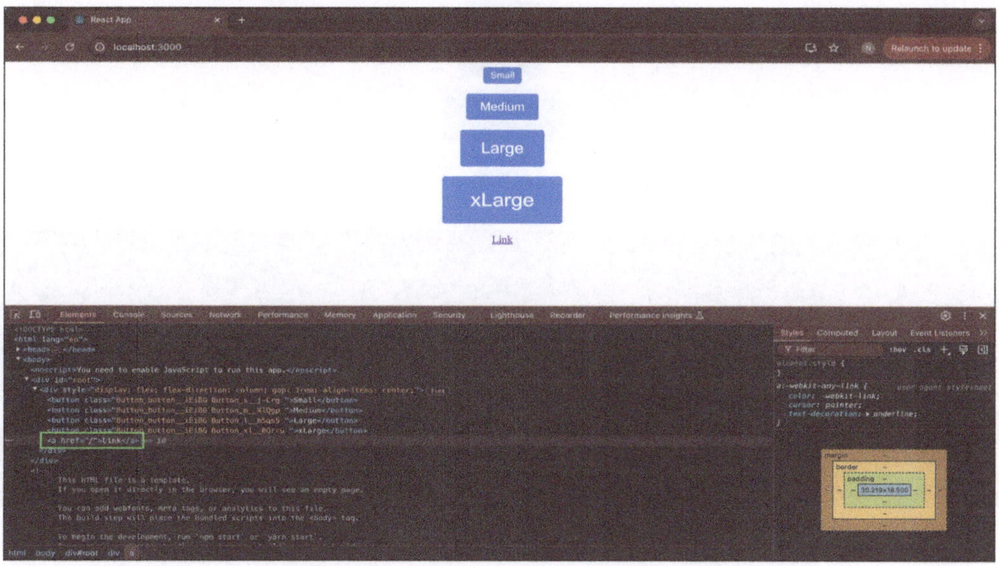

Figure 8.4: *Localhost Showing a Wrong Link*

Now, we want it to look like one of these buttons. We can try to achieve it by wrapping the anchor tag with the **`Button` component** in the **`App.js` file**.

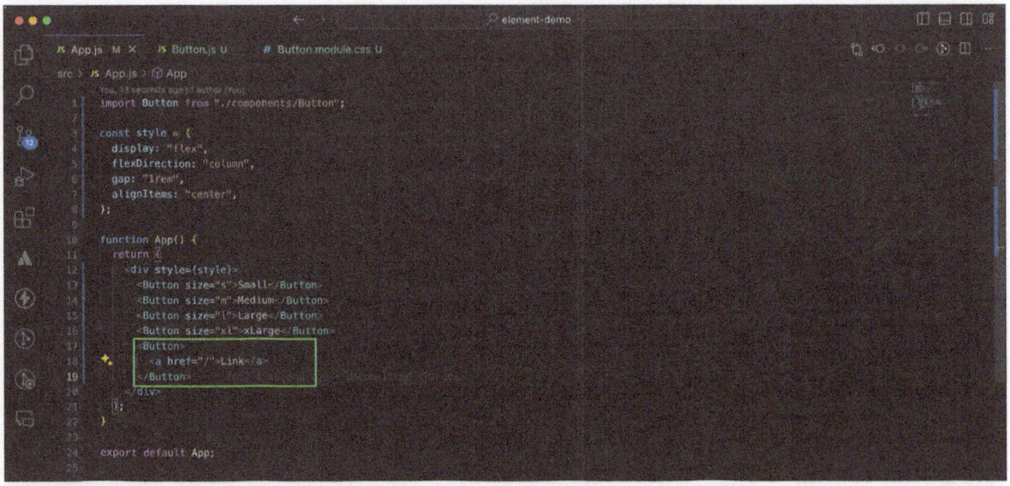

Figure 8.5: *Updating App.js*

Back, in http://localhost:3000/, we can see the anchor tag not taking all the styles of the button. Also, it will also not behave properly.

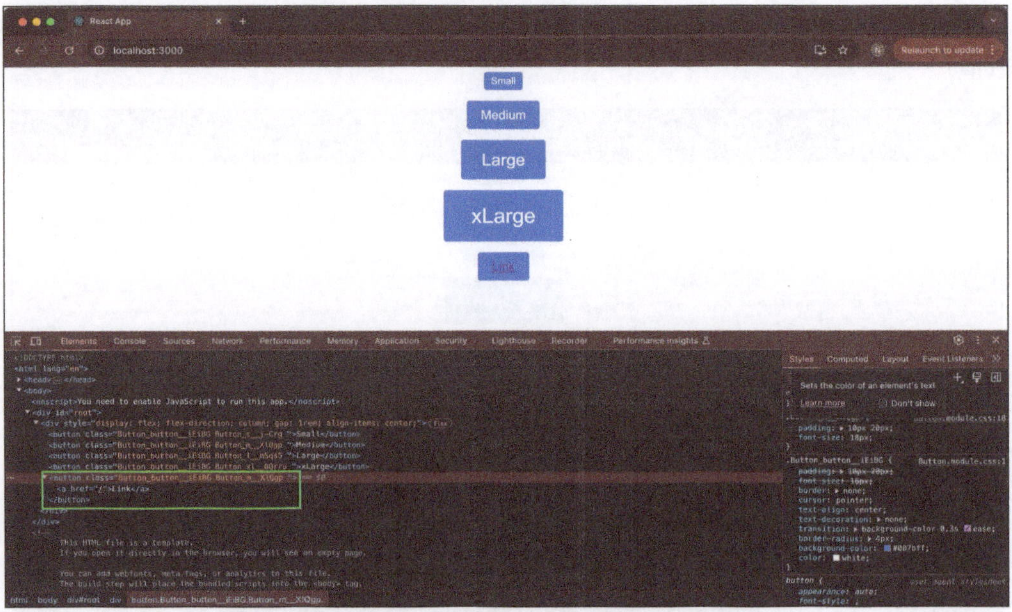

Figure 8.6: *Still Link Showing Wrong in Localhost*

To solve this issue in the **`Button.js`** file, we will pass a new prop called As, and show it instead of the button. It has a default value of button. So, if we do not pass anything, it will be a button.

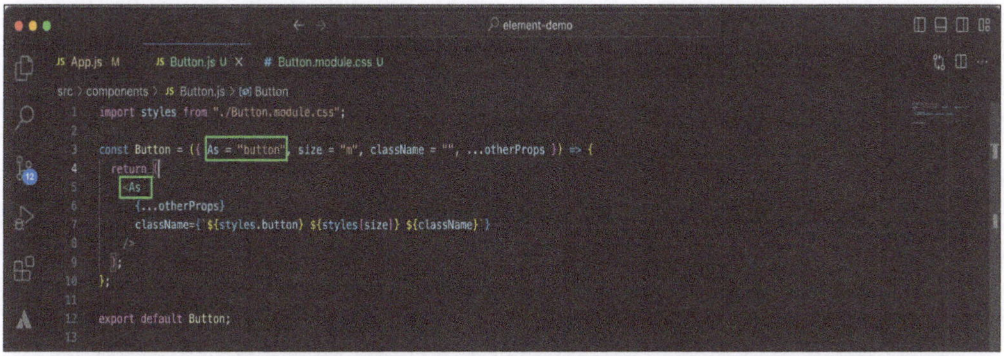

Figure 8.7: *Passing As Prop in Button Component*

Now, in the **`App.js`** file, we will update the anchor tag. Here in the **`Button`** component, we will pass the **`As`** prop as '**a**'.

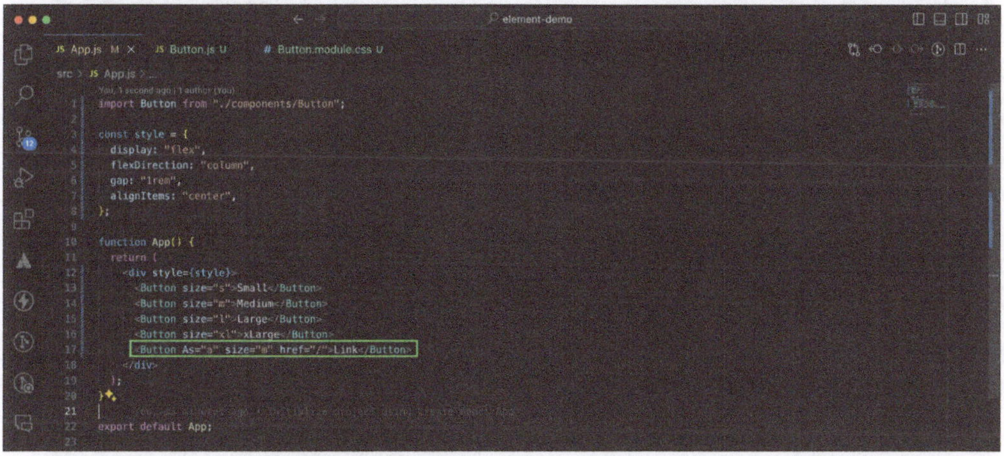

Figure 8.8: *Link Component with As Prop*

Back, in http://localhost:3000/, we can see the anchor tag taking the style properly, and also being shown as anchor tag.

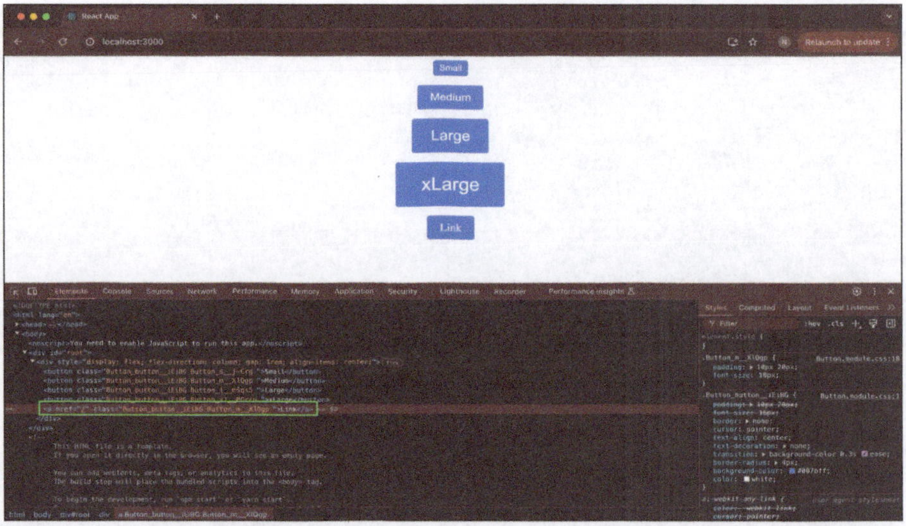

Figure 8.9: *Localhost Showing Link Component Correctly*

Optimizing Context API

We have created a new React TypeScript project for this part. First, add the following code in the **`App.js`** file. Here, we are using the **`Context API`**, along with **`useReducer`** hook. We are wrapping the **`Context Provider`** with two of our components called Display and Buttons.

Also, notice that we have a custom hook called **`useCartContext`** which is using the **`useContext`**, and returning the value.

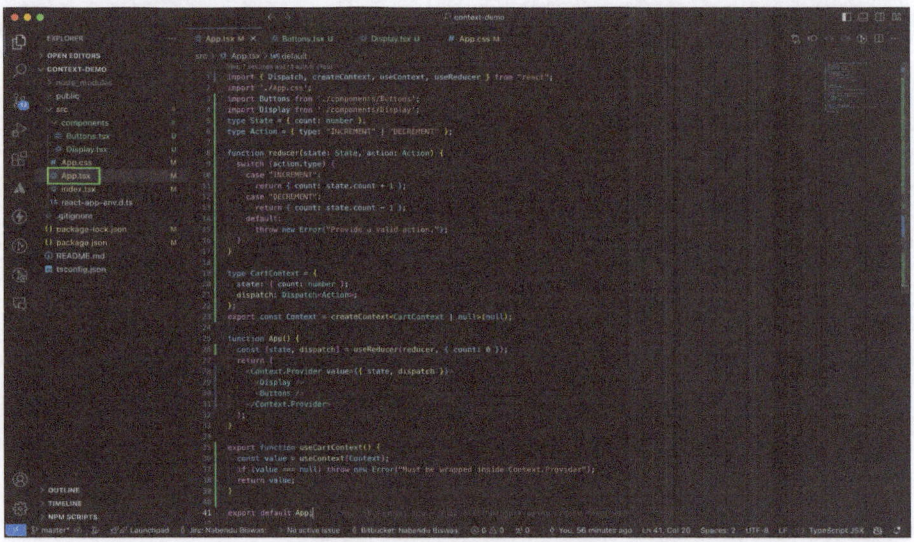

Figure 8.10: *App.tsx File*

Now, inside the **components** folder, we have the **Buttons.tsx** file. Here, we are using the **useCartContext** from the **App** component. Also, we are dispatching different types by clicking the **Decrement** and **Increment** buttons.

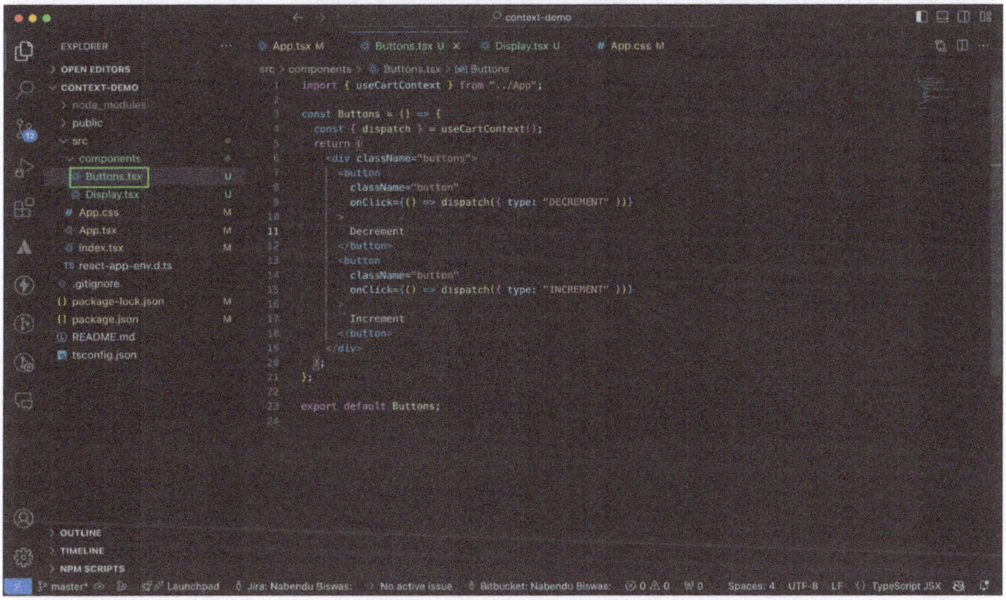

Figure 8.11: *Buttons.tsx File*

Now, inside the **Display.tsx** file, we are again using the **useCartContext** from the **App** component. But here, we are getting the state of count, and displaying it.

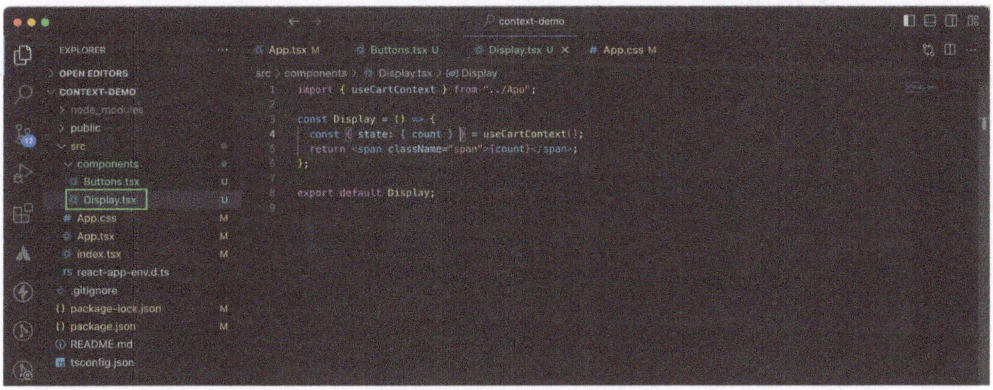

Figure 8.12: *Display.tsx File*

We also have simple styles in the **App.css** file.

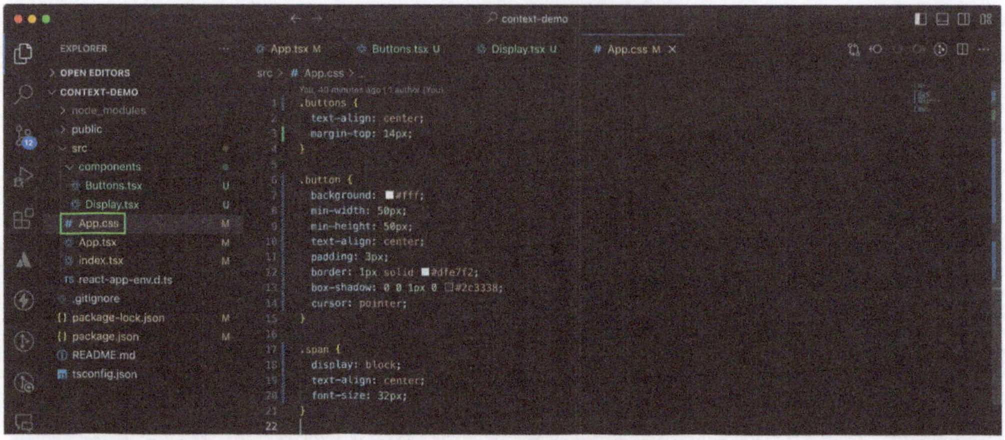

Figure 8.13: *App.css File*

Once, we are running the app in http://localhost:3000/, we have simple **`Increment`** and **`Decrement`** buttons that work quite fine.

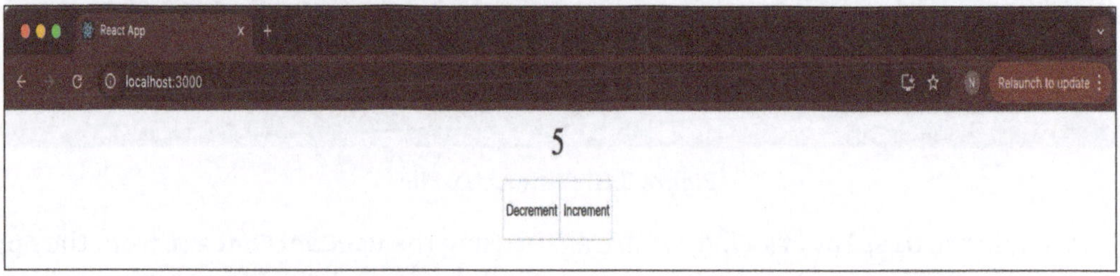

Figure 8.14: *Localhost Showing Increment and Decrement Buttons*

Everything is ok here, but we will make it perfect by separation of logic. Hence, we are not exposing the Context API related codes around our Code base. Separating the Context API logic helps us to migrate easily. For example, if we want to migrate from Context API to React Redux, it will be easier.

For this, we have created a new **`CardProvider.tsx`** file inside the **`components`** folder. We have moved all the codes related to Context from **`App.tsx`** to here. Also, we have added a **`CardProvider`** component which takes a children prop.

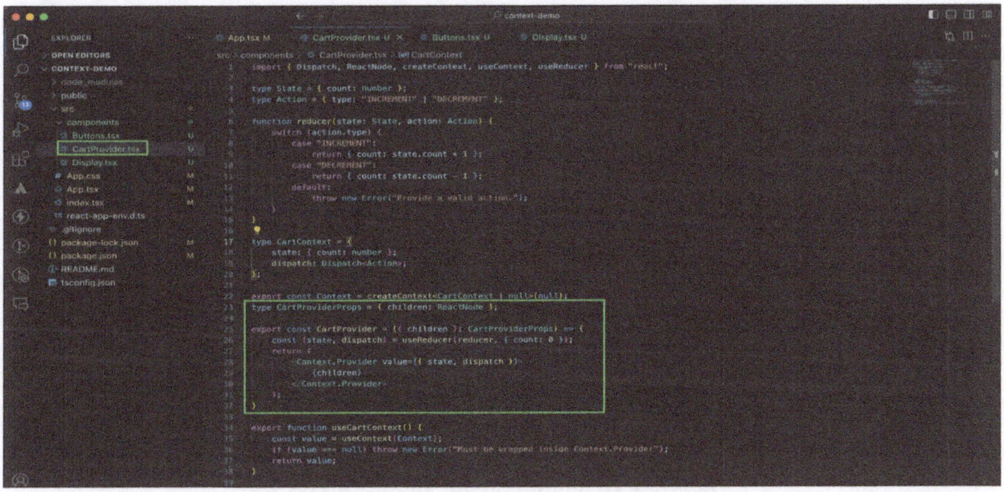

Figure 8.15: *Moving Code to CardProvider.tsx*

The **`App.tsx`** file is now minimalist with calling the **`CardProvider`** component, and passing the **`Display`** and **`Buttons`** components as children.

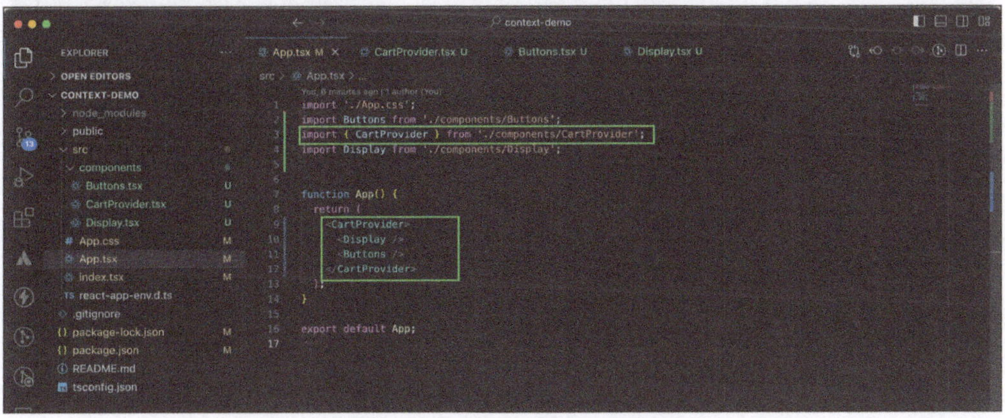

Figure 8.16: *Minimalist App.tsx*

We have to also change the import in the **`Buttons.tsx`** file.

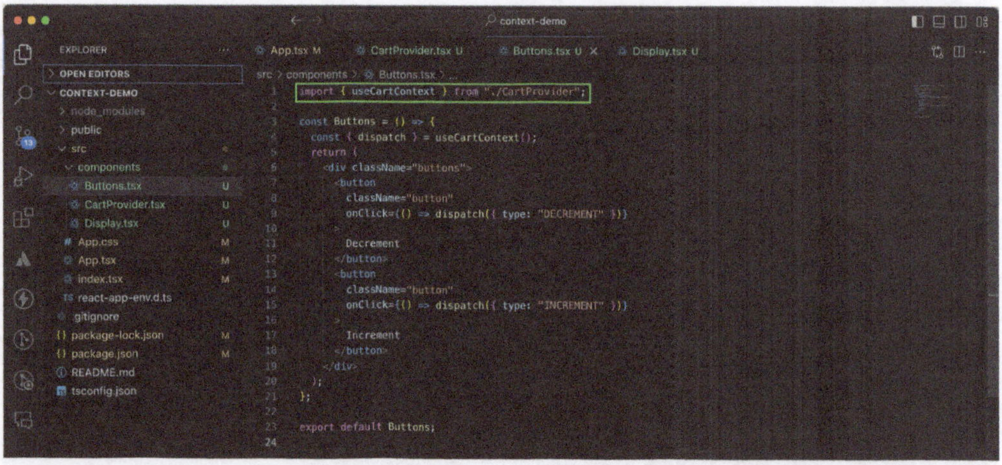

Figure 8.17: *Adding Import in Buttons.tsx*

Adding **`Imports`** in the **`Display.tsx`** file.

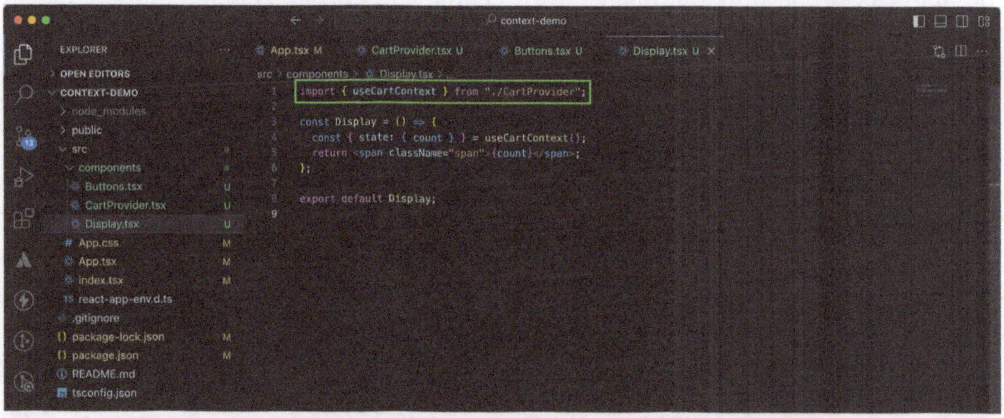

Figure 8.18: *Adding Import in Display.tsx*

Back in http://localhost:3000/, we have the app running as earlier, but the code is more optimized.

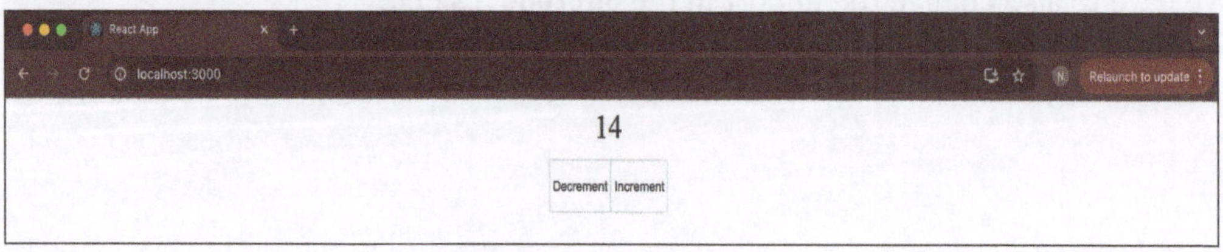

Figure 8.19: Optimized App

General Architecture

In this part, we are going to discuss the directory structure of a React project. You can prefer another structure than what we are going to learn, because it sometimes depends on the nature of the project also.

But we are going to see a standard structure which you can use in your project, and we are also going to understand the reasoning behind the same. We have created another project, and we are going to learn about the directories, from top to bottom.

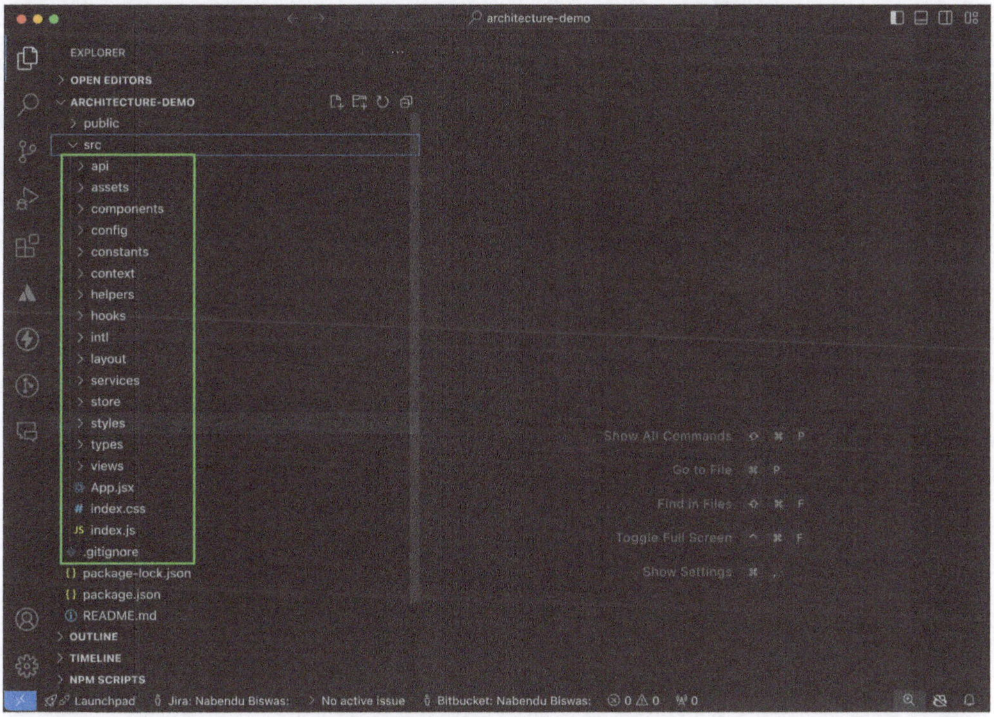

Figure 8.20: *General Architecture*

First of all, we have the **`api`** folder. So, this folder is used to contain the API layer of the application. It will have methods that are responsible mainly for performing API requests, and communicating with a server.

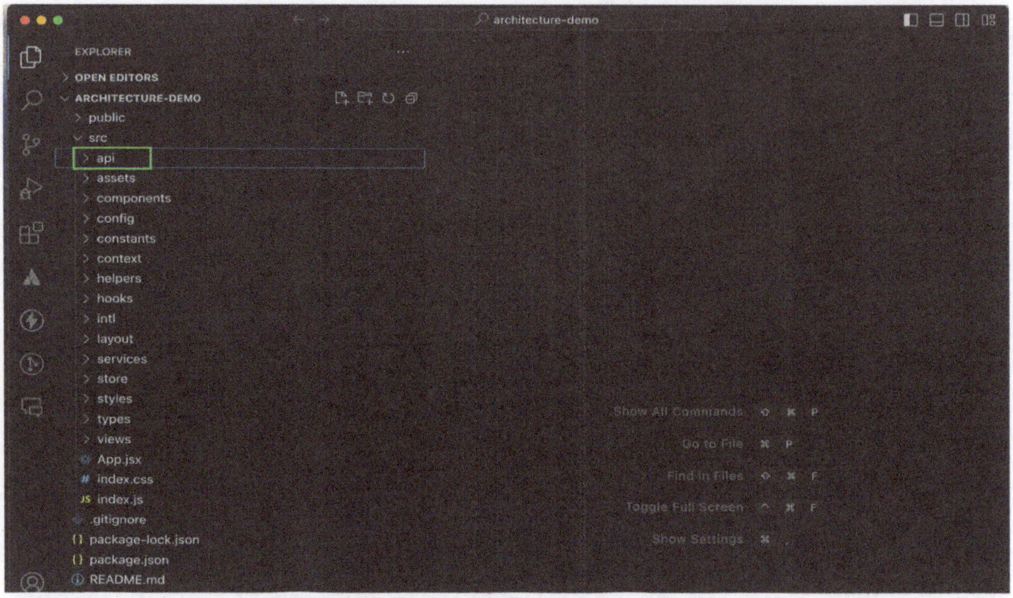

Figure 8.21: *api Folder*

Then, we come to the **`assets`** folder. It contains **`fonts`** and **`images`** folder. In the **`fonts`** folder, you can keep any custom fonts. And in the **`images`** directory, you store any number of pictures that you are going to use throughout the application.

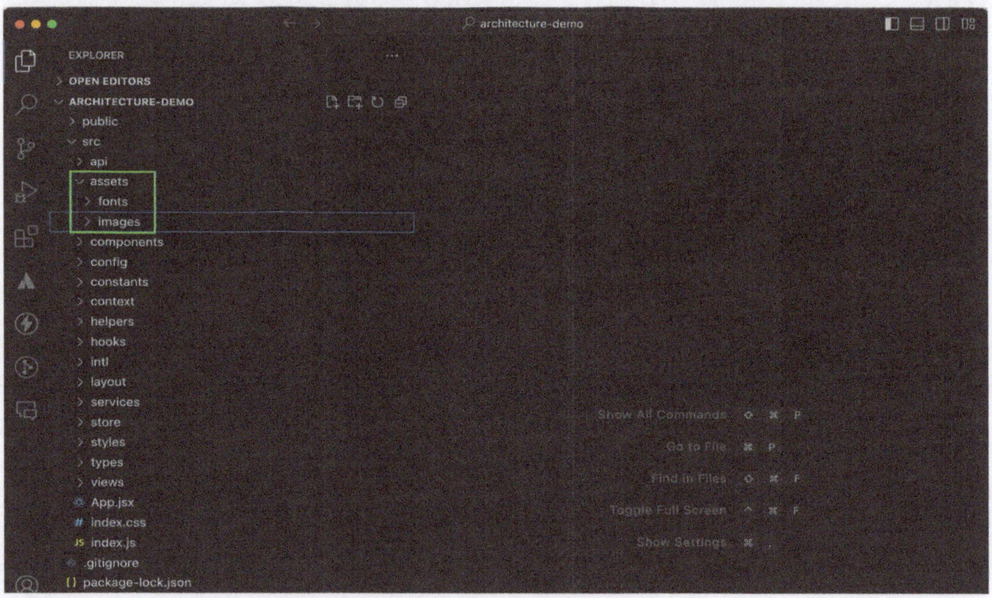

Figure 8.22: Assets Folder

Now, let us move to the **`components` folder**. It comes with a **`common`** and a **`Newsletter` folder**. The **`Newsletter`** can be any other component, and is just an example. The **`common`** directory has more folders such as **`button`**, **`form`** and **`text`** inside it. These again can be anything. It actually contains reusable components that are commonly used throughout the application, as we have used here.

Any components that are not as common would be placed inside the components, but outside the common folder such as the **`Newsletter`** folder.

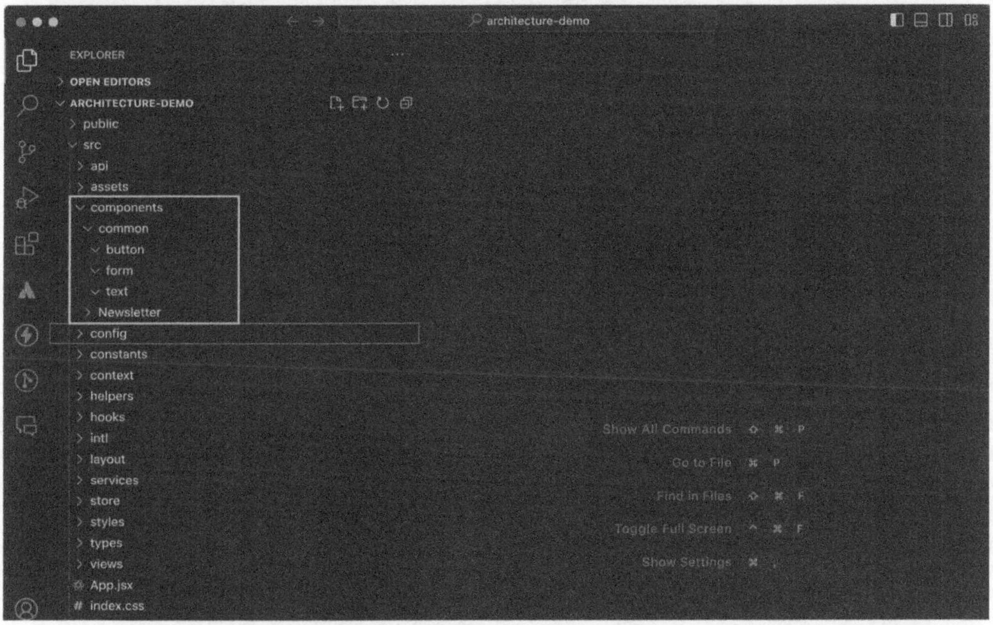

Figure 8.23: *Components Folder*

Next, we have the **config folder**. Here, you can put any runtime config files, and also third party services. For example, if you use Firebase for authentication, you will need to add configuration files, and use them in your application.

We should not confuse it with environmental variables, as anything that goes in here will be present in the build bundle. So, a thing like an environment variable commonly stored as .env should not be kept here.

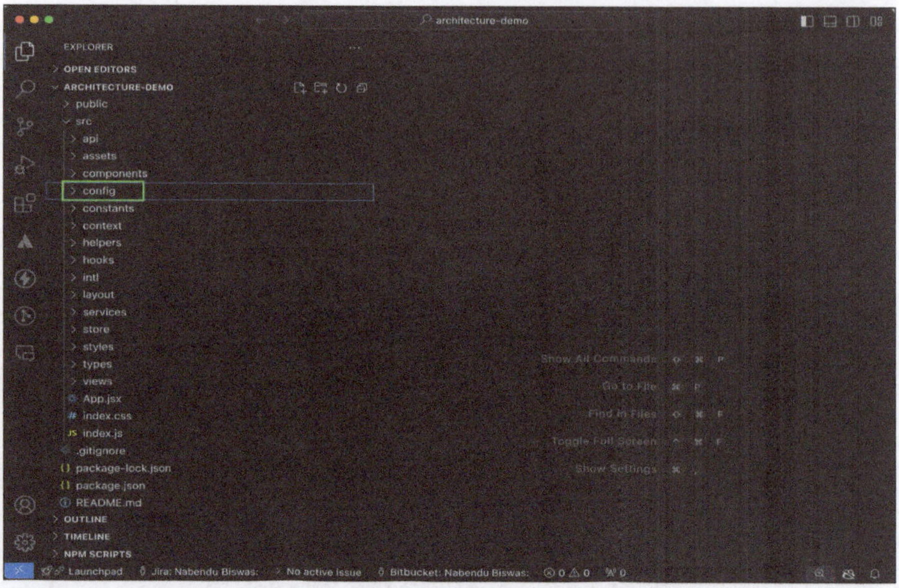

Figure 8.24: *Config Folder*

Next, we have the **`constants` folder** where we can put the constant variables which we use through the app. It is a good practice to capitalize the constants, as we can see in the example, **`app.js`** file.

This we do to distinguish them from other variables and localized constants in our applications.

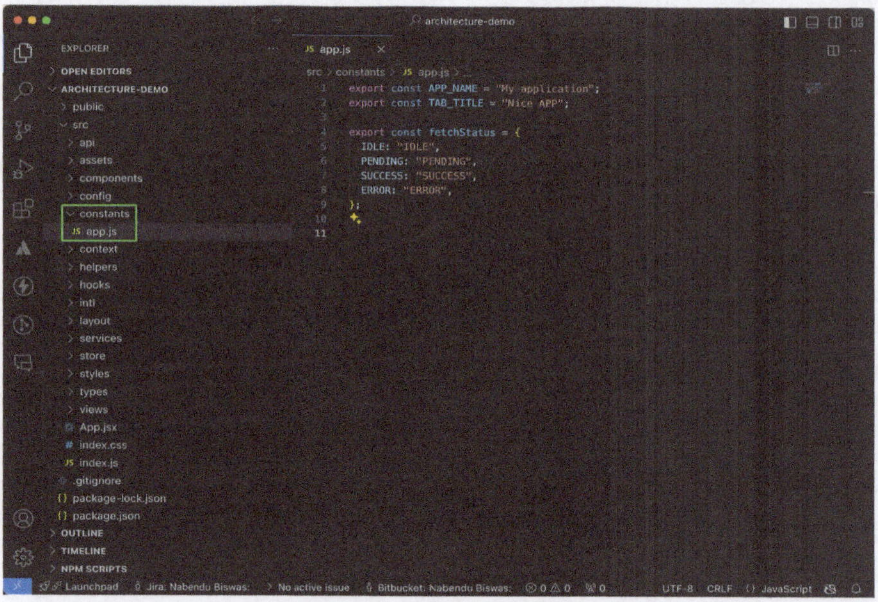

Figure 8.25: *Constants Folder*

Then, we have the **`context` directory**. The context directory should contain any global level context state providers. Therefore, this folder is only for the global state related files.

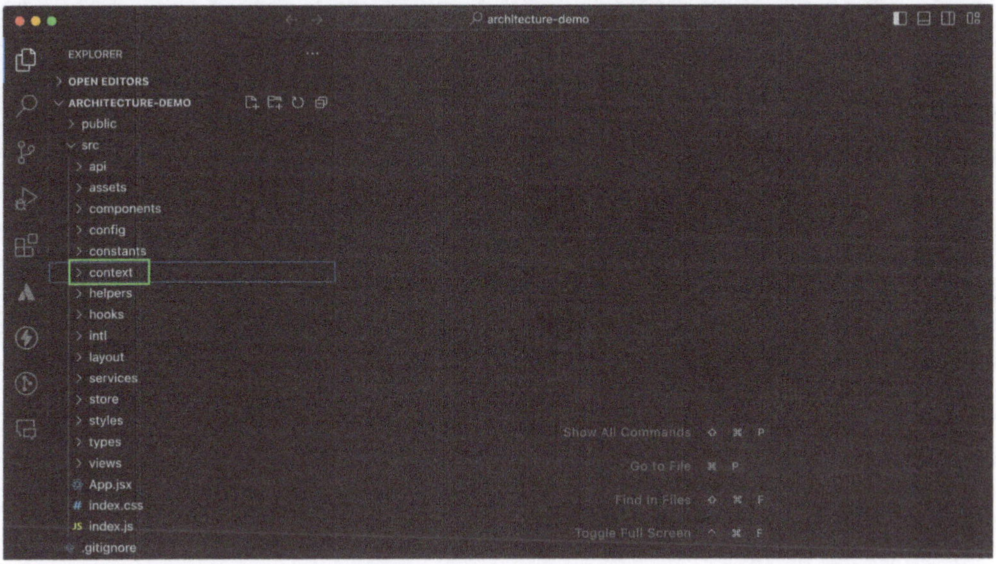

Figure 8.26: *Context Folder*

Next, we have the **`helpers` directory**. Here, we should have all the utilities and small reusable functions. For example, functions to format date, time, currency and so on.

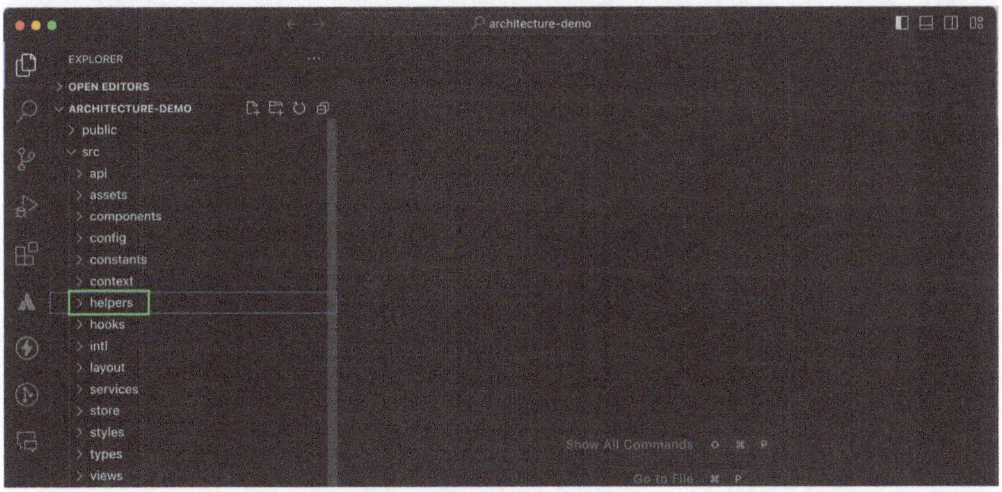

Figure 8.27: *Helpers Folder*

Then, we have the **`hooks` directory**. This will hold any custom reusable hooks which are used throughout the project.

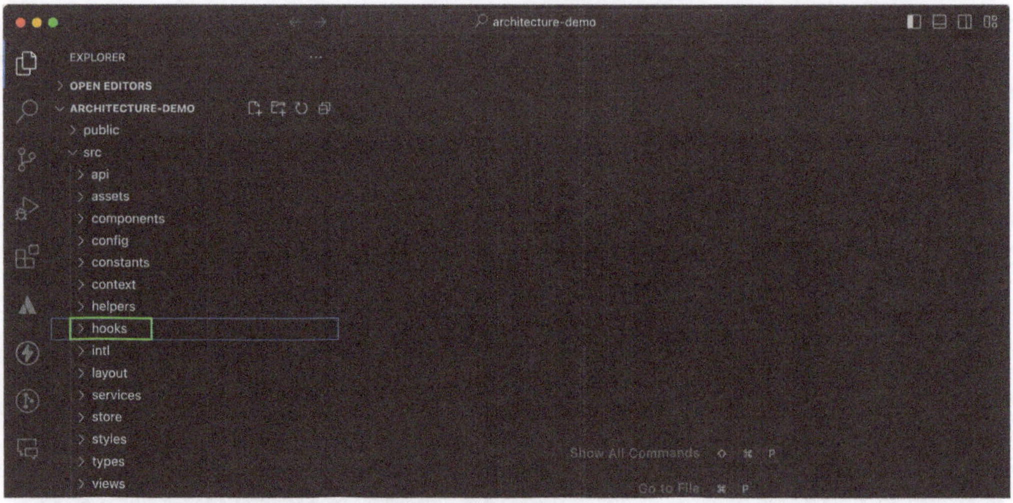

Figure 8.28: Hooks Folder

One of the directories which we use in large projects is the **init directory**, which in some projects, can be optional. It is added, when you require something like internalization support. The packages like **i18n files.**

This is about displaying the content of an app in a format appropriate to the user's local language. This content includes translated text, or specific format of dates, time and currency.

Figure 8.29: intl Folder

Now, we come to the **`layout` folder**. It should have components that provide different layouts for your pages. For example, if you are building a dashboard application, you could render different layouts, depending on if a user is logged in or not.

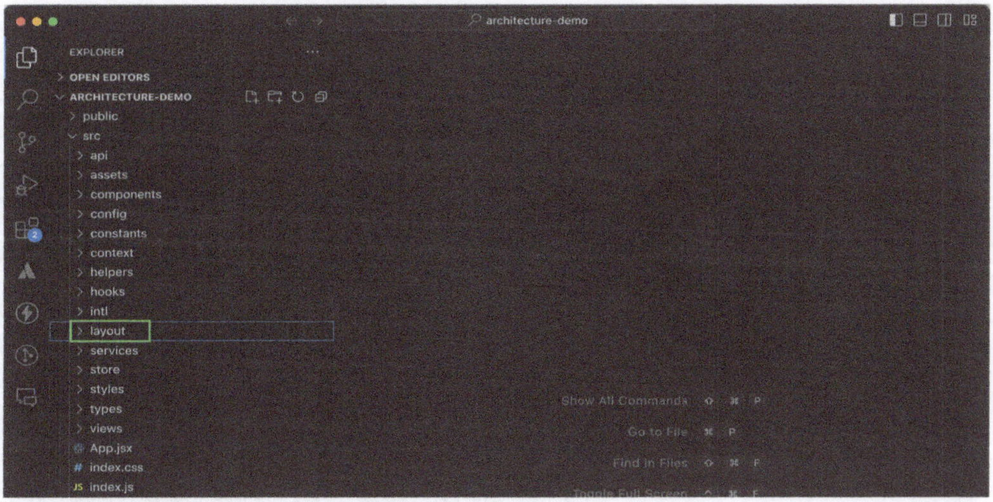

Figure 8.30: *Layout Folder*

So, in larger applications, we might have complex business logic code that is used in a few different places. Codes like these are extracted from **`components`** in places like the **`services`** folder.

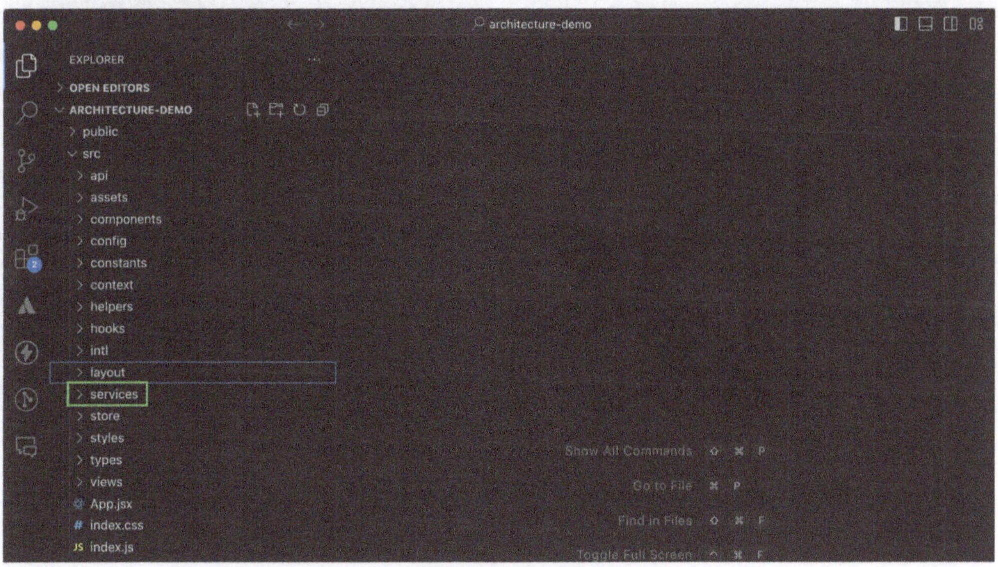

Figure 8.31: *Services Folder*

Next, we will move to the **`store`** folder. The store folder is responsible for files related to global state management. There are many popular state management solutions that can be used for React projects such as Redux, Zustand, Flux, and many more.

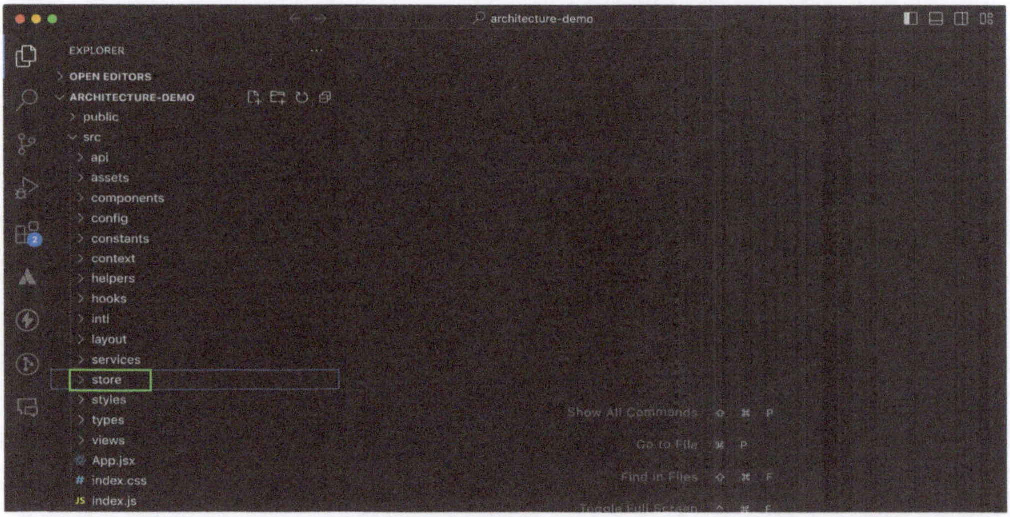

Figure 8.32: *Store Folder*

Now, we will look into the **`styles` folder**. Here, you can put global styles, variables, and theme styles in this folder.

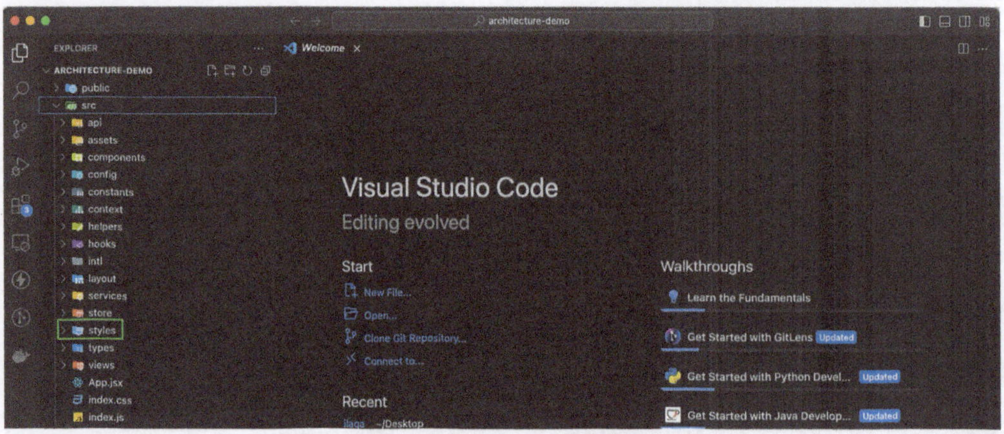

Figure 8.33: *Styles Folder*

Next comes the **types folder** where you can put any global and shareable types of a TypeScript project.

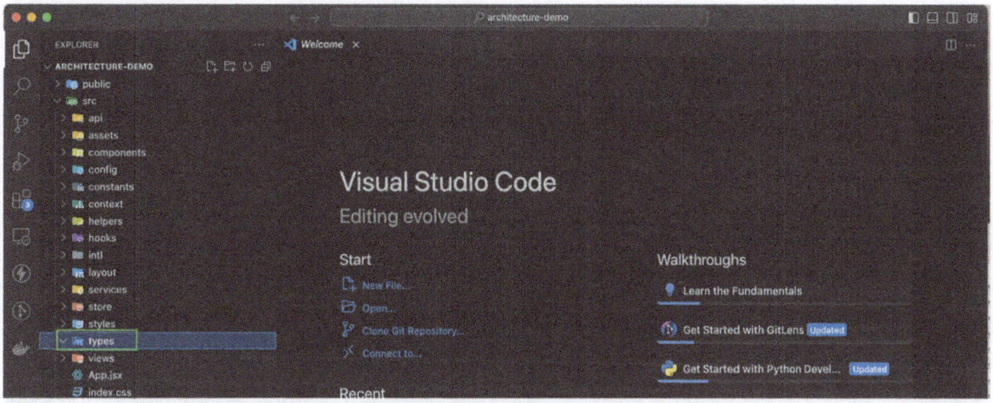

Figure 8.34: *Types Folder*

Lastly, we have the **`views` folder**. It usually contains the root components. For example, if we have a page that is supposed to allow users to view products, we can have a component called **`Products.js`** in this folder, and the **`App.jsx`** will call that as **`Products.js`** component.

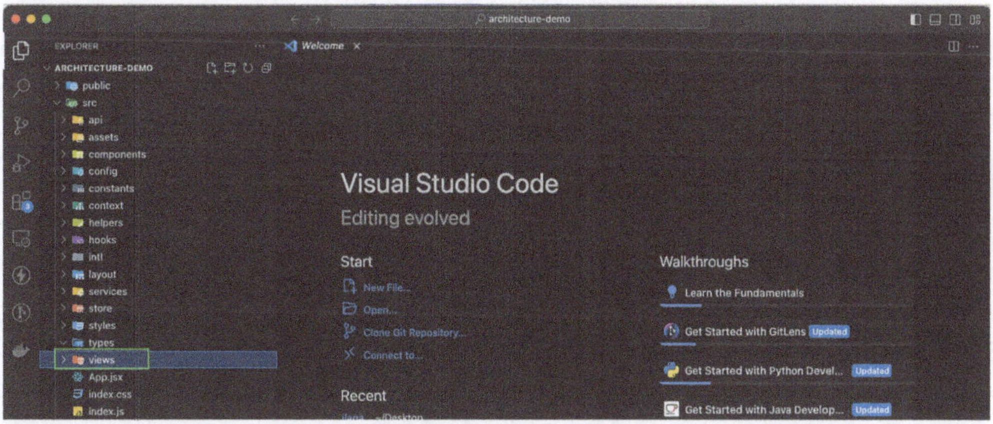

Figure 8.35: *Views Folder*

Route Components

Back in the same project, we have a **`products` folder** inside the **`views`** folder. Here, we have added all the components related to products. Also, in **`App.jsx`**, we are using React router v6. We are calling all these components, based on the route the user hits.

Figure 8.36: *Routes in App.jsx*

The components like **`AddProduct.js`** are illustrated as follows. Here, we will write all the logics to add the product. Similarly, we will have other components to get all the products, edit a product, as well as delete a product, and view a product.

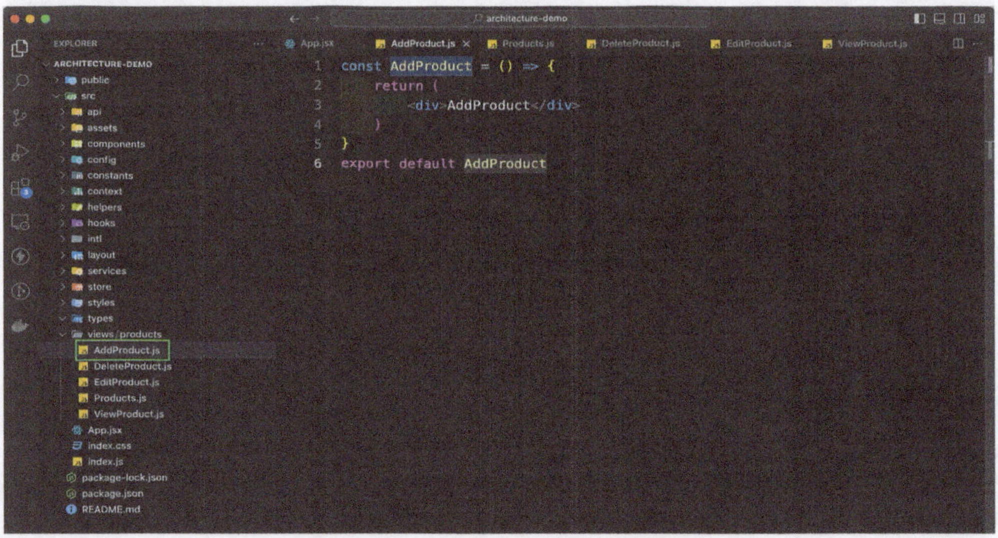

Figure 8.37: *AddProduct.js File*

Encapsulating Components

In the previous part, we have learned to manage root components to keep them more maintainable. But now, let us assume that the root components are going to consume some other components.

So, now we are going to check how to manage those components. For example, in the **`views` folder**, we have **`Edit product`** and **`Add Product`**. For both these components, we are going to have some sort of form.

The form is going to receive some information about the product, so that it is going to insert that product, or update the existing product. Also, let us assume that for both the cases, we are going to consume the same form component. The question is where should we put the product form.

Also, let us assume that the product form will require some utility functions, and also, a service file to contain some business logic. The first thing which comes to our mind is to put these files, based on what they contain.

Thus, the services go to the **`services`** folder, and the utils go to the **`helpers`** folder. Also, the product form goes to the **`components`** folder.

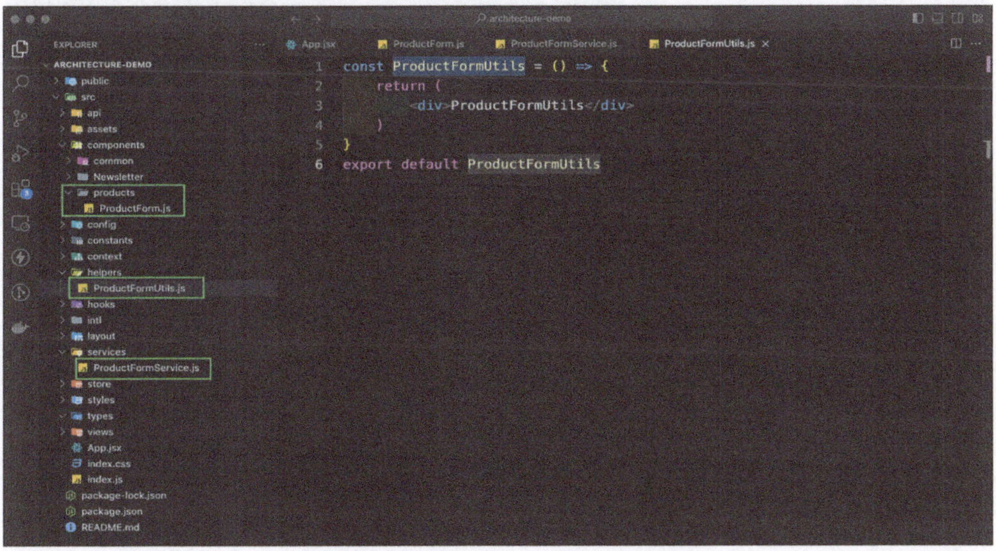

Figure 8.38: *Wrong Addition of Files*

So, is this a really nice structure? Not exactly. Actually, it is not bad, if we have just one feature in our application. However, there are few problems with this practice. First of all, we just created a couple of files, and put them in different folders. With more features, the project will get messy really fast.

Second, when working on a feature, especially in a team, you own that feature, and you are responsible for that feature as well as the code for it. But when working in a team on a larger project, there is a very high chance that your code and features will not be used that much.

Hence, instead of spreading files around the project as we did, we can keep them as close together as possible. So, inside the **`views/products`** folder, we have created a **`components`**, **`helpers`** and **`services`** folder.

The **`components`** folder further has a **`product-form`** folder which contains everything related to the form. The **`helpers`** will contain the general utilities of the products, and the services will contain the **`services`** for the products.

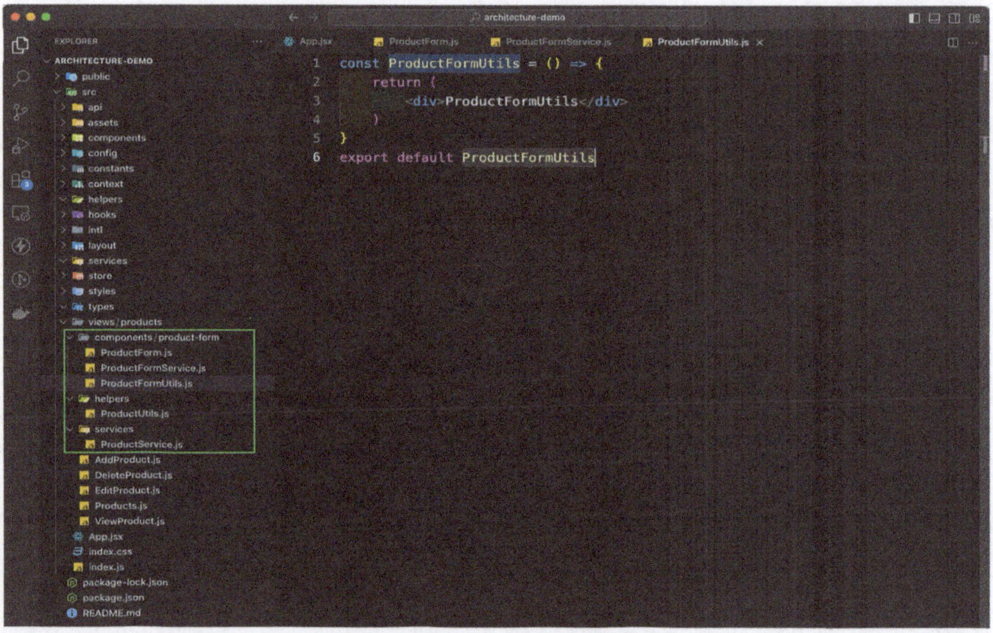

Figure 8.39: *Right Addition of Files*

This approach is known as feature based approach in which components and files are encapsulated, and kept close to where they are actually used.

Conclusion

We have first learned how to use element prop in this chapter. Following that, we discovered how to maximize the well-known context, API. The General Architecture of a sizable React project was then taught to us, and this is quite useful.

Using the overall architecture, we have learned that we may design the major project's path. Finally, we discovered how to incorporate project components.

In the next chapter, we will learn about the **API layer**. With the API layer, we will learn to add the API layer in a React project, while doing API calls.

Points to Remember

- Using element prop.
- Optimizing Context API.
- General architecture of a React project.
- Creating routes, and encapsulating components.
- Using **`useId`** to create random keys.
- Using **`useDeferredValue`** and **`useTransition`** to solve concurrency issues.

CHAPTER 9
API Layer

Introduction

In this chapter, we will learn about the API layer concepts. Here, we will first learn about the API Layer and Async Operations. In all React projects, we do API calls, but there is a better way to do them by converting them into API layers. We are going to learn the same in this chapter.

Structure

In this chapter, we are going to discuss the following topics:

- Building API Layer and API States
- Enhancing the API States
- Avoiding Flickering Loaders
- Abstracting API States
- Adding Request Abort Logic

Building API Layer and API States

Instead of having our components make API calls directly to the backend servers, we want to create an API layer in between them. We are going to use API layer codes that reside in the **`api`** folder under the **`src`** folder. We have also installed **`axios`** and **`styled-components`** through the integrated terminal.

So, we will create a new React project called **`api-layer`**, and further create an **`api`** **folder** inside the **`src`** folder. Inside it, we will create an **`api.js`** file. In this file, we are first importing the axios, and then in **`axiosParams`**, using the **`baseURL`**.

After that we have created an **`axiosInstance`** that will use the method, create, and take the **`axiosParams`**. Next, we have a function **`api`** which will receive a parameter called axios.

Inside the api function, we will return a **get**, **delete**, **post**, **patch**, and **put** functions which takes an **url** and **config**. The **config** can be **empty**. For **post**, **patch**, and **put**, it takes a body parameter also.

In the export, we call the **api function**, and pass the **axiosInstance.**

Figure 9.1: *api.js File*

The second step will be to create a feature based API file which will have several features. Here, we will create a user API that is responsible for fetching users from a backend which will be **jsonplaceholder** in our case.

So create a file **userApi.js** inside the **api** folder. Here, we are using a **fetchUser** function which is calling the **api.get()** from the api.js file. We are passing the end url, and the base **url** in it. Basically, we are passing https://jsonplaceholder.typicode.com/users.

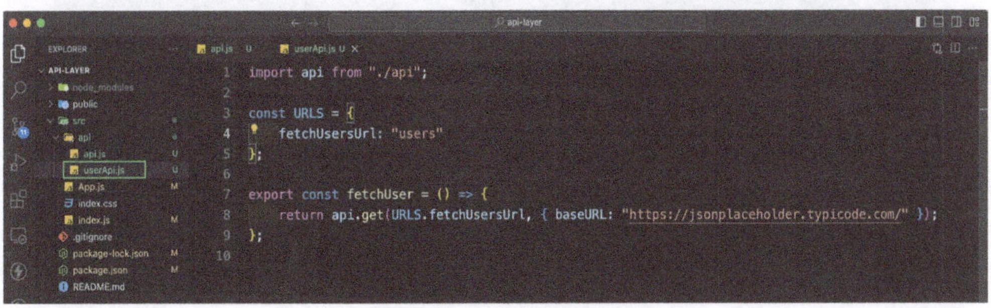

Figure 9.2: *userApi.js File*

Now, create a **components** folder inside the **src** folder, and a file **Users.js** inside it. In this file, we are first creating a custom hook called **useFetchUsers**. Here, we have a user's state first, and then a function called **initFetchUsers**. This async function calls the **fetchUser()** from userApi.js, and sets the response to users. This custom hook returns back users and **initFetchUsers**.

After this, in the main function of Users, we are calling the custom hook, if **useFetchUsers**, and getting the users and **initFetchUsers** from it. Next, inside an **useEffect()**, we are calling the **initFetchUsers()**.

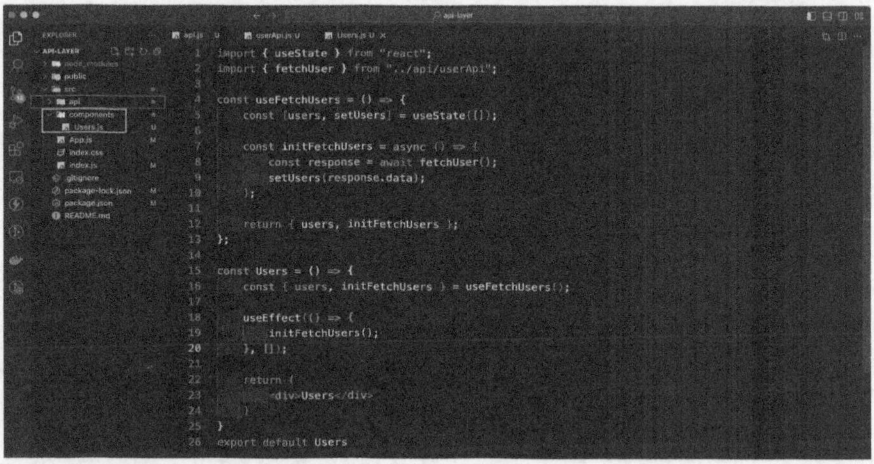

Figure 9.3: *useFetchUsers Hook in Users.js File*

We are using styled components for styling. Hence, we created some styles for the same, using it in the **Users.js** file. We also have styles for the **Container**, **name**, **email** and the **button**.

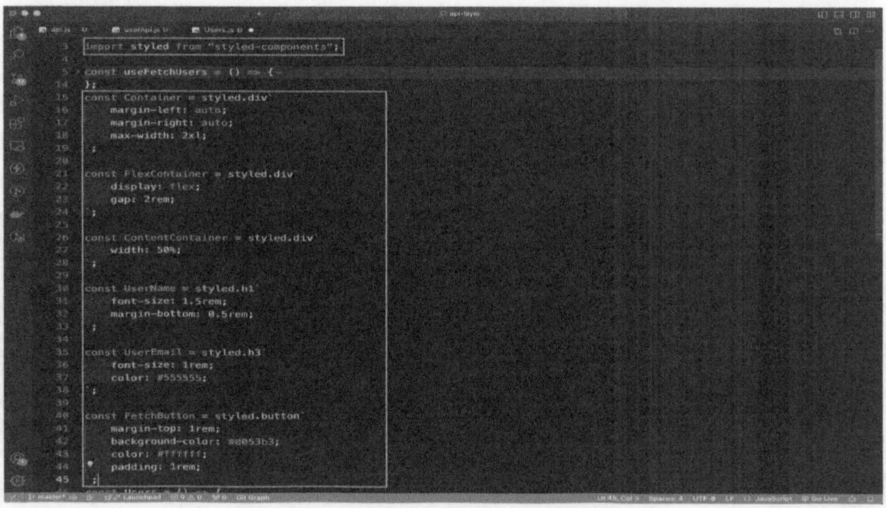

Figure 9.4: *Styled Components in Users.js File*

Next, we are using these styled components to fetch the data. So, inside the return in the **`Users.js`** file, we are first using the Container styled component. After this, we have the styled button, and on clicking it, will call the **`initFetchUsers` function**.

Then after some more styles, we are using the users which we will get from the API call to **`jsonplaceholder`**. Here, we are mapping through it, and showing the name and email.

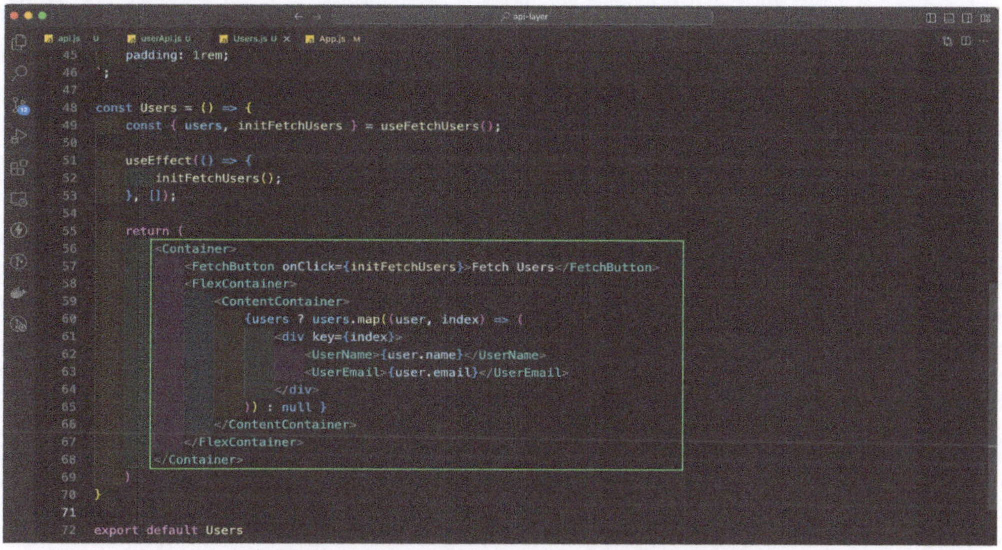

***Figure 9.5:** Users Components in Users.js File*

Next, we will add the **Users component** in the **`App.js` file**.

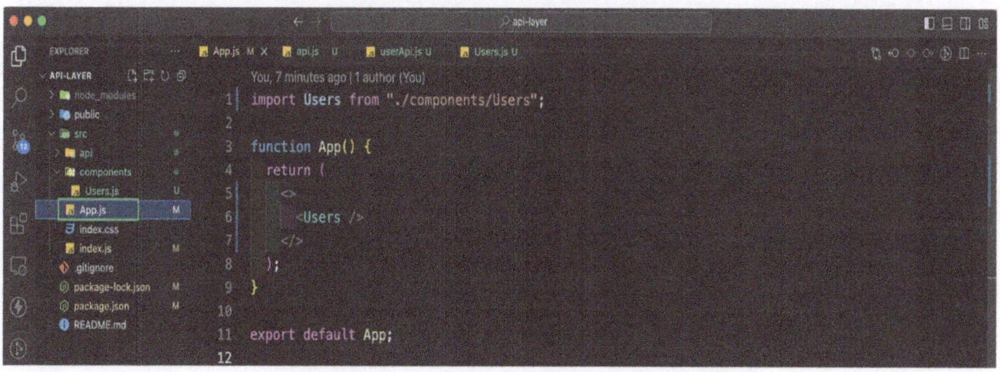

***Figure 9.6:** Users Components in App.js File*

Now, go to http://localhost:3000/ on a browser, and we will see all the data being fetched properly. Also, clicking on the "**`Fetch Users`**" button will fetch all the users from the **`jsonplaceholder`** again.

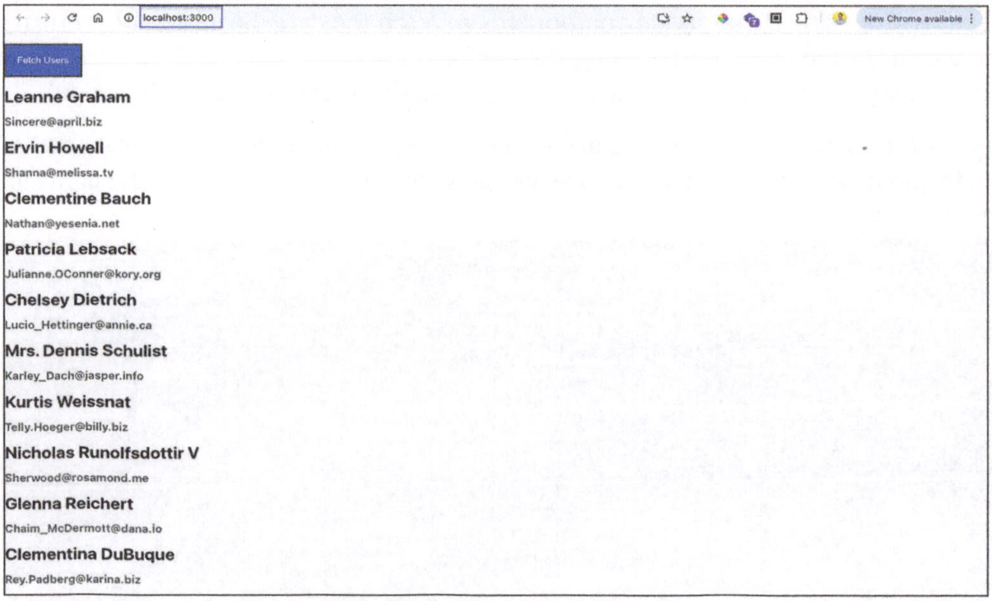

Figure 9.7: *Localhost Showing Users*

There are different API states that we need to handle, when performing asynchronous operations. In this example, when we fetch some data from the server, we want to display a loader so that the user knows something is happening behind the scenes.

In the **`Users.js`** file, we will add a state of **`isLoading`** inside the **`useFetchUsers`** custom hook. Afterwards, inside the **`initFetchUsers`** function, we are setting the loading to true, before the API call, and setting it to false after the API call. We are also returning **`isLoading`**.

Inside the Users, we are also getting the **`isLoading`** in **`useFetchUsers()`**. Also, inside the button, we are showing the message of **`Loading...`** if **`isLoading`** is true.

Figure 9.8: *isLoading in Users.js*

Now, go to http://localhost:3000/, and we will see the message of **`Loading...`** when we click the button briefly, before the message, if **`Fetch Users`**.

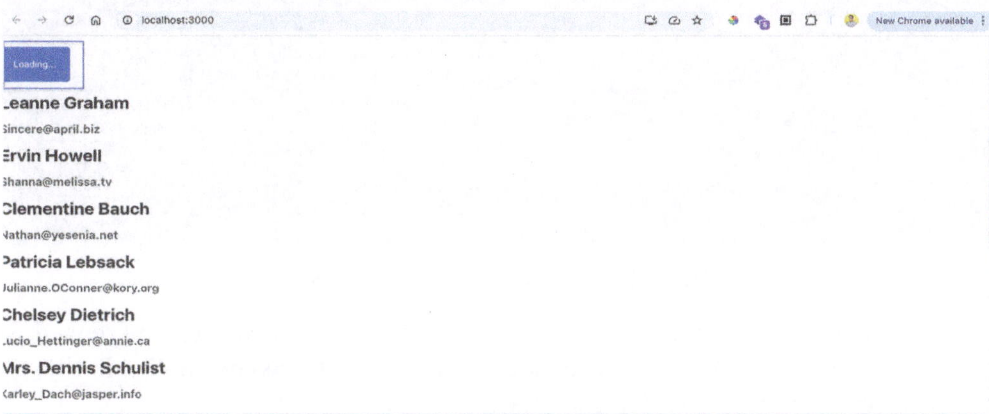

Figure 9.9: *Loading Shown in Localhost*

If we also want to handle the error, we need to do a similar thing. But for doing it, we need another stateful value. Also, to do these, it brings additional complexities. There is a simpler way through which we can reduce the number of stateful values.

We have four main states for performing an action like fetching data. First, we have the idle state, which is the starting point. Then we have the pending, which is an action that is being performed. Also, whenever the action is finished successfully, we call it success. We also have the error state, whenever an action is finished with an error.

So, for all these, we will have one value called the status. As a first step, we will update the **`Users.js`** file. Here, we are using a new state of **`fetchUsersStatus`**, and setting it to **`IDLE`**, **`PENDING`**, **`SUCCESS`**, and **`ERROR`**, depending on where it is.

In the **`Users`** component also, we are updating the **`fetchUsersStatus`**. If we check in http://localhost:3000/, the app is working as earlier.

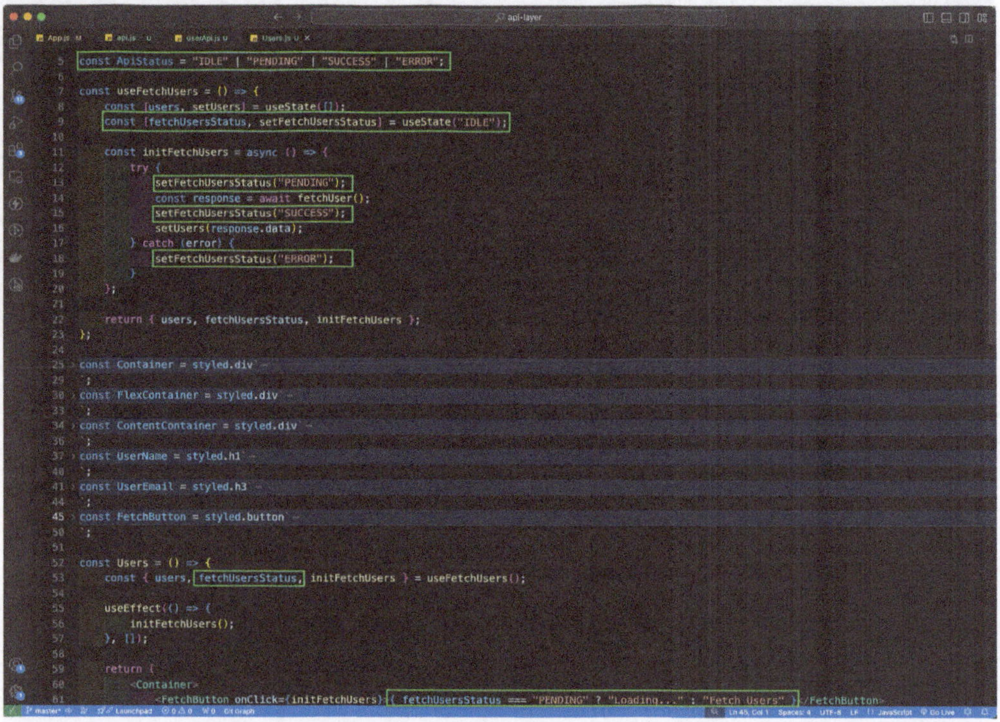

***Figure 9.10:** fetchUsersStatus in Users.js*

Now, we will move the **`try.catch`** block to a new component which can be reused. So, create a new **`helpers`** folder in **`src`**. Inside it is created **`withAsync.js`** file. In this file, we have an async function **`withAsync`** that expects a function.

Inside a **`try.catch`** block, we restructure data in the await. If it is successful, we send the response as data, and error as null. In the catch block, we return the error and the response as null.

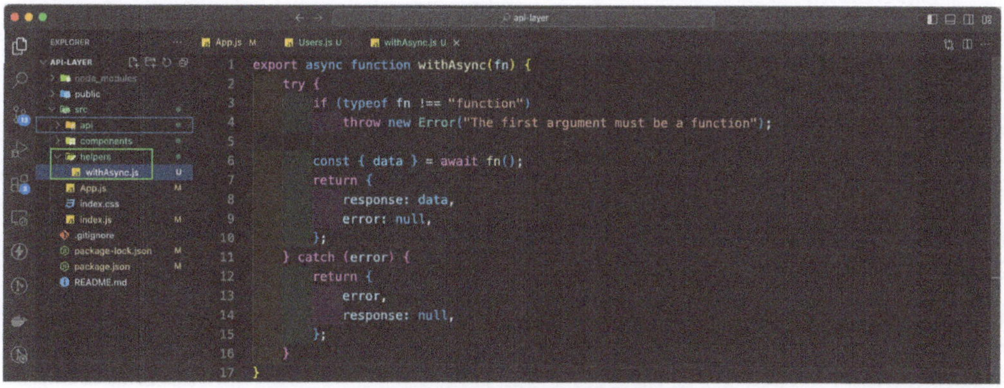

Figure 9.11: *withAsync.js File*

Back in the **Users.js** file, we are first importing **withAsync** function. Then inside the **initFetchUsers**, we are removing the **try.catch** block. Here, we are first calling the **withAsync** function, and passing the **fetchUser()** as a parameter.

Next, in an **if.else** statement, we are checking for errors. If there is an error, we are setting the **fetchUsersStatus** to **ERROR**. And in the else if, we get the response that we are setting the users as response, as well as the **fetchUsersStatus** to **SUCCESS**.

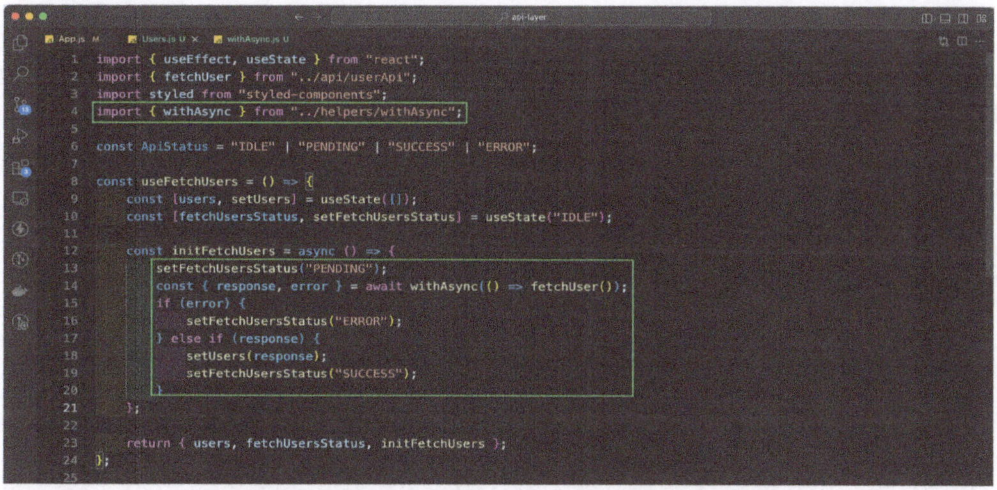

Figure 9.12: *Using withAsync in Users.js File*

If we check in http://localhost:3000/, the app is working as usual.

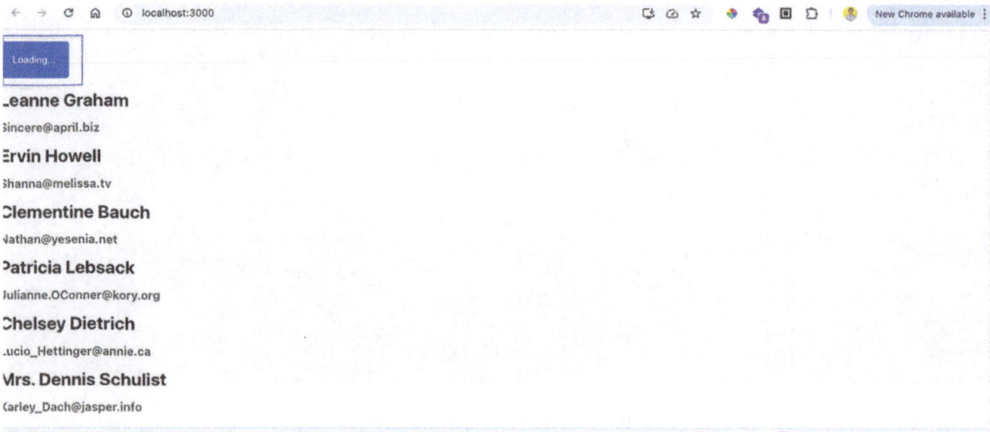

Figure 9.13: *Localhost Working Normally*

Enhancing the API States

In this part, we will first change the strings such as **`setFetchUsersStatus ("ERROR")`** in the **`Users.js`** file. This can possibly lead to typos, and we can improve them. So, we will use constants in its place.

Next, create a new folder called **`constants`** inside the **`src`** folder. Inside it, we will create an **`apiStatus.js`** file. In this file, we have different kinds of exports for **`IDLE`**, **`PENDING`**, **`SUCCESS`** and **`ERROR`**. We are going to use them in different parts of the project.

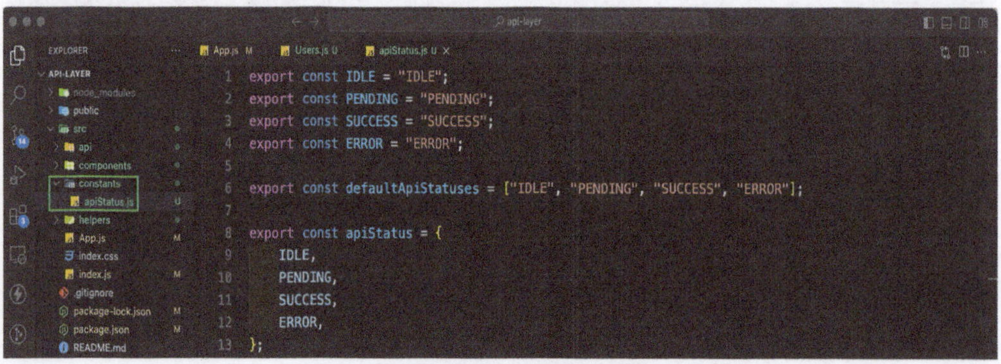

Figure 9.14: *apiStatus.js File*

Back in the **`Users.js`**, we will first import the **`apiStatus`** object. Then we will replace all of the earlier strings with the contents in the **`initFetchUsers`** function. In the return statement of the Users component also, we will replace the string with the constant.

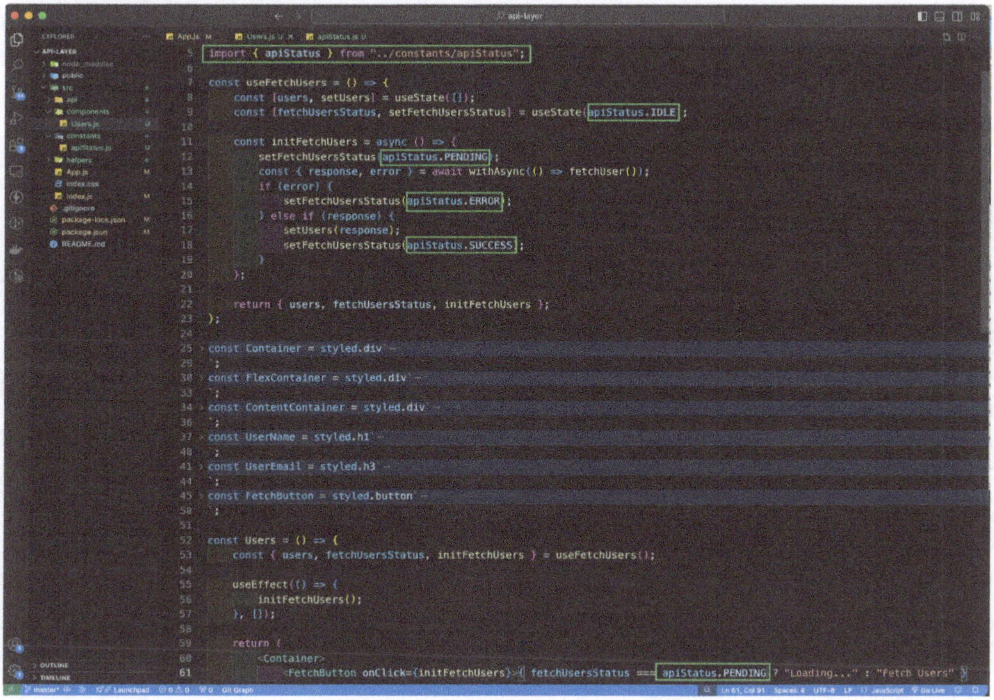

Figure 9.15: *apiStatus in Users.js File*

Next, we will do more enhancement in our code. Here, we will update **`fetchUsersStatus === apiStatus.PENDING`** in Users component return statement to a custom hook. So, we will create a new folder called **`hooks`** inside the **`api`** folder. Inside the hooks folder, we will create a new file called **`useApiStatus.js`**.

Here, we first have a **`prepareStatuses`** function which takes the **`currentStatus`** as a parameter. Inside it, we have an empty statuses object. After this, we have a for loop iterating through the array **`defaultApiStatuses`** from apiStatus.js file.

Inside the for loop, the first step is to take the string like **`IDLE`**, and convert it to **`Idle`** using the function capitalise. Next, we want it to be changed into **`isIdle`** which we are doing through a template string, and storing in a variable called **`normalisedStatusKey`**.

Lastly, we are taking the statuses object, and giving the key as **`normalisedStatusKey`** and value equal to a boolean, which is comparing the status to **`currentStatus`**. Since, our **`defaultApiStatuses`** is ["**`IDLE`**", "**`PENDING`**", "**`SUCCESS`**", "**`ERROR`**"] and maybe, our **`currentStatus`** is **`PENDING`**, we will return the statuses object as **`{isIdle: false, isPending: true, isSuccess: false, and isError: false}`**.

Now, we will use the **`prepareStatuses`** function in the **`useApiStatus`** component. It receives the **`currentStatus`** that has a default parameter of IDLE. Here, we have a status state which is set equal to the **`currentStatus`**. Next, we are calling the

prepareStatuses function, but inside a **useMemo** hook for performance optimization. We also have a console log, showing the status and statuses, which will be helpful later to understand the flow. Finally, from this component, we are returning the status, **setStatus** and statuses as an object.

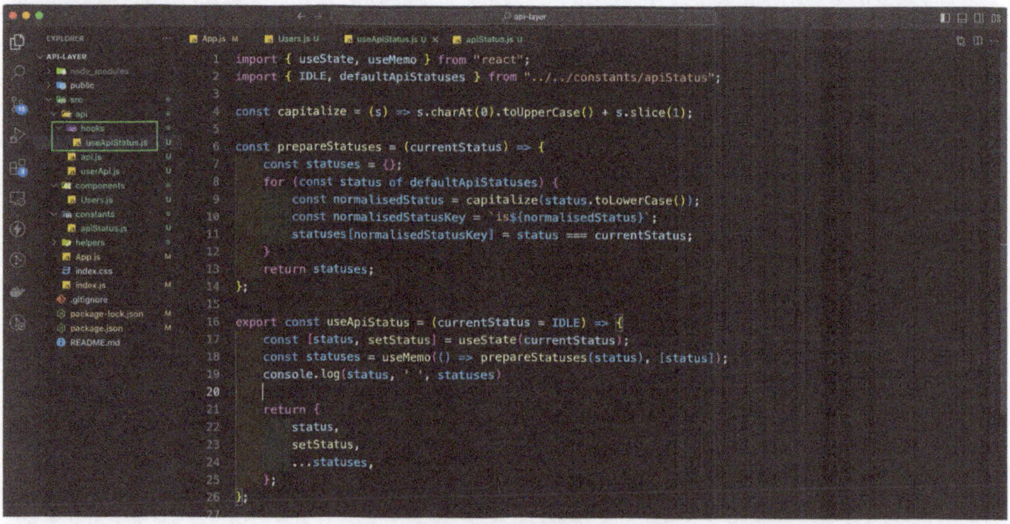

Figure 9.16: useApiStatus.js File

Next, we will go back to the **Users.js** file, and restructure the **useApiStatus** in **useFetchUsers** function to get various constants such as **isIdle**, **isPending**, and others. Notice that we are also changing their names for better readability. We are returning these new constants from the **useFetchUsers** function.

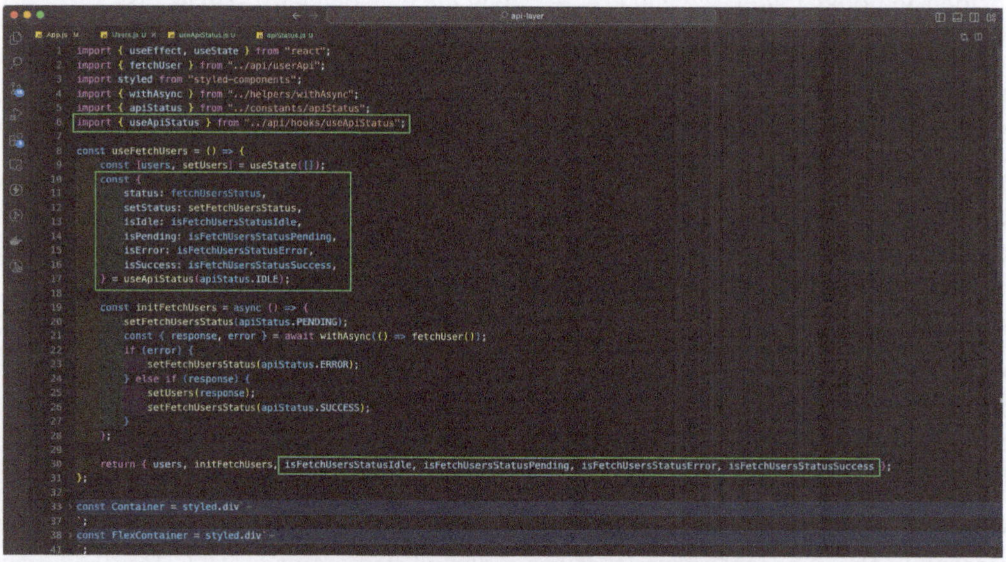

Figure 9.17: useApiStatus in Users.js File

Now, in the **Users** component in the **Users.js** file, we will get these new constants in the call to **useFetchUsers ()**. After this, we will be finally changing the **fetchUsersStatus === apiStatus.PENDING** to **isFetchUsersStatusPending**.

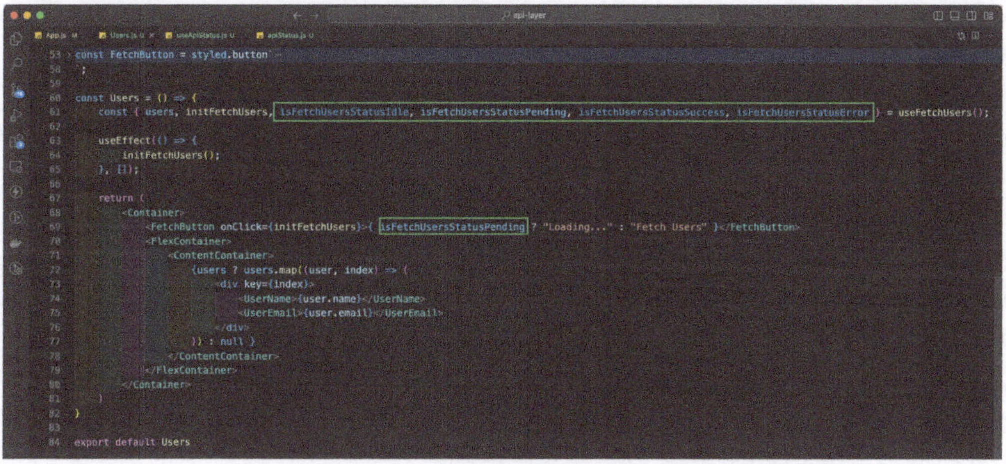

Figure 9.18: *isFetchUsersStatusPending in Users.js File*

If we check in http://localhost:3000/ with the console open, we will see the complete flow which happens from **IDLE** to **PENDING** to **SUCCESS**.

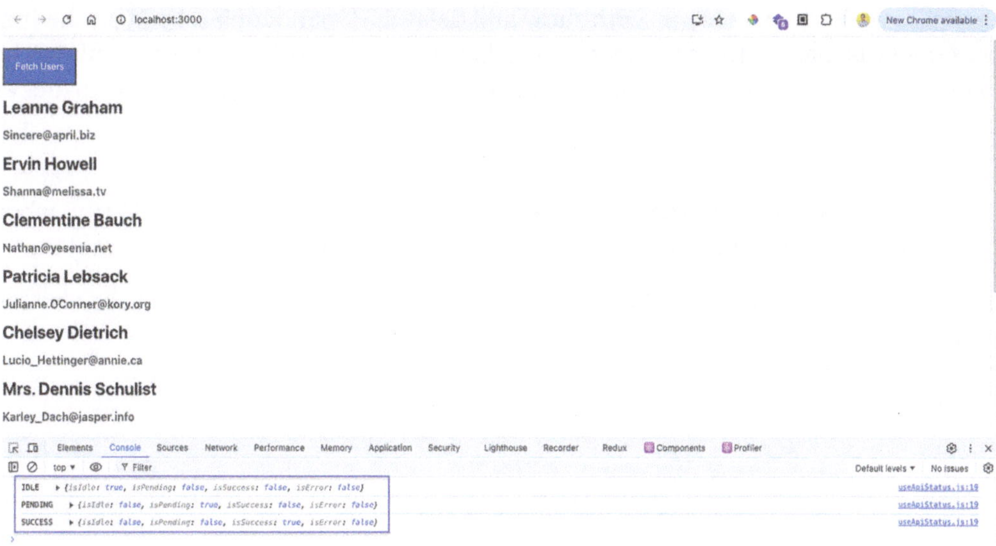

Figure 9.19: *Localhost Showing Different Stages*

Avoiding Flickering Loaders

In this part, we are going to talk about the flickering loaders. We are seeing a loader with **`Loading...`** text, when we click on the **`Fetch Users`** button, or just refreshing the web-app.

However, sometimes that is not the case, and the results are returned very fast, maybe, less than half a second. So, in this scenario, a spinner would be visible only for a split of a second.

This flickering effect is not that great for user experience. Hence, it would be a great idea, if we could add a slight delay before the loader is displayed. For this, we are going to create a component that is in practice called a lazy loader. So, it is going to wait for say, 400 milliseconds.

Now, in this case, if a flag is true, that pending thing is still pending, and then it is going to display that it is loading. Otherwise it is not going to update it, and the fetch users will remain in place. We will see it in practice now.

Thus, create a new file called **`LazyLoader.js`** inside the **`components`** folder. Here, we are getting props which we are destructing to show and delay. Both of these have default values of false and 0 respectively. Next, we have a state called **`showLoader`**.

After this, we have a **`useEffect`**, with show and delay as dependencies. Inside it the first if statement is making the **`showLoader`** as false, if the show is false and returning. The next if statement is checking, if the delay is equal to 0, and making the showLoader as true.

The if statement also has an else which is making the **`showLoader`** as true, after the delay with the help of **`setTimeout`**. We also have the return code that will run, when this component will be destroyed, and uses a **`clearInterval`** to clear the timeout.

Finally, we are checking if **`showLoader`** is true, and then returning **`Loading...`** or else the default props.

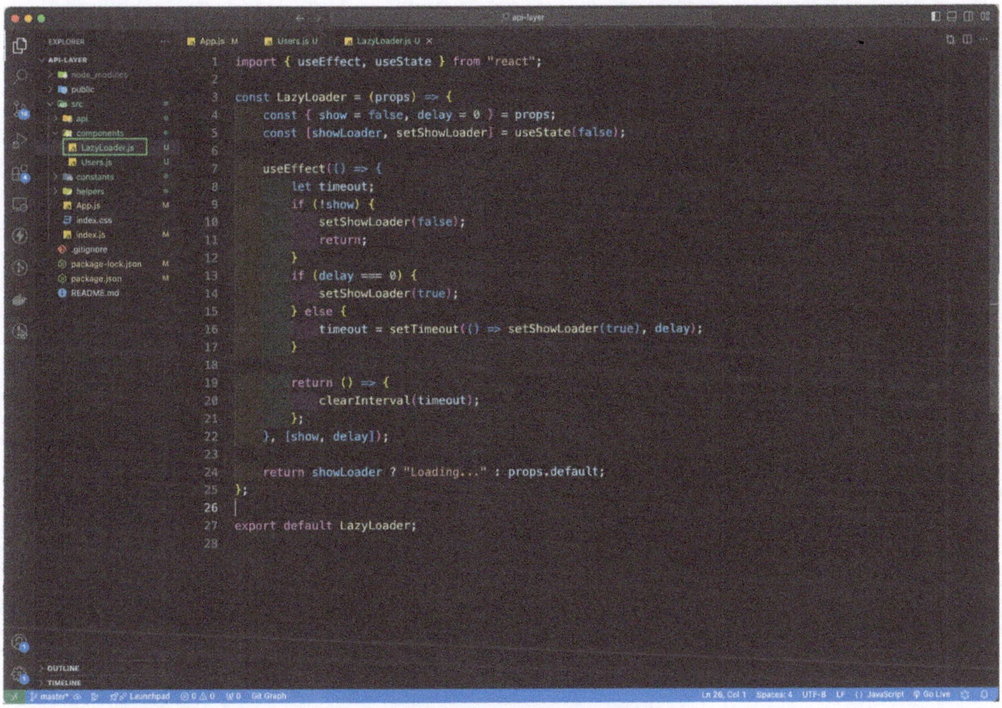

Figure 9.20: *LazyLoader.js File*

Back in the **`Users.js`** file, we will import the **`LazyLoader`** first. After this, instead of our ternary operator code of **`isFetchUsersStatusPending`**, we will use the **`LazyLoader` code**. Here, we are passing the show, delay and default props.

Now, go back to http://localhost:3000/, and refresh it, or hit the **`Fetch Users`** button. It will not show the **`Loading...`** text. Because here in **`LazyLoader`**, we told it to delay for 2000 milliseconds. However, the time it takes to fetch the users is less than this.

But make the delay as 100 milliseconds, and you are going to see the **`Loading...`** text. So, this is an efficient technique to use the **`LazyLoader`**.

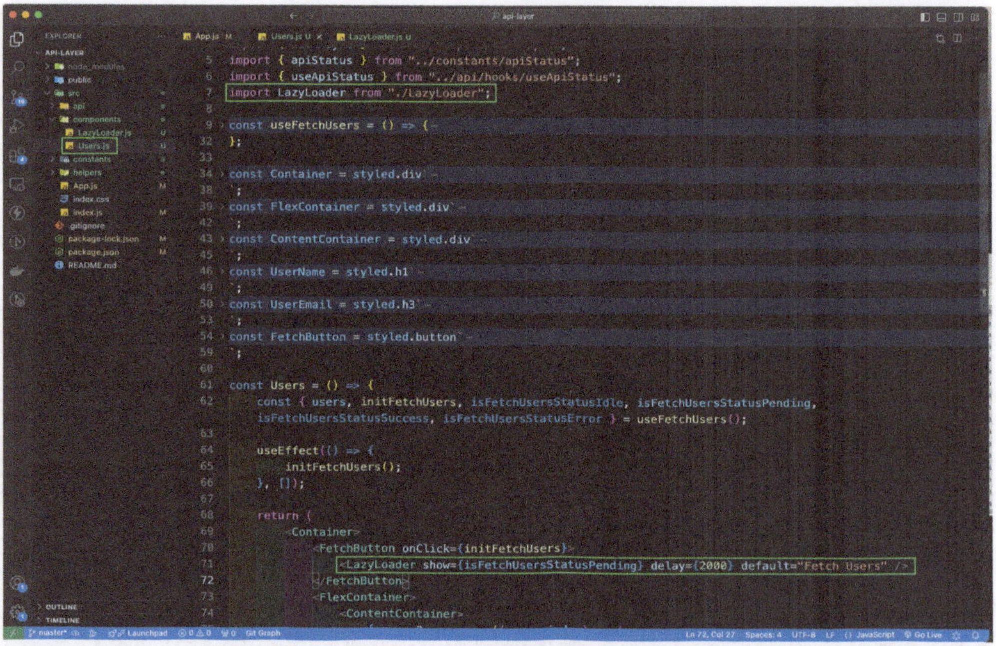

Figure 9.21: *LazyLoader Component in Users.js File*

Abstracting API States

In this part, we are going to do further optimization by lifting up the **`initfetchUsers`** logic, and putting it in a separate custom hook.

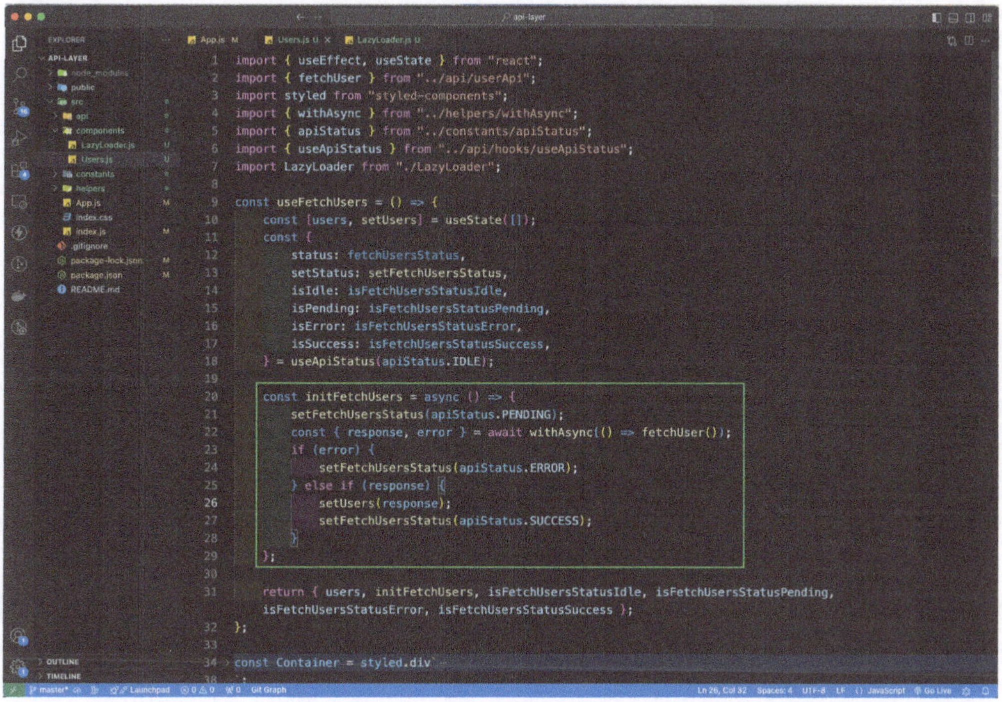

***Figure 9.22:** initFetchUsers in Users.js File*

Now, create a new file called **`useApi.js`** inside the hooks folder. Here, the **`useApi`** function is taking a function and **`config`** as a parameter. After this, restructuring the config to **`initialData`** takes place. Then, we have a state of data and error.

It then utilises the **`useApiStatus`** hook which we created earlier. It is a restructuring status, **`setStatus`** and **`normalisedStatuses`** from here.

The **`exec`** function is responsible for managing the API status, and handling the function that is passed as an argument to this hook. Also, at the start of this function, it clears out the error, and sets the API status to the pending state.

Next, the **`fn`** function is executed. If it resolves successfully, then the API status is set to success. However, if there is an error, it is going to set it to the error state, and the error object is also with the set error method.

The **`useApi` hook** at the end returns an object with the state, their respective setter methods, and of course, the exec method as well as the **`normalisedStatuses`**.

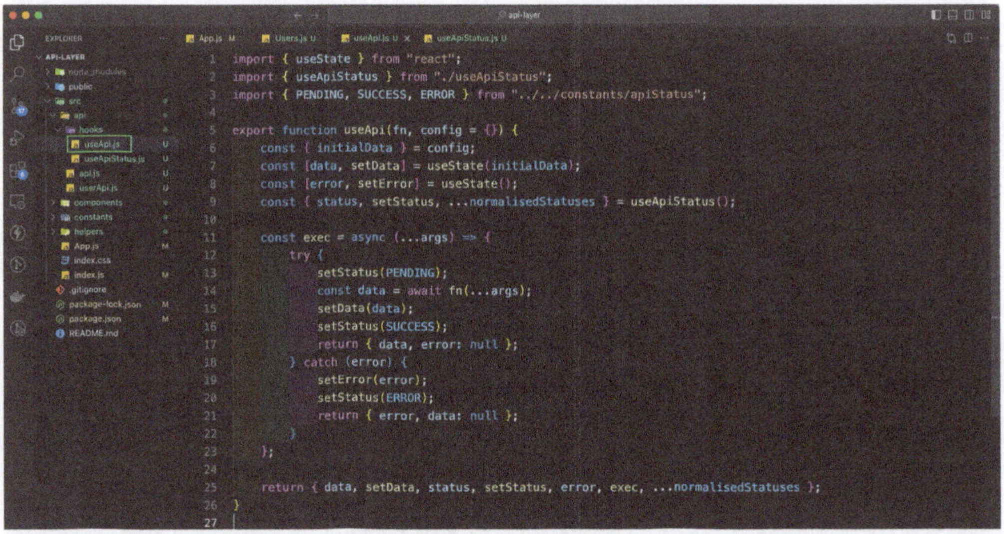

Figure 9.23: *useApi.js File*

Now, we will make use of the **`useApi`** hook that we have created. So, back in the **`Users.js`** file, we will remove the earlier code in **`useFetchUsers`**. Here, we will use the **`useApi`** hook, and pass the required parameters.

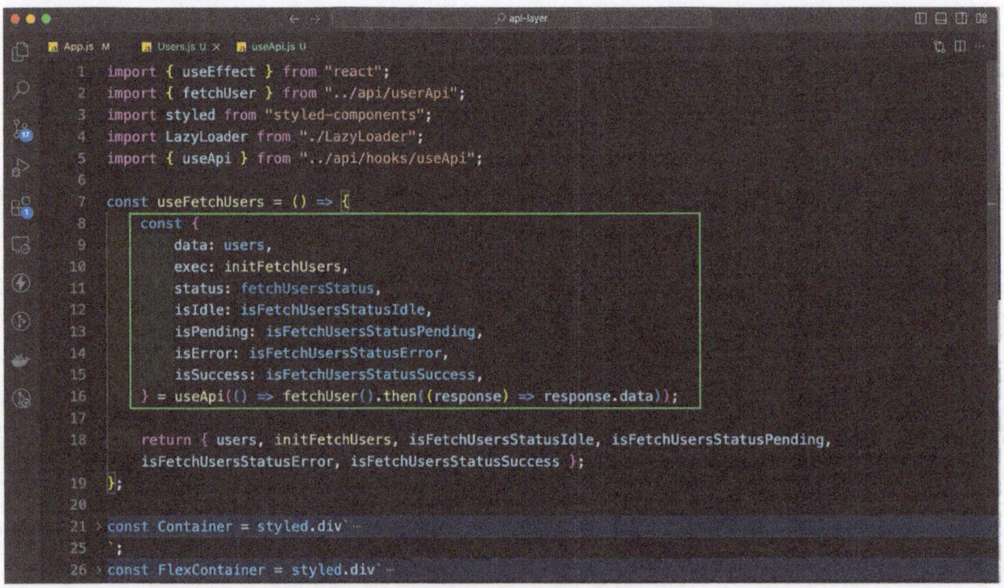

Figure 9.24: *useApi in Users.js File*

Back in http://localhost:3000/, we will see the app working as earlier with no errors.

Figure 9.25: *Localhost Working Fine*

Adding Request Abort Logic

Next, in this part, we will learn about request cancellation. There are a lot of scenarios in which it is a good idea to cancel a request before making another one. A good example is the auto complete functionality.

If you have a massive database, then search queries can take a moment before a response is being sent back from the server. So, imagine we have a food recipes website that allows users to search for meals.

Anytime a user would type something into the search input, an API request would be made. So, upon receiving a response, a list of recipes would immediately be displayed. Let us say the user typed a few characters into the search field, and two API requests were made.

The first request was sent with a query, say **`ta`**, while the second was the **`tandoori`**. However, the first **`ta`** request had a slight delay, and finished after the second one with the **`tandoori`** query.

In such a situation, the search results would not display the data for the latest search, but for the old one instead. That is not a great user experience, but we can solve this problem by ensuring that the first request is cancelled before making the next one.

Thus, so far in our project, we have been using the axios library as the http client for our app. Requests can be cancelled with axios by creating a cancel token that has to be passed to access methods in the config object.

However, we do not want to start creating cancel tokens directly around the application, because it would go against one of the API layers' main principles. It is an application that does not need to know anything about the internal implementation of the API layer.

Hence, we need to make sure that the cancellation is actually made in such a way that it would be easy to replace it, if the application is switched to another method. For example, the fetch method, or any other http client, instead of axios.

To demonstrate how we can add the request cancellation with the API layer, we will implement a feature that allows users to search for the meals. For this, we will use the free meal API website known as https://www.themealdb.com/.

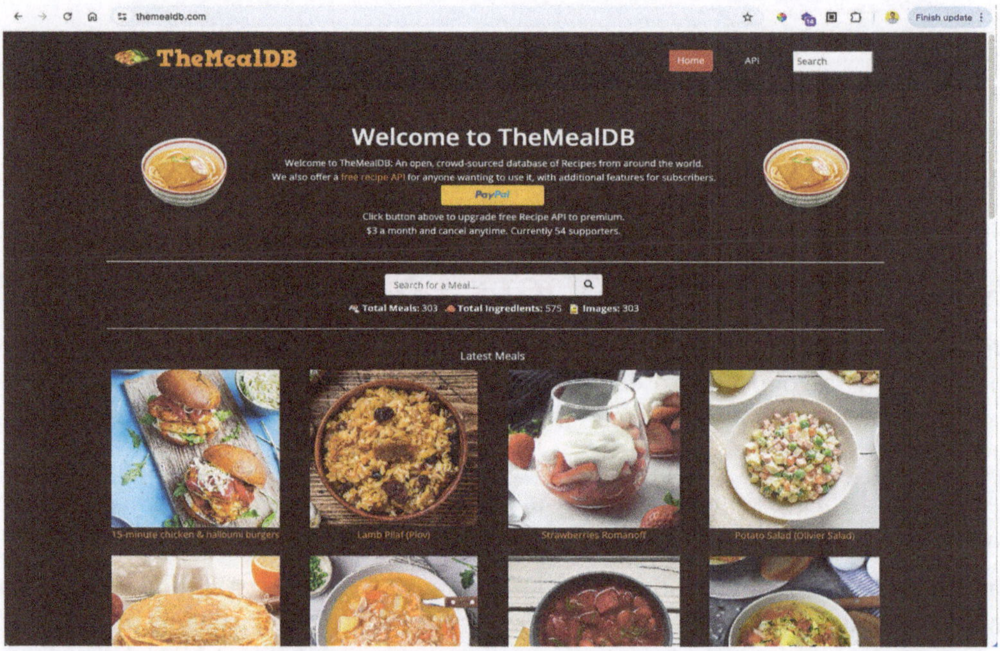

Figure 9.26: *themealdb.com Site*

First of all, we need to modify a base file which is the **`api.js`**. Here, we have first added a function **`didAbort`**. It returns a boolean, if an error object passed is an instance of the cancel error that is thrown by axios. So, if the error is of that type, it will be enhanced with aborted true property.

Also, we have the **`getCancelSource`** function. It creates a new cancel source that contains a cancel method, and a token which has to be passed to a request. Then we have the function **`isApiError`**. It asserts that an error is an axios error.

After this, we have the **`withAbort`** function. We will learn more about it next, but in this function, we are wrapping in all the requests of **`get`**, **`delete`**, **`post`**, **`patch`** and **`put`** created earlier.

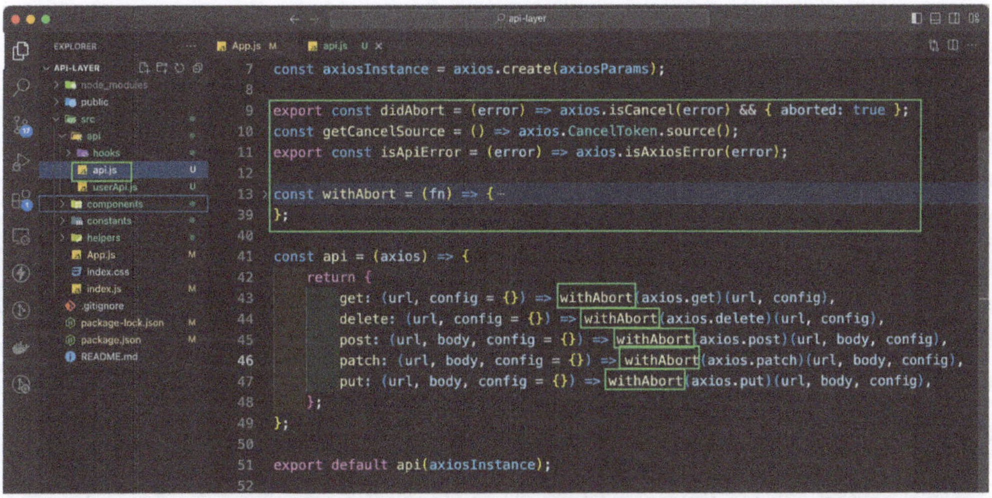

Figure 9.27: *withAbort Addition in api.js*

Now, we have completed the **withAbort** function. It is an HOC (Higher Order Function) that returns another function, and checks if the config object contains an abort property with a function as a value.

If it does, we create a new cancel token, set it on the config object, and pass it to the abort method. This uses both the **didAbort** and **getCancelSource** functions.

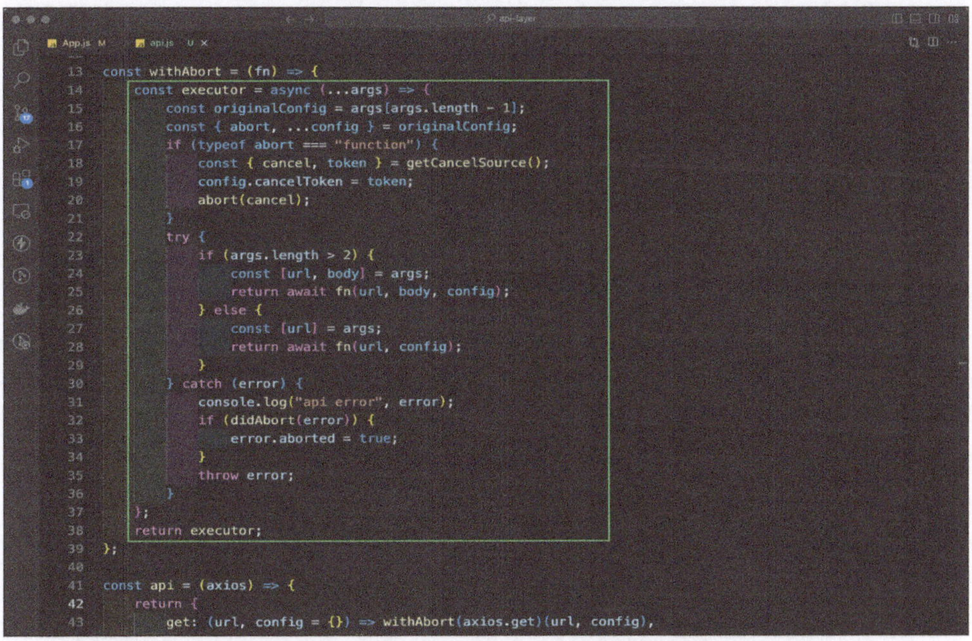

Figure 9.28: *withAbort Details in api.js*

Next, to make use of it, we will create another API. Thus, create a file **mealApi.js** inside the **api** folder. It is similar to the **userApi.js** file, the only difference being the api endpoint.

The complete API endpoint is https://www.themealdb.com/api/json/v1/1/search.php which is a GET api that requires query params also. So, basically we are searching meals with this API endpoint.

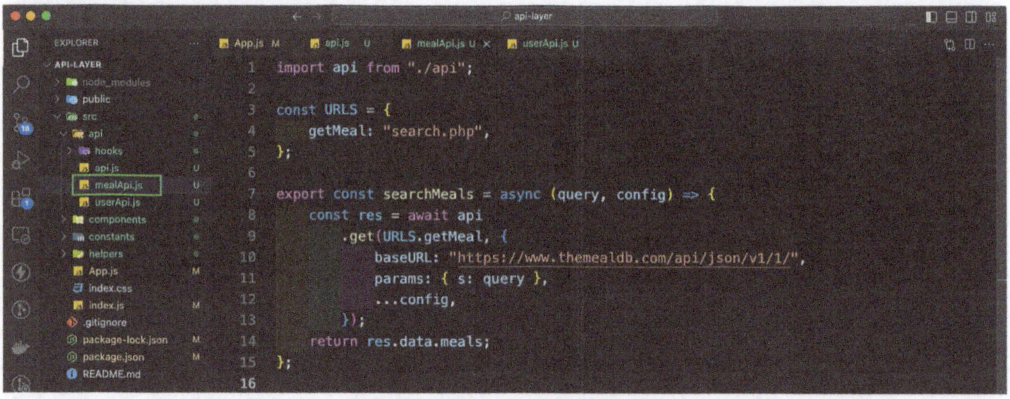

Figure 9.29: *mealApi.js File*

Now, to use it, we will create a new file called **SearchMeal.js** inside the **components** folder. Here, we have imported the required libraries and components. We have also installed the package of **react-toastify** that we are going to use next.

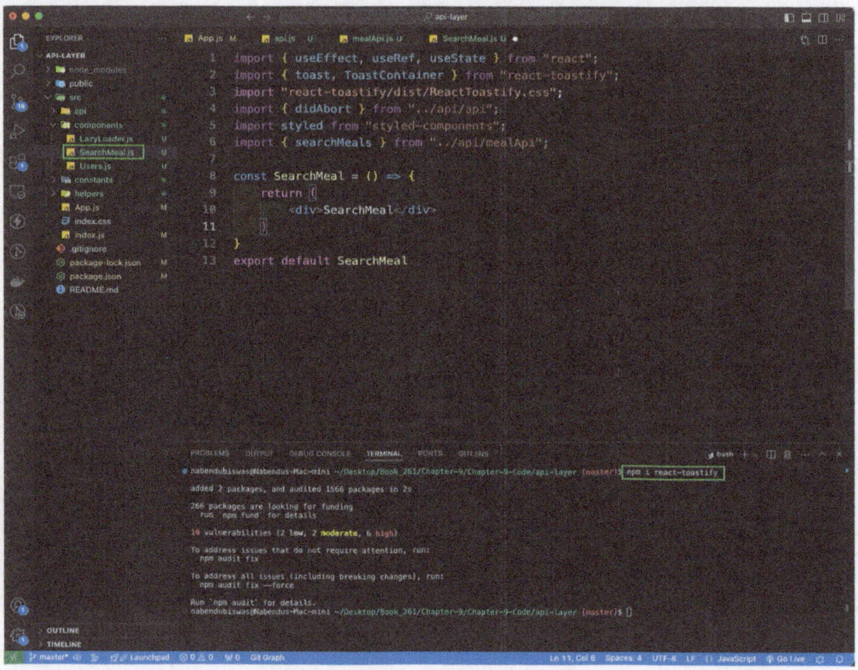

Figure 9.30: SearchMeal.js File

Now, inside this file, the first thing that we want to create is a custom hook, which will be called **useFetchMeals**. First, we will create the state variable of meals that is an empty array. Next, we have a ref called **abortRef**, which will keep a track of the abort function.

We have an async function called **fetchMeals** which receives a query string. The **fetchMeals** is executed every time, we start typing. The first step is to cancel the previous request. We achieve it by the **abortRef.current.abort?.()** in the try block.

After this, we create a **newMeals** variable which calls the **searchMeals** function created earlier with the query. It also needs a config that is an object, and has an abort function. The **abort** function will be called as abort, in which we are making the **abortRef.current.abort** equal to abort. After this, we set the meals equal to the **newMeals**.

Next, in the catch block which executes in case of an error, we are console logging the error. After this, we are calling the **handleQuoteError** function, and passing the error. In the **handleQuoteError** function, we are first passing the error to **didAbort** function. If it is true, then it is an error due to request cancellation. So, in the toast message, we are showing **Request aborted**. Otherwise, it is just a normal error, and we are showing a normal message.

Finally, in the **useFetchMeals**, we are returning the state **meals** and **fetchMeals** function.

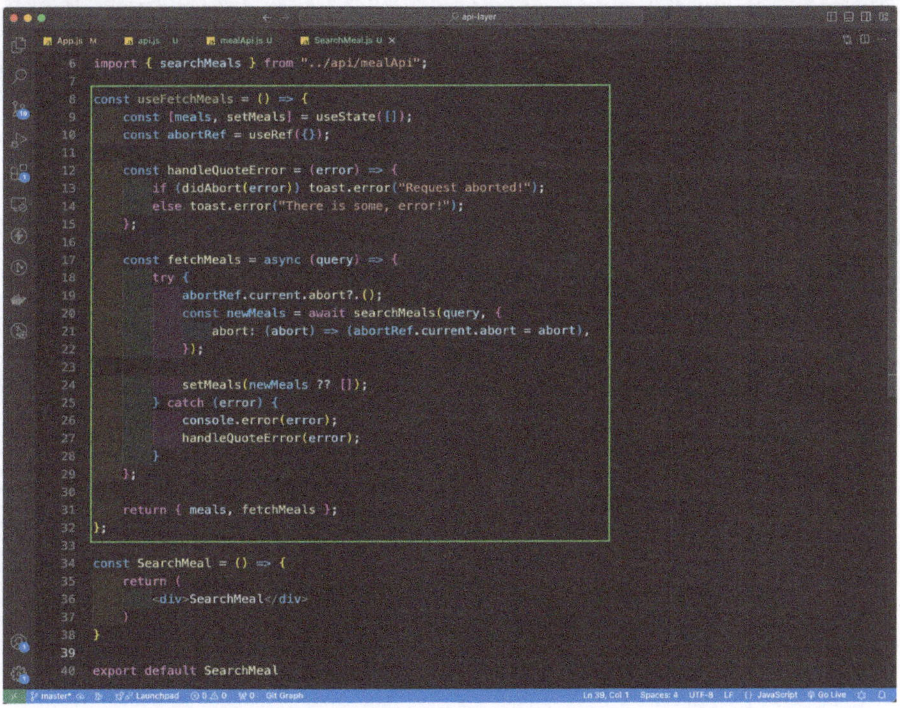

Figure 9.31: *useFetchMeals in SearchMeal.js File*

Before creating the **SearchMeal** component, we will again add the styled components for styling in **SearchMeal.js** file.

Figure 9.32: *Styled Components in SearchMeal.js File*

Next, we will complete the **SearchMeal** component in the **SearchMeal.js** file. Here, we have a query state first. After this, we get the meals and **fetchMeals** from the **useFechMeals** hooks.

Now, in a **useEffect**, we are calling the **fetchMeals**, and passing the query. It also has a dependency on query. Next, in the **return** statement, we will use some styled component created earlier for styling. Here, we have an input that has a value of query. It also changes the query once to write anything in it.

After this, inside a styled component of **MealContainer**, we are showing all the meals through a map, because it is an array of objects.

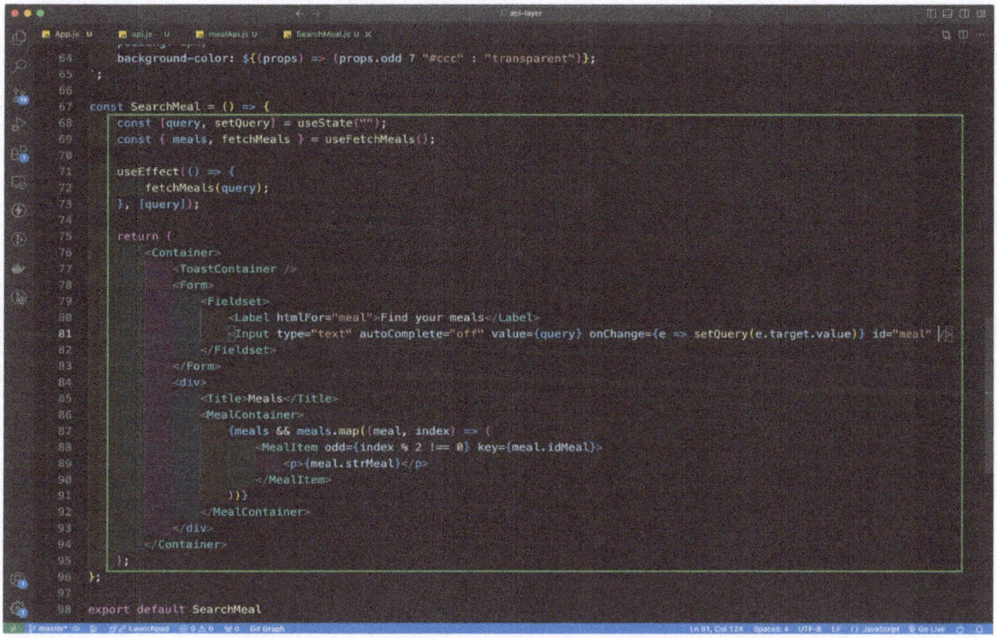

Figure 9.33: *SearchMeal Components in SearchMeal.js File*

Now, in http://localhost:3000/, we will first see all the meals.

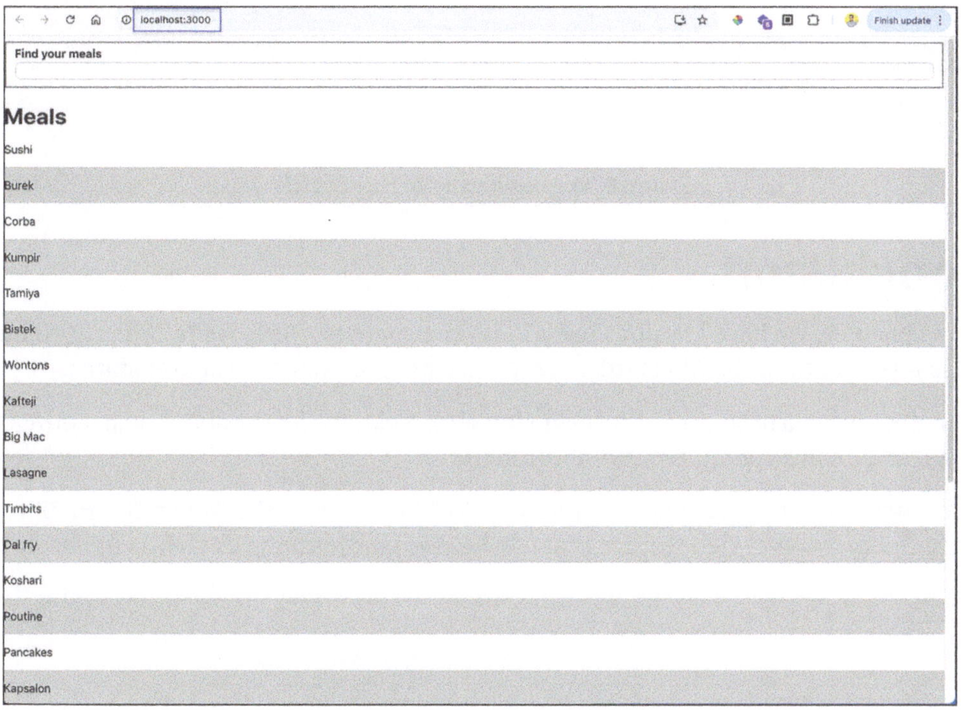

Figure 9.34: *Initial Localhost*

Now, write something slowly in the input box. In this case, we have written **s** and **u**, after a time gap. Here, we will successfully see every meal that contains **su**.

Figure 9.35: *Localhost with Slow Search*

Now, we have typed **`shi`** very fast, that is within 2 seconds. Here, we got the result, but also a toast containing **`Request aborted`** text.

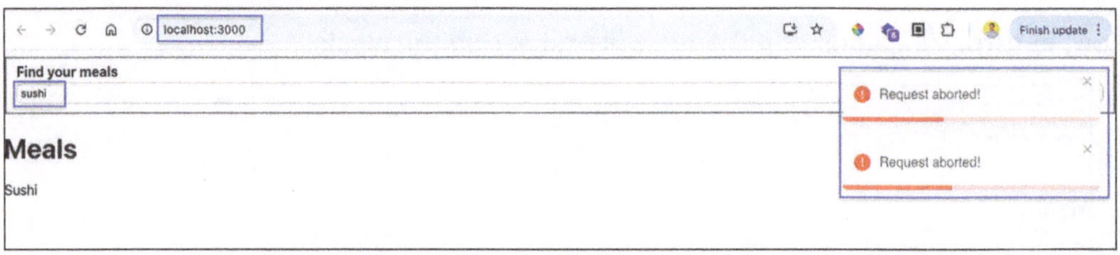

Figure 9.36: *Localhost with Fast Search*

Conclusion

In this chapter, we have learnt to use API layer concepts. Here, we first learnt to build API layers, and then the API states. Next, we learnt to enhance the API states.

After this, we learnt to avoid flickering loaders. Next, we learnt about abstracting API states, and finally, adding request abort logic.

In the **next chapter**, we will **combine the API Layer with the React Query library**. React Query is a very rich feature that can be used for fetching as well as updating the data.

Points to Remember

- API Layer acts as a middle layer between React components and backend servers, ensuring cleaner and reusable code.
- API States (`IDLE`, `PENDING`, `SUCCESS`, `ERROR`) help manage asynchronous operations efficiently.
- Using constants for API states avoids typos and improves readability.
- The `useApiStatus` hook abstracts API state management for better reusability.
- The `LazyLoader` component prevents flickering loaders by adding a delay before displaying loading indicators.

CHAPTER 10
API Layer with React Query

Introduction

In this chapter, we will continue to learn about API layer concepts, but with React-Query library. Here, we will first learn about React Query, and different operations with it.

Structure

In this chapter, we are going to discuss the following topics:

- Server Setup
- Fetching Data with React-Query
- Updating Data with React-Query
- Pagination with React-Query
- Infinite Scroll with React-Query

Server Setup

In this section, we are going to combine the API layer with the React-Query library. React query is a feature rich in performance solution that can be used for fetching as well as updating data. It can also be used for catching, and background re-fetching data.

We are taking the code from the previous chapter, but have added a **`server`** folder in it. The start script is pointing to an **`index.js`** file in the **`package.json`** file. We also have the dependencies of **`cors`**, **`express`**, and **`nanoid`** in it.

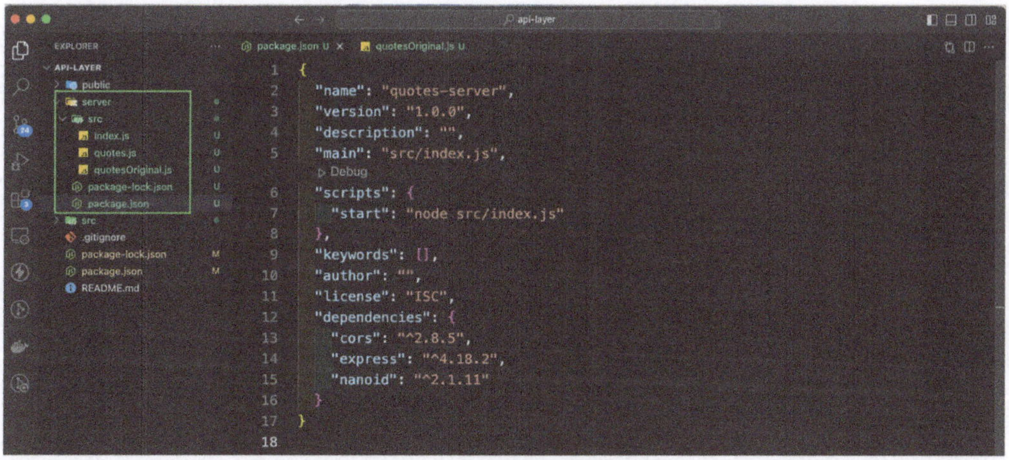

Figure 10.1: *package.json File*

We have a **`quotesOriginal.js`** file inside the **`src`** folder. We have also the constant **`quotesOriginal`**. It has an array of objects called quotes which have an object with **`quote`**, **`author`**, and **`id`**.

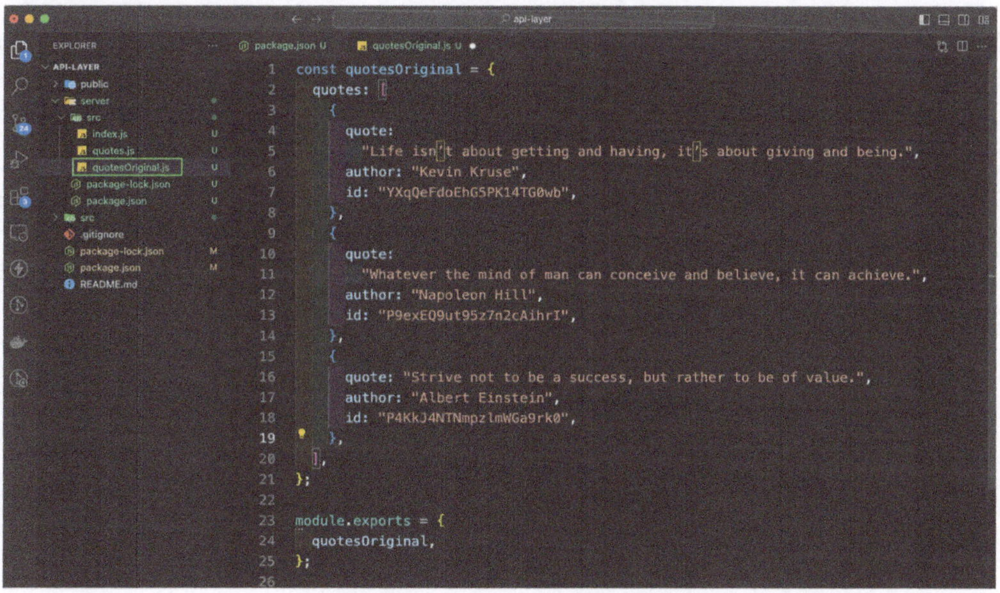

Figure 10.2: *quotesOriginal.js File*

We also have a **`quotes.js`** file inside the **`src`** folder, along with constant quotes. It has an array of objects called quotes that have an object with **`quote`**, **`author`**, and **`id`**.

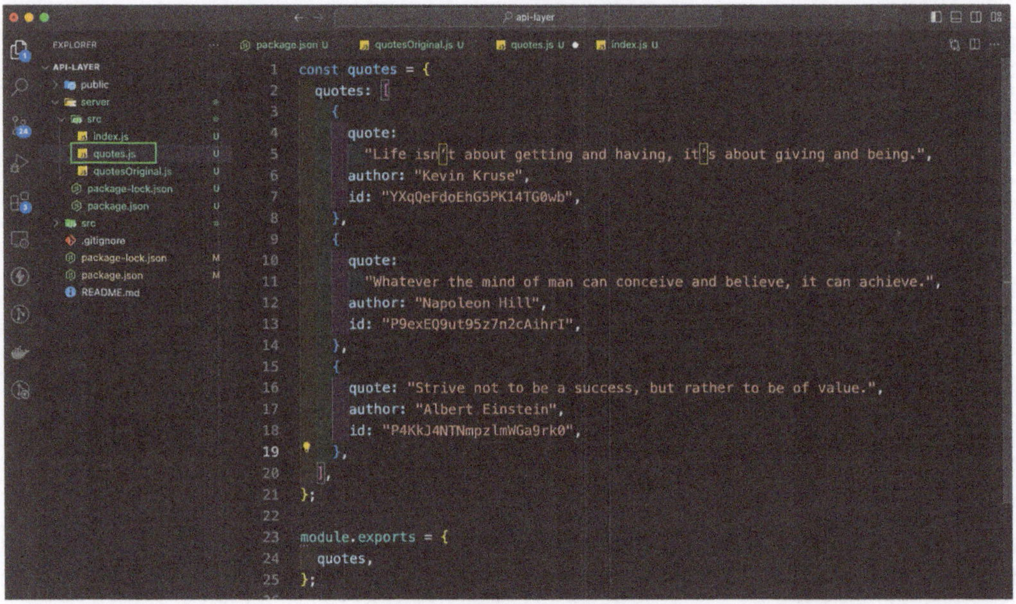

Figure 10.3: *quotes.js File*

Now, the main **`index.js`** file inside the **`src`** folder of the server, first contains the required imports. Then we have a **`sleep`** function which resolves a promise after a time. After this, we have a **`readQuotes`** function that gets the quotes from the quotes file.

Next, we have the **`addQuote`** function which adds the passed quote and the author, which has a unique id. It adds it at the start of the quotes array. Next, we have a function **`getQuotesByPage`** which uses **`readQuotes()`** to get the paginated quotes. Lastly, we have a similar function called **`getQuotesByCursor`**.

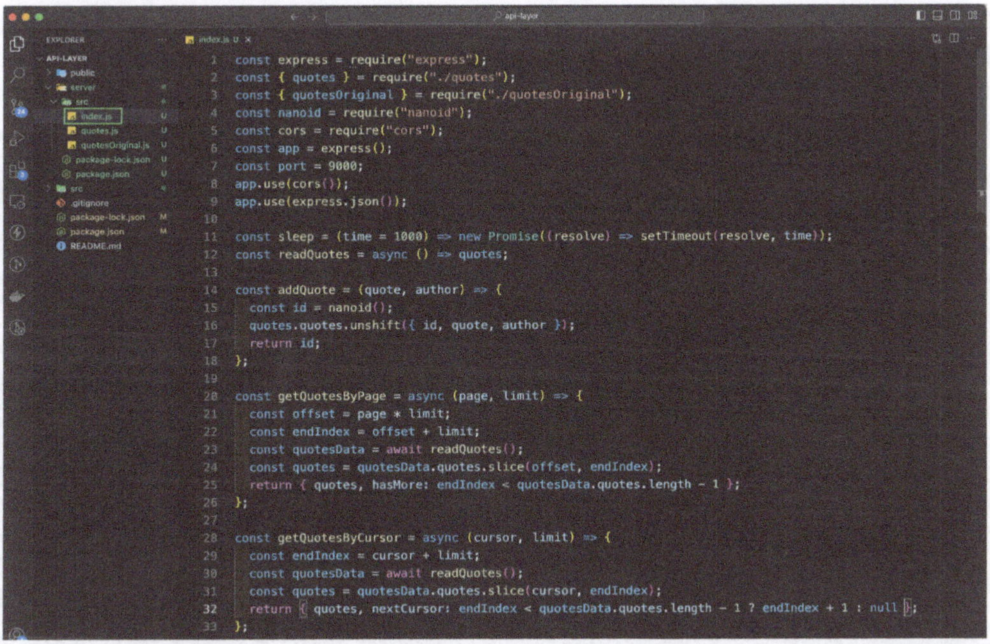

Figure 10.4: *index.js File with GET APIs*

Next, we will add a **`GET api`** of **`/top_quotes`** which uses **`readQuotes()`** to get all the quotes. Then in response, send the top five (5) quotes by using a javascript slice to get the first five (5) quotes.

After this, we have GET for **`/`** in which we get a page or cursor in the query. If it is a page, we use **`getQuotesByPage`** to get all the quotes. And if it is a cursor, then we use **`getQuotesByCursor`** to get the quotes.

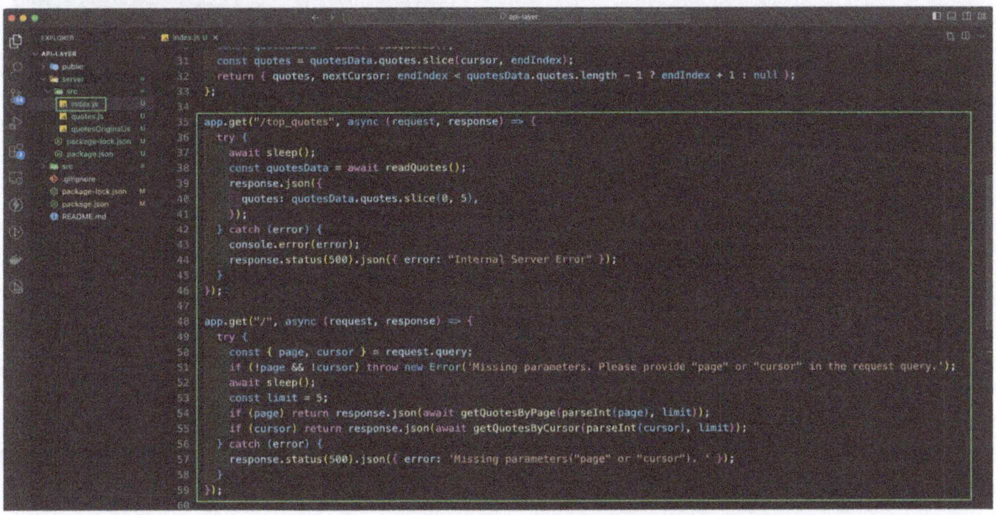

Figure 10.5: *index.js File with More GET APIs*

Now, we have a POST to **/** which uses **addQuote()** to add the quote and the author. We also have a **/reset** which takes all the **quotesOriginal**, and pushes it to quotes. Finally, we are using **app.listen()** to listen on a port.

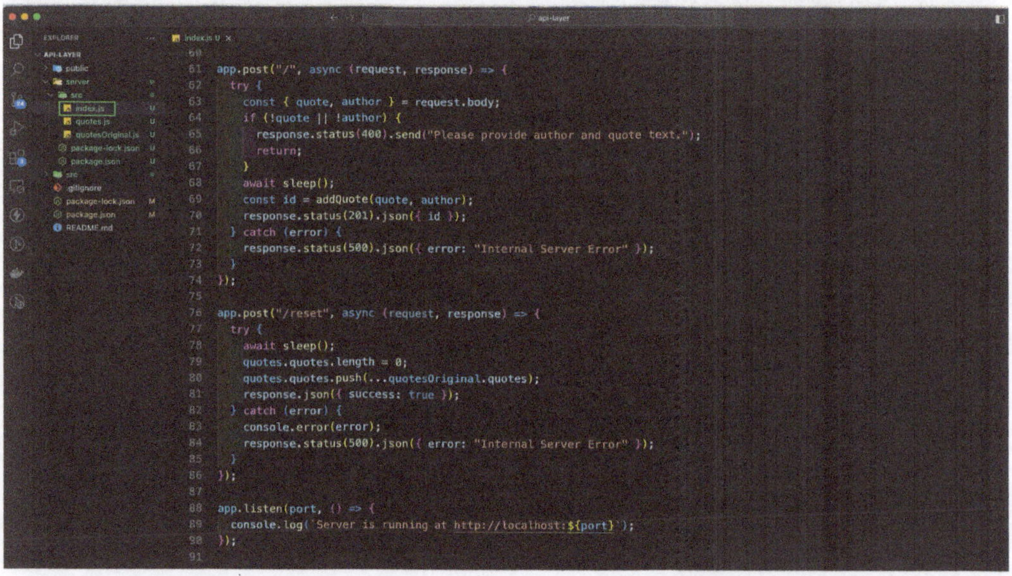

Figure 10.6: *index.js file with POST APIs*

Now, inside the server, first install all the packages using **npm i**, and then start the server using npm start. It will start the server on http://localhost:9000/.

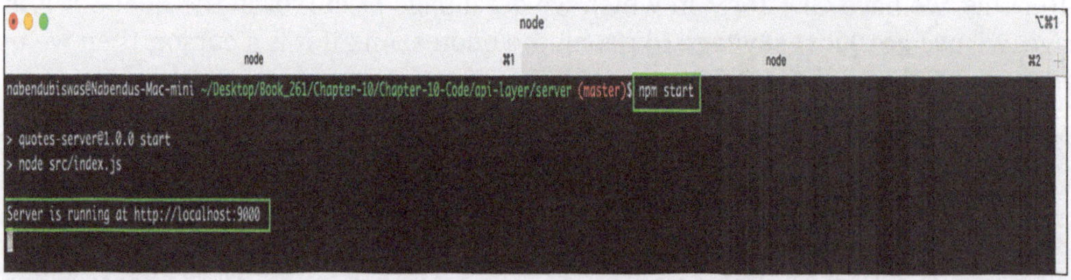

Figure 10.7: *Starting the Server*

Fetching Data with React-Query

So, let us start the implementation of react-query with our API layer. First by creating a simple component that is going to display some quotes. We will first go to the **api.js** file inside the **api** folder.

Here, we will change the **baseURL** to http://localhost:9000/ because that is where the server is running.

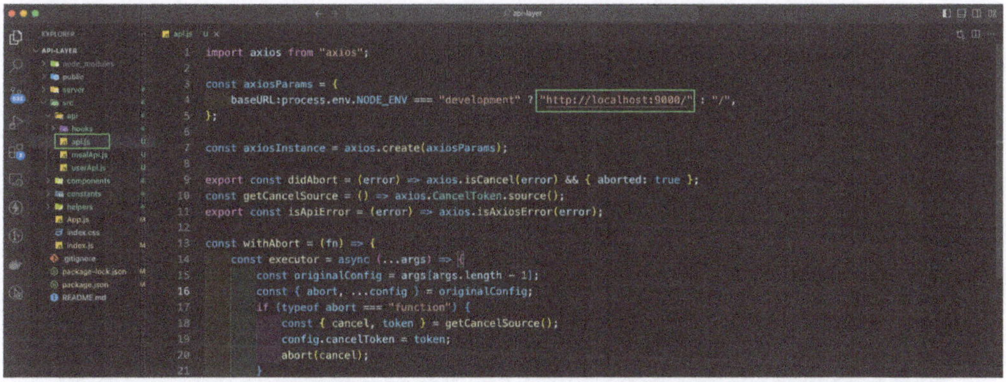

***Figure 10.8**: Changing API Endpoint in api.js*

Next, we will create a file, **`quoteApi.js`** inside the **`api`** folder. Here, we will use **`api.get ()`** to hit the **`/top_quotes`** endpoint, we recently created. Here, we are getting all the quotes, and returning it.

We have also installed **`react-query`** library through the integrated terminal that we are going to use soon.

***Figure 10.9**: quoteApi.js File and React-Query Installation*

Now, we will create a component called **`FetchTopQuotes.js`** inside the **`components`** folder. Here, we are first importing the **`useQuery`** from react-query. We are also installing the styled component, and the **`fetchTopQuotes`** created previously.

After this, we created some styled components for the **`Container`**, **`Title`**, **`ErrorMessage`**, **`LoadingMessage`**, **`QuotesContainer`** and **`QuoteBlock`** which we shall use them soon.

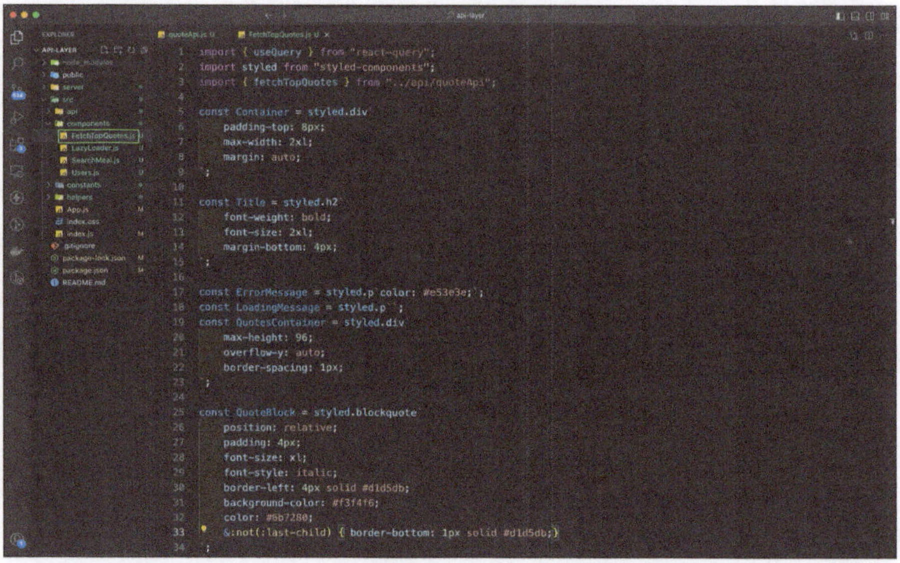

Figure 10.10: *FetchTopQuotes.js File with Styled Components*

Next, we have added some more styled components for **`QuoteText`**, **`AuthorCite`**, **`AuthorInfo`**, and **`AuthorName`**. After this, in the main **`FetchTopQuotes`** function, we have first extracted the data, **`isLoading`**, **`isSuccess`**, and **`isError`** by using **`useQuery`**.

Here, we are passing top-quotes endpoint and **`fetchTopQuotes`** which we had imported earlier. Next, we have a return statement that is empty now, and we are going to fill it next.

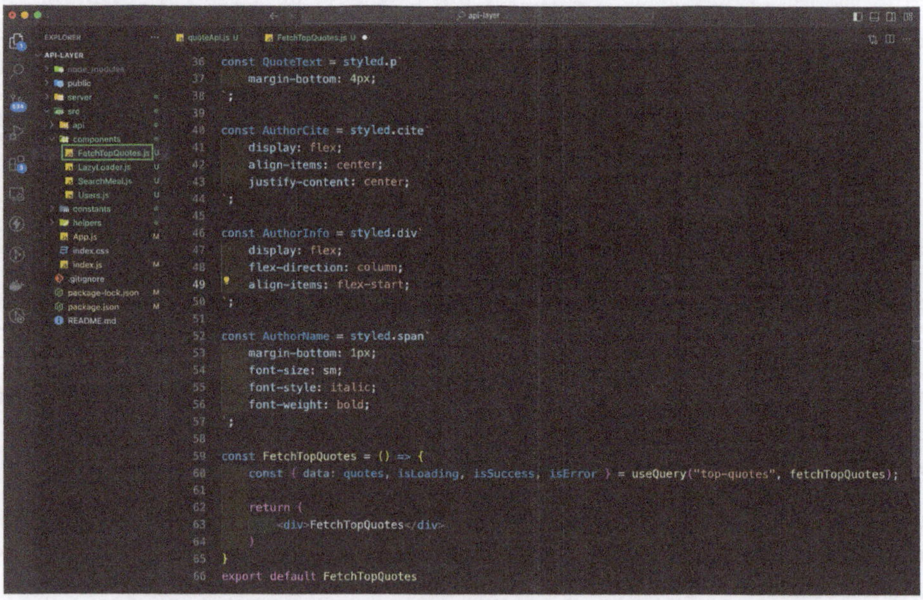

Figure 10.11: *FetchTopQuotes.js File with More Styled Components*

Now, in the **FetchTopQuotes.js** file, we will add the styled components created earlier in the **return** statement. Here, after having the appropriate styled component, we are checking **isError** and **isLoading** first, and displaying the message, if they are true.

After this, if **isSuccess** is true, then we are looping through the quotes array, and then displaying the quote as well as the author.

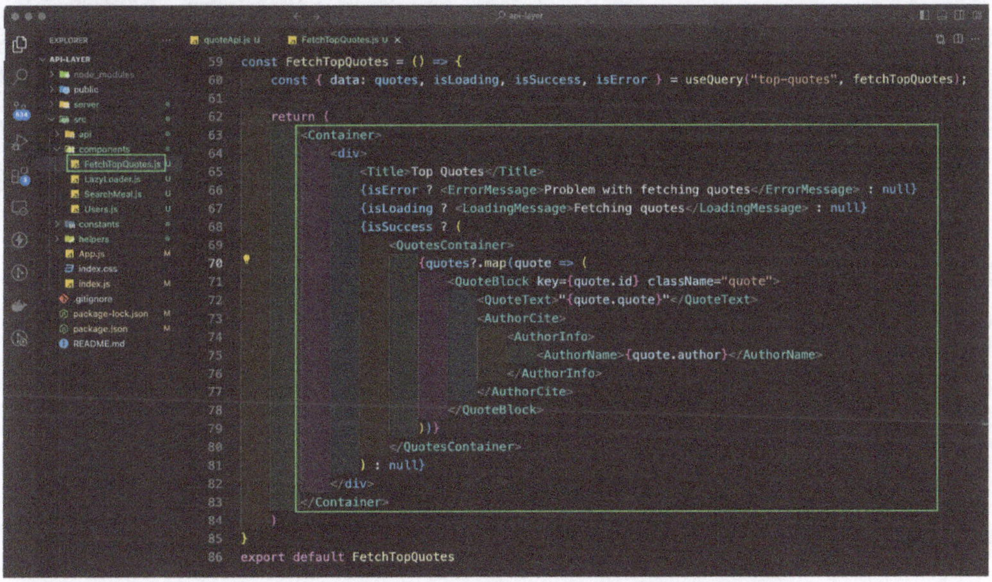

Figure 10.12: *FetchTopQuotes.js File Return Statement*

Next, to show the **FetchTopQuotes**, we will change the earlier code in the **App.js** file. Here, we will also add the code for using react-query and toast. We are first importing the **QueryClient** and **QueryClientProvider** from react-query.

After this, we have imported the **ToastContainer**, and the required CSS. Finally, we have imported the **FetchTopQuotes**. Next, we have created a constant **queryClient** using **QueryClient**.

Inside the return, we are wrapping everything with **QueryClientProvider**, and passing the client as props. Inside it, we are calling the **ToastContainer** and **FetchTopQuotes**.

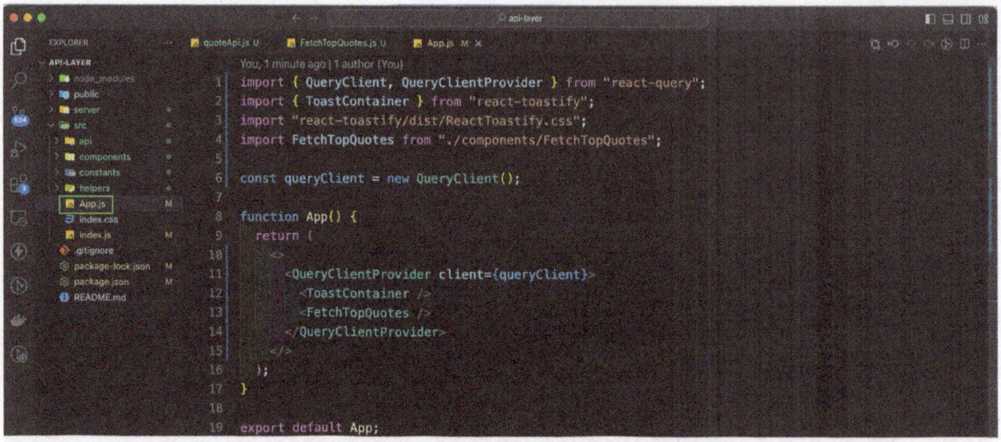

Figure 10.13: *FetchTopQuotes in App.js File*

Now, going to http://localhost:3000/ will show the top five (5) quotes.

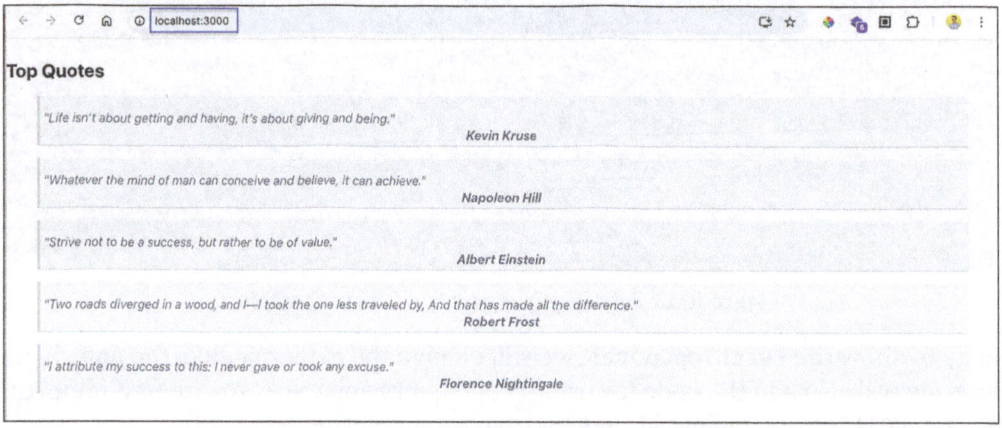

Figure 10.14: *Localhost Showing Quotes*

Updating Data with React-Query

So, any requests that are supposed to update data on the server can be performed with the `useMutation` hook that is provided by the react-query library. First in the `quoteApi.js` file, we will add two new APIs for `postQuote` and `resetQuotes`.

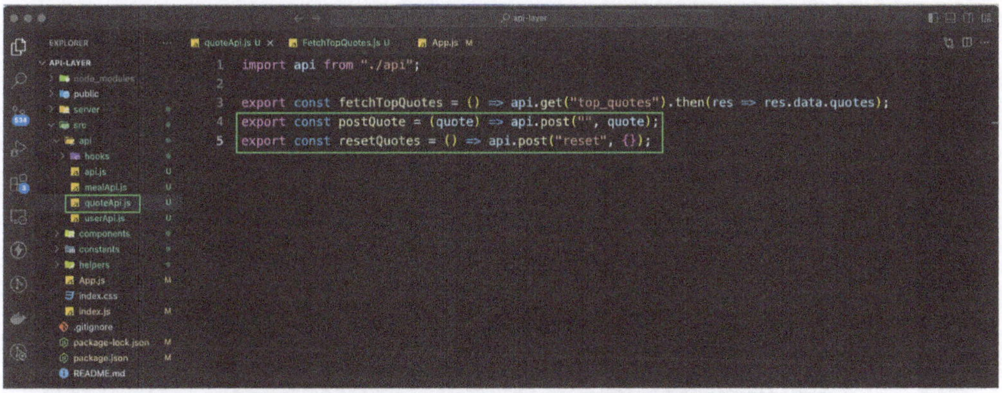

Figure 10.15: *postQuote and resetQuotes in quoteApi.js*

Next, create a new file **`UpdateQuotes.js`** inside the **`components`** folder. Here, we will first import the **`useMutation`** and **`useQueryClient`** from react-query. After this, we have also imported **`postQuote`** and **`resetQuotes`** from the previous file, and imported the **`useState`** from react.

In the next step, inside the **`UpdateQuotes`** function, we have first created a constant **`queryClient`** using **`useQueryClient`**. Then we created the constant **`createQuoteMutation`** and **`resetQuotesMutation`** using **`useMutation`**, and passing **`postQuote`** and **`resetQuotes`** respectively.

Next, we have a state of form that has an object with the keys of the author and quote. After this, an **`onChange`** function will set the form with the earlier value updated with new value. Then we have the async function of **`onSubmit`** which takes the author and the quote from the form.

After doing a check with the if statement that both are there, it uses **`createQuoteMutation`** on the **`mutate`** function to submit the form. It takes a second parameter that sets the form back to an object with the keys of the author and quote. Next, it calls the API top-quotes, and also shows a toast message.

Next, we have an **`onReset`** function which uses **`resetQuotesMutation`** on the **`mutate`** function. After doing the reset, it calls the API top-quotes, and shows a toast message.

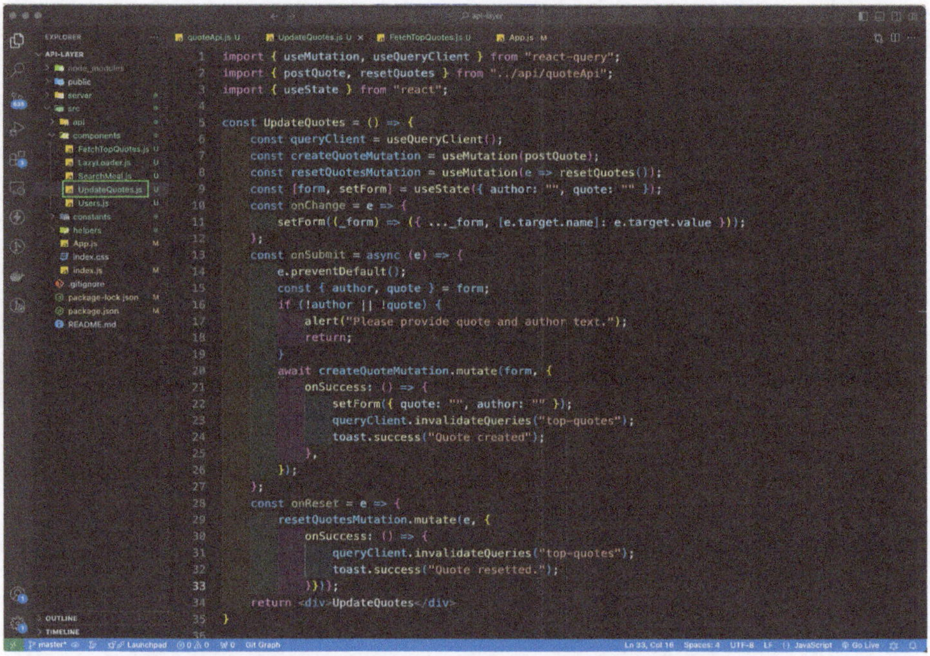

Figure 10.16: *UpdateQuotes.js Imports and Functions*

Now, in the same **`UpdateQuotes.js`** file, we have imported the toast and styled components. After this, we have added some styles for the **`Container`**, **`Title`**, **`Form`**, **`FormGroup`**, **`Label`**, **`Input`**, and **`Button`**.

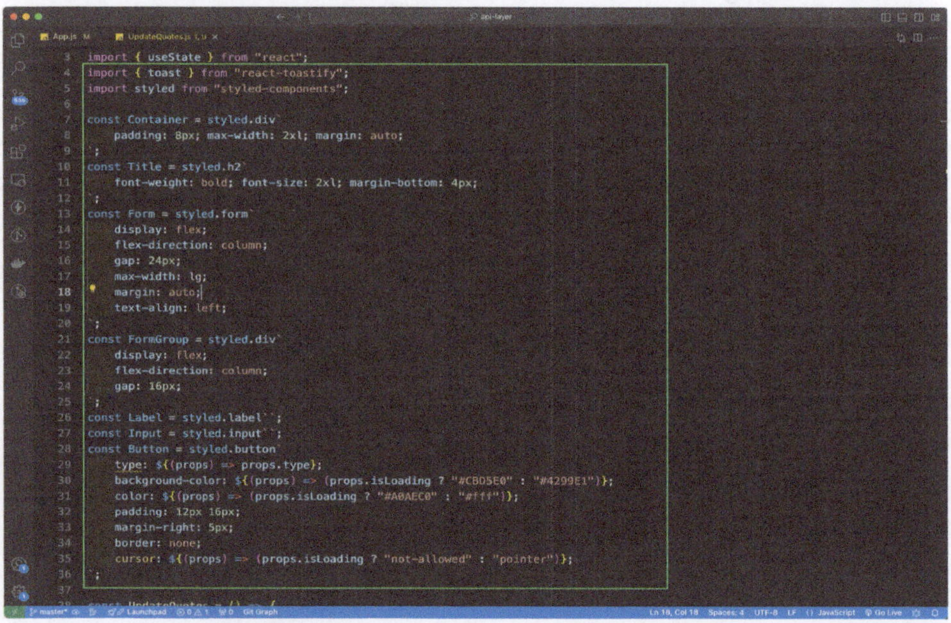

Figure 10.17: *UpdateQuotes.js Styled Components*

Next, in the **return** statement, we have added the styles created earlier. Here, we have input for the Author and the Quote. Next, we have two buttons. The first button calls the **onSubmit,** and also uses **isLoading** state to show different messages.

The next button calls the **onReset,** and also shows different messages depending on **isLoading**.

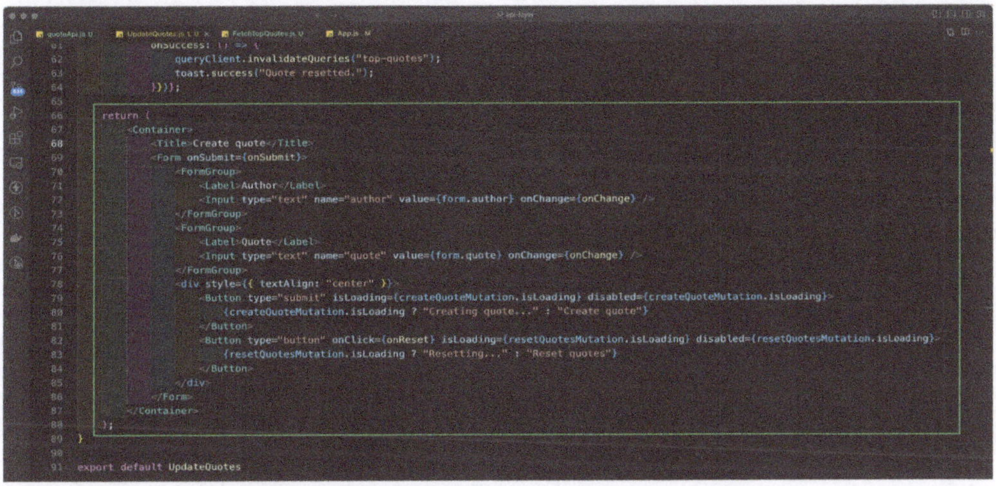

Figure 10.18: *UpdateQuotes.js Return Statement*

After this in the **App.js** file, we shall import **UpdateQuotes** also.

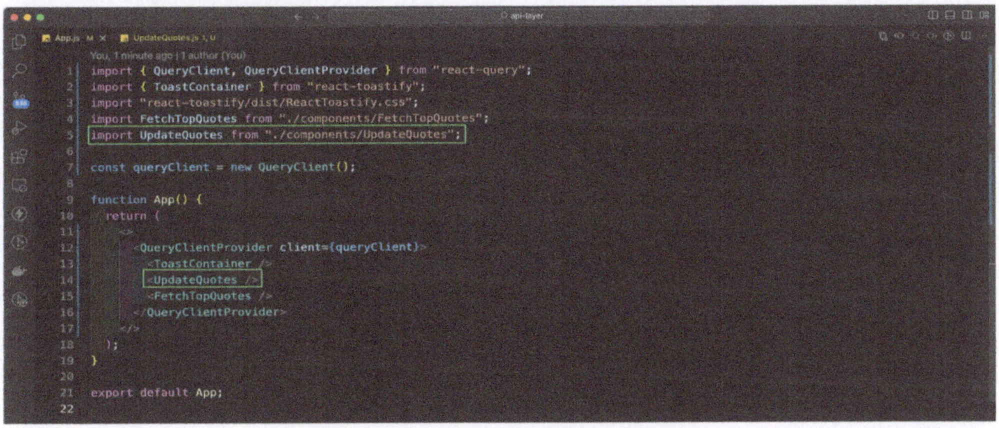

Figure 10.19: *UpdateQuotes in App.js File*

Now, in http://localhost:3000/, we will see a form. We have entered an **Author** and a **Quote**, and hit the **Create quote** button.

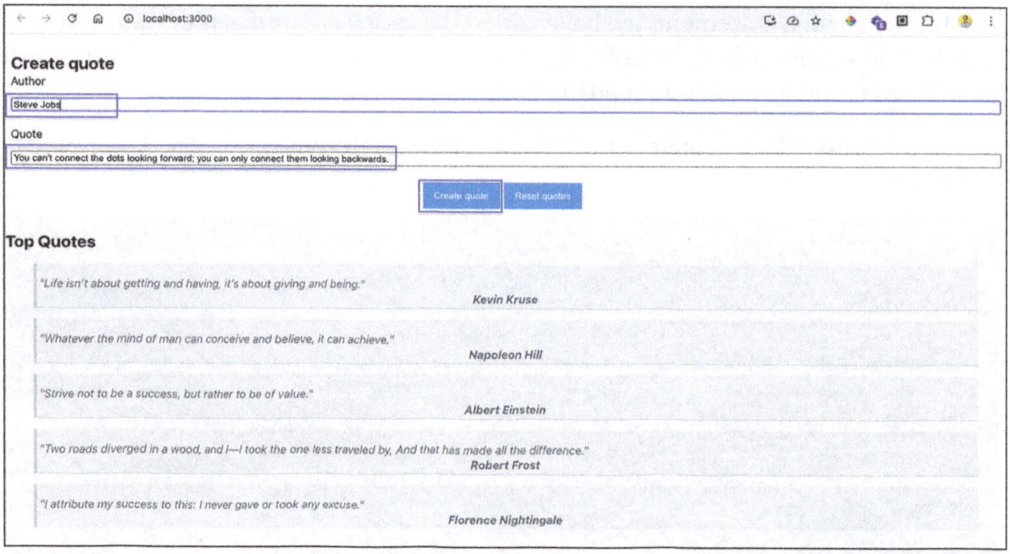

Figure 10.20: *Author and Quote in Localhost*

Now, the new quote will be shown, and also a toast message of **`Quote created`**.

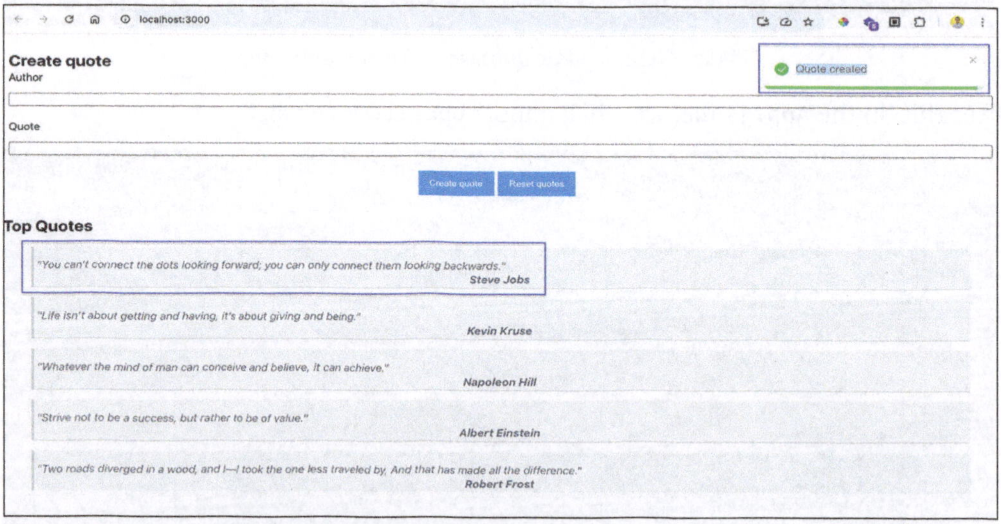

Figure 10.21: *Successful Quote Created in Localhost*

If we click on the **`Reset Quotes`** button, the last quote will be cleared, and we will also get the toast message of the **`Quote reset`**.

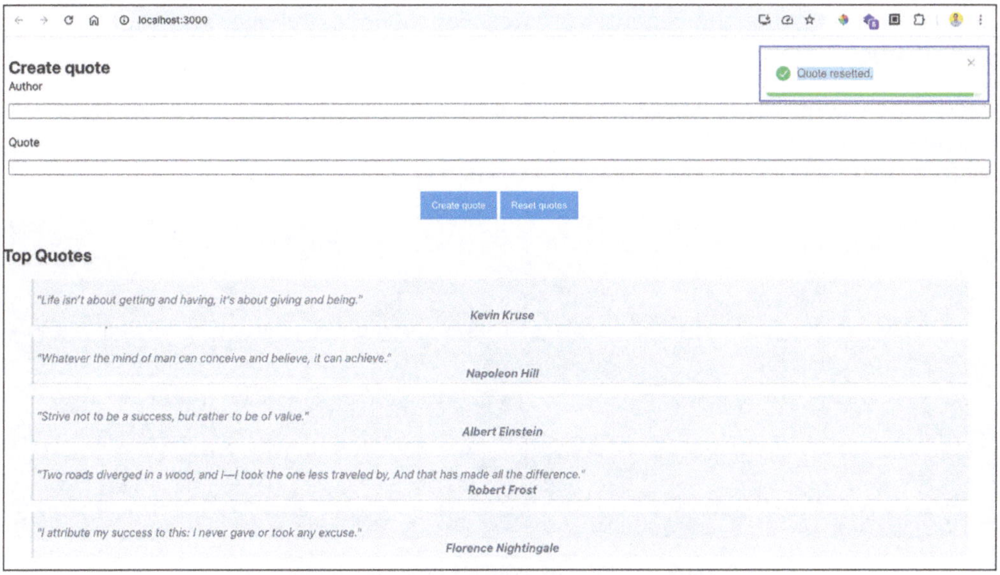

Figure 10.22: *Reset Successful in Localhost*

Pagination with React-Query

Pagination is quite simple to implement with React-Query. We can use the same **useQuery** hook. But instead of passing the query key string, we should pass an array that contains the query key as the first item, and the page number as the second item.

Firstly, we are going to get back to **quoteApi.js**, and then create **fetchQuotesByPage** that will do an API of GET to /, and pass the params of the page. We are getting back the response.

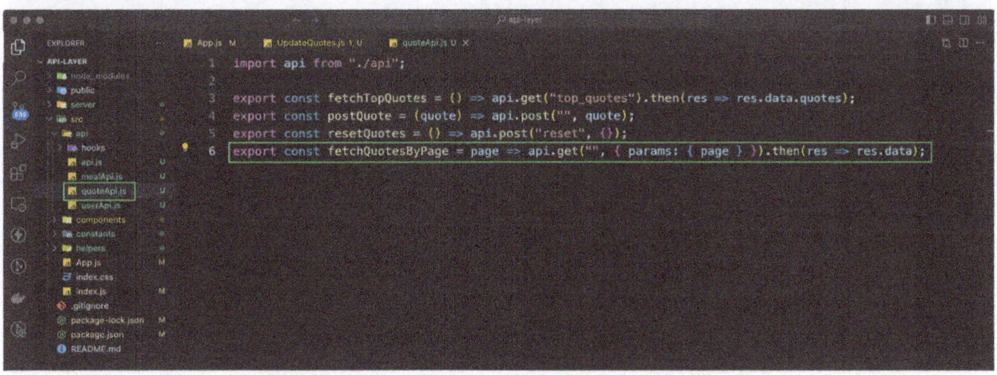

Figure 10.23: *fetchQuotesByPage in quoteApi.js*

Now, we will create a new component of the **PaginatedQuotes.js** file. Here, we are first importing **useState** from react, and then **useQuery** from react-query. After this, we are importing the recently created **fetchQuotesByPage**, and then the style components.

Next, inside the function, **PaginatedQuotes** we are creating a state of page. Next, with **useQuery**, we are passing the quotes and page as well as passing the **fetchQuotesByPage** in the page. We are also passing **keepPreviousData** as true.

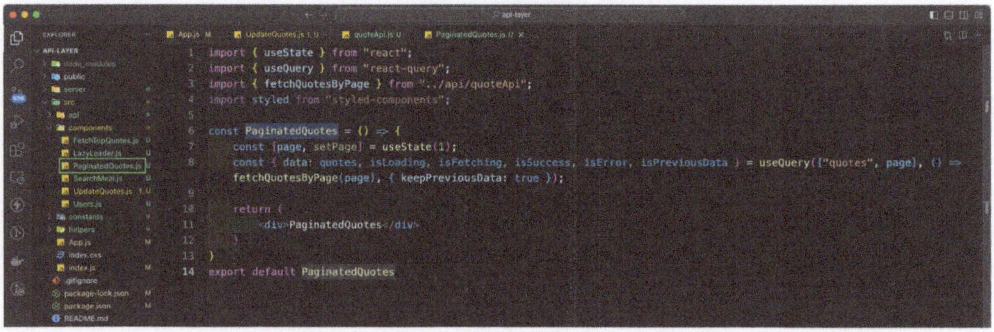

Figure 10.24: *PaginatedQuotes.js Imports and useQuery*

Next, we will add styled components in the **PaginatedQuotes.js file** for **Container**, **Title**, **ErrorMessage**, **LoadingMessage**, **LoadingMessage**, **QuotesCOntainer**, **QuoteBlock**, **QuoteText**, **CiteContainer**, and **AuthorText**.

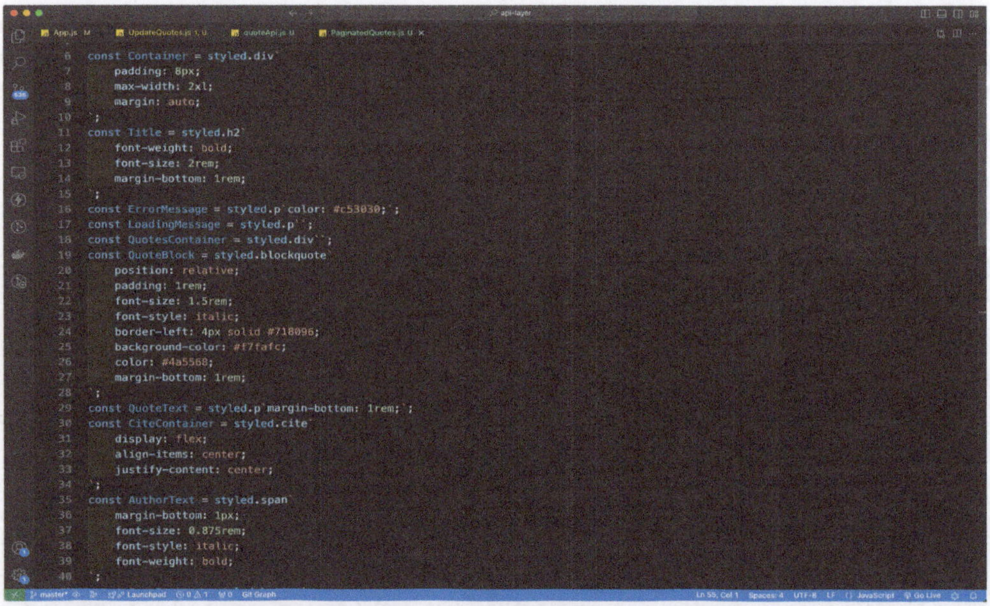

Figure 10.25: *PaginatedQuotes.js Styled Components*

Next, we will add the styled components for **PageButton**, **PageNumber**, **NextPageButton** and **LoadingSpan** in the **PaginatedQuotes.js** file.

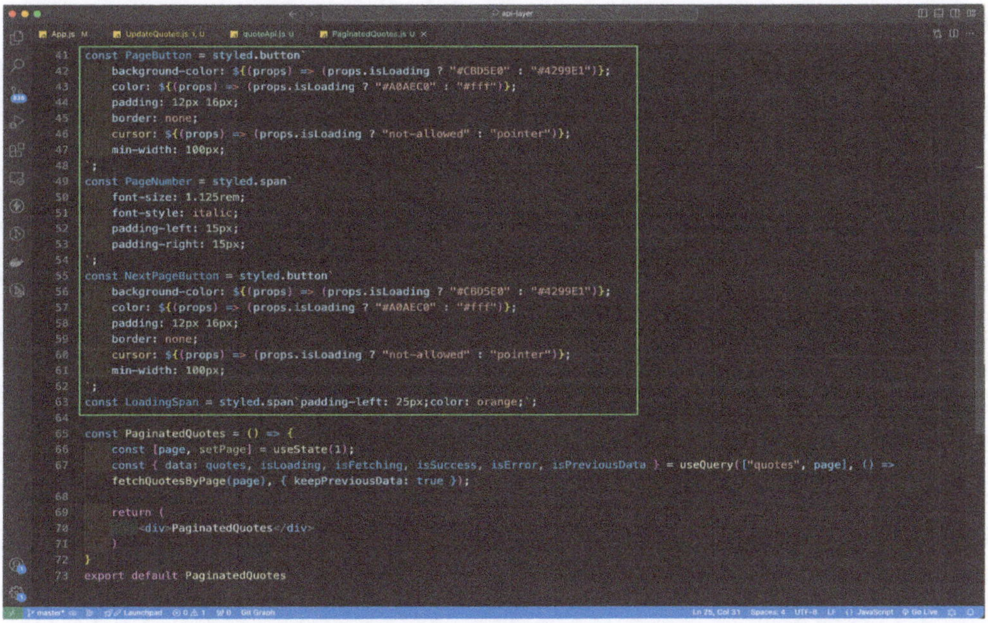

Figure 10.26: *PaginatedQuotes.js More Styled Components*

Next, inside the return statement in the **`PaginatedQuotes.js`** **file**, we will add the styled components created earlier. Inside it, if **`isError`** or **`isLoading`** is there, we will show the respective message.

The main code is in **`isSuccess`** which will loop through the quotes and show the quote and author. Lastly, we have the code to take to the next page from both the **`Previous`** and **`Next`** buttons. Here, we are changing the page state to take to the next or previous page.

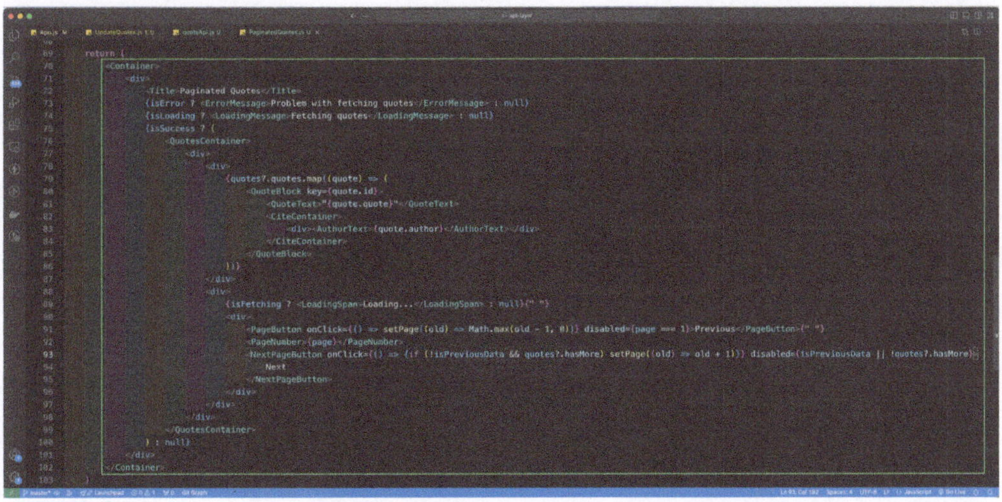

Figure 10.27: *PaginatedQuotes.js Return Statement*

Finally, we will add the **PaginatedQuotes** in the **App.js file**.

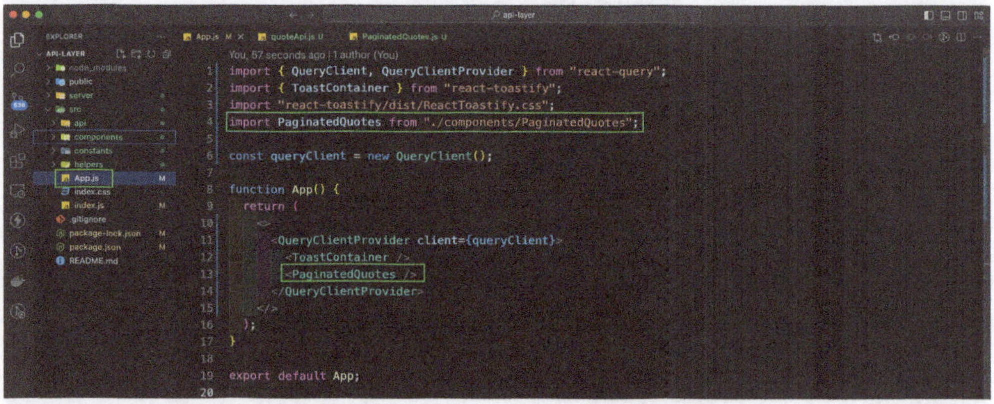

Figure 10.28: *PaginatedQuotes in App.js*

Now, in http://localhost:3000/, we will see the pagination buttons of **Previous** and **Next** at the bottom-left. It also shows the page number at the centre.

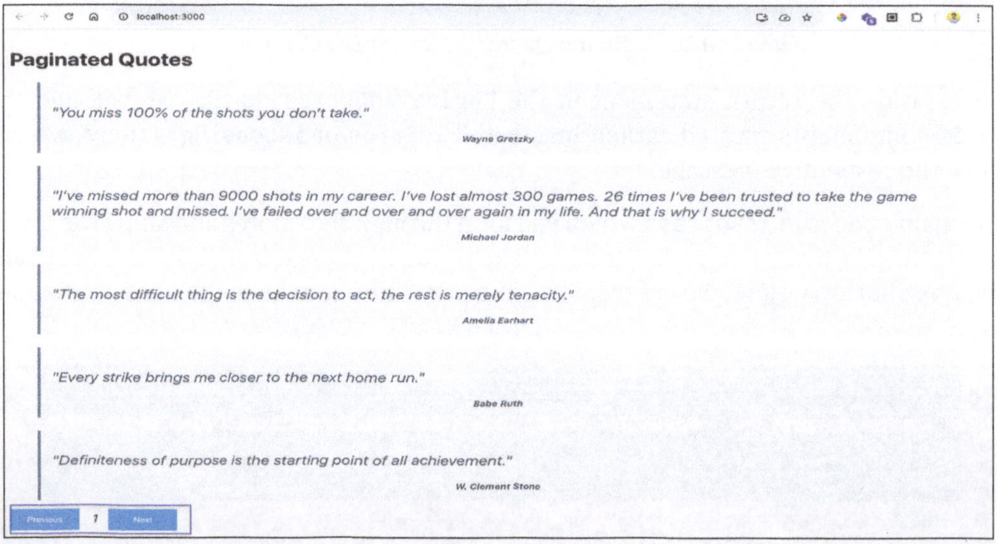

Figure 10.29: *Localhost Showing Pagination Buttons*

Now, click on the **Next** button, and it will take us to the next page. Clicking on the **Previous** button, will take us to the previous page.

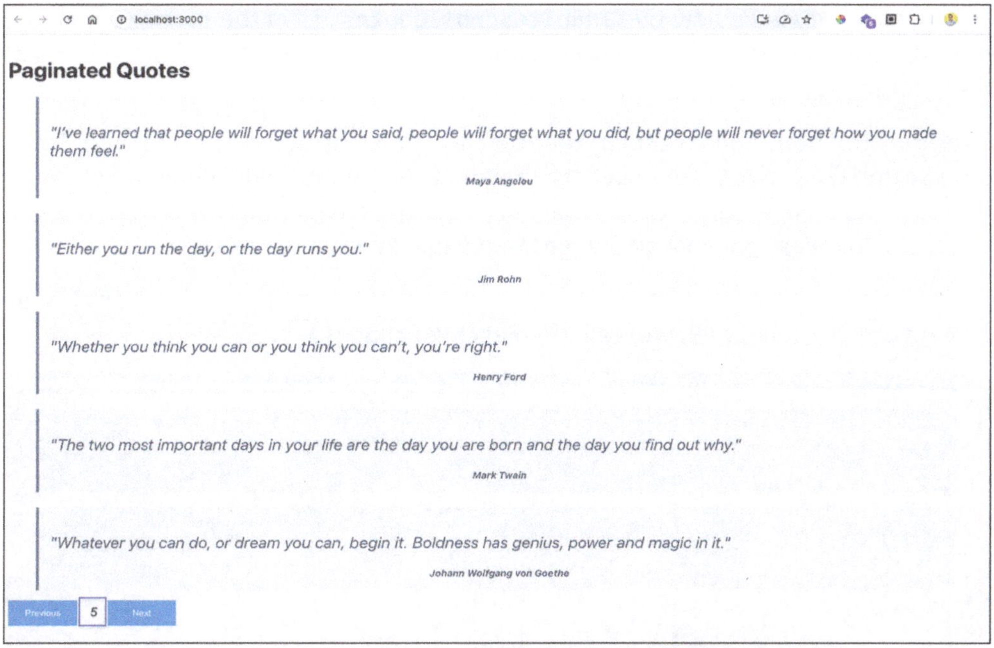

Figure 10.30: *Localhost Pagination Buttons Working*

Infinite Scroll with React-Query

Infinite scroll is another technique that is usually used to load more data on demand. We are going to combine react-query's **`useInfiniteQuery`** hook, with intersection observer.

Here also, we will add a constant in the **`quoteApi.js`** file. The constant is **`fetchQuotesByCursor`**, and it will take a parameter cursor which will do an **`api.get()`**. It will pass the params cursor, and get back the data.

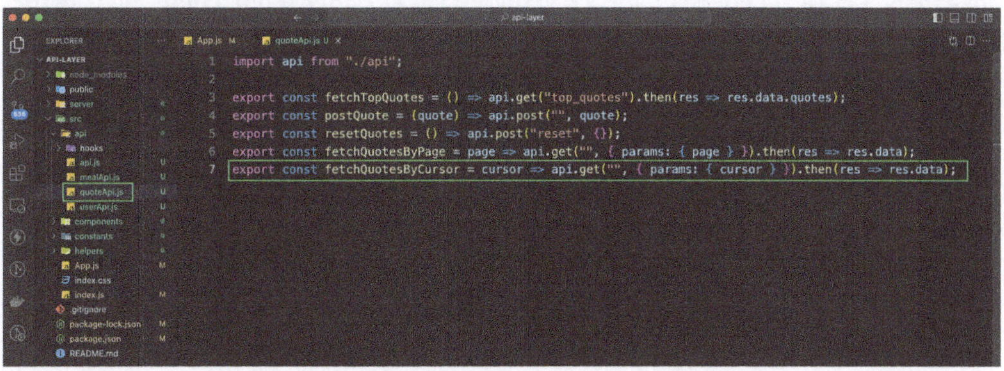

Figure 10.31: *fetchQuotesByCursor in quoteApi.js*

We also need to install the **`react-intersection-observer`** in the terminal. After this, we have created a new file, **InfiniteScrollQuotes.js** in the **components** folder. Here, we have imported the required things, including **useInView** from the **react-intersection-observer**.

Inside the function, **InfiniteScrollQuotes**, we first extracted the **ref** and **inView** from **useInView()**. Next from **useInfiniteQuery**, we extracted the data, **isLoading**, **isFetchingNextPage**, **isSuccess**, **isError**, **fetchNextPage**, **hasNextPage**. Here, we passed the "**quotes**", **pageParam** and **getNextPageParam** as parameters.

Next, we have an **useEffect** that changes when **inView** changes. If the **inView** and **hasNextPage** are true, then we call the **fetchNextPage()**.

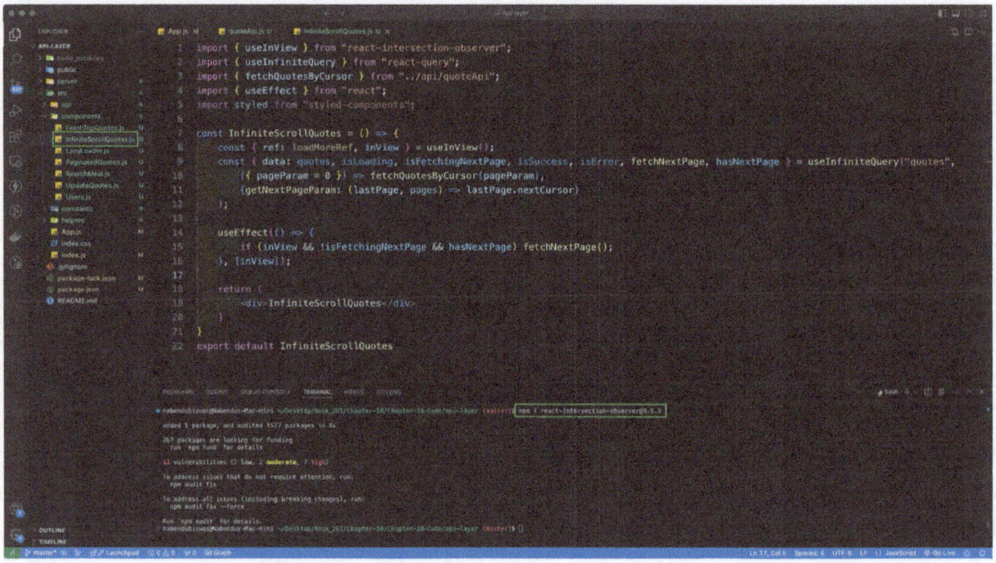

Figure 10.32: *InfiniteScrollQuotes.js Imports and Constants*

After this in the file, **InfiniteScrollQuotes.js** we add styled components for **Container**, **Title**, **ErrorMessage**, **LoadingMessage**, **QuotesContainer**, **QuoteBlock**, **QuoteText**, **CiteContainer**, and the **AuthorText**.

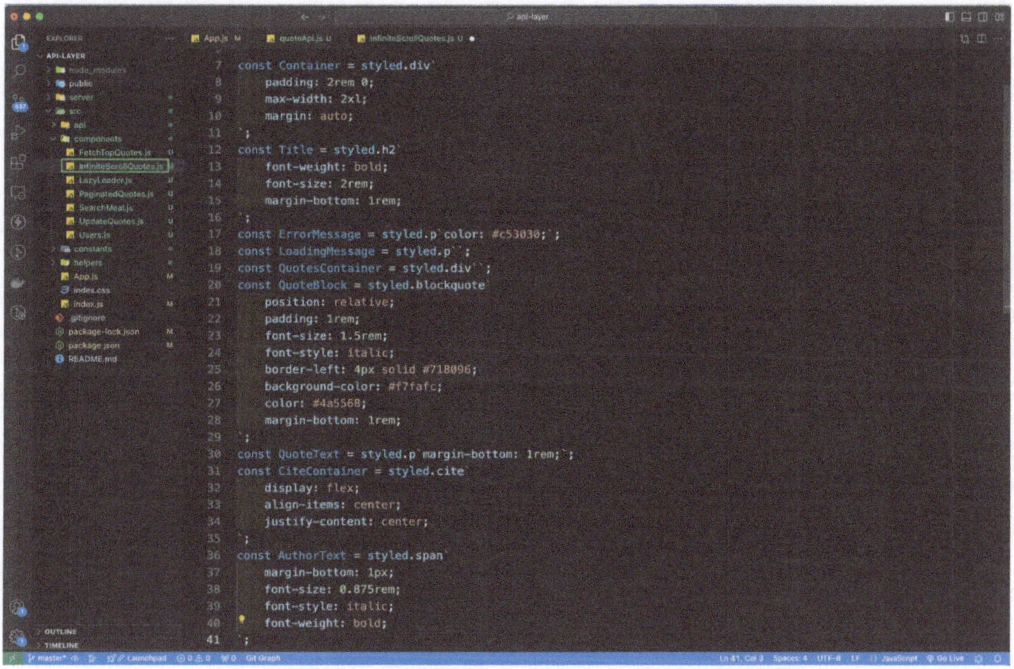

***Figure 10.33:** InfiniteScrollQuotes.js Styled Components*

Now, inside the **`return`** statement in the file **`InfiniteScrollQuotes.js`**, we have the styled components created earlier. We also have the messages shown in case of error or loading. If the case is isSuccess, we have most of the logic.

Here, we are looping through the quotes, and showing each quote with the author. We also have an empty **`div`** with the **`ref`** of **`loadMoreRef`**, and this is where the logic of infinite scroll works. Lastly, if **`isFechingNextPage`** is true, we are showing the Loading text.

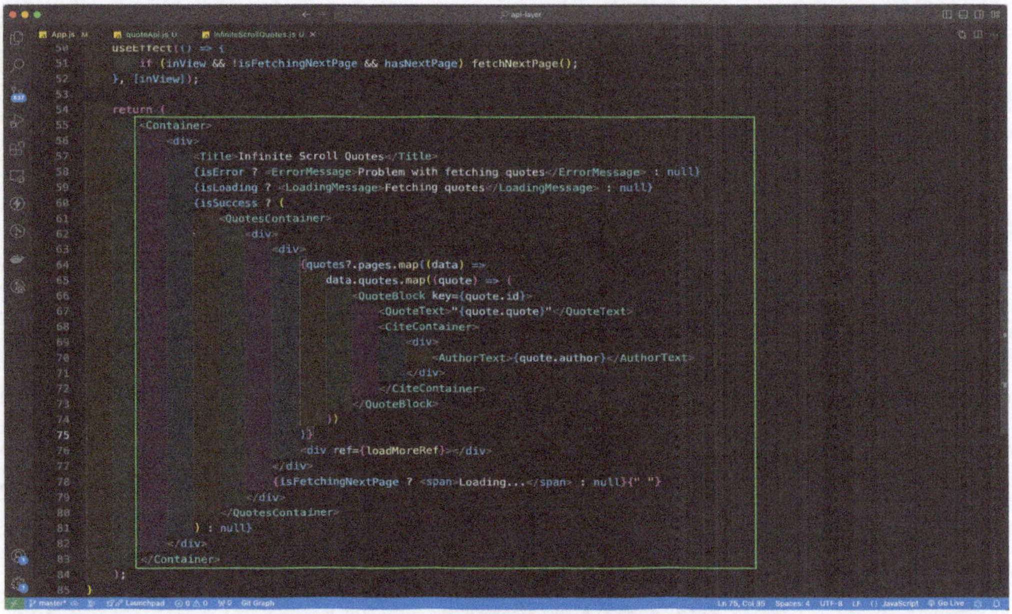

Figure 10.34: *InfiniteScrollQuotes.js Return Statement*

Next, we will add the **`InfiniteScrollQuotes`** in the **`App.js`** file.

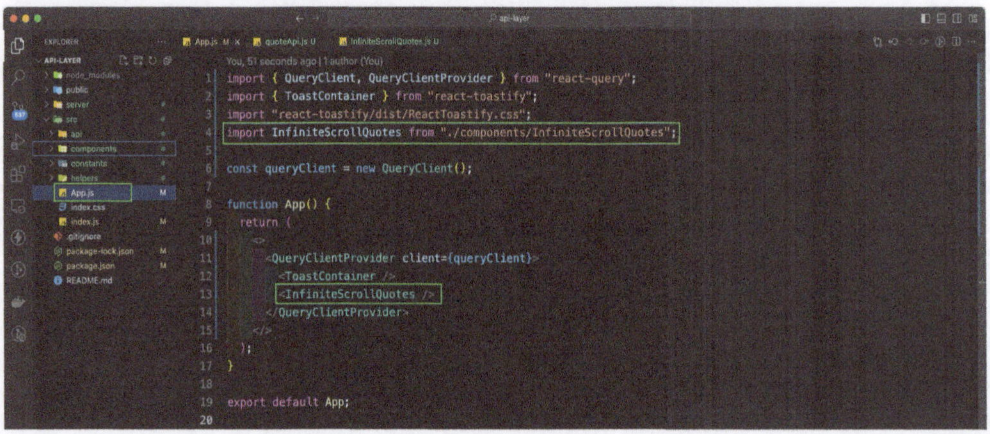

Figure 10.35: *InfiniteScrollQuotes in App.js*

Now, go to http://localhost:3000/, and all the items that can be on the screen will be shown.

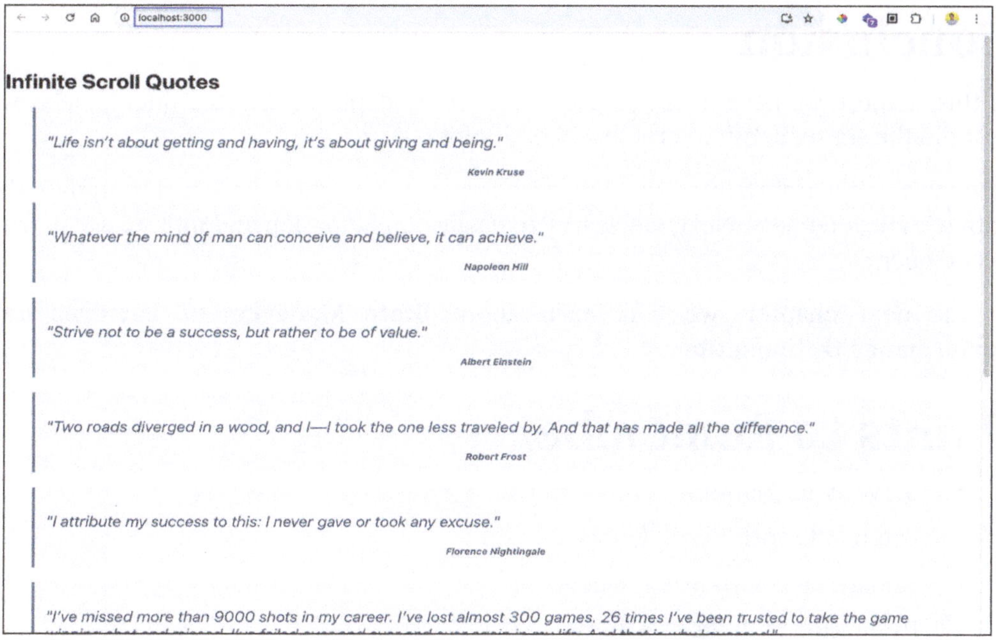

Figure 10.36: *Localhost with Infinite Scroll*

Now, scroll down, and we will see the `Loading`, followed by the new items.

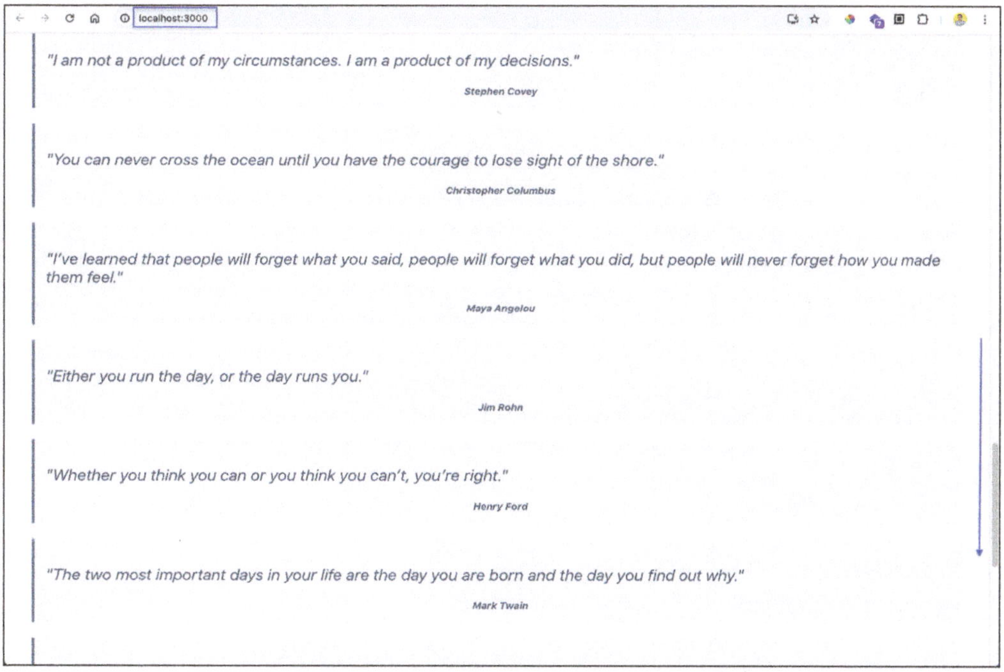

Figure 10.37: *Localhost Infinite Scroll Successful*

Conclusion

In this chapter, we have learnt to use API layer concepts with React-query. Here, we first did the server setup to create API endpoints.

After this, we learnt to fetch the data with React-query. Then we learnt to update the data with React-query. Next, we learnt to easily do pagination and infinite scroll with React-query.

In the next chapter, we will learn about **State Management Patterns and Performance Optimization**.

Points to Remember

- Server with NodeJS.
- Fetch data with React-Query.
- Update data with React-Query.
- Pagination with React-Query.
- Infinite Scroll with React-Query.

Chapter 11
State Management Patterns

Introduction

In this chapter, we will learn about State Management Patterns with the **`use-immer`** library. We can handle a lot of react code base with **`useState`** hook, but the code can become complicated in some cases. This can be solved with the **`use-immer`** library, which we are going to discuss in this chapter elaborately.

Structure

In this chapter, we are going to discuss the following topics:

- Immutable updates with **`useImmer`**
- Cleaner reducer with **`useImmerReducer`**

Immutable Updates with `useImmer`

A lot of states and React code bases can be handled with the **`useState`** hook. However, there are some situations where they could be improved by using some other syntax such as **`useEmitter`** hook.

In this section, we are going to cover how to improve state handling using the useImmer hook. To get an idea of the concept that we are going to work on, we have created a new React project.

Now, open the **`App.js`** file. Here, we have a very basic state variable called **`person`**. It has an initial property of name called Tony. So, here, if you want to update the state, you need to use a function called **`onChange`**. Now, we want to add a property called age.

But, we cannot do it with **`person.age = 24`**, because we are mutating the state object, and React does not allow that. If you want to update the person variable, you have to create a new object using the spread operator with **setPerson({ …person, age: 44 })**.

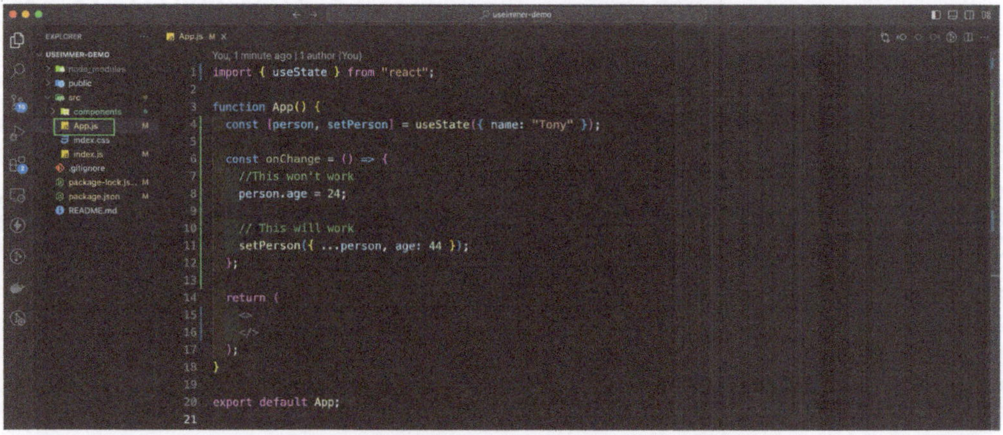

Figure 11.1: *Problem with useState in App.js File*

This is done because React encourages the functional paradigm, and object immutability. This approach makes the code easier to follow, and it helps to avoid potential issues. But in some cases, we are forced to write more codes.

Let us take an example in which we are forced to write unnecessary, complicated pieces of syntax. We will create a small Trello or Jira type of application. Here, we will have a dummy data. So, create a file **boardData.js** and put the following data in it.

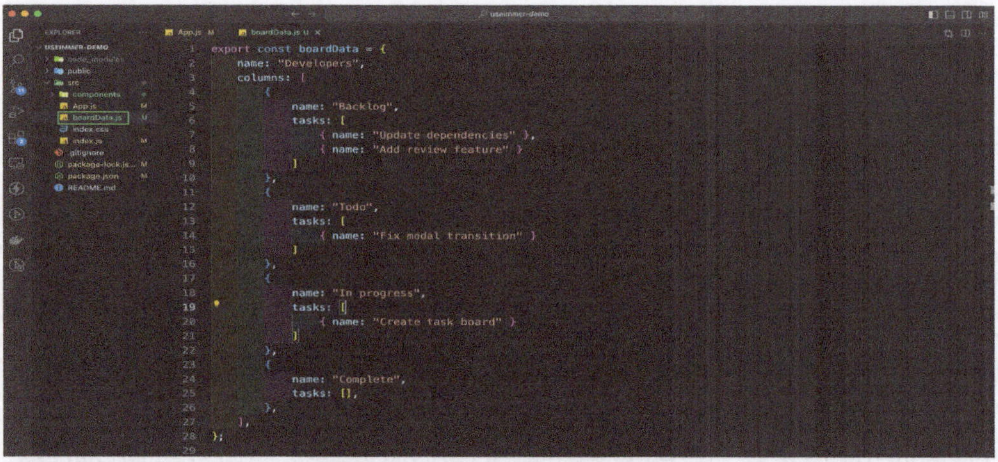

Figure 11.2: *Data in boardData.js File*

Now, create a **components** folder inside **src** and a file, **TasksBoard.jsx** inside it. Here, we are first importing **useState**, then **boardData**, and the styled components, which we have installed through the terminal.

Inside the **TasksBoard** function, we have a state of board and the **selectedTask**. We have the skeleton of two functions such as **onSelectTask** and **onTaskNameChange** that we are going to complete soon.

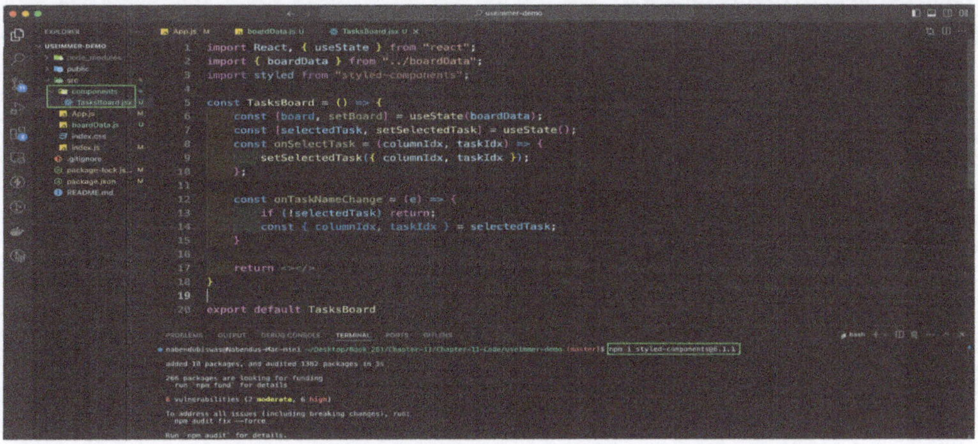

***Figure 11.3:** Imports and States in TasksBoard.jsx File*

Next, we will add some styles, using the styled components in the file, **TasksBoard.jsx**.

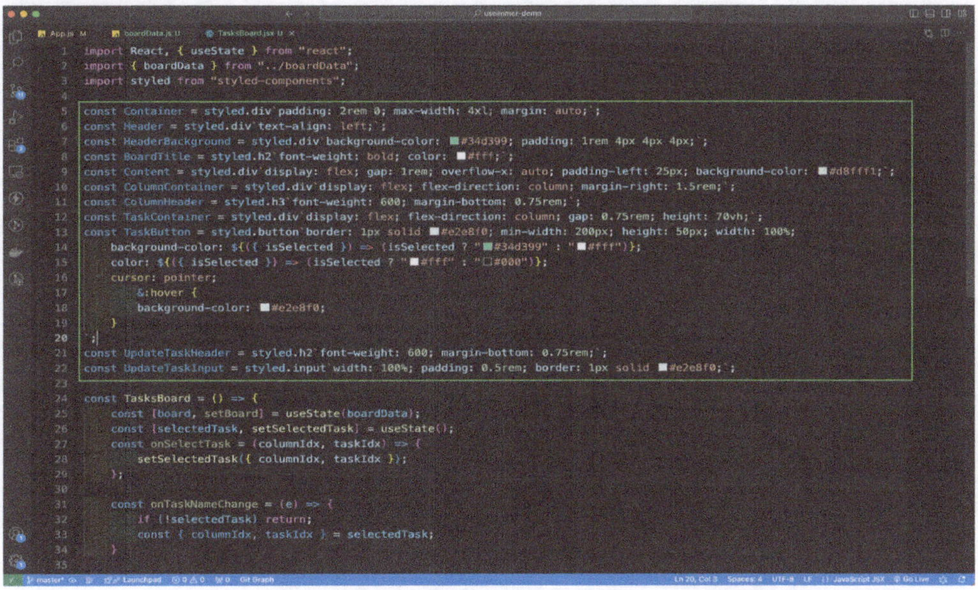

***Figure 11.4:** Styled Components in TasksBoard.jsx File*

Now, inside the **return** statement, we will use the previously created styled components to first show the name. After this, we will loop through the columns to show the column name. We are further looping through the tasks, to show the tasks of each column.

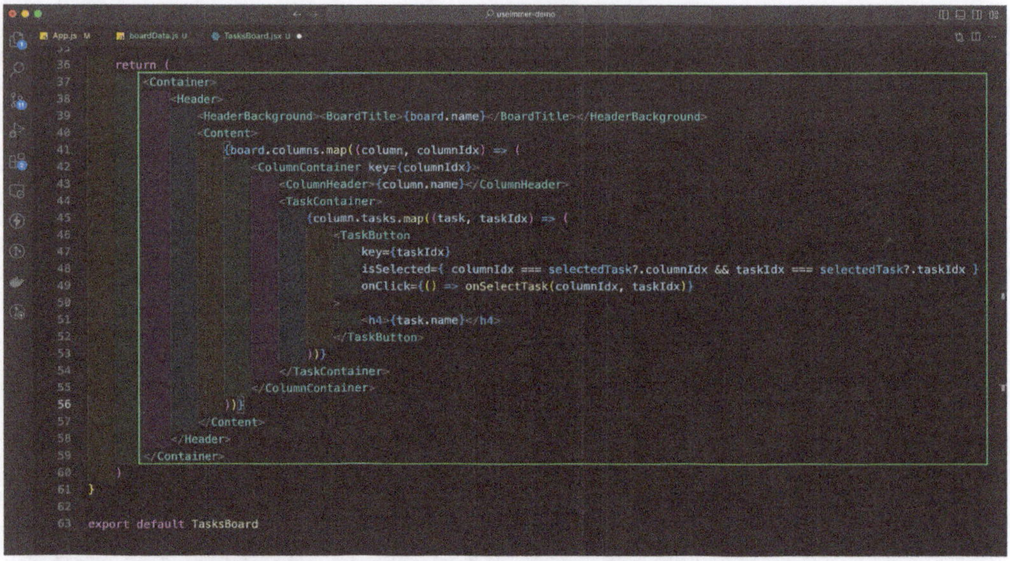

Figure 11.5: *Using Styled Components in TasksBoard.jsx File*

We are further adding a **div** to show the selected task. This has an **onChange** handler which calls the **onTaskNameChange** function created earlier.

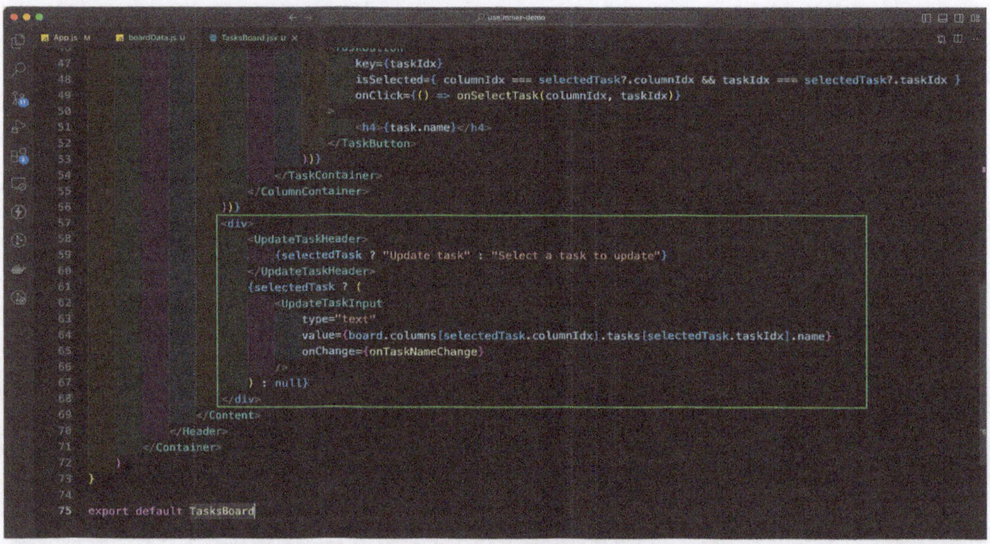

Figure 11.6: *Update the Task Input in TasksBoard.jsx File*

Now, we will add the **TasksBoard** component in the **App.js** file. We have also commented on the earlier person code.

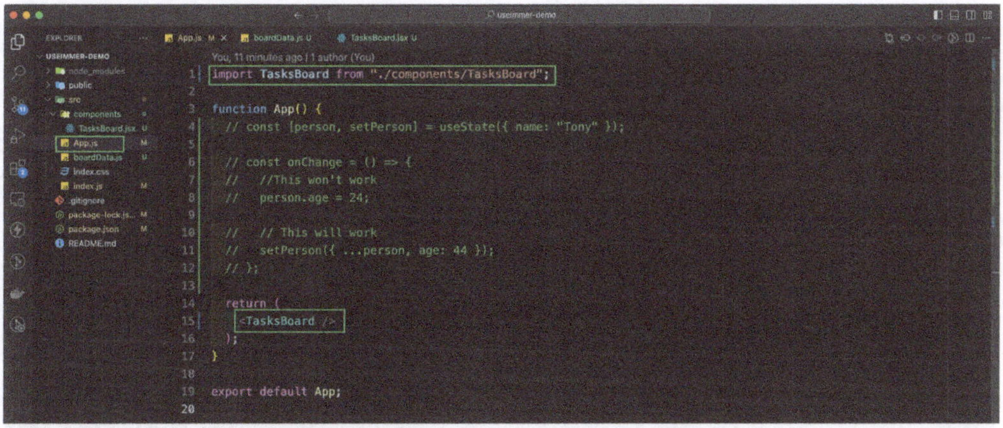

Figure 11.7: *Importing TasksBoard in App.js File*

Now, in http://localhost:3000/, we will see our styled app. Here, we have the columns of **`Backlog`**, **`Todo`** and **`In Progress`**.

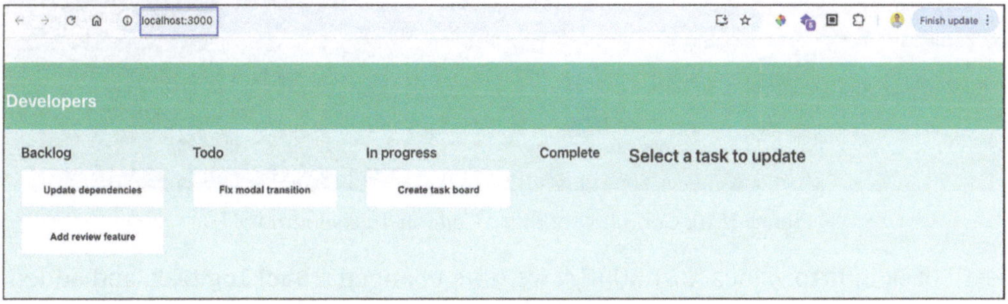

Figure 11.8: *Localhost Showing All Columns*

Next, clicking on any of the tasks, will change the '**`Select a task`**' to update to '**`Update task`**'. It will also put that task in an input box. But we will not be able to update it, as we have to write further a code for it.

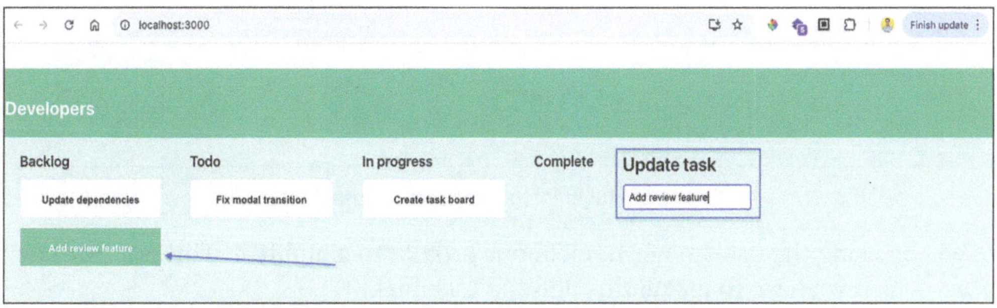

Figure 11.9: *Selecting Column in Localhost*

Now, back in the file **`TasksBoard.jsx`**, and inside the **`onTaskNameChange`** function, we will add the code to change the board. Here, with setBoard, we shall get the board, and first using the spread operator as **...board**, to get every element.

After this step, we will go through the columns, looping through it. Then looping through the tasks, and looping through it. We then finally get the task with the task **id**, changing its value. You can see a lot of use of spread operators here that complicates the code.

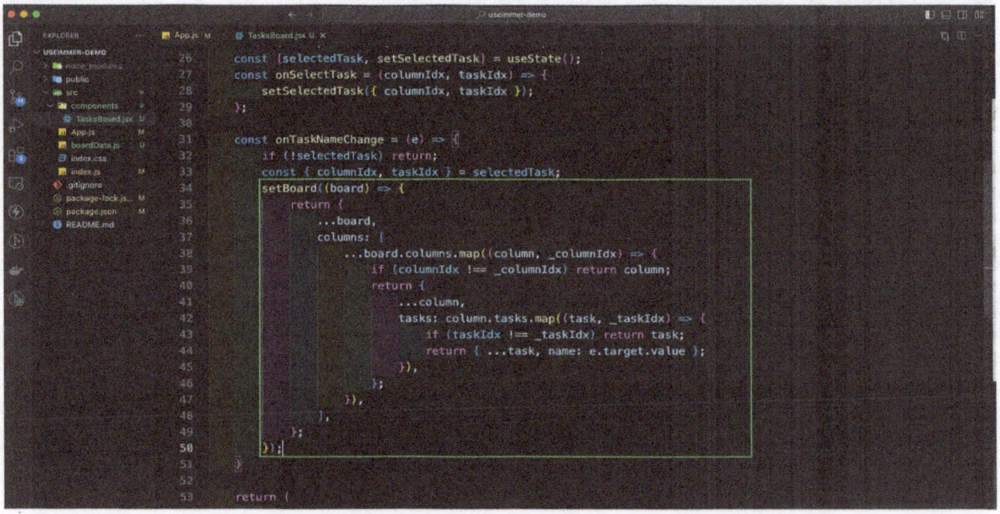

Figure 11.10: *Complex setBoard Code in TasksBoard.jsx File*

Next, back in http://localhost:3000/, we have changed a **Backlog** task, and added it to it. Next, we clicked on a **Todo** task, and changed it.

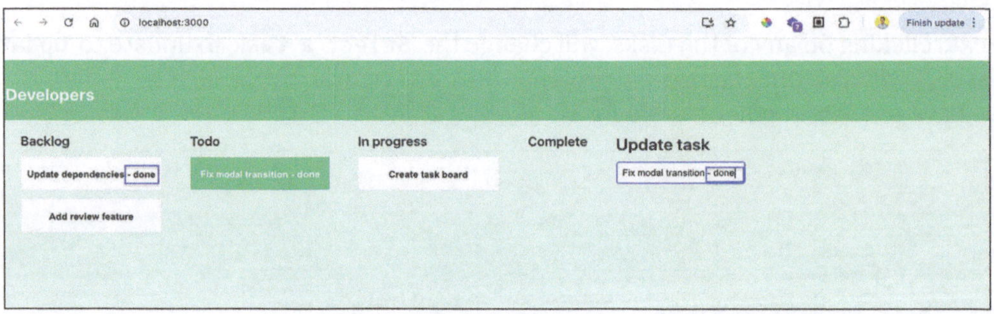

Figure 11.11: *Updating Column in Localhost*

We will be using the use-immer hook in our project to simplify it. This is a third party library which we have to install through the terminal.

***Figure 11.12:** Installing use-immer Library*

Next, back in the **`TasksBoard.jsx`** file, we will first import **`useImmer`**, and then use it in place of **`useState`**. After this in **`onTaskNameChange`**, we have commented out the setBoard complex code, and replaced it with a one line code.

With **`useImmer`**, we can directly navigate through a complicated array of objects, which again contains an array of objects.

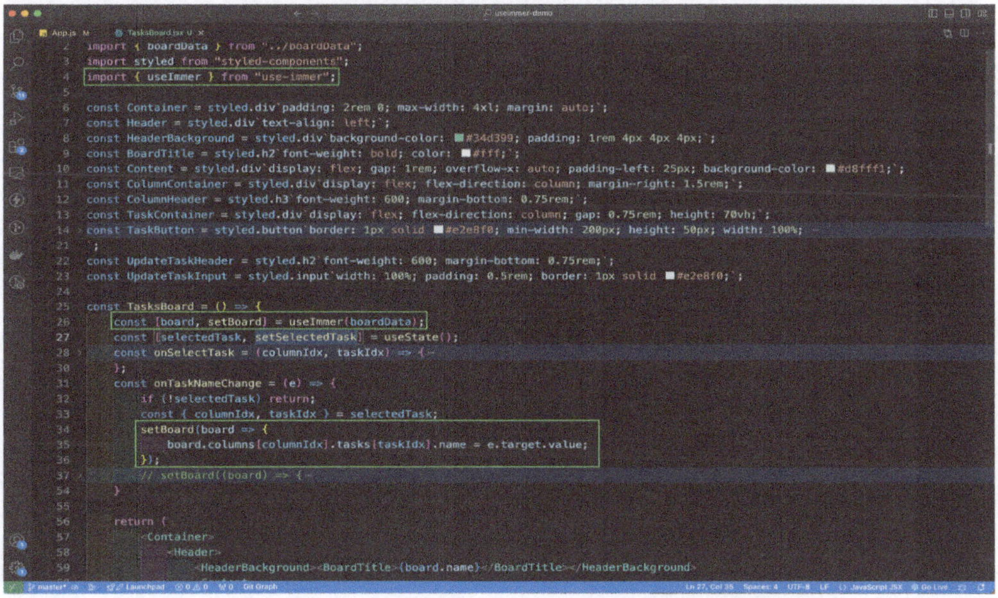

***Figure 11.13:** Using use-immer in TasksBoard.jsx File*

Back in http://localhost:3000/, we are getting the same features.

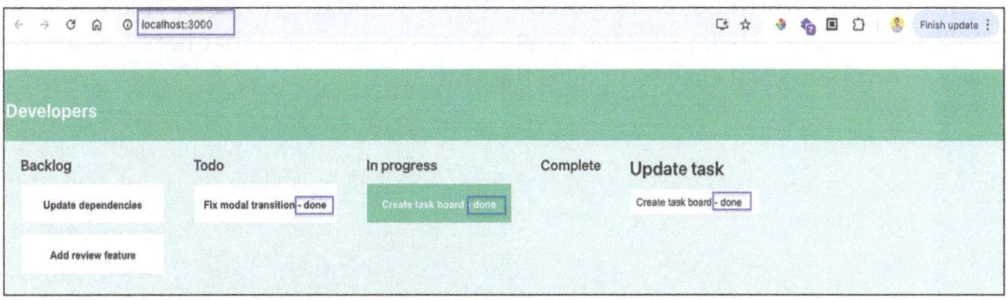

***Figure 11.14:** Localhost Working as Earlier*

Cleaner, Reducer with `useImmerReducer`

Beside the **useState** hook, there is a hook called **useReducer** that is used when dealing with complex data sets. We will see how to implement it, using a basic shopping list application.

So, let us first walk through the basic code, for which we have again created a new react app. We have first created a **components** folder inside **src** folder, and inside it created a **ShoppingList.jsx** file.

First, we have imported the **useReducer** and styled components which we have also installed in the terminal. After this, we have written some styles, using styled-components.

Next, we have a function to get a random number. Also, we have created a constant called **shoppingItems** that contains the initial state for the reducer.

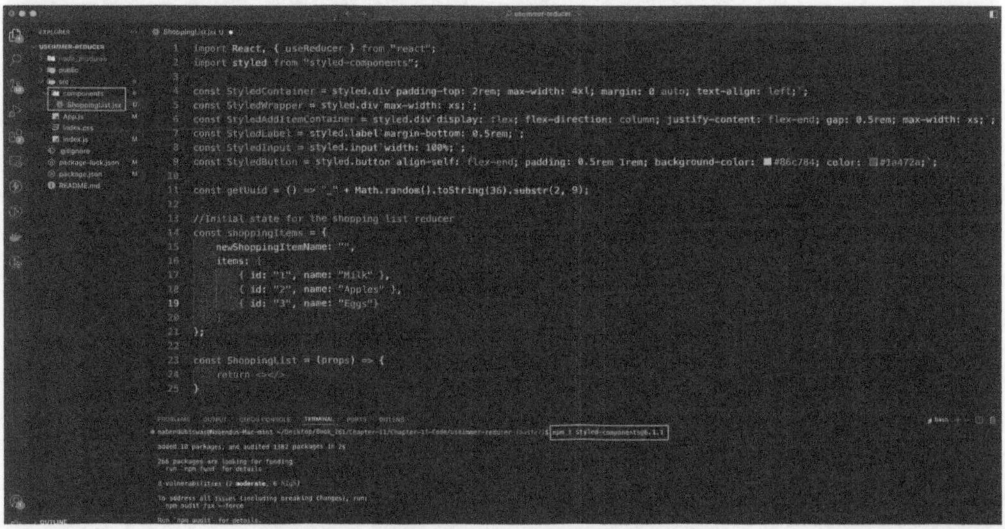

Figure 11.15: *Initial ShoppingList.jsx File*

Next, we will have the reducer constant which will take the state and action. It will have switch cases, which depending on the type will update the state. This is a normal reducer that we use, while using the **useReducer** hook. Notice that here we are using spread operators in each case to update the state.

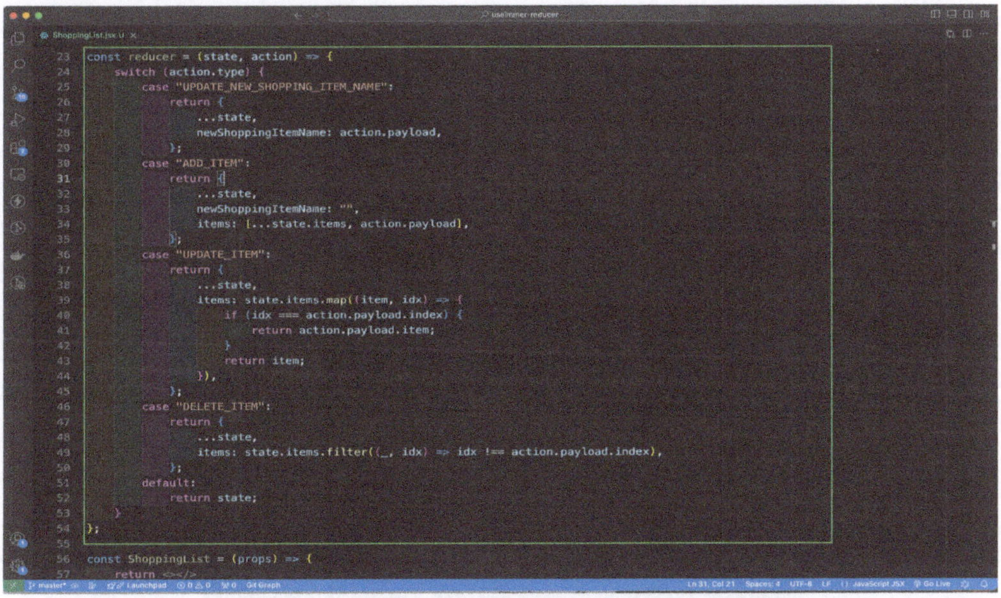

Figure 11.16: *Complex Reducer in ShoppingList.jsx File*

Now, inside the **ShoppingList** function, we will have a **shoppingList** constant, and with the useReducer hook, will pass the reducer and **shoppingItems** created earlier.

Next, we will have the **addItem**, **deleteItem**, **updateItem** and **onChangeShoppingListItemName** functions. These functions dispatch to the cases declared earlier with the payload.

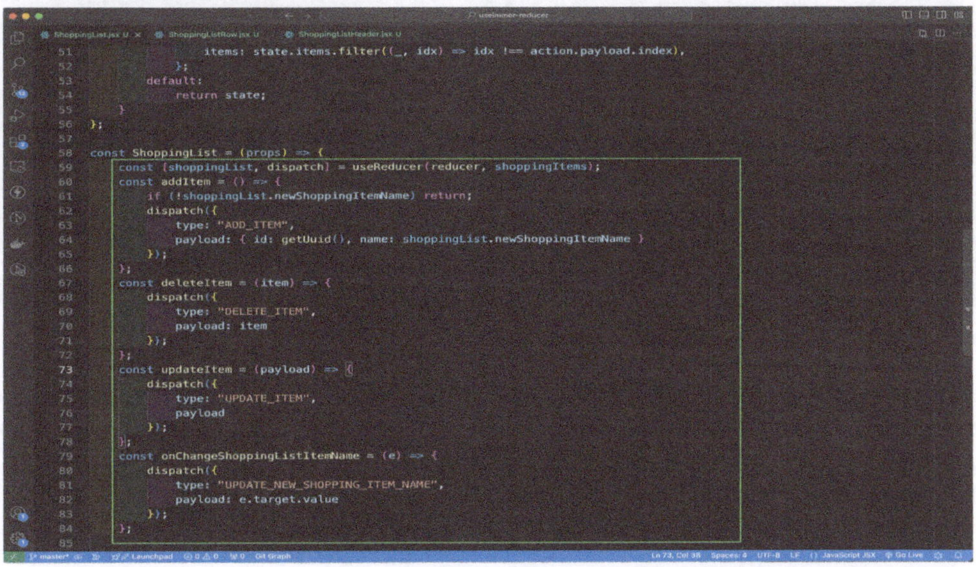

Figure 11.17: *useReducer in ShoppingList.jsx File*

Now, inside the return statement of the **ShoppingList.jsx** file, we will use the styled components created earlier. Here, we are also calling a component of **ShoppingListHeader**, and passing a prop of the **shoppingList**.

We are also looping through items of **shoppingList**, and passing each item to the **ShoppingListRow** component.

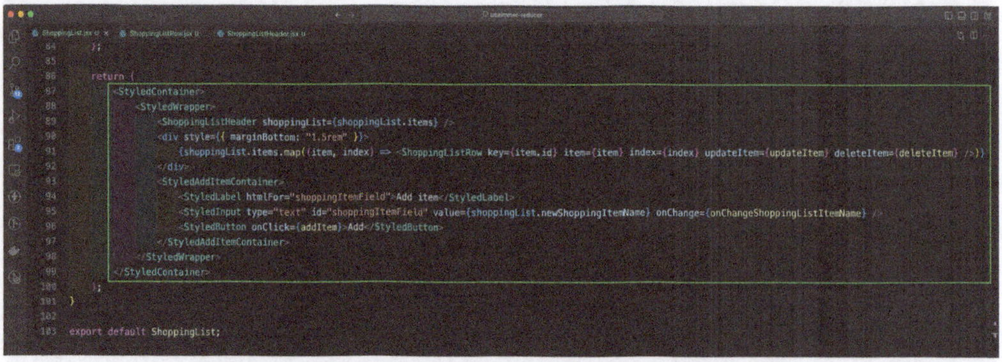

Figure 11.18: Styled Components in ShoppingList.jsx File

Next, create a new file called **ShoppingListHeader.jsx** inside the **components** folder. Here, after importing the styled components, and using it, we are using the **props.shoppingList.length** to show the length.

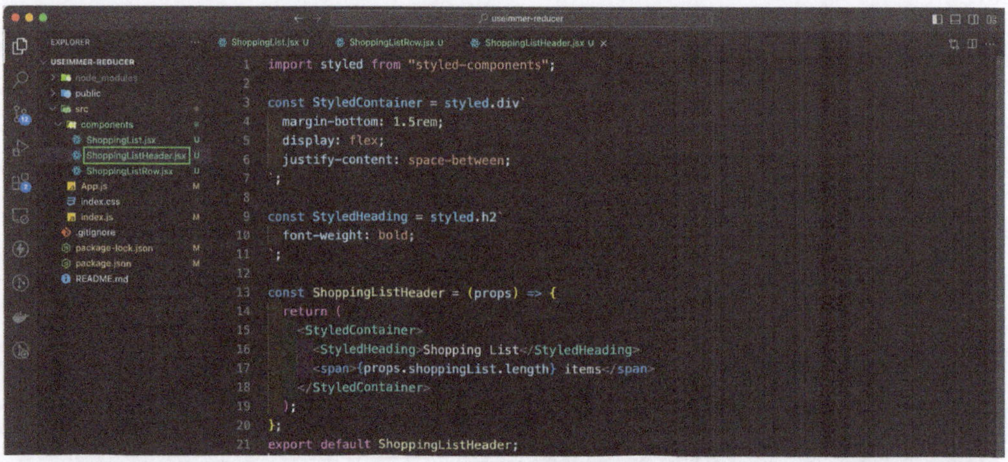

Figure 11.19: ShoppingListHeader.jsx File

Next, create a new file called **ShoppingListRow.jsx** inside the **components** folder. Here, we are first importing the **useEffect** and **useState** hook, and also the styled components. After this, using the styled components, we create the styles for this component.

Next, we have a function called **useEditShoppingItem** which takes the item,

updateItem, and index from the props, and then **useState** to set the name. Also, have a state variable of **isEditing** that is initially set to false.

Then there is an **useEffect** hook which sets the name to **props.item.name**. After this, we have an **onSaveItem** function which uses **updateItem** to update the item, and also change the **isEditing** to false.

Next, we have the **onEditItem** function that changes the **isEditing** to true. Then we have a **cancelEdit** function which changes the **isEditing** to false, and also changes the name back to the original name.

Finally, we are returning name, **isEditing**, **cancelEdit**, **setName**, **onSaveItem**, and **onEditItem** from this **useEditShoppingItem** function. After this, we have the main **ShoppingListRow** function that we will update next.

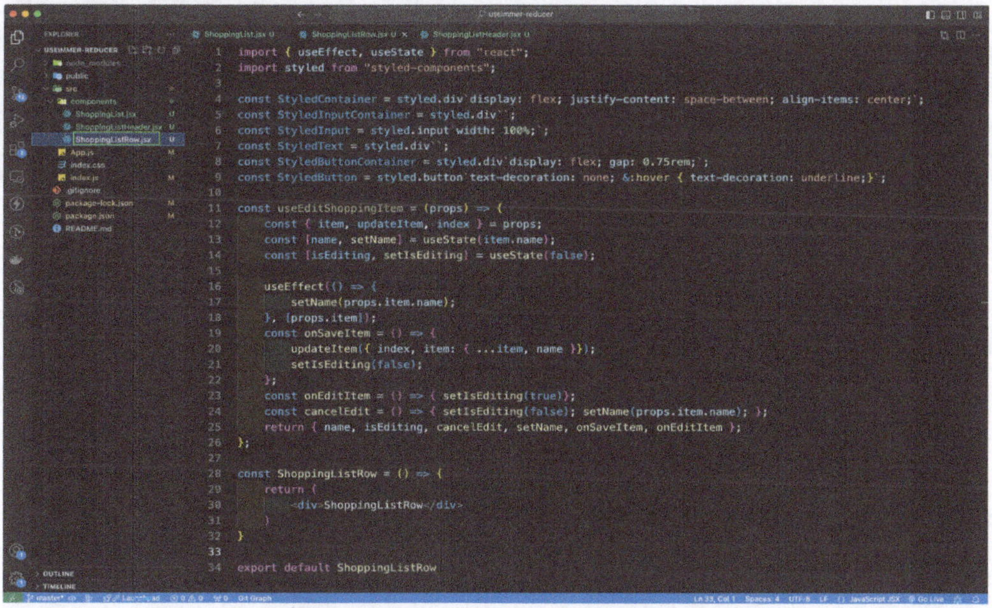

Figure 11.20: *Initial ShoppingListRow.jsx File*

Now, in the **ShoppingListRow** function, we are getting the props, and extracting the items, **deleteItem** and index from it. After this, we are calling the **useEditShoppingItem** function, and getting the name, **isEditing**, **cancelEdit**, **setName**, **onSaveItem**, and **onEditItem** from it.

Next, inside the **return** statement, we are using styled components. Here, first if the **isEditing** is true, we are changing the name, or else keeping it as the passed name. Again, if the **isEditing** is true, we will show the **Save** and **Cancel** button that will call **onSaveItem**, and **cancelEdit** respectively.

If the **isEditing** is false, we will show the **Edit** and **Delete** buttons, which will call **onEditItem** and **deleteItem** respectively.

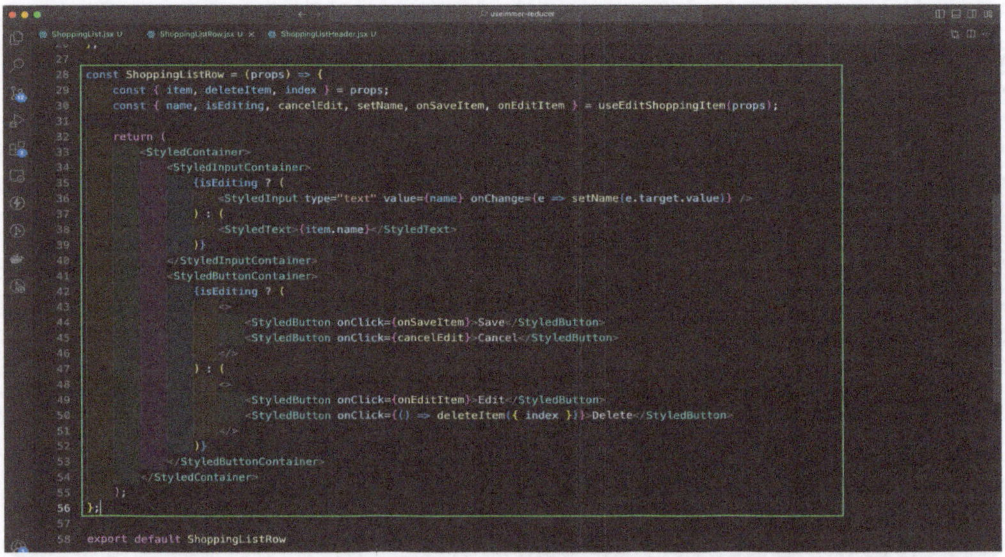

Figure 11.21: *Styled Components for ShoppingListRow.jsx File*

Finally, in the **App.js** file, we will add some styles, and then call the **ShoppingList** component.

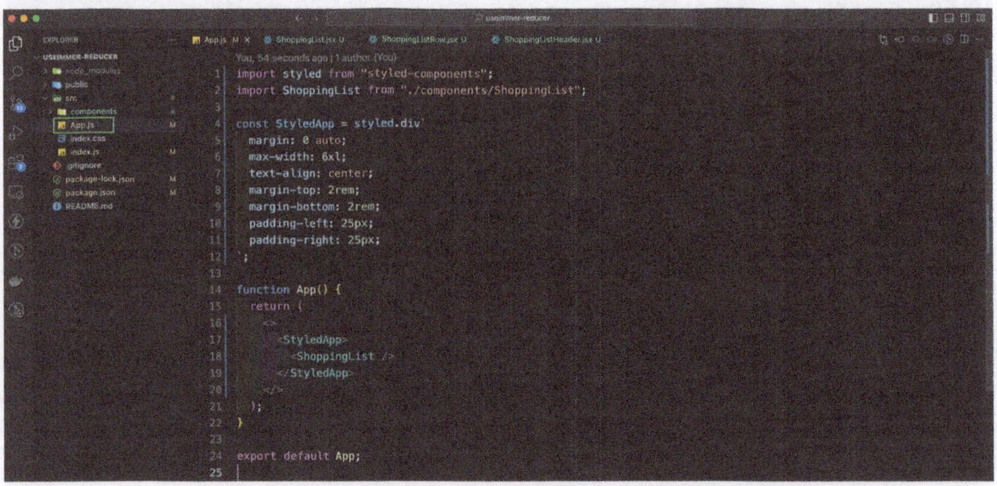

Figure 11.22: *Importing ShoppingList Component in App.js File*

Now, go to http://localhost:3000/, and we will see the initial shopping list with the pre-defined items.

Figure 11.23: *Localhost Showing Shopping List*

Now, all the functionalities such as '**`Add item`**', '**`edit`**', '**`save`**', as well as the item are working fine.

Figure 11.24: *Updating and Adding in the Shopping List*

Our main problem as told earlier, was the complex reducer syntax in the **`ShoppingList.jsx`** file. Here, we are first importing **`useUmmerReducer`**, which we had already installed in the integrated terminal.

After this, instead of the **`useReducer`** hook, we are using the **`useImmerReducer`** hook inside the **`ShoppingList`** function.

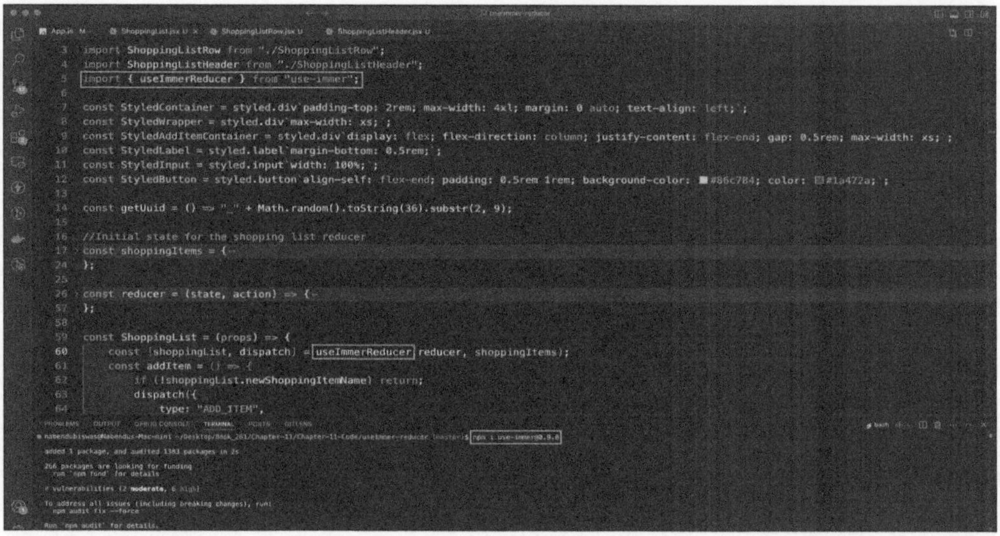

Figure 11.25: *Using useImmerReducer Hook in ShoppingList.jsx File*

Now, in the reducer, we have updated the cases. Here, the main thing is that we can use the push, splice and other array methods. We can also update the object, '**`shoppingItems`**' directly with statements like **`state.newShoppingItemName = action.payload`**.

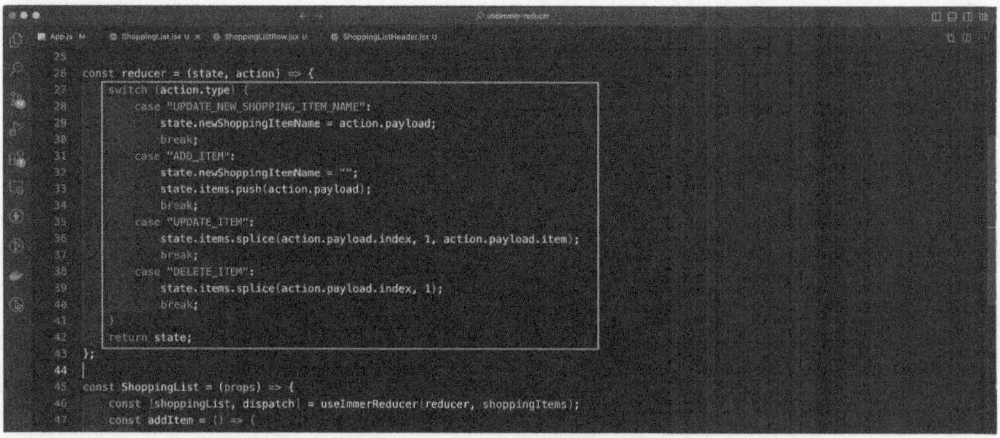

Figure 11.26: *Updated Cases in ShoppingList.jsx File*

Back in http://localhost:3000/, all the functionalities are working as usual.

***Figure 11.27:** Localhost Working as Earlier*

Conclusion

In this chapter, we have learnt to use the use-immer library. This library is used to uncomplicate the code of **`useState`** and **`useReducer`** hook.

Here, we learnt to use the **`useImmer`** hook, instead of **`useState`** hook. After this, we learnt to use the **`useImmerReducer`**, instead of **`useReducer`** hook. However, in both cases, the code was simplified a lot.

In the next chapter, we will learn about **performance optimization** using lazy loading, **`useMemo`**, **`useCallback`**, and other methods.

Points to Remember

- Using **`useImmer`** in place of **`useState`** hook.
- Using **`useImmerReducer`** in place of **`useImmerReducer`** hook.

CHAPTER 12
Performance Optimization

Introduction

In this chapter, we will learn about **Performance Optimization techniques in React**. This includes various techniques such as Code-Splitting, Lazy Loading, **`useCallback`**, **`useMemo`** and many others.

These techniques increase the performance which means that the web-app will be faster. Also, it will take less time to render, and the user experience will be enhanced.

Structure

In this chapter, we are going to discuss the following topics:

- Code-Splitting and Lazy-Loading
- **`useCallback`** and **`useMemo`** hook
- State Collocation and Lifting Components up
- Throttling
- Debouncing

Code-Splitting and Lazy-Loading

One of the best techniques that can be used to improve an application loading performance is code splitting and lazy loading. In the past, it was quite common to create one big bundle file that would contain all the JavaScript codes for an application.

However, the problem is that, when a user visits a website's home page, they would need to download all the codes for the whole website. Even though it is not really necessary on the first visit.

There is a way to avoid this, and **code splitting is a technique** that helps avoid this specific problem. Modern applications often have their code split into multiple chunks. So, if a user visits a home page, they only get the code for that home page.

Then, if they go to another page, like a register page, then the code of the register page would be loaded on demand. Now, we will look at **how to implement code splitting and lazy loading in a React application**. We have created a new react app, and also installed React Router v6 in it. We have also added **`BrowserRouter`** in the **`index.js`** file.

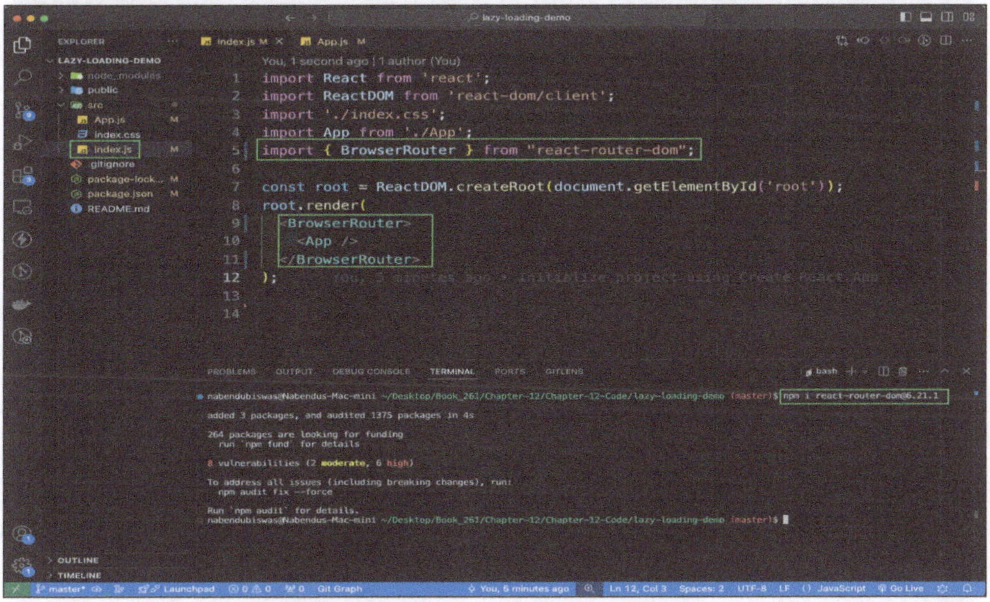

Figure 12.1: *index.js File with React Router*

After this in the **`App.js`** file, we have imported the Link, Route, and Routes from the react router. Also, we have installed and imported the styled components. Next, we have added some styled components, and we have also added an **`AppContainer`** inside the **`App`** function.

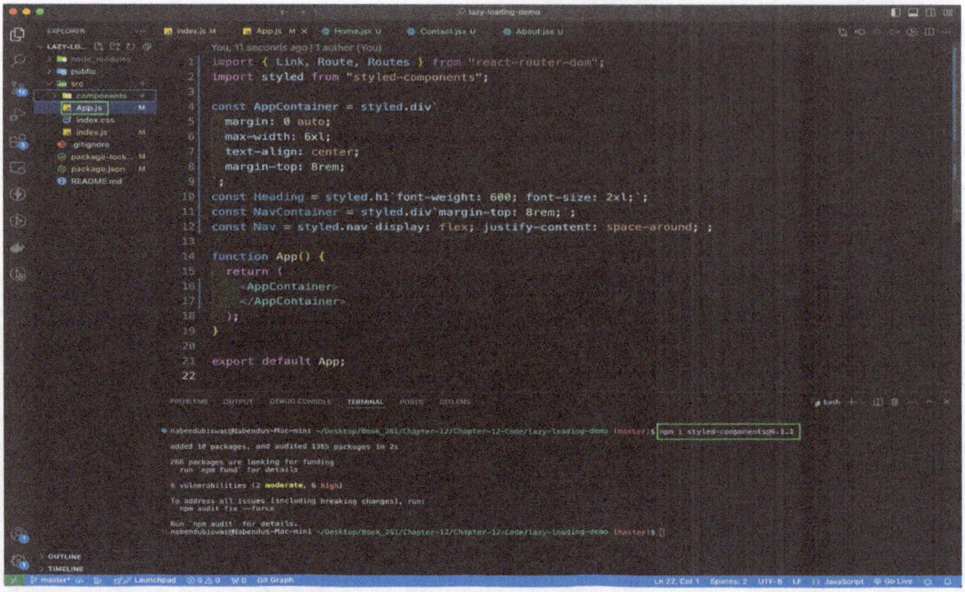

Figure 12.2: *App.js File with Styled Component*

Next, we have updated the **`App.js`** file. Here, we have first imported the Home, **`About`** and **`Contact`** components that we will create soon.

Next, inside the **`AppContainer`**, we have added more styled components created earlier. We have **`Nav`** and **`Routes`** inside it, which takes us to **`Home`**, **`About`** and **`Contact`** components.

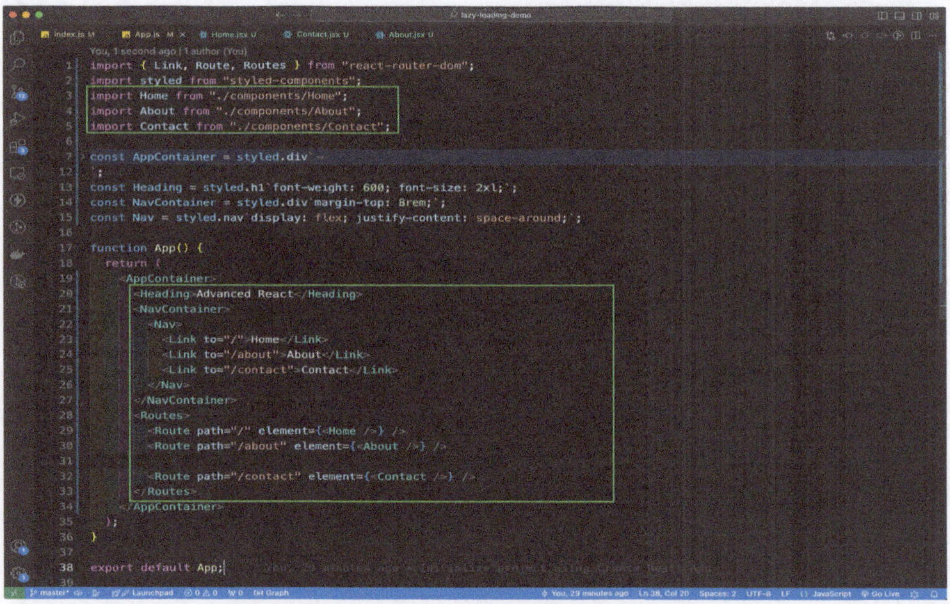

Figure 12.3: *App.js File with Styled Component*

Next, create a **components** folder inside the **src** folder. We have created **About.jsx**, **Contact.jsx**, and **Home.jsx** files inside it. We have a simple component for Home that just shows a div. Similarly, create the **Contact**, and **About** components also.

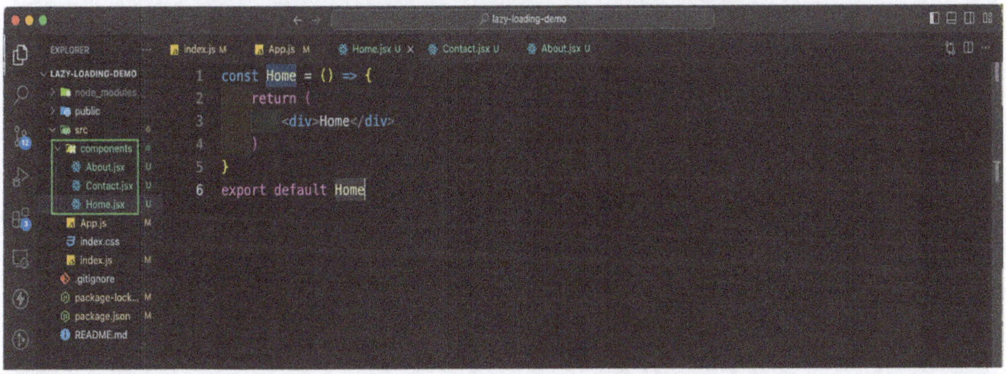

Figure 12.4: *Home.jsx File*

Now, go to http://localhost:3000/, and it will show '**Home**'. Clicking on **Contact**, it will show the '**Contact**'. But the problem is that when we visit the **home** page, then also the **Contact** and **About** will be downloaded.

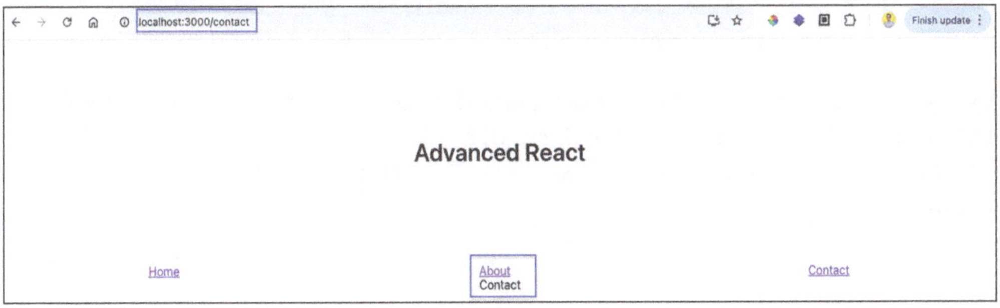

Figure 12.5: *Localhost with Routing*

Now, to fix this issue, we are going to use a function called **lazy**, and also a component that is called the **suspense** component. Back in the **App.js** file, instead of static imports, the routes component will pass a **callback** method to the **lazy** method that returns an import.

We have already imported the **Lazy** and **Suspense** method from the React, earlier. The suspense component is used to provide a loading indicator, until a component is up and ready. In our case, we will wrap all the routes with our suspense because we do not want to show anything, until we have that component loaded.

In Suspense, we have fallback props which show an **h3** of loading.

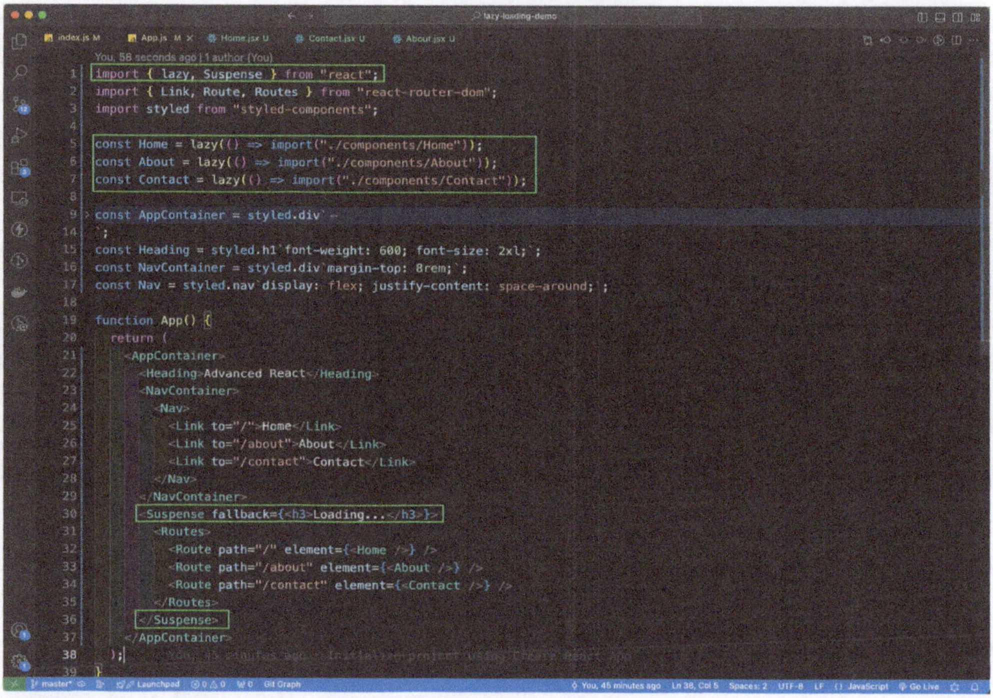

Figure 12.6: *Lazy Loading with Suspense in App.js*

Next, you go to http://localhost:3000/, and the **`home`** will be loaded. You will also see a **`Loading`** text for a millisecond. Similarly, in the **`goto`** http://localhost:3000/contact, you will see a **`Loading`** text. It will also show the **`About`**. This indicates that the **`Lazy Loading`** is working properly.

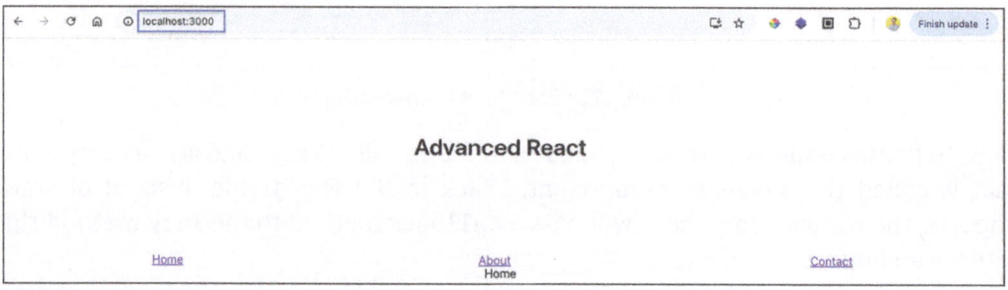

Figure 12.7: *Lazy Loading Working in Localhost*

`useCallback` and `useMemo` Hooks

Next, we will understand different performance improvement techniques which include **`useCallback`** and **`useMemo`** hooks. For this, we have created a new project, and installed styled-components in it.

Figure 12.8: *index.js and Styled Components Added*

Now, in the **`App.js`** file, we will render an **`Ingredients`** component.

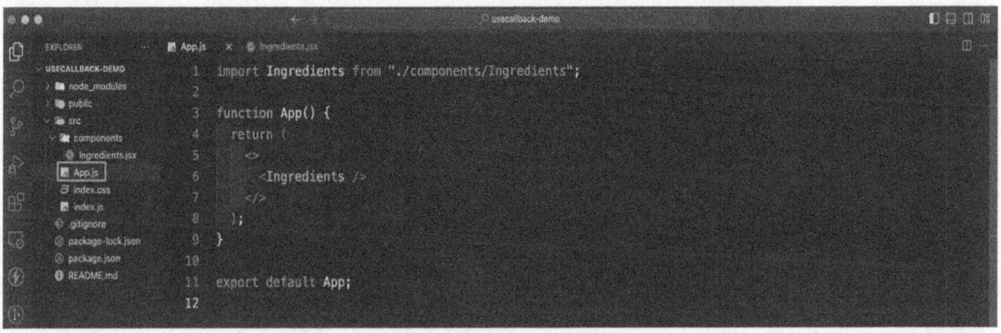

Figure 12.9: *App.js Calling Ingredients Component*

Now, create a **`components`** folder inside the **`src`** folder. Inside it, create an **`Ingredients.jsx`** file where we have imported **`useState`**, **`nanoid`**, and **`styled`** components. After that, we have written some styles through the styled components.

We have an **`initialIngredients`** array that contains an array of objects containing three ingredients. After this, inside the **`Ingredients`** function, we have the state of the ingredients We also have an **`addIngredient`** function, which adds the new ingredient to the existing ingredients array.

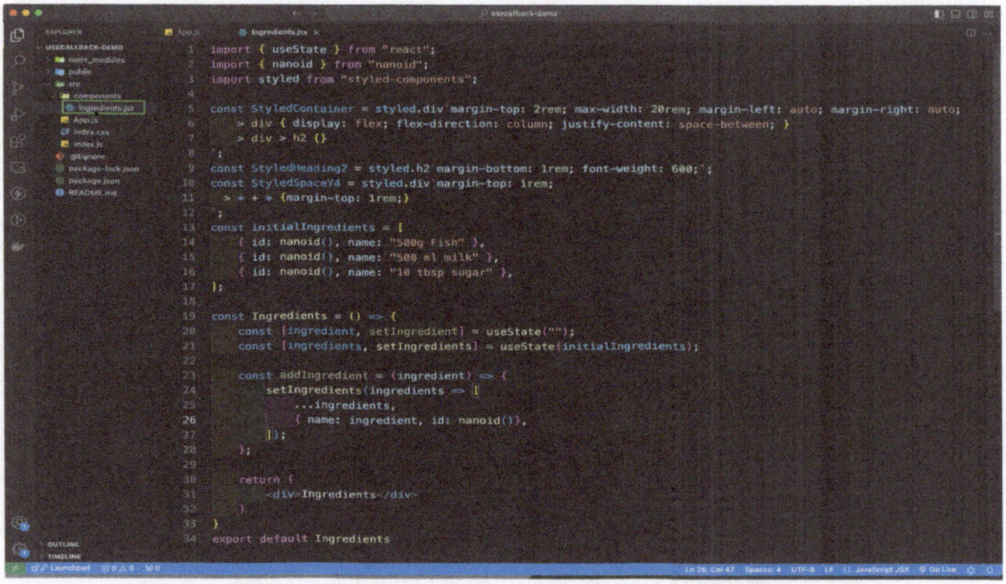

Figure 12.10: *Ingredients.jsx File with the Usage of Styled Components*

Back inside the **`Ingredients`** function, we have added a console log at the start. Next, we have added the **`deleteIngredient`** which changes the ingredients array by filtering the passed id.

Next, we have a **`HeaderText`** function that console logs and returns an header text. Inside the **`return`** statement, we are calling three components of **`IngredientsInfo`**, **`IngredientsList`** and **`AddIngredient`**.

Figure 12.11: *Ingredients.jsx File with the Usage of Styled Components*

Now, we will create the file, **`IngredientsInfo.jsx`** inside the **`components`** folder. It is a simple component showing just styled icons. But note the console log here.

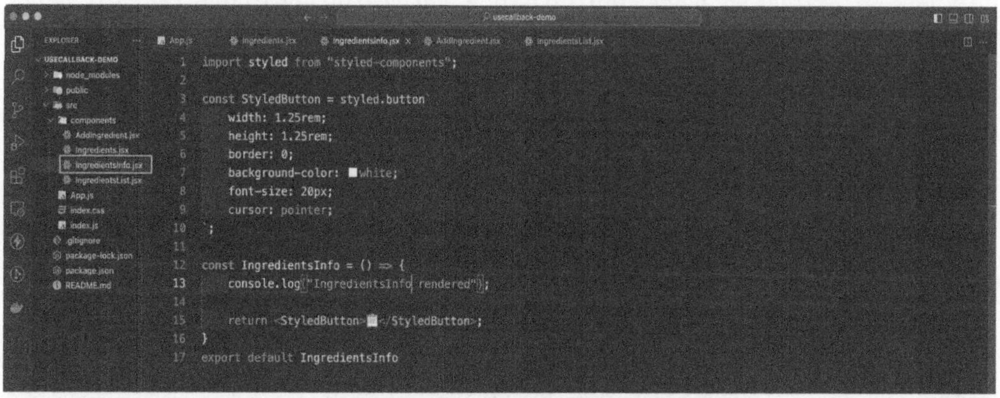

Figure 12.12: *IngredientsInfo.jsx File*

Next, we will create the file, **`IngredientsList.jsx`** inside the **`components`** folder. Here, we have some styled components, first. After this, inside the **`IngredientsList`** function, we have a console log first. Then, we get the **ingredients** and **`deleteIngredient`** from the props.

Inside the **`return`** statement, we are looping through the ingredients array, and showing the ingredient name. We are also showing an X, clicking on which will pass the id to the **`callback`** function **`deleteIngredient`**.

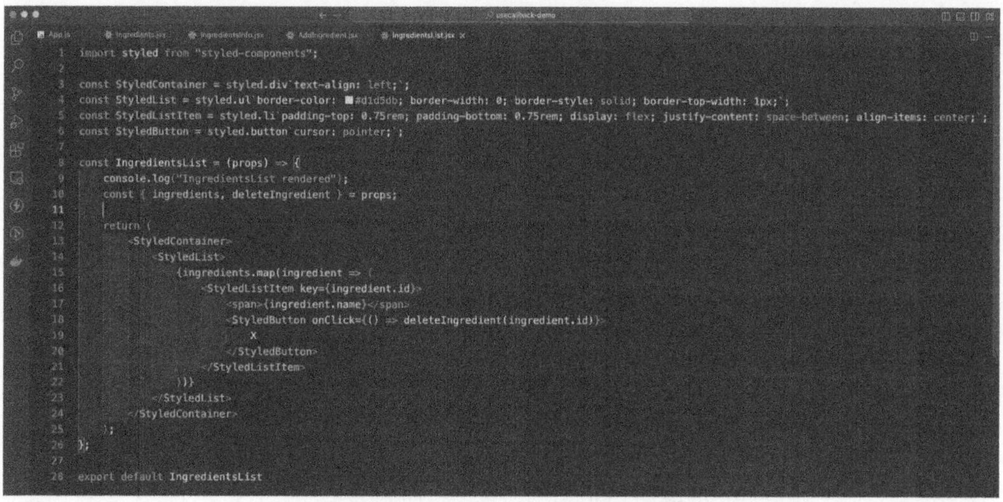

Figure 12.13: *IngredientsList.jsx File*

Next, inside the **`components`** folder, create an **`AddIngredient.jsx`** file. Here, after importing the styled components, we have written some styles through it. After this, inside the **`AddIngredient`** function, we have a console log.

Next, we are restructuring **addIngredient**, **ingredient**, and **setIngredient** from props. Inside the **return**, we have a form where we have an input to take the ingredient. After this, we have a button which will call the **addIngredient** to call back the function.

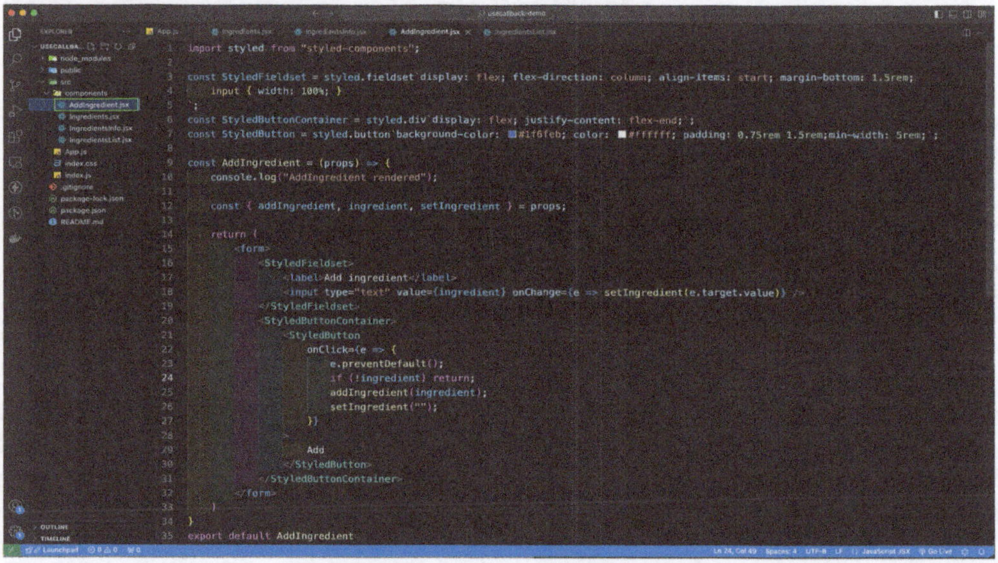

Figure 12.14: *AddIngredient.jsx File*

Now, go to http://localhost:3000/, and open the console. Here, we will see all of the console logs from all the components.

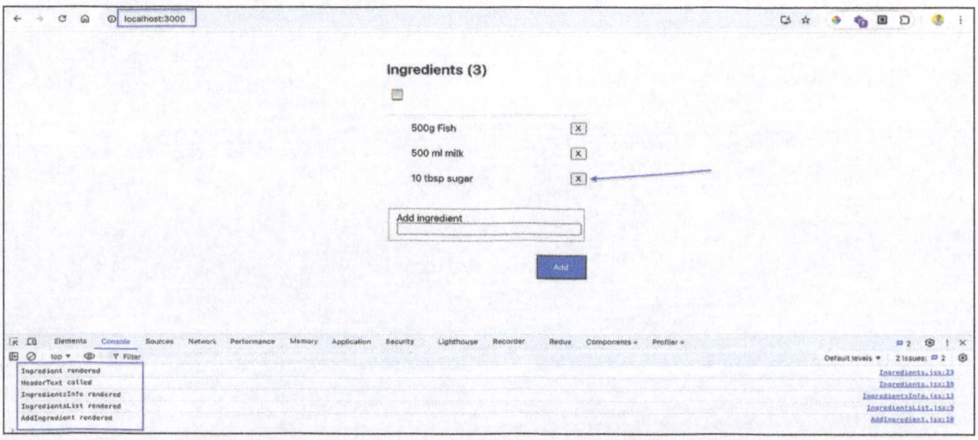

Figure 12.15: *Localhost Rendering All the Components*

Now, we have removed an item, and it is also showing all of the console logs.

Figure 12.16: *Remove Items Rendering All Components*

Next, we have written "**`10 kg Potatoes`**" in the input box. And it rendered all the components that many times.

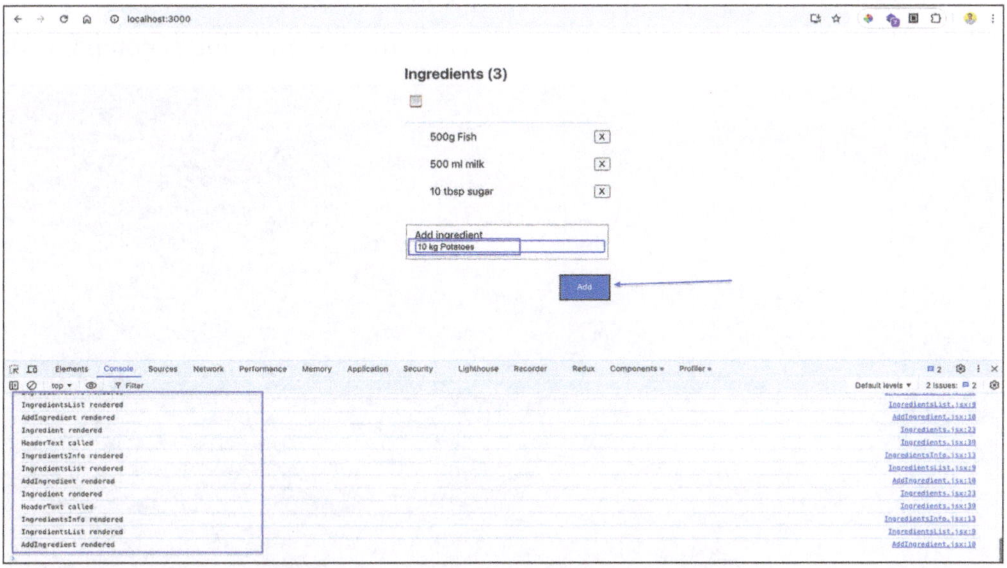

Figure 12.17: *Writing Rendering All Components*

Even clicking on the **`Add`** button is rendering all of the components that is shown in the console log. We have the issues of all components being rendered with each operation, and this is a huge performance issue.

Figure 12.18: *Adding Rendering All Components*

We will solve these issues in this section, and the next section. First, we will solve the **`IngredientsList`** rendering issue. So, in the **`IngredientsList.jsx`** file, we will import a memo from the react, and then wrap it in the export.

The use of **`memo`** function is a popular react way to stop re-rendering of components.

Figure 12.19: *Adding Memo in IngredientsList*

Going back to http://localhost:3000/, we have again written text "**10**" in the input field. However, still the console log of "**IngredientList rendered**" was called two times.

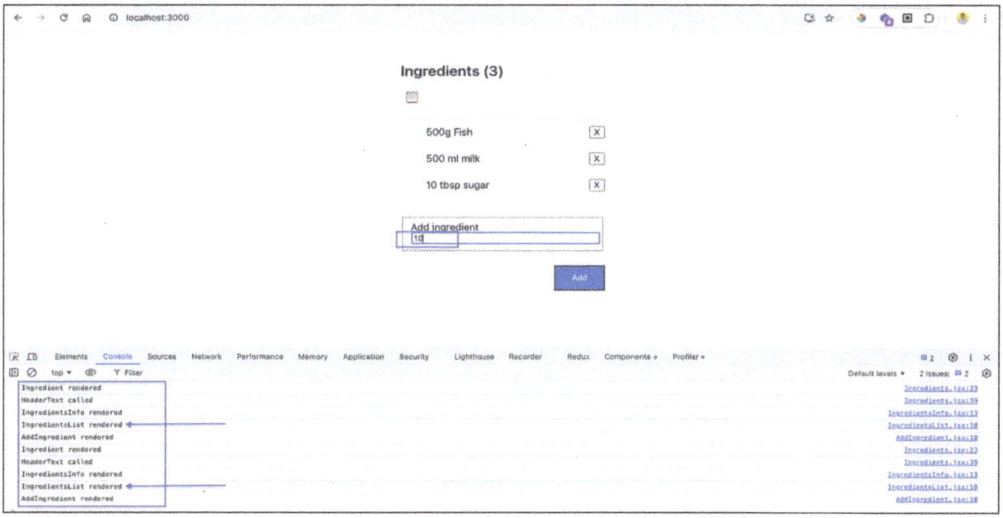

***Figure 12.20:** Localhost Still Rendering IngredientsList*

But why did not this work? We have **two props of ingredients** and **`deleteIngredient`** in the **`IngredientsList.jsx`** file. This **`deleteIngredient`** function is recreated every time the **`Ingredients`** component is re-rendered.

The memo actually performs a shallow props comparison. So, the **`deleteIngredient`** function as a prop in the previous props is different than the one in new props. To fix this issue, we have to change the export of **`IngredientsList`**. In the memo, beside passing the **`IngredientsList`**, we are going to receive a function.

This function will take the **`prevProps`** and **`nextProps`**, and then it is going to compare the **`prevProps.ingredients`** with **`nextProps.ingredients`**.

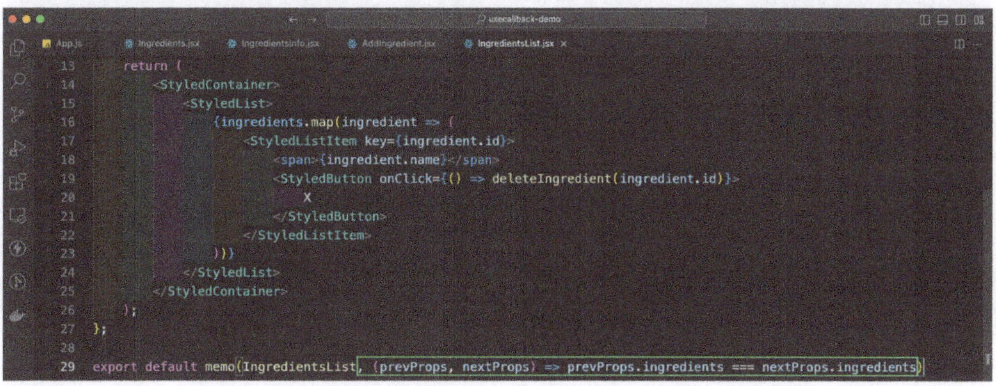

***Figure 12.21:** Adding prevProps in IngredientsList.jsx File*

Now in http://localhost:3000/, we have again written the text "**`10`**" in the input field. But this time, we did not get the console log of "**`IngredientList`** rendered".

Figure 12.22: *IngredientsList Not Rendered*

Next, instead of comparing **`prevProps`** and **`nextProps`** in memo, we have a better option to use the **`useCallback`** in the parent component. Hence, in the **`Ingredients.jsx`** file, the **`deleteIngredient`** function will be through the **`useCallback`** hook.

It also does the deep comparison as done with the **`prevProps`** and the **`nextProps`**.

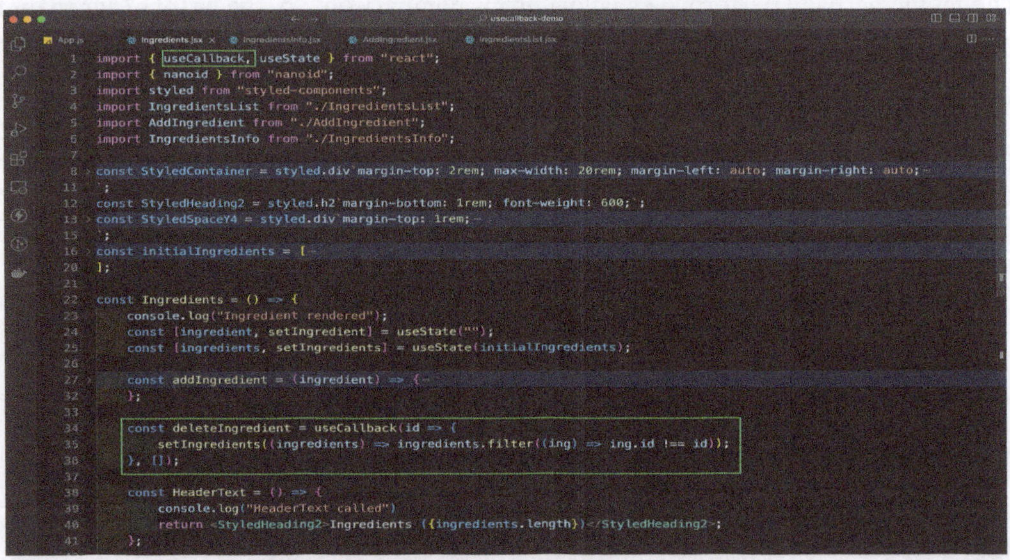

Figure 12.23: *useCallback in Ingredients.jsx File*

Again in http://localhost:3000/, we have written the text "**`10`**" in the input field. But this time, we did not get the console log of "**`IngredientList rendered`**".

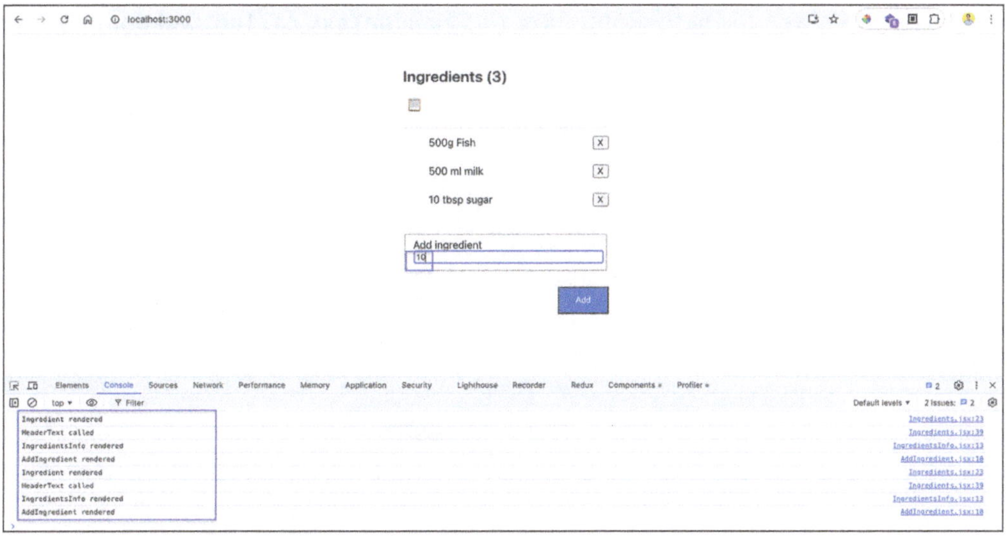

Figure 12.24: *IngredientsList Not Rendered*

The **useMemo** hook can be used to memorize state values. However, it can be used for more than just preserving or memorizing values. We can use it to memorize react elements as well.

Every time we used to type in the input box, the "**HeaderText called**" was called, but we do not want it. So, we will use the **useMemo** hook in the **HeaderText** function, and give the dependency on the change of ingredients' array length.

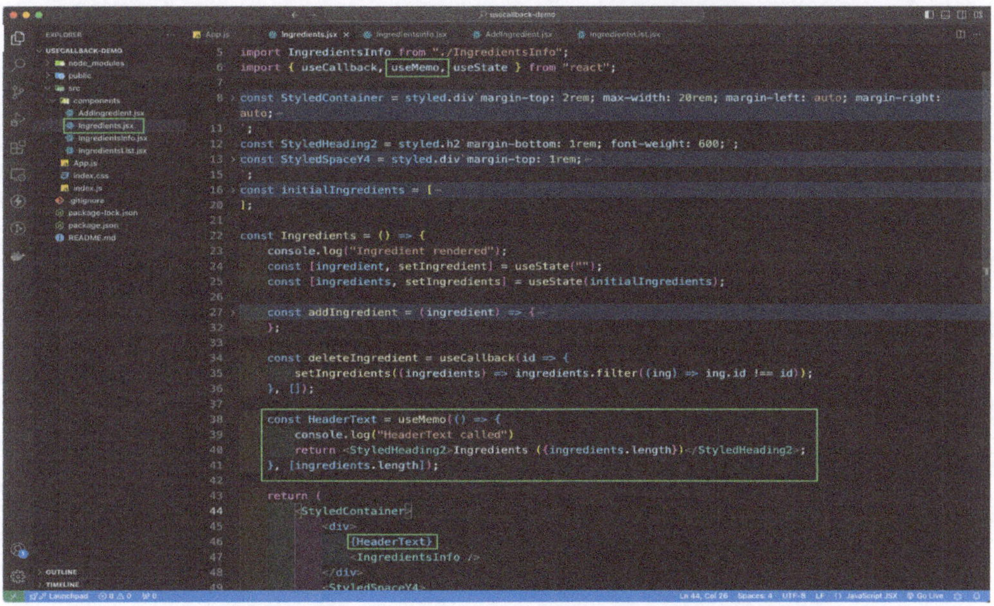

Figure 12.25: *Adding useMemo in Ingredients.jsx File*

Now, even when we type in the input box, the "**HeaderText called**" will not be shown in the console.

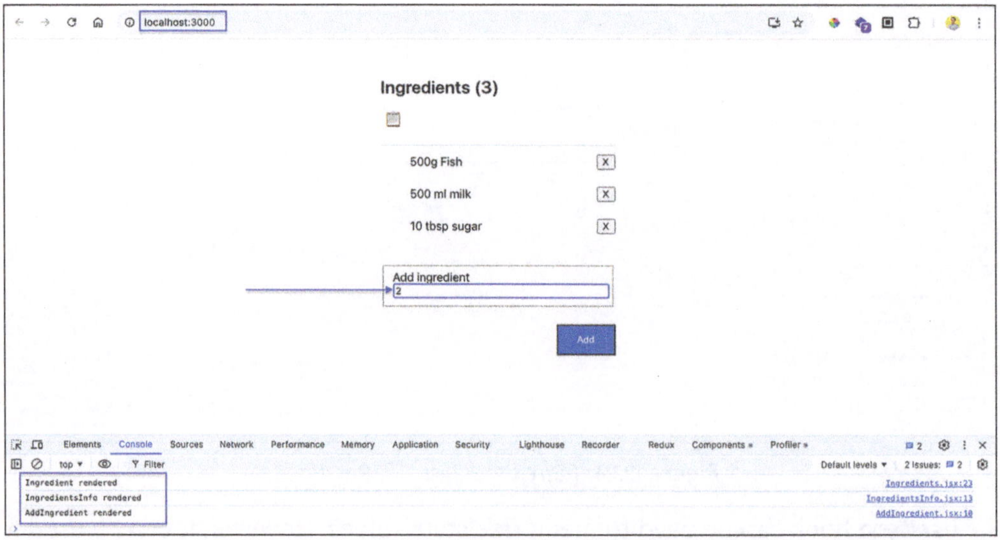

Figure 12.26: *HeaderText Not Called While Writing*

We have removed one ingredient, and the function **HeaderText** will be called, because the length of the ingredients is changed. Similarly, if we add an ingredient, it will also be shown.

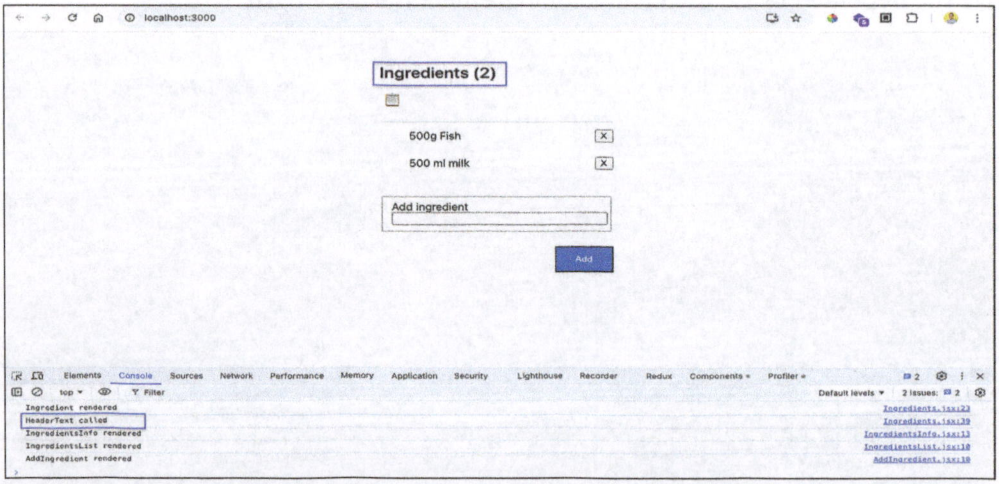

Figure 12.27: *HeaderText Called While Removing*

State Collocation and Lifting up Components

We are still with the ingredients application optimization. When we type something in the input box, we have three components re-rendered. Out of this, only the **`AddIngredient`** should be re-rendered, and the rest two should not be re-rendered.

***Figure 12.28:** Three Components on Typing*

This is happening because we are receiving an **`ingredient`** as a prop in the **`AddIngredient.jsx`** file. To fix it, we will use a technique called **State Collocation**. It, basically means moving the state down.

We will do this by first going to the **`Ingredients.jsx`** file. Here, we have removed the **`ingredient`** state, and also removed the props being passed to the **`AddIngredient`** component.

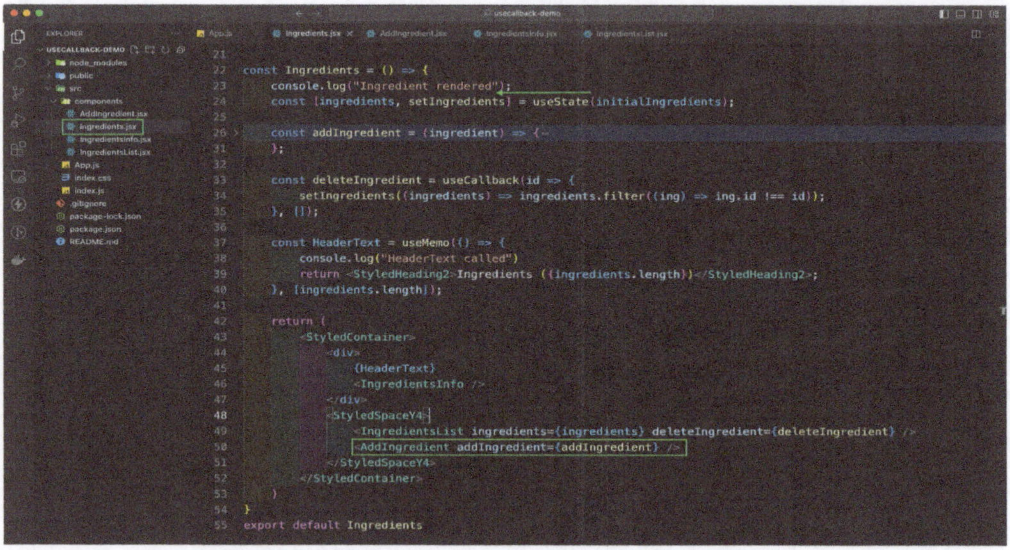

Figure 12.29: *Ingredient State Removed in Ingredients.jsx*

Now, in the **`AddIngredient.jsx`** file, we have added the state of the ingredient, and also removed it from the props.

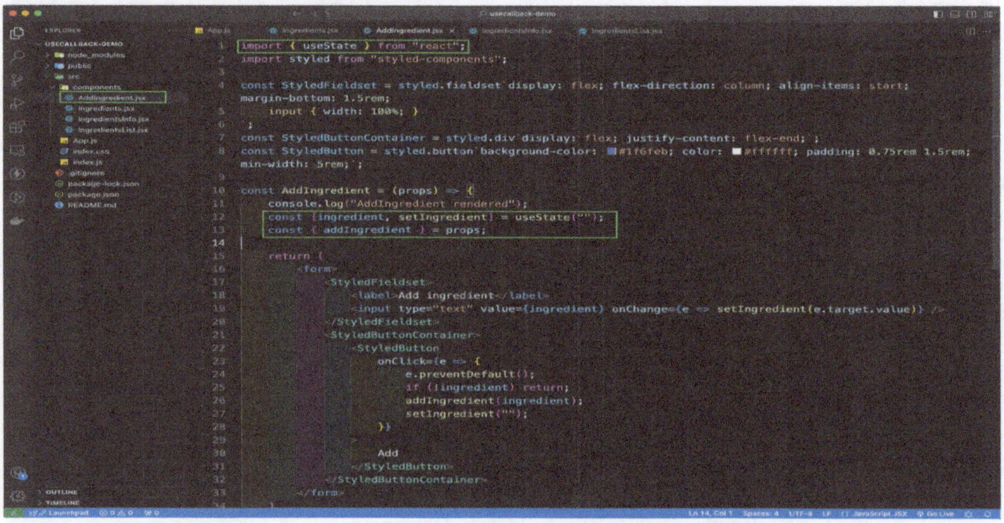

Figure 12.30: *Ingredient State Added in AddIngredient.jsx*

Back in http://localhost:3000/, we have typed in the **`Add Ingredient`** input box, and only the **`AddIngredient`** component has been rendered.

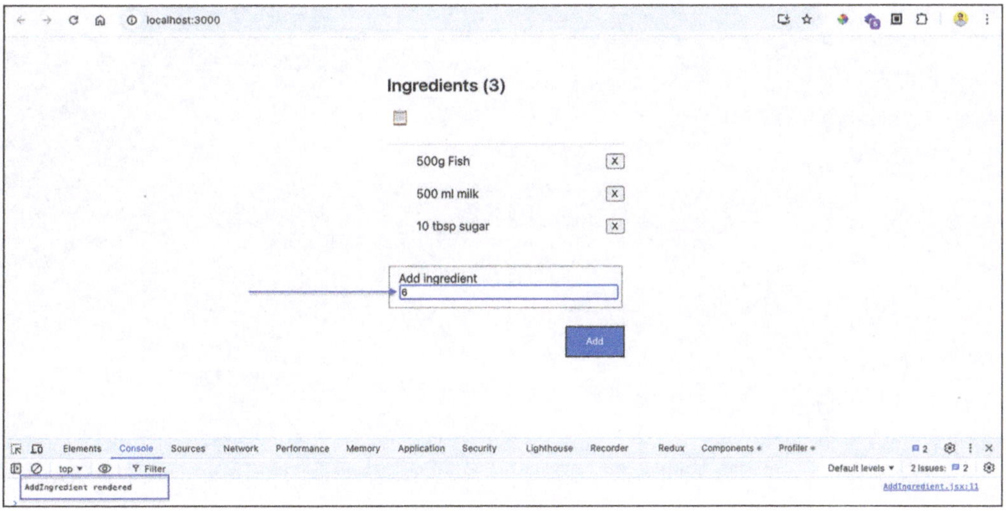

***Figure 12.31:** Only AddIngredient Rendered in Localhost*

Now, we will prevent components from unnecessarily re-rendering by lifting it up. Thus, we have removed an ingredient in http://localhost:3000/, and it rendered all components, because the ingredients state was changed.

***Figure 12.32:** Removing Ingredients, and Rendered All Components in Localhost*

Hence, to use the technique of lifting components up, we will first add a props of **`ingredientsInfo`** in the **`Ingredients.jsx`** file. Next, we will show it, instead of the **`IngredientsInfo`** component.

Figure 12.33: *ingredientsInfo Props in Ingredients.jsx*

Now, in the **`App.js`** file, we will pass the props of **`ingredientsInfo`**, which will be the **`IngredientsInfo`** component.

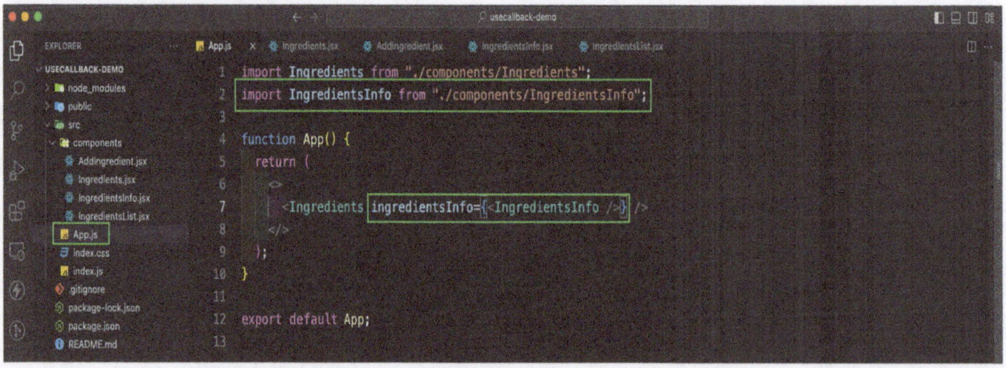

Figure 12.34: *ingredientsInfo props in App.js*

Next, in http://localhost:3000/, we have removed an item, and the **`IngredientsInfo`** component was not re-rendered.

Figure 12.35: *Removing Item, but not Rendering IngredientsInfo*

Similarly, in http://localhost:3000/, we have added an item, and the **`IngredientsInfo`** component was not re-rendered.

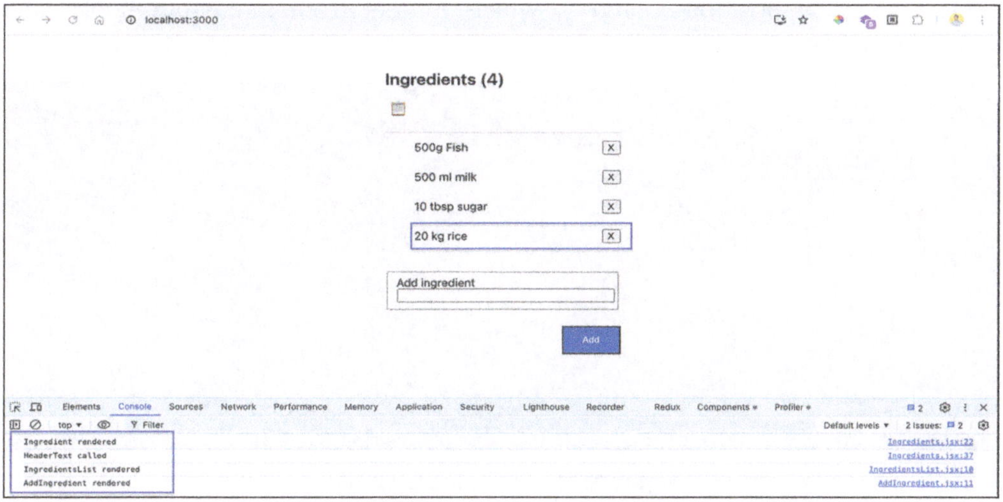

Figure 12.36: *Adding Item, but not Rendering IngredientsInfo*

Throttling

There might be situations where it might be a good idea to limit how many times a callback function is initialized. Most of the time, there are two types of techniques which can be applied - **throttling and debouncing.**

We will look into throttling in this section, and debouncing in the next section. '**Throttle**' means how often a function is executed. To check this, we have created a new react project.

Here, in the **App.js,** we are calling a component, **TrackMouse**.

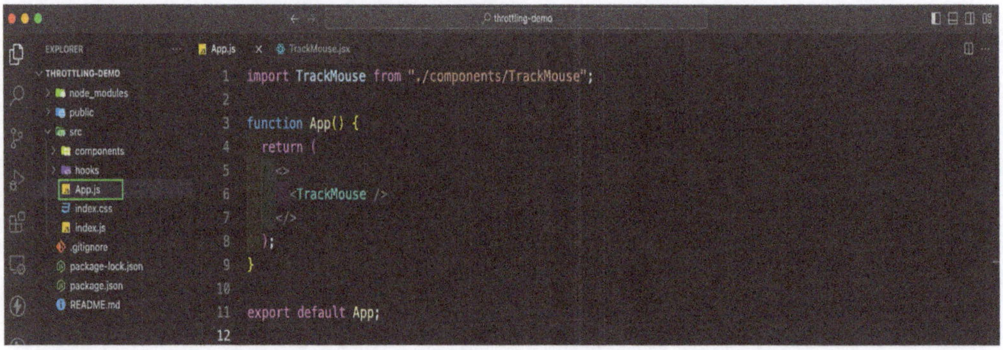

Figure 12.37: *App.js Rendering TrackMouse Component*

Now, create a **components** folder, and inside it a **TrackMouse.jsx** file. This component simply displays a position x and y, which it gets from a custom hook called **useMousePosition**.

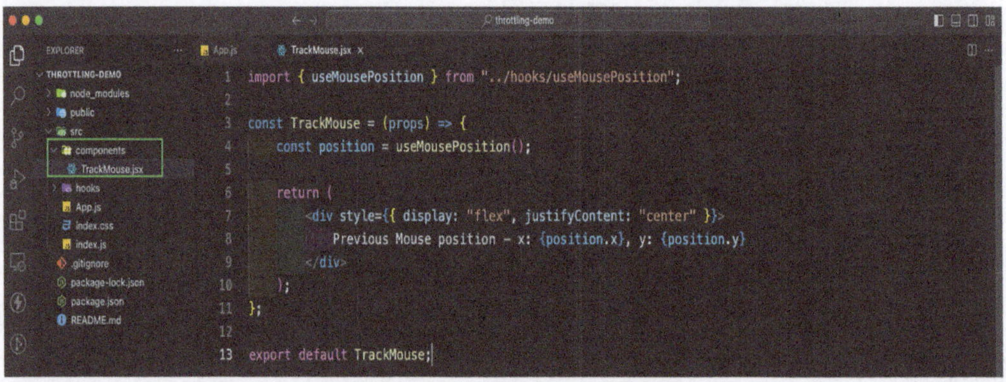

Figure 12.38: *TrackMouse.jsx File*

Next, create a **hooks** folder, and inside it **useMousePosition.js** file. This has a state of position that is initially an object with x and y as 0. Inside the **useEffect**, which will run once, we have an **eventlistener**, which tracks the **mousemove**.

The **eventlistener** calls a function **onMouseMove**, which using **clientX** and **clientY** gets the mouse position. It then updates the position to the latest x and y. We also have a **return** statement inside **useEffect** that removes the **eventlistener**.

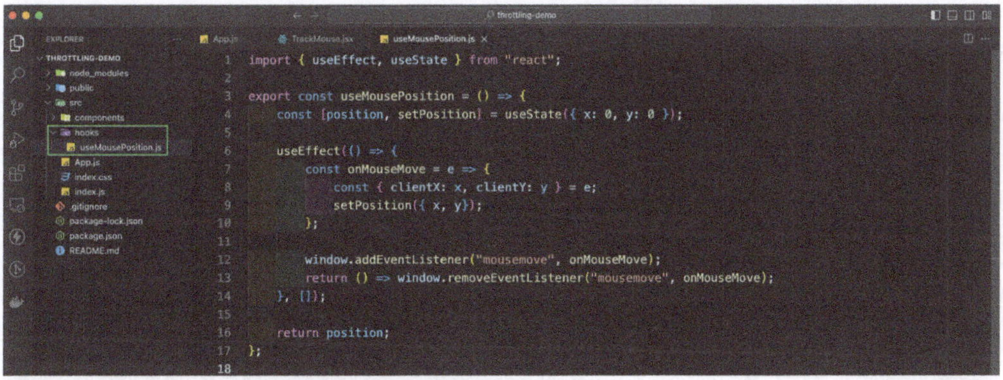

Figure 12.39: *useMousePosition.js File*

Now, go to http://localhost:3000/, and move your mouse. It will update the position for even a pixel value change. It means that the **`setPosition`** is called at a very fast pace in the **`useMousePosition.js`** file, and we will have a lot of renders.

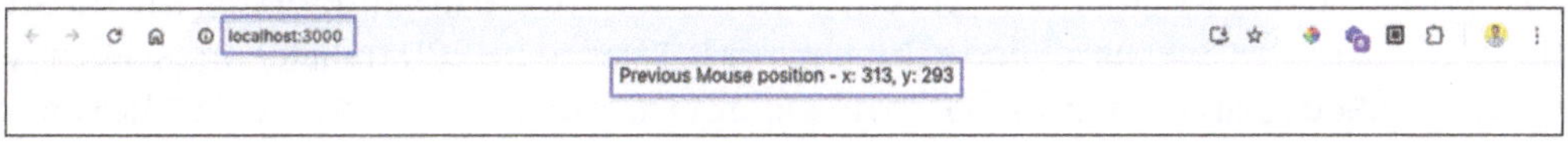

Figure 12.40: *Localhost Showing Mouse Movements*

We will limit through throttling, how long before it displays the next position of the mouse. For this, we will create a **`helpers`** folder, and inside it a **`throttle.js`** file. The throttle is a Higher Order Function that accepts a function and waits arguments, and then returns another function.

So, our throttle code receives a function and waits for arguments. Inside it, we will have three variables. First is **`timerId`**, which is for holding the **`setTimeout`** reference. Second is **`inThrottle`**, which is just a boolean value. It indicates if we are throttling or not.

The third variable is **`lastTime`**, which shows the last time of throttle that happened. After that, we are going to return another function, and it will have all the arguments it received.

Inside the **`return`**, we have an **`if`** statement to check if we are not throttling. Then, we will make the **`lastTime`** to be the current time. After that, we are making the **`inThrottle`** to be true.

In the else part, we are first clearing the **`timerId`** with **`clearTimeout ()`**. The **`timerId`** here is the reference of the last **`setTimeout`**. Then, the new **`timerId`** will be **`setTimeout`** which will run after "**`wait - (Date.now() - lastTime`**" or 0.

Now, inside the **`setTImeout`**, we have another if statement which will check if enough time has passed since the last throttle. It will run when the "**`Date.now () - lastTime`**" will be greater than or equal to the wait.

Inside the if, we will run the passed **function(fn)** with all the arguments that we have. After that, the **lastTime** will be **Date.now ()**.

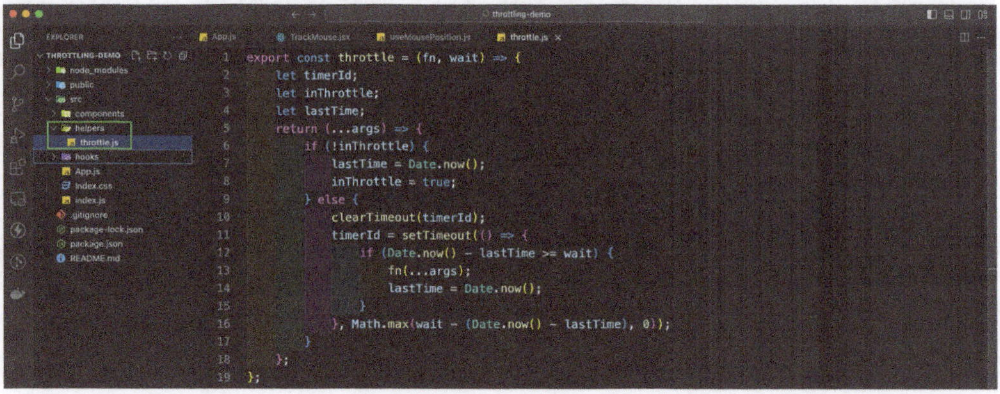

Figure 12.41: *throttle.js File*

Next, go back to the **useMousePosition.js** file. Here, we are first importing the throttle function. After this, we hard-code the **throttleTime** to be 200 milliseconds. Next, we wrap the **onMouseMove** function with the **throttle**, and pass the **throttleTime** as the second argument.

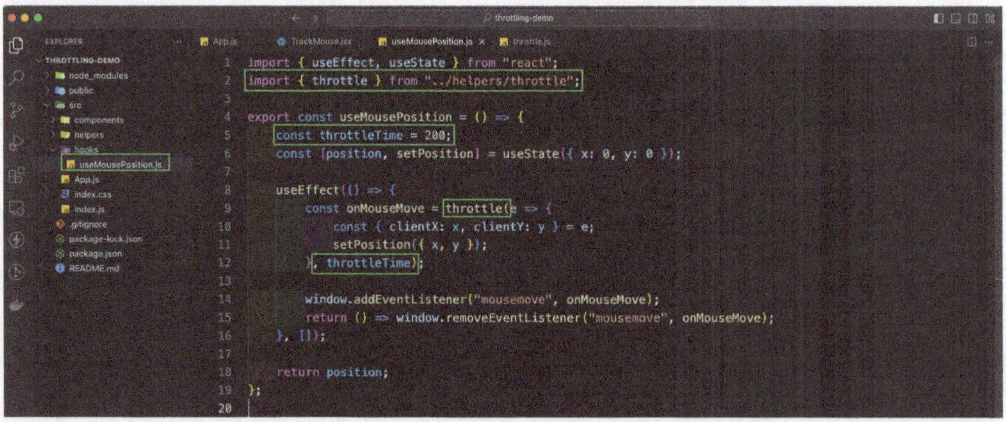

Figure 12.42: *Using Throttle in useMousePosition.js File*

Now, go to http://localhost:3000/, and move the mouse. Here, we will see the position being updated a bit slower than the earlier time. Actually, it updates after every 200 milliseconds, and with this the rendering happens less, and performance optimization has been done.

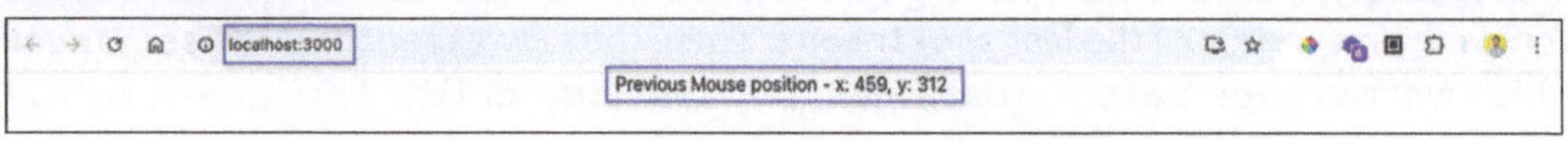

Figure 12.43: *Mouse Position after Delay in Localhost*

Debouncing

One of the great examples for debouncing is a search field that provides autocomplete results. Let us have a website that offers search meals functionality. For instance, if a user types fish, it will result in four (4) API requests.

But we should not do the API request on every keystroke. Instead, we can let the user type, and then fetch new results, only when a specific amount of time has passed, since the last keystroke.

We have created a new project, and updated the **`App.js`** to display a component called **`Search`**.

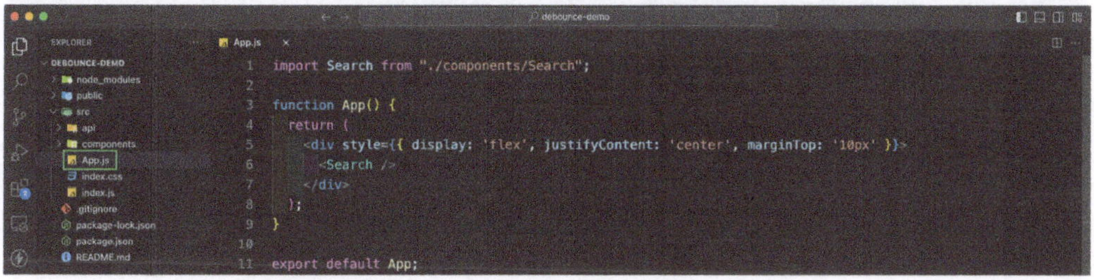

Figure 12.44: *App.js Rendering Search Component*

Now, create a **`components`** folder inside the **`src`** folder. Within it, we have created a **`Search.jsx`** file. Here, we are importing **`searchMeals`** from an **`api`** file. Inside the **`search`** function, we have a query and meals state. After this, we have an **`initSearchApiRequest`** function that uses the **`useMemo`** hook to call the **`searchMeals`**.

Next, we have an **`onChangeQuery`** which takes the value, and calls the **`initSearchApiRequest`** with this value.

Inside the **`return`** statement, we have the input to enter the text. Every time the meals array is updated, we loop through it, and show each item.

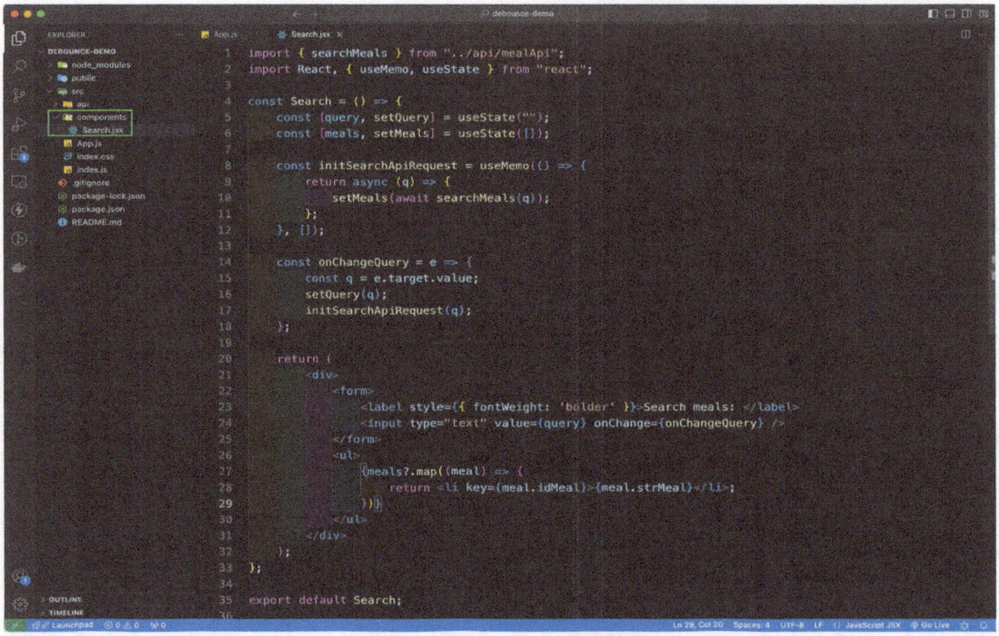

Figure 12.45: *Search.jsx File*

Next, create an **`api`** folder inside the **`src`** folder. Inside it, we have created a **`mealApi.js`** file. Here, we are first importing **`api`** that we will create next. Within the **`searchMeals`** function, we get the query.

After this, we use **`api.get()`** to call **`search.php`** with the passed params. We are basically returning back the meals array. Also, we do have an error handling feature to do a console log, and return an empty array.

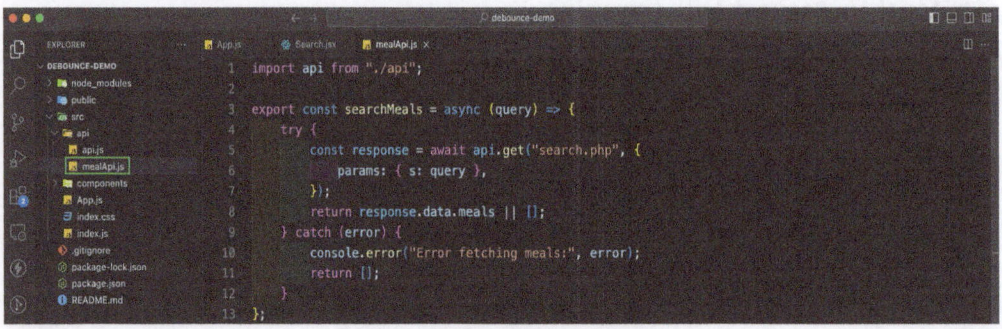

Figure 12.46: *mealApi.js File*

Now, create an **`api.js`** file inside the **`api`** folder. Inside it, we are importing **`axios`** which we need to install by npm. Next, using the **`axios.create()`**, we are calling the api of themealdb.com.

After this, we have a variable **api** that has an object which has a '**get**' function. It uses **axiosInstance.get()** with the passed **url** and **config**.

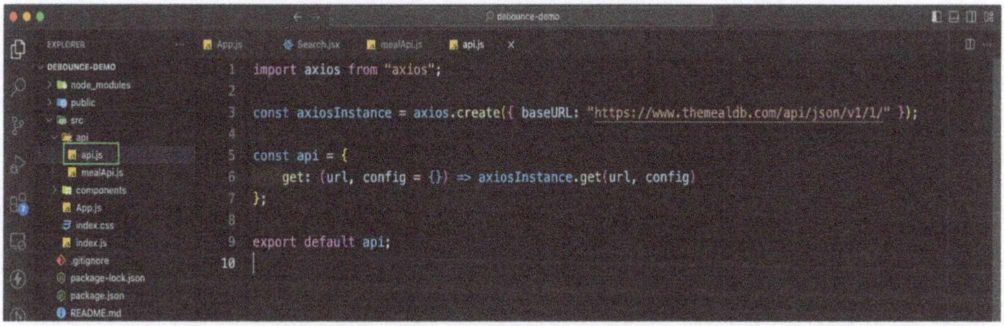

***Figure 12.47:** An api.js File*

Now, in http://localhost:3000/, in the input field, write eggs. In the **Network** tab, we can see that four (4) API requests have been made.

Once with **e**, then with **eg**, then with **egg**, and lastly with **eggs**. This is not completely right, and we will fix the same with debounce.

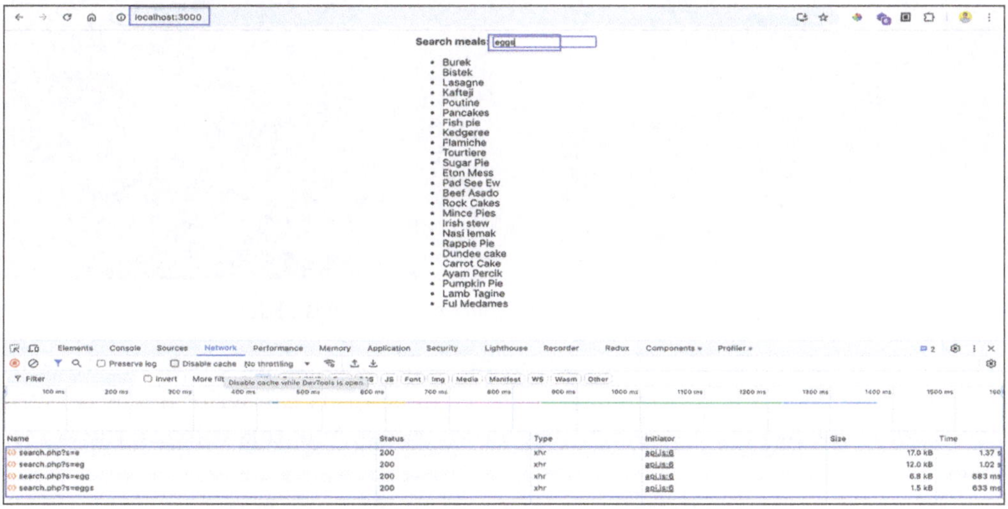

***Figure 12.48:** Localhost Doing Multiple API Requests*

Next, create a **helpers** folder inside the **src** folder. Inside it, we have created a **debouncs.js** file. The debounce is also a Higher Order Function like throttling. It takes a function, and delays as arguments.

Inside the function, it has a variable **timerId**. Then it returns all the arguments which it receives. Now, inside the return, we first check if we have a **timerId**. Then by clearing it with **clearTimeout()**, we proceed further.

After this, the **timerId** is initialized with **setTimeout**. Inside this **setTimeout**, we call the **fn** with the **argos**, after the delay.

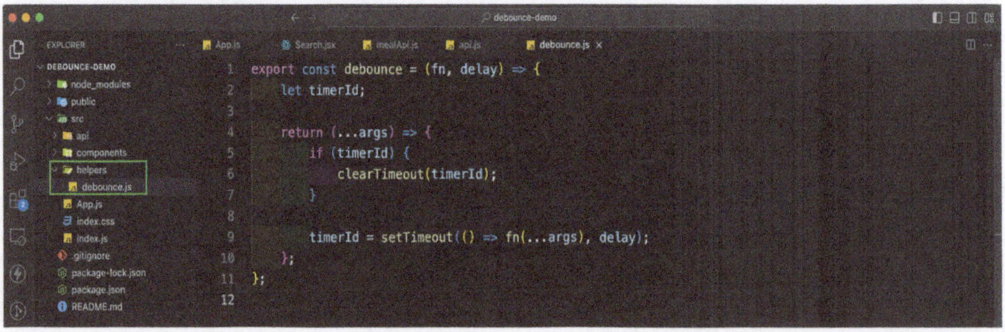

Figure 12.49: *debounce.js File*

Now, back in the **Search.jsx** file, we first import the debounce. After that, we wrap the debounce in the return function, and add a second argument for delay. It is 500 milliseconds in our case.

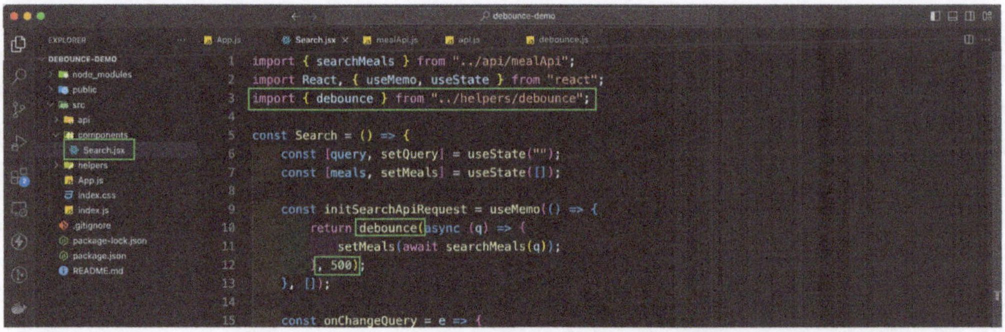

Figure 12.50: *Adding Debounce in Search.jsx File*

Next, back in http://localhost:3000/ in the input field, write **eggs**. This time the api call will be done after 500 milliseconds. As most of us can write this within that time, so only one API request will be made with "**eggs**". And this will give the correct result.

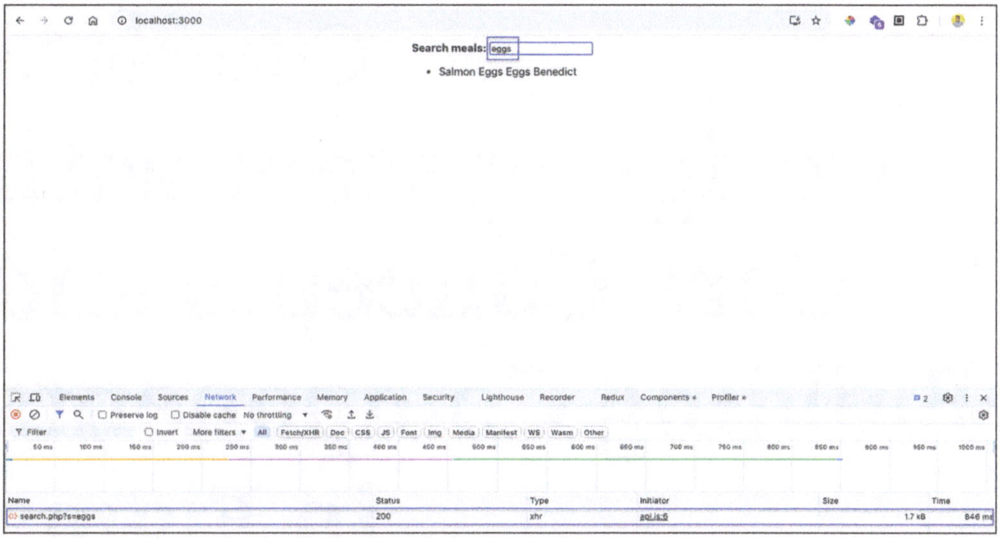

Figure 12.51: *Localhost Doing One API Request*

Conclusion

In this chapter, we have learnt to use various performance optimization techniques. First, we have learnt to load only the component visited by the user by using Lazy Loading.

Next, we have optimized a project using **`useCallback`**, **`useMemo`**, state collocation, and lifting components up. After all these, we learnt to delay function and api calls, using throttling and debouncing.

In the next chapter, we will start a new section of the design system. Here, we will learn the **core concepts and building components with Figma**.

Points to Remember

- Using lazy-loading with suspense.
- Using **`useCallback`** and **`useImmerMemo`** hook.
- Using state collocation and lifting components up.
- Throttling and Debouncing.

CHAPTER 13
Design System with Core Concepts and Building Components in Figma

Introduction

In this chapter, we will learn about Design systems. We will first understand what a Design system is. After this, we will learn about the downside of design systems and then about the audience of design systems.

We will learn about the key concepts and mistakes to avoid. Finally, we will get hands-on on Color Palette in Figma, and also design a Modal.

Structure

In this chapter, we are going to discuss the following topics:

- Understanding Design System
- Down Sides of Design Systems and Team Structure
- Audience of Design Systems and Example
- Key Concepts and Practical Checklist
- Mistakes to Avoid
- Hands-on on Color Palette in Figma
- Hands-on Designing a Modal

Understanding Design System

There is no exact definition of a Design System. If it is a UI/UX design system, they most probably refer to design language such as color palettes, topography, UI kits and tools like Figma.

But if a developer talks about a design system, they usually mean a component library in React or Angular, or a style guide via tools such as GatsbyJS and Storybook. In fact, design systems include all of these pillars together - Design language, UI Kit, component library, and style guide.

Design systems help companies to define their own brand identity, and turn them into accessible, consistent and reusable components. And this comes with a bunch of benefits, like everyone should be able to use your product the same as others.

Design systems make sure that your app has enough colors with proper contrast ratios, and type scales with large sizes so that the contents of your application is easy to explore. It also ensures that different parts of your application can be accessed with keyboards, and the important alerts are detected by screen readers for users who need that.

When you work for an enterprise company, it is quite possible that they have a suite of products. A very good example of this is Google. They have a suite of products that look and feel like they have come from the same family. When you use Gmail, Google Drive, you see the same web-components each time.

This is what we mean by consistency here. All the products should showcase the brand of the company. Consistency is a primary focus of design systems. One of the other benefits of the design system is cascading updates.

You can change the style as simple as doing a single click, and the whole design system will be alerted. And when it comes to onboarding new members into the team, design systems provide a central style guide. It can help the UI developers in your team find the information, they need to start.

This is also a benefit for cross-team collaboration, because all teams use the same system. Like a developer from Team A can help fix a bug in Team B as the design system is the same.

Now, once your design system is in place, and it is stable, designers can use the UI kit for instantly prototyping new components. It is followed by the developers, who can use the component library, and develop these components very fast.

Down Sides of Design Systems and Team Structure

There are also some drawbacks with Design Systems. Building a solid design system from scratch can take time. In some cases, it can even last several years. And for companies, time is a very valuable resource.

For handling this issue, you need to set the right team structure for your design system. We are going to learn about the team structure, next to handle some issues like time.

The process of developing a design system lasts forever. It lasts as long as your product exists, and continues to progress over time. The main reason behind this is it is just a product that serves other products.

Then, we have the maintenance issue. Every product needs maintenance, and a design system is a product that serves other products. It has a complete lifecycle, as a product which requires a team to maintain it.

Now, we will learn about a proper team structure for the design system. You need to sell your design system to all the team members. For promoting that adoption, you build a team in three different ways.

The first way is having a central team. In this model, there is a core team responsible for everything. They work on building and maintaining the design system from zero to 100. They define the foundations of the system, along with UI Kits, developing the component library and style guides. The team consists of designers, engineers and product managers.

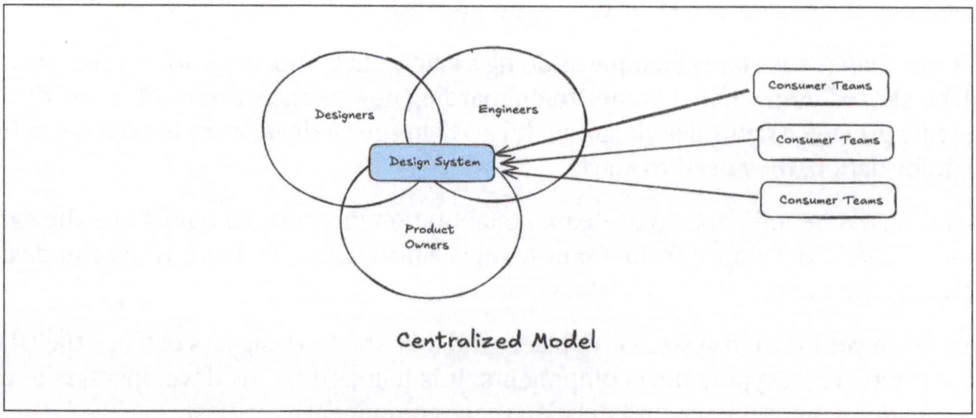

Figure 13.1: *Centralized Model*

The opposite model to the centralised one is the distributed team. Instead of having a core single team in charge of everything, the consumer teams of the design system are responsible for developing and maintaining it. People usually like systems that they are part of creating. This way distributed models increase the popularity of the design system, and a wider adoption of it.

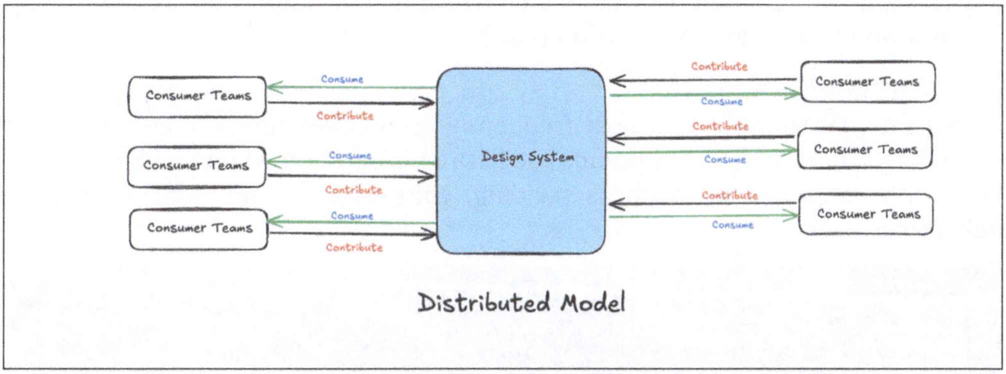

Figure 13.2: *Distributed Model*

The final model is the hybrid model which brings the best of both these earlier models. It has a core team dedicated to the design system that leads to faster development and delivery. It also welcomes contributions from consumer teams, which in return bring more innovation.

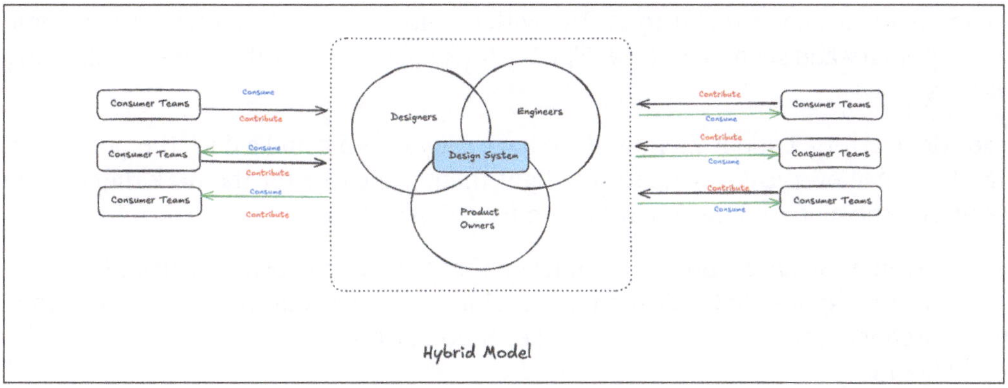

Figure 13.3: *Hybrid Model*

Audience of Design Systems and Example

We should not copy, paste open source design systems because the primary audience of the design system is the team, and the company that created it in the first place. It means for their brand and identity.

Now, if a design system is open source or shared with members outside the company, it should accept contributions from outside members. Also, it should also be a source of learning and inspiration for others.

You need to know how to build and develop the design language and foundation, based on a specific brand, and then Figma, React and Storyboard will be easy parts. Next, we will see a real life example that will convince us how important having a design system is, and how it can save your time, effort and money.

We all are familiar with buttons. They are pretty simple, and easy to develop components. Buttons are the most frequently used components in an application, so that they can showcase our brand. The first consideration when building a button starts with its properties such as padding, **`font-size`**, **`color`**, **`font-family`** and **`background-color`**.

```
button {
  font-size: 16px;
  font-family: sans-serif;
  color: grey;
  background-color: white;
  padding: 6px;
}
```

Figure 13.4: *Button Style*

Then, we have to consider different states such as hover, active, clicked and maybe, disabled. We also have more than one button type usually in our code bases. They are often primary and secondary buttons, if not the third type of buttons.

We might need some icon buttons also, with or without text. Each one of them comes with a primary and secondary type. The buttons may come in different sizes like small and large.

Also, do not forget about themes. If we have a light theme and a dark theme, then we should double everything. One for the light theme, and one for the dark theme. Now, we will do the math of how much this simple thing will cost.

Let us assume, we have a product team, and that team has a designer, an engineer and a QA. All are responsible for designing, developing and testing the button component in the product team. If each member takes $100 per hour, they will finish processing in 150 hours.

It means every team member is spending about 50 hours on average, working on the project. So, this is a total of $15,000 for building buttons. Yet there is one team working on buttons in an enterprise corporation. If we assume that there are 50 such teams working on building buttons for their products, they will end up spending about $1 million.

Also, as each team works in its own design, the final quality of each set of buttons will be different. So, here the design system comes to the rescue as it sinks all the product teams, and provides them with a single source of design foundations. This means that the costs will be dramatically dropped.

Key Concepts and Practical Checklist

What we mean by design language is a set of standards and elements that define the identity of a brand via a product. You can think of a design language as the personality of a component, a brand, and the related design elements.

Design language consists of two parts - foundation and components. The foundation includes some principles that describe how your product can showcase the personality of your brand. It consists of stuff like color, typography, icons and some graphic motions.

A component library is a bunch of components developed in frameworks and libraries like ReactJS or VueJS. It brings the design language and UI kits into a live final product. The style guide is simply the documentation for everything, you have in your design system. It starts from design language and UI kits up to the component library. There are different tools with which you can build your style guides like storybooks.

Before we flag a component as fully delivered, we need some design and development checklist. This is to make sure that the component meets the requirements. First, let us see the checklist related to the design phase.

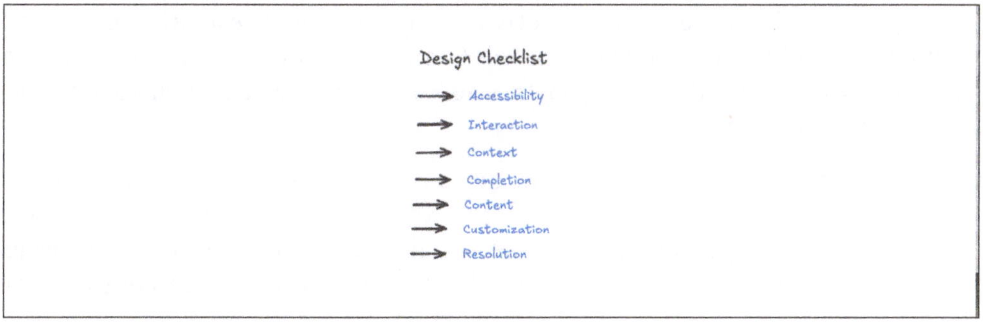

Figure 13.5: *Design Checklist*

All users, despite their conditions, must be able to navigate the product with the same experience. The design system should take into account the requirements needed by users with visual disabilities. It should make sure they can consume the product easily, whenever the user interacts with that specific component.

What interaction is supposed to happen? Is there feedback that must be shown to the user? All the interactions need to be defined. The context is about where and how a component should be used. For instance, if we have a secondary button component and a link component, we should define when to go with any of them.

Check that all states such as hover, clicked, and disabled are defined for that component. What kind of content should that component display? Is this showcasing the brand identity efficiently?

Then, we should check if this component is customizable? For example, if a button component is consumed by several products, then it may have different colors in every product. You must define these customizable parameters very well.

How does the component display on different screen resolutions? How does the layout change? You have to also consider all these factors. Now, when we go to the development phase, we need to consider the following checklist.

Figure 13.6: *Development Checklist*

For accessibility, you should develop the product with Semantic HTML, to make sure it complies with the assistive technologies, and you should consider features like keyboard navigation.

Your component should respond properly to screen size and resolution changes. Do you implement all the customizable properties of this element? You have to check in the case of customization that you have followed, and see that you have properly implemented all of them.

In case something goes wrong, how do the components respond? Have you considered type checking to make sure that the component receives the correct props, and all the dependencies we use should work the same on all browsers. In case, they do not work the same on all browsers, you need to consider using polyfills.

Mistakes to Avoid

Let us see a list of mistakes that we should avoid in our journey. The following is the complete list diagram.

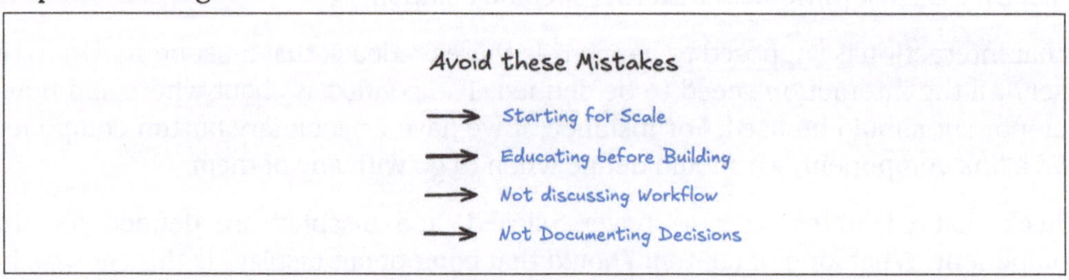

Figure 13.7: *Mistakes to Avoid*

Do not imply large-scale considerations at the beginning of the task. This can really frustrate the system. First, deliver something, then scale it up. That is the rule, you should always keep in mind.

Do not talk to your teammates about your design system with nothing. First design and develop some components, and then engage others, so that they have something to work on, right after you educate them.

Hence, when you want to collaborate with others about your design system, it is very important that you set up a workflow. Something that is clear, or just a procedure for that. The path to collaboration should be very clear and understandable by all the members.

The last one is really important. When you work on design systems, you will be provided with many resources, and this means more people are watching you. Documenting decisions will save you and your team from having to explain to each stakeholder why you are doing something a certain way.

Hands-on Color Palette in Figma

In this part, we will use Figma as it is the most popular design tool. We will learn how to build a design foundation for a project, starting from the color palette, up to designing components and complex UIs.

First, we define the color styles, and then we move on building the states of buttons for our projects. Finally, we will be using all the components to build a modal for an authentication form.

The first thing we did is to log into https://www.figma.com/ through the browser.

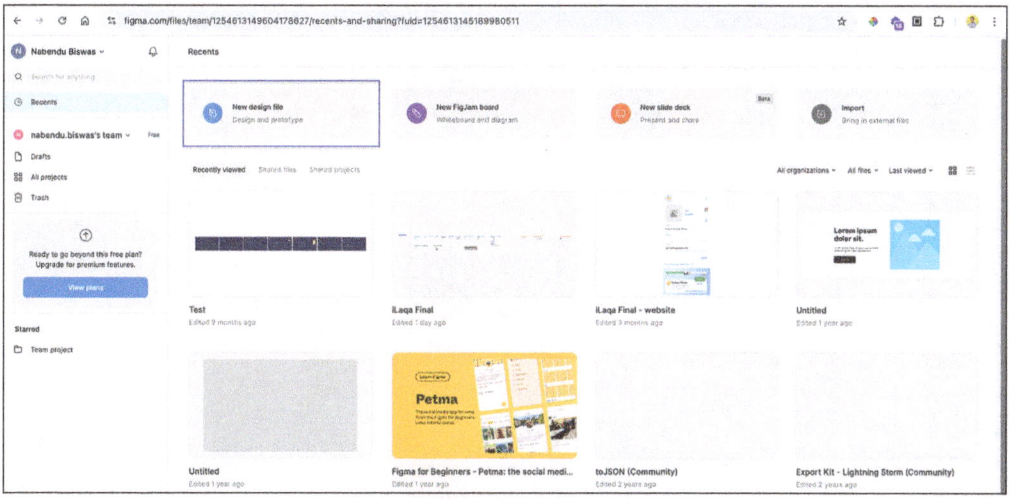

Figure 13.8: Figma

The first thing we are going to do is to create a color palette. Click on the **`New design file button`** in Figma. It is going to create a new file.

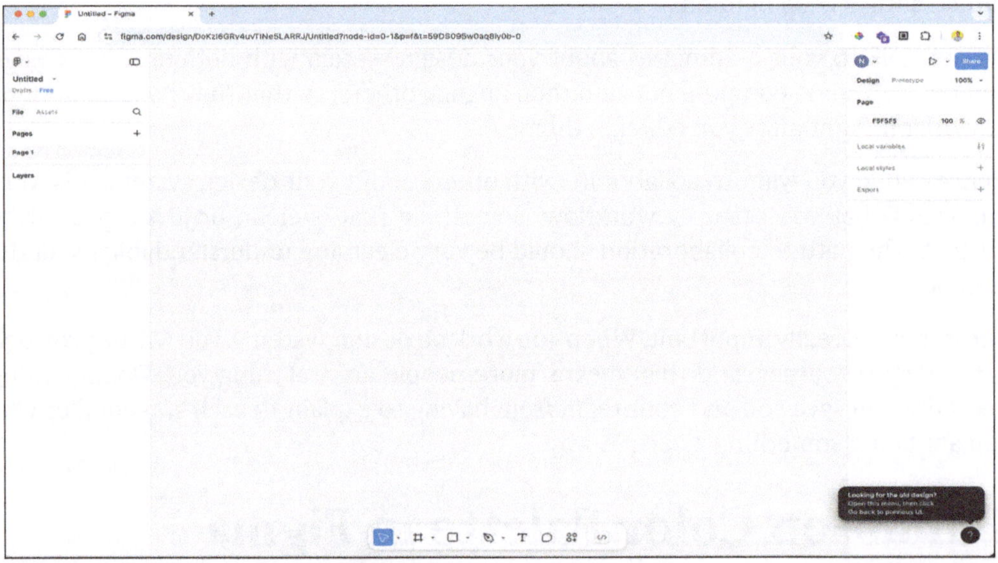

Figure 13.9: *New Project Figma*

We have named the document as Figma-design and the page as Colors. We have also added new artworks in it.

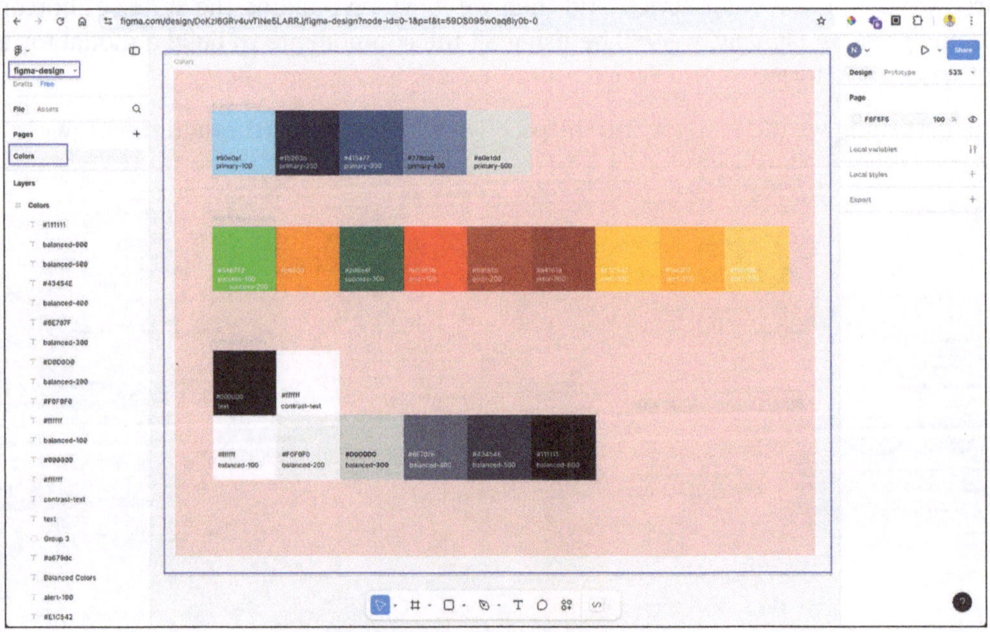

Figure 13.10: *Color Palette Figma*

This artwork is our color palette, and we can change it from sites like https://coolors.co/, or the designer can decide the colors in the color palette. We have visited the site, and logged into it, and then clicked on **`Explore trending palettes`**.

Figure 13.11: *Color Palettes Site*

The next screen will show a lot of awesome palettes. We have chosen a palette pattern. Here click on the first color pattern to copy it.

Figure 13.12: *Color Palettes Site*

Back in figma, click on the text for the first item, and change it with the hex-code of the color, which we just copied from the coolors.com site.

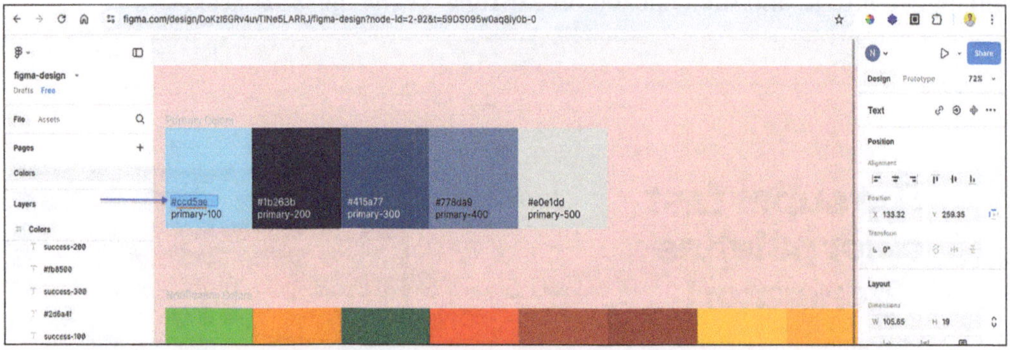

Figure 13.13: *Changing hex-code Figma*

We also need to change the actual color. For this, double click on the item, and copy it in the **`Fill`**.

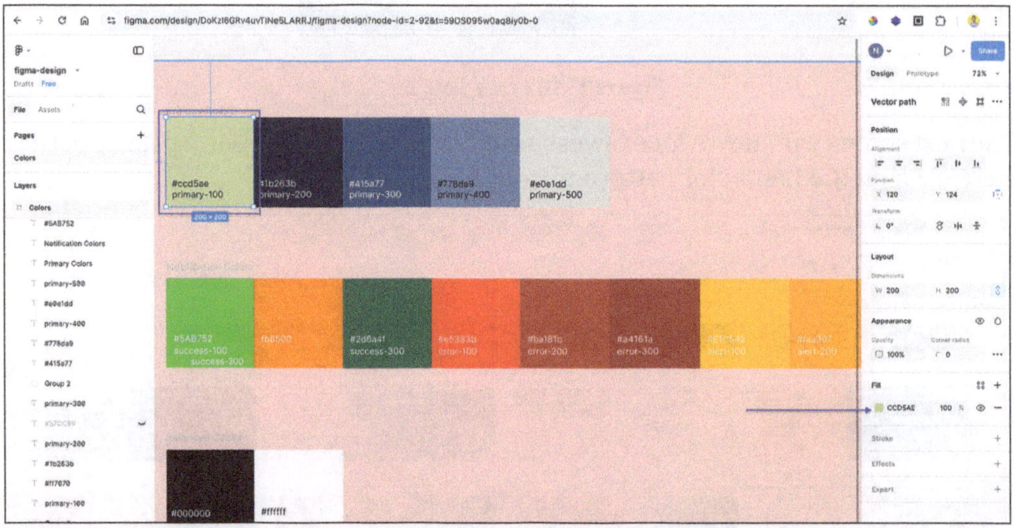

Figure 13.14: *Changing hex-code Component*

Following the same process of changing the text and the item, we changed the whole palette.

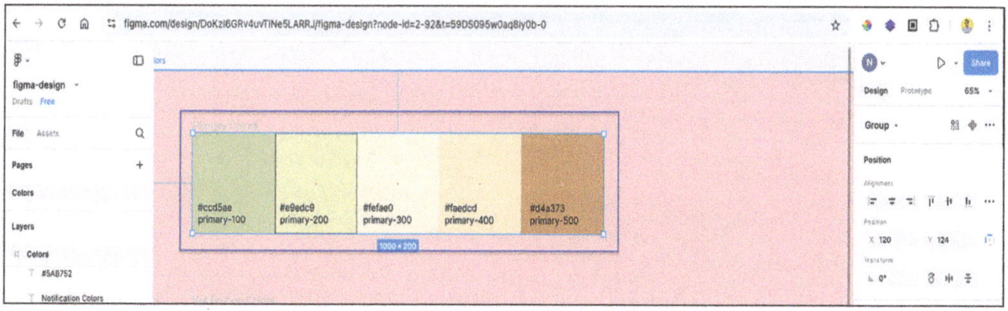

***Figure 13.15:** Changing hex-code of all Components*

There are colors in figma artwork that we are going to use for other purposes in our applications. For example, the **`Notification Colors`**, which we are going to use for alarm messages, or error messages.

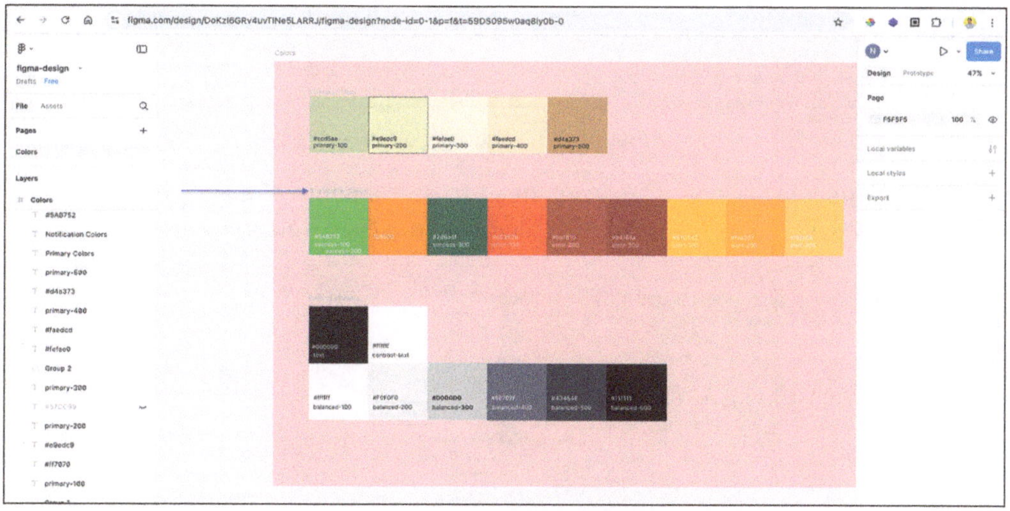

***Figure 13.16:** Notification Colors*

Now, we will see the real benefit of this color palette system in our project. For this, first click on an item, and then in **`Fill`**, click on the four round circle icon. It will open a modal, in which, click on the **+** icon.

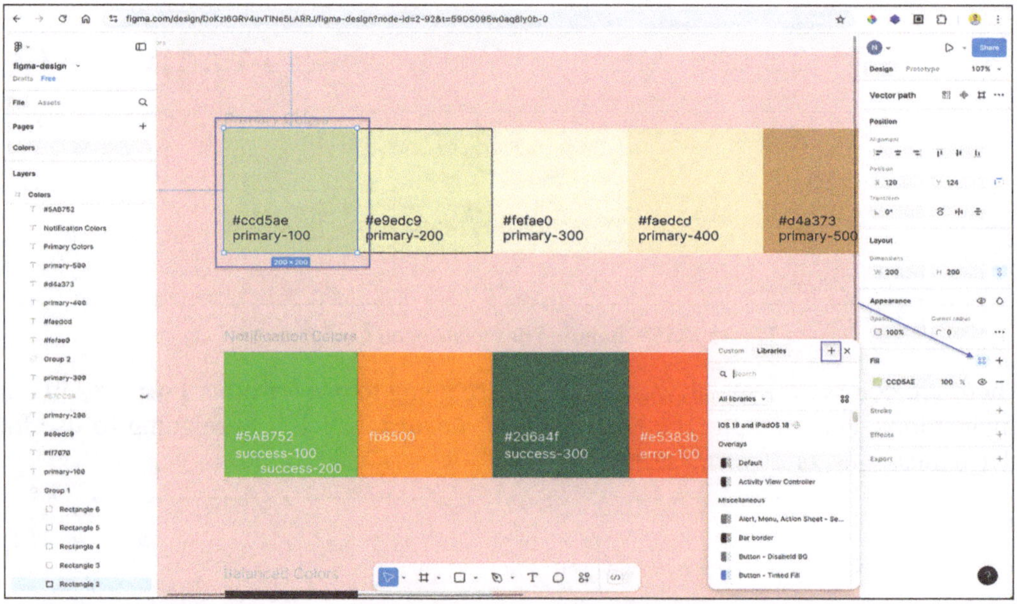

Figure 13.17: *Adding Colors*

Another pop-up will open and here, we need to give a name. We are giving the name of **`primary-100`** to it, and then click on the **`Create style`** button.

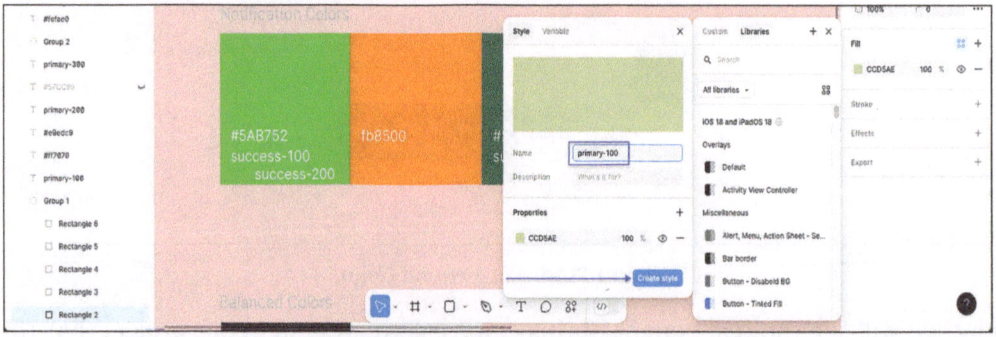

Figure 13.18: *Adding Color pop-up*

Now, we want to create an item of **`Ellipse`**. So, click on the bottom menu, and select an **`Ellipse`**.

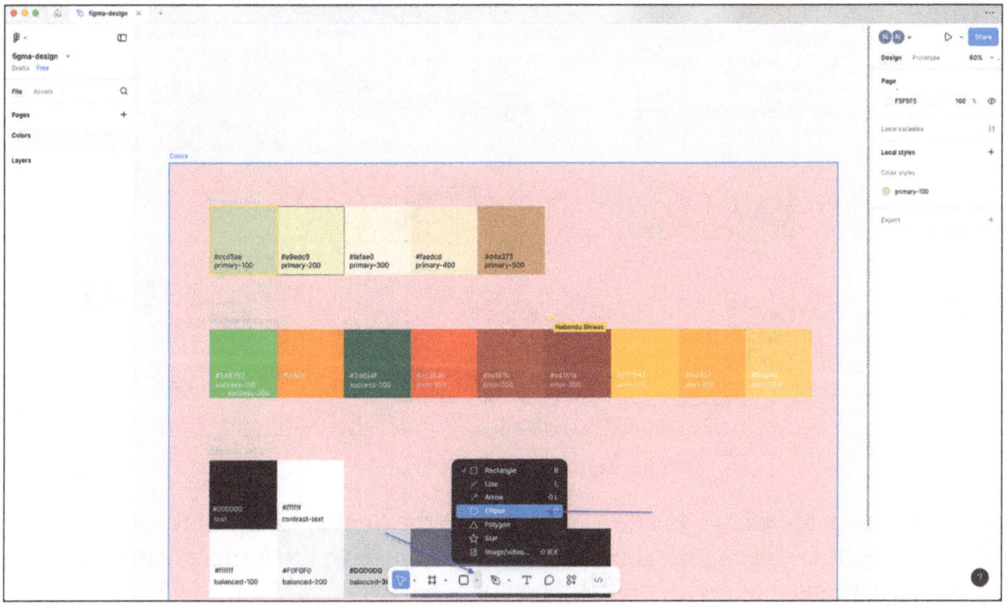

Figure 13.19: *Creating Ellipse*

After the **`Ellipse`** is created, in the **`Fill`**, click on the four-circle icon again. Here, we will see a color of **`primary-100`** present. Clicking on it will update the color of the **`Ellipse`**, and this is how easy it is to add a color to an item.

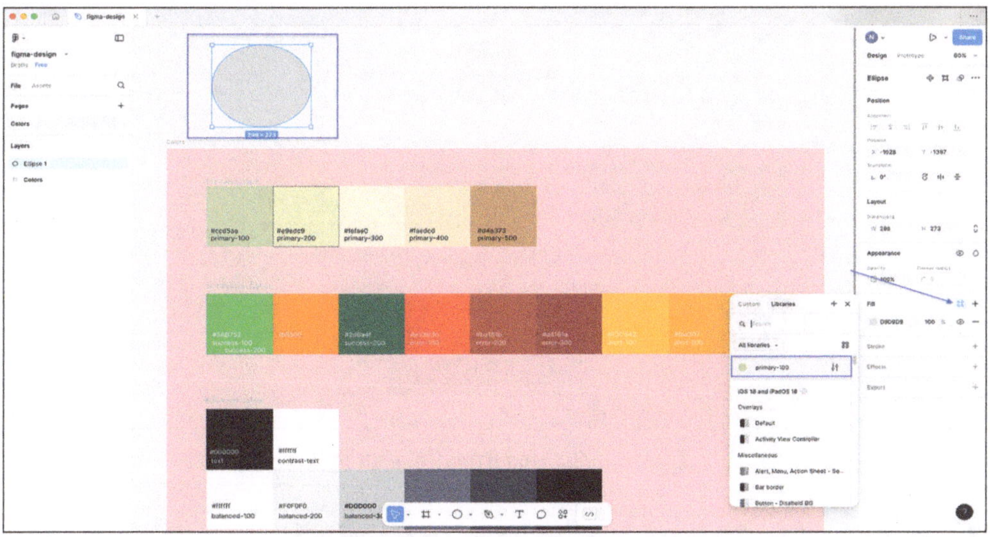

Figure 13.20: *Adding Color Ellipse*

There is one more feature which we can use. Go back to the original item. Here **right-click** on **`primary-100`**. After this, click on **`Edit style`**.

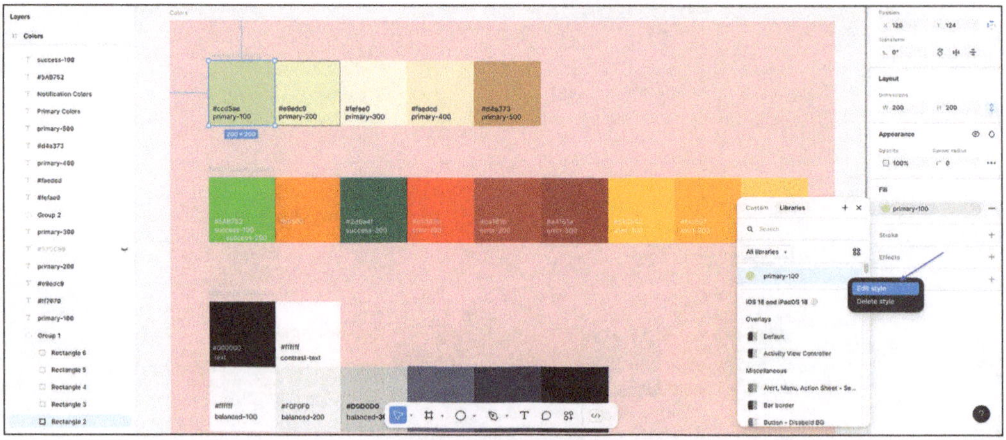

Figure 13.21: Edit Style

In the next pop-up, just give a new hex-code in the **`Properties`**. All the items related to the parent item will change the color. Suppose, we have 100 items created out of the parent item, then all of their color will be changed.

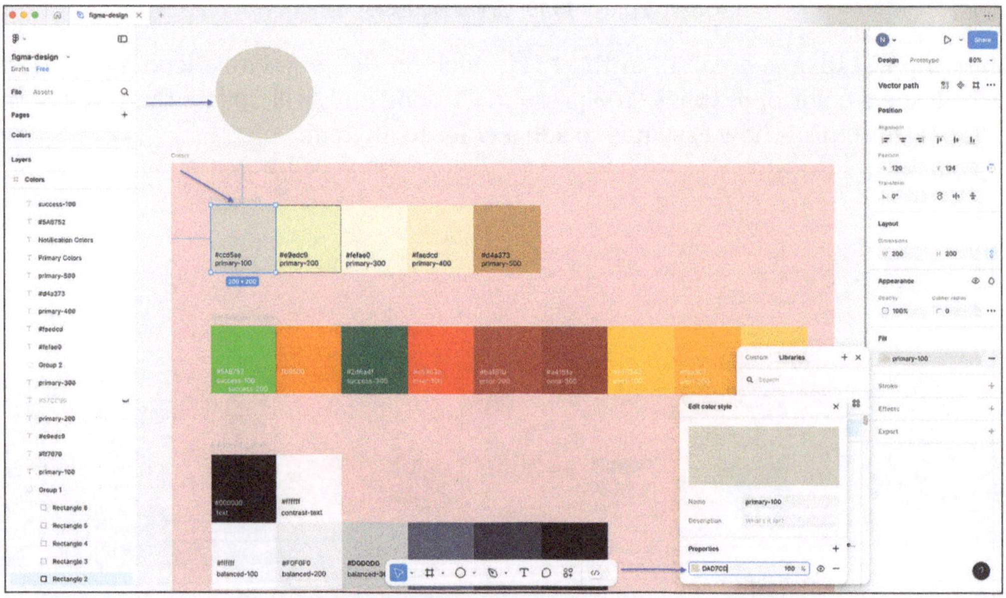

Figure 13.22: *Updating Color in Style*

Hands-on Designing a Modal

In this part, we are going to create a modal using Figma. We have created two new pages called **`Text Inputs`** and **`Pop-ups`**. Next, we will create a Frame from the toolbar at the bottom.

***Figure 13.23:** Creating the Frame*

We have created a Frame of 1152×707 which is large enough for our design.

***Figure 13.24:** Inserting the Frame*

Next, we will create a rectangle, and give it a predefined color of **`Balanced-200`**, which we have learnt to create in the previous section.

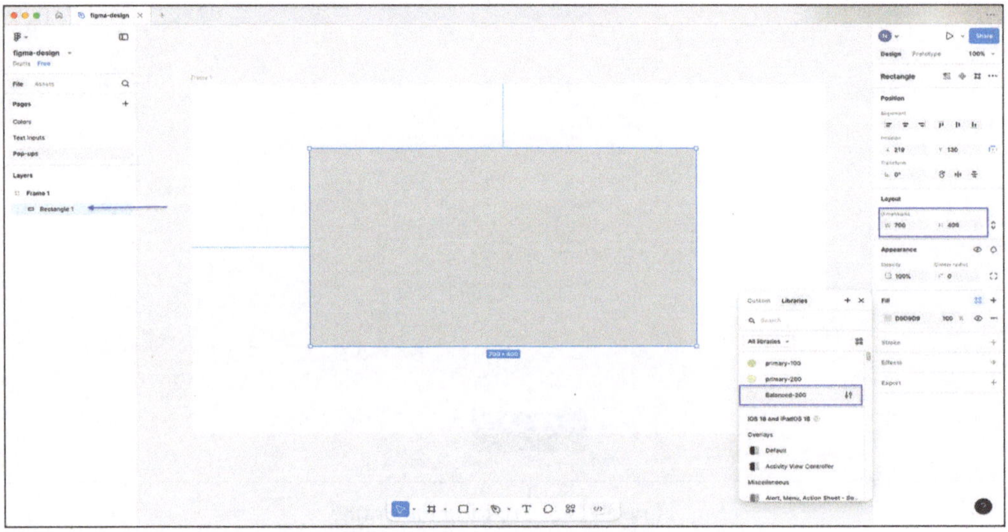

Figure 13.25: *Adding a Rectangle*

Now, we will first center this rectangle by clicking on the **`Alignment`**. Next, we will also lock the rectangle by right-clicking, and selecting **`Lock/Unlock`**.

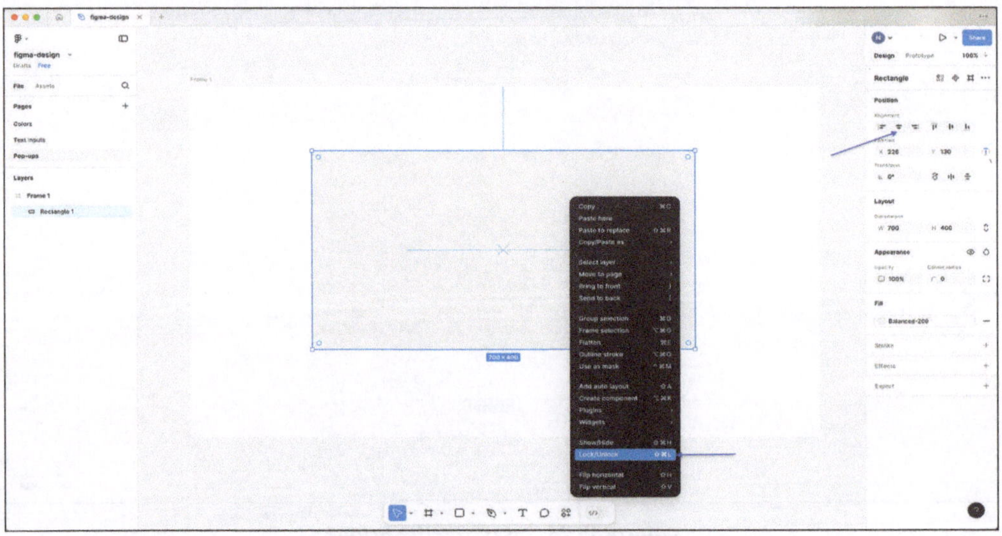

Figure 13.26: *Locking the Rectangle*

We have added a new page called **`Buttons`** which has pre-build buttons in it. Now, we want to use a button in our **`Pop-ups`** page, so right-click on the button. Then click on **`Group`** selection.

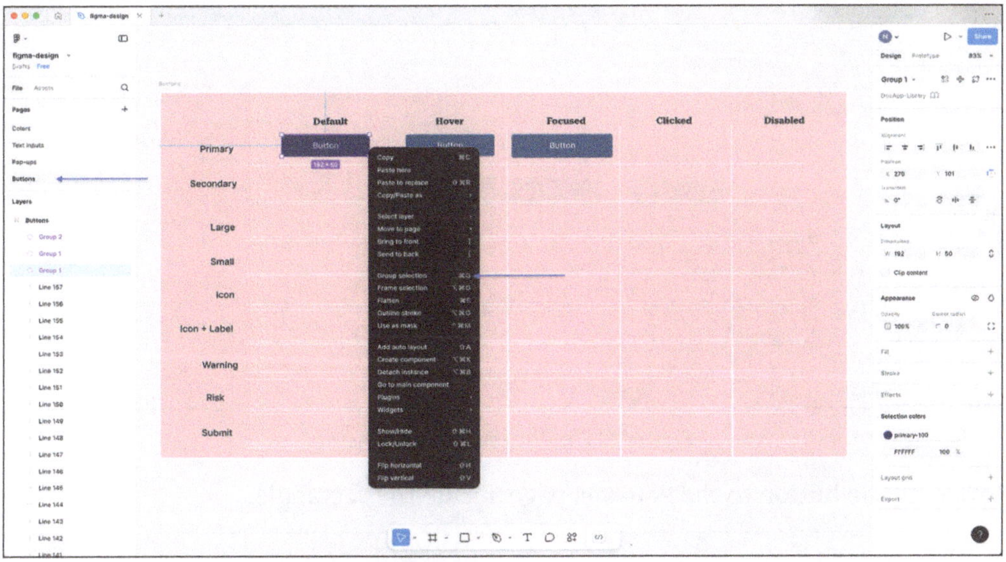

Figure 13.27: *Group Selection of the Button*

Again, right-click on it, and then click on **`Create`** component to make it a reusable component.

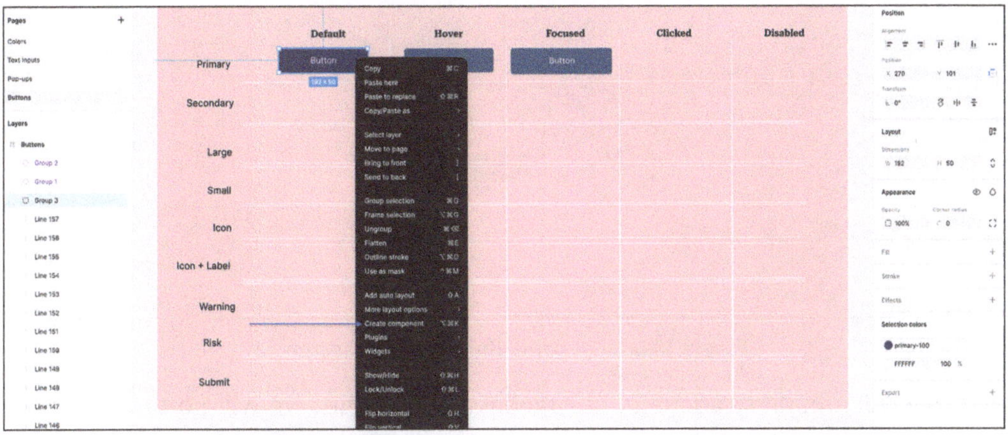

Figure 13.28: *Create Component of the Button*

Now, click on **`Assets`**, and then search for **`Buttons`**, and our component will be there.

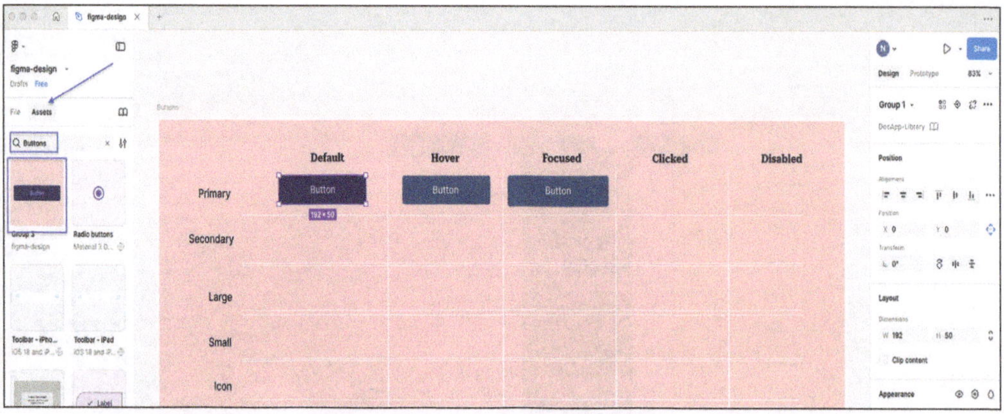

Figure 13.29: *Buttons Become Assets*

Now, drag the button to the **`Pop-ups`** page, inside the rectangle.

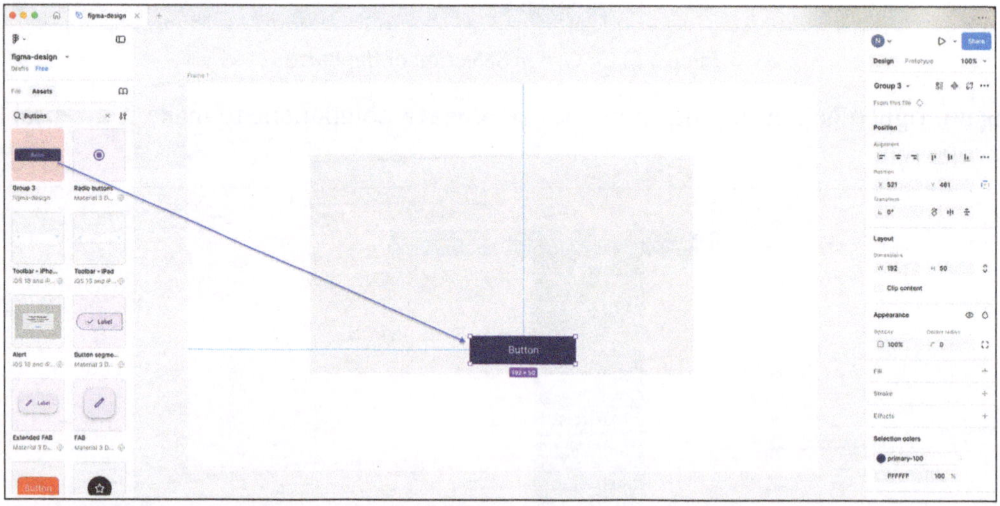

Figure 13.30: *Dragging Button to the Rectangle*

Next, we will add illustrations in our modal, and for this, we will go to the https://undraw.co/ site. Here, we have also changed the illustration color to our button color, by giving its hex code.

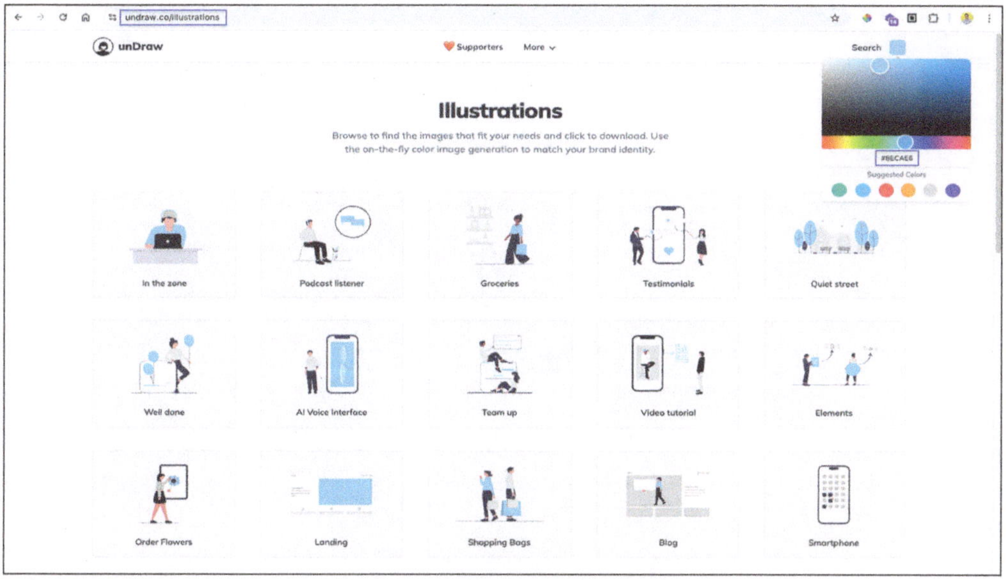

Figure 13.31: *Illustrations Site*

Once, we have selected the illustration, just click on it. Then click on the **`Download SVG`** button.

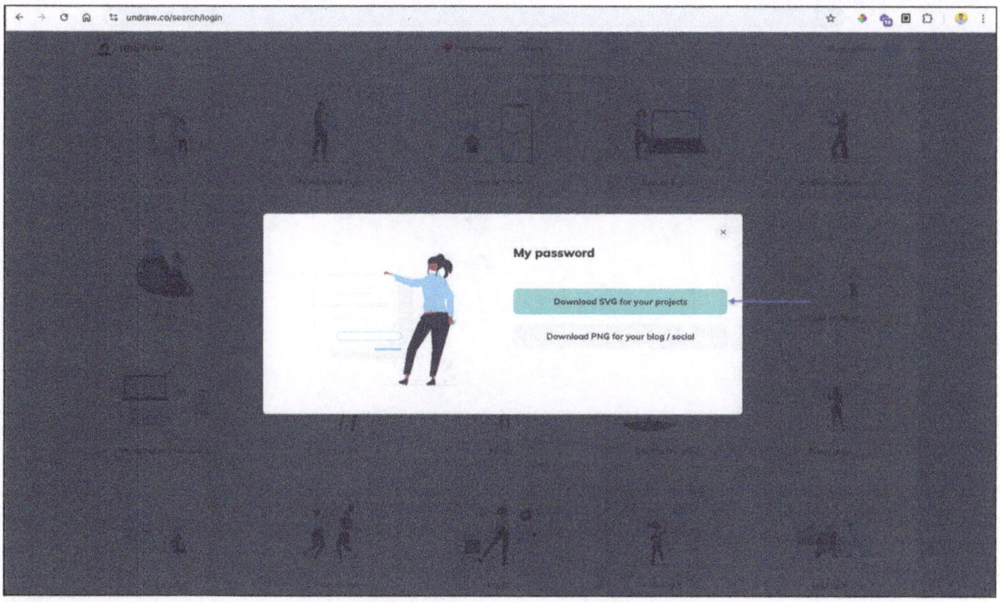

Figure 13.32: *Download SVG*

Next, drag the image from the **`download`** folder to the rectangle in Figma.

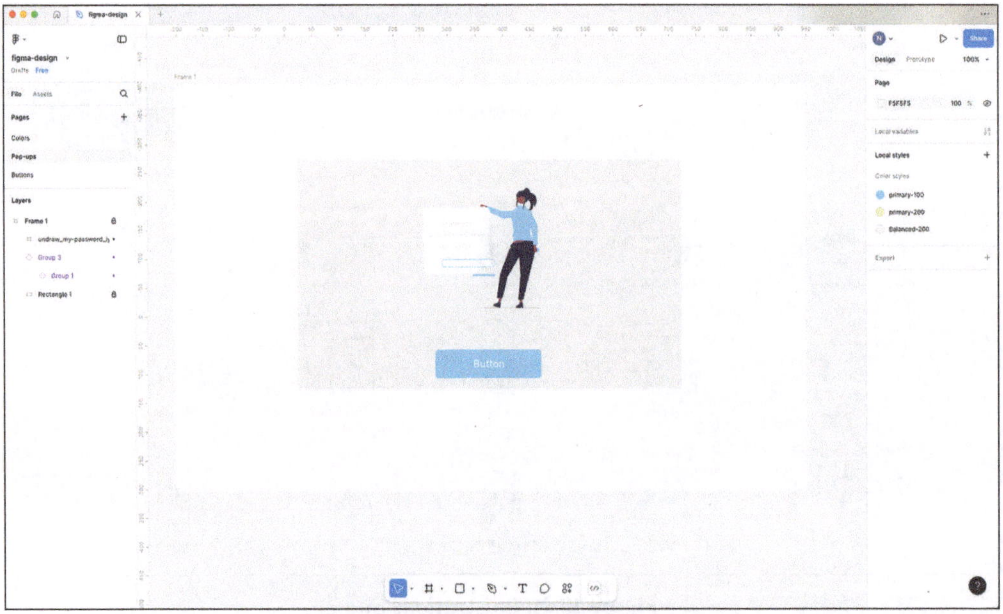

Figure 13.33: *Illustration inside Rectangle*

We will also add a **`Close`** button from the **`Assets`** tab. Again, we have to drag it, and put it in the correct place.

Figure 13.34: *Closed Icon inside Rectangle*

Conclusion

In this chapter, we have learnt about design systems. First, we had learnt the core concepts that started with understanding the design system. Then we talked about the downside of design systems, and the three types of team structures used for design systems.

Next, we learnt about the key concepts and practical checklist to follow. Lastly, we have learnt about the mistakes to avoid creating a design system. After this, we moved to Figma, and used this design tool to create a Color Palette as well as a modal.

In the next chapter, **we will continue with the design system, and learn to create a component in React**. We will also learn style compositions, and encapsulating styles.

Points to Remember

- Core concepts of Design Systems.
- Three types of teams to create a Design system - Centralized, Distributed and Hybrid.
- Creating a color palette and modal with Figma.

Chapter 14
Design System with Developing Components and Encapsulating Styles

Introduction

In this chapter, we will continue our Design Systems journey. We will first learn to develop components in React, from the Figma design created in the previous chapter. After this, we will learn about style compositions, and encapsulating styles.

Structure

In this chapter, we shall discuss the following topics:

- Extensible Foundations
- Creating Button Component
- Building a Modal
- Style Compositions
- Encapsulating Styles

Extensible Foundations

Now, we are going to create react components from figma files, created in the previous chapter. So, we are going to create the button created in the previous chapter. Following that, we are also going to build the whole modal.

In this section, we are going to write the initial setup, for button and modal components.

Figure 14.1: *Button in Figma*

We have created a new react app with **`create-react-app`**, and removed the files which are not required. In the **`App.js`** file, we have removed the earlier code, and just put an h1 with text.

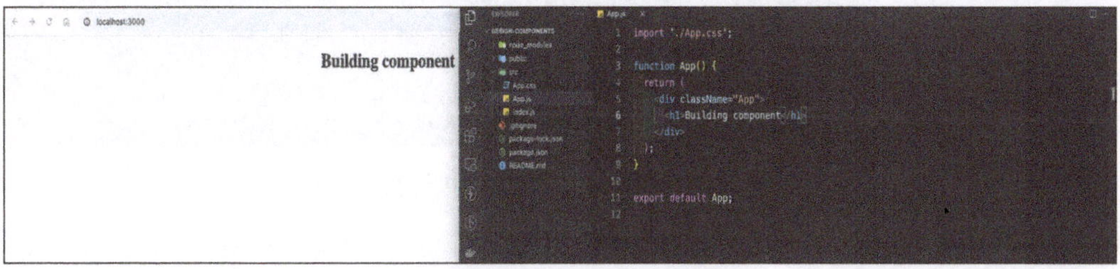

Figure 14.2: *New React Project*

Now, create an **`assets`** folder inside **`src`**, and inside it, create an **`images`** folder. We have kept the **`register.svg`** file within it which we have downloaded in the previous chapter. Next, we have created an **`utils`** folder inside **`src`**, and created a **`GlobalStyles.js`** file inside it.

Next, we have installed styled-components from the integrated terminal. In the **`GlobalStyles.js`** file, we have imported **`createGlobalStyle`** from **`styled-components`**, first. Next, we have used it to create styles for **`html`**, **`*`**, and **`body`**.

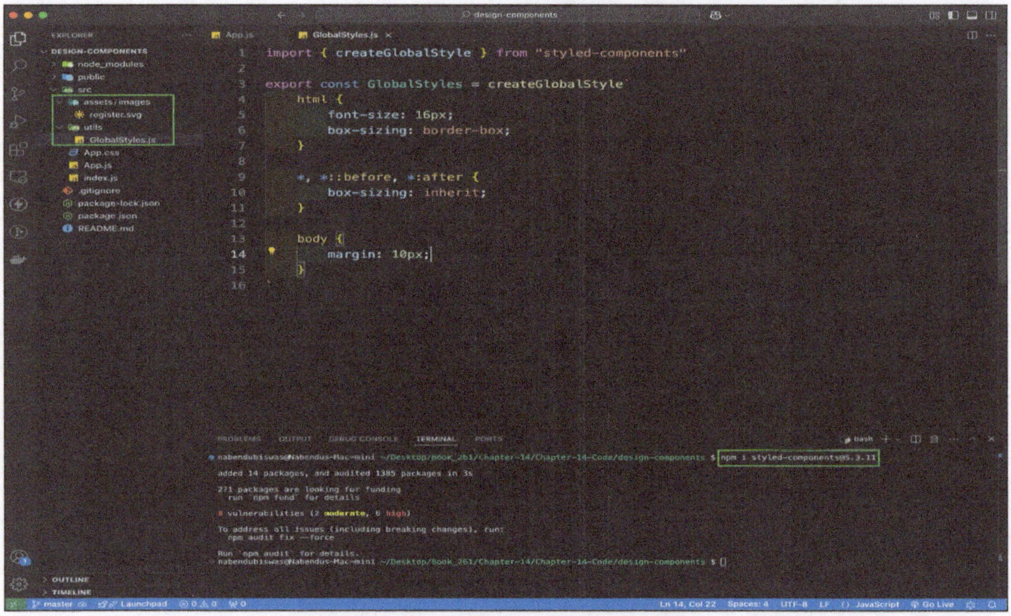

Figure 14.3: *Image and GlobalStyles*

Now, we will import **`GlobalStyles`** in **`App.js`**, and use it.

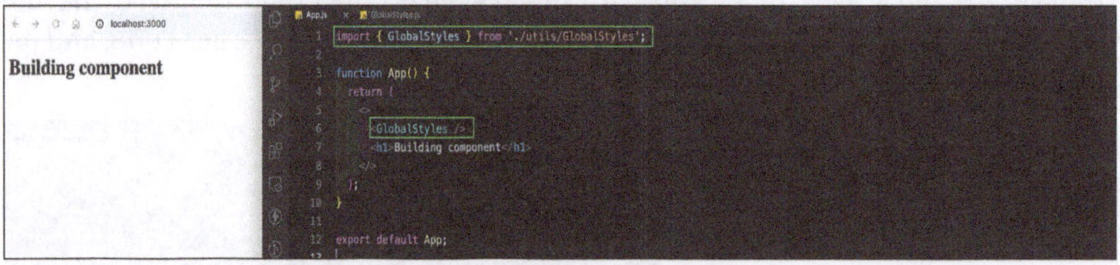

Figure 14.4: *GlobalStyles in App.js*

In the **`utils`** folder, we will create a new file called **`colors.js`**. Here, we have put all the colors from the figma palette from the previous chapter. All the colors are in objects with the color depth as key, and hex code as value.

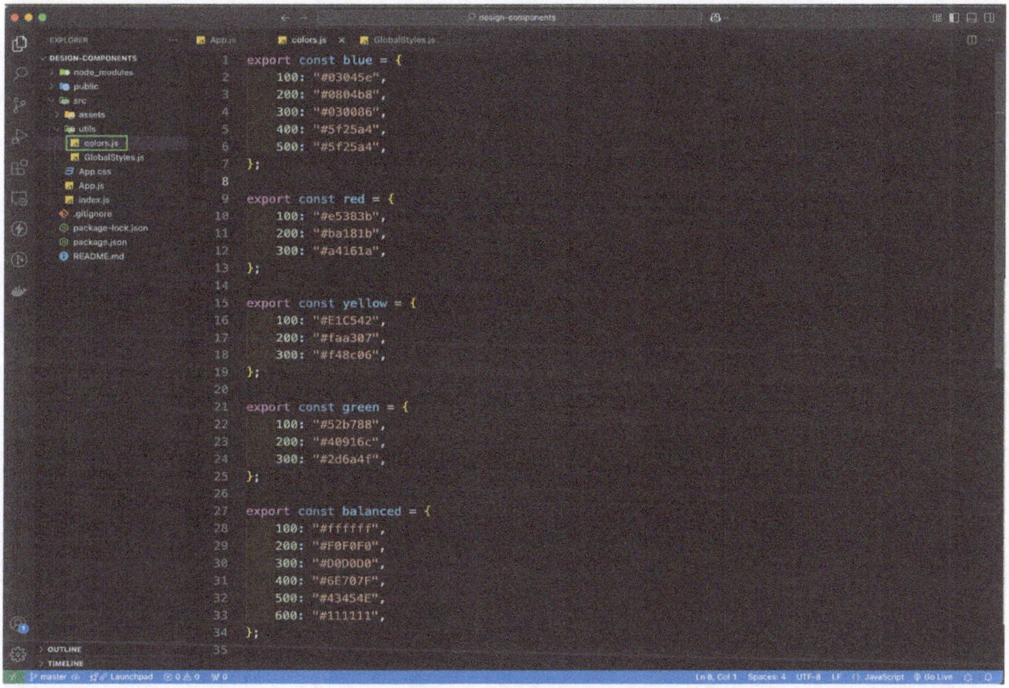

Figure 14.5: *Colors in colors.js*

Now, create a file called **`typescales.js`** in the **`utils`** folder. Here, we have an object, **`typescales`** which contains keys as **`header1`**, **`header2`** and others, and value in different **`rem`** units.

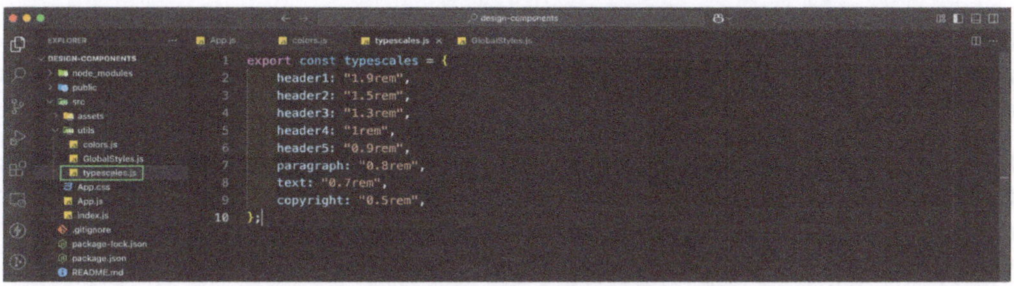

Figure 14.6: *typescales.js File*

Next, we will create an **`index.js`** file in the **`utils`** folder which will export the **`colors`**, **`typescales`** and **`GlobalStyles`**.

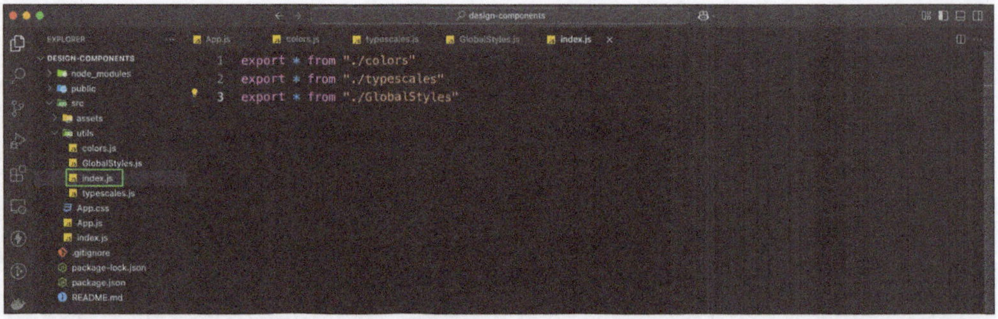

Figure 14.7: *index.js file for Utils*

Back in the **`App.js`**, we will now import from utils.

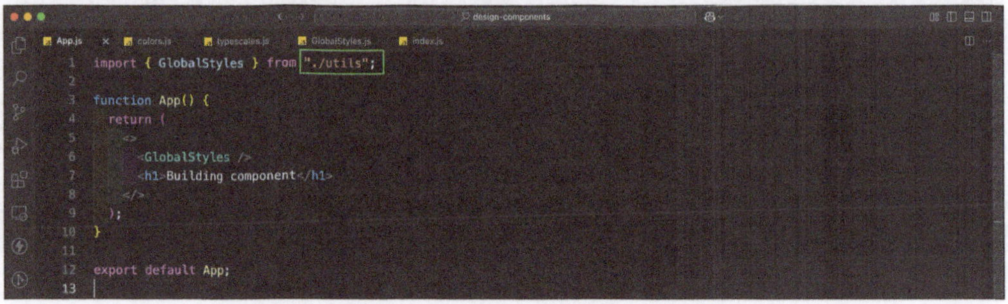

Figure 14.8: *Importing GlobalStyles from Utils*

Creating Button Component

Now, we will create the **`Button`** component, and use the elements created in the previous part. So, create a new **`components`** folder inside the **`src`** folder. Here, create a **`Buttons.jsx`** file.

Inside it, we are first importing the styled components and balanced, blue **`typescales`**. Next, we have created a **`Button`** through the styled components, with different required styles. These styles are **`font-size`**, **`border-radius`**, **`padding`**, **`cursor`** and **`transition`** that are required in a button.

Next, we have styles for hover, focus, active and disabled for the button.

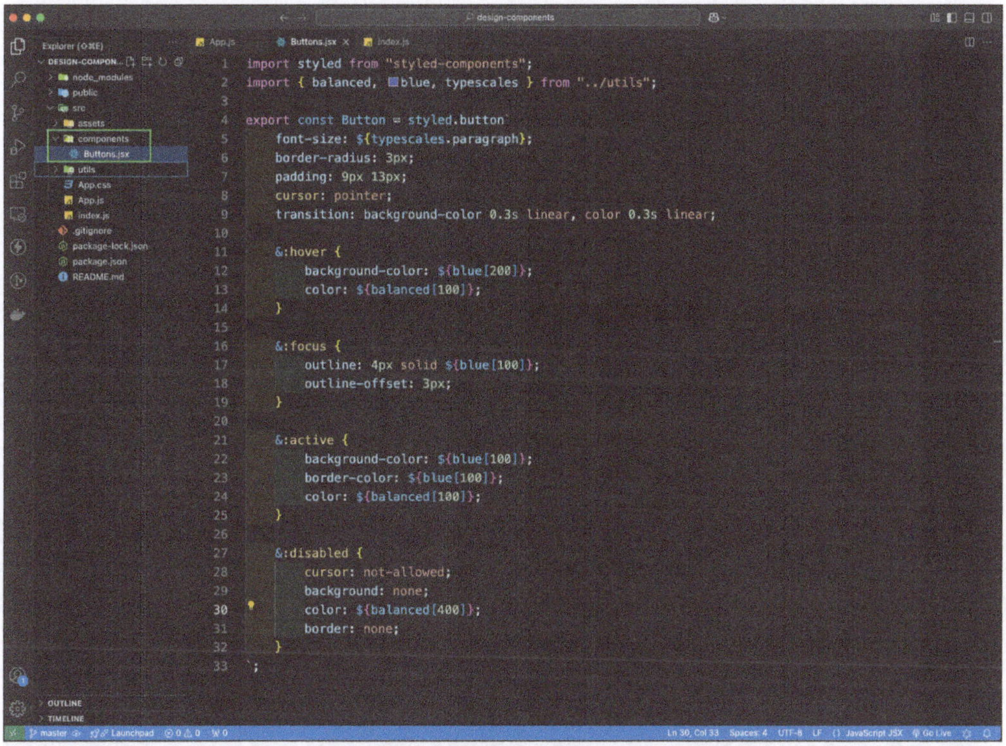

Figure 14.9: *Styles in Buttons.jsx File*

Now, just add the **`Button`** component in the **`App.js`** file. In http://localhost:3000/, we will see the button with all the styles.

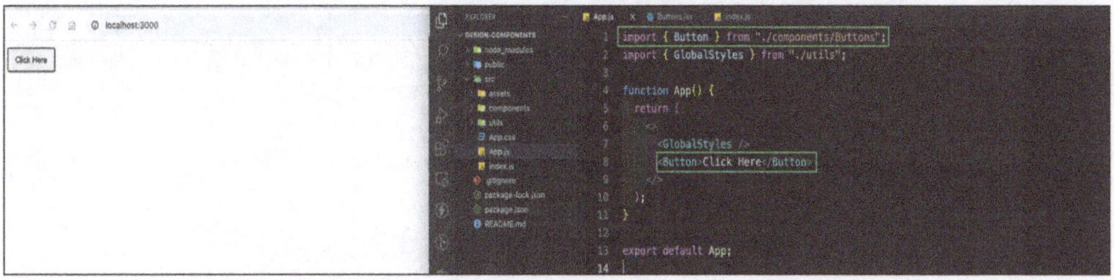

Figure 14.10: *Rendering Button Component in App.js File*

Take the mouse over it, and you will see the hover style.

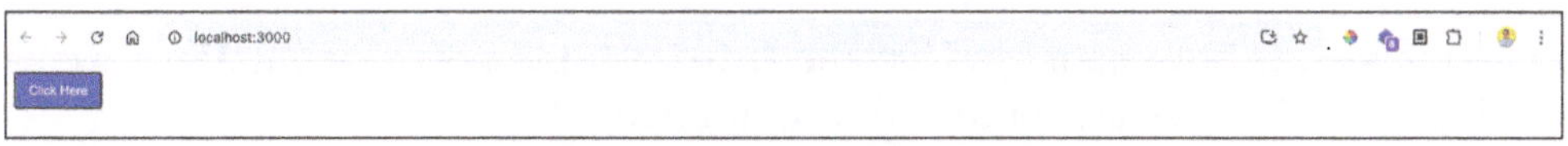

Figure 14.11: *Hover Style of Button*

Click over the button, or go to it by pressing the tab, and you will see the focus styles.

Figure 14.12: *Focus Style of Button*

Back in the **`App.js`** file, we have added disabled attribute to the **`Button`** component. Now, in http://localhost:3000/, we will see the disabled styles of the button.

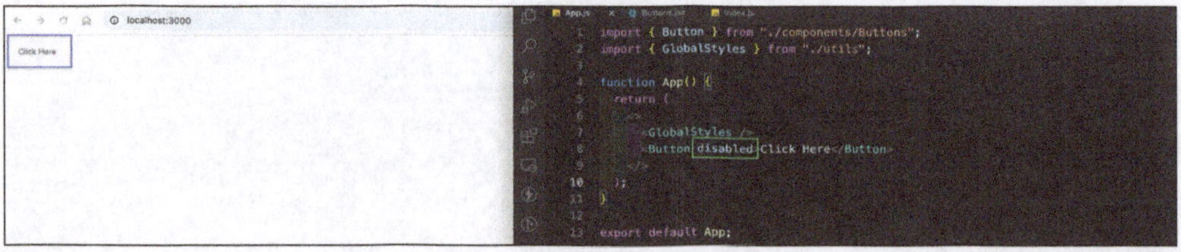

Figure 14.13: *Disabled Style of Button*

Next, in the **`Buttons.jsx`** file, we will create a new **`PrimaryButton`** which will inherit all the styles from the **`Button`**. On the top of it, there will be its own styles. We will have the disabled styles, and beside this, a large, small and warning styles.

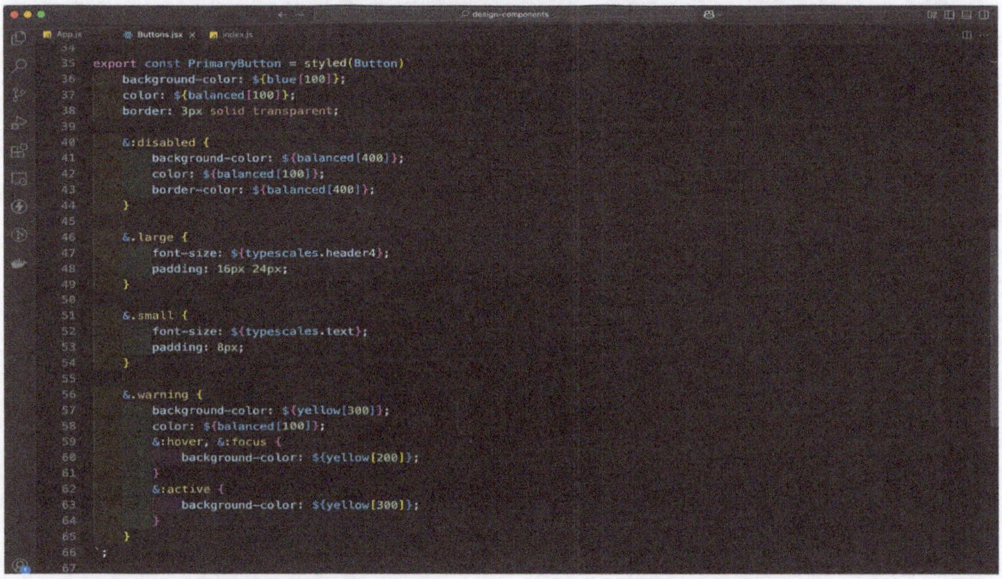

Figure 14.14: *PrimaryButton Component in Buttons.jsx*

Now, in the **`App.js`** file, import and use the **`PrimaryButton`** component. Here, we have also added the **`disabled`** attribute in the component.

Notice that in http://localhost:3000/, we have a different disabled style than the **`Button`** component.

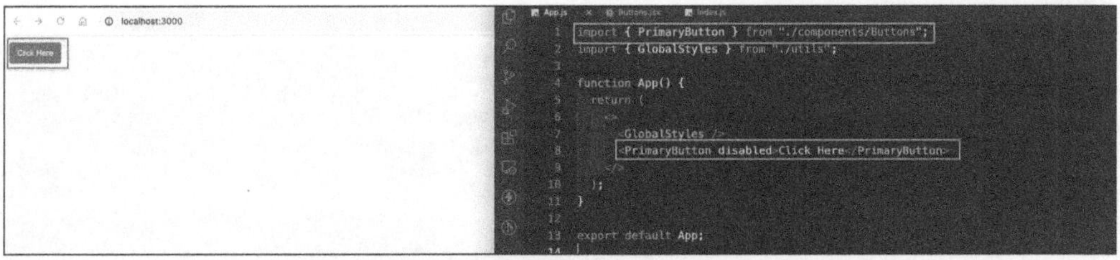

Figure 14.15: *Disabled Style in PrimaryButton*

Next, we have removed the **`disabled`** attribute from the **`PrimaryButton`** component, in the **`App.js`** file. Also, in http://localhost:3000/, we will see the styles for the **`PrimaryButton`.**

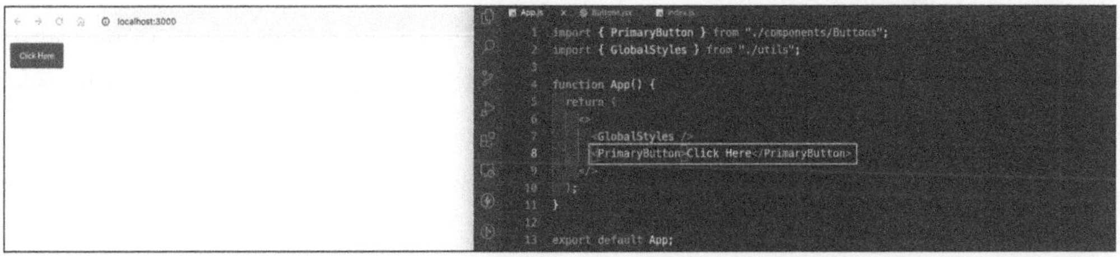

Figure 14.16: *Normal Style in PrimaryButton*

To use the styles for large, we need to add a **`className`** of **`large`** in the **`PrimaryButton`** component. The button will be large now.

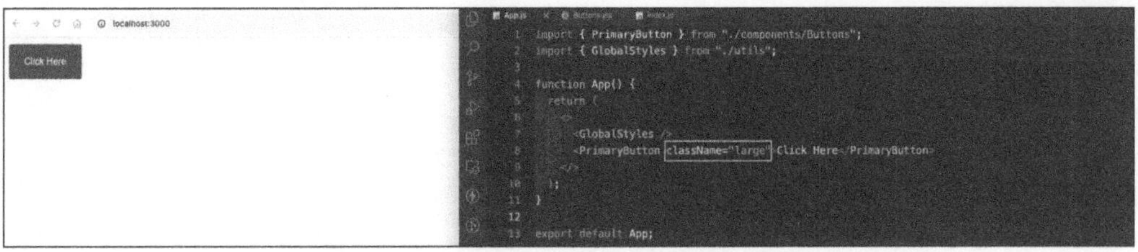

Figure 14.17: *Large Style in PrimaryButton*

To use the styles for small, we need to add a **`className`** of **`small`** in the **`PrimaryButton`** component. The button will be small now.

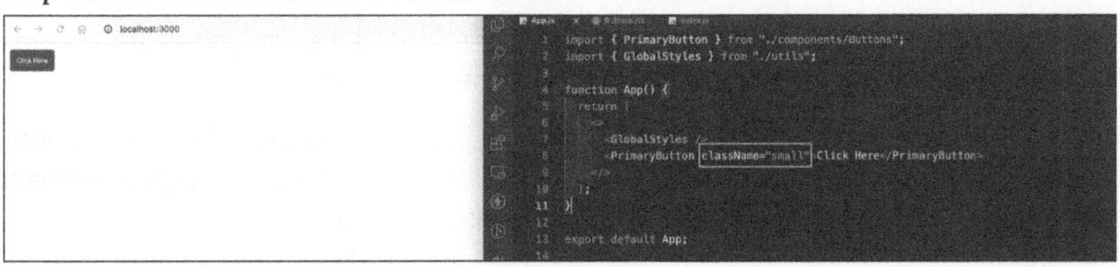

Figure 14.18: *Small Style in PrimaryButton*

Lastly, to use the styles for warning, we need to add a **className** of **warning** in the **PrimaryButton** component. The button will be warning style now, with a color of yellow.

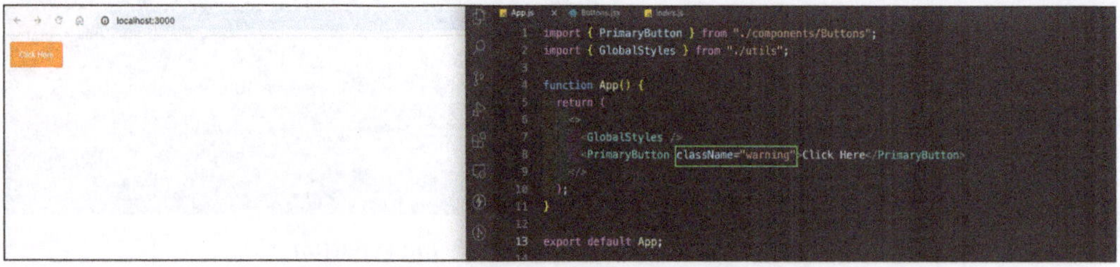

Figure 14.19: *Warning Style in PrimaryButton*

Building a Modal

Now, we will create the **Modal** component in React that we have created in Figma in the previous chapter. We will also add some additional topics in it like text and a box shadow for the modal.

Figure 14.20: *Modal in Figma*

First, create a **Register.js** file in the **components** folder. Here, we have again imported the styled components, and balanced and typescales from utils.

Next, we have created styles for the main **RegisterContainer** which will contain everything. It also has a box-shadow. After that, we have styles for **RegisterHeader** and **RegisterHelper** which will be used in the text in our modal.

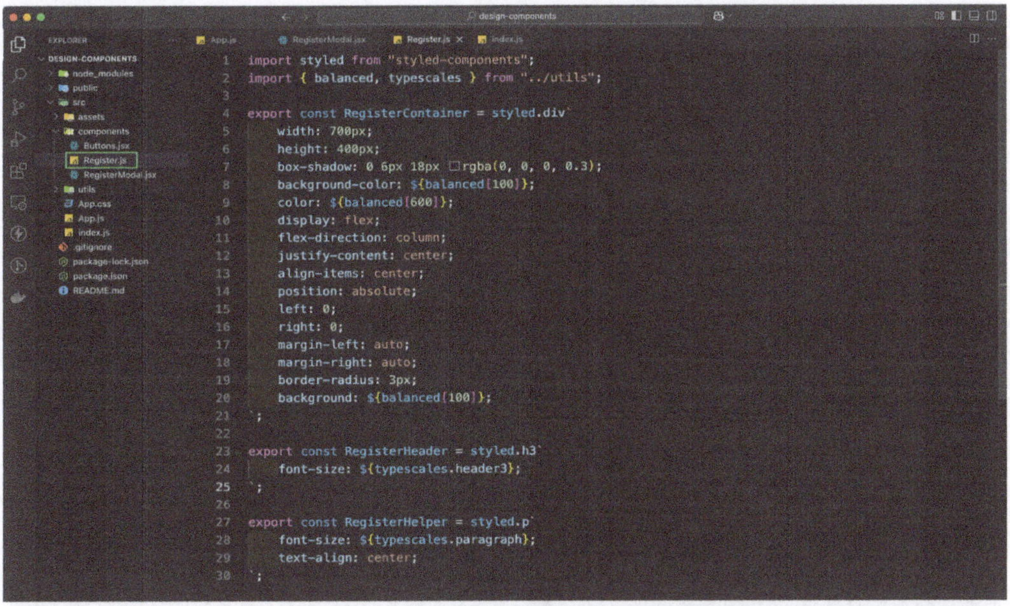

***Figure 14.21:** Styled-components in Register.js File*

Now, create a **`RegisterModal.jsx`** file in the **`components`** folder. Here, we are first importing **`PrimaryButton`** from the **`Button`** component. After this, we are importing **`RegisterContainer`**, **`RegisterHeader`** and **`RegisterHelper`** from **`Register.js`** file.

Next, inside the return of **`RegisterModal`**, we are wrapping everything with **`RegisterContainer`**. Then, we use **`RegisterHeader`** and **`RegisterHelper`** to show the texts. After this, we use the **`PrimaryButton`** component with a simple alert and **`Register`** text.

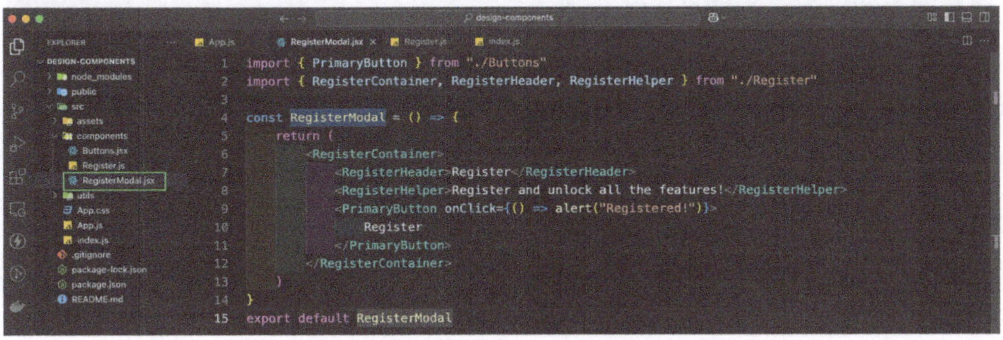

***Figure 14.22:** RegisterModal.jsx File*

Now, in http://localhost:3000/, we will see the modal with the three elements.

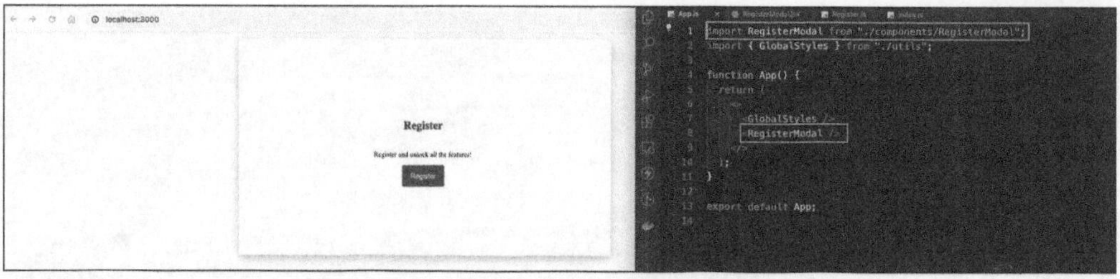

Figure 14.23: *Rendering RegisterModal from App.js File*

Next, we will write the logic to show the close icon. For this, first create an **icons** folder inside the **assets** folder. Here, create a file **close.js**, and inside it put the following code.

In this simple component, we are using the **svg** image of a close icon, and giving it 100% width and height with **styled-components**.

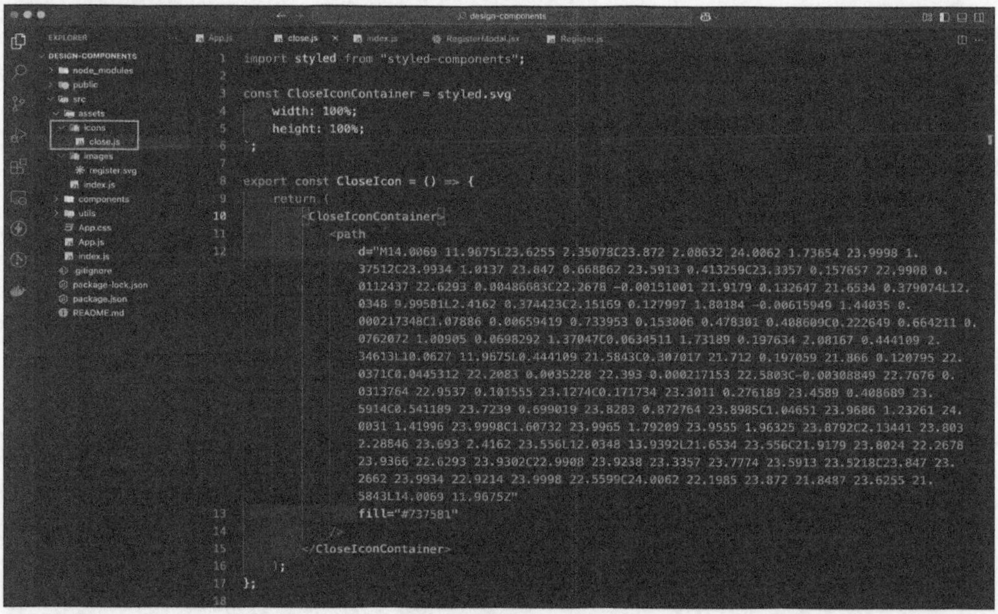

Figure 14.24: *close.js File*

Next, create an index.js file in the **assets** folder. Here, we are exporting the close icon created earlier.

Figure 14.25: *index.js file for Assets*

Back in the **Register.js** file, we will add styles for **CloseIconContainer**. These styles are for placing the close icon at the right place which is top right for us.

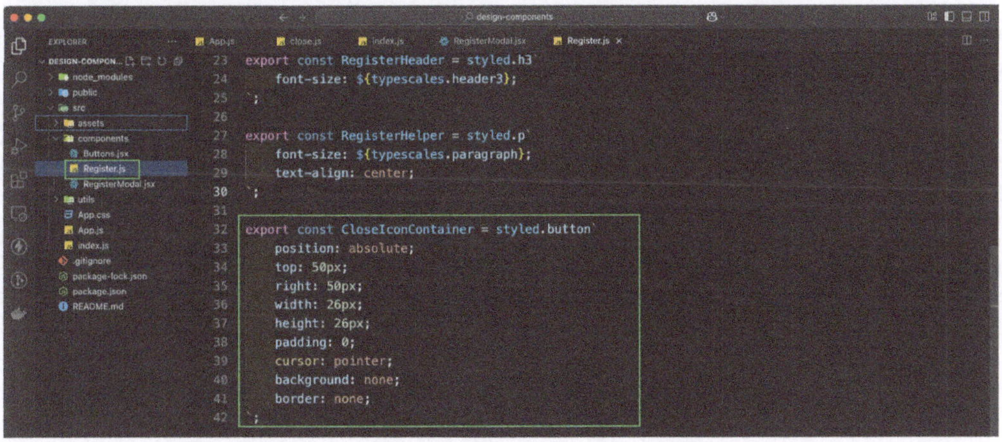

Figure 14.26: *Adding CloseIconContainer Styles in Register.js File*

Now, in the **RegisterModal.jsx** file, we will import the **CloseIcon** from the assets, first. After this, we will import **CloseIconContainer** from the **Register**. Now, inside the **return** statement, we will put the **CloseIcon** wrapped inside the **CloseIconContainer**. In the **CloseIconContainer**, we will also show a simple alert on clicking it.

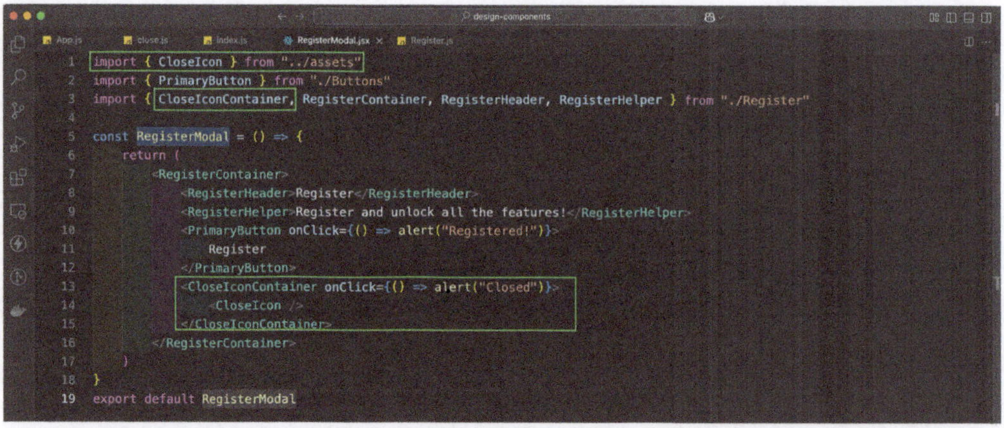

Figure 14.27: *Rendering CloseIconContainer and CloseIcon in RegisterModal.js File*

Next, we have a close icon in the modal in http://localhost:3000/, and on clicking it, an alert is shown.

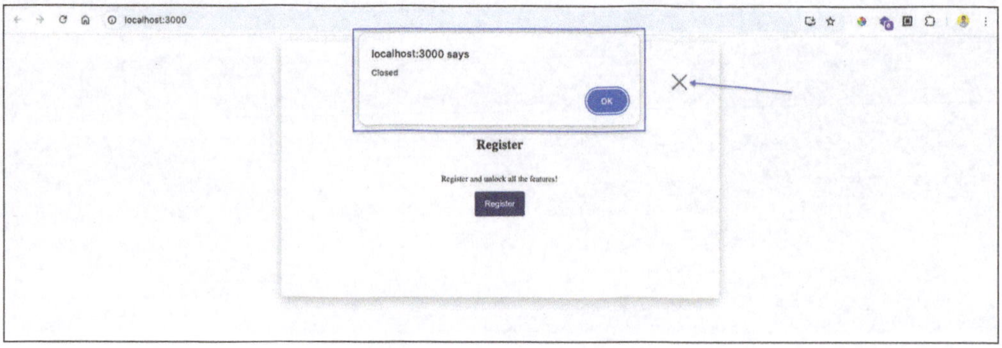

Figure 14.28: *CloseIcon in Localhost*

Now, we will add the logic to show the **`register.svg`** image. For this, back in the **`index.js`** file inside the **`assets`** folder, we will import the **`register.svg`** image, and also export it as Images.

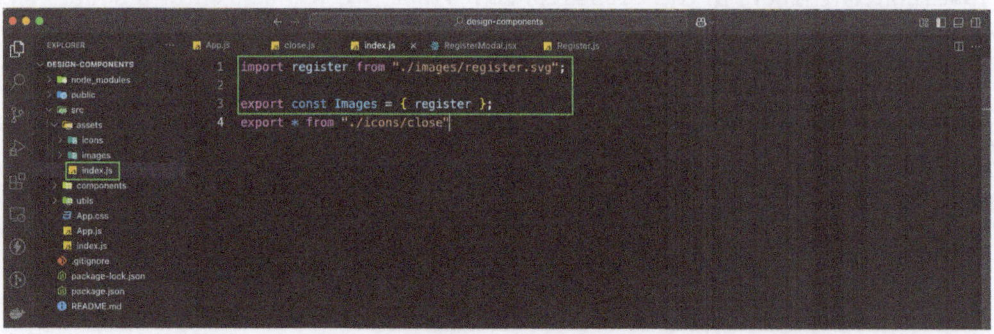

Figure 14.29: *Updating index.js of Assets*

Next, in the **`RegisterModal.jsx`** file, we will show an image with the **`img`** tag. Inside it, we will have a **`maxWidth`** style, and in **`src`**, we will use **`Images.register`** to use the **`register.svg`** image.

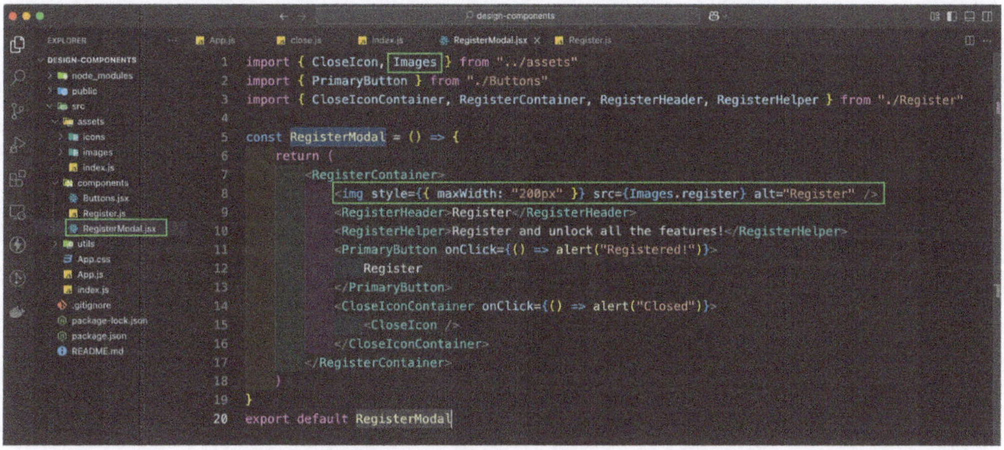

Figure 14.30: *Adding Image in RegisterModal.jsx File*

Next, in http://localhost:3000/, our modal is complete with the **`Register`** image shown.

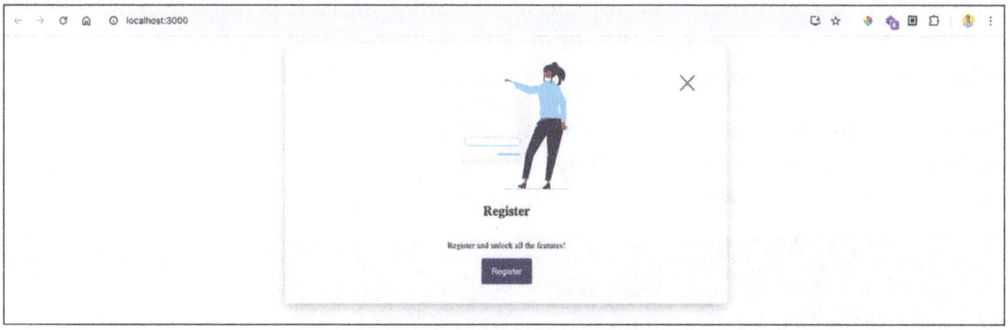

Figure 14.31: *Register Modal in localhost*

Style Compositions

So, in this session, we are going to learn about style composition. What does it mean exactly to compose a style, and how exactly, is it going to help us in building our component libraries?

If we want to talk about composition, it means that every component is composed of several smaller components or entities, in the case of ReactJS, or any other library, or framework that have something in common in terms of styles. It can be padding or background color, or aspect ratio.

All these things are repeating. They are common among components that we build. For instance, look at this very basic layout.

***Figure 14.32:** Basic Layout*

It is a hero page, which has a menu bar. This has two buttons at the top, and then we have a call to action section. Then, of course, a hero image in here. The very usual solution for building such a page is having a CSS class like the following figure.

Here, we have a **`container`** class for the whole thing, and a top, left, right and bottom sections. At first, this is actually working. But the thing is that by building such a CSS architecture, you are creating unique styles that are unique to the component.

Hence, for example, every time you want to build a top section in a different page, you have to rewrite such a unique style over and over. Also, this breaks the reusability principle, which is why ReactJS was made in the first place.

```
.container {
    /* Styles of hero container */
}

.top {
    /* Styles of top section */
}

.left {
    /* Styles of left section */
}

.right {
    /* Styles of right section */
}

.bottom {
    /* Styles of bottom section */
}
```

***Figure 14.33:** Basic Styles*

So, what is the alternative to this? Actually, this is the style composition that we are talking about in this course. It is about breaking the styles into smaller single purpose components.

For example, you create a component layer which vertically layers the children on top of each other, or you can also create an inline pattern component that is going to horizontally layer the children in row. Also, we have the split or cover that are just examples. Thus, this is what we mean by the style composition.

```
function Layers() {
    // Vertically layer children on top of each other
}

function Inline() {
    // Horizontally layer children in row
}

function Split() {
    // Split the width of the parent between two children
}

function Cover() {
    // Vertically center children
}
```

Figure 14.34: *Layer Styles*

Thus, by taking a bunch of such component patterns that we can build for specific CSS purposes, we will build the following `jsx` file. In fact, you need to simply wrap the elements, like menu items or buttons.

```
const HeroPage = () => {
    return (
        <Layers>
            <Inline>Top</Inline>
            <Split>
                <Cover>
                    <Layers>
                        <h1>Title</h1>
                        <p>Subtitle</p>
                        <Inline>
                            <button>Register</button>
                            <button>Login</button>
                        </Inline>
                    </Layers>
                </Cover>
                <img src="" alt="" />
            </Split>
        </Layers>
    )
}

export default HeroPage
```

Figure 14.35: *Using Layer Styles in the Component*

This is the hero page that we just talked about. The idea is that for every layout, for every component or page that we want to create, we have a bunch of elements. These elements share some common styles.

For instance, in the menu bar, all these elements are inline, that is they are in a single row. Also, here we have the layers, where we have the menu and the rest of the hero page. They are layers on top of each other. We can see the layers being used again for the left part, which is the '`Call to Action`' section.

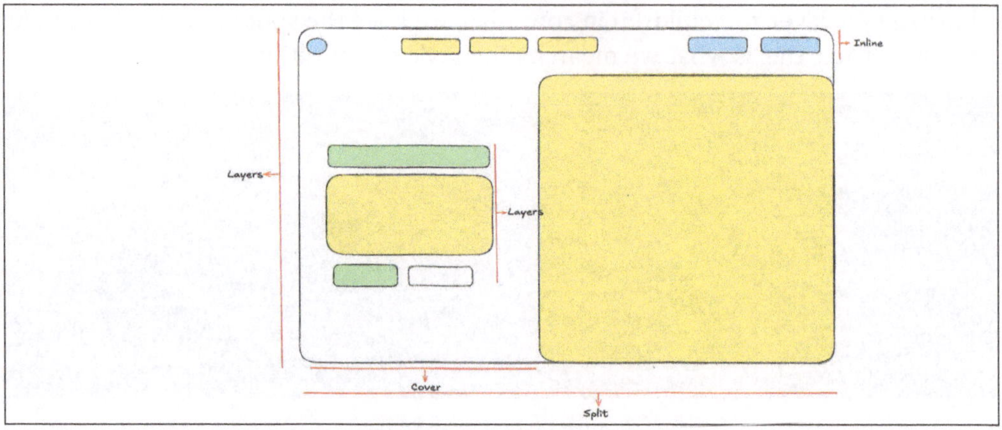

Figure 14.36: *Layer Styles Updated in the Figure*

So, this is what style composition is all about, that is making use of reusable components. And that is because most of the layouts that you build in your applications consist of these common styles. We are separating these styles into smaller styled components, and simply composing them to achieve the final layout that we desire.

Encapsulating Styles

In this section, we are going to see encapsulating styles, and learn how it is going to help us to build a more robust design system. We are going to see two main principles that you should keep in your mind.

We will first check the encapsulation concept, which means that if we have a piece of code, it can be a class or an object, and we want to restrict the access to some parts of it, and only expose them through a specific channel like a function.

Let us see a `Car` example in TypeScript. We have a public class of `Car`, and it has a private string variable called model. This string model is not accessible directly from outside the Car class.

You only need to create an instance of the `Car` class, and then in case you want to read the value of the model variable, you need to call the function `getModel()`. This applies a layer of safety and consistency.

```
class Car {
    private model: string;

    constructor(model: string) {
        this.model = model;
    }

    public getModel(): string {
        return this.model;
    }
}

const myCar = new Car("Tata Tiago");
console.log(myCar.getModel());
```

Figure 14.37: *Encapsulation*

Now, why do we need the encapsulated thing with the styles? The main issue that we face during styling our element and layouts, is the conflicts we get between different elements. We need to build our components in our patterns in a way that they only should care about their own styles.

They should not expose any styles that are going to affect the environment that they are going to be used in. So, the first principle is that components should not lay themselves out. The components should only set the CSS that are inside of it. So, properties such as position, size and margin, which affects the outer space of a component, should be decided by the parent component.

Also, as you know, the margin, size and the position are not considered part of the content. The properties which are considered belonging to the component is the border. So, remember the position, size and margin are not set by the component itself. The parent component is responsible for modifying them. And by this, we are going to guarantee that the component is going to be highly reusable.

The second principle, which is linked to the first one, is that each component should only style itself and its immediate children. You cannot style the deep children, or even grandchildren.

Conclusion

In this chapter, we have first created a React project, and added global styles using styled-components in it. After this, we have created the **Button** component in React from the Figma design in the previous chapter.

Next, we created the Modal in React, again from the Figma design in the previous chapter. After this, we learnt about the concept of Style Compositions and Encapsulating styles.

In the next chapter, we will **continue with the design system, and learn about patterns for spacing**. Here, we will learn about different spacing patterns such as Layers pattern, Split pattern, Column Pattern, and others.

Points to Remember

- Creating Global Styles with styled-components.
- Converting a Figma design of a button to `Button` component in React.
- Converting a Figma design of a modal to `Modal` component in React.
- Dividing the component to smaller components, using Style Compositions.
- Restricting access by Encapsulating Styles.

CHAPTER 15
Design System with Patterns for Spacing

Introduction

In this chapter, we will continue our Design Systems journey. We will learn about different patterns for spacing. These patterns include Layers pattern, Split pattern, Column pattern and many more.

Structure

In this chapter, we shall discuss the following topics:

- Overview
- Layers Pattern
- Split Pattern
- Column Pattern
- Grid Pattern
- Inline-Bundle Pattern

Overview

In this chapter, we are going to talk about the various patterns for spacing. We are going to create some pattern components that will help us apply different types of spacing strategies.

So, we are going to start building pattern components that are used for applying common styles. We will use these styles in our layouts and components, so that we can achieve more simplicity and reusability.

For the rest of the chapter, we are going to work with styled-components. We have worked with it earlier in the book.

Layers Pattern

In this part, we are going to talk about **Layers** pattern. '**Layers**' means stacking different elements on top of each other, with consistent spaces between them. It can be several paragraphs of text, or social media feeds.

These elements will be vertically stacked on top of each other with custom or uniform spaces between them. For this, we have created a new React project. The **App.js** is rendering a **SubscribeForm** component.

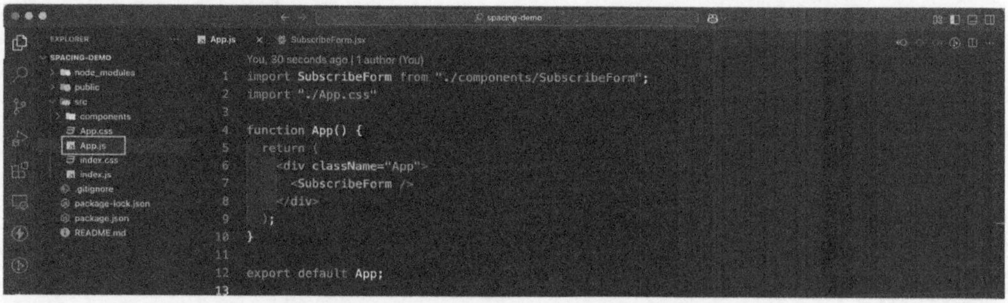

Figure 15.1: *App.js Rendering SubscribeForm*

We have created a **components** folder inside the **src** folder. Inside it, we have created a **SubscribeForm.jsx** file. This file has a basic form with several **divs**, separating each part.

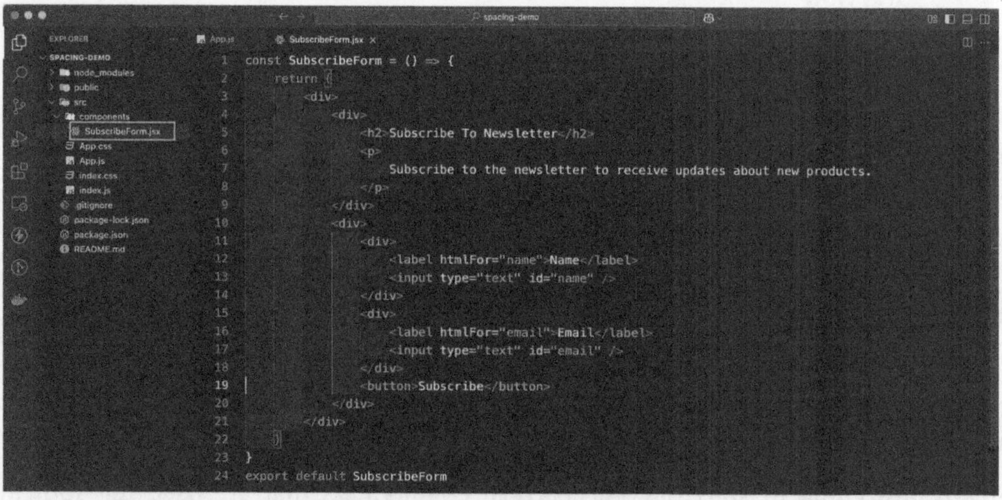

Figure 15.2: *SubscribeForm.jsx File*

Right now, the form looks like the following in http://localhost:3000/:

Figure 15.3: *Localhost Showing Subscribe Component*

Now, we will style the form with **`Layers`**. And for this, we have installed and imported **`styled-components`** first. Next, we created a style called **`Layers`** for **`div`**, in which we will have a display of grid.

Also, we have a gap which is equal to **`props.gutter`** or 1rem. This is a styled component feature in which if we pass an attribute of **`gutter`**, and then it will be taken or **`1rem`** will be taken.

Now, inside the **`return`** statement, we have changed two **`divs`** with **`Layers`**, and also passed the attribute of **`gutter`** with **`0.25rem`** as value.

Figure 15.4: *Adding Layers in SubscribeForm.jsx*

Now, in http://localhost:3000/, we can see that the form is better styled with Layers.

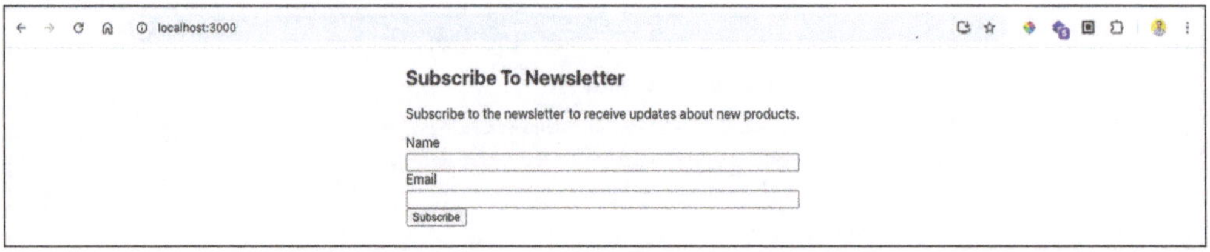

Figure 15.5: *Localhost Showing Layered Form*

Next, we will replicate all **divs** with Layers in the **SubscribeForm.jsx** file. Some have attribute gutter, and others do not. .

This is the power of Layers which can be used in different configurations.

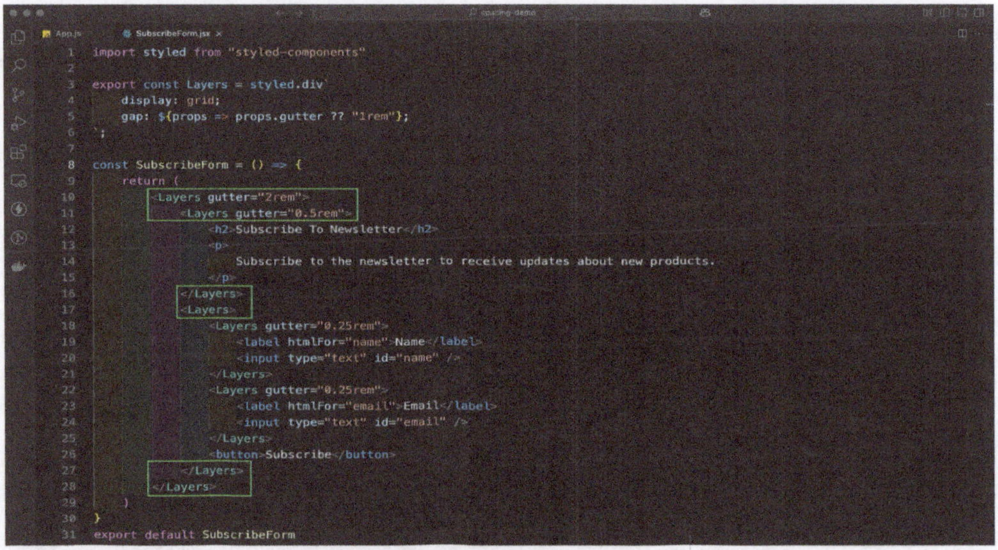

```
import styled from "styled-components"

export const Layers = styled.div`
    display: grid;
    gap: ${props => props.gutter ?? "1rem"};
`;

const SubscribeForm = () => {
    return (
        <Layers gutter="2rem">
            <Layers gutter="0.5rem">
                <h2>Subscribe To Newsletter</h2>
                <p>
                    Subscribe to the newsletter to receive updates about new products.
                </p>
            </Layers>
            <Layers>
                <Layers gutter="0.25rem">
                    <label htmlFor="name">Name</label>
                    <input type="text" id="name" />
                </Layers>
                <Layers gutter="0.25rem">
                    <label htmlFor="email">Email</label>
                    <input type="text" id="email" />
                </Layers>
                <button>Subscribe</button>
            </Layers>
        </Layers>
    )
}
export default SubscribeForm
```

Figure 15.6: *Adding More Layers*

Now, our form is completely styled in http://localhost:3000/.

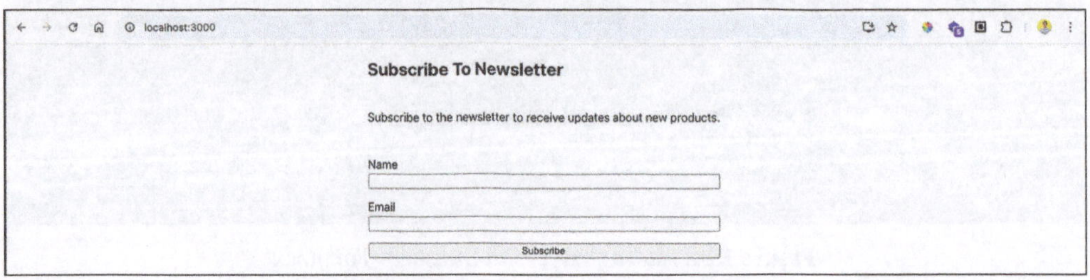

Figure 15.7: *Localhost with Better Layers*

Our style is complete, but we will make this even more efficient by having a consistent gutter value. For this, create a **common** folder inside the **src** folder, and inside it, create a **spaceSchema.js** file.

Here, we are exporting **spaceSchema,** which is an object. It contains the key as **xs**, **s**, **m**, and other similar sizing element names, and values contain size in rem.

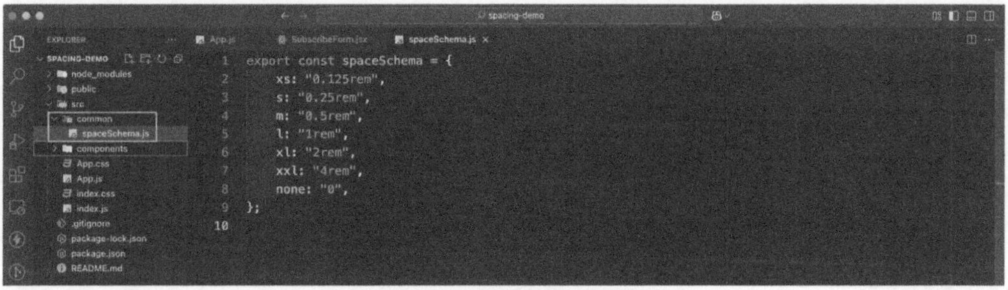

Figure 15.8: *spaceSchema.js File*

Back in the **SubscribeForm.jsx** file, we are first importing **spaceSchema**. After this in the gap, we have changed the code to take **props.gutter**, and make it equal to the value from the **spaceSchema** file. If it is not provided, then take the **large(l)** value.

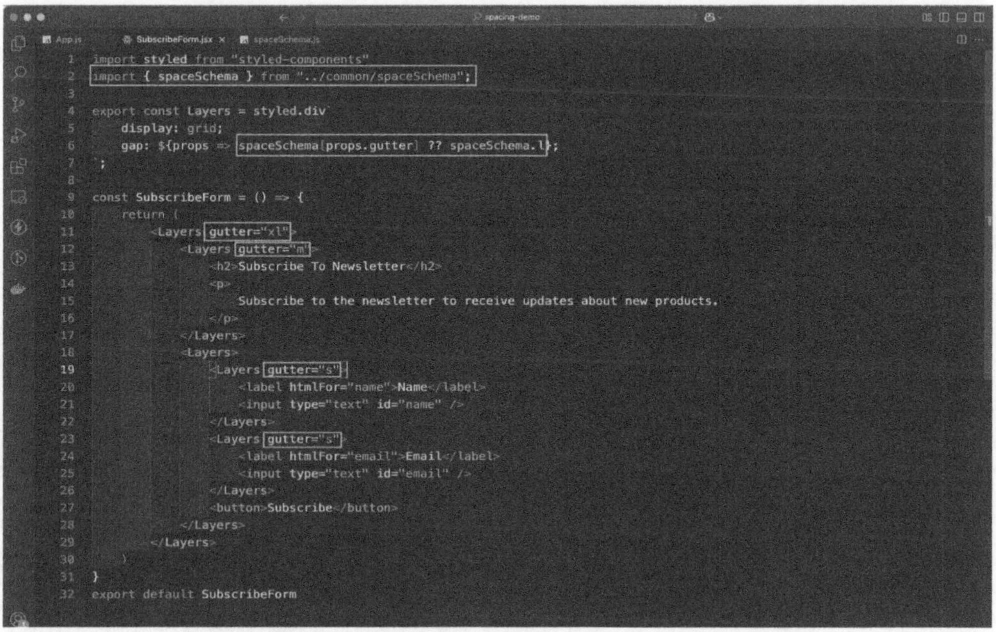

Figure 15.9: *Using spaceSchema in SubscribeForm.jsx File*

Our layout is still the same in http://localhost:3000/.

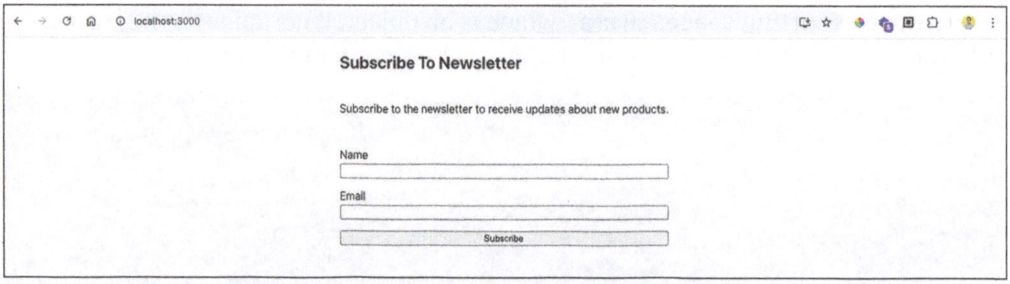

Figure 15.10: *Localhost Showing Layered Components*

Split Pattern

In this part, we are going to talk about **`split`** pattern. **`Split`** pattern basically divides the screen. This pattern allows splitting the screen into left side and right side, with customizable space in-between.

Here, we are going to style a different form. For this, first create a **`Form.jsx`** inside the **`components`** folder. Here, we are using Layers from the earlier part to create a form with different fields.

We are also wrapping everything in **`InputGroup`**, and the code for it will be shown next.

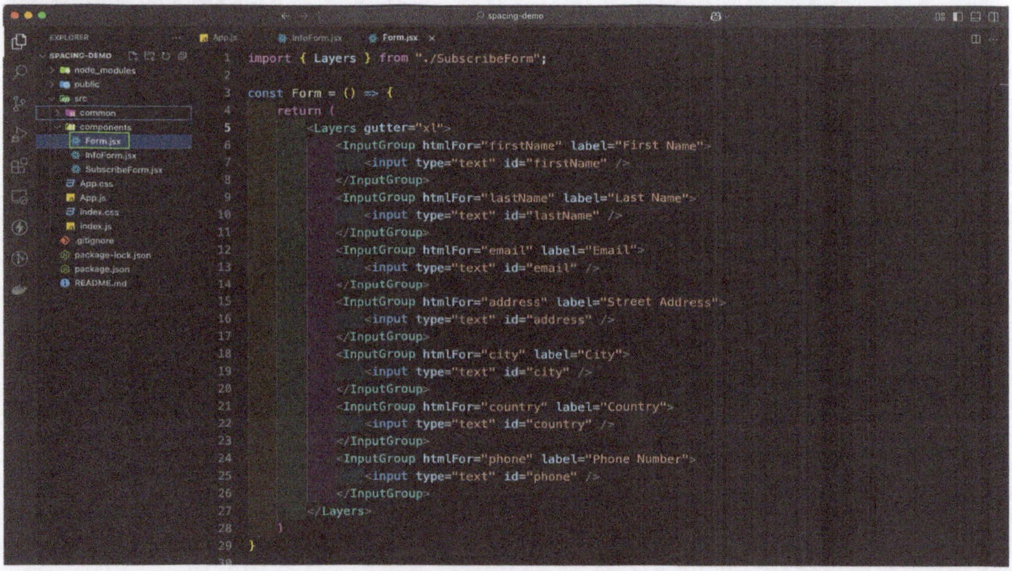

Figure 15.11: *Form.jsx File*

The code for **`InputGroup`** again consists of **`Layers`** with medium gap. Also, it consists of a label element with html Form, the content of the label taken from props.

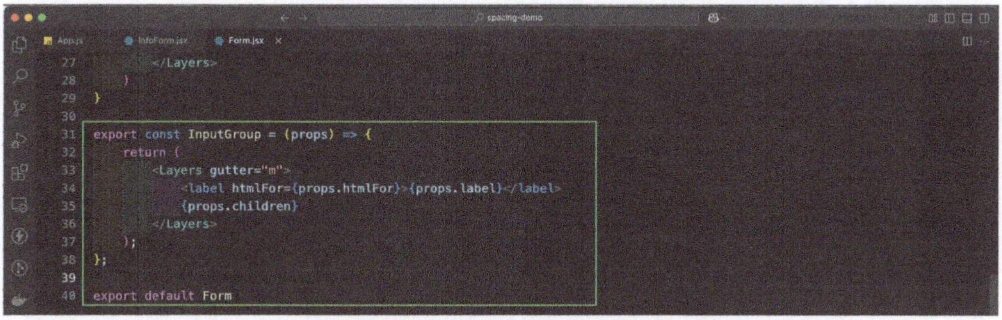

Figure 15.12: *Return in Form.jsx File*

Now, create a file, **InfoForm.jsx** inside the **components** folder. This file has a main **div** which wraps a **div** and **Form** component. The **div** component contains text in **h3** and **span**.

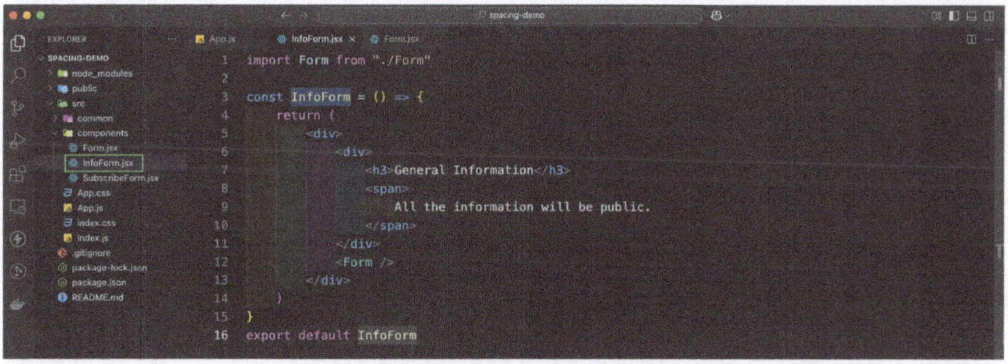

Figure 15.13: *Initial InfoForm.jsx File*

Back in the **App.js** file, we will call the **InfoForm** component.

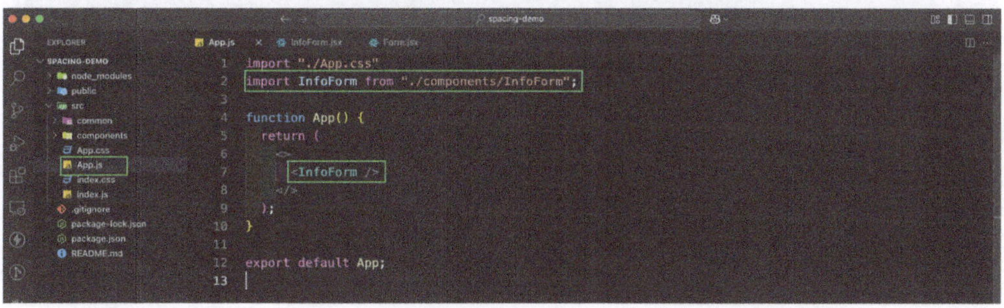

Figure 15.14: *App.js Rendering InfoForm*

Now, in http://localhost:3000/, we will see everything one after the other. Our main target is to split the first **div** from **InfoForm** on the left side, and the **Form** component on the right side.

Figure 15.15: *Localhost Showing InfoForm*

Back in the **InfoForm.jsx** file, we will first import the **spaceSchema**, and then the styled components. After this, we are writing a code for div, and naming it as **Split**. This will again be a grid, and the gap will be taken from **spaceSchema**.

Next, it has **grid-template-columns** as **1fr 1fr**. It means that the two elements in the grid will be divided into equal columns. We also have some padding of 20px.

Now, the main **div** has been changed with the **Split**, and also passing a gutter of **xl**.

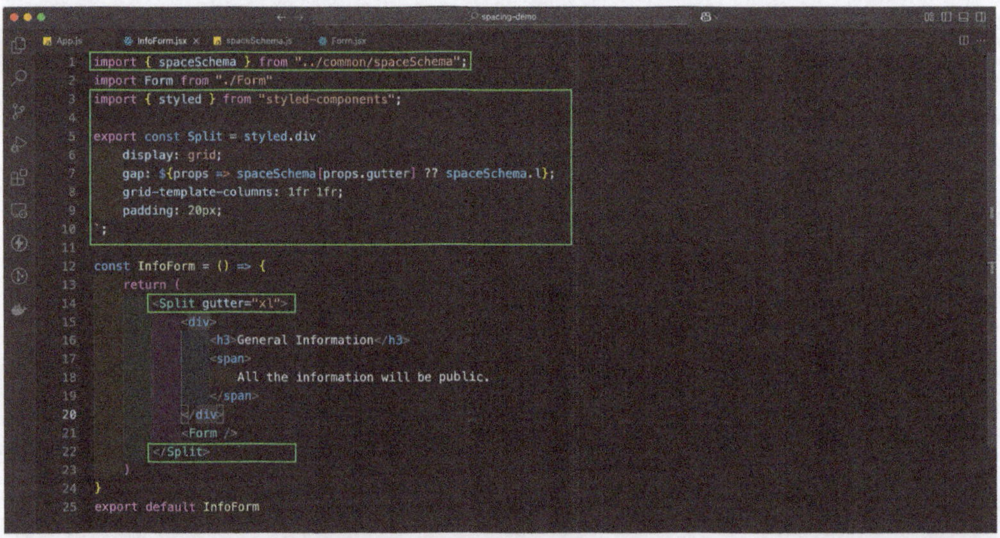

Figure 15.16: *Split in InfoForm.jsx*

Now, in http://localhost:3000/, the two parts are divided into equal ratios.

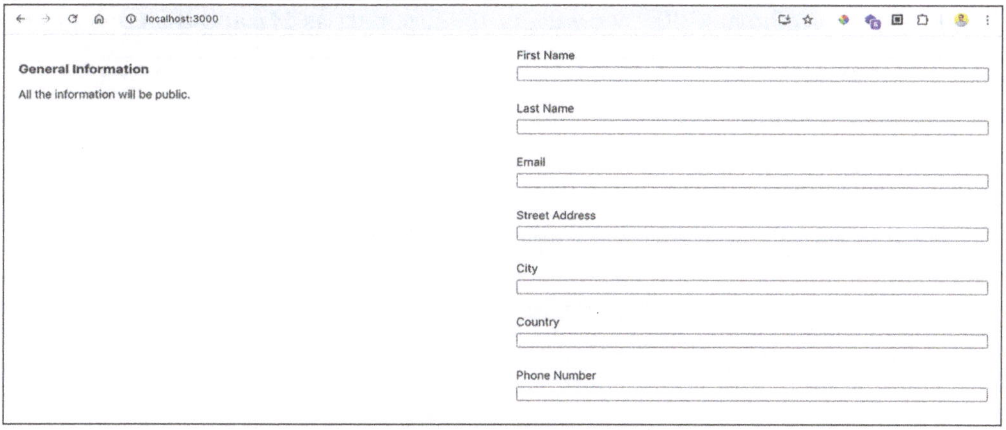

Figure 15.17: *Localhost Showing Splitted Components*

Our code is done, but we are going to make it more reusable. Here, we have created a fractions object. Inside it, we have different keys like ¼, ⅓, and ½ which give different **fr** values.

Now, in the **Split** code, we are removing the hard-coded **1fr 1fr** with a props of fraction. Depending upon it, the **fr** value will be taken. If we do not pass the fraction props, we will get the default key of ½ which will give the **fr** of **1fr 1fr**.

Inside the **return** statement, we are passing the fraction **props** as ½ and **gutter** props as **xl**.

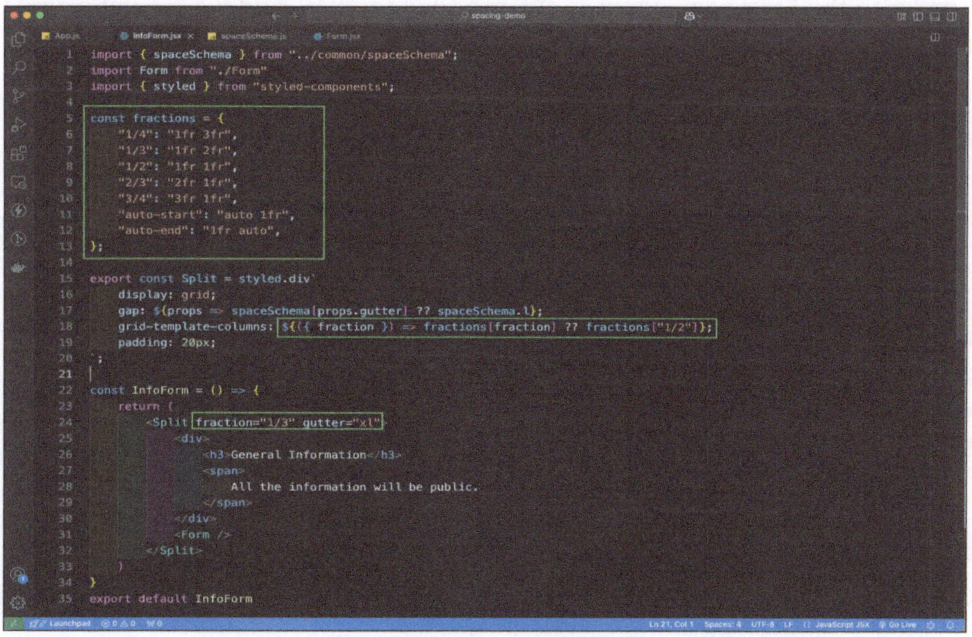

Figure 15.18: *Adding Fraction in InfoForm.jsx*

Now, in http://localhost:3000/, we will get the first part as **1fr** and the **Form** as **2fr**.

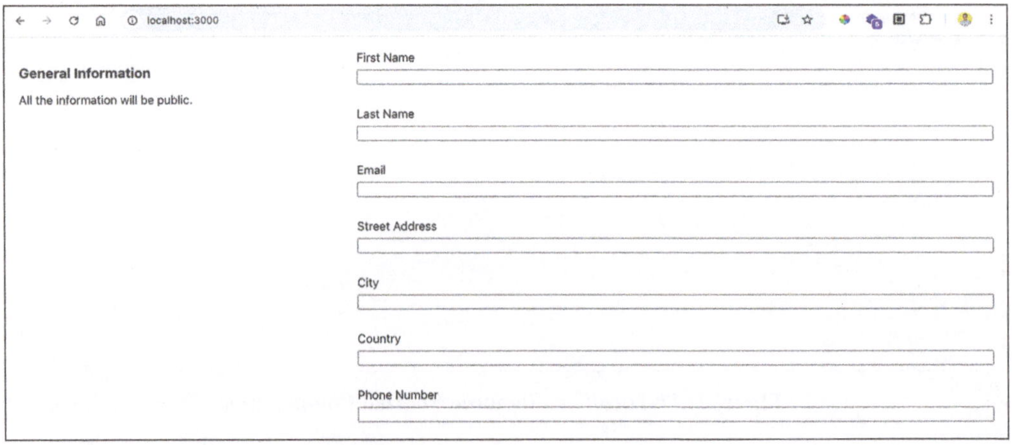

Figure 15.19: *Localhost with Fraction*

Column Pattern

In this part, we are going to talk about **column** pattern. When you wrap a group of elements inside this pattern, it is going to allow you to sort them in several columns.

So, we are going to work with the previous component, from the previous section. First, create a new component called **FormCols.jsx** inside the **components** folder. This is similar to the **Form** component in the previous section, and we are importing the **InputGroup** from it.

Figure 15.20: *FormCols.jsx File*

Next, create a new file **`InfoFormCols.jsx`** inside the **`components`** folder. It is similar to the **`InfoForm`** component, and we are also importing **`Split`** from it.

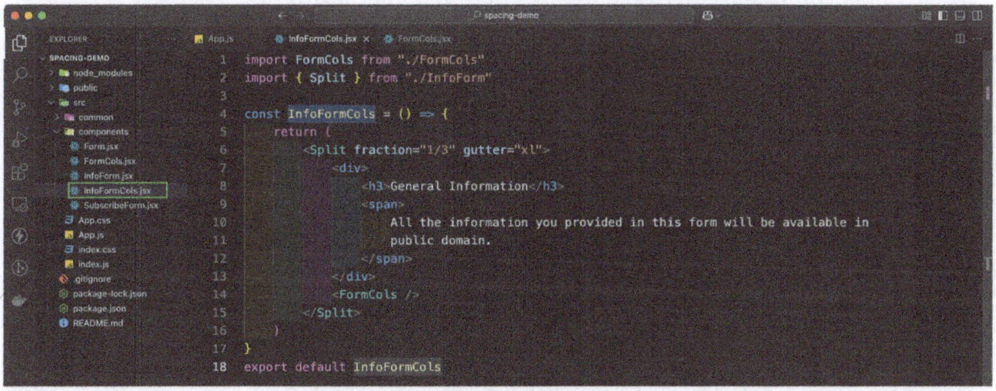

Figure 15.21: *InfoFormCols.jsx File*

Now, import the **`InfoFormCols`** component from **`App.js`**, and render it.

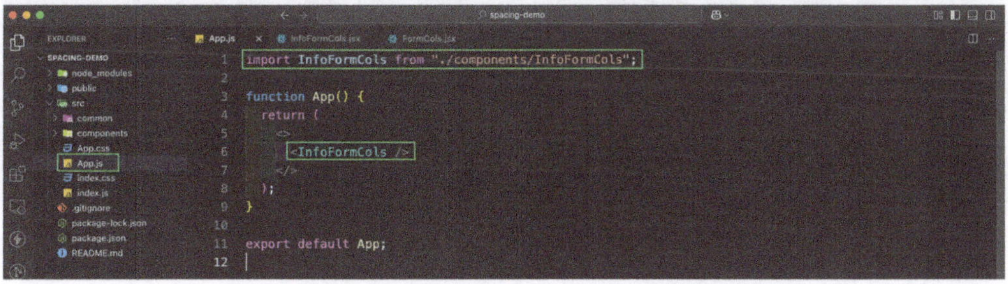

Figure 15.22: *Rendering InfoFormCols from App.js File*

Now, in http://localhost:3000/, the form is similar to the previous section.

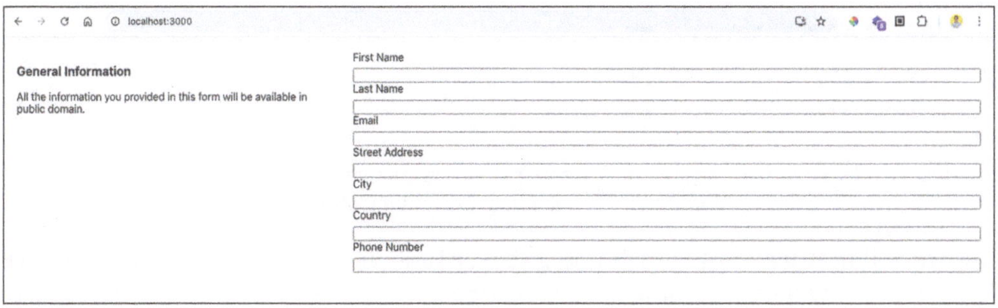

Figure 15.23: *Localhost Showing InfoFormCols*

Back in the **`FormCols.jsx`** file, we will first import the **`styled-components`**. After this, we have imported **`spaceSchema`**, as we are going to use the gutter. Then, we have created a new styled component called Columns.

It has a display of **grid** and **gap**, as in the previous section, but has one more thing of **grid-template-columns** of **repeat(2, 1fr)**, which means **1fr 1fr**. Next, we have wrapped everything with **Columns** inside the **return** statement.

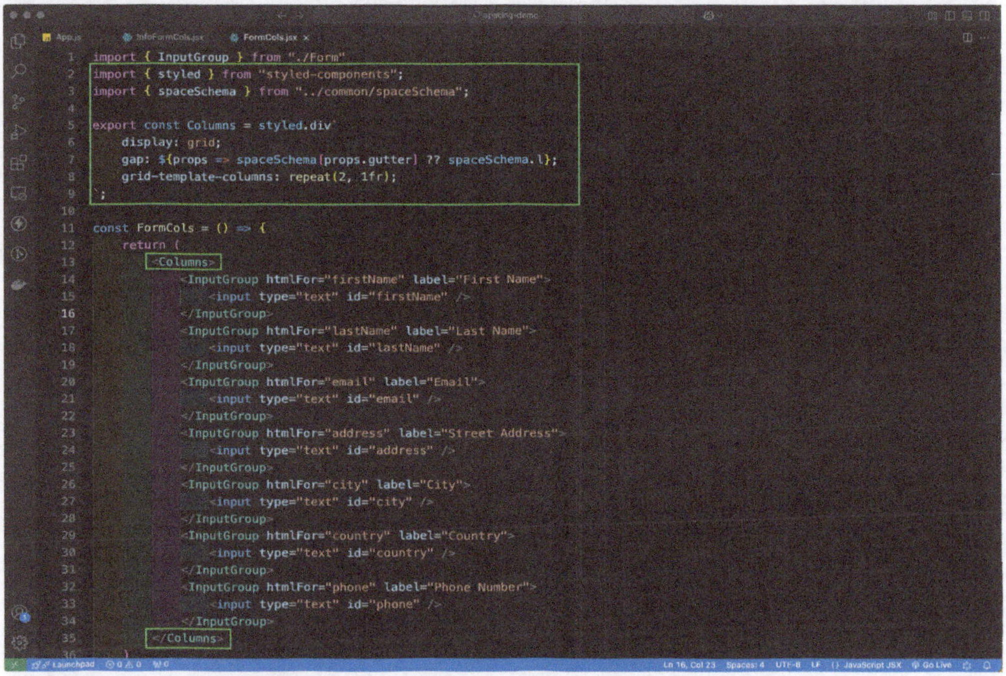

Figure 15.24: *Adding Columns in FormCols.jsx File*

Now, in http://localhost:3000/ we will see two columns.

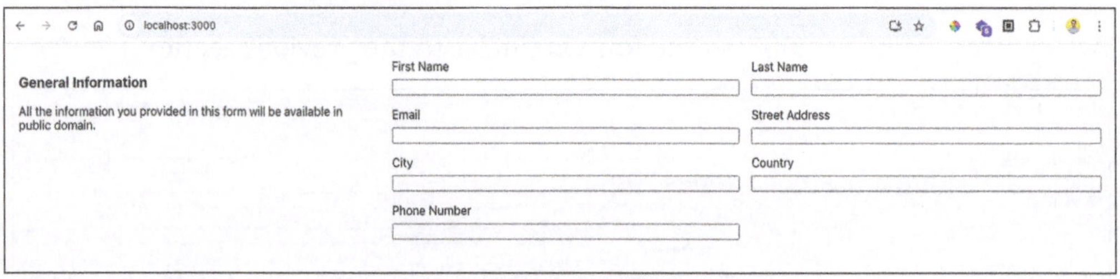

Figure 15.25: *Localhost Showing Columns*

Now, we will first make the **grid-template-column** inside the **Columns** as **repeat(6, 1fr)**. Next, we will make a new **styled-component** of the **Column** which has a **grid-column** with span 3.

Lastly, we have wrapped all the **InputGroup** with the **Column**.

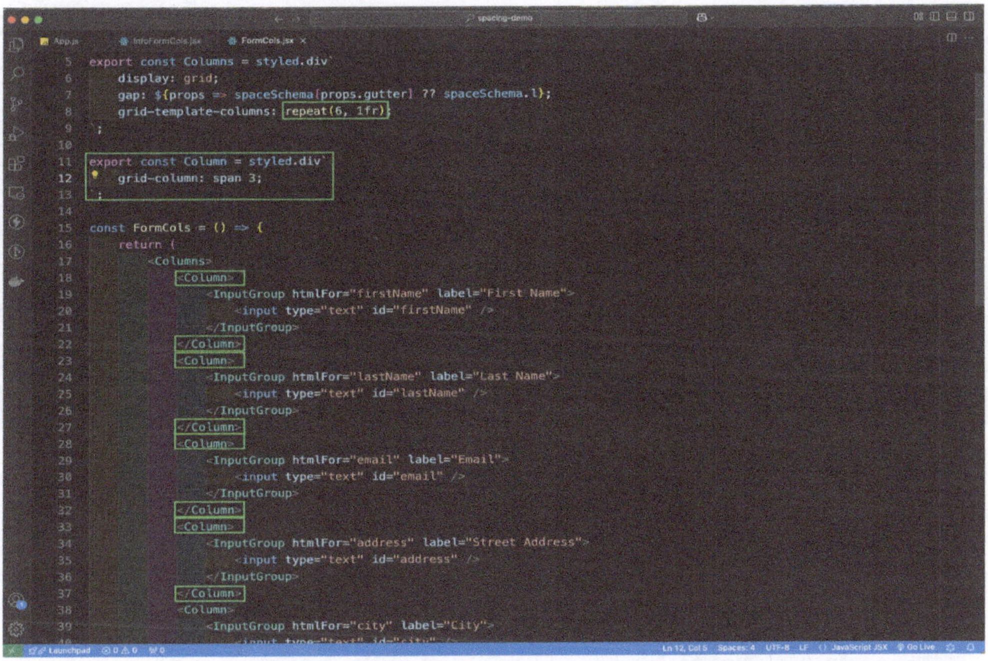

Figure 15.26: *Adding Column in FormCols.jsx File*

Back in http://localhost:3000/, we will see a similar layout because with columns of **`1fr 1fr 1fr 1fr 1fr 1fr`** and span of 3, it means each column will be of 2 parts.

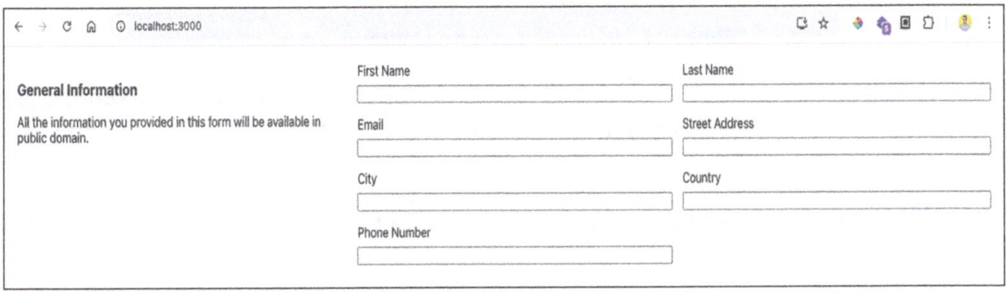

Figure 15.27: *Localhost Showing Columns*

We have everything hard-coded, and now, we will make it generic. So, first in the Columns styled component, we will change the **`grid-template-columns`**. We will also make the repeat get columns props, with a default value of 1.

Now, in the **`Columns`**, we will pass a column props with a value of 6.

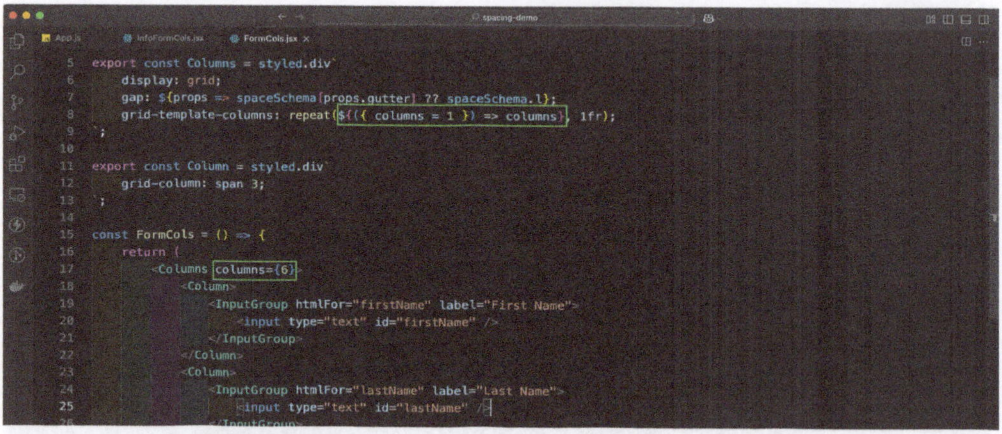

Figure 15.28: *Adding Columns Props in FormCols.jsx File*

Back in http://localhost:3000/, we will get the same UI.

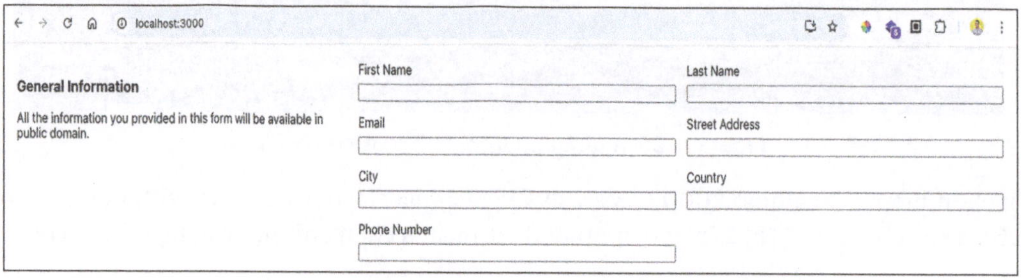

Figure 15.29: *Localhost with Columns Props*

Next, we will also remove the hard-coded span 3 from the **`Column styled-component`**. Here instead of 3, we are passing props of **`spanSize`** which again have a default value of 1.

Inside the **`return`** statement, we are passing **`spanSize`** props in all **`Columns`**, but they are of different sizes.

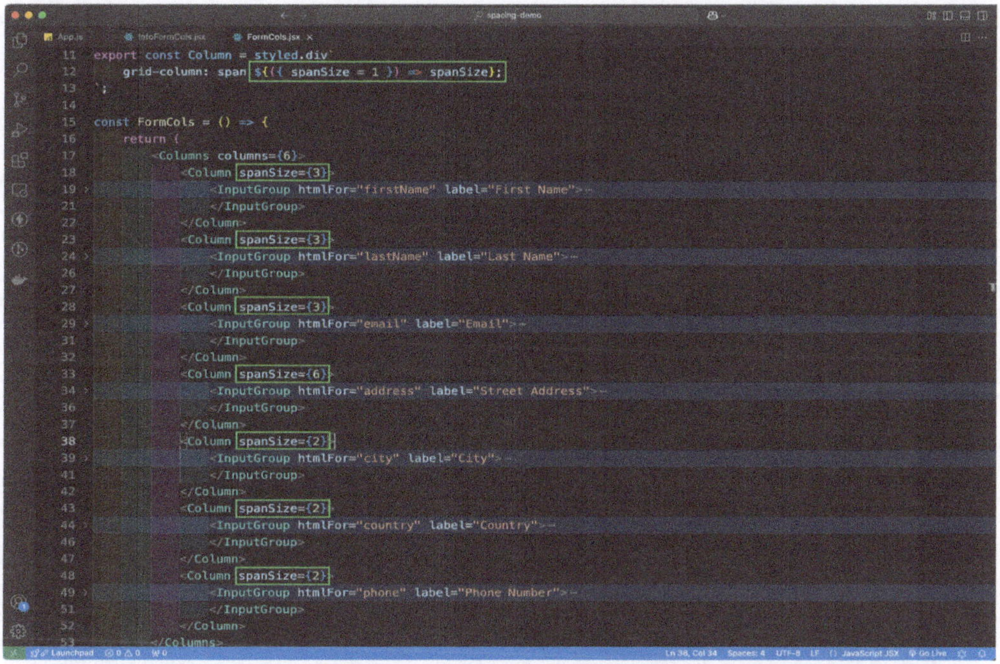

Figure 15.30: *Adding spanSize in FormCols.jsx File*

Now, in http://localhost:3000/, we will see columns of different sizes.

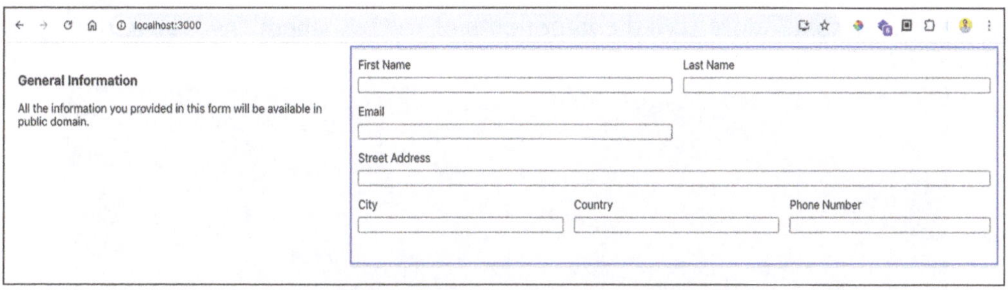

Figure 15.31: *Localhost with spanSize*

Grid Pattern

In this part, we are going to learn about **grid** pattern. This pattern will allow building grid lists with customizable spaces between items. In this part, we are also going to create a beautiful contact list.

In this part, we are going to use a **Card** component. The way we will create this card component is not the main thing of this part, but how we still use it, using the grid is important. For this, first create a **Card.jsx** file inside the components folder.

Here, we have imported some required elements, and after this, we have styled the components of **`InlineBundle`** and **`Pad`**.

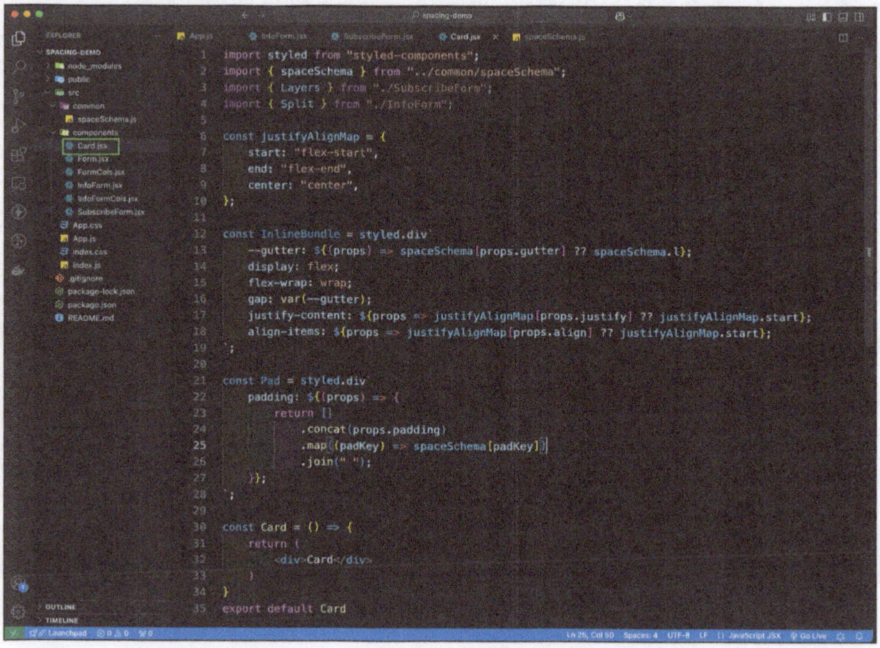

Figure 15.32: *Card.jsx File with Styled-components*

Next, we have some more styled components of **`MediaWrapper`**, **`Avatar`** and **`Wrapper`** in the **`Card.jsx`** file.

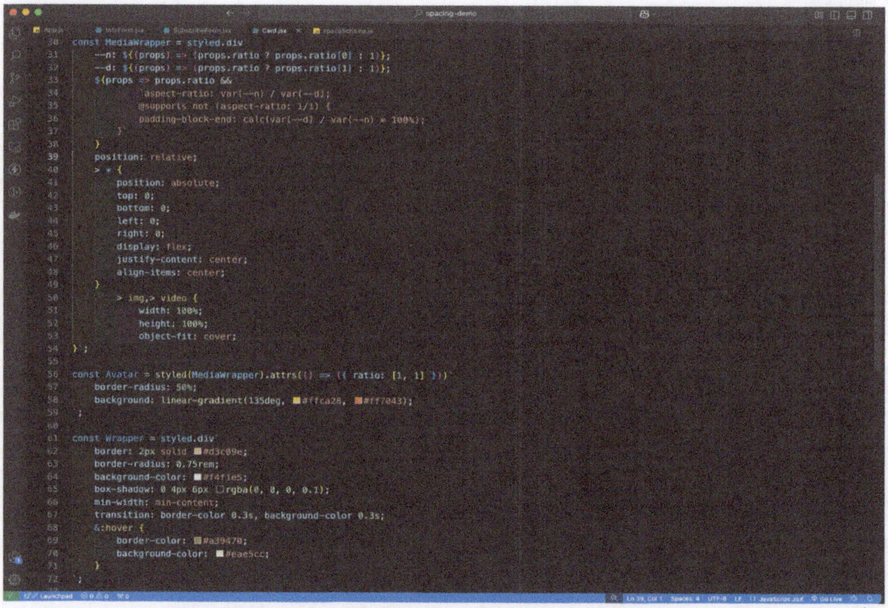

Figure 15.33: *Card.jsx File with More Styled-components*

Next, we added more styled components of **`ButtonsContainer`**, **`CurvedSpan`**, **`DetailsContainer`**, and **`CallMessageButton`** in the **`Card.jsx`** file.

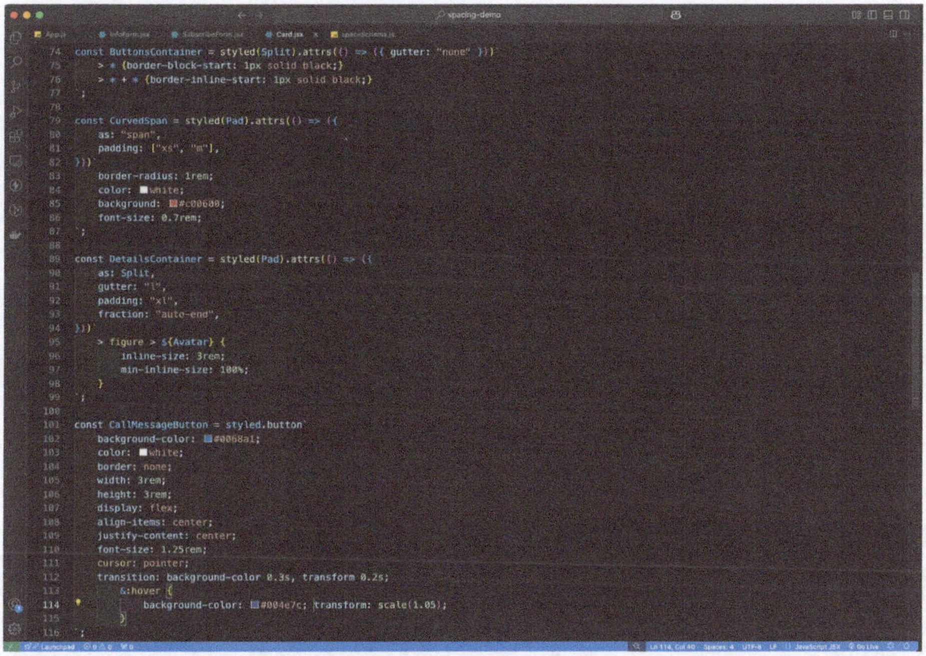

Figure 15.34: *Card.jsx File with More Styled-components*

Now, inside the return statement of the **`Card`** component, we are using all of these styled components to create a rectangle.

Figure 15.35: *Return Statement of Card.jsx File*

Now, create a **`Cards.jsx`** file, and render **`Card`** components from it for more than 5 times.

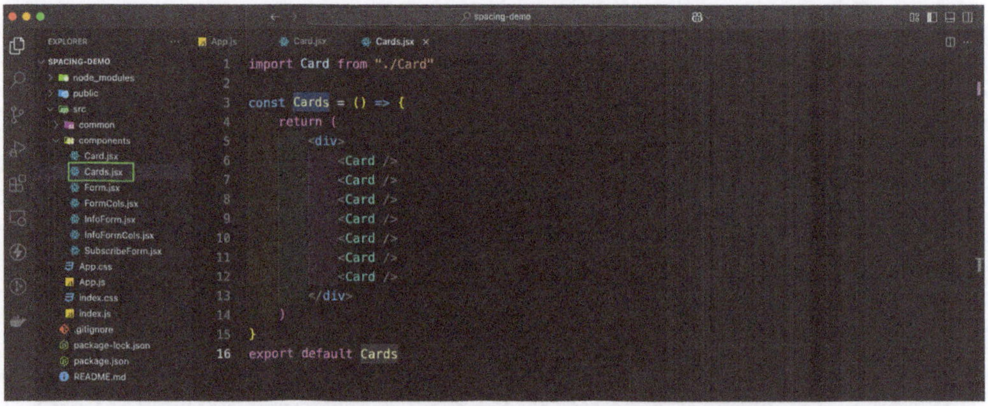

Figure 15.36: *Cards.jsx File Rendering Card Components*

Now, in the **`App.js`** file, we will render the **`Cards`** component.

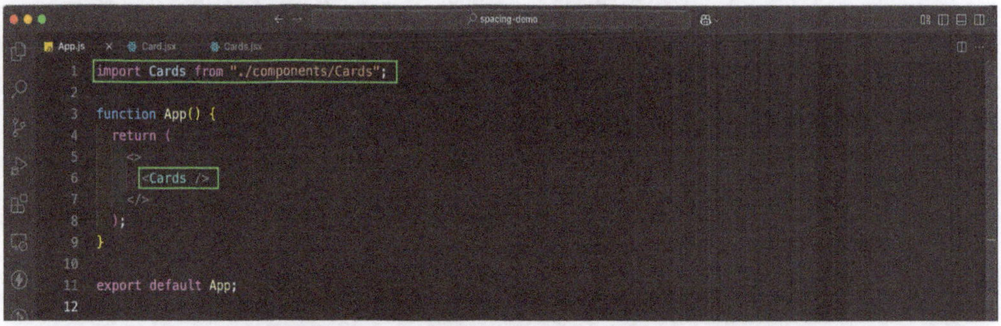

Figure 15.37: *App.js File Rendering Card Components*

Now, in http://localhost:3000/, we will see all the **`Card`** components shown, one after the other.

Figure 15.38: *Localhost Initial Desktop View*

In the **`Mobile`** view also, they are shown one after the other.

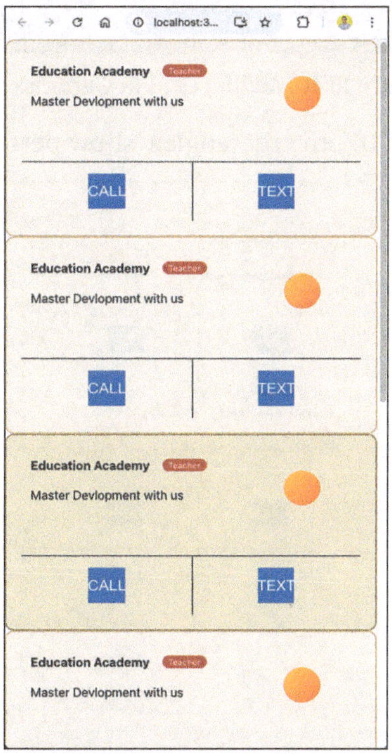

Figure 15.39: *Localhost Initial Mobile View*

Now, back in **`Cards.jsx`** file, we will first import **`styled-components`** and **`spaceSchema`**. After this, we have created a styled component called **`Grid`**. It has a display of a grid, and the gap taken from **`spaceSchema`**, as earlier.

In the **`grid-template-columns`**, we are using **`repeat`**, but with **`auto-fit`**. We are also using **`minmax`** which is **`24rem`** or **`1fr`**, whichever fits. After this, we have replaced the **`div`** with **`Grid`**, inside the **`return`** statement.

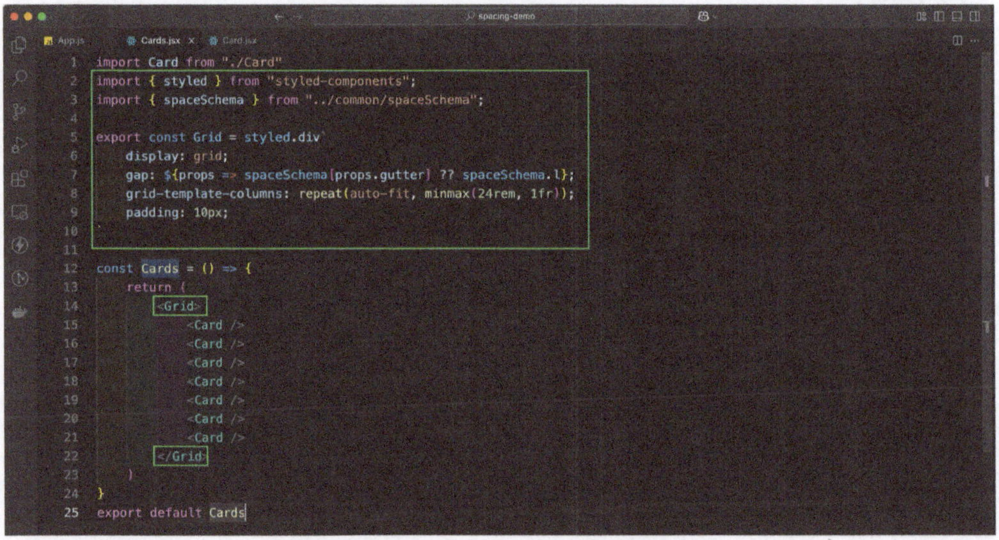

Figure 15.40: *Adding Grid in Cards.jsx File*

Back in http://localhost:3000/, the rectangles show perfectly in the desktop view.

Figure 15.41: *Localhost Desktop View with Grid*

Also, it shows perfectly in the mobile view.

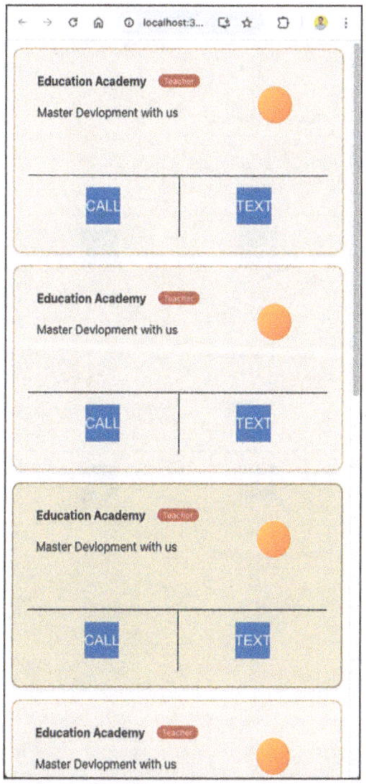

Figure 15.42: *Localhost Mobile View with Grid*

Now, we will remove the hard-coded data in the **`Cards.jsx`** file. Here, in the minmax, we are passing a props of **`minWidth`**, and if it is not passed, then take **`310px`**. Inside the **`return`** in **`Grid`**, we are passing the props of **`minWidth`** and **`gutter`**.

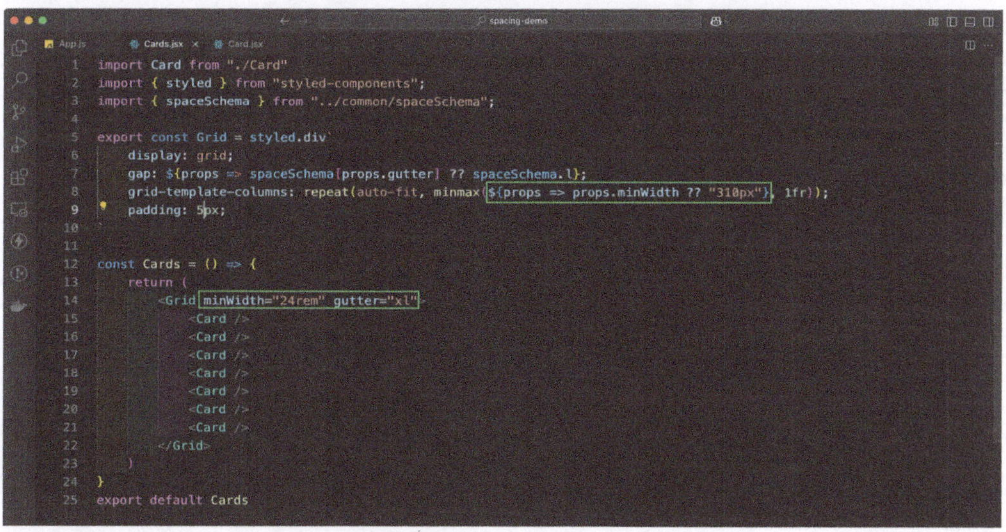

Figure 15.43: *Minmax in Grid of Cards.jsx File*

Now, in http://localhost:3000/ the desktop view is as earlier. Also, check the mobile view which is also as earlier.

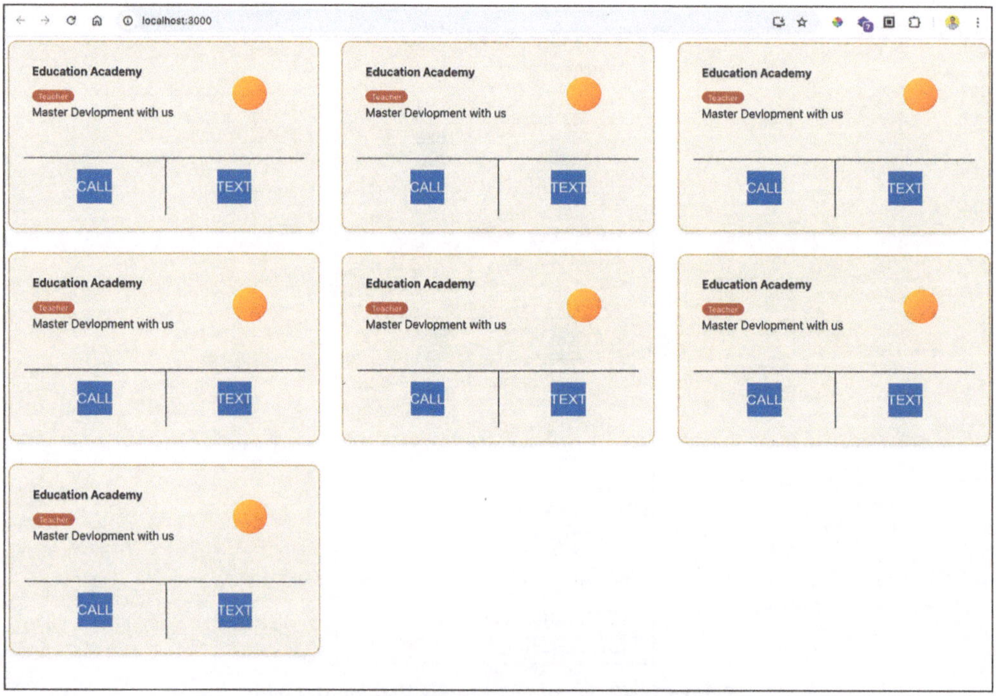

Figure 15.44: *Final Desktop View*

Inline Bundle Pattern

In this part, we are going to learn about the **`Inline Bundle`** pattern. This pattern will allow restoring inline elements in several lines similar to resizing of a text. For this, we will create a **`helper`** component of **`MenuBasis.jsx`** inside the **`components`** folder.

Here, we have some styled components of **`Pad`**, **`Logo`**, **`MenuWrapper`**, **`Menu`**, and **`MenuItems`**.

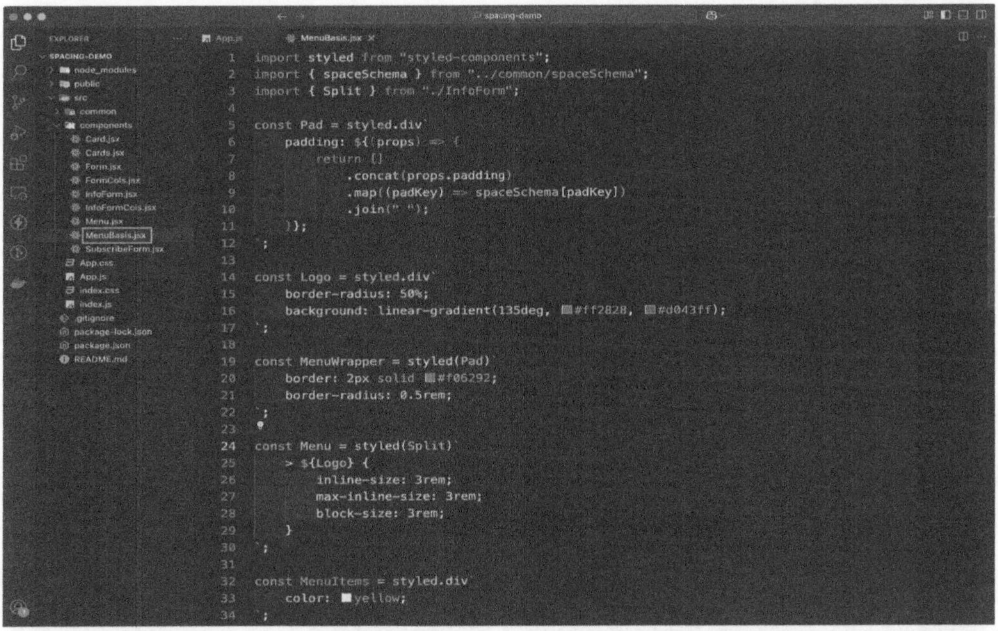

Figure 15.45: *MenuBasis.jsx File*

Now, inside the **return** statement, we are using the various styled components. Also, we are getting props for children, which we are using.

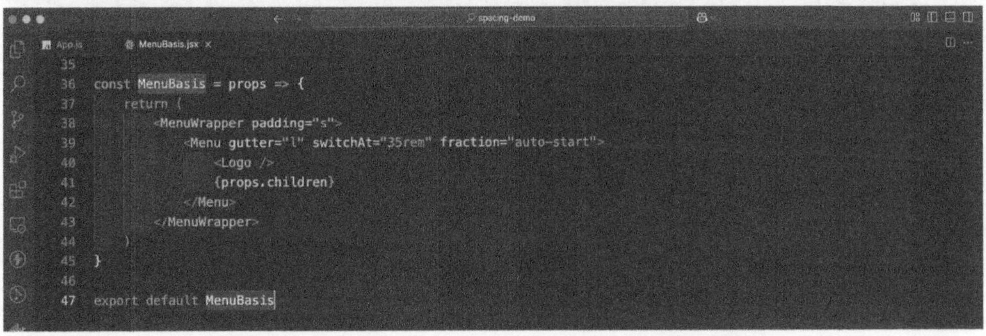

Figure 15.46: *Return Statement of MenuBasis.jsx File*

Now, create a **Menu.jsx** file inside the **components** folder. Here, we are using the **MenuBasis** component to wrap everything. Inside it, we have a **div** with 5 spans showing five elements.

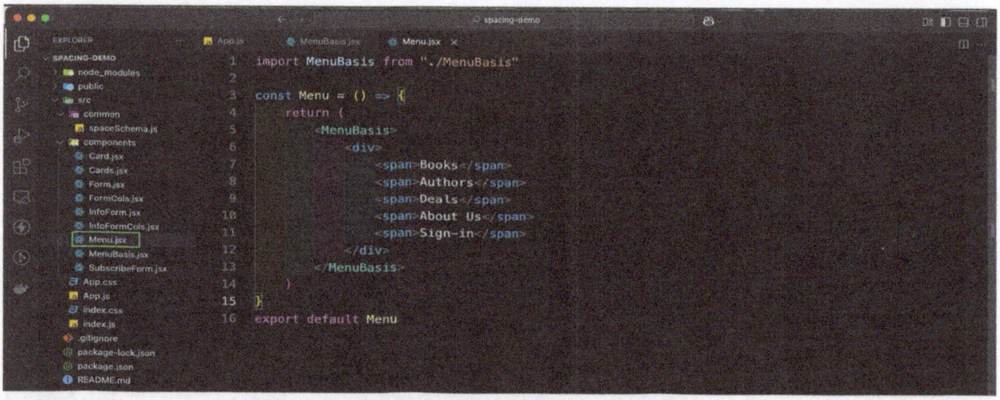

Figure 15.47: *Initial Menu.jsx File*

Now, we are rendering the **`Menu`** component from the **`App.js`** file.

Figure 15.48: *App.js Rendering Menu Component*

In http://localhost:3000/, we will see all the elements not styled properly.

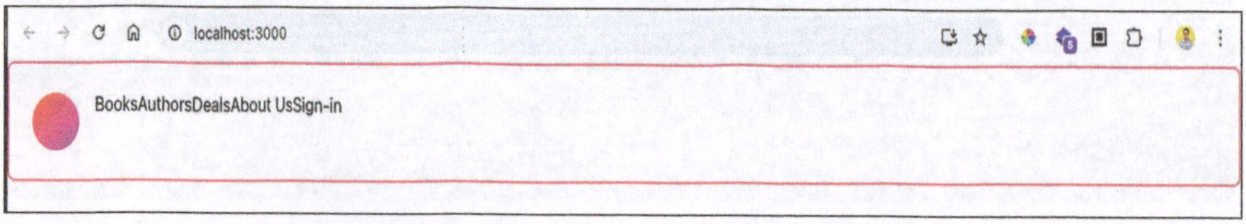

Figure 15.49: *Localhost Showing Initial Menu Component*

Back in the **`Menu.jsx`** file, we are first importing **`spaceSchema`** and styled-components. After this, we create a styled component called **`InlineBundle`** which has a display of **flex** and **flex-wrap** as wrap.

It also has a gap of **`1rem`** which will give some gap between the elements. Then **`justify-content`** as **flex-end** which will move all elements to end in x-axis. Next, we have **`align-items`** as center, which will move all elements to the center in the y-axis.

Inside the **`return`** statement, we have replaced the **`div`** with the **`InlineBundle`** styled component.

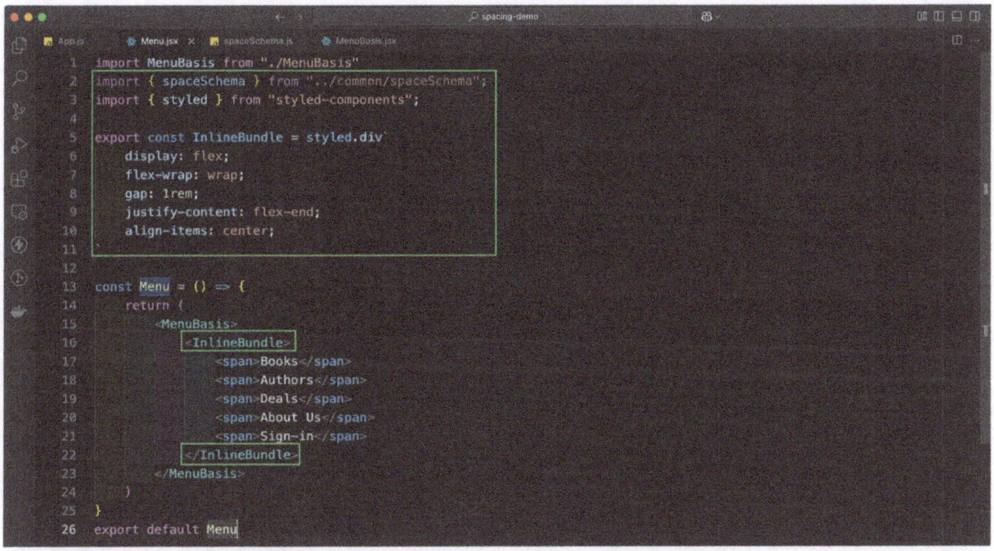

***Figure 15.50:** Adding InlineBundle in Menu Component*

The mobile view in http://localhost:3000/ is perfect now.

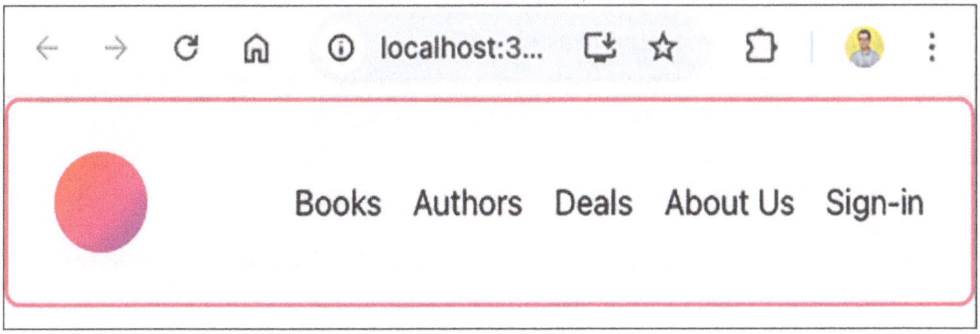

***Figure 15.51:** Mobile View of Menu Component*

Again, we will replace the hard-coded values to props value. So, in the **`Menu.jsx`** file, we will have a CSS variable of gutter which will get the props, and use the **`spaceSchema`**. The gap will use the CSS variable of the gutter.

The **`justify-content`** and **`align-items`** will get props. Then, we will use a **`justifyAlignWay`** function, which through the props of justify or align will get a value of start, end or center. These values will be converted to **`flex-start`**, **`flex-end`** or **`center`**.

If no value is provided, we will take the **`flex-start`** as default. Lastly, from the **`InlineBundle,`** we will pass the props of the **`gutter`**, justify and align with values of 1, and end with the center, respectively.

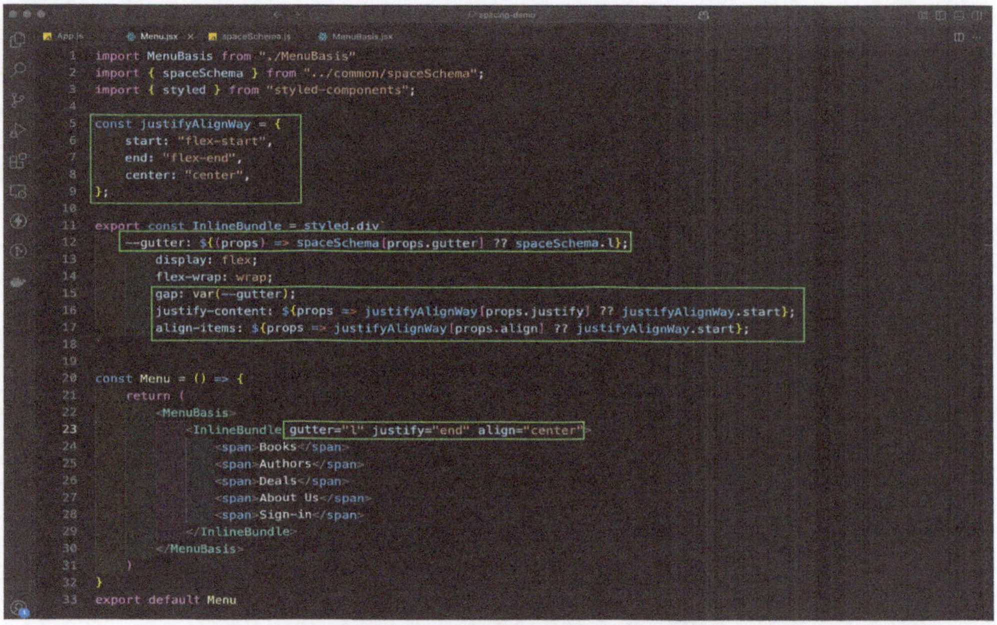

Figure 15.52: *Adding Props in InlineBundle*

The mobile view is still perfect, and as earlier.

Figure 15.53: *Final Mobile View*

The desktop view is also perfect.

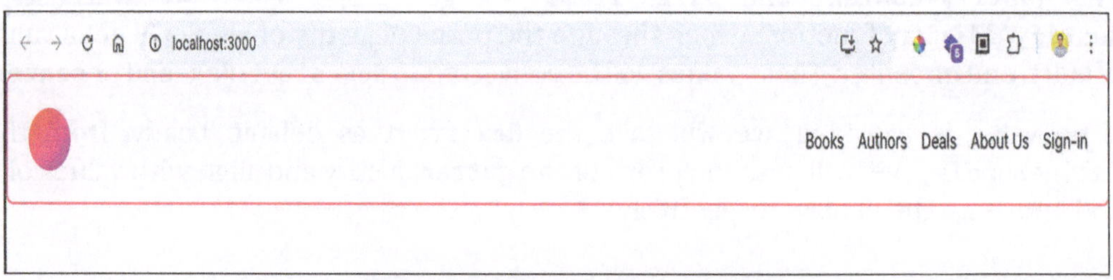

Figure 15.54: *Final Desktop View*

Conclusion

In this chapter, we have learnt about different patterns for spacing. We have first learnt about Layers pattern which is used to stack different elements on top of each other. Then, we learnt about the Split pattern that allows splitting the screen into left and right sides.

After this, we learnt about column patterns which allow us to sort several columns. Next, we learnt about Grid pattern that allows us to build grid lists. Lastly, we learnt about the Inline Bundle pattern which allows restoring inline elements in several lines.

In the next chapter, **we will continue with the design system, and learn about complex styles**. Here, we will learn about patterns like Pad pattern, Center pattern and others.

Points to Remember

- The meaning for spacing.
- Layers Pattern used to stack different elements on top of each other.
- Split Pattern to divide the screen.
- Column Pattern to sort elements in columns.
- Grid Pattern to build grid lists with customisable spaces between items.
- Inline Bundle Pattern to allow restoring inline elements in several lines.

CHAPTER 16

Design System with Patterns for Complex Styles

Introduction

In this chapter, we will continue our Design systems journey. We will learn about complex design patterns. These patterns include Pad pattern, Center pattern, Cover pattern and much more.

Structure

In this chapter, we are going to discuss the following topics:

- Overview
- Pad Pattern
- Center Pattern
- Media-Wrapper Pattern
- Cover Pattern

Overview

In this chapter, we are going to check the wrapper component patterns. We are going to have some components that are going to be used as wrappers. They wrap other elements and components, so that we can produce the desired layout we want.

In the previous chapter, we focused on spacing, but we need some more low-level styles. In the previous chapter, we explored a concept called nested components pattern.

It can be seen in the following code, in which we needed to nest the patterns in the **Menu** component.

```
const Menu = () => {
    return (
        <MenuBasis>
            <InlineBundle gutter="l" justify="end" align="center">
                <span>Books</span>
                <span>Authors</span>
                <span>Deals</span>
                <span>About Us</span>
                <span>Sign-in</span>
            </InlineBundle>
        </MenuBasis>
    )
}
export default Menu
```

Figure 16.1: *Nested Component Pattern*

However, sometimes layout components need to be on the same level so that it can give us the desired styles, we want. In this case, having a pattern component at the same level, it is advised to use the as prop pattern. It is also known as **polymorphic react**.

```
const Menu = () => {
    return (
        <MenuBasis as={InlineBundle}>
                <span>Books</span>
                <span>Authors</span>
                <span>Deals</span>
                <span>About Us</span>
                <span>Sign-in</span>
        </MenuBasis>
    )
}
export default Menu
```

Figure 16.2: *Polymorphic React*

Pad Pattern

The pattern which we are going to create is called the **Pad pattern**. It is going to apply padding spaces to any component that it wraps. The padding spaces are part of the element itself, and they also need to be consistent.

For example, we have gutters as the gaps in the display grid in the previous chapter, and we want to create a combination of gutters and paddings. A padding of large should be equal to the gutter of large.

So, for this we are going to need a kind of pattern that is going to allow us to create such settings. For this chapter, we have again created a new React project. Here, we have created a **common** folder inside the **src** folder, and created a **spaceSchema.js** file in it. This is the same file which we have used in the previous chapter, with the same content.

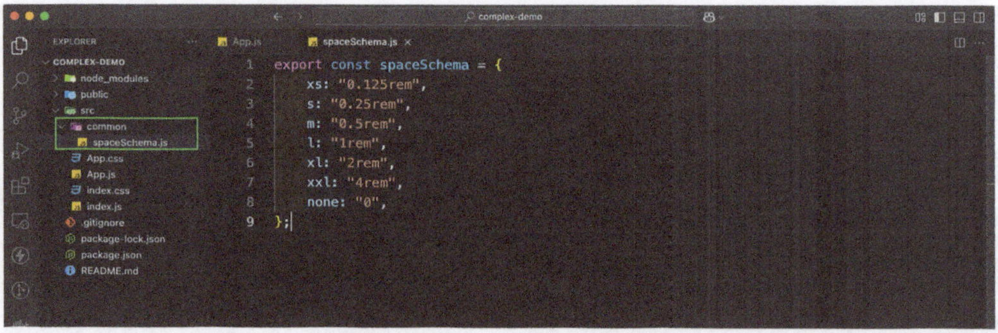

Figure 16.3: *spaceSchema.js File*

After this, create an **utils.js** file inside the **common** folder. Again, it has got the **Layers**, **Grid** and **InlineBundle** from the previous chapter. We have also installed **styled-components** in the integrated terminal.

Figure 16.4: *utils.js File*

Now, we have created a **styled.js** file inside the **common** folder. It has the styled components of **Card**, **Top**, **Button**, **Description**, **Price** and **Name**.

Also, it has a **Top** component which is taking the **props**, and adding it in the **Layers** component.

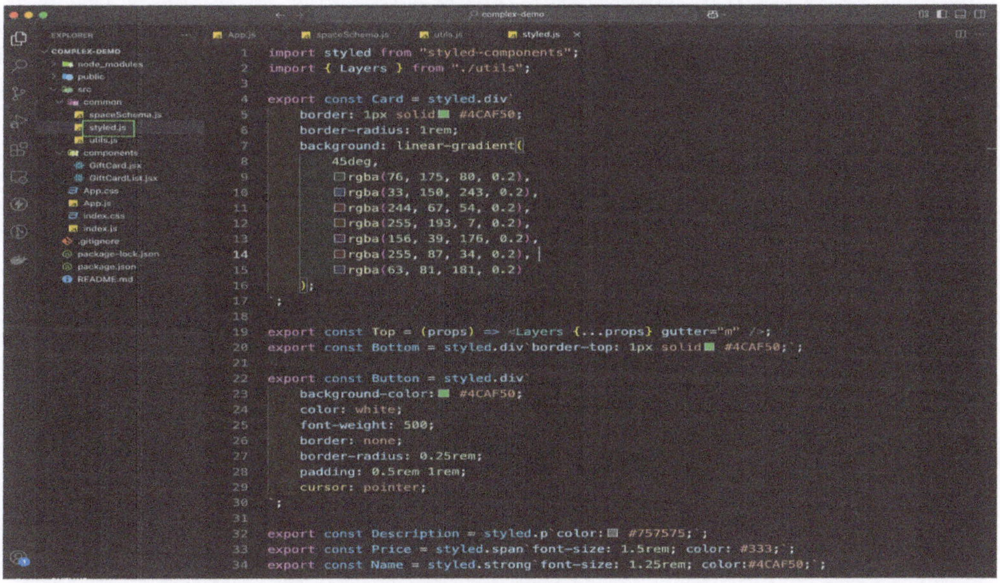

Figure 16.5: *styled.js File*

Now, create a file, **`GiftCard.jsx`** inside a **`components`** folder. It is using the various elements from the styled and utils file. In this, we are creating a **`Card`** with **`Top`** and **`Bottom`** containing different items.

Figure 16.6: *GiftCard.jsx File*

Next, create a **`GiftCardList.jsx`** file inside the **`components`** folder. Here, we are rendering the **`GiftCard`** component four times, and we have wrapped everything with a Grid.

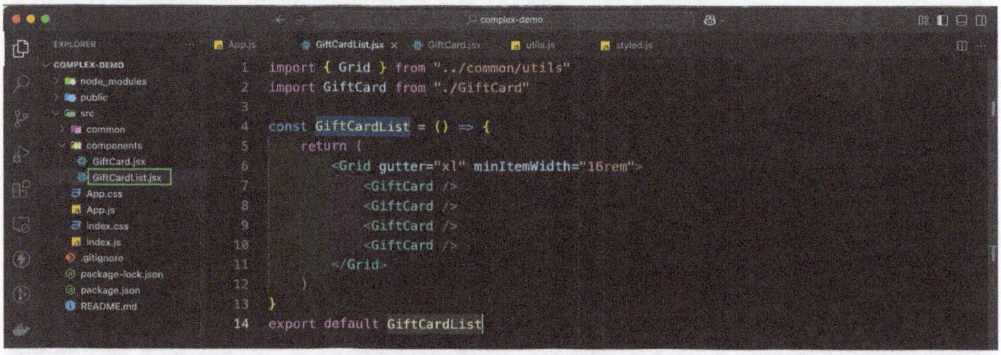

Figure 16.7: *GiftCardList.jsx File*

Now, in the **`App.js`** file, we are rendering the **`GiftCardList`** component.

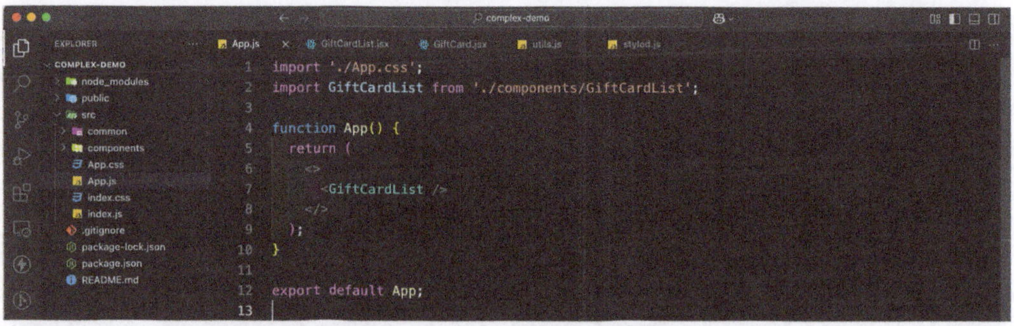

Figure 16.8: *Rendering GiftCardList from App.js File*

Now, in http://localhost:3000/, we will see four **`Cards`**, but they are not styled properly.

Figure 16.9: *Localhost with Initial GiftCardList*

The following is the mobile view in http://localhost:3000/.

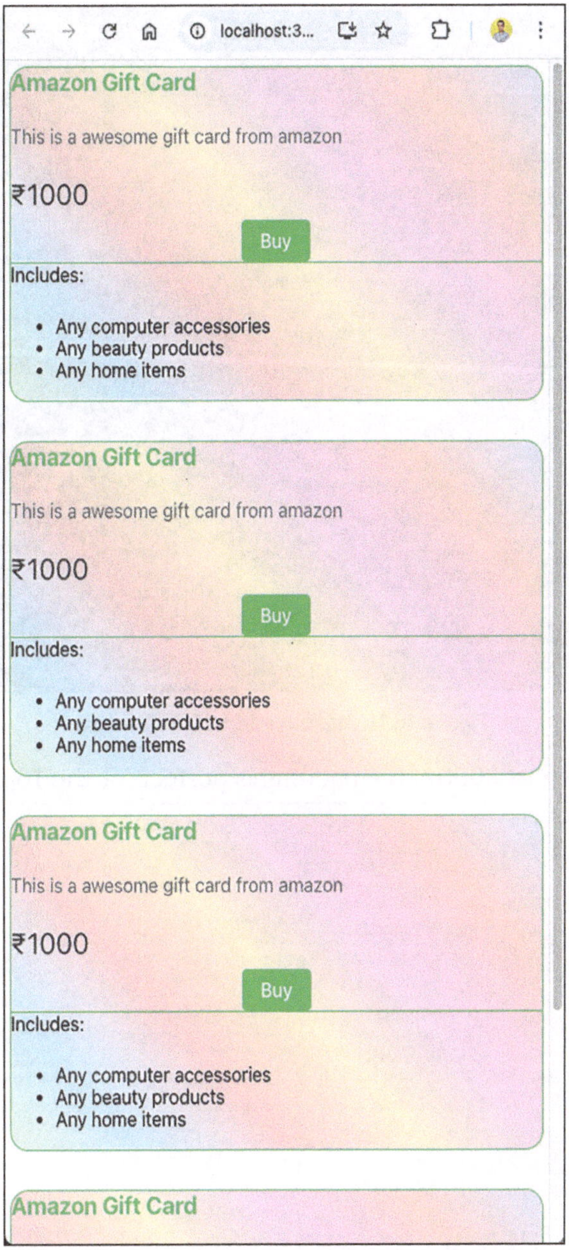

Figure 16.10: *Mobile View with Initial GiftCardList*

As we can see in both the views, the padding is not proper. So, in the **`GiftCard.jsx`** file, we will create a new styled component of Pad. Here, the padding is according to the props, and we are taking it from **`spaceSchema`**.

After this, we have wrapped the **`Top`** with the **`Pad`** component, and passed the padding props as 1. Also, we have wrapped the Layers with a **`Pad`** component, with **`props`** of **`1`**.

Figure 16.11: *Adding Pad in GiftCard.jsx*

Now, in http://localhost:3000/, the padding is perfect for the `Top` and `Bottom` parts.

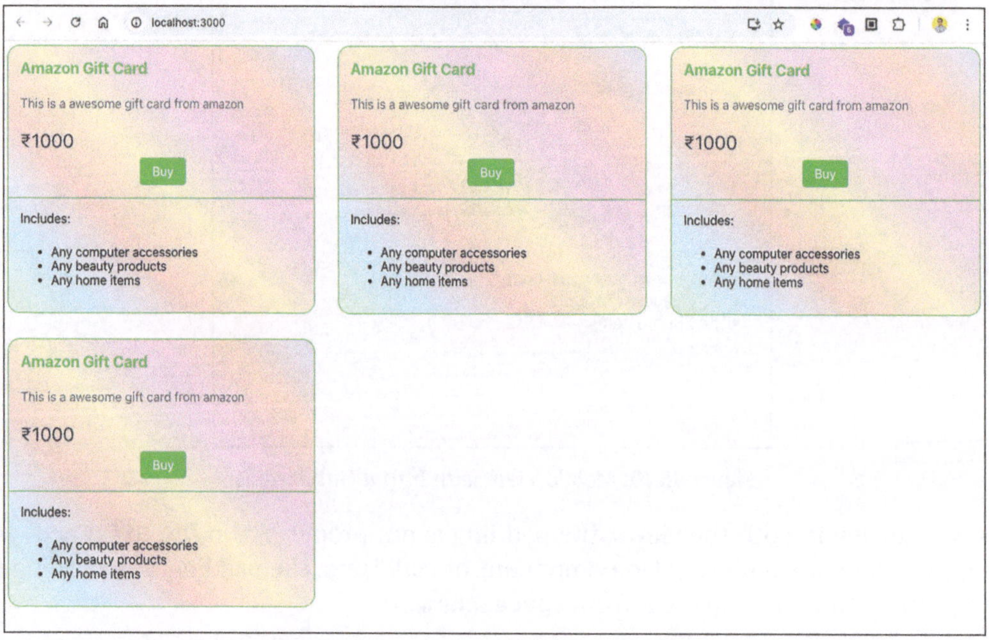

Figure 16.12: *Padding Added in Localhost*

Now, we will add a logic for giving multiple elements in padding. For example, in padding, we can give 2 or 4 items also like padding: **`0.5rem 4rem`**.

So, we have updated the **`Pad`** in **`GiftCard.jsx`** to check if an array is passed, and then mapping through the array using **`join`**. Next, we are passing the padding in the **`Button`** with the **`Pad`** and an array.

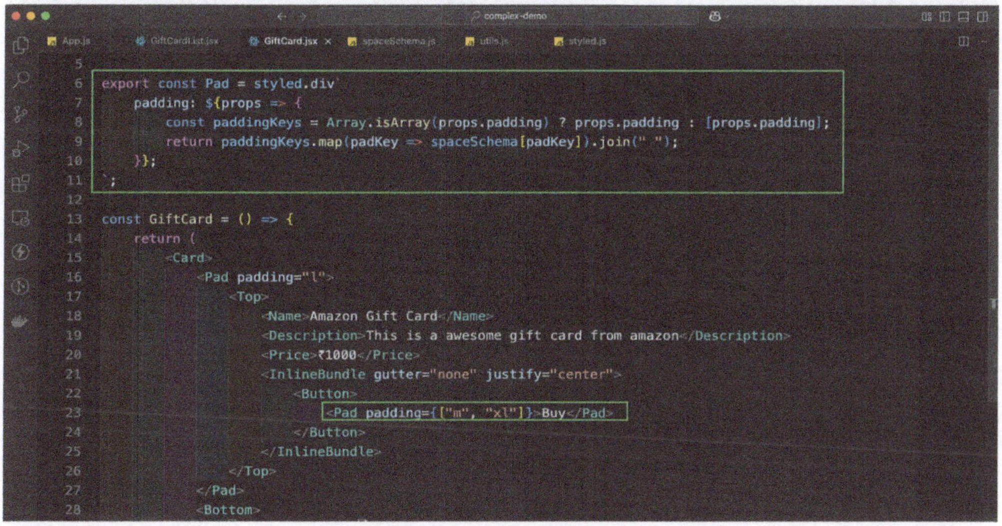

Figure 16.13: *Multiple Padding in Pad*

Now, the button is much better in http://localhost:3000/.

Figure 16.14: *Padding in Buttons*

Now, we will use polymorphic react and the **`Button`** component **`Pad`** component with as.

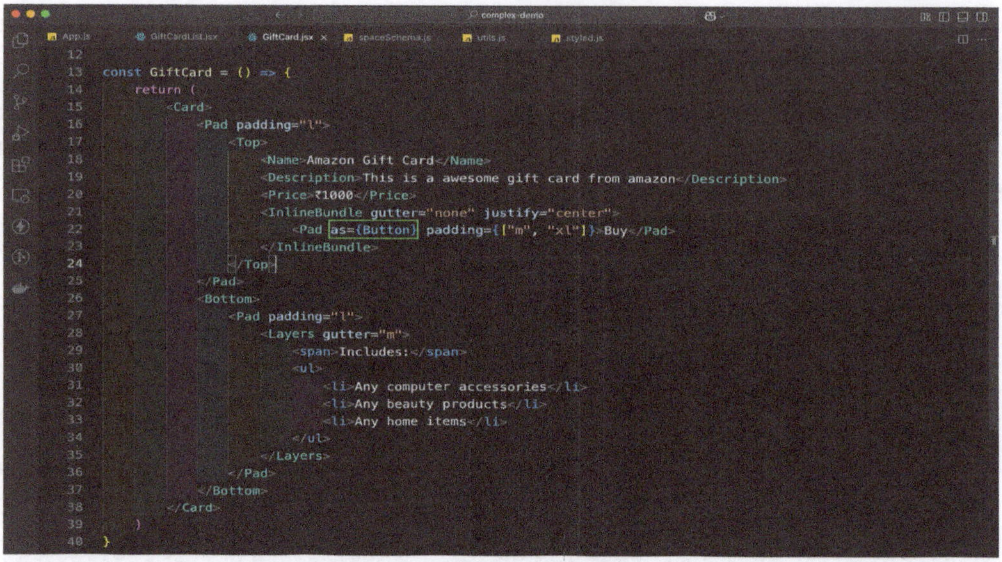

Figure 16.15: *Pad with Button and as Props*

Now, still the button is perfect in http://localhost:3000/.

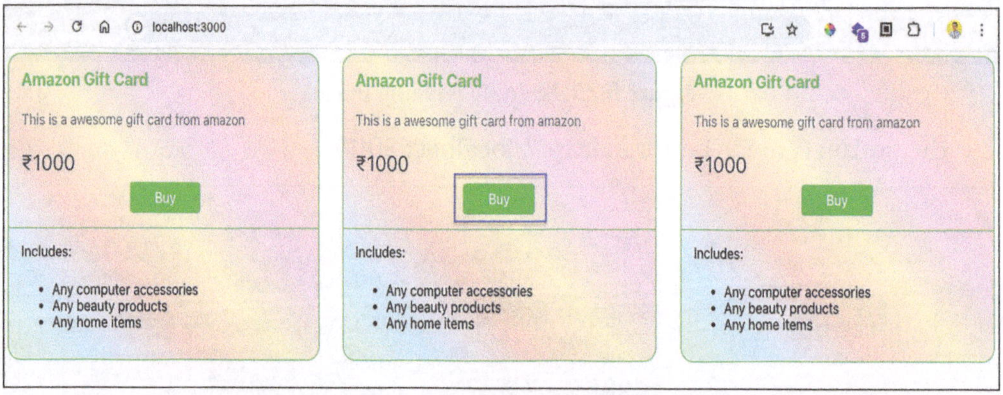

Figure 16.16: *Localhost with Final Pad Pattern*

Center Pattern

The pattern which we are going to create is called the **`Center`** pattern. Whenever we wrap some elements, with this **`center`** component pattern, it is going to center all those children. It will also **`center`** itself horizontally.

Again, we need to add some old **`styled-components`** from previous chapters first. So, in the **`utils.js`** file, we will add the **`Split`** styled component. It also needs the function fractions.

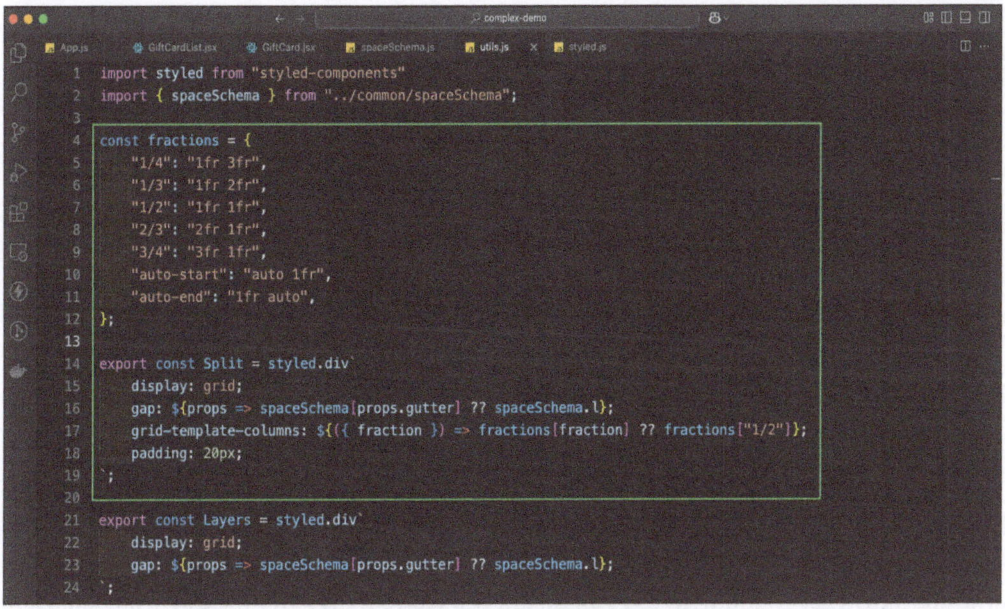

Figure 16.17: *Adding Split in utils.js*

Back in the **`styled.js`**, we will add a **`MediaWrapper`** component. We have also imported **`Split`**, and an image.

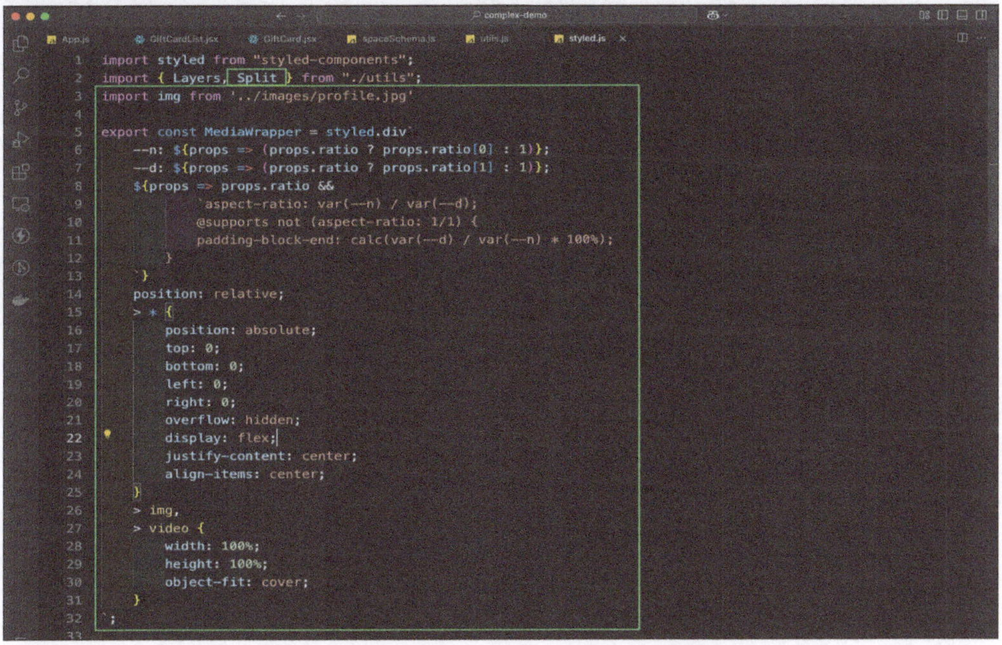

Figure 16.18: *Adding MediaWrapper in styled.js*

In the **`styled.js`**, we will add more styled components of **`LogoImg`**, Wrapper and then, we will use all of them in the **`Extras`** component.

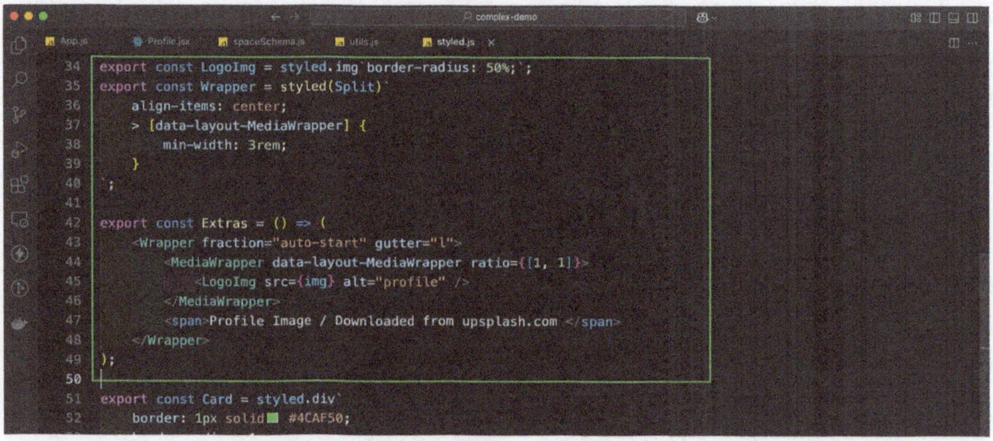

Figure 16.19: *Adding LogoImg, Wrapper, and Extras in styled.js*

Now, we will create a **`Profile.jsx`** file inside the **`components`** folder. Here, we have a div wrapping a **`h2`** and **`p`** text. After this, we are rendering the **`Extras`** component.

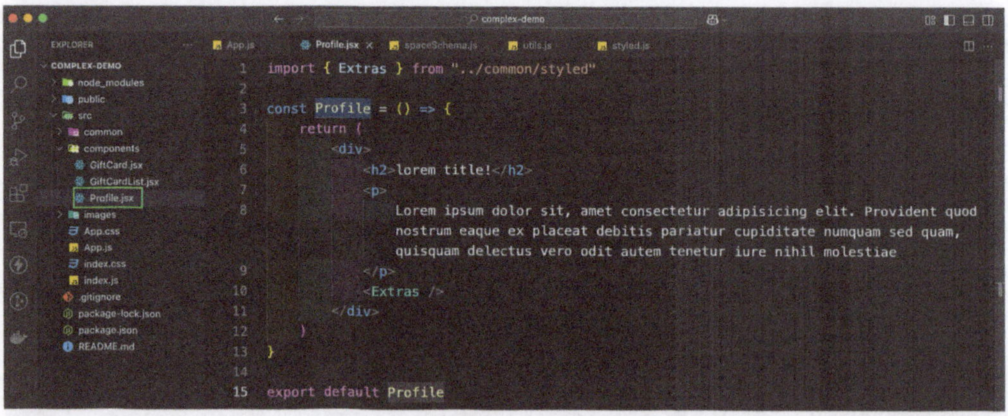

Figure 16.20: *Profile.jsx File*

Next, we will render the Profile component from the **`App.js`** file.

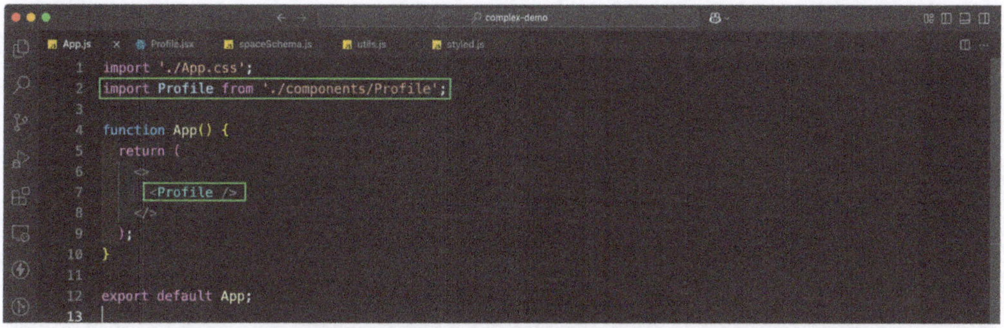

***Figure 16.21:** Rendering Profile from App.js File*

Now, in http://localhost:3000/, we will see the **`Profile`** component, which is not centered.

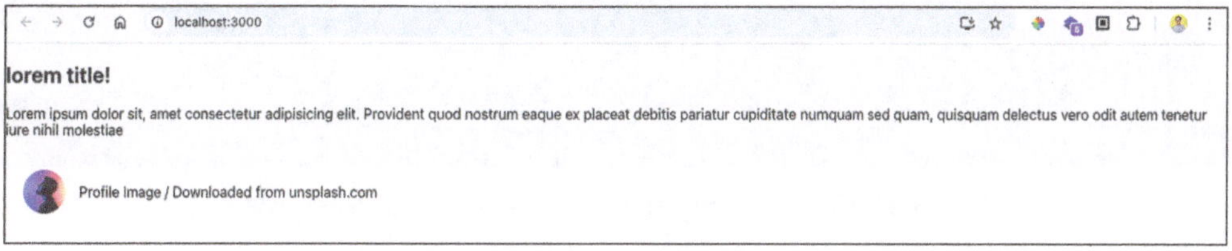

***Figure 16.22:** Initial Profile Component in Localhost*

To centre the elements, we will go back to **`Profile.jsx`** file. Here, we will create a Center styled component. It has **`margin-inline-start`** and **`margin-inline-end`** as auto to center the elements.

Then, we have max-inline-size which will take the size from a **`props`** called **`maxWidth`**. Next, we have a props of **`centerText`** to make the text-align to **`center`**. Also, the props of **`centerChildren`** will use flex to **`center`** all the children.

After this, inside the **`return`** statement, we have replaced the **`div`** with **`Center`**. Also, we are passing the **`props`** of **`maxWidth`**, **`centerText`** and **`centerChildren`**.

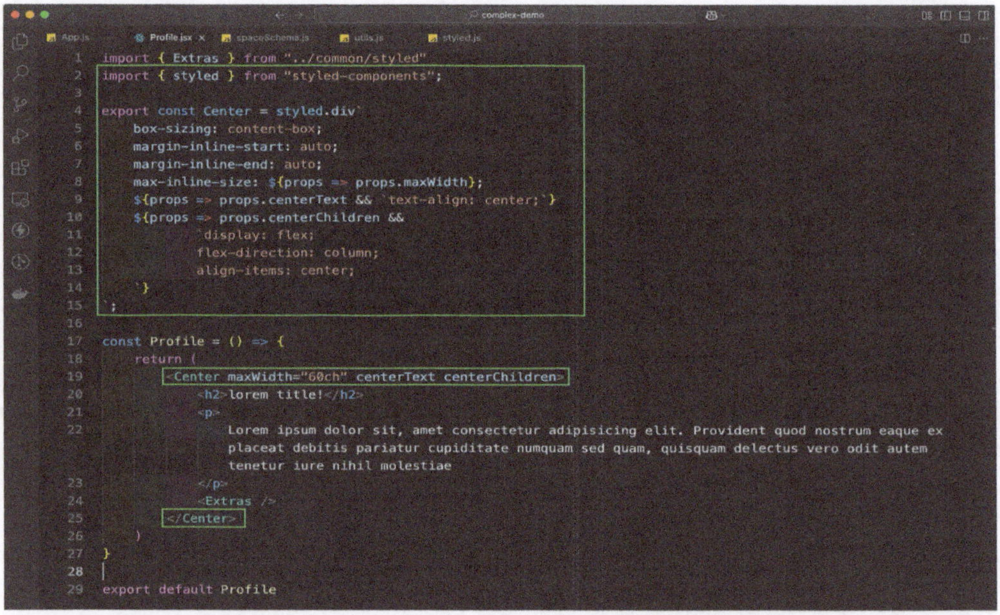

Figure 16.23: *Center Styled Component in Profile.jsx File*

Back in http://localhost:3000/, everything is centered and almost perfect.

Figure 16.24: *Elements Centered in Localhost*

We will again use polymorphic react, and use as in **`Center`** to add **`Layers`**. We have also added a gutter required in **`Layers`**.

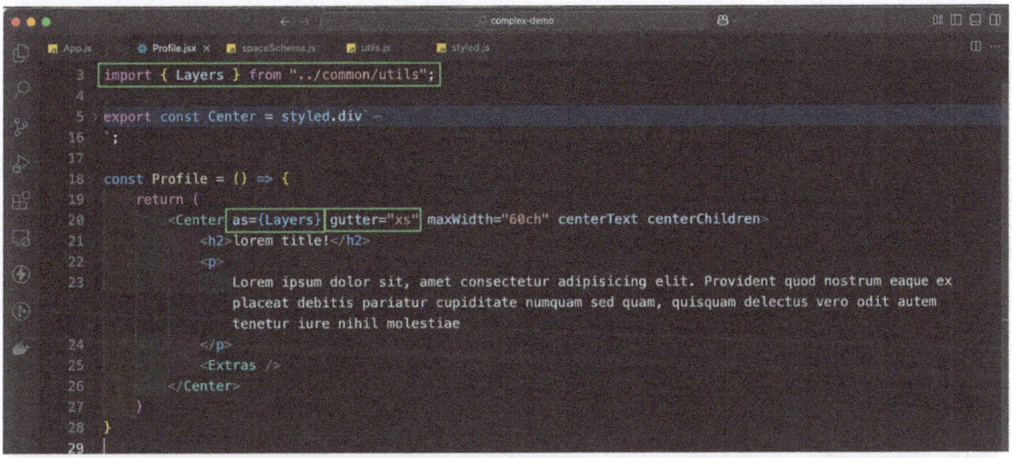

***Figure 16.25:** Adding Layers in Center*

This completes our **`Center`** design pattern, and the output is completely centered in http://localhost:3000/.

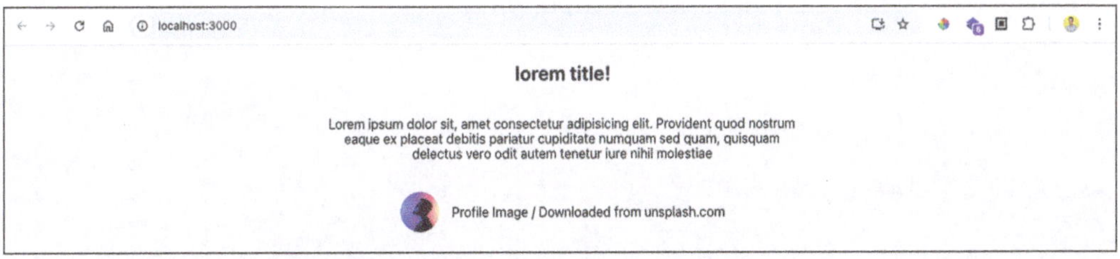

***Figure 16.26:** Final Centered Elements in Localhost*

Media-Wrapper Pattern

The pattern which we are going to learn about is the Media-Wrapper pattern. It is used, when it comes to display images and videos. Making images responsive can be tricky, and we will learn to do so in this section.

Our media wrapper pattern helps us set the aspect ratio based on the size. This pattern can be very much helpful, if we have to display images several times in our code base. So, again we will do some setting first.

Here in the **`utils.js`** file, we will add the code of Pad and Center, which we have created earlier in this chapter.

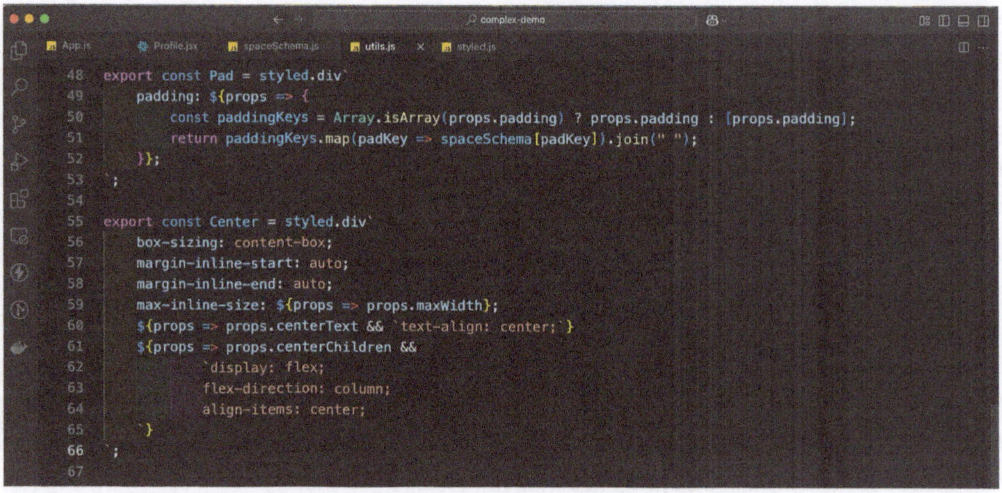

Figure 16.27: *Adding Pad and Center in utils.js*

Now, in the **`styled.js`** file, we will create a new component called **`DescriptionMedia`**. It will use the **`Center`** and **`Pad`** styled-components.

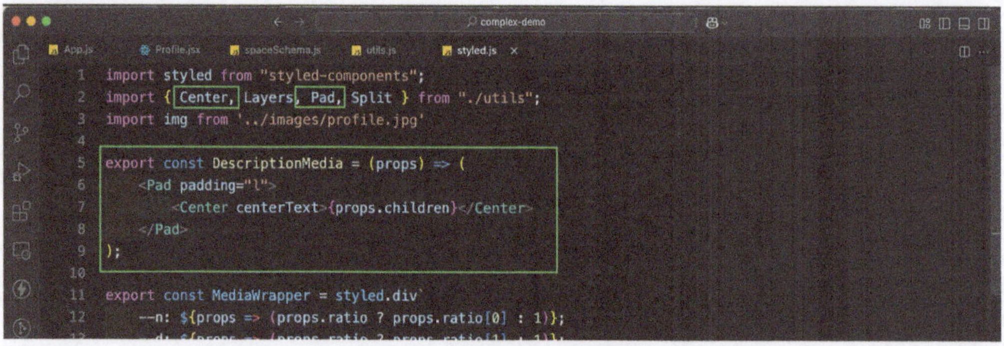

Figure 16.28: *Adding DescriptionMedia in styled.js*

Now, we will create a **`Product.jsx`** file inside the **`components`** folder. It will show a t-shirt image which we have just added, and also the **`DescriptionMedia`** component. In the **`DescriptionMedia`** component, we are passing a text that is taken by a child.

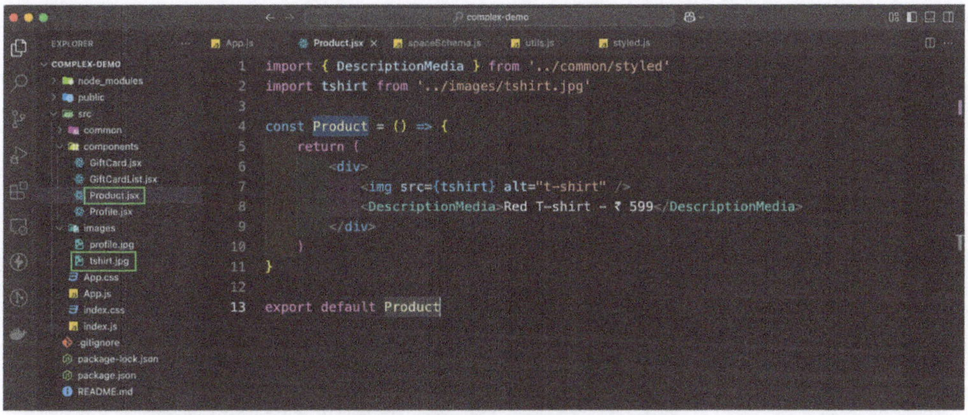

Figure 16.29: *Product.jsx File*

Now, create a **ProductList.jsx** file in the **components** folder. Here, we are rendering the **Product** component four times. We have also wrapped the **Product** components with **Grid** styled components, and passed props of gutter as well as **minItemWidth** in it.

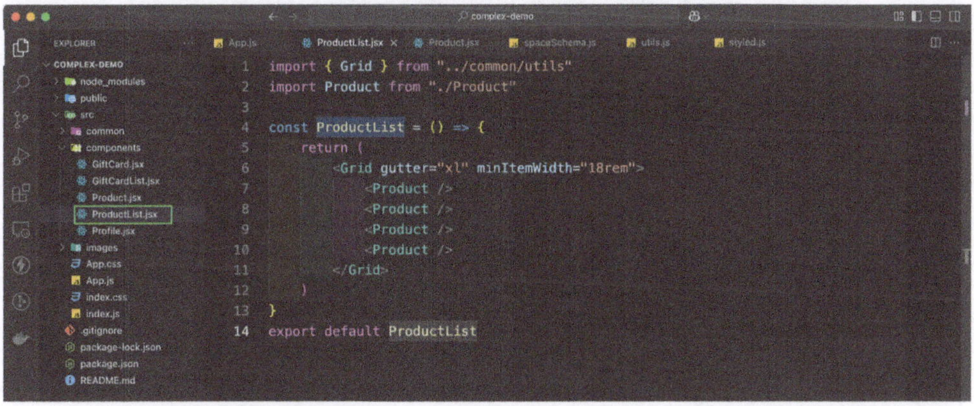

Figure 16.30: *ProductList.jsx File Rendering Product*

Now, we are rendering the **ProductList** component in the **App.js** file.

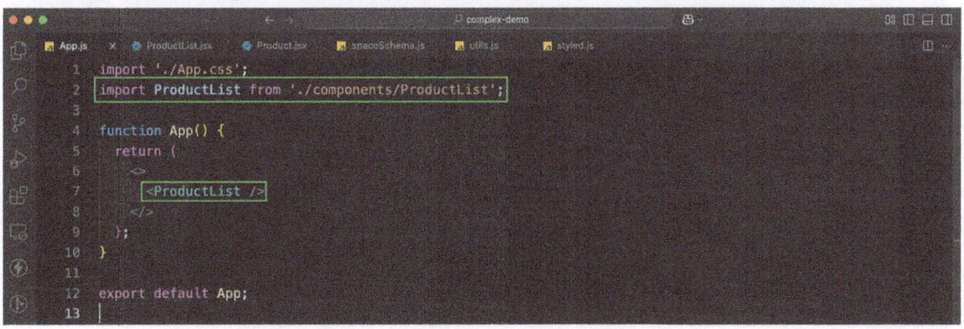

Figure 16.31: *App.js File Rendering ProductList*

Now, the mobile view in http://localhost:3000/ will show the without styled image.

Figure 16.32: *Localhost Showing ProductList*

Back in the **`Product.jsx`** file, we will create a styled component called **`MediaWrapper`**, and wrap the image. We are making it as position relative, and giving a width and height.

The **`> *`** is targeting the children, which is the **`img`** tag in our case. By this, we are making the position absolute, and the width and height as 100%.

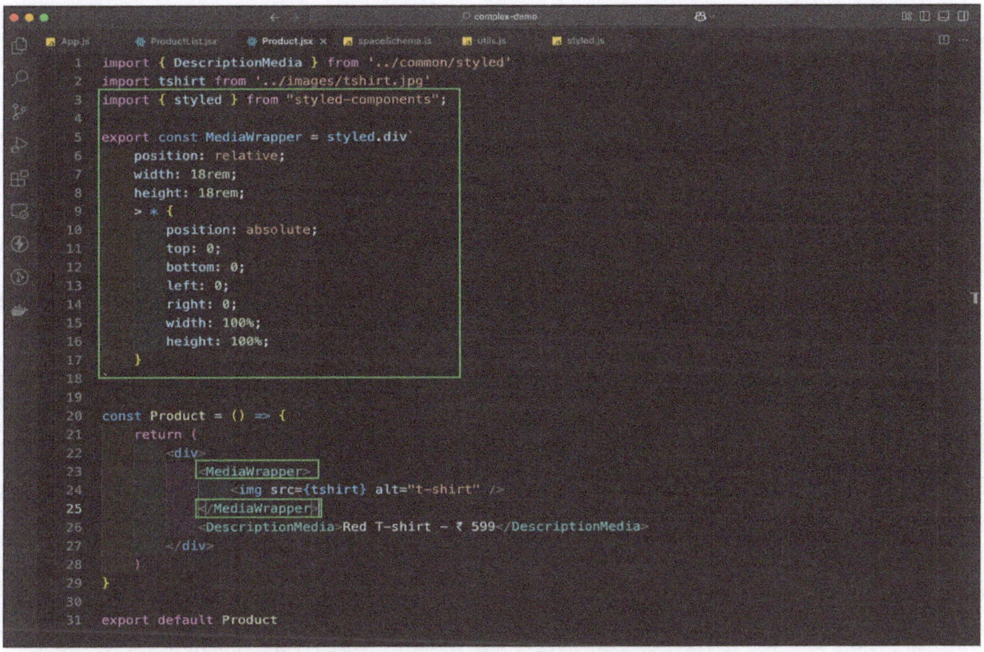

Figure 16.33: *MediaWrapper Styled Component in Product.jsx*

Now, the mobile view in http://localhost:3000/ will show the following content. The image is fixed, but the text is not ok now.

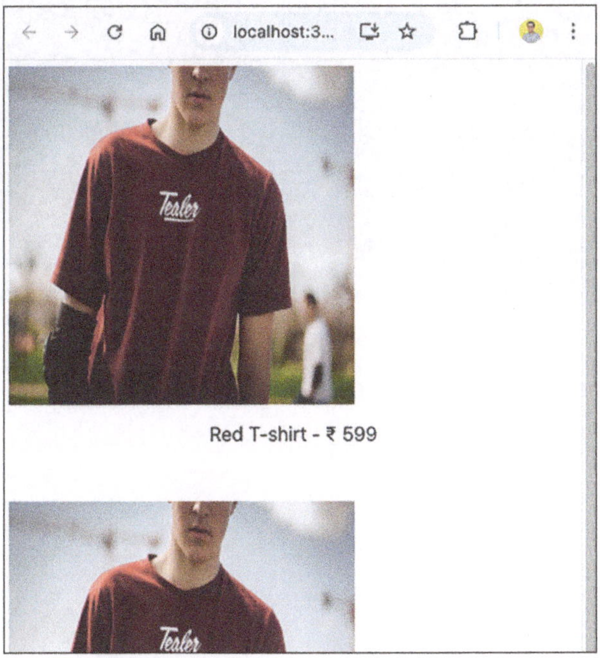

Figure 16.34: *Localhost with MediaWrapper*

Back in the **`Product.jsx`** file, we will add the concept of aspect-ratio, which is the width and height ratio. We are going to pass it through a props named ratio as an array of two elements.

So, inside the **`MediaWrapper`**, we have created two variables **`–n`** and **`-d`**, and stored the first value of the array as well as the second value of the array in them. After this, we are making the aspect-ratio equal to them.

There are also some browsers like Safari which do not support the aspect-ratio. We are checking the same with **`@support`** not, and then using padding-bottom to do the same.

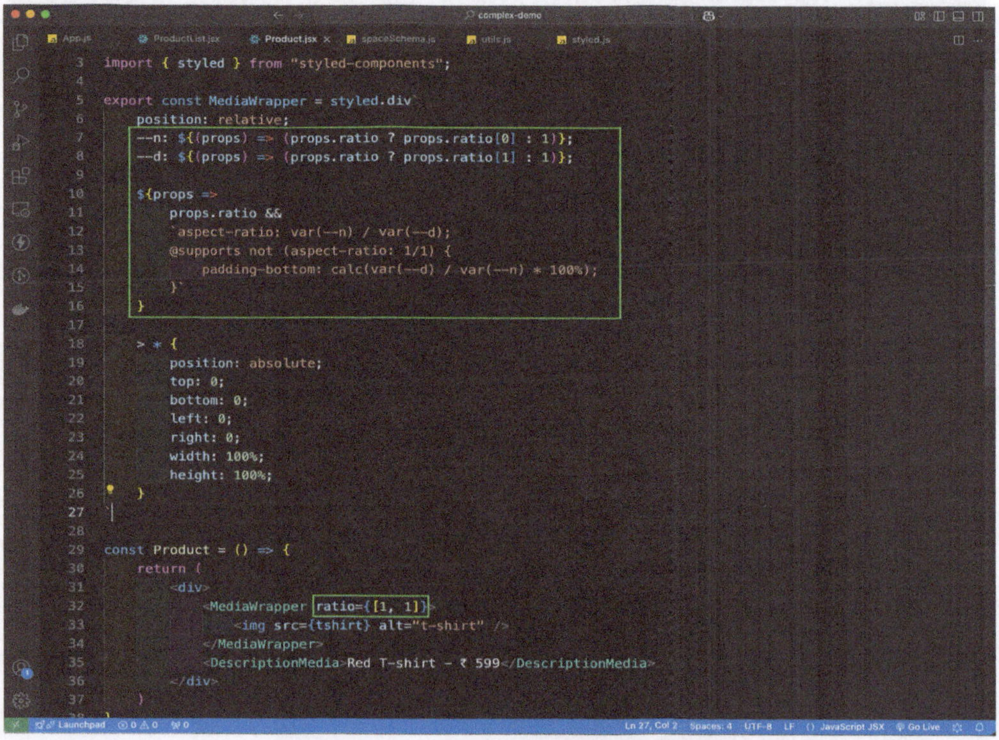

Figure 16.35: *Ratio Prop in MediaWrapper*

Now, our image and text are perfect in the mobile view.

***Figure 16.36:** Mobile View with Ratio in MediaWrapper*

We have one more thing remaining, and for it, we will make the **`image`** and **`video`** tag as width and height to 100%. Also, make the object-fit to cover.

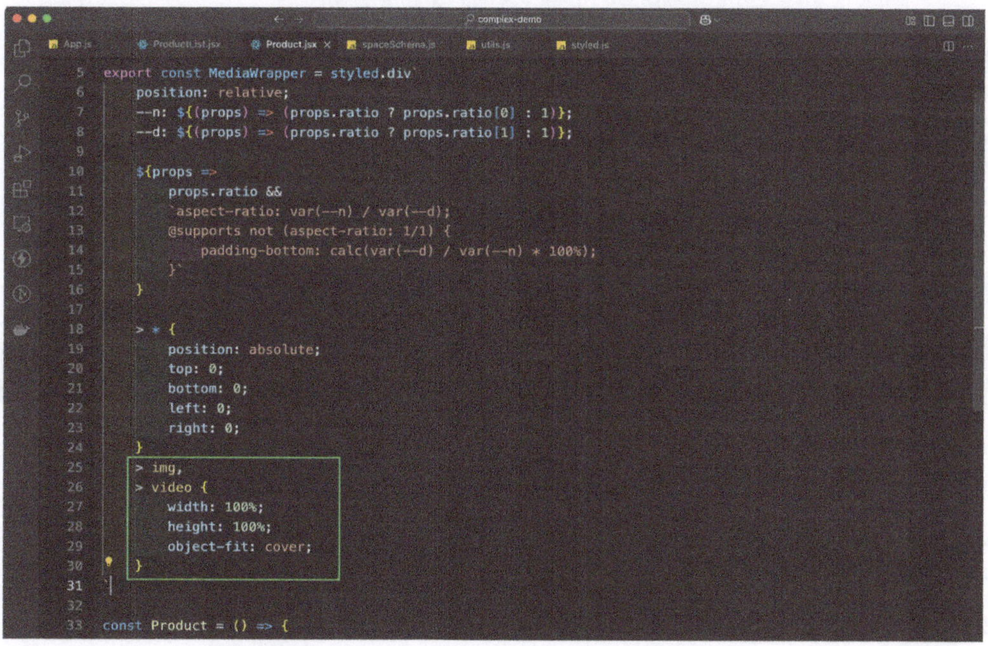

***Figure 16.37:** img and video styles in MediaWrapper*

The movie view is now perfect for all size images.

Figure 16.38: *Perfect Mobile View*

The desktop view is also perfect.

Figure 16.39: *Perfect Desktop View*

Cover Pattern

The pattern which we are going to learn now is the **`Cover Pattern`**. It is about vertically centering the elements. So, we are going to build a **wrapper** component. Whenever it wraps some children, it is going to center them vertically.

Also, we are going to add a feature that allows us to inject a top section and a bottom section. First, we are going to create a new helper function called **CoverButton** in the **styled.js** file. It is a simple button which also uses the **Pad styled-component**. We can create two types of buttons here - one primary and other normal.

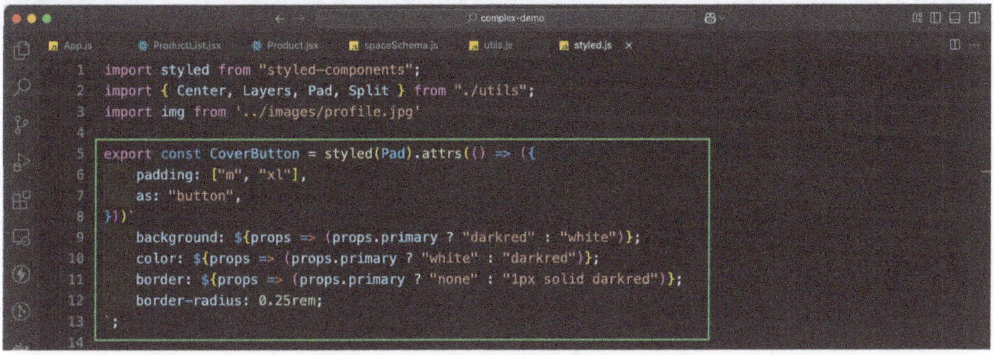

Figure 16.40: *CoverButton in styled.js*

Now, create a **HeroPage.jsx** file inside the **components** folder. Here, we are first importing the **CoverButton**, **InlineBundle** and **Layers**, and then creating two simple components of **Top** and **Bottom**.

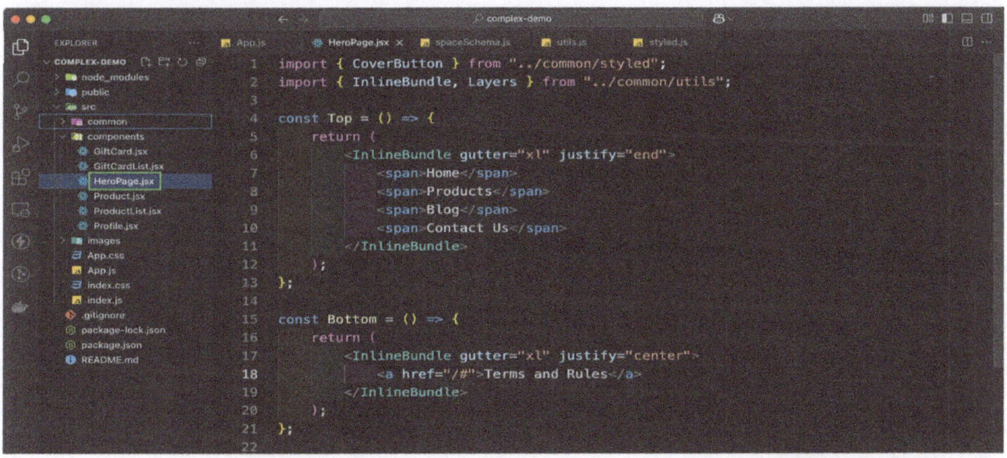

Figure 16.41: *Top and Bottom Components in HomePage.jsx File*

Next, inside the return statement in the **HeroPage.jsx** file, we are first rendering the **Top** component. After this, with **Layers** styled components, we are showing an **h1** and **span** text, and also two buttons wrapped with **InlineBundle**.

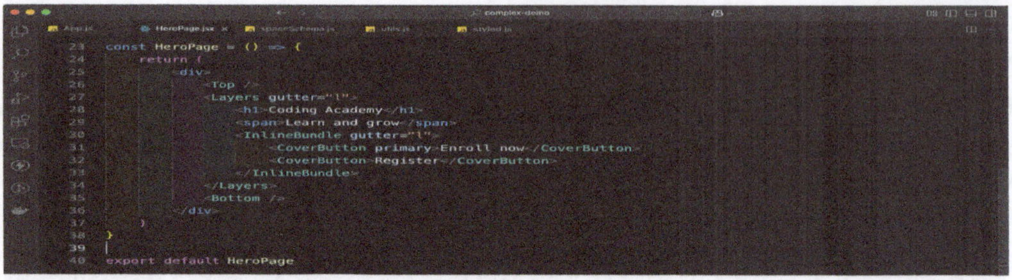

```
const HeroPage = () => {
  return (
    <div>
      <Top />
      <Layers gutter="1">
        <h1>Coding Academy</h1>
        <span>Learn and grow</span>
        <InlineBundle gutter="1">
          <CoverButton primary>Enroll now</CoverButton>
          <CoverButton>Register</CoverButton>
        </InlineBundle>
      </Layers>
      <Bottom />
    </div>
  )
}

export default HeroPage
```

Figure 16.42: *Return in HomePage.jsx File*

Now, in http://localhost:3000/, our desktop view without any **Cover** styles will look as follows: .

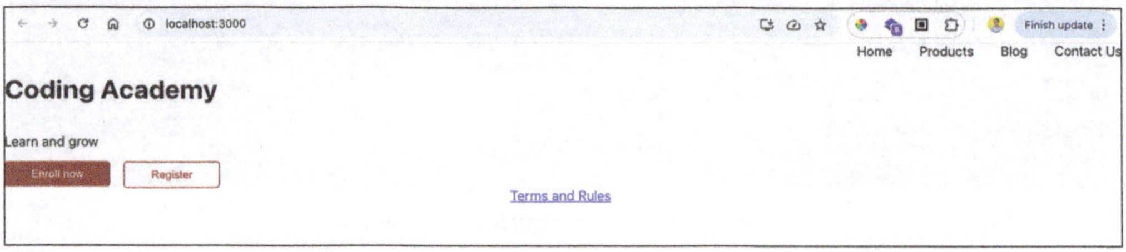

Figure 16.43: *Localhost Showing HomePage Component*

And, in http://localhost:3000/, our mobile view without any **Cover** styles will look as follows:

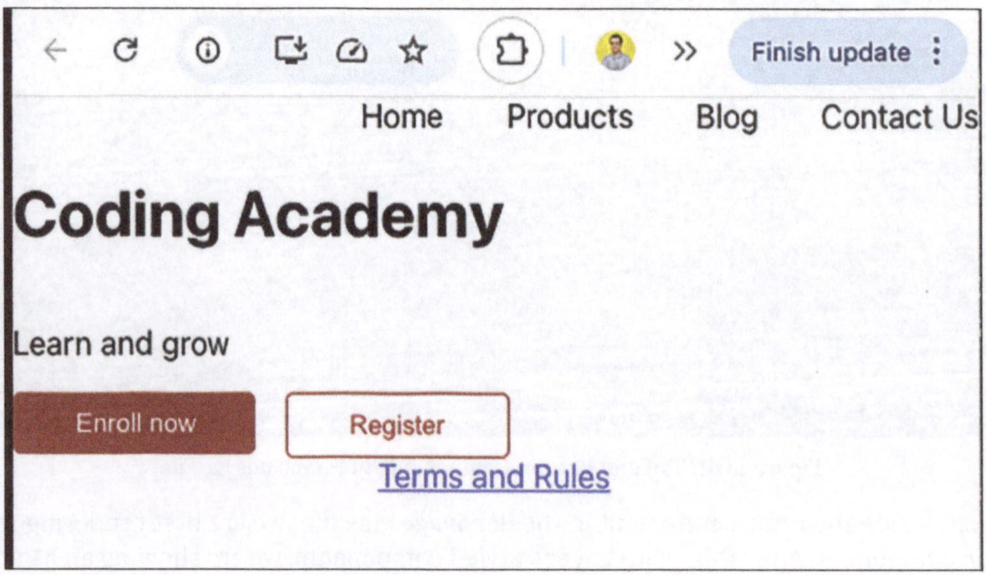

Figure 16.44: *Localhost in Mobile View*

Now, we will add the styled component of **Cover** in the **HeroPage.jsx** file. Here, we are using a grid and **centering** the children.

After this, we change the **div** with **Cover**, and also comment **Top** and **Bottom** for the moment.

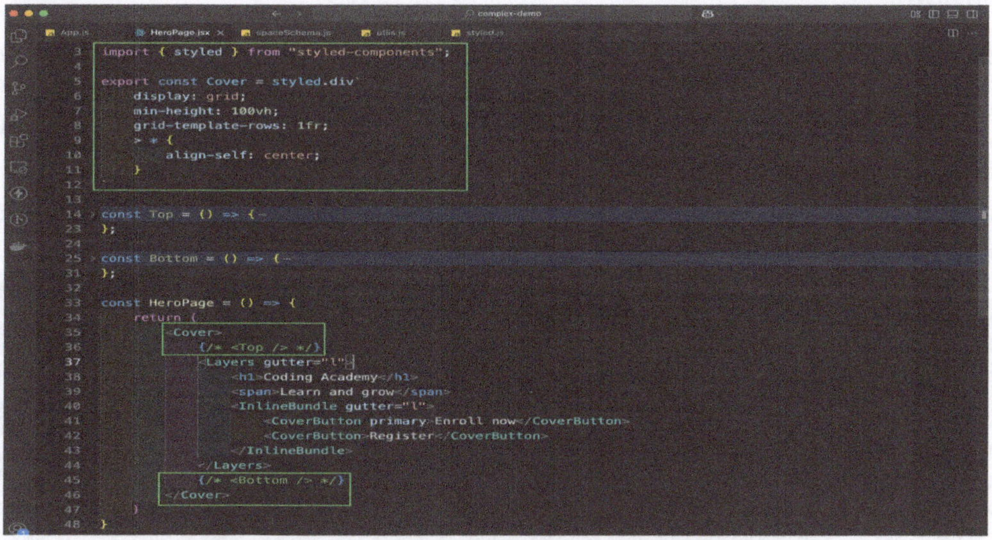

Figure 16.45: *Cover Styled Component in HomePage.jsx File*

Now, in http://localhost:3000/, we will see the main content centered. But we need to add logic to use the **Top** and **Bottom** components also, and we are going to do that next.

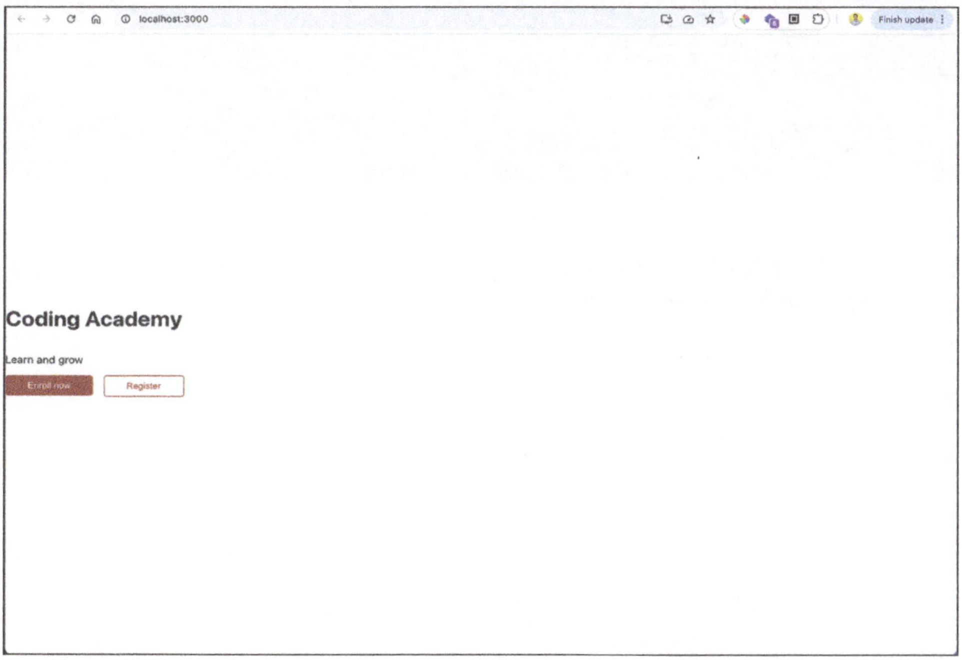

Figure 16.46: *Centered Elements in Localhost*

We have changed the **`Cover`** styled-component to take the children, **`top`** and **`bottom`** props. We are then returning the children and sending the **`top`**, **`children`** and **`bottom`** with a **`div`**.

After the return, we also have a display of **`grid`** and **`gap`** with **`spaceSchema`**. We have a **`min-block-size`**, which if not passed, is **`100vh`**. Then the **`grid-template-row`** takes the top and bottom props. We are using multiple ternary operators to change the style for top and bottom, top only, bottom only, and no top or bottom.

Lastly, in the **`return`** statement in the **`Cover`**, we are passing the **`top`** and **`bottom`** as the respective components.

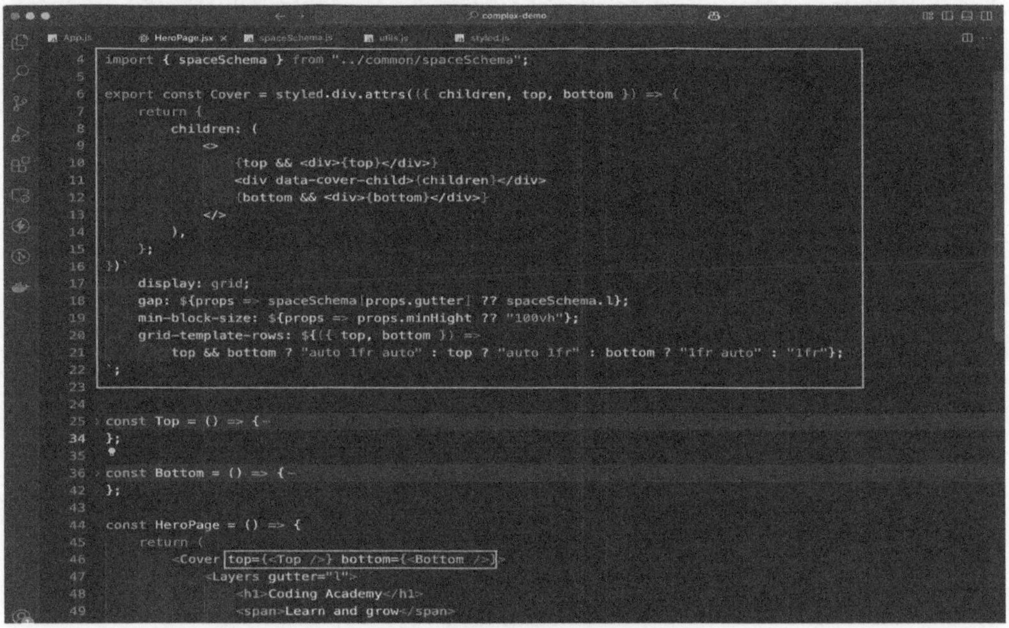

Figure 16.47: *Cover with Props*

In http://localhost:3000/, our component is almost perfect as we want. But there is one thing left, and that is to center the main element.

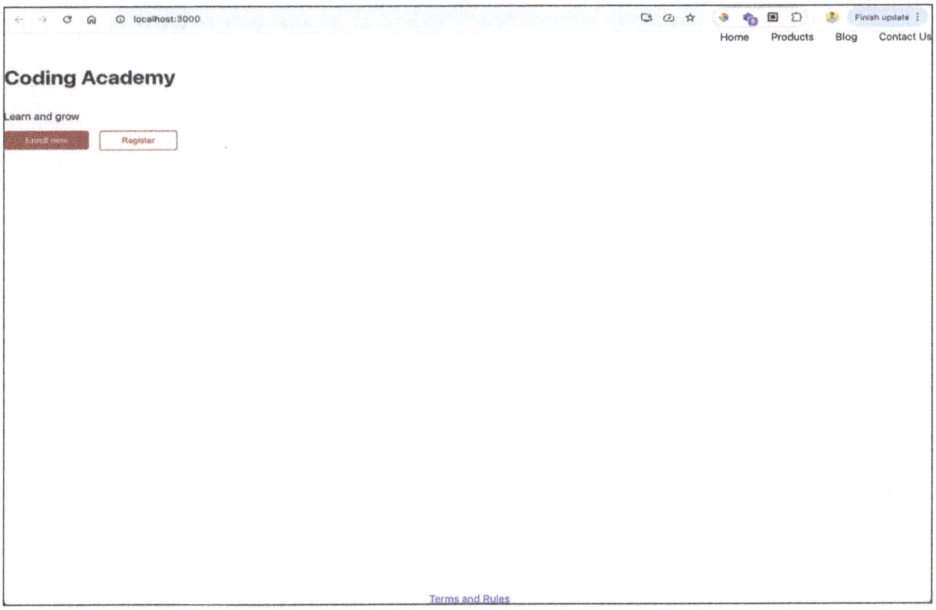

Figure 16.48: *Localhost with Updated HeroPage*

Back in the **HeroPage.jsx** file in the **div** for children, we already have **data-cover-child**. We are using it to give the style of **align-self center**. Also, we are using the **Pad styled component** in **Cover** with as, and passing the padding.

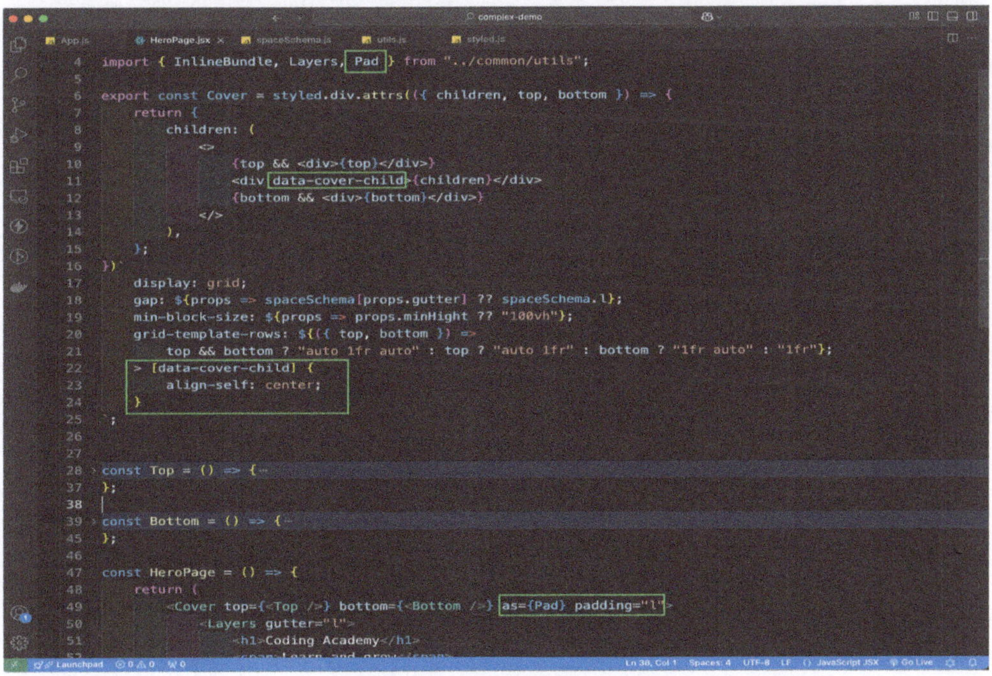

Figure 16.49: *Centered Children*

Now, our desktop view in http://localhost:3000/ is as we want, with centered main elements as well as header and footer at correct places.

Figure 16.50: *Final Desktop View*

And, our mobile view in http://localhost:3000/ is as we want.

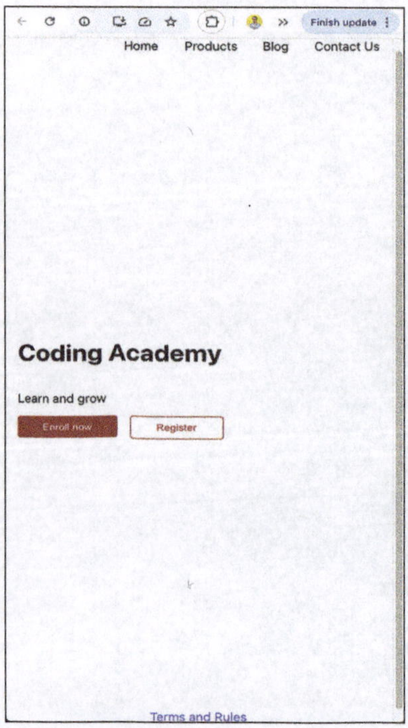

Figure 16.51: *Final Mobile View*

Conclusion

In this chapter, we explored a few advanced and powerful design patterns in React that can help build more reusable and flexible UI components. So, let us walk through what we learned – with relatable use cases.

Pad Pattern: Adds consistent padding around any wrapped component.

Use case: Apply spacing to Card components, without modifying internal layout.

Center Pattern: Centers child content, both vertically and horizontally.

Use case: Align a spinner or modal content in the middle of the screen.

Media Wrapper Pattern: Ensures consistent layout for media like images and videos.

Use case: Use in galleries or media blocks for clean alignment.

Cover Pattern: Vertically centers content in a flexible container.

Use case: Center a login form or hero section regardless of screen height.

In the next chapter, **we will complete the design system, and create a final project** with it.

Points to Remember

- Polymorphic React with as keyword
- Creating Pad Pattern
- Creating Center Pattern
- Creating Media-wrapper Pattern
- Creating Cover Pattern

CHAPTER 17
Design System (Final Project)

Introduction

In this chapter, we will complete our design system section. Here, we will work on a final project using the design system to consolidate everything we have learned so far. This hands-on project will bring together multiple design system concepts, helping you understand how to organize and structure components in a real-world scenario.

You will learn how to combine reusable elements such as the Navbar, Sidebar, Forms, and Buttons into a cohesive interface that follows consistent design principles. This chapter will not only strengthen your understanding of styled-components and layout utilities but also demonstrate how a design system improves scalability and collaboration in larger projects.

By completing this chapter, you will gain practical experience in implementing a full-featured mini-application that adheres to design system standards – an essential skill for professional React developers building maintainable and visually consistent applications.

Structure

In this chapter, we shall discuss the following topics:

- Overview
- Navbar with Menu and Header
- Sidebar Menu
- Building Form
- Finishing Buttons

Overview

In this chapter, we are going to do the final project with all the design system patterns we have learned in the earlier chapters. Here, we are going to build a small website that will have a Navbar and header. It will also have a sidebar menu and form. Finally, we will finish the website with a nice button.

Navbar with Menu and Header

Create a new React project, and in the **`App.js`** file, add the **`MainPage`** component.

Figure 17.1: *App.js Rendering MainPage*

Next, create a **`components`** folder in the **`src`**, and inside it, create a **`MainPage.js`** file.

Now, the **`MainPage`** will render a **`MenuBar`** component.

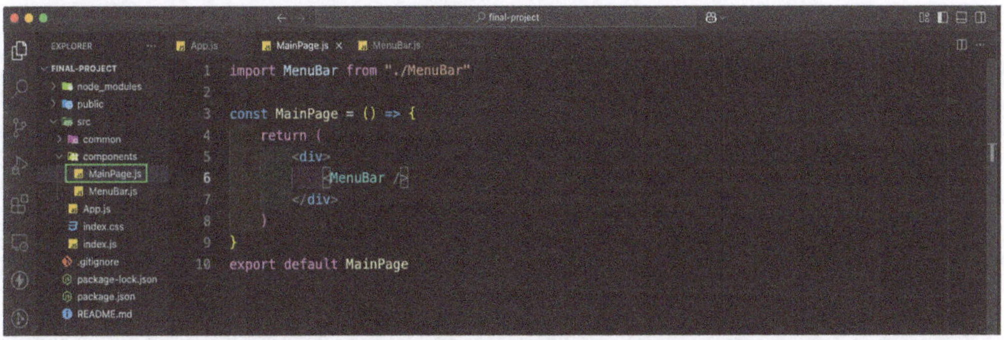

Figure 17.2: *MainPage.js Rendering MenuBar*

Now, create a **`MenuBar.js`** file inside the components folder. Here, we have a **`div`** that contains other elements such as the logo, nav, and input.

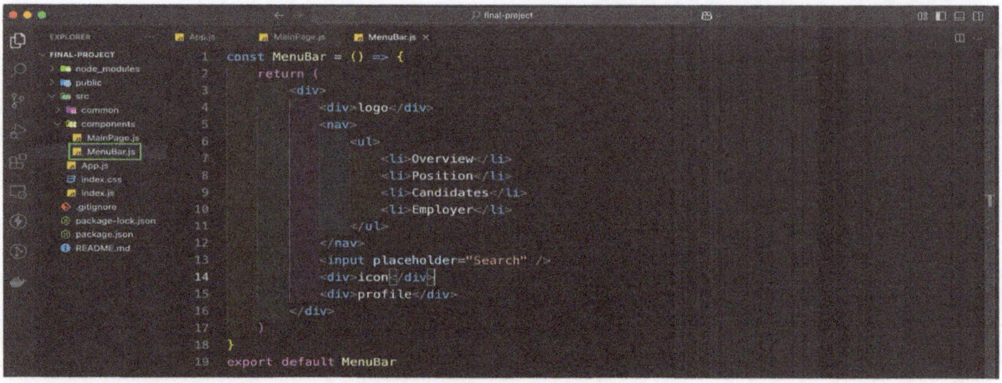

Figure 17.3: *Skeleton Code in MenuBar.js*

Now, when we open our app at http://localhost:3000/, we will see a menu with no styles.

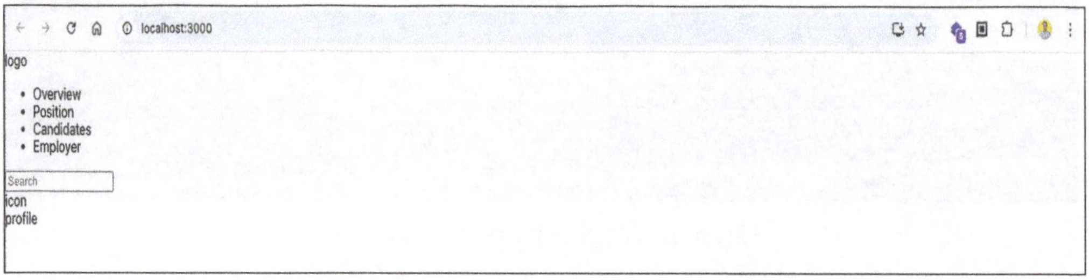

Figure 17.4: *Localhost Showing MenuBar*

Next, inside the **`src`** folder, create a folder called **`common`**. Inside this folder, create the file **`spaceSchema.js`**, which is from the earlier design system chapters.

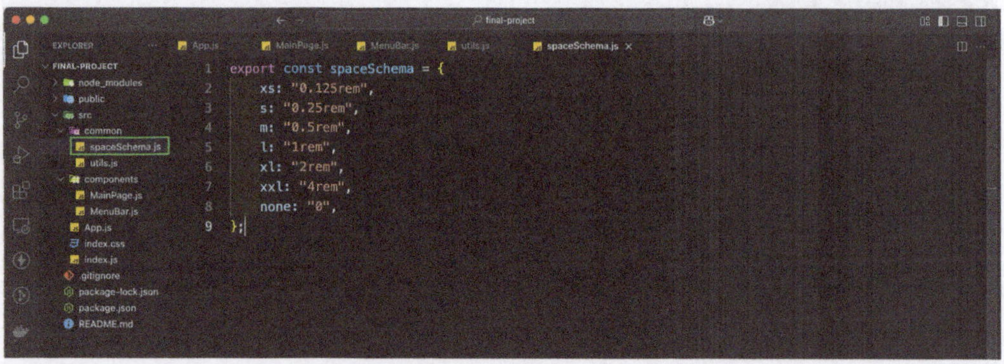

Figure 17.5: *spaceSchema.js File*

Now, create the file **`utils.js`** inside the **`common`** folder. Here, we will import styled and **`css`** from styled components. We are also importing **`spaceSchema`** which was created earlier.

Now, we have added the styles for **`responsive`**, **`stretchMap`** and **`justifyAlignWay`** that we created in the earlier chapters.

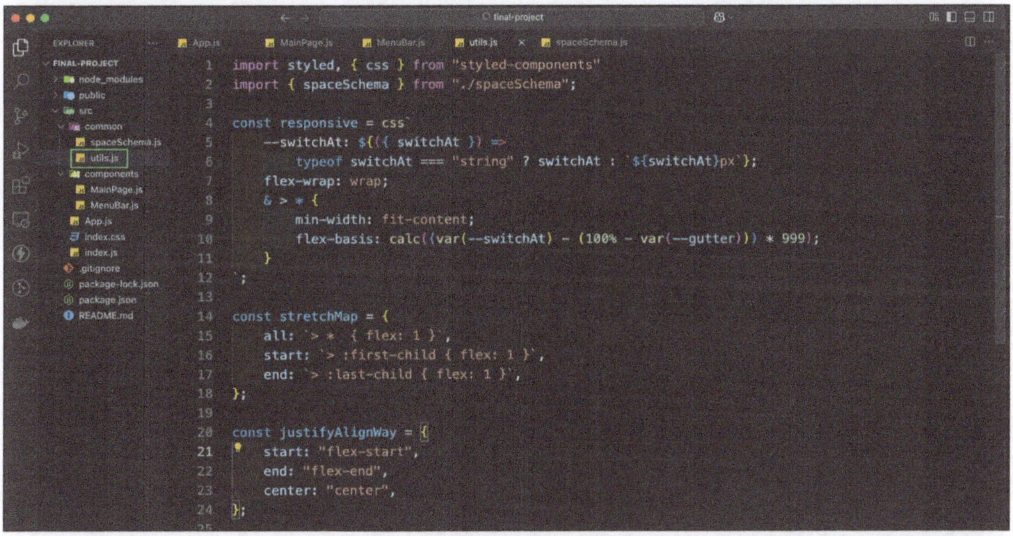

Figure 17.6: *utils.js File*

We have added more styles for **`InlineBundle`**, **`Inline`** and **`Pad`** in the **`utils.js`** file from the earlier chapters.

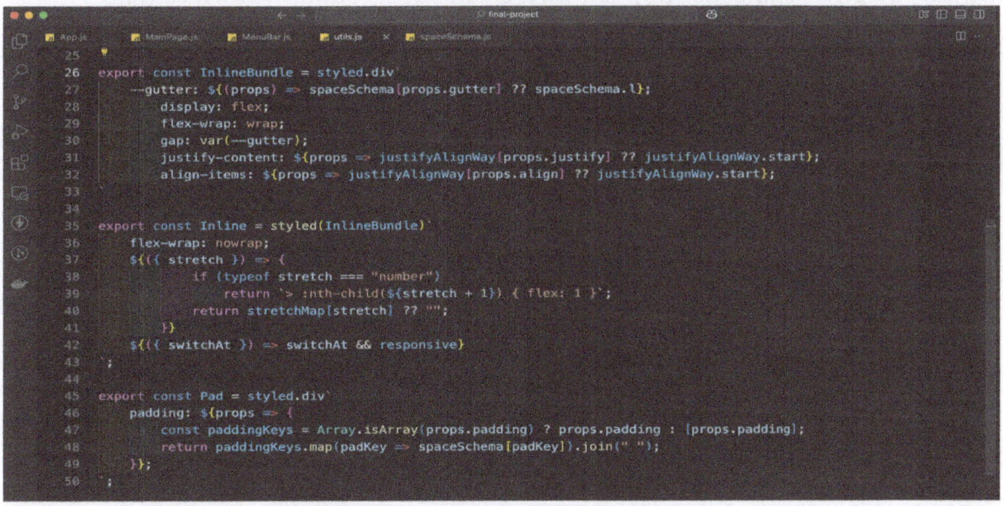

Figure 17.7: *More Styles in utils.js File*

In the **`MenuBar.js`** file, import **`styled-components`** first. After this, create the styled component for the **`Menu`**. We are using the **`Inline`** and **`Pad`** components from **`utils.js`**, and passing some props. Then, set the background, color and border styles.

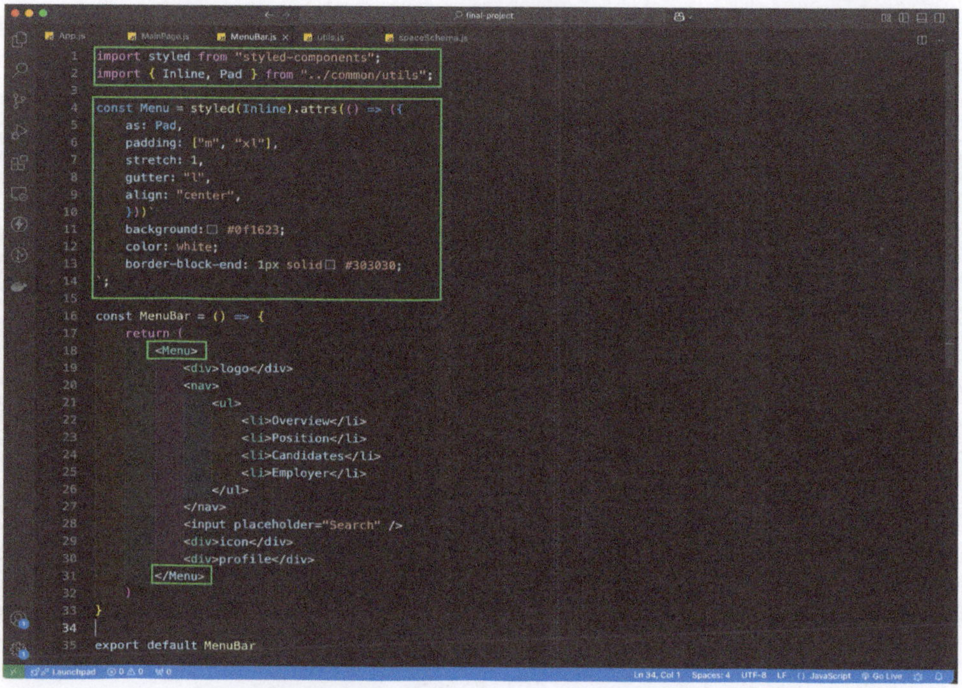

Figure 17.8: *Using Menu in MenuBar.js File*

Now, the http://localhost:3000/ shows a clean background with white text.

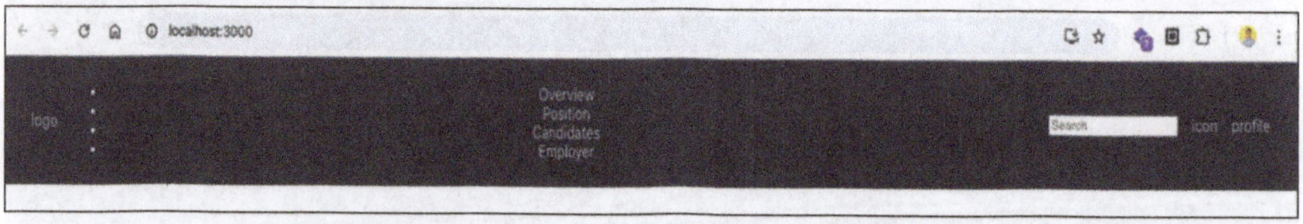

Figure 17.9: *MenuBar Styled in Localhost*

Now, add a file **`Logo.js`** inside the **`components`** folder. Here, based on the size props, change the width and height.

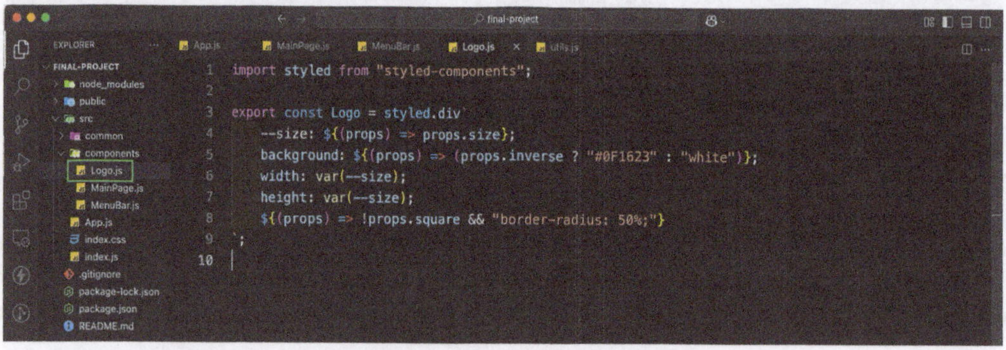

Figure 17.10: *Logo.js File*

In the **`MenuBar.js`** file, import the **`Logo`** component. Add the **`Logo`** in place of various **`divs`**, and also give the size props. Besides this, change the **`ul`** with the Inline components, with some props.

***Figure 17.11:** Styled Component in MenuBar.js File*

In http://localhost:3000/, our **`Navbar`** is styled better.

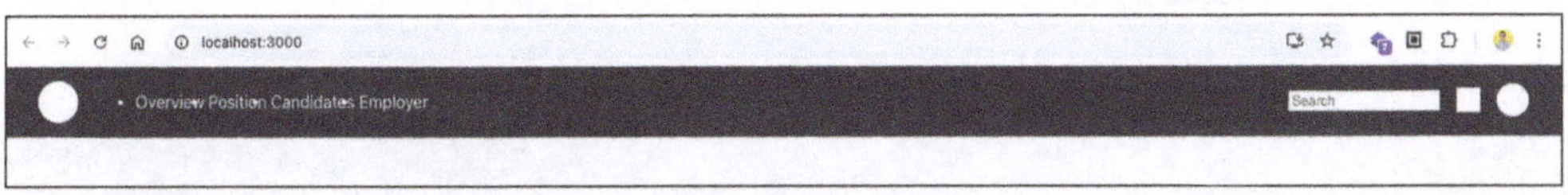

***Figure 17.12:** MenuBar Better Styled in Localhost*

In the **`MenuBar.js`** file, add a styled component for **`Item`** and **`SearchBar`**. Here, we are also using the Pad-styled component. Now, instead of the **`li`**, we are using **`Item`**, and the input has been replaced with **`SearchBar`**.

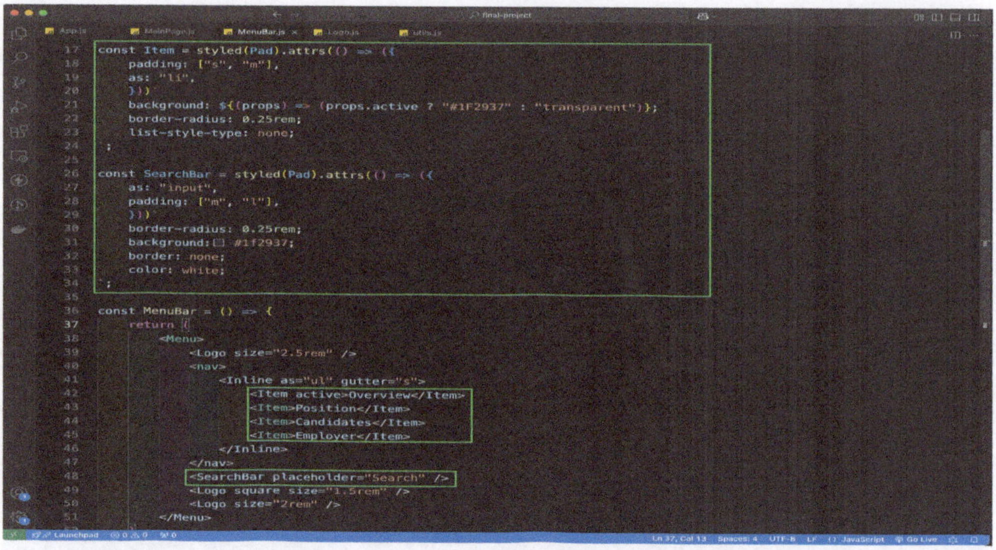

Figure 17.13: *Styled Component in MenuBar.js*

In http://localhost:3000/, the **`Navbar`** is displayed perfectly.

Figure 17.14: *MenuBar Completely Styled in Localhost*

Sidebar Menu

In the **`MainPage.js`** file, add the **`Content`** component.

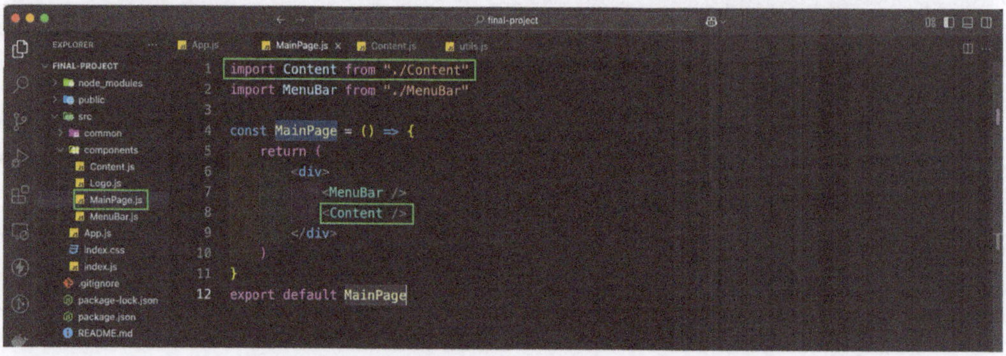

Figure 17.15: *Rendering Content from MainPage.js*

Now, create a **`Content.js`** file inside the **`components`** folder. It contains the basic skeleton with **`div`**, **`header`**, **`main`**, and **`nav`** tags.

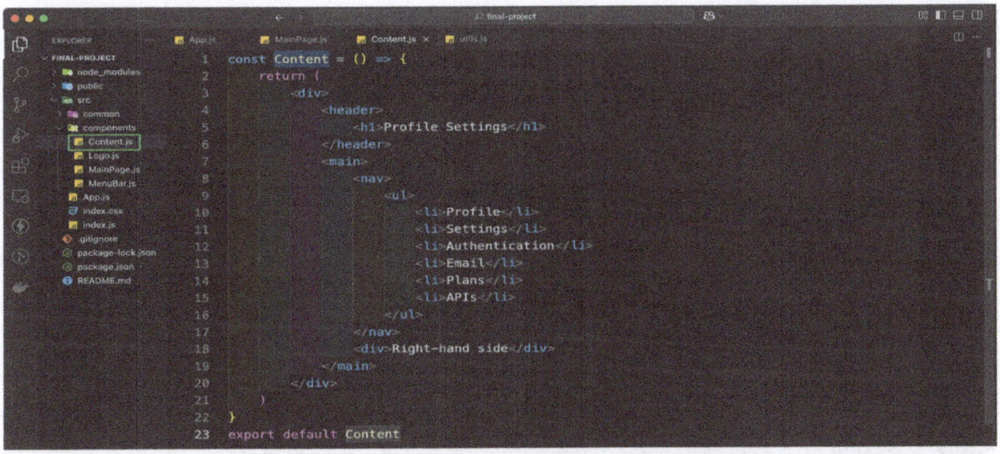

Figure 17.16: *Skeleton Code in Content.js*

In http://localhost:3000/, we will see the basic content.

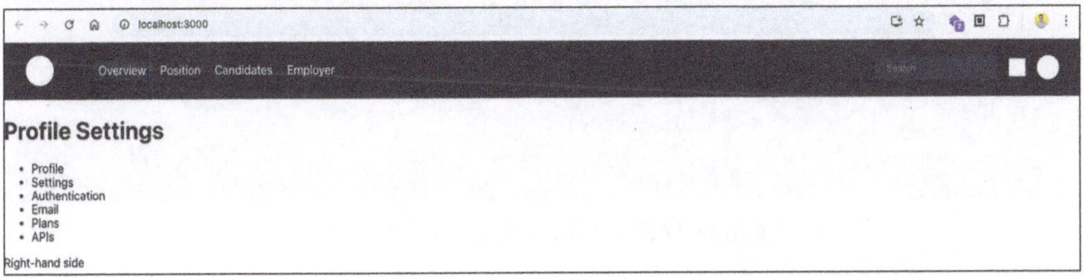

Figure 17.17: *Localhost Showing Content*

We will also change the overall background in the **`index.css`** file.

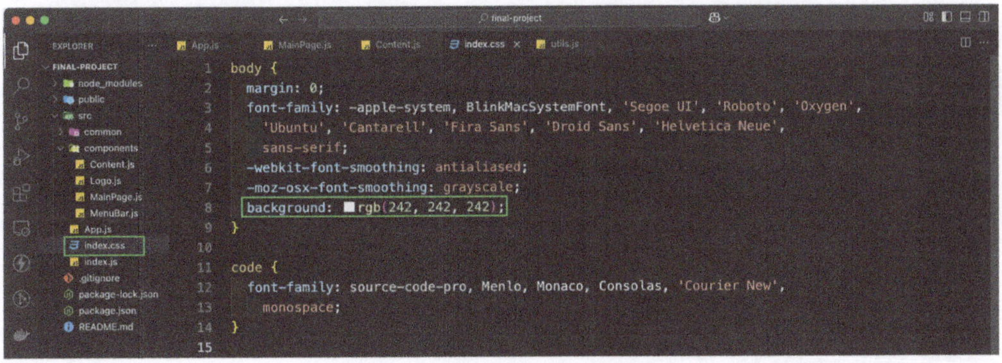

Figure 17.18: *Updating index.css*

In the **`Content.js`** file, use the Pad-styled component to create a new styled component called **`ContentArea`**. Also, create another **`styled`** component called **`SettingsHeader`**.

Next, replace the root **div** with **ContentArea**, and the **header** with **SettingsHeader**.

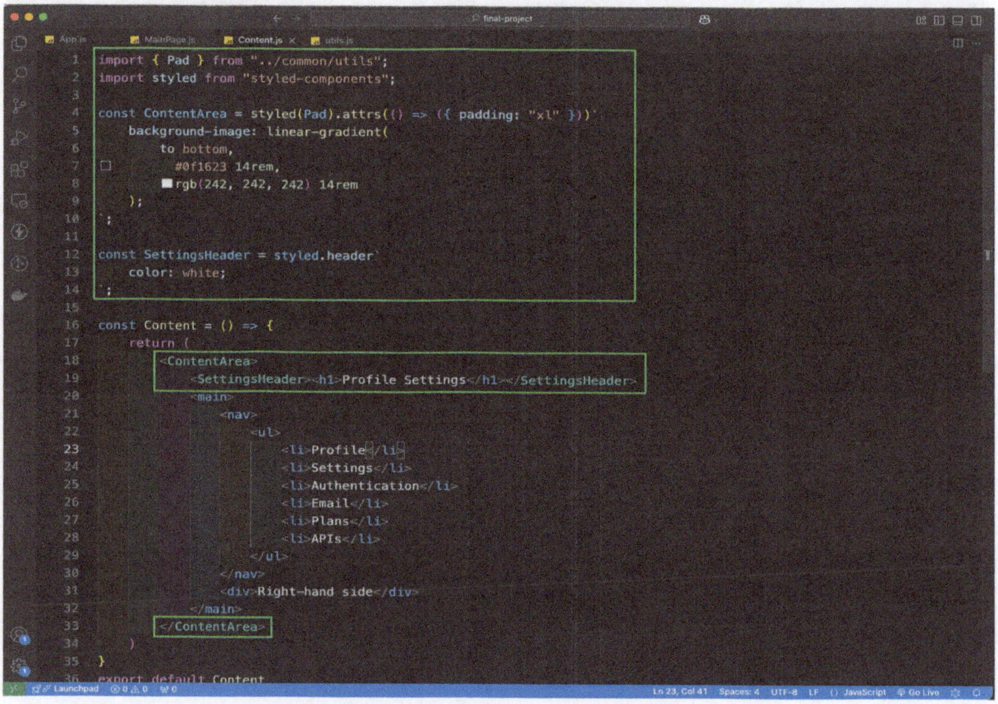

Figure 17.19: *ContentArea in Content.js*

Now, in http://localhost:3000/, the background and text of the content have changed.

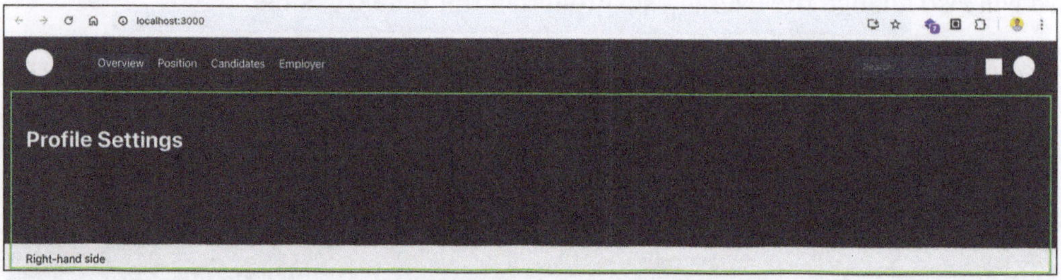

Figure 17.20: *ContentArea Styled in Localhost*

In the **utils.js** file, add **Fractions**, **Split**, **Layers** and **Center** from the earlier chapters.

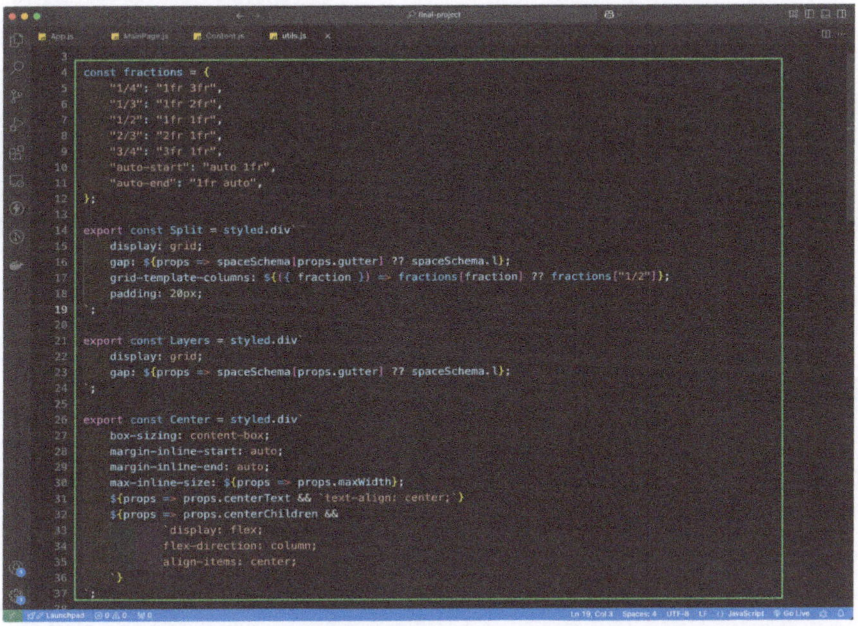

Figure 17.21: *Adding More Styled Components in utils.js*

In the **`Content.js`** file, add one more styled component, **`SettingsPane`** which uses the Split-styled component. We have wrapped everything with **`Center`**, and also replaced the **`main`** tag with **`SettingsPane`**.

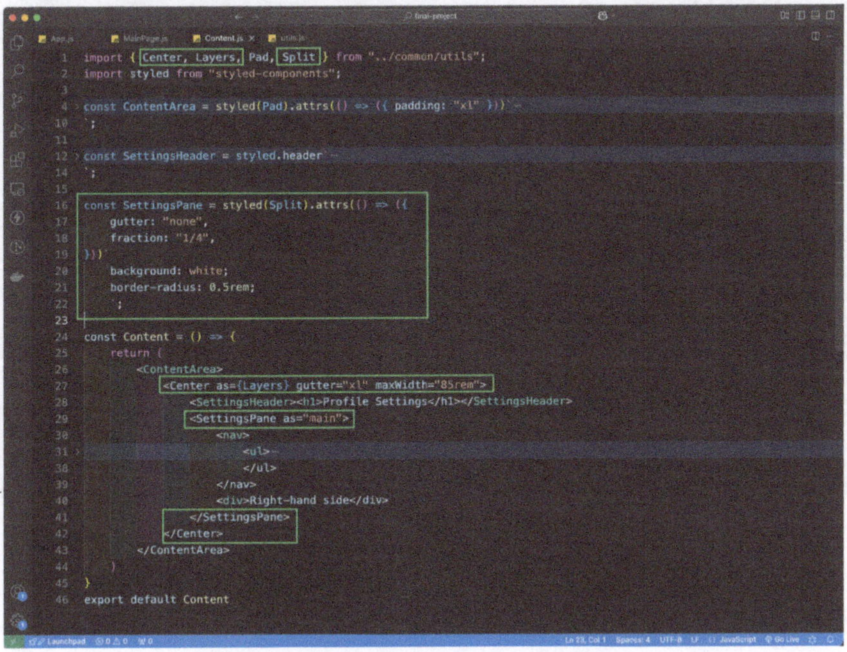

Figure 17.22: *SettingsPane in Content.js*

Now, the **li** elements are showing correctly on the left side in http://localhost:3000/.

Figure 17.23: *ContentArea More Styled in Localhost*

Now, for the **nav**, including the **ul** and **li** from **Content.js**, we will create a different component. So, create a **SideBar.js** file in the **components** folder. Here, first, import the required elements.

Next, create the styled components, **SideMenu** and **SideMenuItem** in the **SideBar.js** file.

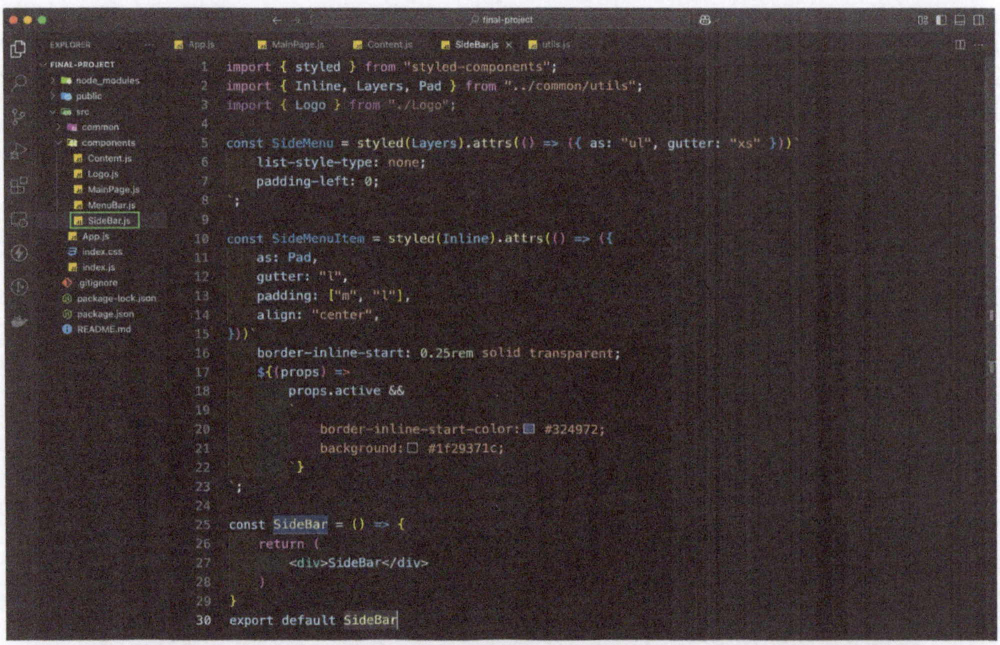

Figure 17.24: *SideBar.js File*

Now, inside the return statement in the **SideBar.js** file, wrap everything with a Pad-styled component. Then, we have the **SideMenu**, and all the items as **SideMenuItem**.

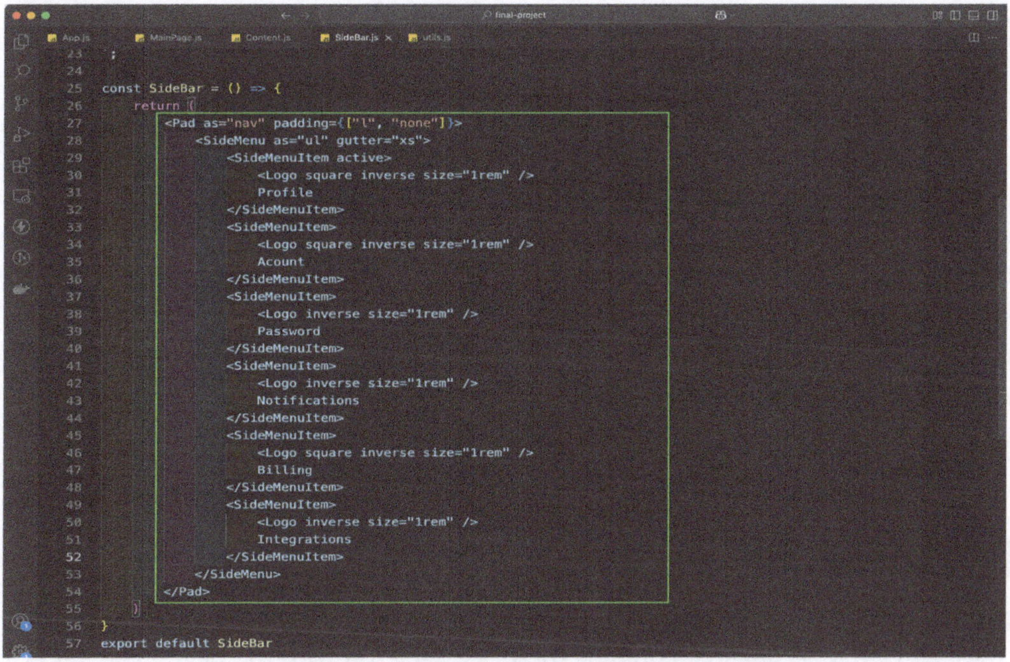

Figure 17.25: *Styled Components in SideBar.js File*

Now, in the **`Content.js`** file, remove the **`nav`** code, and render the **`SideBar`** component.

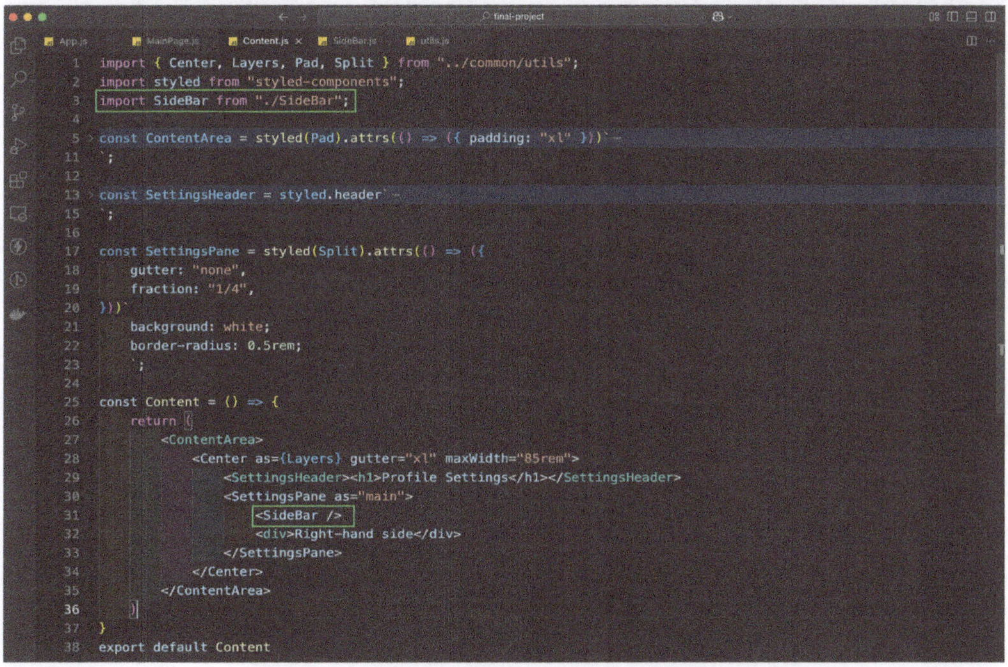

Figure 17.26: *Rendering SideBar from Content.js File*

Now, our **Sidebar** menu is perfect in http://localhost:3000/.

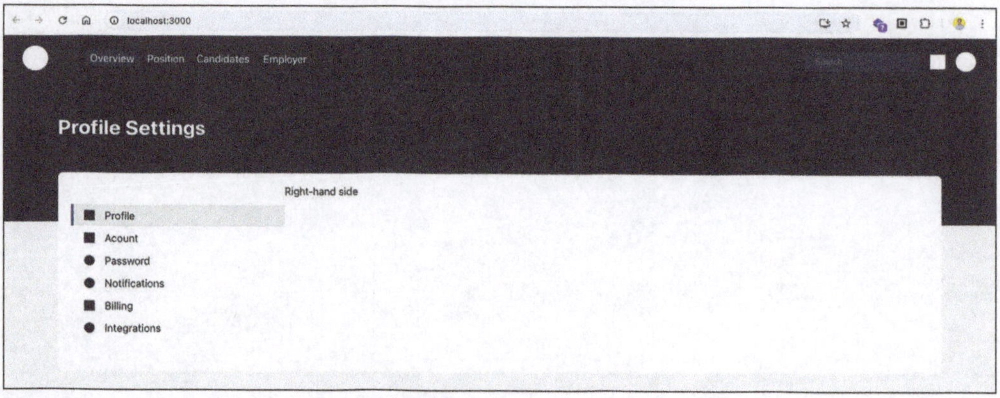

Figure 17.27: *SideBar Menu in Localhost*

Building Form

The right-hand side will contain a form. For this, create a **RightSide.js** file in the **components** folder. This file contains the basic skeleton with the **main div**, **section** and **button**.

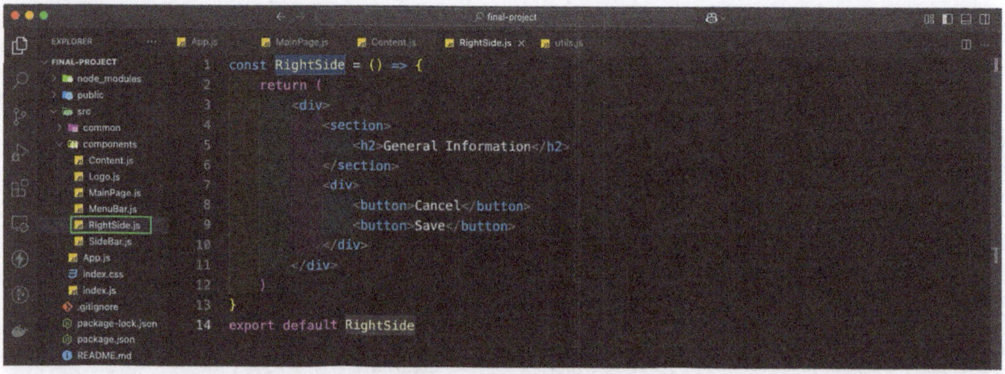

Figure 17.28: *RightSide.js File*

Now, in the **Content.js** file, replace the **div** in the following **SideBar** with the **RightSide** component.

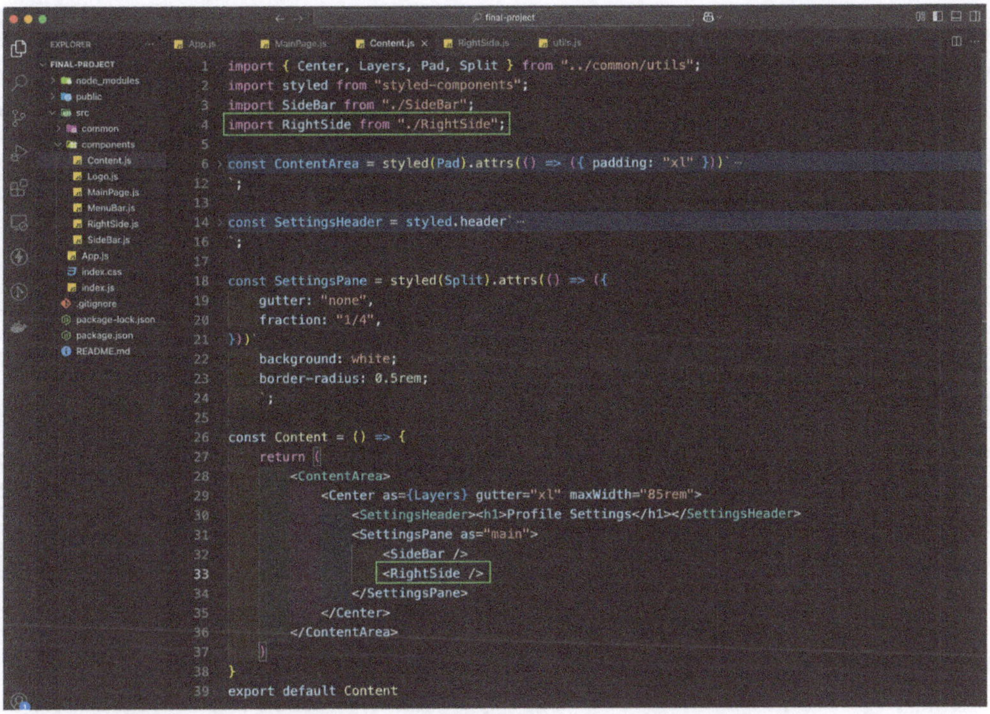

Figure 17.29: *Rendering RightSide in Content.js File*

Now, in http://localhost:3000/, we have a basic text and two buttons on the right side.

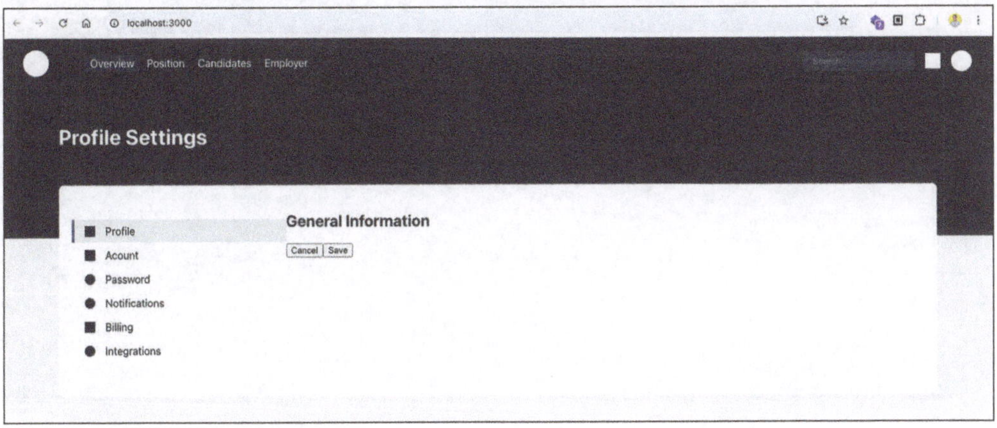

Figure 17.30: *Localhost Showing Basic RightSide*

In the **`RightSide.js`** file, add styled components for **`Form`**, **`InputGroup`**, **`SubLabel`** and **`Input`**.

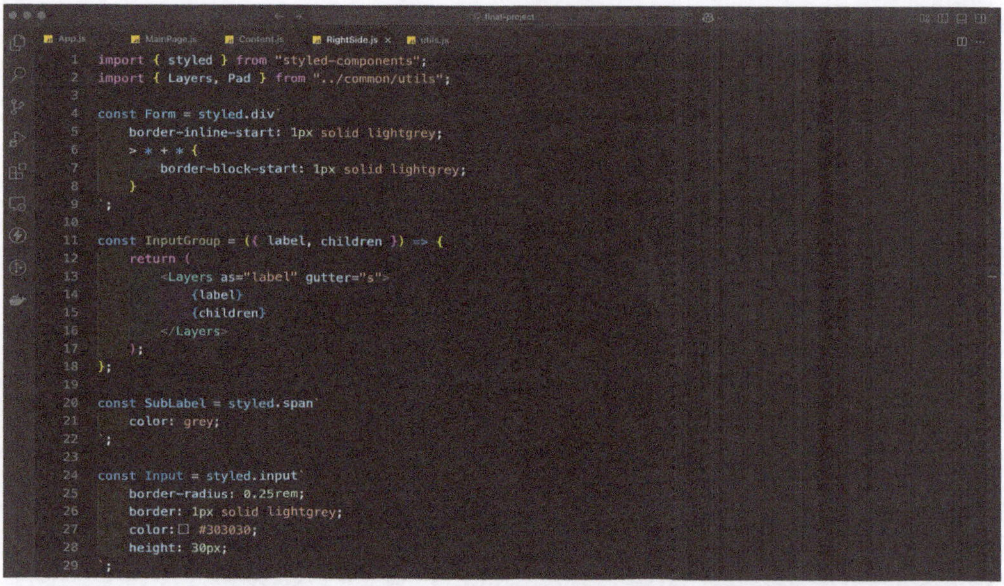

Figure 17.31: *Adding Styled Components in RightSide.js*

Within the **`return`** statement in the **`RightSide.js`** file, wrap everything with the **`Form-styled`** component. Then, use the **`Layers`** and **`SubLabel`**-styled components to wrap the content.

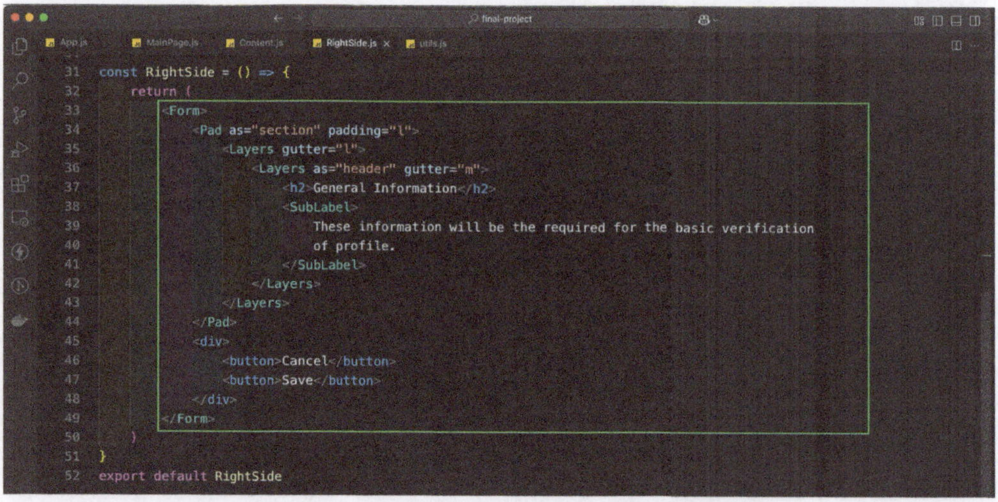

Figure 17.32: *Using Styled-components in RightSide.js*

Now, in http://localhost:3000/, our **`RightSide`** component is displayed better.

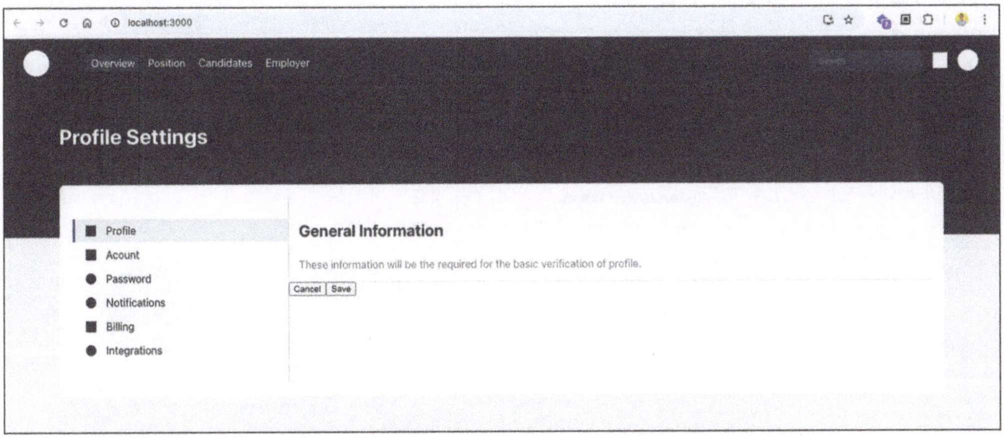

Figure 17.33: *Localhost Showing Basic RightSide*

In the following internal **`Layers`** in the **`RightSide.js`** file, add a **`Split-styled`** component. Inside it, place another **`Layers`**, and then add two **`InputGroup`** components containing Input.

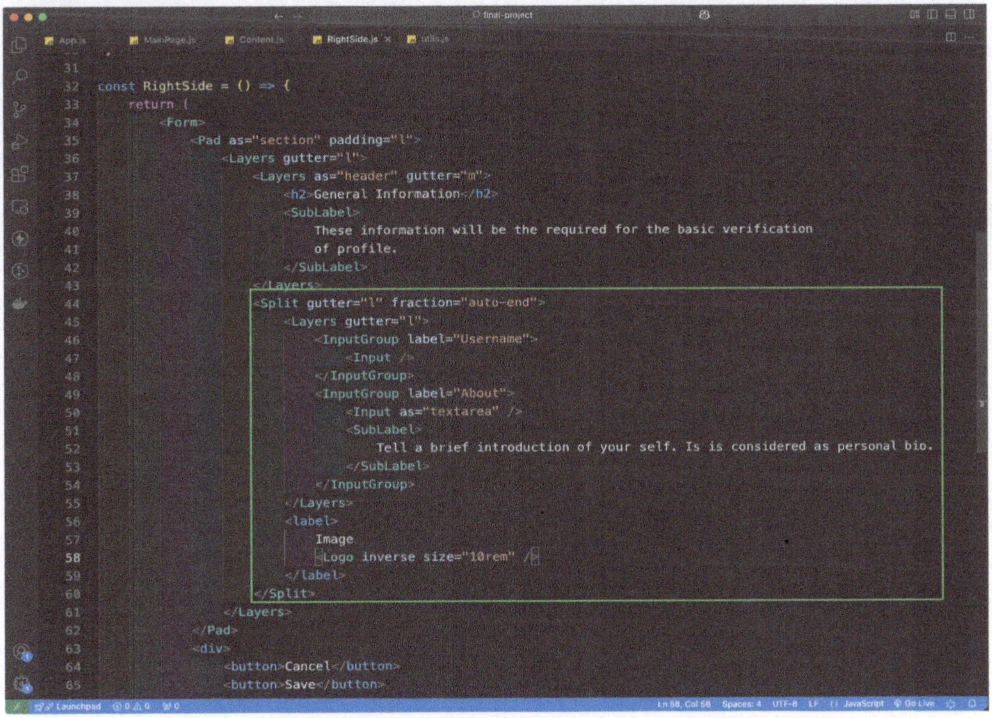

Figure 17.34: *Adding More Styled Components in RightSide.js*

Now, in http://localhost:3000/, we will see a nice form.

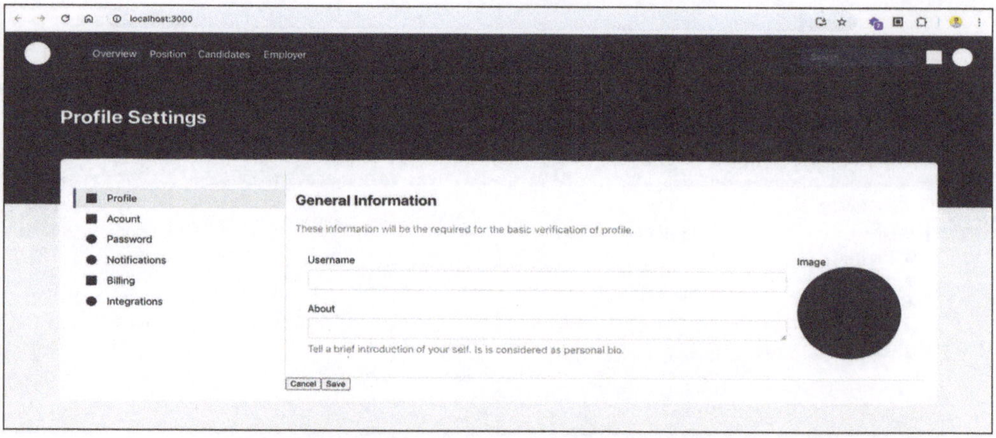

Figure 17.35: *Localhost Showing Better RightSide*

In the **utils.js** file, add **Columns** and **Column-styled** components.

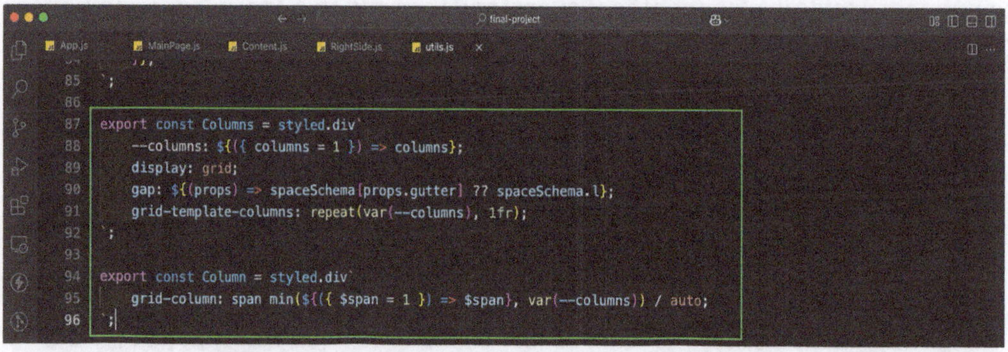

Figure 17.36: *Adding More Styled Components in utils.js*

Now, in the **RightSide.js** file, after the **Split** component, add the **Columns**-styled component. After this, use various **InputGroup** components with Input.

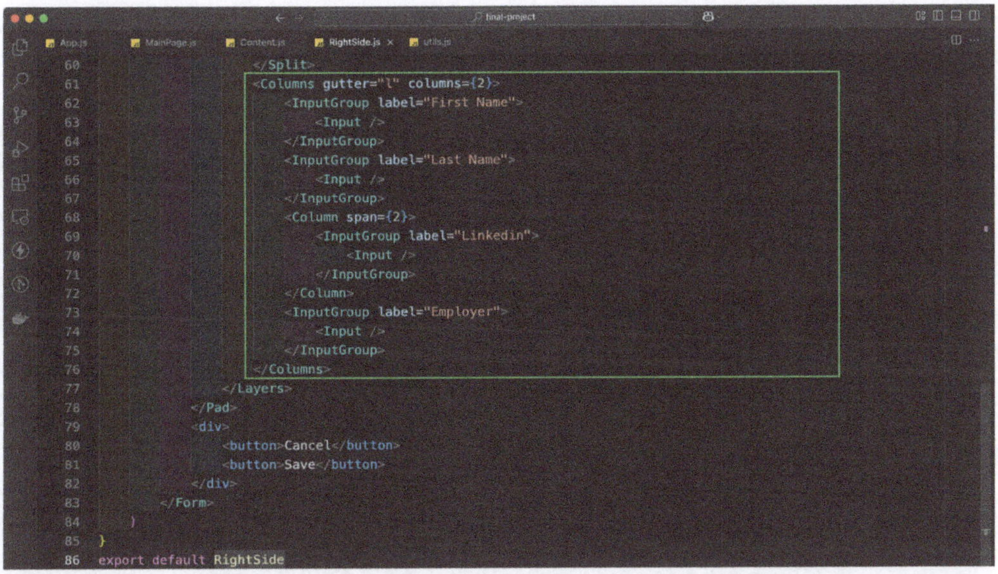

Figure 17.37: *Using More Styled Components in RightSide.js*

In http://localhost:3000/, we have all the input fields displayed.

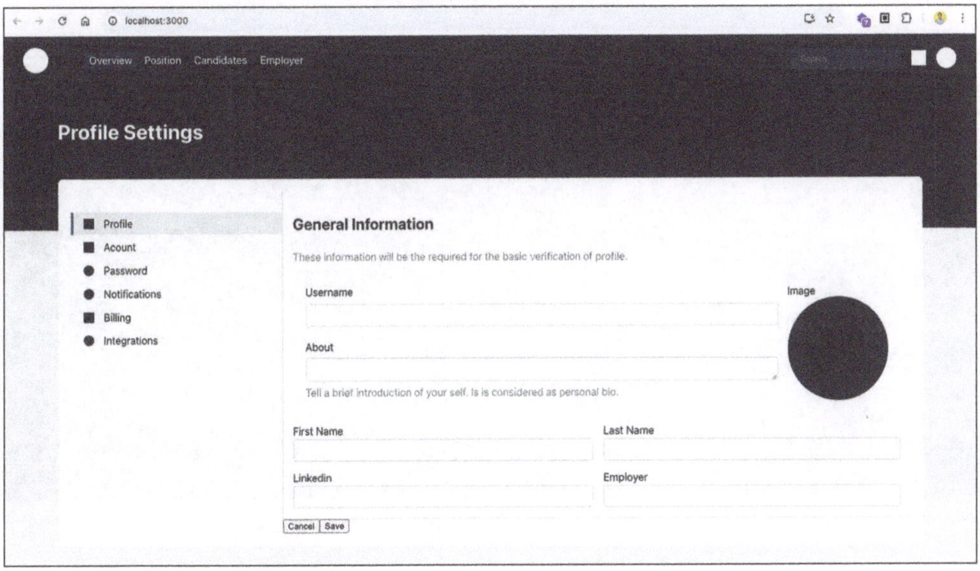

Figure 17.38: *Localhost Showing Completed RightSide*

Finishing Buttons

The last thing remaining is the two buttons in our form. For that, create a **`Controls.js`** file in the **`components`** folder.

Here, create a **Button-styled** component, which has the button parameters, and also takes props. Inside the **return** statement, create two buttons inside the inline-styled component.

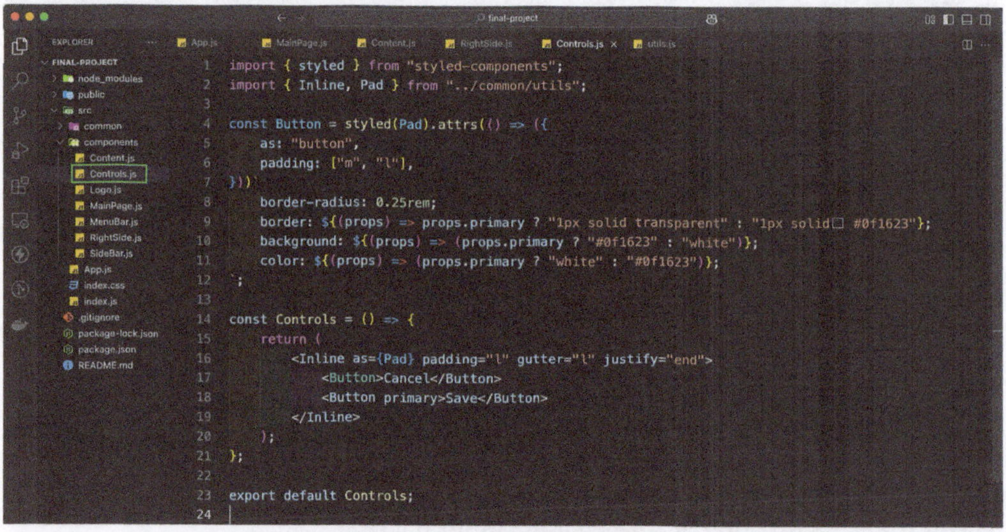

Figure 17.39: *Controls.js File*

In the **RightSide.js** file, remove the buttons, and render the **Controls** component.

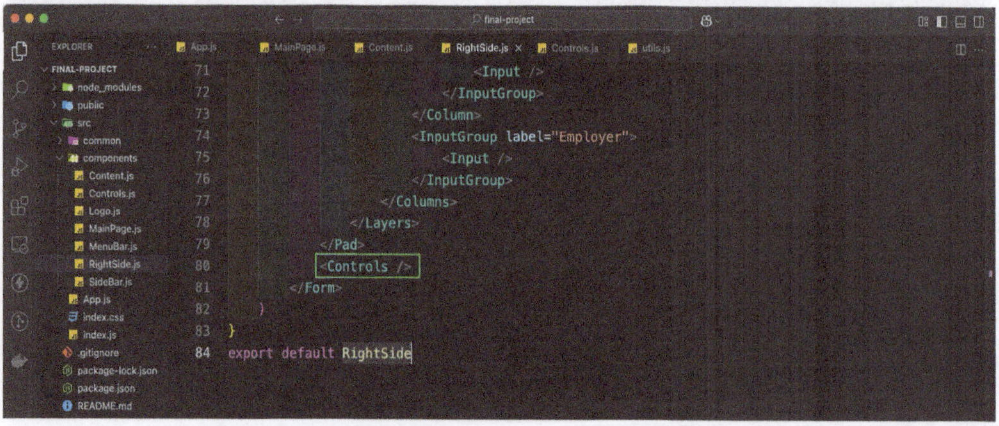

Figure 17.40: *Rendering Controls from RightSide.js File*

Now, in http://localhost:3000/, our final project is complete, and everything is visible.

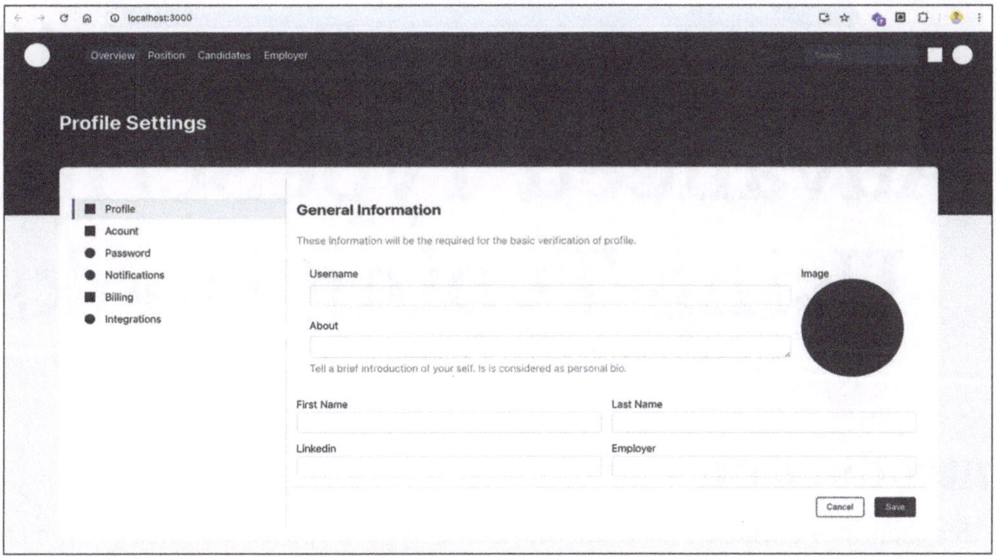

Figure 17.41: *Completed Project*

Conclusion

In this chapter, we completed our final project using the Design System. First, we built a Navbar with a **`Menu`** and **`Header`**. After that, we created the left sidebar in the project.

Next, we worked on the right-hand side, where we created a form. Finally, we added two buttons to the form.

In the next chapter, **we will start a new section on TypeScript**.

Points to Remember

- Create **`Navbar`** with **`Menu`**, using the design system.
- Create **`Left sidebar`**, using the design system.
- Create a **`Form`**, using the design system.
- Create a **`Button`**, using the design system.

CHAPTER 18
Advanced TypeScript Using Typing Hooks

Introduction

In this chapter, we will start with the **Advanced TypeScript** section. Here, we will be learning about **Typing Hooks**. By typing hooks, we mean the type of hooks. Also, we will learn to write the types of hooks in typescript, and some advanced types in hooks.

Structure

In this chapter, we are going to discuss the following topics:

- Overview
- Typing `useState`
- State without Initial State
- Passing States and Events
- Typing `useRef`
- Typing Custom Hooks
- Complex States
- Tuples with Custom Hooks

Overview

In this chapter, we will learn about typing hooks. Here, we will first learn about `useState` and state without initial state. After this, we will learn about passing states and events.

Next, we will learn about typing `useRef` and custom hooks. Further, we will learn about complex states. Lastly, we will learn about tuples with custom hooks.

Typing useState

First, we will look into **`useState`**, and check if we have any challenges in setting the default types of **`useState`**. We have first created a new react typescript project, and in the **`App.tsx`** file, we have added the **`ShoppingCard`** component.

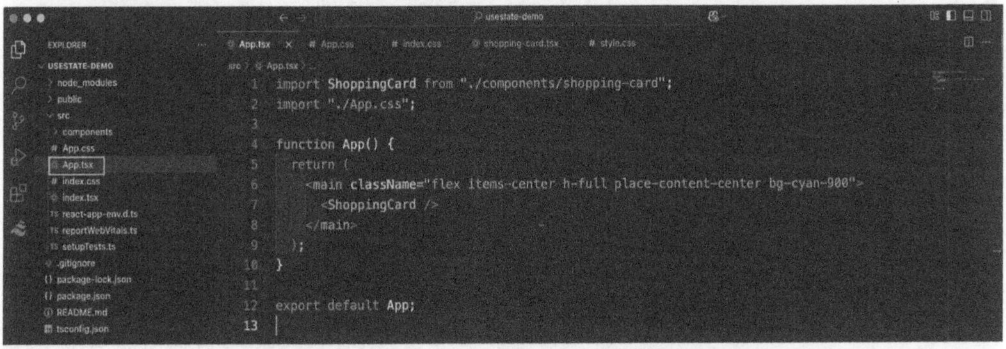

Figure 18.1: *App.js Rendering ShoppingCard*

Next, in the **`App.css`**, we have updated the basic styles.

Figure 18.2: App.css Styles

Also, updated the styles in the **`index.css`** file. All of these codes can be taken from the referenced project.

Figure 18.3: *index.css Styles*

Now, we will create a **`shopping-card.tsx`** file inside the components folder. Here, we will create the **`ShoppingCard`** component which will use the styles from the **`style.css`** file.

In this simple component, we are showing a value. It has an increment, decrement and reset button. We also have a form through which we can add a number, and click a button to update the value.

Note that we have not added any types. But these types are implicitly defined in this file.

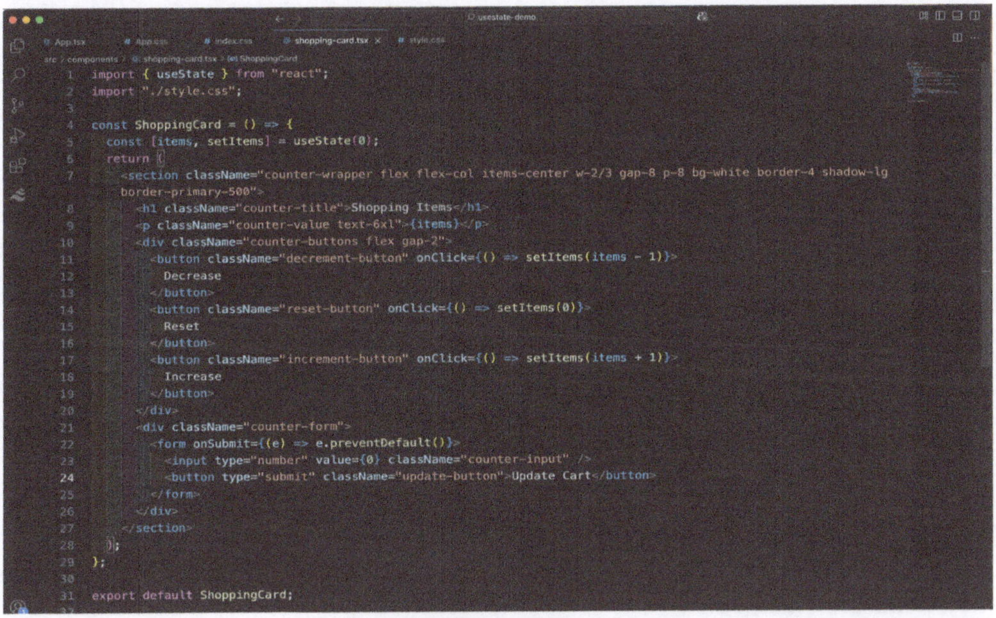

Figure 18.4: *shopping-card.tsx File*

Now, we have added the code for this component in the **`style.css`** file.

Figure 18.5: *style.css File*

In http://localhost:3000/, we have a nice looking Shopping Items component.

***Figure 18.6:** Localhost Showing Shopping Items*

The code for our form was not added. So, we have added the same in the **`shopping-card.tsx`** file. For this we also need an **`useEffect`** changing the state of **`inputItems`** when items are changed.

Notice, we are also explicitly defining the typescript in both of the **`useState`**. The items state is a number and the **`inputItems`** state can be a string or number.

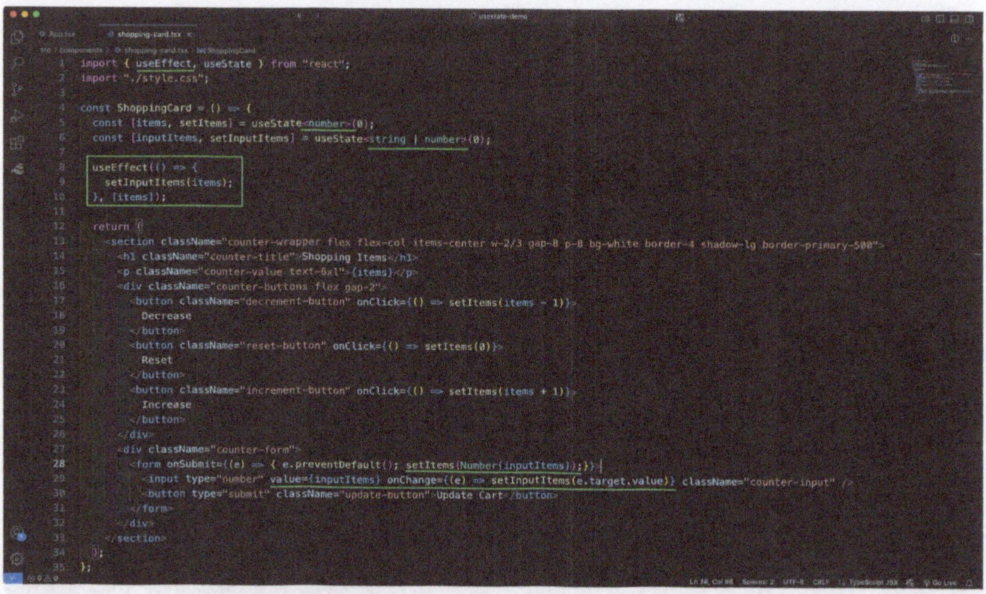

***Figure 18.7:** Form Logic in Shopping-card.tsx File*

Now, in http://localhost:3000/, when we change the text in the input field, and click on the **`Update Cart`** button, the item value also gets changed.

***Figure 18.8:** Form Update in Localhost*

There is a TypeScript shortcut which is **valueAsNumber**. If we change it in the **onChange** of input, we can get rid of Number in the **setItems**. Also, we have removed the explicit types in the **useState**.

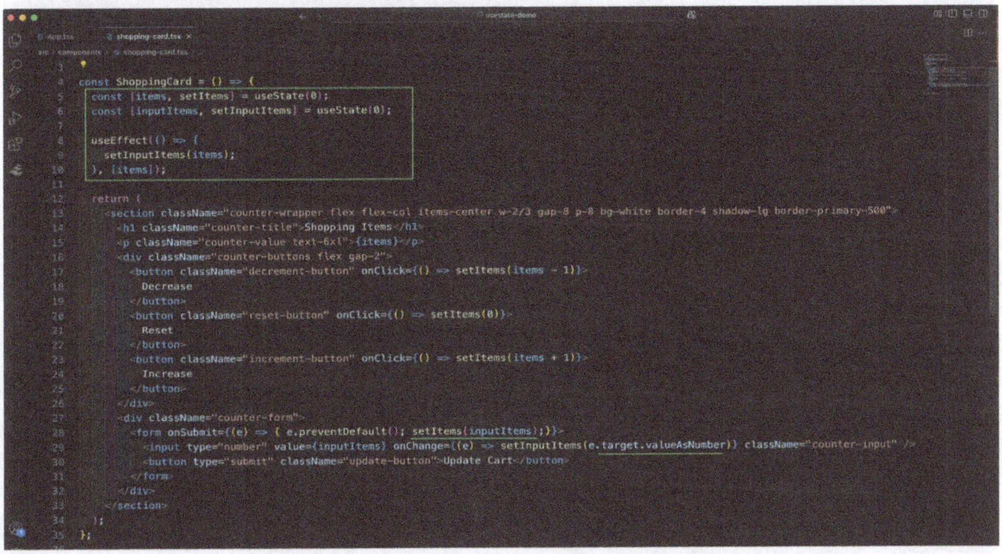

***Figure 18.9:** valueAsNumber in shopping-card.tsx*

Back in http://localhost:3000/, everything works the same.

Figure 18.10: *Localhost with Shopping Items*

State Without Initial State

Now, for this section, we have a new project. So, in the **`index.tsx`** file, we have removed the unrequited things.

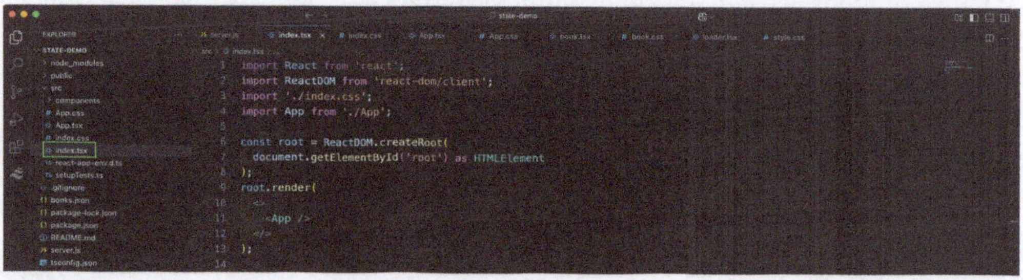

Figure 18.11: *index.tsx File*

Next, we have updated the **`index.css`** file.

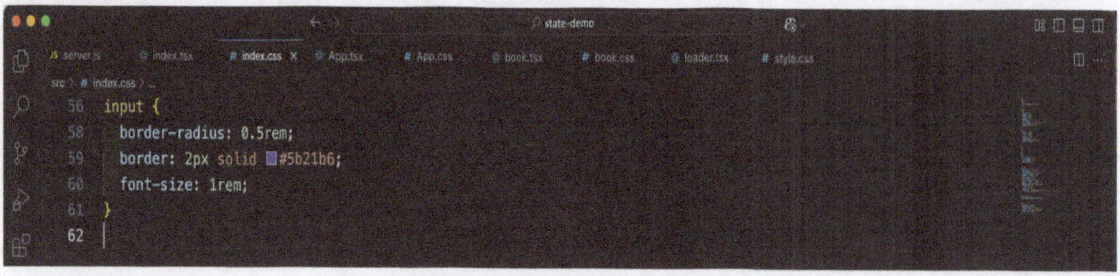

Figure 18.12: *index.css File*

Now, in the **`App.tsx`** file, we have first imported the required things, including **`axios`** and **`Book`** components. Next, we have created a type for **`Book`**, which has an **`id`**, **`title`** and **`author`**.

We also have a function called **`fetchRandomBook`**, which is calling an API endpoint that we are going to create soon.

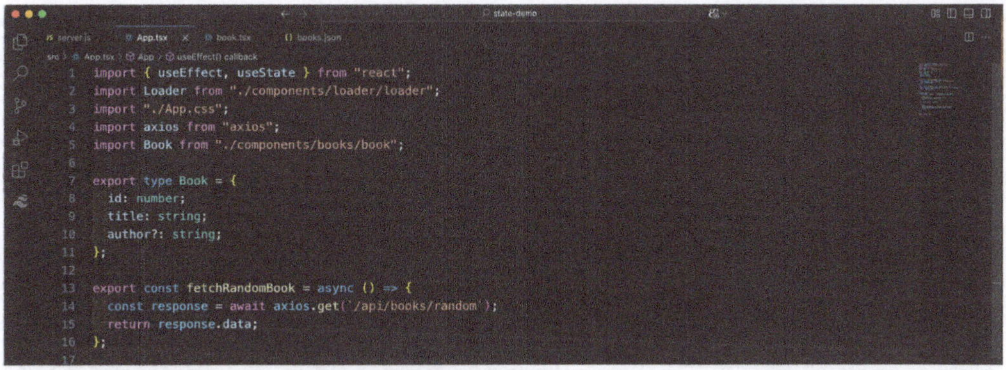

Figure 18.13: *App.tsx File with Type Book*

Inside the **App()**, we are having a state of the book, first. Here, we are keeping its type as Book or undefined. Next, the **useEffect()** is calling the function **fetchRandomBook()**.

Also, inside the **return** statement, we are rendering the **Book** component. We are passing the props of title and author here.

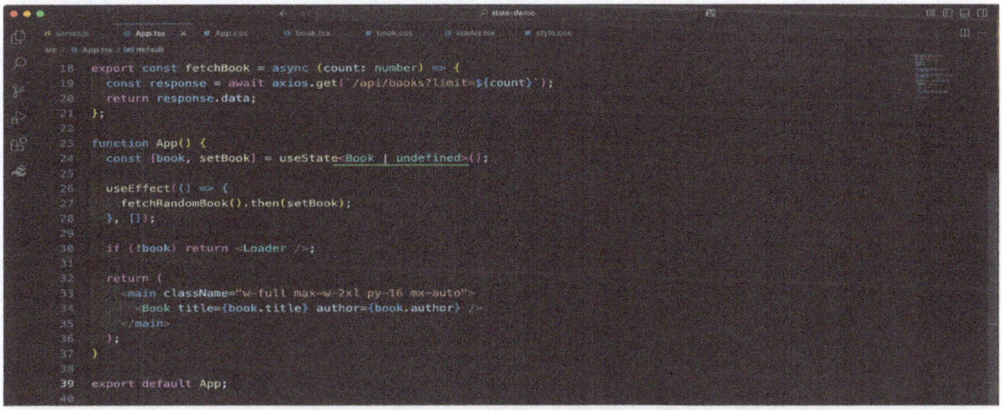

Figure 18.14: *App.tsx File Rendering Book Component*

Now, we will add styles in the **App.css** file.

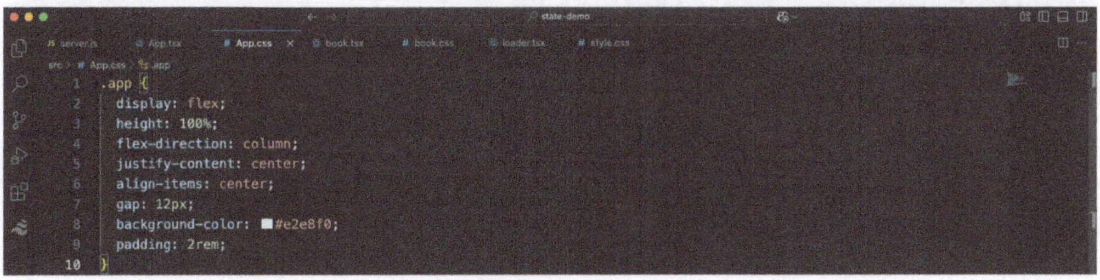

Figure 18.15: *App.css File*

Next, we are going to create the **book.tsx** file. Here, we are getting the title and the author props. And for these props, we have to create a type of **BookProps**, which have title and author as string.

Inside the **return** statement, we are just showing the **title** and **author** with some styles.

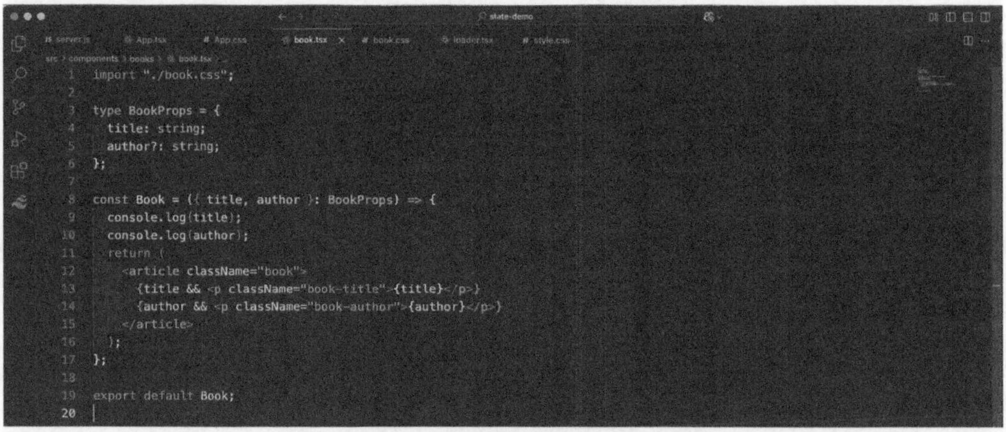

Figure 18.16: *Book.tsx File*

We are creating the styles for the **Book** component in the **book.css** file.

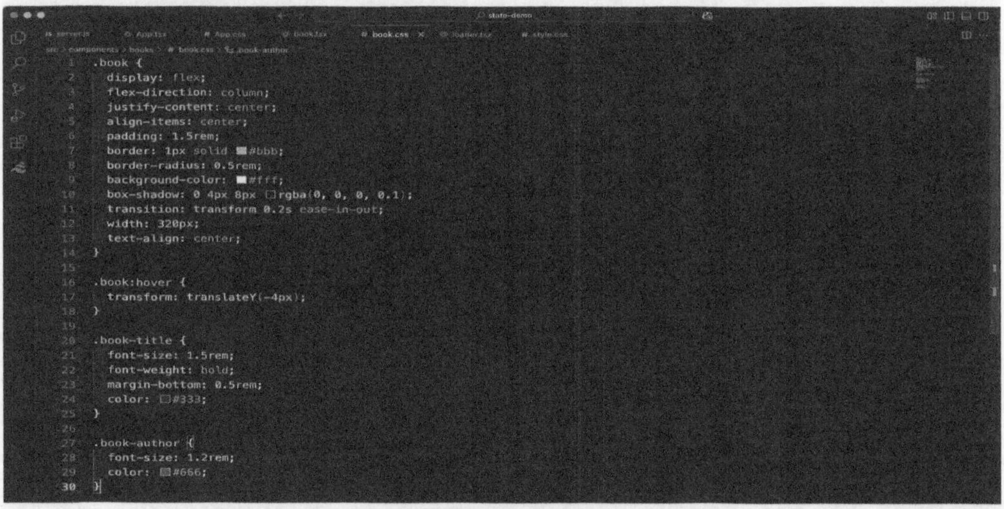

Figure 18.17: *Book.css File*

We also have a **Loader** rendered in the **App.tsx** file. So, we will create a **loader.tsx** file, and have a simple **Loader** here.

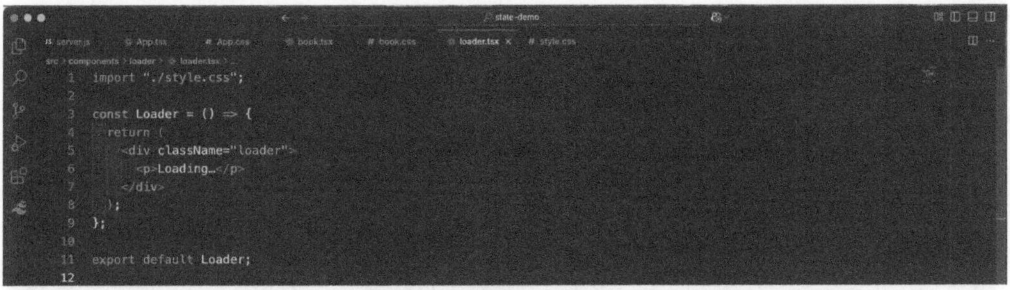

Figure 18.18: *Loader.tsx File*

We will also add the styles for the **`Loader`** component now in the **`style.css`** file.

Figure 18.19: *Style.css File*

Now, we will create a **`books.json`** file, which will be used to do the API call from a simple server. This contains an array of objects, which have **`title`** and **`author`**.

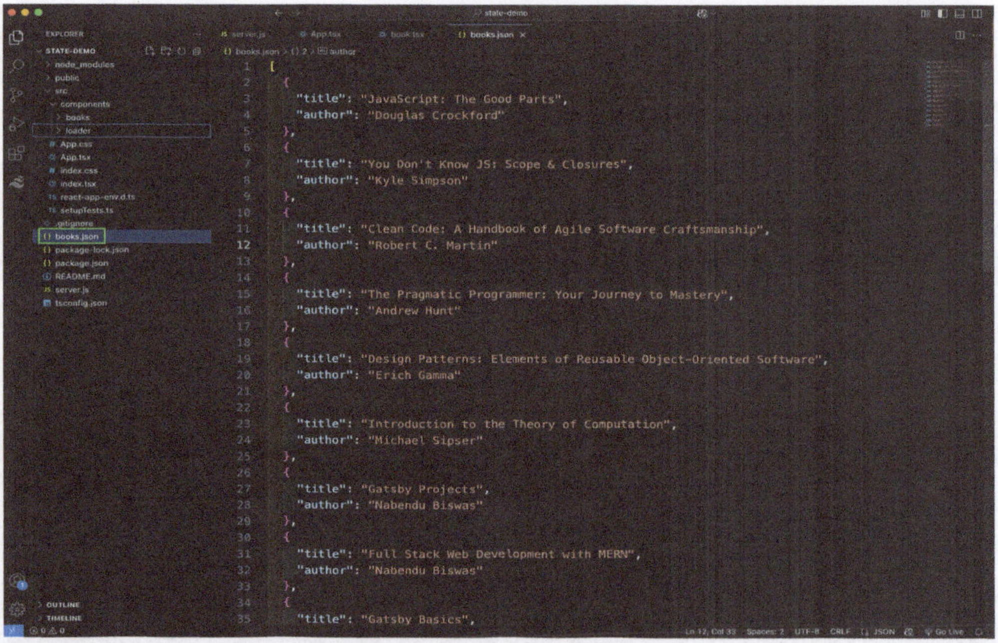

Figure 18.20: *Books.json File*

Now, we will create a simple node server with **`server.js`** file. It contains the API logic required from our frontend.

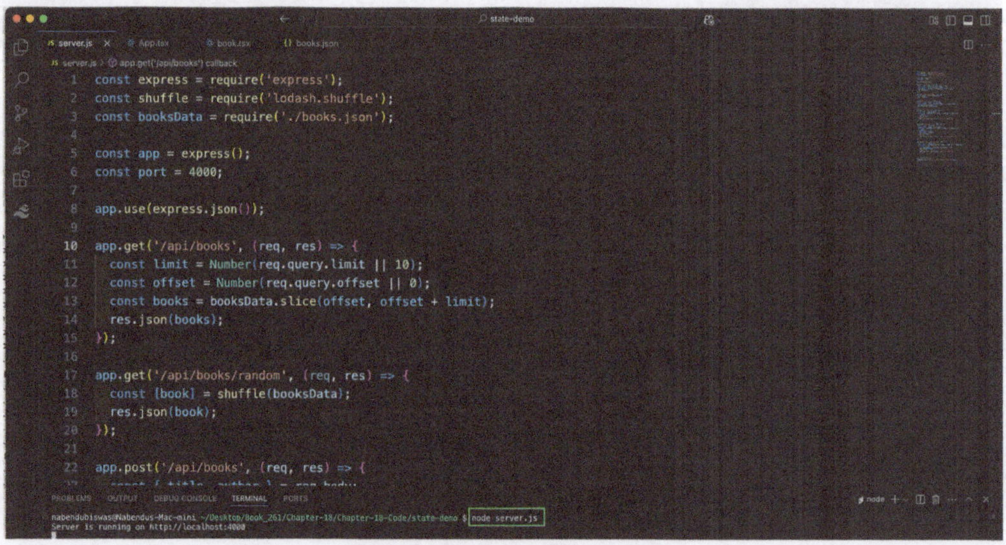

Figure 18.21: *Server.js File*

Now, in http://localhost:3000/, we will see a random book title with the author.

Figure 18.22: *Localhost Showing Title with Author*

Passing States and Events

Now, we will add the logic in the same project for passing states and events. For this, first we need to update the **`index.css`** file as follows:

Figure 18.23: *Index.css File*

Next, we will also update the styles in the **`App.css`** file.

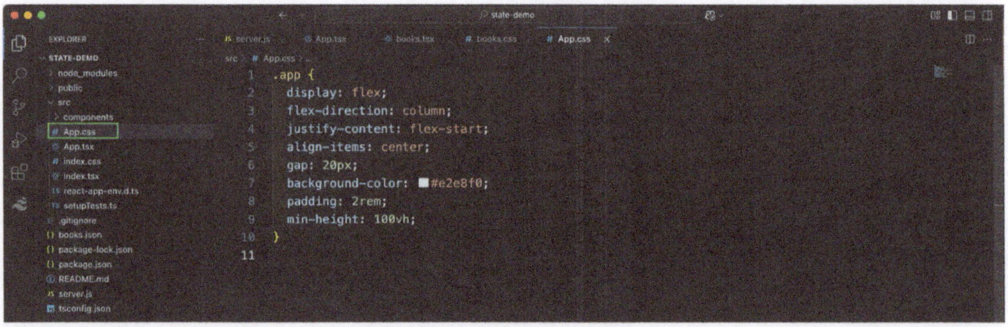

***Figure 18.24:** App.css File*

Now, we will create a new **books.tsx** file. Here, we are again taking a type of **BooksProps**, first. It has a count, **onSubmit** and **onChange** type. This includes count, **onSubmit**, **onChange**, and the **children** prop.

Inside the **Books** component, we have a form which takes an input, and has a **submit** button. Below the form, we render the children using **{children}**, which in this case, refers to the list of **Book** components passed from the **App** component.

***Figure 18.25:** Books.tsx File*

Now, we will create a **books.css** file, and add styles to it.

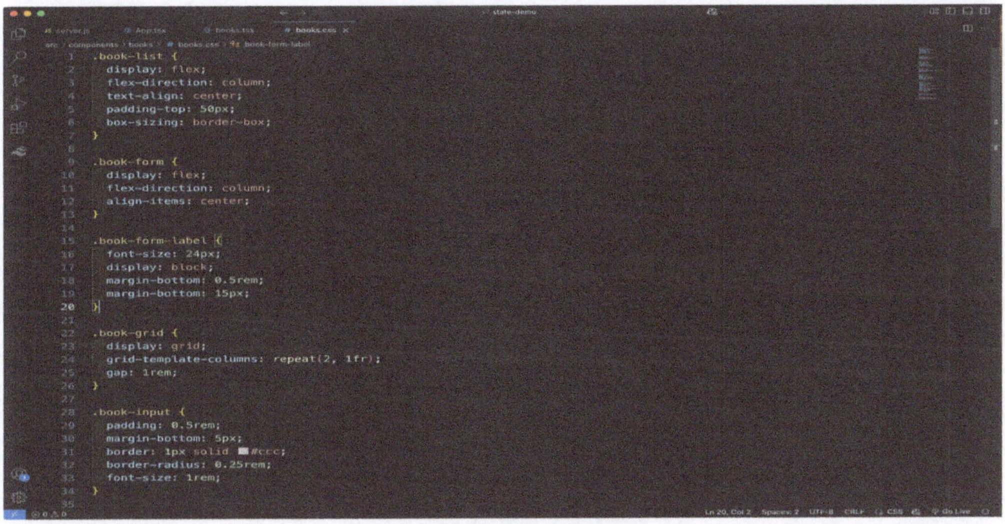

Figure 18.26: Books.css File

Back in the **App.tsx** file, we have added a state of books in which we have also given the type as a **Book** array. Next, we also have a count state, with the initial value of 5.

Inside the return statement, we are having the **Books** component, which have the count, **onChange** and **onSubmit** props. We are also passing each book, which we had received by map through the received data.

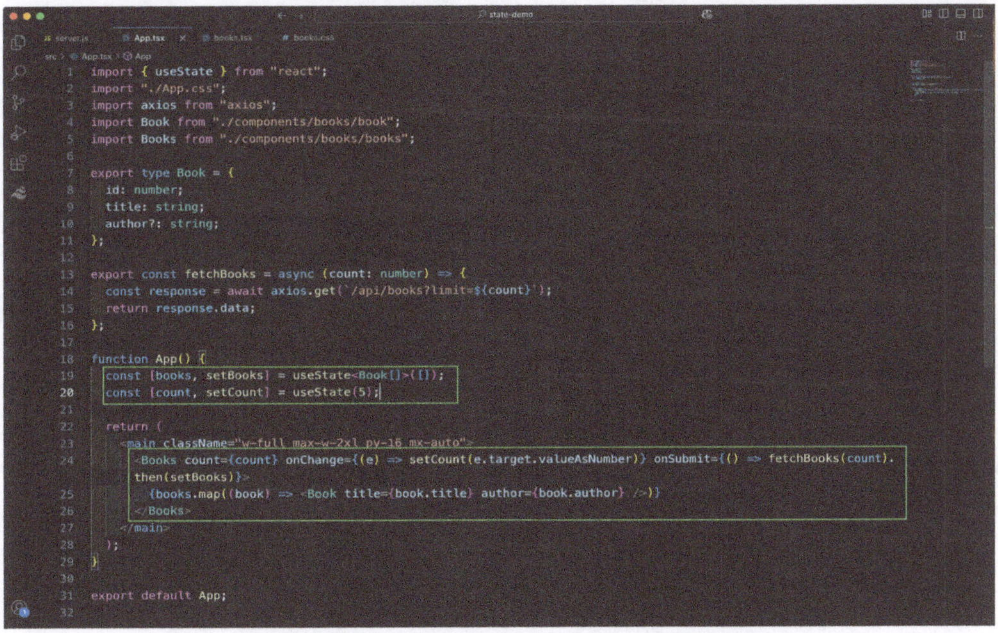

Figure 18.27: *Books Component in App.tsx File*

Now, in http://localhost:3000/, we can give a number in the input, and hit the **`Load Books`** button. It will load the number of books such as 2 in this case.

Figure 18.28: *Localhost with Two Books*

If we type 4, and click on **`Load Books`**, we will get four books.

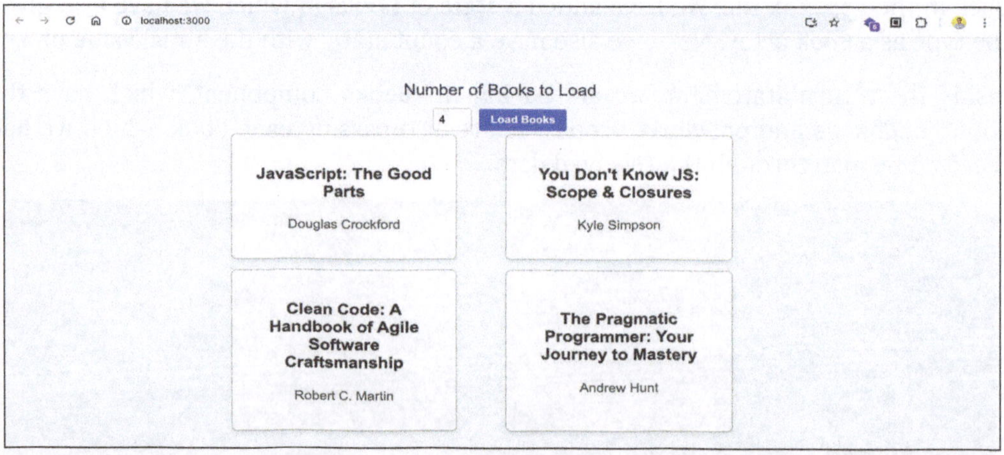

Figure 18.29: *Localhost with Four Books*

Typing `useRef`

Now, we will look into typing **`useRef`** hook. We have created a new project, and the **`App.tsx`** file has two **`refs`**. But we can see some errors here. These errors are coming because we cannot have refs without any values.

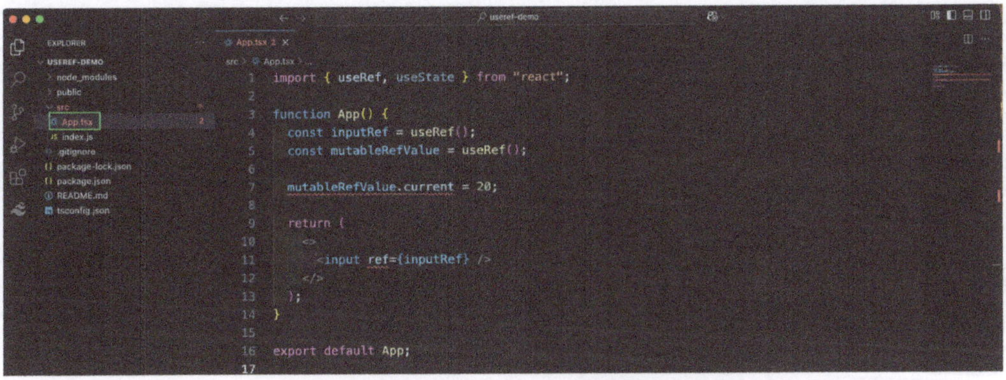

Figure 18.30: *App.tsx with useRef Issue*

So, to fix it, we have given the first ref as **`HTMLInputElement`** type and the value of null. Also, the second ref, the input type of number and the value of 20.

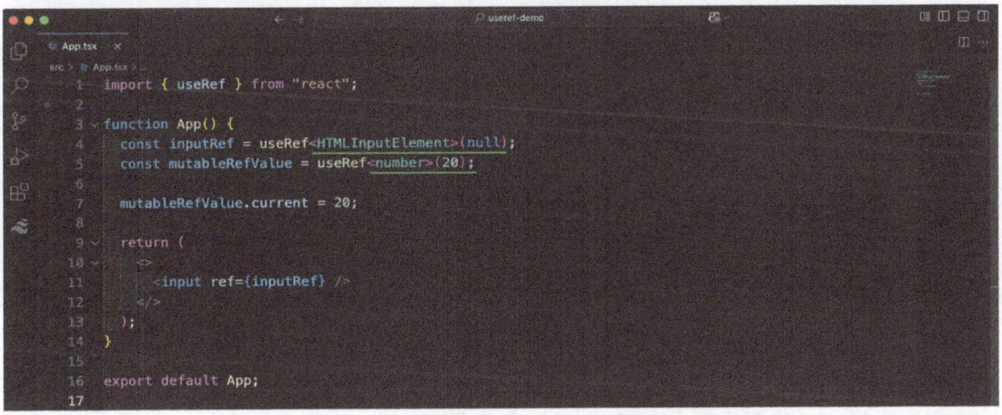

Figure 18.31: *App.tsx with useRef Fixed*

Typing Custom Hooks

Now, we will look into typing a custom hook. We have created a new project for the same. Here, inside the **`App.tsx`**, we have a custom hook of **`useUrl`**. It takes a **`defaultUrl`**, and returns the **`url`** as well as **`setUrl`**.

Inside the **`App()`**, we are just using this simple custom hook of **`useUrl`**.

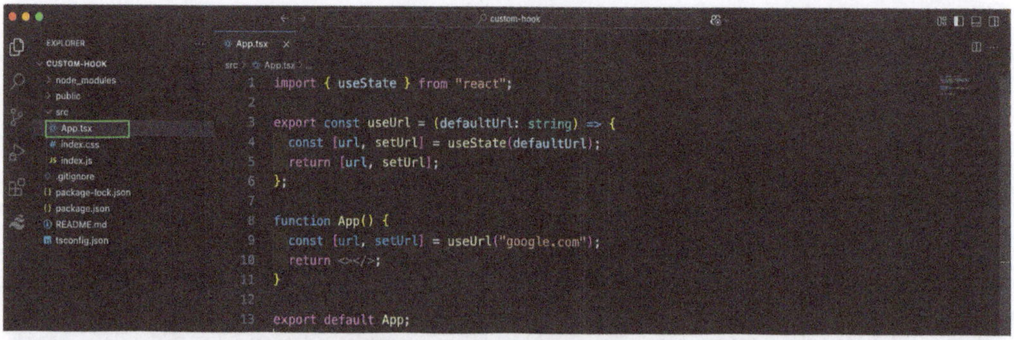

Figure 18.32: *App.tsx with useUrl Custom Hook*

Now, if we hover the mouse over the url, it will tell us that it should be a string. So, we have updated the same in the **`return`** statement.

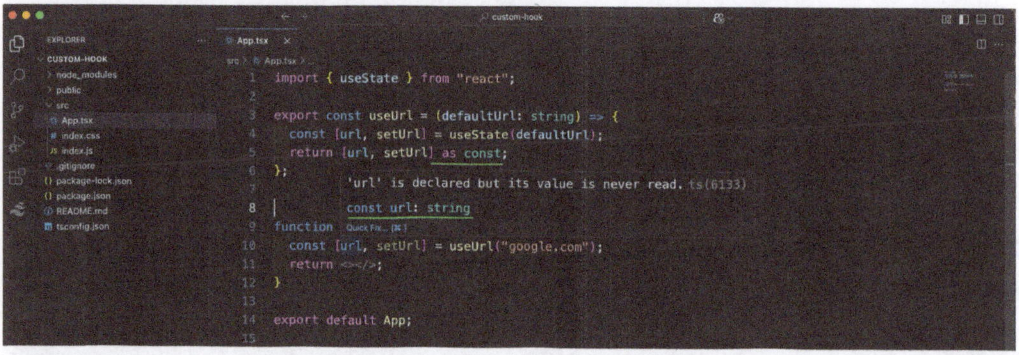

Figure 18.33: *App.tsx with useUrl Custom Hook Fixed*

Typing Complex States

Next, we will look into writing types for complex states. For this, we have created a new project, which has an **`use-user.tsx`** file. This file has a **`useUser`** custom hook that is taking a string.

It has a state with the initial value of fetching. Within the **`useEffect`**, the state is changed to fetched and error. Finally, we are returning to the state.

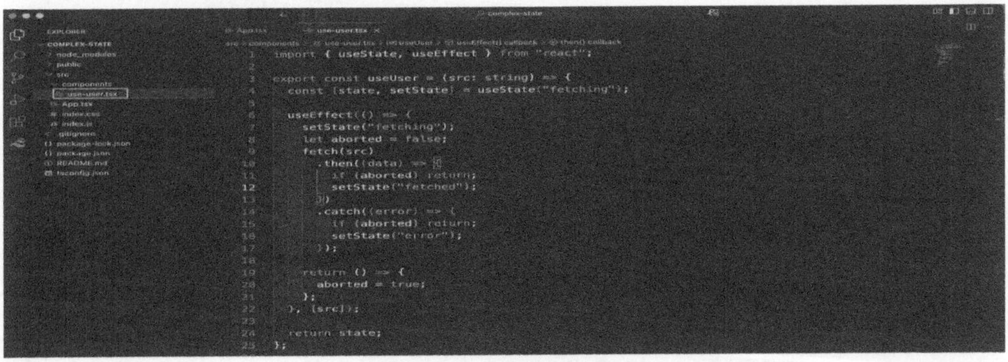

Figure 18.34: *Use-user.tsx File*

Now, in the **`App.tsx`**, we are calling the **`useUser`** hook. The state of fetching, fetched and error are doing different operations. But we can also have a state like non-existing-state, which is wrong.

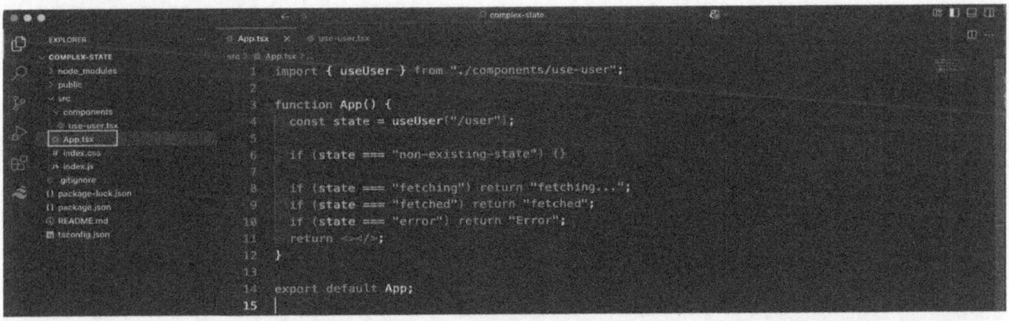

Figure 18.35: *App.tsx File*

To fix this, we will go back to **`use-user.tsx`** file, and have a type of **`State`** which can be fetching, fetched or error only. Next, we are using this **`State`** in the **`useState`**.

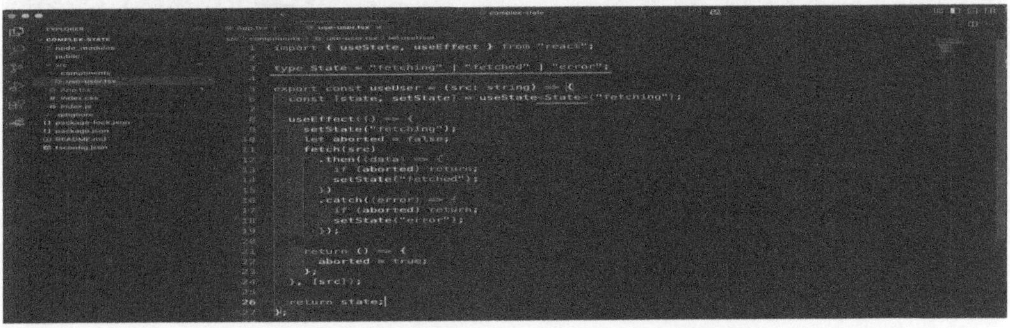

Figure 18.36: *Type State in use-user.tsx File*

Now, going back to **`App.tsx`**, we will see the perfect error for the **`non-existing-state`**.

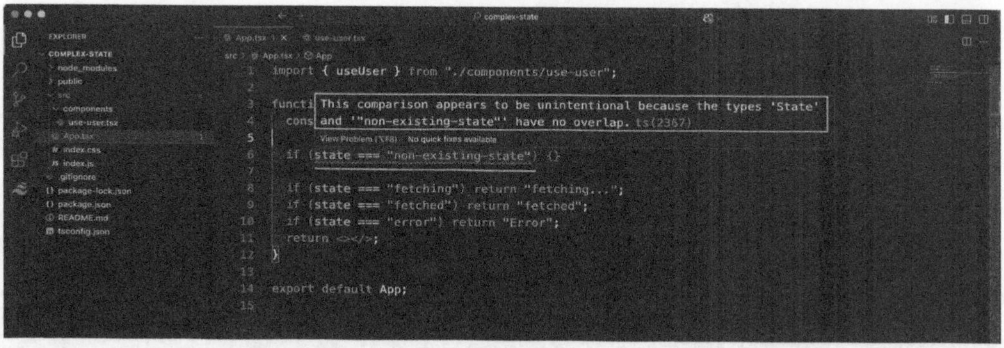

Figure 18.37: *Correct Error in App.tsx File*

We will change the **`use-user.tsx`** file to check a more complex state. Here, we have changed the **`useState`** to have an object of key status and value fetching as initial state.

We have changed the **`useEffect`** for fetching and fetched. But for status of error, we also want to pass the error. Here, we are getting an error for the same.

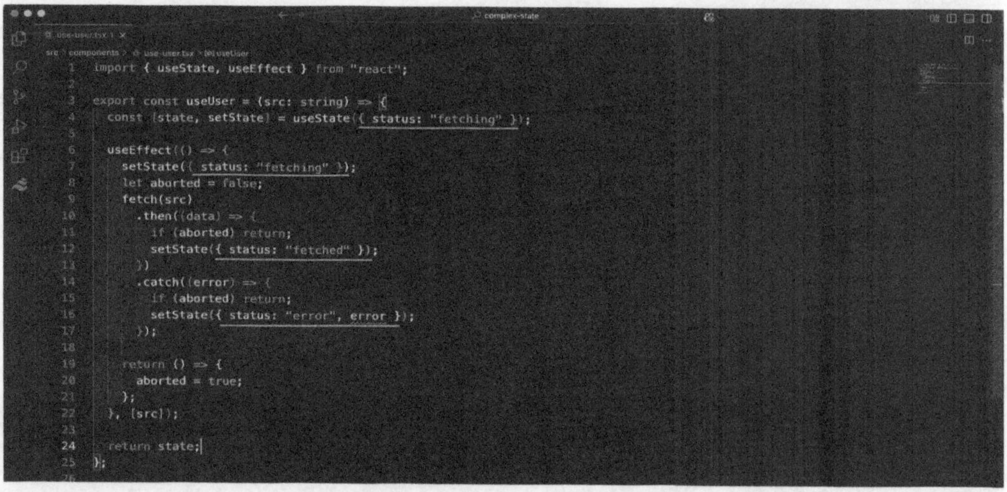

Figure 18.38: *Updating Use-user.tsx File*

To fix this issue, we will first go to **`App.tsx`**, and have the **`if`** statement. Then compare **`state.status`**, instead of state.

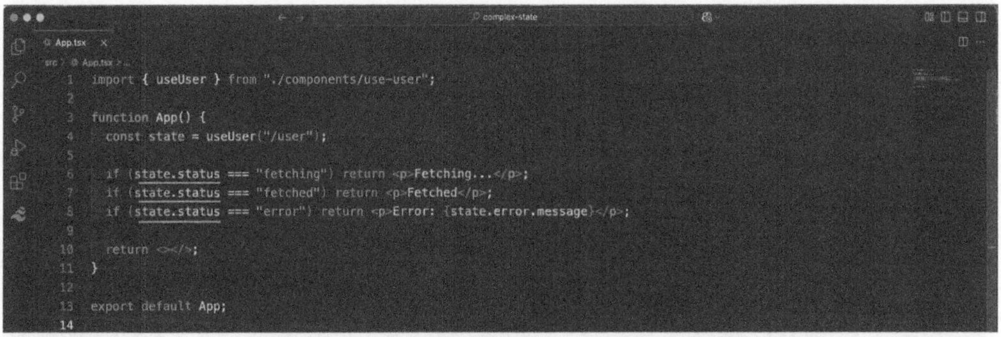

Figure 18.39: *Changing State in App.tsx File*

Next, back in the **`use-user.tsx`** file, we have a new type of **`State`** which takes different objects with status as key. Now, the status is not giving any error.

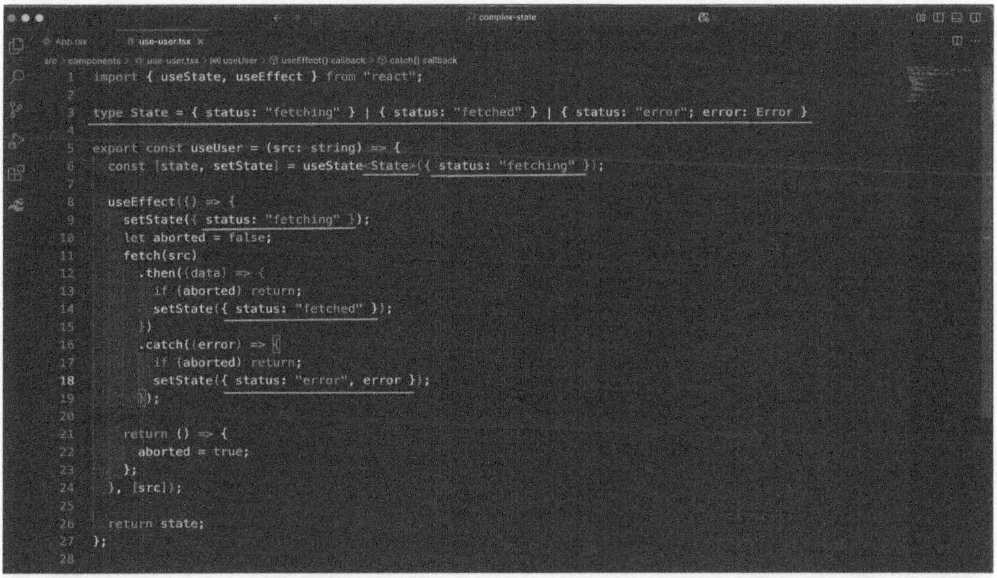

Figure 18.40: *Updating Use-user.tsx File*

Tuples with Custom Hooks

Lastly, we will see an example of tuples with custom hooks. We are again in a new project. Here, in the **`App.tsx`** file, we are calling the **`useUser`** custom hook. But the **`value.message`** and value.name are giving errors. This is giving an error, because we have used wrong type in **`useUser`** file.

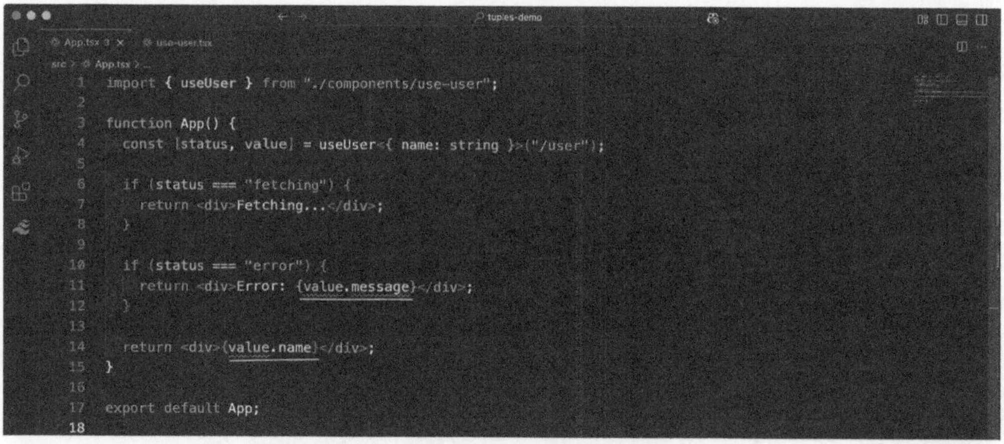

Figure 18.41: *Error in App.tsx File*

Now, in the **use-user.tsx** file, the **type** is an array with value as fetching or success, or error, or **Error**, or undefined. The data initial value is fetching and undefined.

If the fetch is successful, it is an array of success and data. In the case of error, it is "**error**" and error.

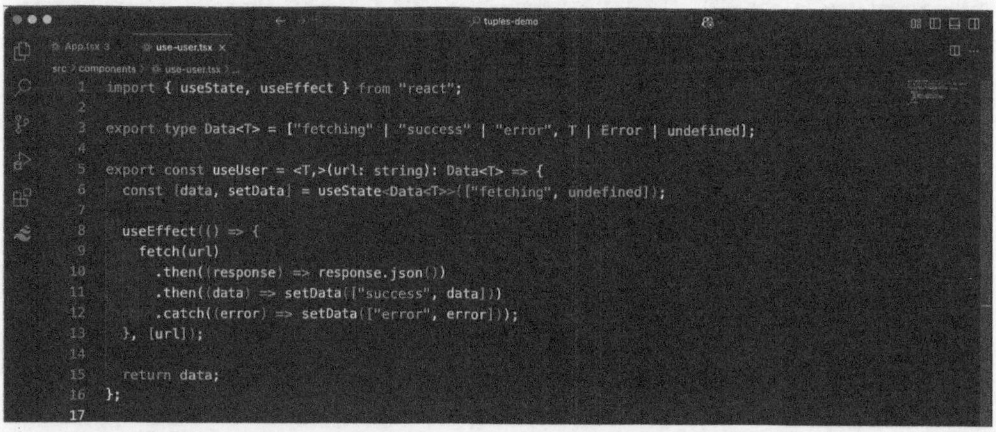

Figure 18.42: *Array Type in Use-user.tsx File*

We will update our Data type to tuples containing fetching, undefined or success, and T or "**error**" and error. We can also see that the **App.tsx** now has no error.

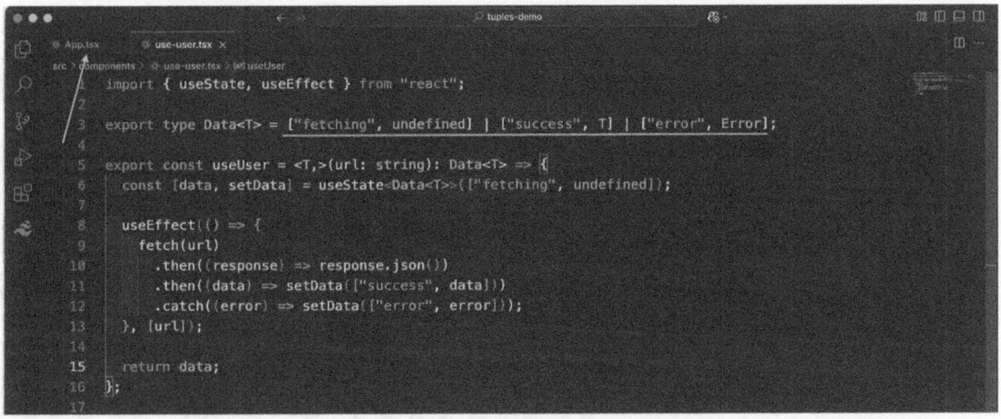

Figure 18.43: *Tuple Type in Use-user.tsx File*

Conclusion

In this chapter, we have started a new section of Advanced TypeScript. Here, we learned about types in different hooks. First, we learnt about typing **`useState`**, and to write type, while using **`useState`**.

Next, we learnt to write a type of state, without initial state. After that we learnt about passing states and events, and writing types in the same. Next, we learnt about typing custom hooks and complex states.

Lastly, we learnt about tuples with custom hooks. In the next chapter, **we are going to learn how to write the type for reducers and context API in typescript**.

Points to Remember

- Typing **`useState`**
- Typing state without initial state
- Passing states and events
- Typing **`useRef`**
- Typing custom hook and complex states
- Tuples with custom hooks

CHAPTER 19
Advanced TypeScript Using Typing Reducers and Context API

Introduction

In this chapter, we will continue with the Advanced TypeScript section. Here, we will be learning about Typing Reducers and Context API. We will also learn about writing types of reducers.

Additionally, we will also be passing dispatch as a prop in reducers, and writing types for the same. Next, we will learn to write the types of action and reducers. Lastly, we will learn to write the types for Context API.

Structure

In this chapter, we shall discuss the following topics:

- Overview
- Typing Reducers
- Passing Dispatch as a Prop
- Action and Reducer Types
- Context API with Types

Overview

In this chapter, we will learn about typing reducers and Context API. Here, we will first learn about typing reducers. After that, we shall learn about passing dispatch as a Prop.

Next, we will learn about action and reducer types. Lastly, we will learn about Context API with types.

Typing Reducers

First, we will look into typing reducers. We have first created a new react typescript project, and the **index.tsx** file looks like *Figure* 19.1.

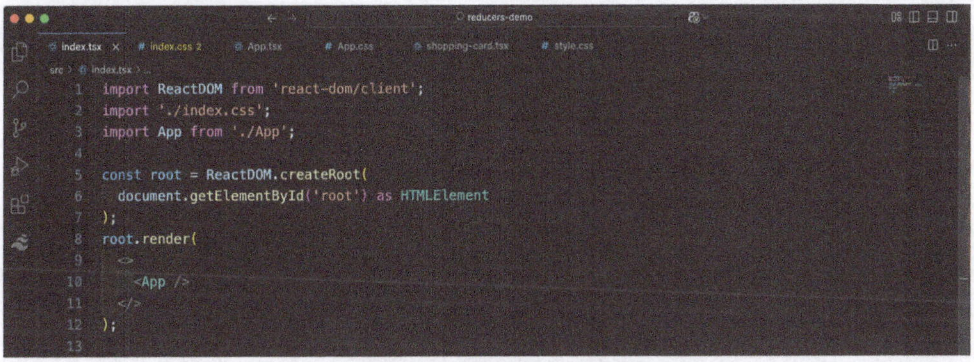

Figure 19.1: *Index.tsx File*

Also, we have updated the styles in the **index.css** file. All of these codes can be taken from the referenced project.

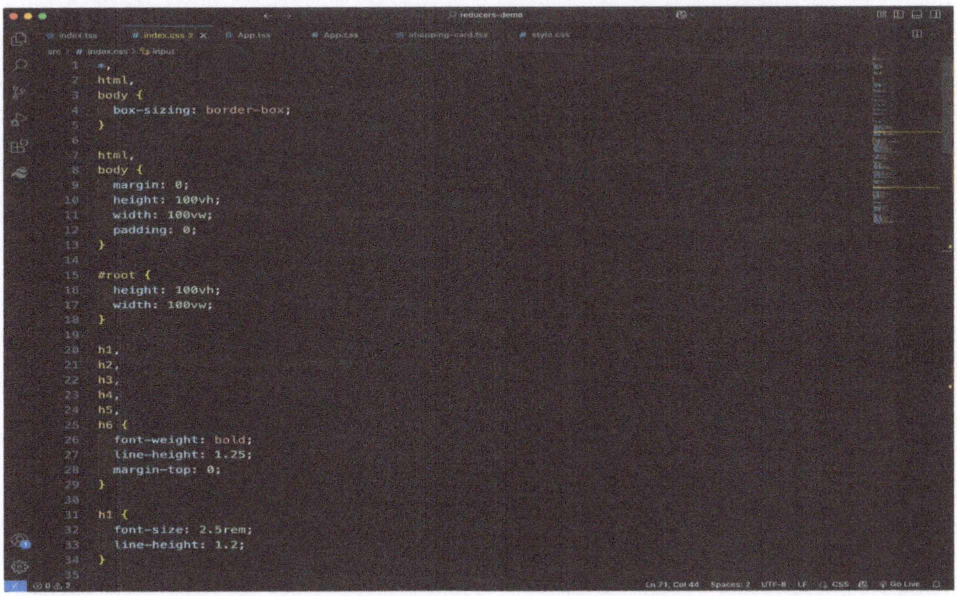

Figure 19.2: *Index.css File*

In the **App.tsx** file, we have added the **ShoppingCard** component.

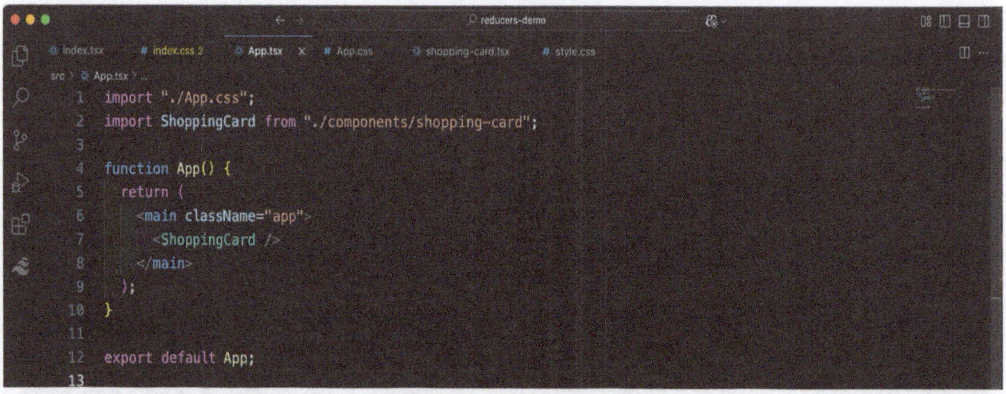

```
import "./App.css";
import ShoppingCard from "./components/shopping-card";

function App() {
  return (
    <main className="app">
      <ShoppingCard />
    </main>
  );
}

export default App;
```

Figure 19.3: *App.tsx File*

Next, in the **App.css**, we have updated the basic styles.

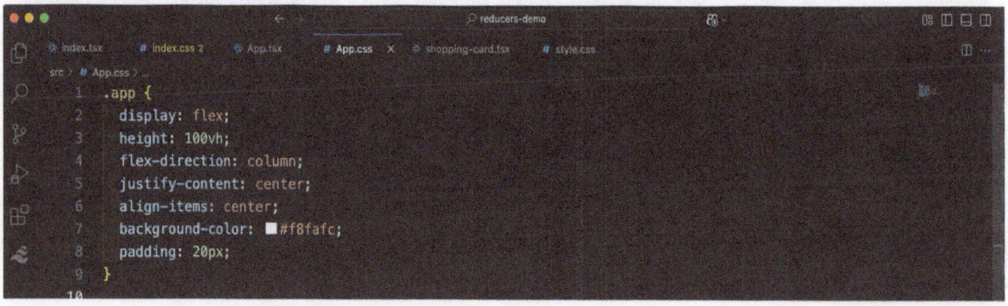

```
.app {
  display: flex;
  height: 100vh;
  flex-direction: column;
  justify-content: center;
  align-items: center;
  background-color: #f8fafc;
  padding: 20px;
}
```

Figure 19.4: *App.css File*

Now, in the **shopping-card.tsx** file, we have a **cartReducer** which takes the state and action as parameters. It has a switch case that takes different action types, and updates the items as well as the **inputItems** accordingly.

```tsx
import { useState, useReducer } from "react";
import "./style.css";

type InitialState = {
  items: number;
  inputItems: string | number;
};

const initialState: InitialState = {
  items: 0,
  inputItems: 0,
};

const cartReducer = (state = initialState, action: any) => {
  const { items, inputItems } = state;

  switch (action.type) {
    case "increase":
      const newItemsInc = items + 1;
      return { items: newItemsInc, inputItems: newItemsInc };
    case "decrease":
      const newItemsDec = items - 1;
      return { items: newItemsDec, inputItems: newItemsDec };
    case "reset":
      return { items: 0, inputItems: 0 };
    case "updateInputItems":
      return { items, inputItems: action.payload };
    case "updateItemsFromInput":
      return { items: Number(inputItems), inputItems };
    default:
      return state;
  }
};

const ShoppingCard = () => {
```

Figure 19.5: *cartReducer in Shopping-card.tsx File*

Inside the **`ShoppingCard`**, in the **`shopping-card.tsx`** file, we are using the **`useReducer`** hook. This is used to dispatch different types with a click of different buttons.

```tsx
const ShoppingCard = () => {
  const [{ items, inputItems }, dispatch] = useReducer(cartReducer, initialState);

  return (
    <section className="counter-wrapper">
      <h1 className="counter-title">Shopping Cart Items</h1>
      <p className="counter-value">{items}</p>
      <div className="counter-buttons">
        <button className="decrement-button" onClick={() => dispatch({ type: "decrease" })}>Decrease</button>
        <button className="reset-button" onClick={() => dispatch({ type: "reset" })}>Reset</button>
        <button className="increment-button" onClick={() => dispatch({ type: "increase" })}>Increase</button>
      </div>
      <div className="counter-form">
        <form onSubmit={(e) => {e.preventDefault(); dispatch({ type: "updateItemsFromInput" });}}>
          <input type="number" value={inputItems} onChange={(e) => dispatch({types: "updateInputItems", payload: e.target.value,})}
            className="counter-input"
          />
          <button type="submit" className="update-button">
            Update cart
          </button>
        </form>
      </div>
    </section>
  );
};

export default ShoppingCard;
```

Figure 19.6: *ShoppingCard in Shopping-cart.tsx File*

We have the basic styles for the **`shopping-card.tsx`** file, in the **`style.css`** file.

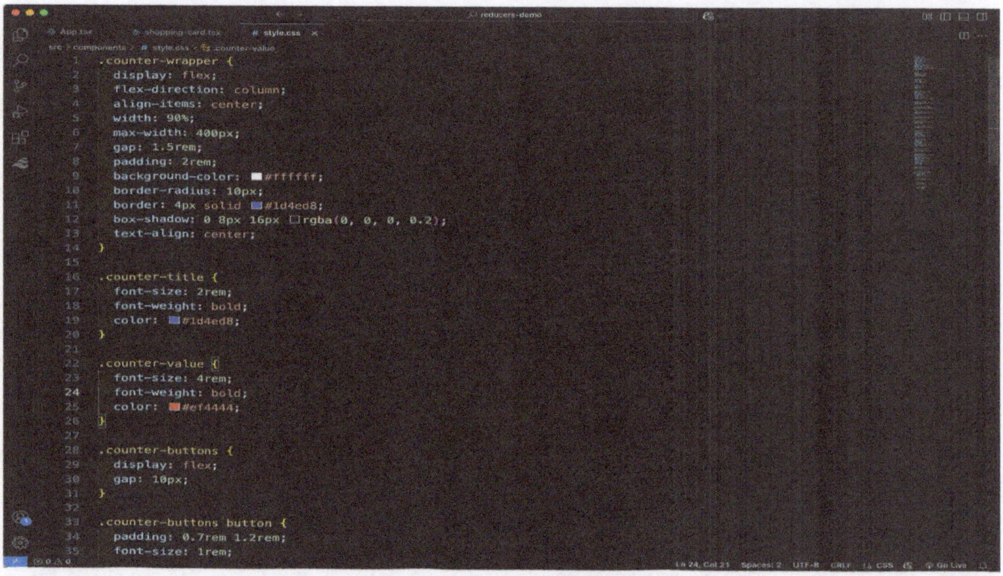

Figure 19.7: *Style.css File*

In http://localhost:3000/, we can see the nice **`Shopping Cart items`**.

Figure 19.8: *Localhost Showing Shopping Cart*

Now, we need to add the proper types in the file, **`shopping-card.tsx`**. So, first we have removed the action of any, and then we have added a type of Action and **`ActionWithPayload`**.

We have replaced the action of any with Action or **`ActionWithPayload`**. But we are getting an error in payload, and that type string is not assignable to type number.

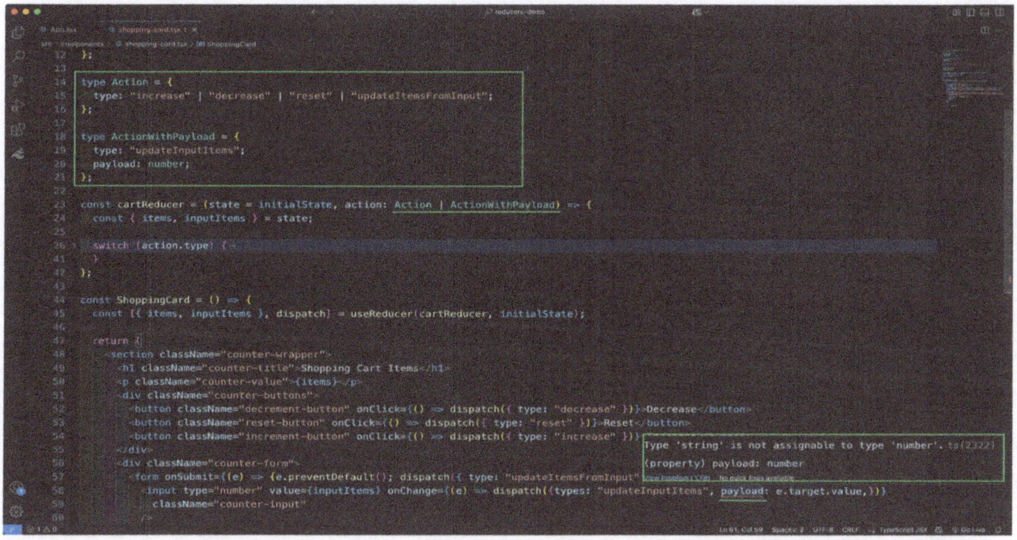

Figure 19.9: *Types and Payload Error in Shopping-card.tsx*

To fix the issue, we had made the payload to **`e.target.valueAsNumber`**. But we are getting another error of types. Actually, this error was kept intentionally by giving a wrong spelling.

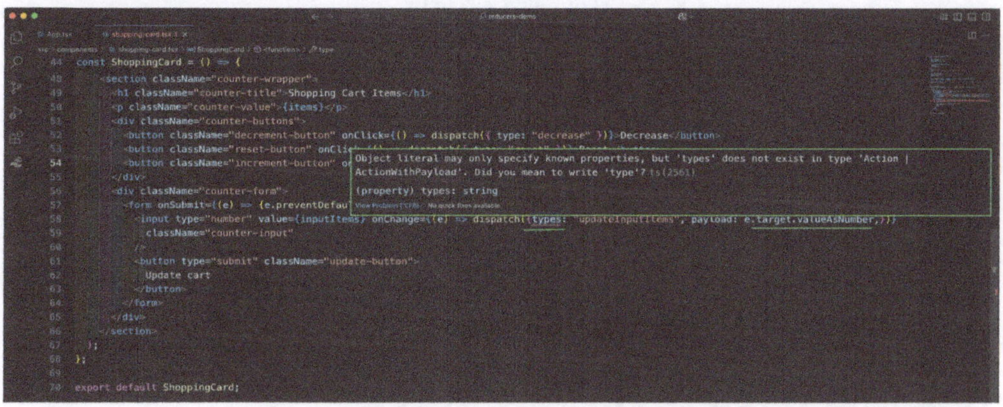

Figure 19.10: *Types Error in Shopping-card.tsx*

We have made it to **`type`**, and the error is resolved in the file, **`shopping-card.tsx`**.

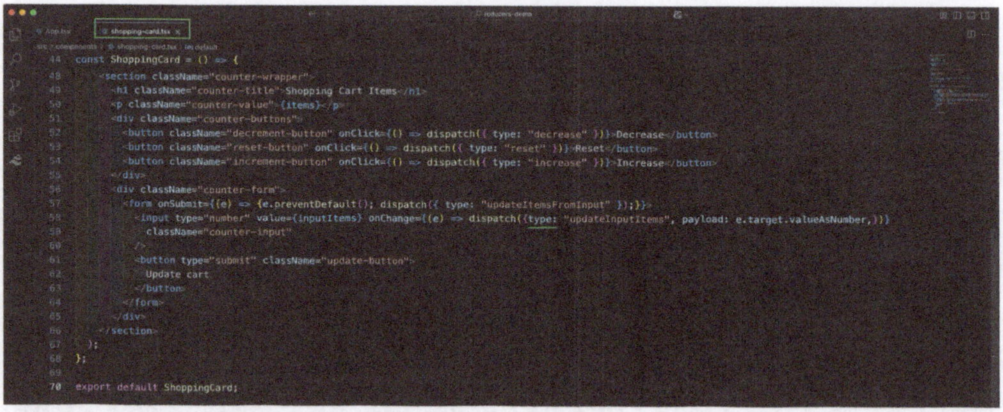

Figure 19.11: *No Error in Shopping-card.tsx*

Now, in http://localhost:3000/, every feature of the small app is working correctly.

Figure 19.12: *Localhost Showing Shopping Cart*

Passing Dispatch as a Prop

Next, we will look into passing the dispatch as a prop. Thus, we have created a new react typescript project, and the **`index.tsx`** file looks like the following figure.

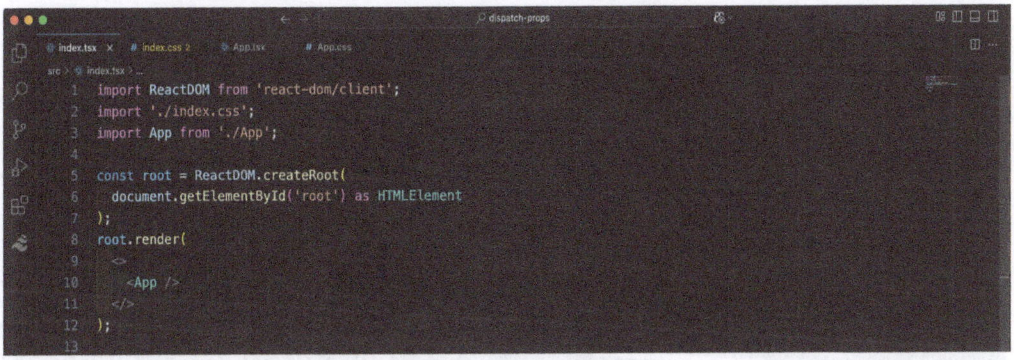

Figure 19.13: Index.tsx File

Also, updated the styles in the **`index.css`** file. All of these codes can be taken from the referenced project.

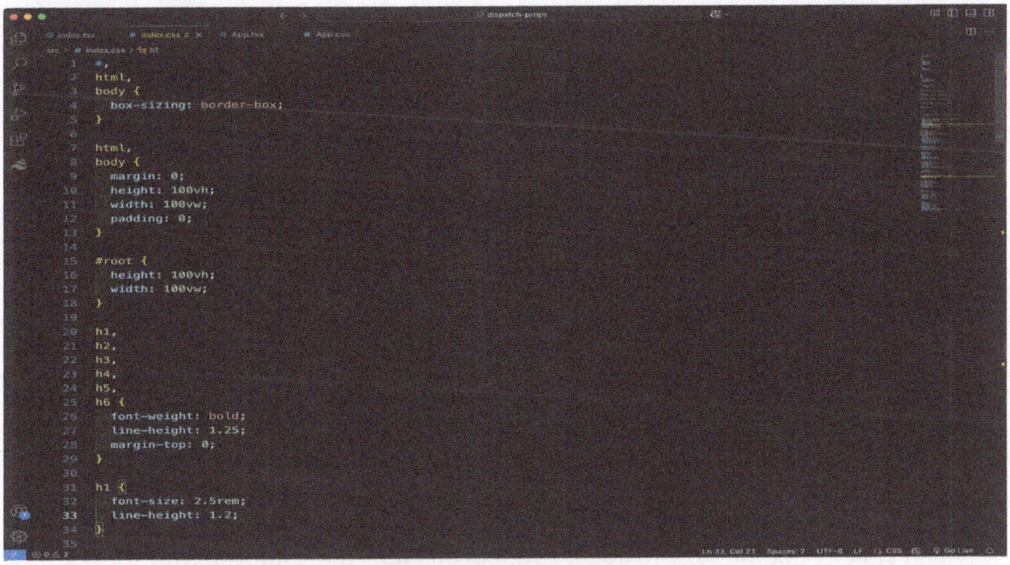

Figure 19.14: Index.css File

In the **`App.tsx`** file, we have added several components such as **`ColorSelect`**, **`SetColors`**, **`ColorGroups`** and **`Saved Colors`**.

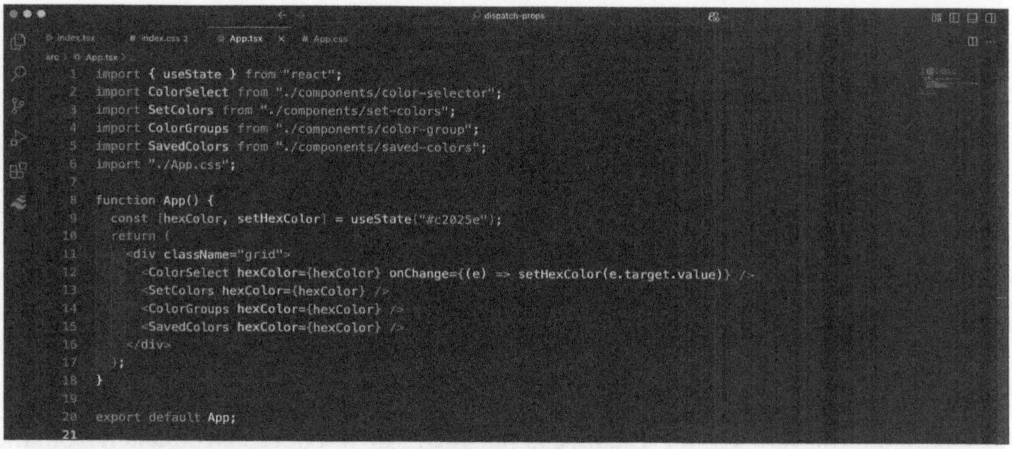

Figure 19.15: *App.tsx File*

Next, in the **`App.css`**, we have updated the basic styles.

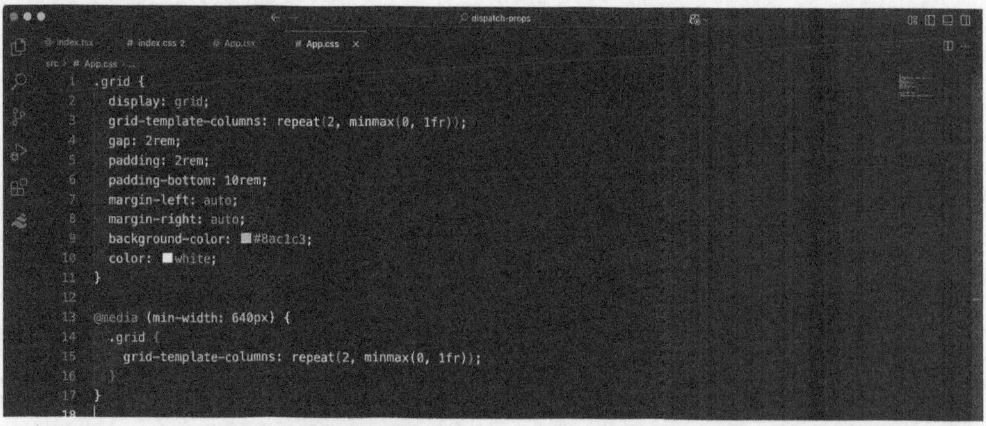

Figure 19.16: *App.css File*

The main **`index.tsx`** file for the **`color-selector`** looks like *Figure* 19.17.

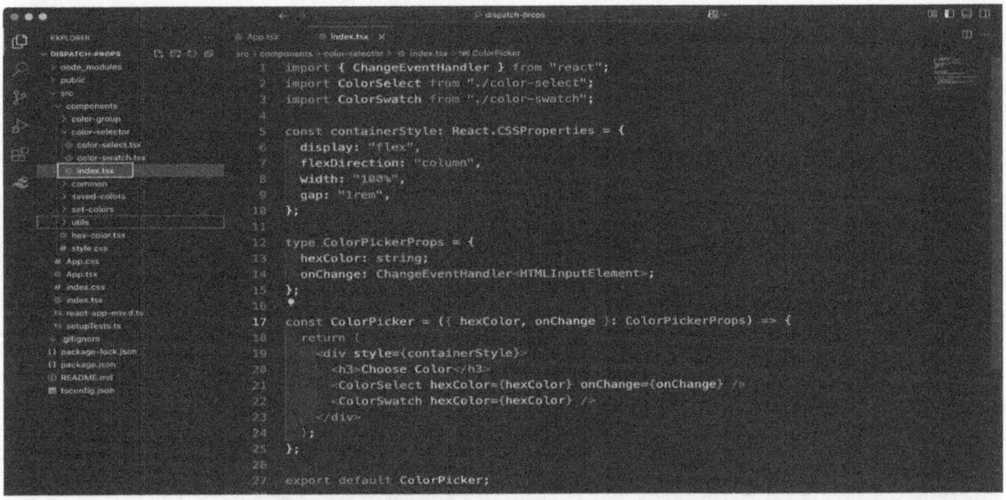

***Figure 19.17:** ColorPicker Component*

The main **index.tsx** file for the **set-colors** looks like *Figure* 19.18.

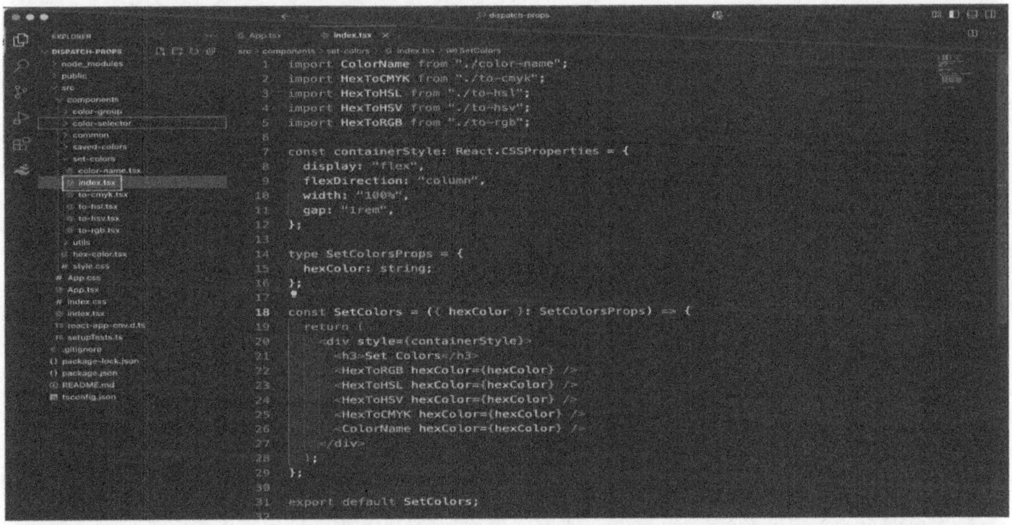

***Figure 19.18:** SetColors Component*

The main **index.tsx** file for the **color-group** looks like *Figure* 19.19.

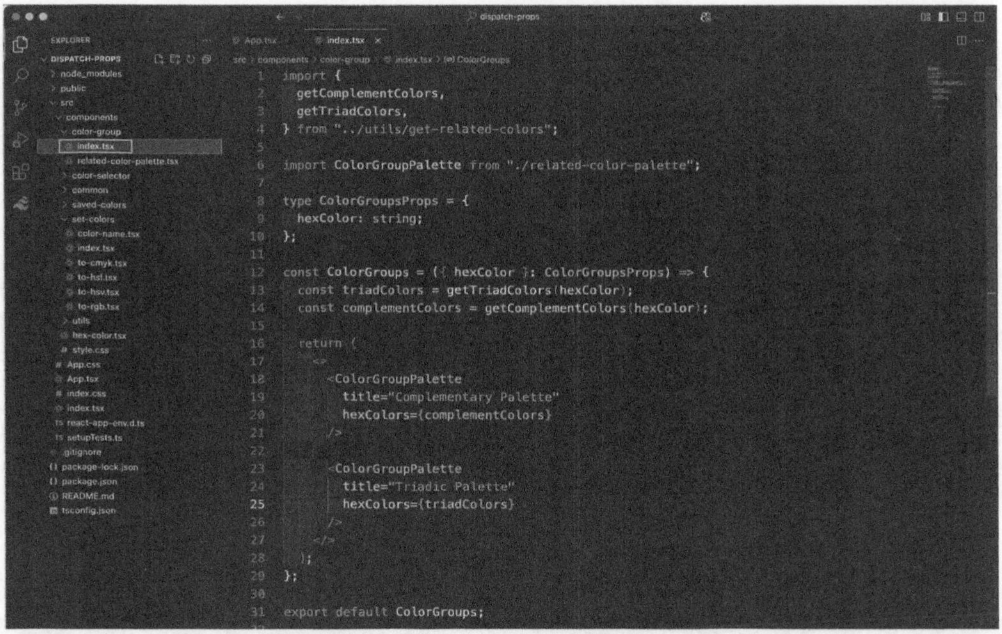

Figure 19.19: *ColorGroups Component*

The main **`index.tsx`** file for the saved-colors looks like *Figure* 19.20.

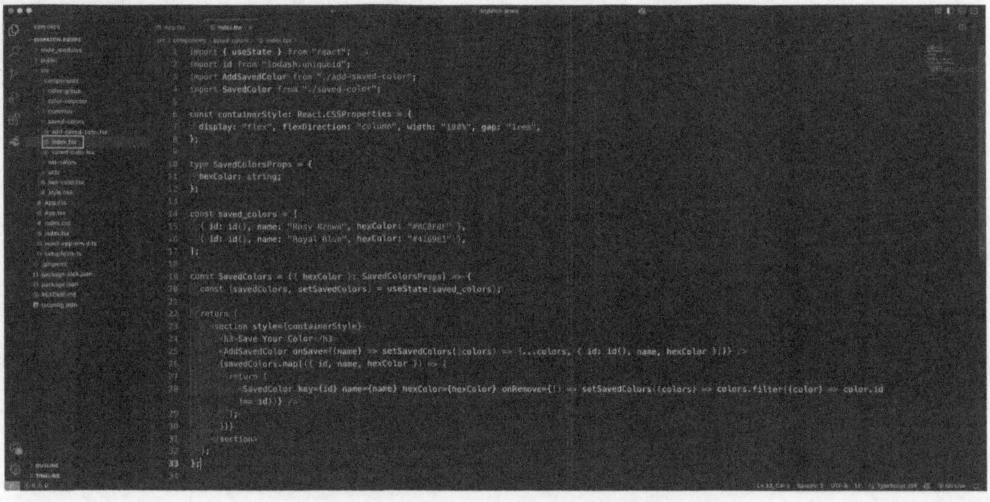

Figure 19.20: *SavedColors Component*

Rest of the files can be taken from the referenced project. The project in http://localhost:3000/ looks like the following *Figure* 19.21.

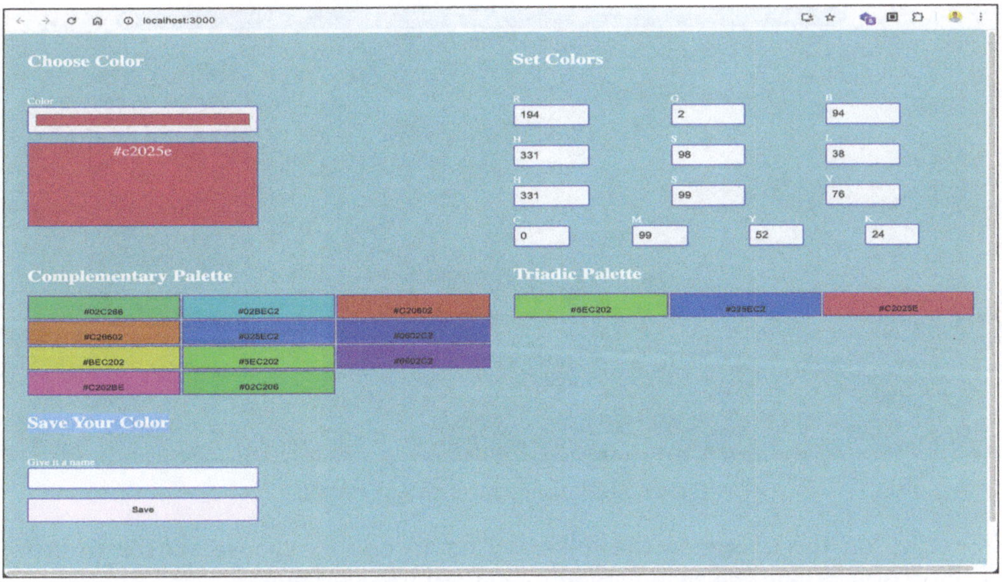

Figure 19.21: *Localhost Showing Color Palette Project Component*

Now, we are going to create a reducer called **`colorReducer.ts`**. It is like a normal redux reducer, but we also have the type for all the required things.

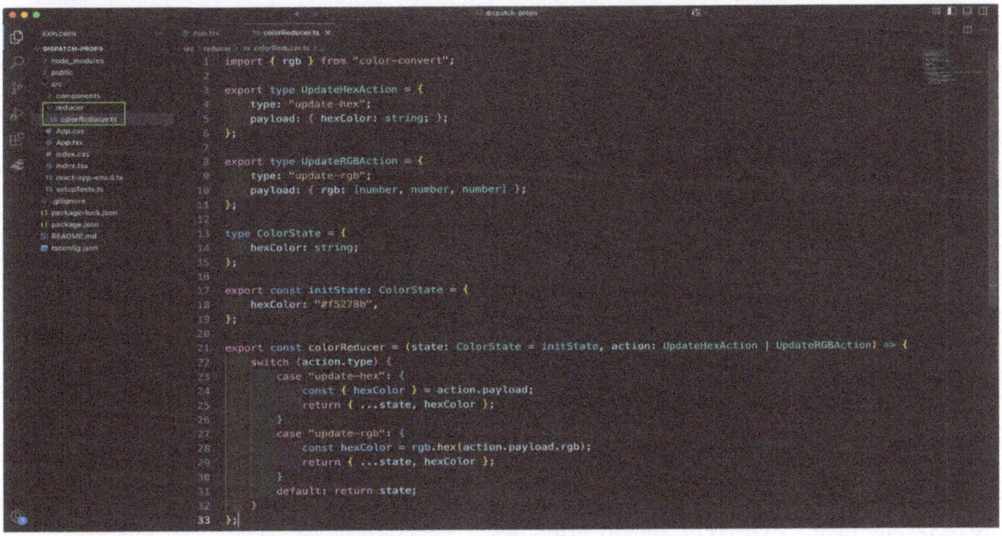

Figure 19.22: *colorReducer.ts File*

Next, in the **`App.tsx`**, we will change the **`useState`** with the **`useReducer`** hook. Here, we are importing the **`colorReducer`** and **`initState`**. We have also changed the **`onChange`** of the **`ColorSelect`** to dispatch the type of update-hex and the payload.

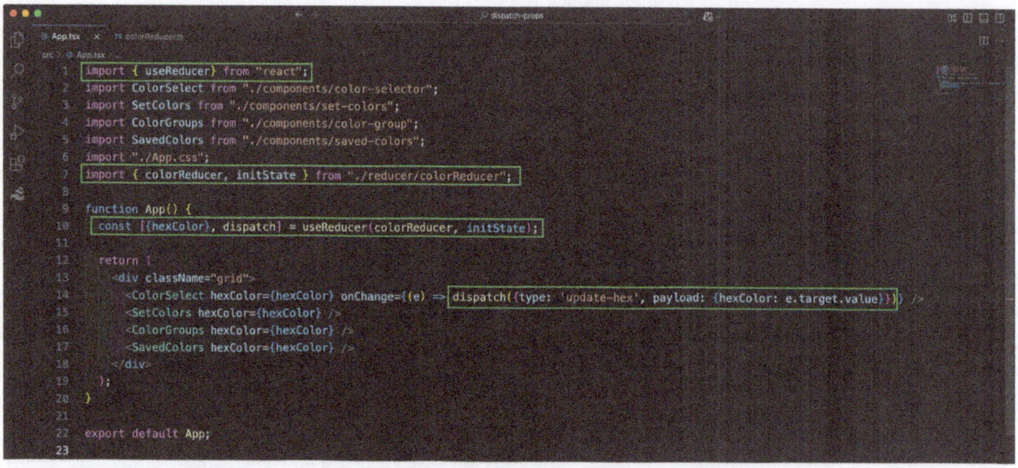

***Figure 19.23:** useReducer in App.tsx File*

Now, click on the **`Color`** in the following figure option, **`Choose Color`** in http://localhost:3000/, and the change functionality starts working.

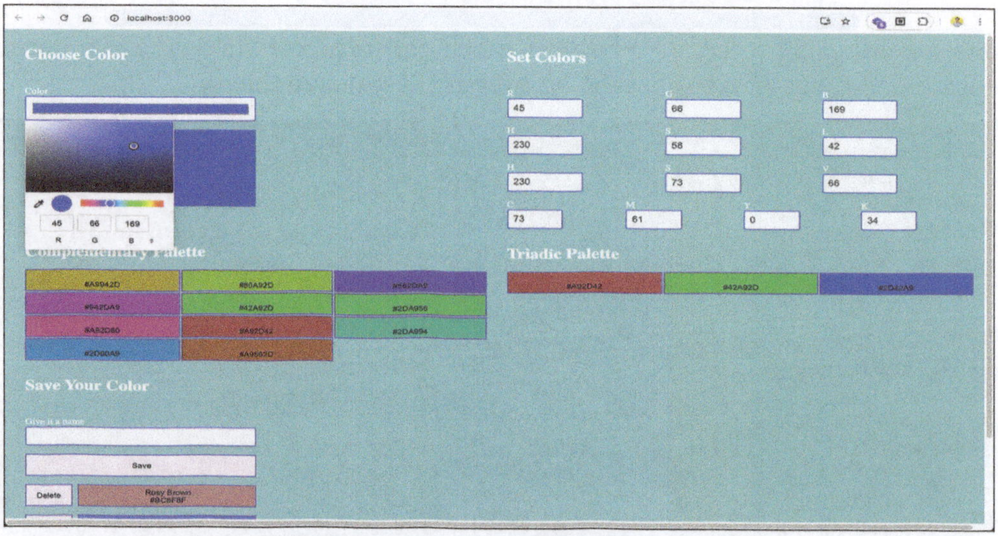

***Figure 19.24:** Localhost Showing Color Palette*

Next, we will check one more example of passing dispatch as props. So, in the **`App.tsx`**, we will pass a **`dispatch`** parameter.

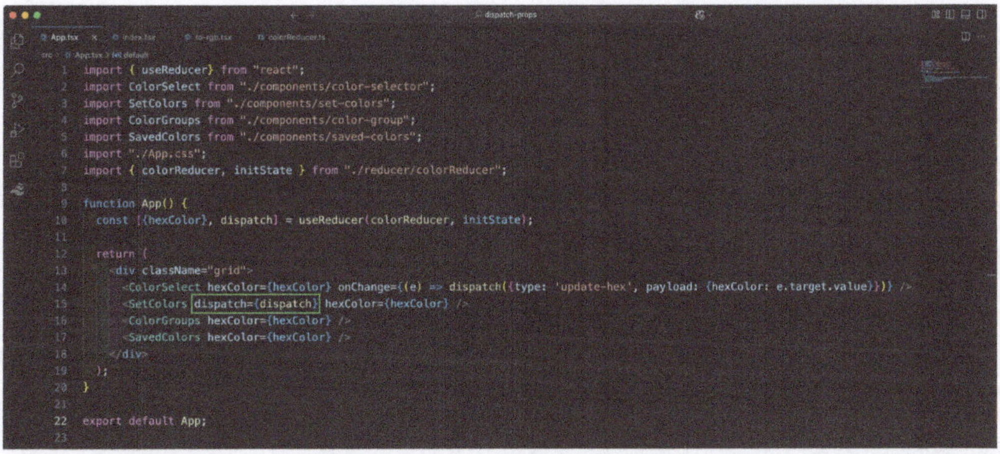

Figure 19.25: *Dispatch Prop from App.tsx*

In the **`colorReducer.ts`**, we have added a type of **`ColorActions`**, and added the earlier type of **`UpdateHexAction`** as well as **`UpdateRGBAction`** to it. Also, in **`update-rgb`**, we have added #, so that the **`hexColor`** can be taken correctly.

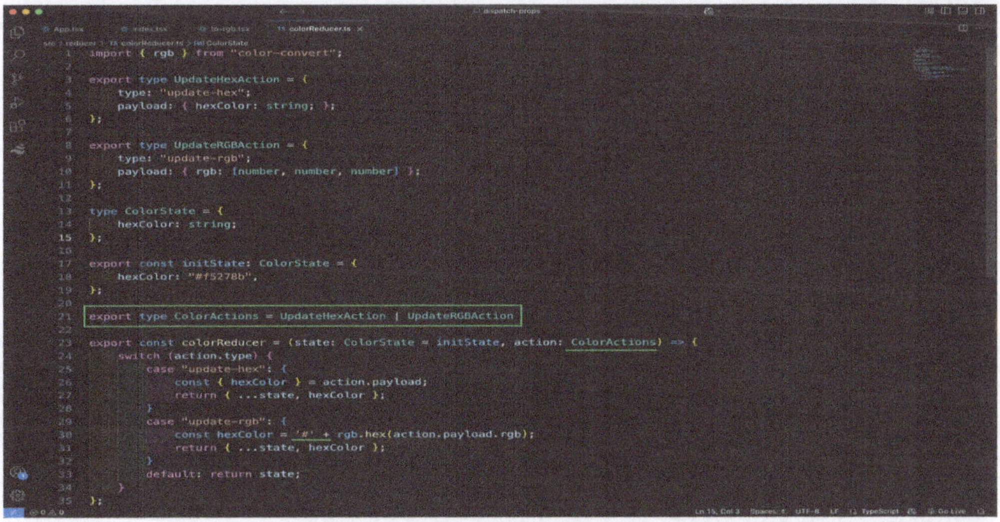

Figure 19.26: *ColorActions in colorReducer.ts*

Now, in the file, **`index.tsx`** of **`set-colors`**, we are importing the **`Dispatch`** and **`ColorActions`**, first. In the type of **`SetColorsProps`**, we are giving the type for dispatch. Also, in the **`HexToRGB`** component, we pass the **`props`** of dispatch.

Figure 19.27: *Dispatch from SetColors Component*

Next, in the **`to-rgb.tsx`** file, we have added a type of dispatch to the **`HexToRGBProps`**. Then, we have a function of **`updateRGB`** which is taking an object with red, green and blue as parameters.

Next, we dispatch the type of **`update-rgb`** and a payload. In the **`LabeledInput`** component, the **`onChange`** is calling the **`updateRGB`** function, and passing the values according to the red, green or blue colors.

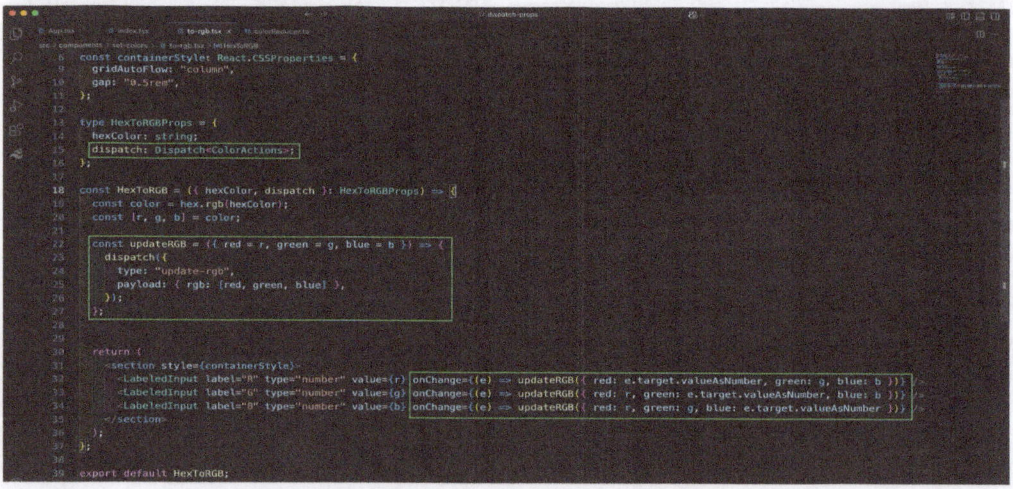

Figure 19.28: *Updating to-rgb.tsx File*

Now, in http://localhost:3000/, the following **`Set Color`** changes the R, G or/and B, and this will reflect.

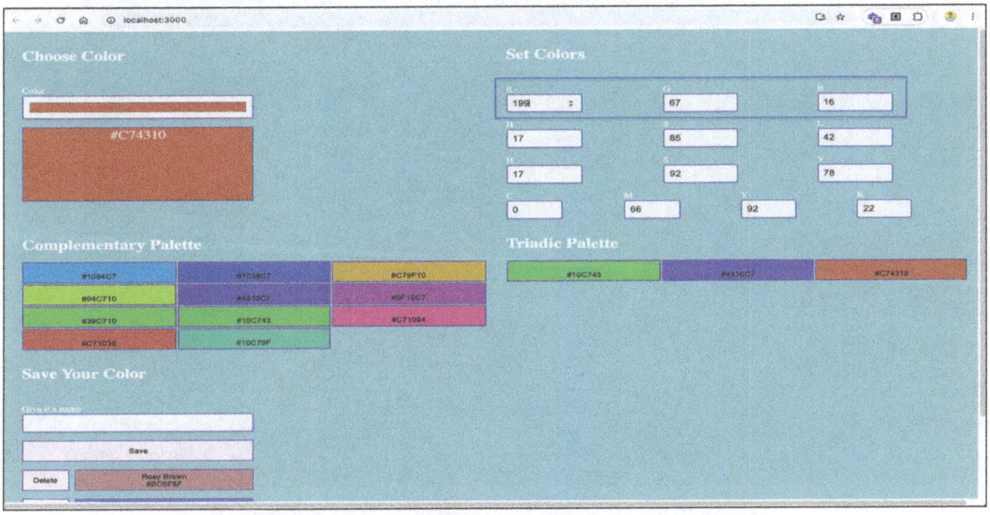

Figure 19.29: *Updating R, G, and B in Localhost*

Action and Reducer Types

Next, we will look into action and reducer types. For this, we will use the same project from the previous section. Here, in the **`SavedColors`**, we will pass a dispatch props.

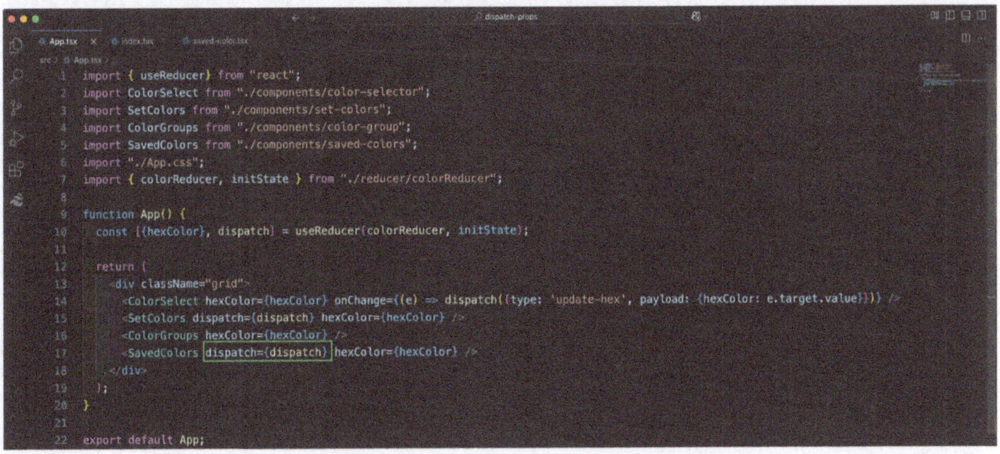

Figure 19.30: *Dispatch from App.tsx*

Next, in the **`index.tsx`** of **`saved-colors`**, we will have a type of dispatch. We also pass the dispatch as a prop in the **`SavedColors`** component.

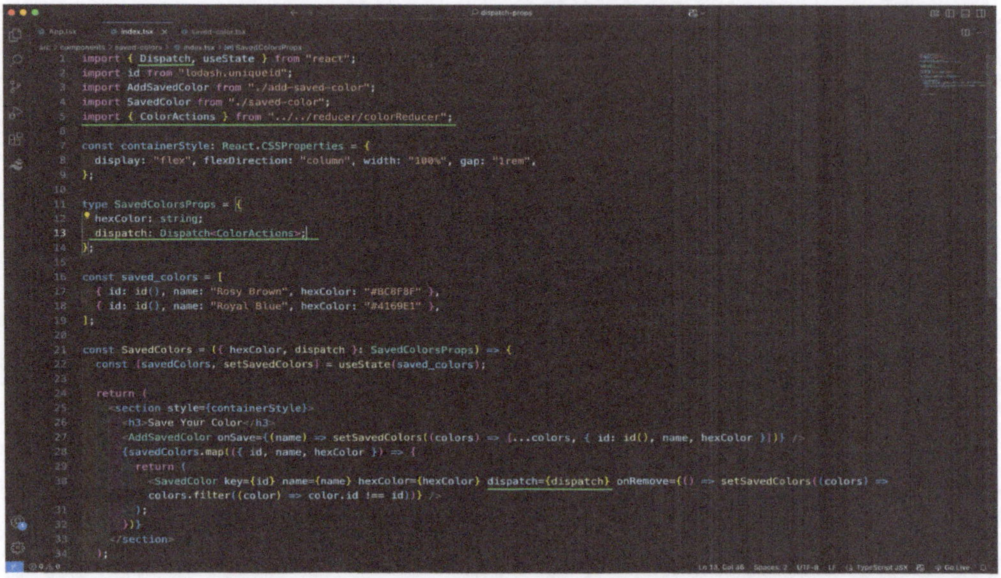

Figure 19.31: *Dispatch from SavedColors Component*

Now, in the **saved-color.tsx** file, we will first import **Dispatch** and **ColorActions**. Next, in the type of **SavedColorProps**, we will add a type of dispatch.

Inside the **return** statement of **SavedColor**, we change the **onClick** for the **ColorChangeSwatch** component. Here, we dispatch the type of **update-hex**.

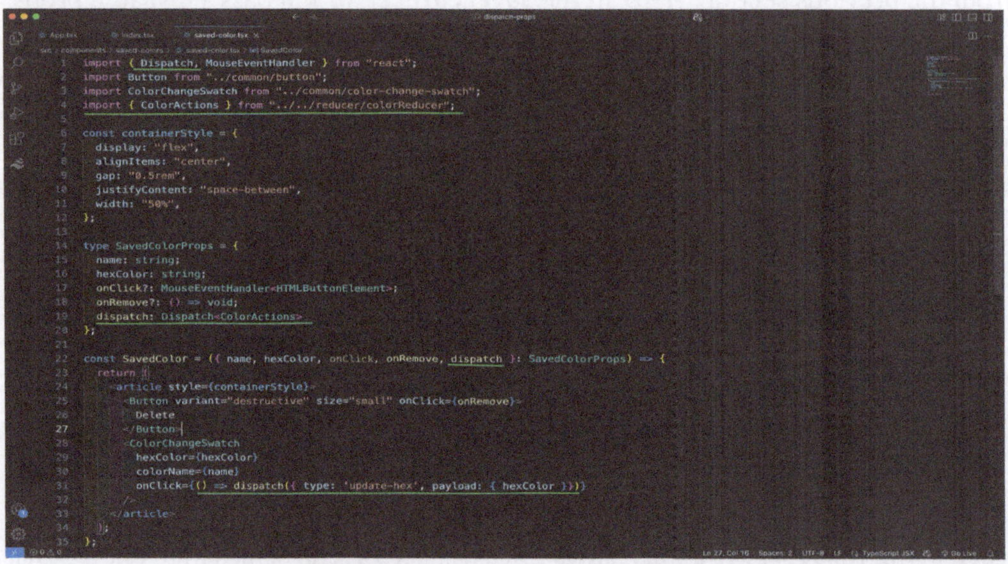

Figure 19.32: *Dispatch from SavedColor Component*

Next, in http://localhost:3000/, click on Royal Blue color in the bottom left, and it will change the main **color** in the top left.

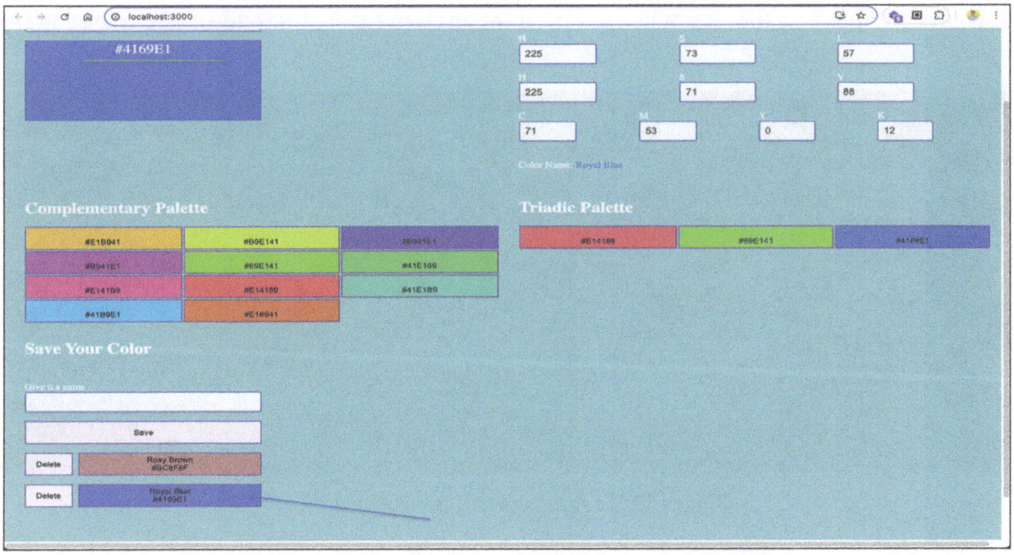

Figure 19.33: *Localhost with Saved Color Features*

Context API with Types

Now, we will look into Context API with types. For this, we will use the same project from the previous section. Here, we are first creating a **context** folder inside the **src** folder. Within it, we have created the **context.tsx** file, and here, we are using the usual context **api** code in React.

Here, we are also exporting **ColorProvider** that takes a children prop. The type of this children prop is **PropsWithChildren**, which we have imported from React. Inside the **ColorProvider**, we are using **useReducer**, and passing the **colorReducer** as well as initState to it.

In the return statement in the **Provider**, we are passing the **children** prop.

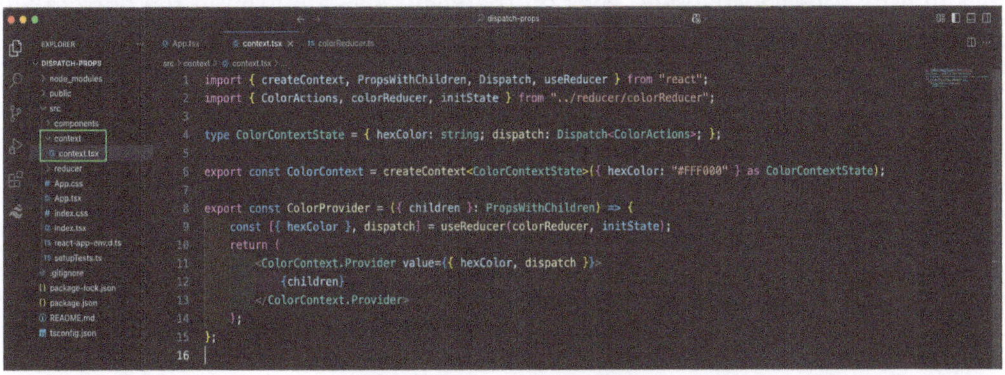

Figure 19.34: *Context.tsx File*

Now, in the **App.tsx** file, we will use the **useContext** hook, instead of the **useReducer** hook.

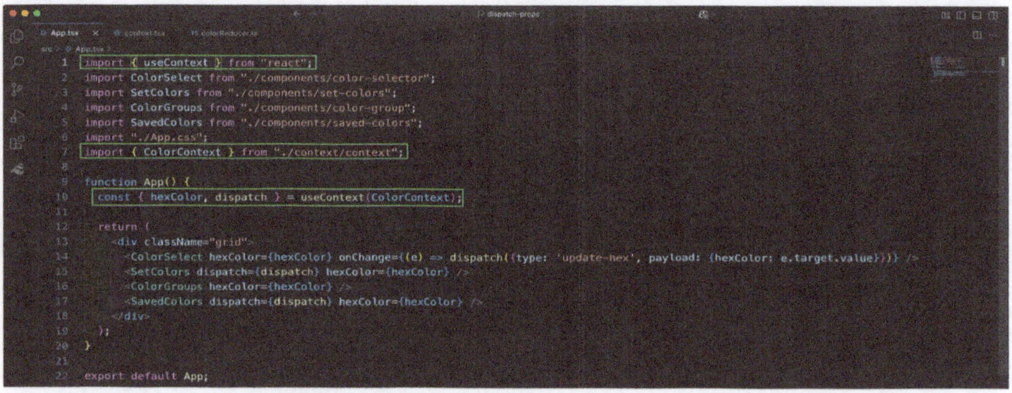

Figure 19.35: *App.tsx with useContext File*

To use the Context API, we also need to wrap the **App** with **ColorProvider** in the **index.tsx** file.

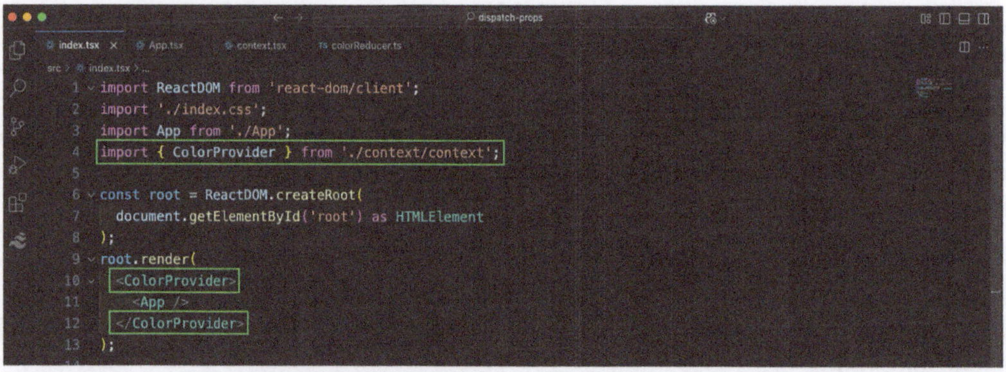

Figure 19.36: *Index.tsx with ColorProvider*

Now, in http://localhost:3000/, click on the **Rosy Brown** button in the bottom left, and it will change the main color in the top left.

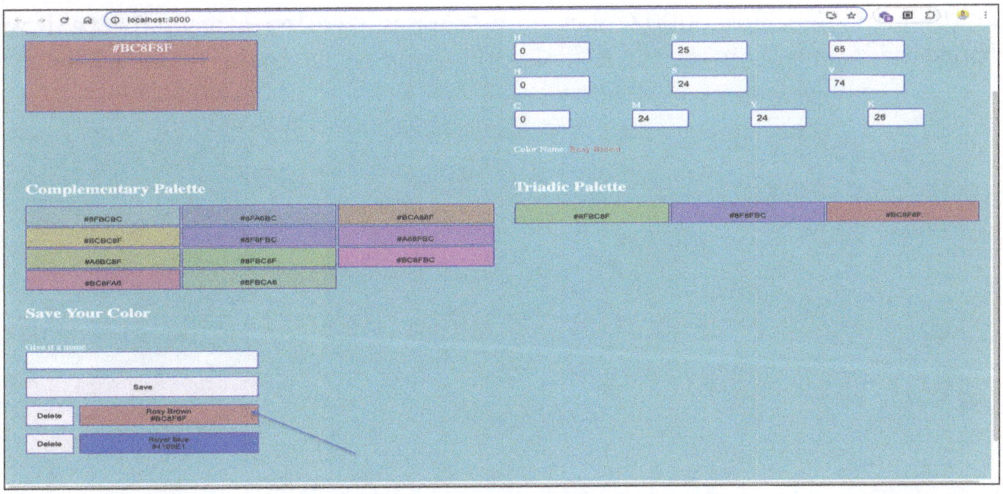

***Figure 19.37:** Localhost Working with Context*

We will see one more Context API example. Here, in the **`color-change-swatch.tsx`** file, we will import **`useContext`** and **`ColorContext`**, first. Next, we are going to use dispatch from **`useContext`**, and pass the **`ColorContext`** to it.

We are also changing the **`Button`** component **`onClick`** to dispatch update-hex.

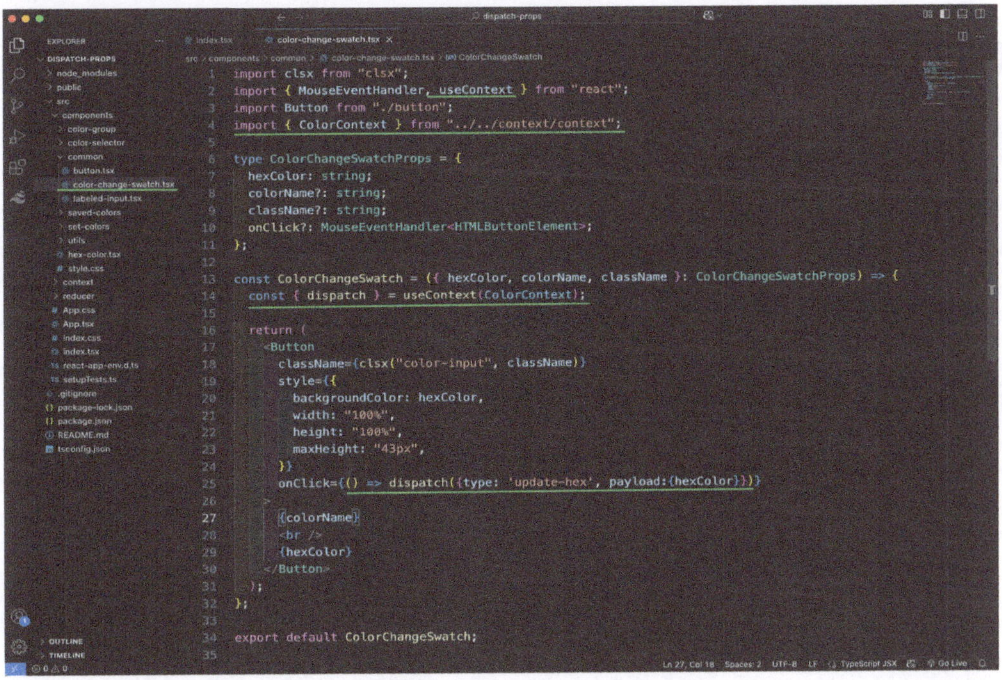

***Figure 19.38:** Color-change-swatch.tsx File*

Now, in http://localhost:3000/, click on a **`Color`** in **`Complementary Palette`**, it will change the main color in the top left. Also, this color will go to the **`Triadic`** Palette.

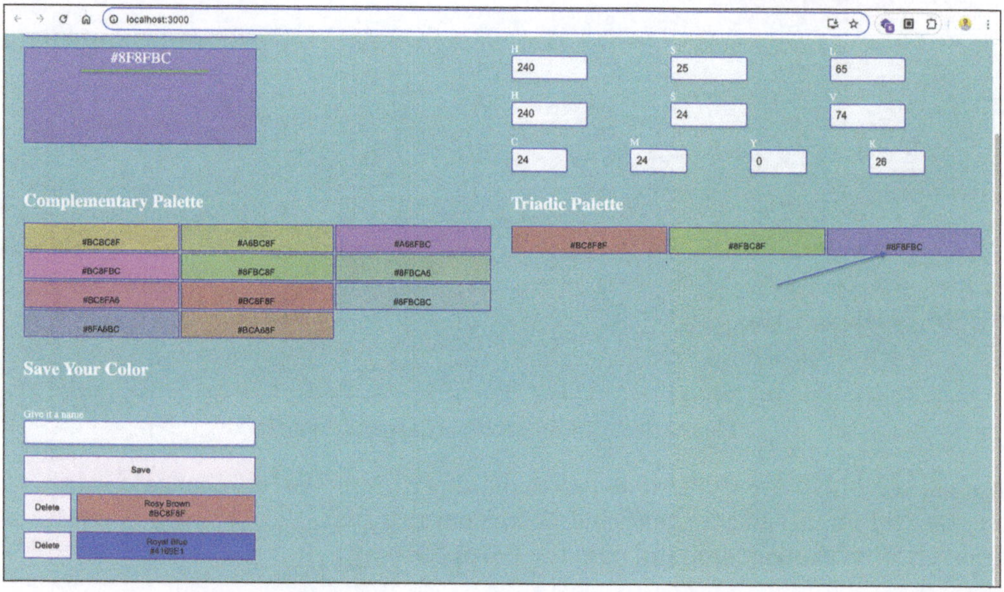

Figure 19.39: *Localhost Working with Context*

Conclusion

In this chapter, we continued with Advanced TypeScript concepts. Here, we also learned about typing reducers, first.

Next, we learnt to pass dispatch as a prop in reducers. In the next step, we learnt about action and reducer types. Lastly, we learnt about types in Context API. In the next chapter, **we will continue our Advanced TypeScript journey**, and learn about writing types in Generics.

Points to Remember

- Typing Reducers
- Passing dispatch as props
- Action and reducer types
- Context API with types

CHAPTER 20
Advanced TypeScript with Typing Generics

Introduction

In this chapter, we will continue with the Advanced TypeScript section and focus on one of its most powerful concepts – *Typing Generics*. Generics allow us to write flexible, reusable, and strongly typed code without sacrificing type safety. They are widely used in modern React and TypeScript projects, especially in scenarios where components, hooks, or utilities must work with various data types while maintaining type correctness.

By the end of this chapter, you will understand how to apply generics to contexts, helper types, custom hooks, and reusable components. You will also learn how to infer generic types automatically and use them effectively in real-world React projects. Understanding generics is essential for writing scalable, maintainable, and bug-resistant TypeScript code, especially in large enterprise-level applications.

Structure

In this chapter, we will cover the following topics:

- Overview
- Context with Generics
- Building a Type Helper
- Another Type Helper
- Hook with Generics
- Inferring Generic Types
- Generic Components

Overview

In this chapter, we will learn about typing generics. Here, we will first learn about context with Generics. After that, we will learn about building type helpers with two examples.

Next, we will learn about hooks with generics. In the next step, we will learn about interfering generic types. Lastly, we shall learn about Generic components.

Context with Generics

First, we have taken the project from the earlier chapter. Here, in the **`context.tsx`** file, we are currently using the **`createContext`** from React.

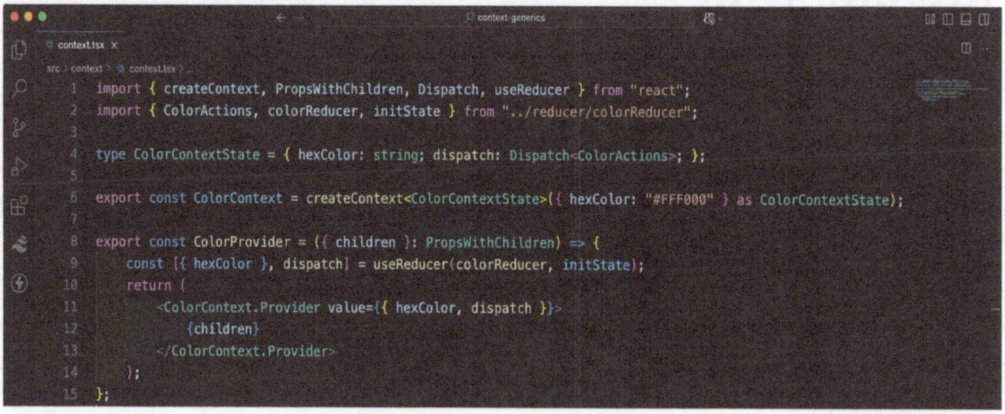

Figure 20.1: *Context.tsx File*

We have created a new file called **`create-context.tsx`,** and here we have created a **`createContext`** function. Also, we are using the generic type which is given by **`T`** that is further given in the argument, first. We have also given it in the **`React.useContext`**.

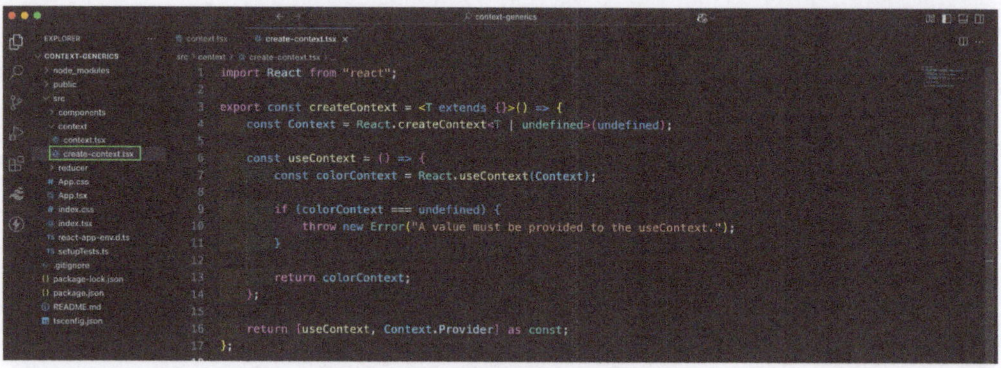

Figure 20.2: *Create-context.tsx File*

Back in the **context.tsx** file, we are first importing **createContext** from the **create-context.tsx** file. Next, we are restructuring the **useContext** and **ContextProvider** from **createContext** as well as getting rid of the '**as**' keyword.

Also, the **ColorContext.Provider** is now **ContextProvider**.

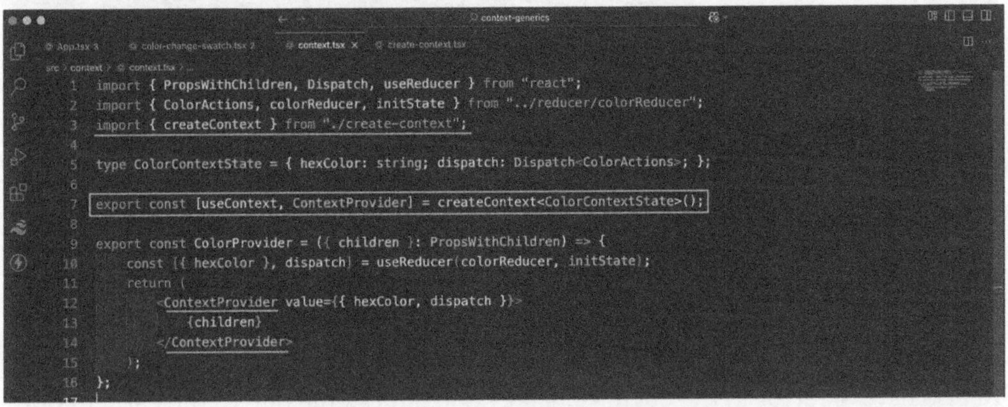

Figure 20.3: *Updated Context.tsx File*

In the **App.tsx,** we will find some errors in the earlier code, as we have changed the logic in the **context.tsx** file.

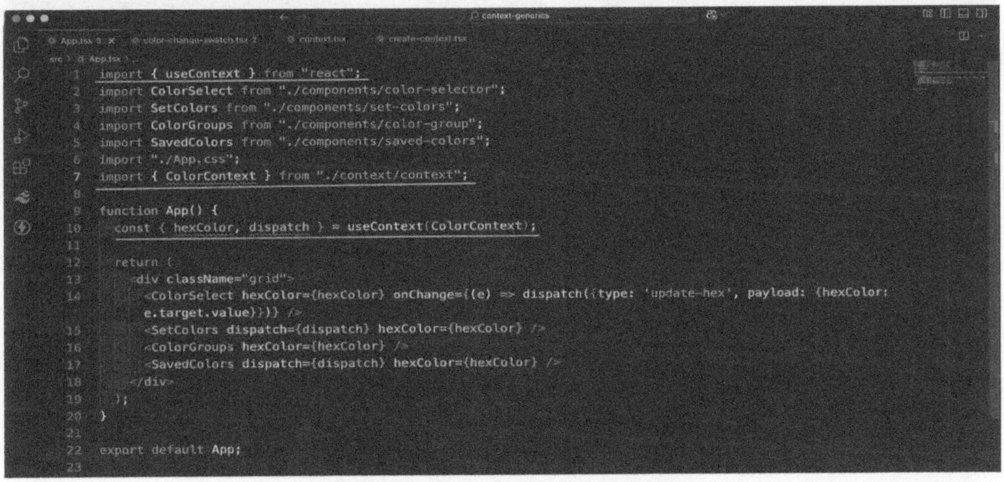

Figure 20.4: *Error in App.tsx File*

Now, instead of getting **useContext** from react, we are getting it from the **context.tsx** file in the **App.tsx** file.

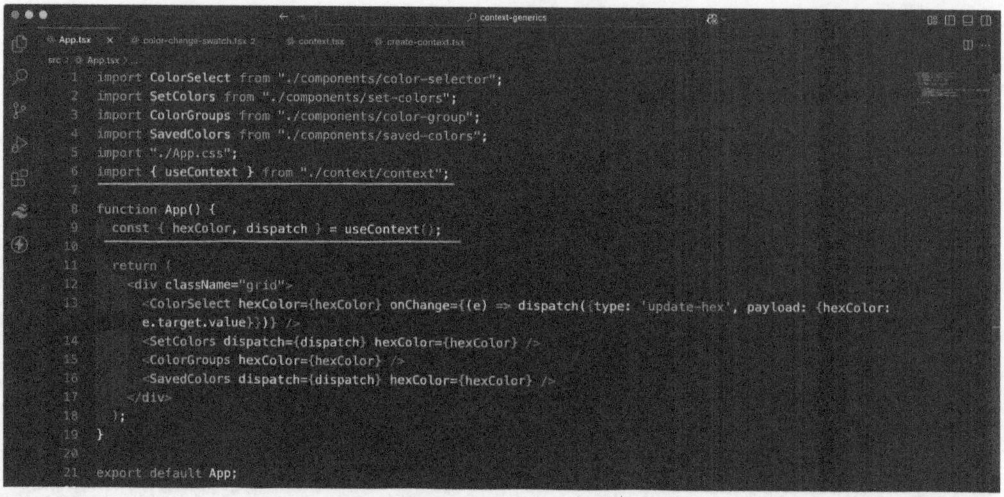

Figure 20.5: *Updated App.tsx File*

We also have an error in the **`color-change-swatch.tsx`** file due to the earlier code.

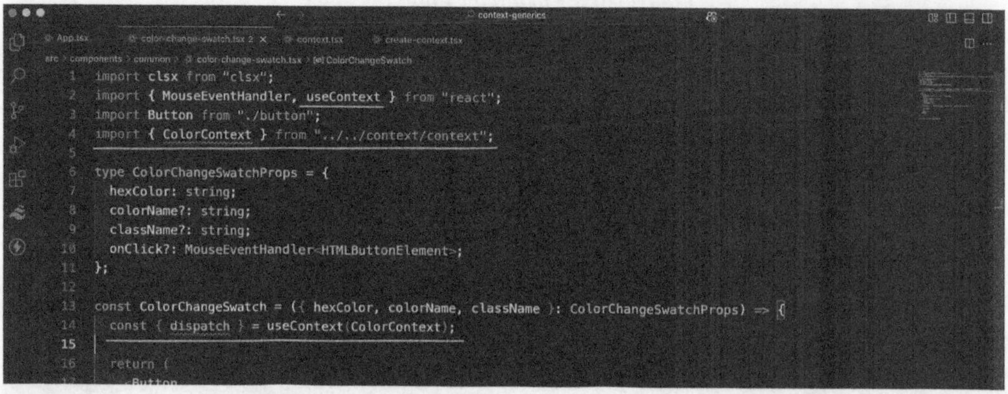

Figure 20.6: *Error in Color-change-swatch.tsx File*

Again to fix it, we will get the **`useContext`** from the **`context.tsx`** file, instead of react in the **`color-change-swatch.tsx`** file.

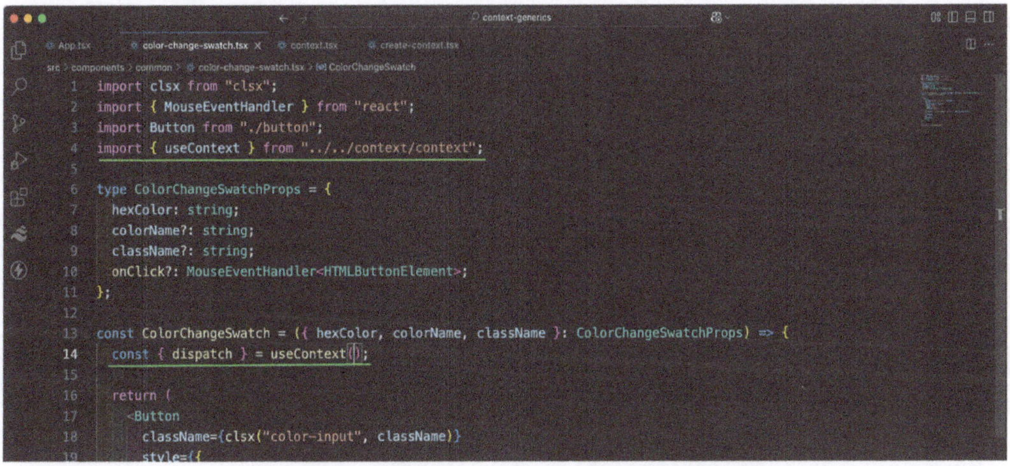

Figure 20.7: Updated Color-change-swatch.tsx File

Our app functionality is working as earlier in http://localhost:3000/.

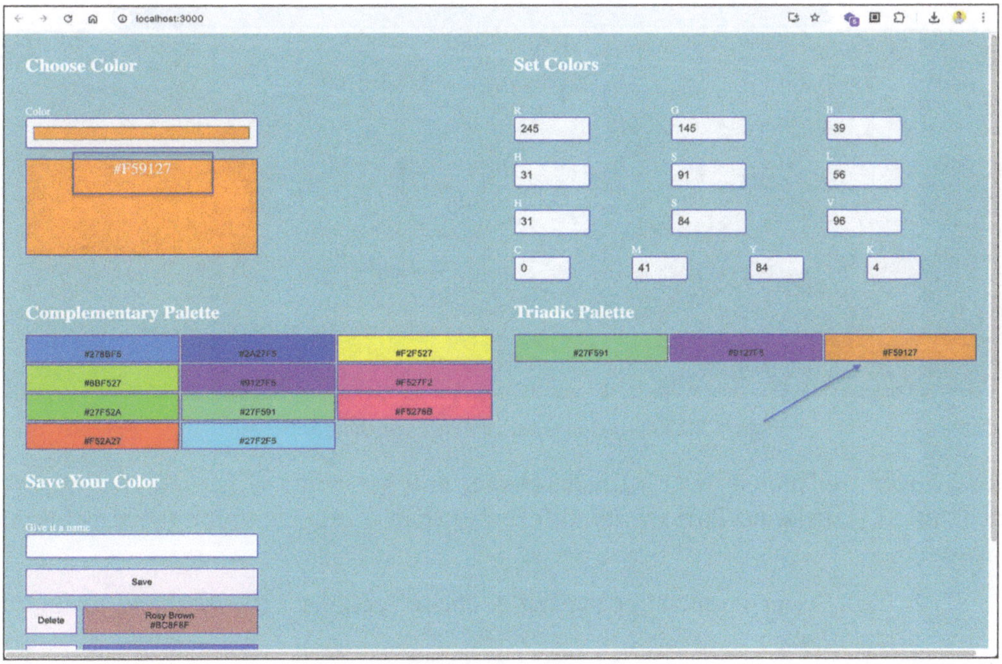

Figure 20.8: Localhost WorkingFine

Building a Type Helper

Now, we will learn to build a type helper, and for this, we have created a new project. Here, we have a **`type-helper.tsx`** file. It has two different types of **`FlexibleMenu`** and **FlexibleButtonVariant**, which have been used in **menus** and **buttonVariants** respectively.

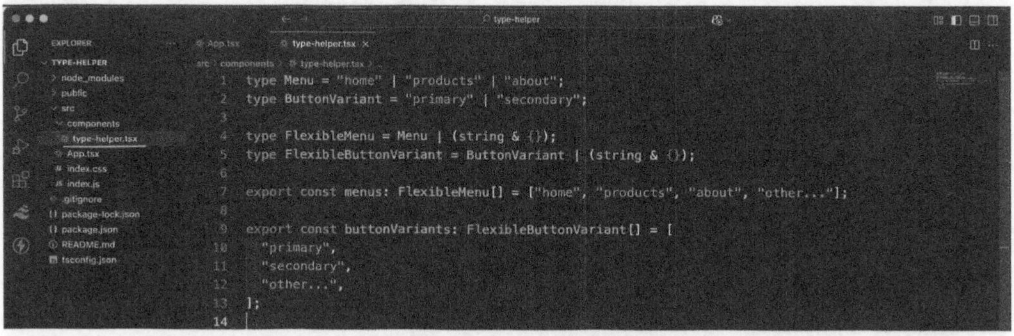

Figure 20.9: *Type-helper.tsx File*

We have created a common type of **FlexibleAutoComplete** in which we are using a generic type. This common type, we are passing in the **FlexibleMenu** and **FlexibleButtonVariant**.

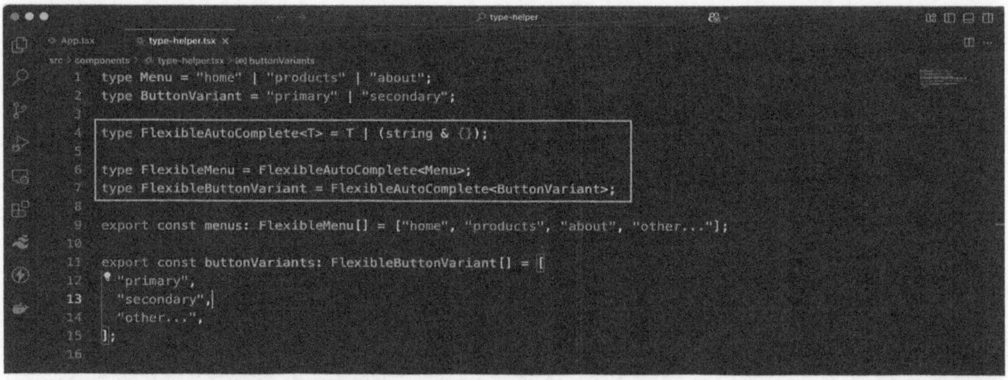

Figure 20.10: *Adding Generics in Type-helper.tsx File*

Now, hover the mouse over **FlexibleMenu**, and we will see the correct type of (**string &{}**) or **Menu**. This works differently than a regular union (**string** | **Menu**) because:

- In TypeScript, a union like **string | "home"** collapses to just string, losing the literal type.
- But by using **string** and **{}** instead of just string, we are telling TypeScript: "**keep this as a flexible string but do not collapse literal types into just string**".
- So (**string & {}**) | "**home**" preserves "**home**" as a valid value instead of treating it as just a string. **string** & **{}**

This trick ensures autocomplete, and literal types like "**home**" or "**products**" are preserved, while still allowing arbitrary strings like "**other**..."

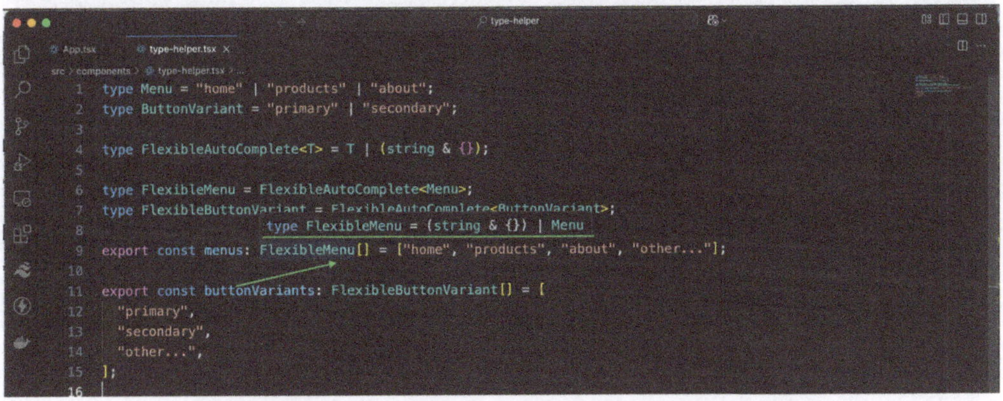

Figure 20.11: *Type of FlexibleMenu in Type-helper.tsx File*

Next, hover the mouse over **FlexibleButtonVariant**, and we will see the correct type of (**string** and **{}**) or **ButtonVariant**.

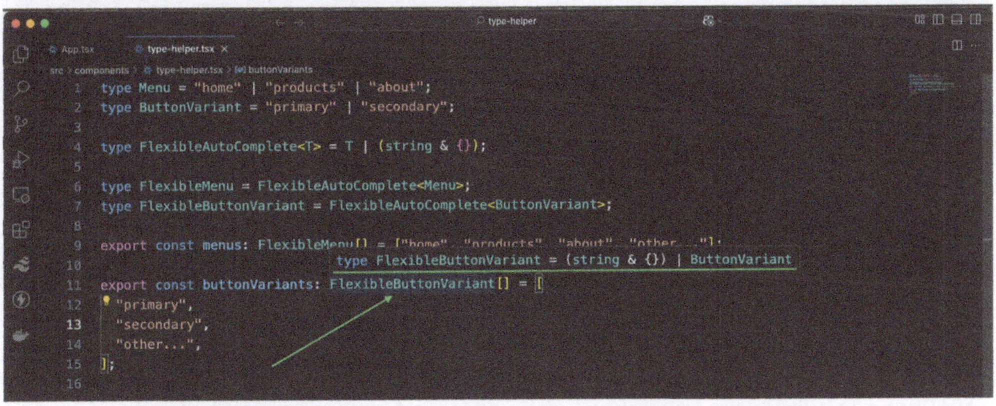

Figure 20.12: *Type of FlexibleButtonVariant in Type-helper.tsx File*

Another Type Helper

Now, we have created a new project in which the **App.tsx** file is rendering the Input component, and passing some props. However, two of them are giving errors.

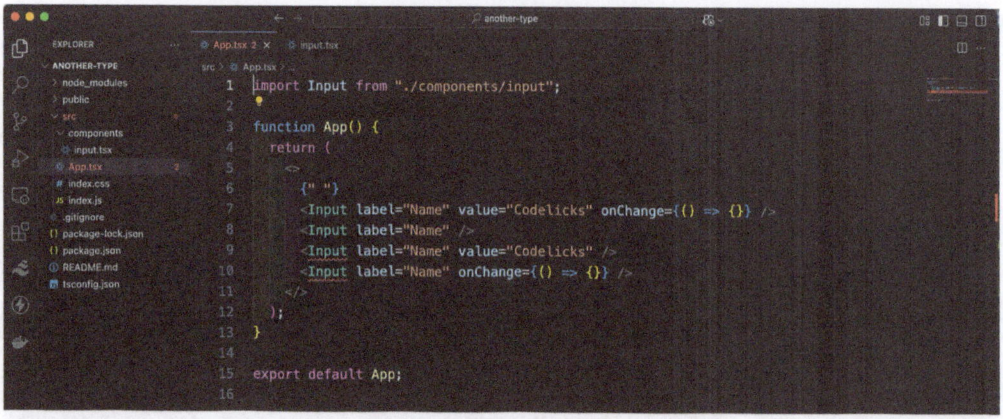

Figure 20.13: *App.tsx File*

Now, hover the mouse over Input, and we will get the correct error.

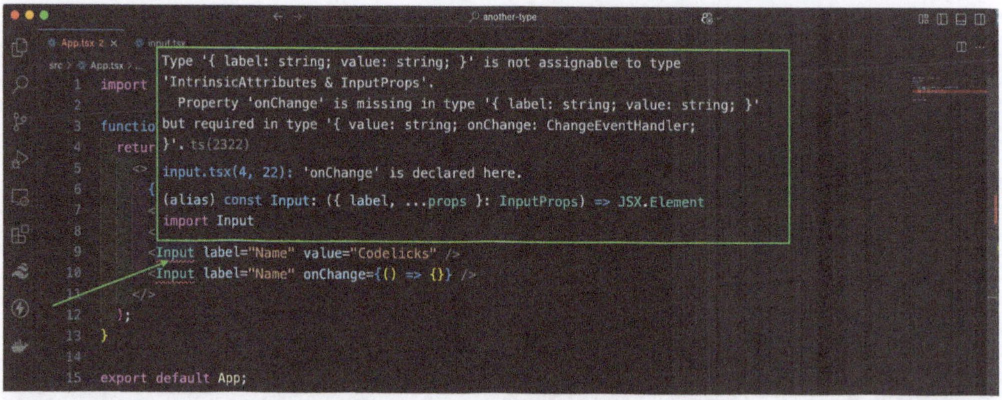

Figure 20.14: *Error in Input in App.tsx File*

Next, we have the **`input.tsx`** file containing the **`Input`** component. Here, we have **`InputProps`** in which we must have the value and **`onChange`**, or both should not be present.

The label is a must in the **`props`**, and that was the reason, we got errors in the last two **`Input`** component renderings.

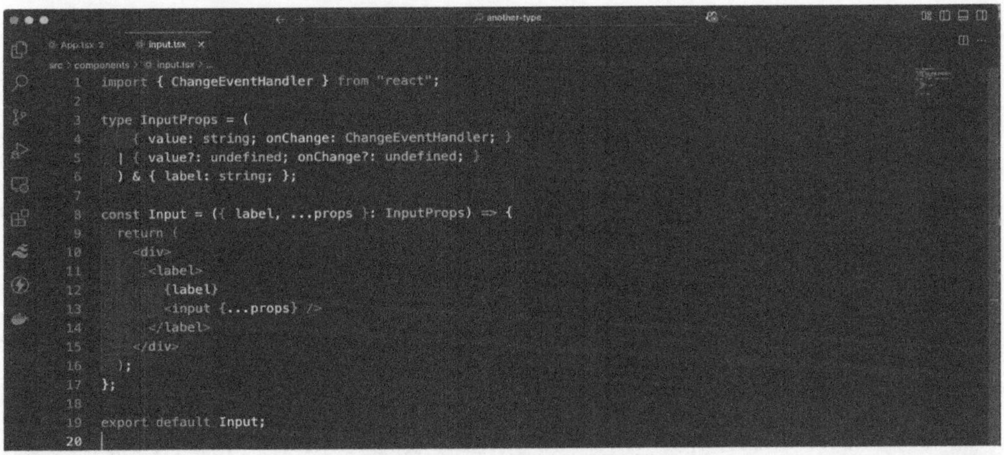

Figure 20.15: *Input.tsx File*

Now, we will change the logic to use Generics. Here, we have first a type of **`TightProps`** which takes T or a type of **`OptionalUndefined`**. Next, we have declared the type of **`OptionalUndefined`** which is using the TypeScript concept of **`Partial`** and **`Record`** to make T undefined.

Then, we update the **`InputProps`** to use the **`TightProps`**.

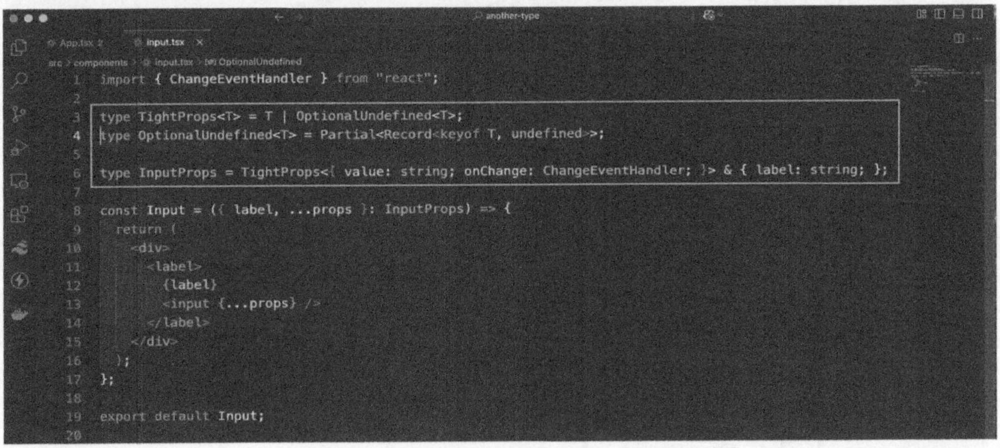

Figure 20.16: *Generics in Input.tsx File*

We still have an issue here. We have created a new type of test that uses **`TightProps`**, but takes string only.

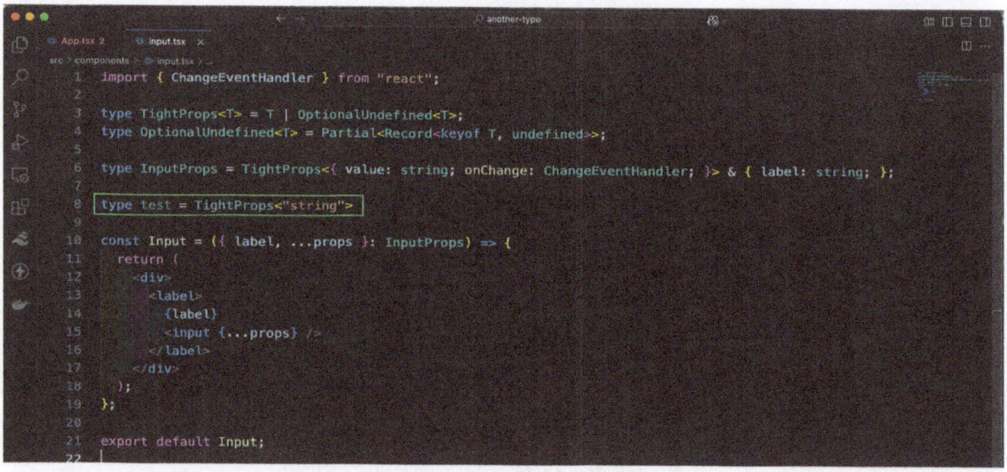

Figure 20.17: *Issue in Input.tsx File*

To fix this issue, we have to extend the **`T`** with **`Record`** of string, or any in both **`TightProps`** and **`OptionalUndefined`**. Now, we are getting the correct error in the test.

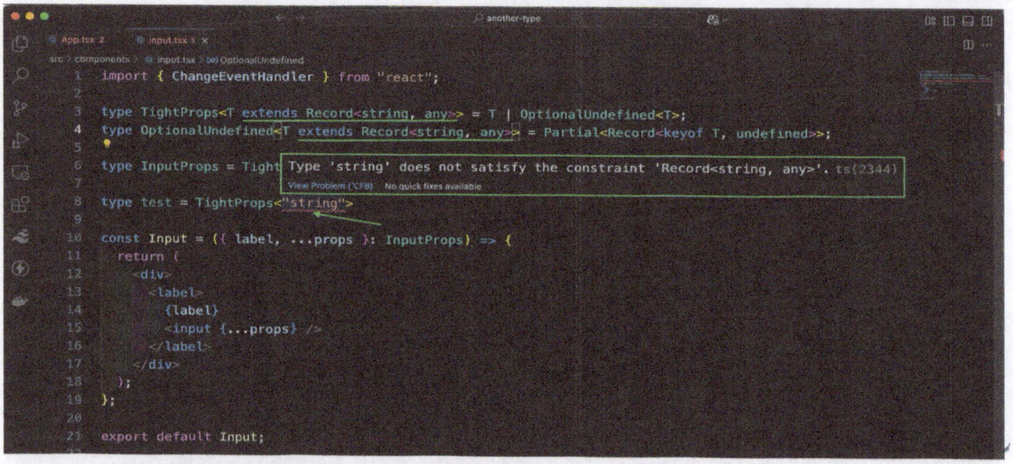

Figure 20.18: *Issue Fixed in Input.tsx File*

Hook with Generics

Now, we have created a new project, and here we have a custom hook of **`useLocalStorage`**. It has a get and set function, and returns the same.

Now, inside the App, we are using the type of **`{level: string}`** in **`useLocalStorage`** but getting the error.

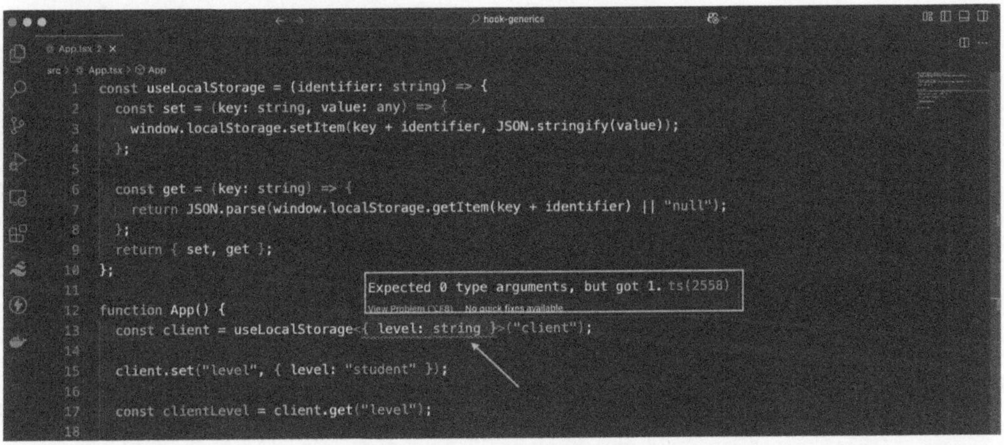

Figure 20.19: *Error in App.tsx File*

To fix this issue, we will use generics to make the parameter to take **<T>**. Also, the set to take the value of **T**, and get a return type of **T** or **null**.

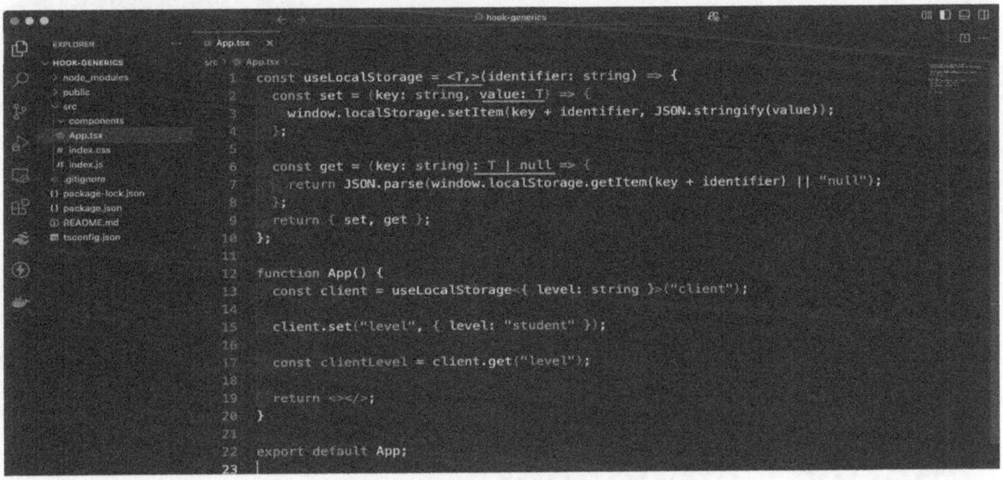

Figure 20.20: *Generics in App.tsx File*

Inferring Generics Types

Now, we will look into inferring generics types. For this, we have again created a new project. Here, we have a custom hook of **useStateObject** that returns a value and set. It is being used inside the **App** component in which we pass it as an object.

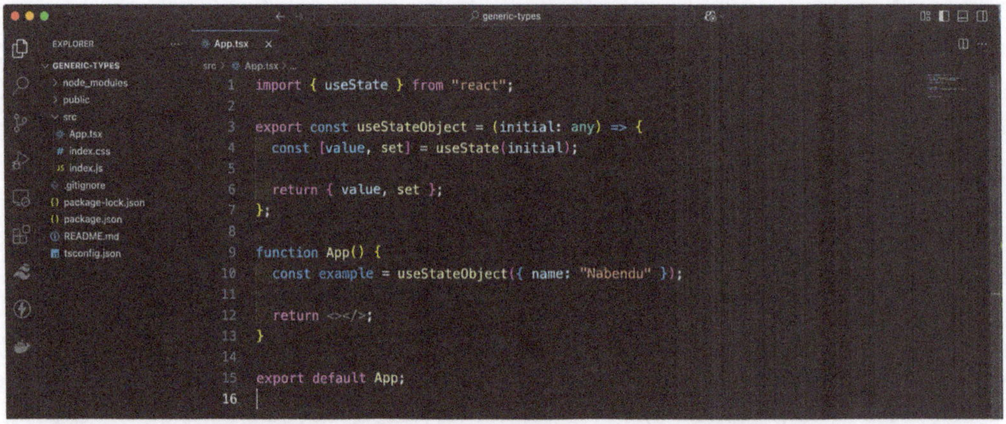

Figure 20.21: *App.tsx File*

Next, instead of passing any object which is not a good practice, we will pass the generic of T, and our component works the same.

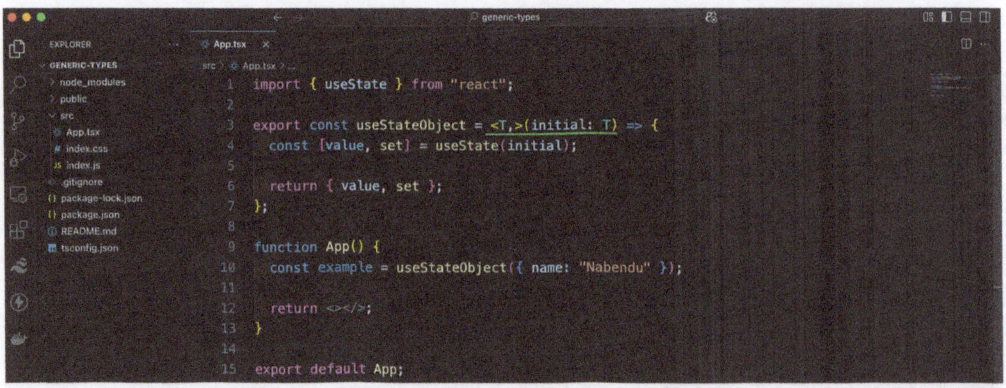

Figure 20.22: *Generics in App.tsx File*

Generics Components

Finally, we will learn about generic components. We have created a new project for the same. Here, we have an interface of **`ProductListProps`** in which the rows are of **`any[]`** type, and the **`renderRow`** parameter is of row type.

One of the issues here is that the second **`ProductList`** inside the **`App`** is not giving any error. The accepted things here are id and title.

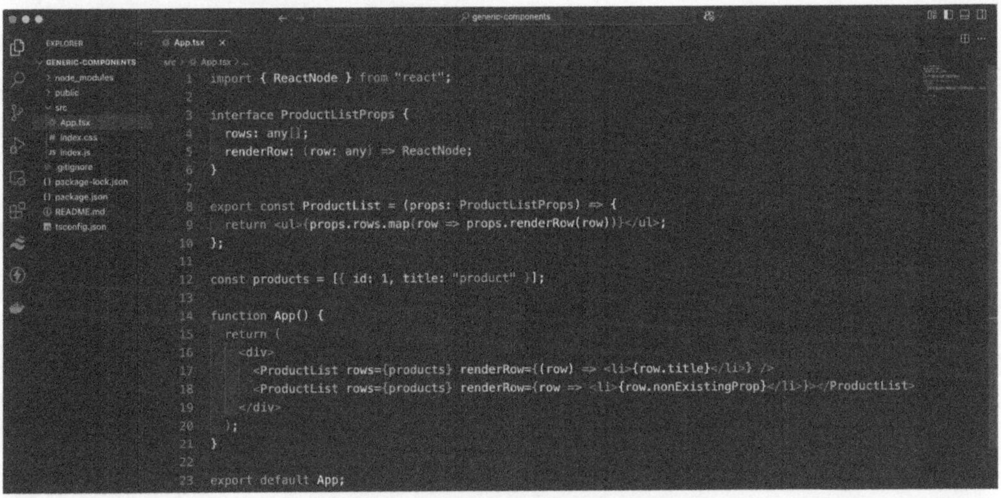

Figure 20.23: *Issue in App.tsx File*

Now, to fix this issue, we will make the interface **`ProductListProps`**, and take a generic of **`T`**. Now, the rows will take the **`T`**, and also the **`renderRow`**. Next, we get the correct error in the **`row.nonExistingProp`**.

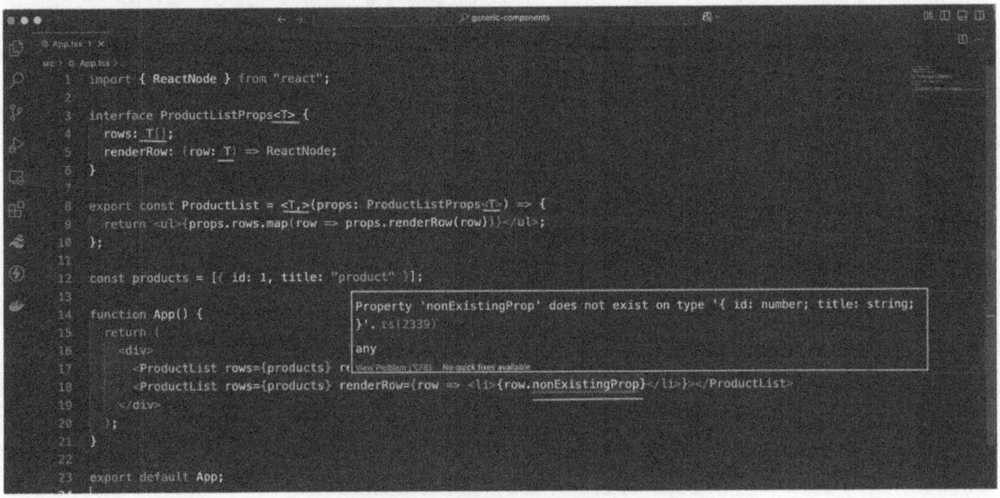

Figure 20.24: *Generics in App.tsx File*

So, instead of taking the rows from the products, we will directly add them. Here, in the first **`ProductList`**, we have taken the rows props as an array which is wrong, and hence, we are getting an error for the same.

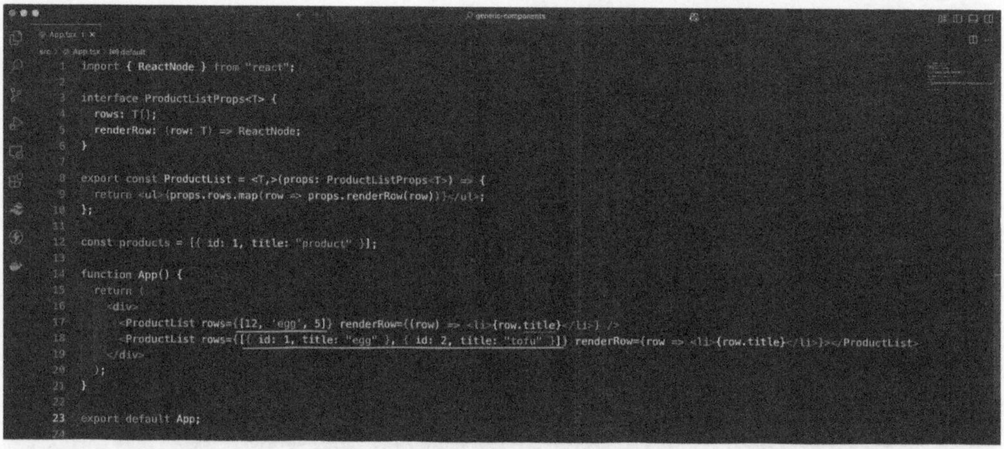

Figure 20.25: *Using Rows in App.tsx File*

Now, we will make the code even more usable by having an interface of **`Product`** that has an id, title, and price. Next, both of the **`ProductList`** are giving errors which is right.

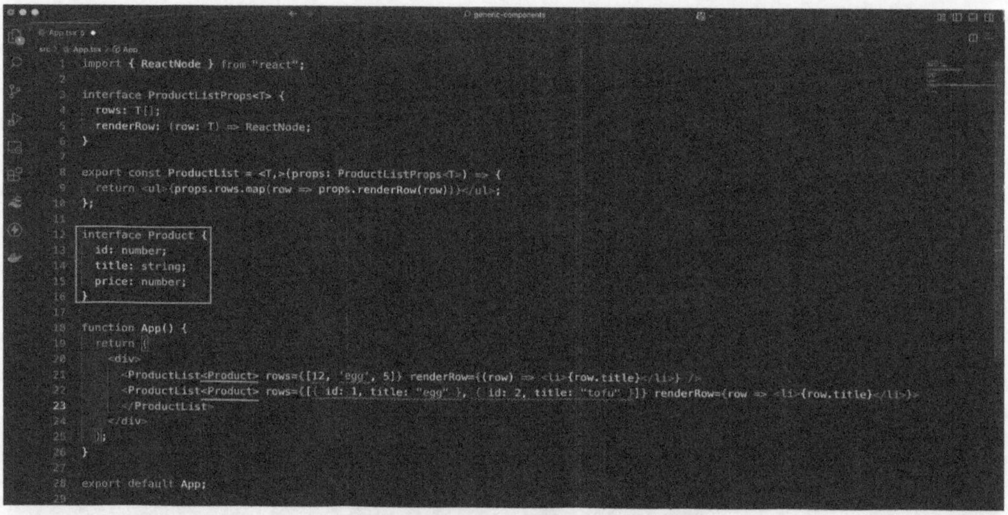

Figure 20.26: *Interface in App.tsx File*

Next, we will make the **`secondProductList`** have rows as an array of objects, having **`id`**, **`title`** and **`price`** and the error is resolved.

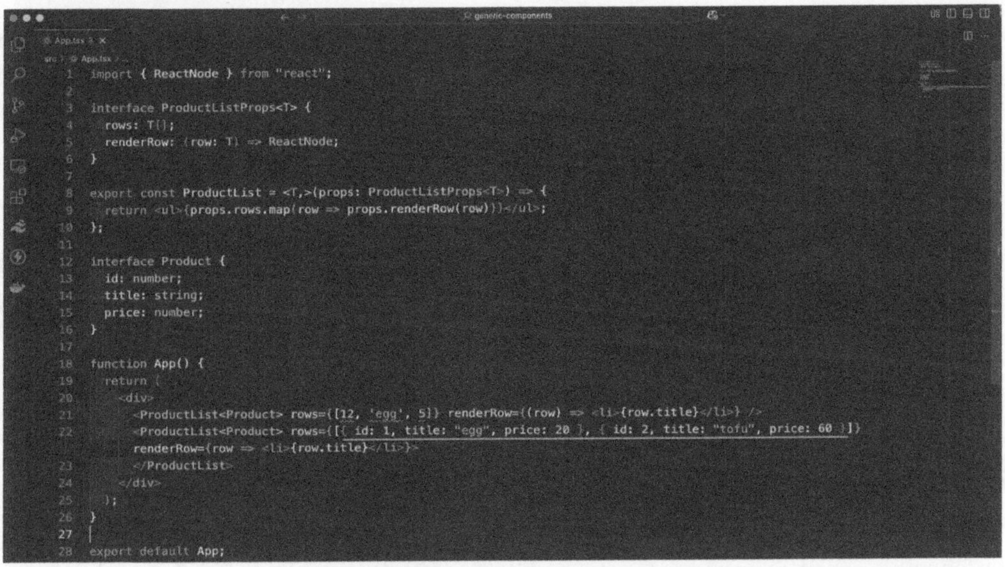

Figure 20.27: *Error Fixed in App.tsx File*

Conclusion

In this chapter, we are continuing with the Advanced TypeScript concept of types in Generics. Here, we first learned about context with generics. Next, we learnt about building two Type Helpers.

In the next step, we learnt about hooks with Generics. After that, we learned about inferring Generic Types. Lastly, we learnt about Generic Components. **In the last chapter of the book, we will learn about component patterns in TypeScript.**

Points to Remember

- Context with Generics
- Building Type Helpers
- Hook with Generics
- Inferring Generic Types
- Generic Components

CHAPTER 21

Advanced TypeScript (Component Patterns)

Introduction

In this chapter, we will continue with the Advanced TypeScript section. Here, we will be learning about Component Patterns in TypeScript such as HOC, Render Props, Custom Hooks and Prop Composition.

Structure

In this chapter, we are going to discuss the following topics:

- Overview
- Higher Order Components
- Render Props
- Custom Hooks
- Limiting Prop Composition
- Requiring Prop Composition

Overview

In this chapter, we will learn about **`Component Patterns`** in TypeScript. Here, we will first learn to use Higher Order Components. After that, we will learn to use **`Render`** Props.

Next, we will learn to use **`Custom Hooks`**. Finally, we will learn to use Limiting Prop Composition and Returning Prop Composition.

Higher Order Components

For using Higher Order Components, we have created a new React TypeScript project. In the **`App.tsx`**, we are rendering a component called **`MousePosition`**.

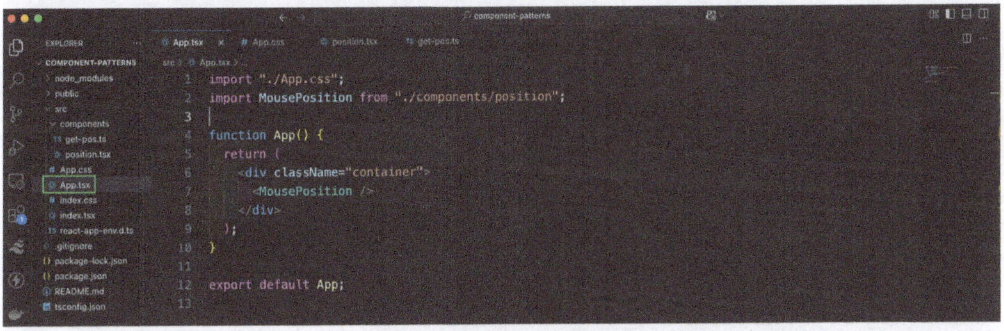

Figure 21.1: *App.tsx File*

Next, we have also added some styles in the **`App.css`** file for **`body`**, **`container`** and **`relative-container`**. We are going to use them in various components.

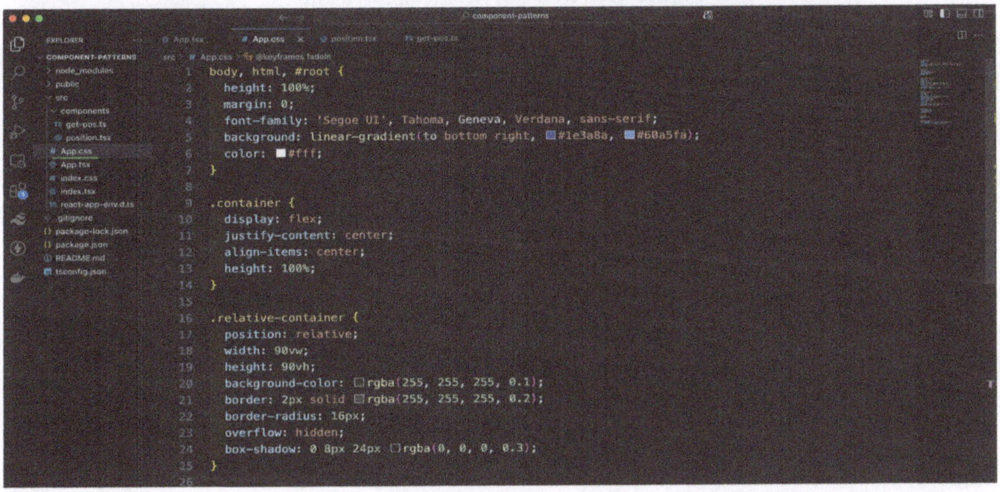

Figure 21.2: *App.css File*

Now, we have also added some more styles for **`absolute-section`**, **`bold-span`**, and paragraph in the **`App.css`** file.

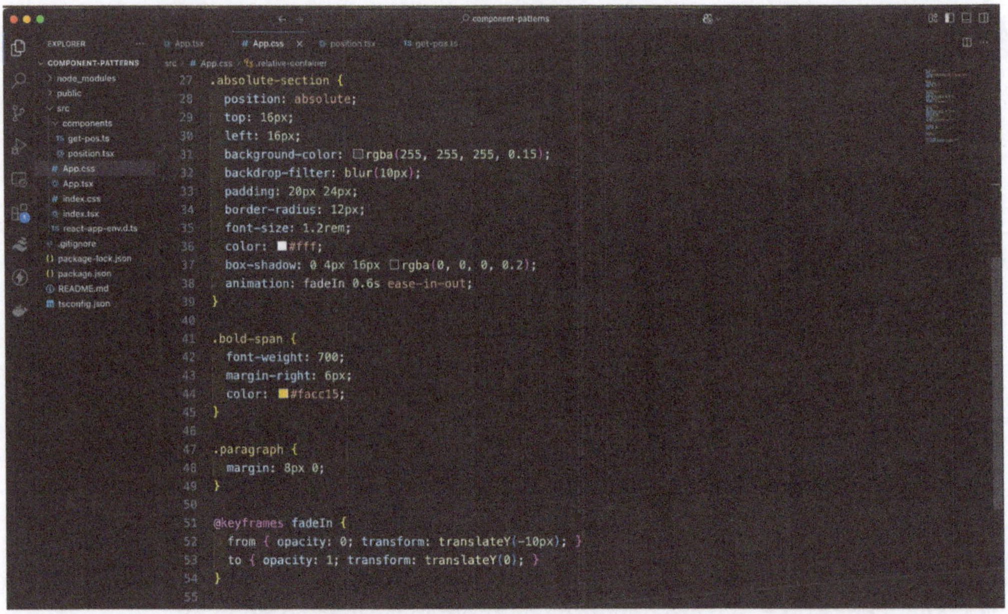

***Figure 21.3:** More Styles in App.css File*

Now, we have created a new file called **`position.tsx`** inside the **`components`** folder. Here, we are first importing **`MouseEventHandler`**, then **`useCallback`** and **`useReducer`** hook from React.

After this, we have an **`initialState`** of x and y. Next, we also have a type of **`UpdatePositionAction`** that has a type and payload. Next, we have created a reducer in which we are passing the state and action.

Finally, in the **`MousePosition`** function, we are using the **`useReducer`** hook, and passing the reducer and the **`initialState`**. In the **`return`** statement, we are calling the **`updatePosition`** function on detecting the mouse move.

From the **`updatePosition`** function, we are dispatching the type and payload. In the payload, we are dispatching the event to the **`getPosition`** function from the **`get-pos`** file.

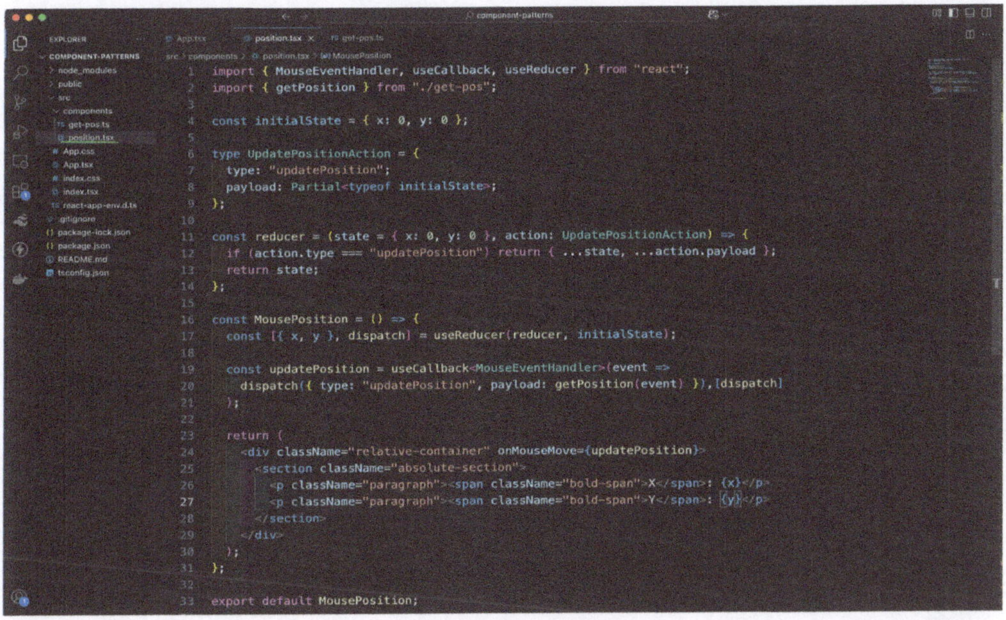

Figure 21.4: *Position.tsx File*

In the **`get-pos.ts`** file, we have a function called **`getPosition`** which is taking the event, and returning the x with **`event.clientX`**, and y with **`event.clientY`**. These **`clientX`** and **`clientY`** are actually used to get the exact mouse position.

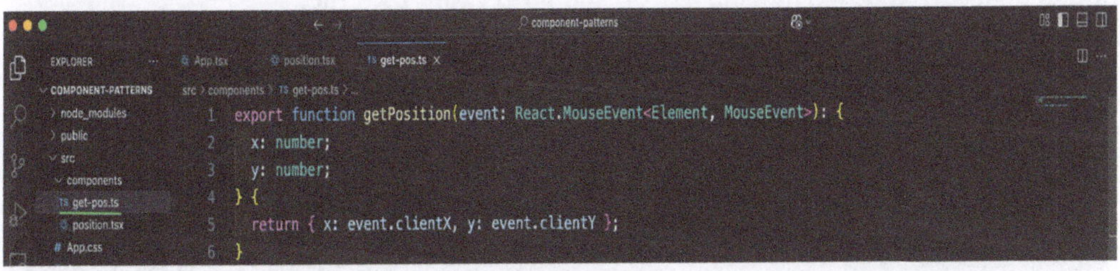

Figure 21.5: *Get-pos.ts File*

In http://localhost:3000/, when we move the mouse, we are able to get the location of the mouse, and it also updates.

Figure 21.6: *Localhost*

Now, we are going to convert the earlier code to an HOC (Higher Order Component). For this, inside the **`components`** folder, we have created an **`ad hoc`** folder. Here, we have also created a **`displayMousePosition.tsx`** file. We have the code to display the mouse position that we had earlier on the **`position.tsx`** file.

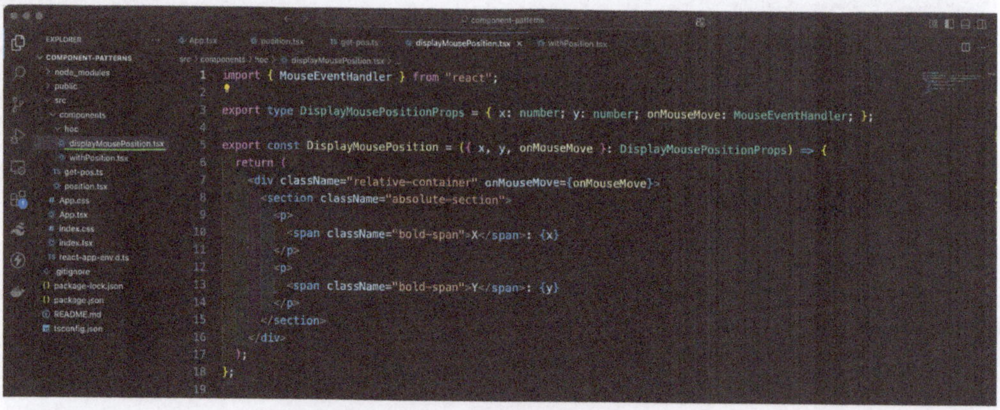

Figure 21.7: *displayMousePosition.tsx File*

Next, we have created the HOC in the **`withPosition.tsx`** file. Here, we have moved the code for **`updatePosition`**. Also, notice that we are returning the **`Component`** with x, y and **`onMouseMove`** props.

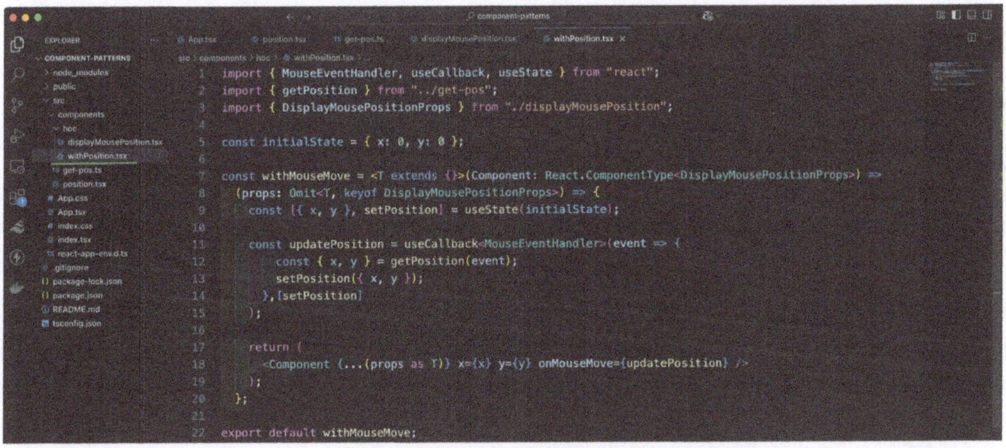

Figure 21.8: *withPosition.tsx File*

Now, in the **`App.tsx`** file, we will create a **`Wrapper`** variable. This will render the **`withMouseMove`**, and pass the **`DisplayMousePosition`** to it. Inside the **`return`**, we will call the **`Wrapper`** component.

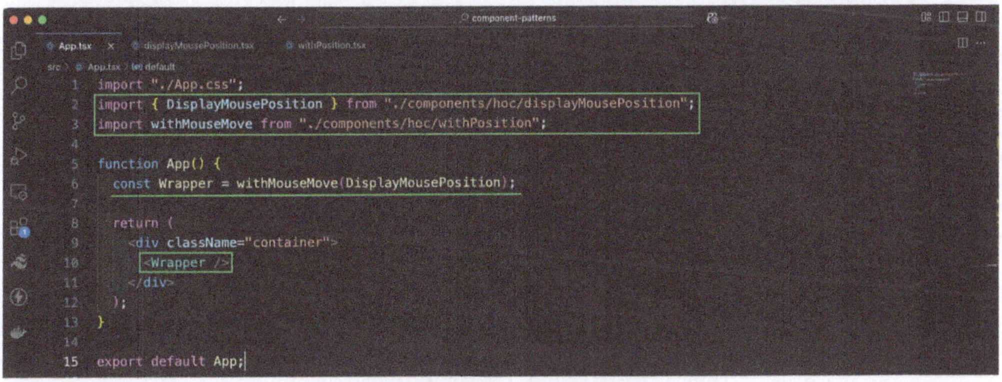

Figure 21.9: *App.tsx File*

Back in http://localhost:3000/, our app works like earlier.

Figure 21.10: *Localhost*

Render Props

Now, we will convert the same project to use **Render Props**, instead of HOC. Here, we have created a **render-props** folder. Inside it, we have created a **RenderPositionProps.tsx** file.

In fact, we have first imported the **MouseEventHandler** and **useState** from react. Then we have a type of **RenderPositionProps**, in which we give the type of children.

In the **RenderPositionProps** function, we are getting the children props. Inside it, we are creating a state of position with initial values of x and y to 0. Next, in an **updatePosition** function, we are updating the x and y, based on **one.clientX** and **e.clientY**.

Inside the **return** statement, we are just showing the x and y.

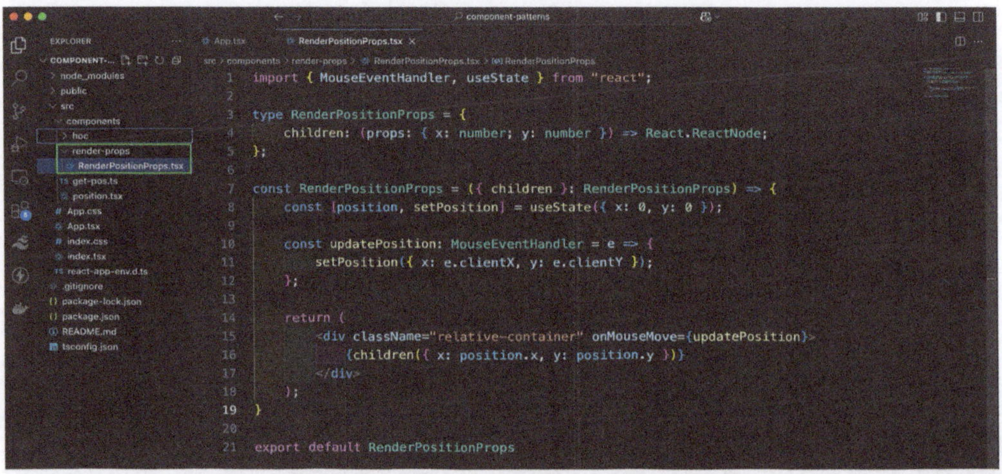

Figure 21.11: *RenderPositionProps.tsx File*

Next, in the **App.tsx**, we will create the component of **DisplayMousePos** which will take the parameters of x and y. Inside the return of the **App** function, we will use the **RenderPositionProps** component, and pass the x and y to the **DisplayMousePos** inside it.

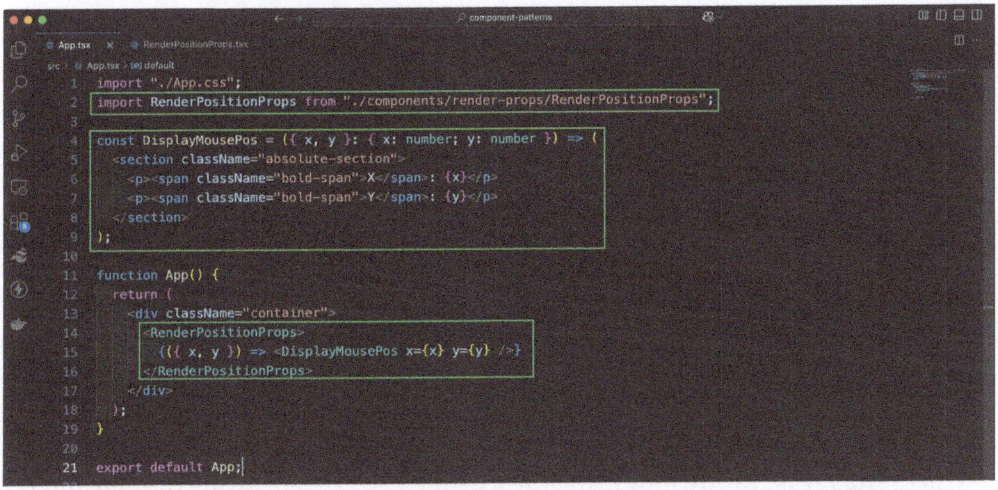

***Figure 21.12:** App.tsx File*

Back in http://localhost:3000/, our app will work as earlier.

***Figure 21.13:** Localhost*

Custom Hooks

Now, we will convert the earlier app to use hook. So, we have created a **`hook`** folder inside the **`components`** folder. Inside it, we have created a **`useMousePosition.ts`** file.

Here, we are first importing **`MouseEventHandler`**, **`useCallback`** and **`useState`** from react. Then we are also importing **`getPosition`** from **`get-pos`**. Inside the **`useMousePosition`** function, we have a variable of **`initialState`** having an object of x and y equal to 0.

Next, we have a **`useState`** in which we have **`setPosition`**, and use the **`initialState`**. After this, we have a function of **`updatePosition`** in which we are using **`useCallback`** that takes the event and calls the **`getPosition`** event. Also, use **`setPosition`** to update the x and y.

Lastly, we are returning the x, y and **`onMouseMove`**. The **`onMouseMove`** is the **`updatePosition`**.

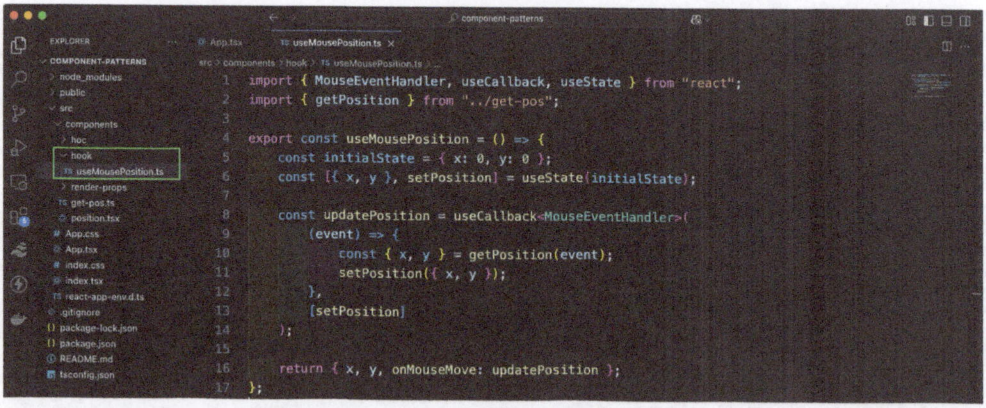

Figure 21.14: *useMousePosition.ts File*

Now, in the **`App.tsx`**, we are importing the **`useMousePosition`**. Inside the **App** function, we are using the **`useMousePosition`**, and restructuring x, y and **onMouseMove**. Inside the **`return`** statement, we are rendering the x and y.

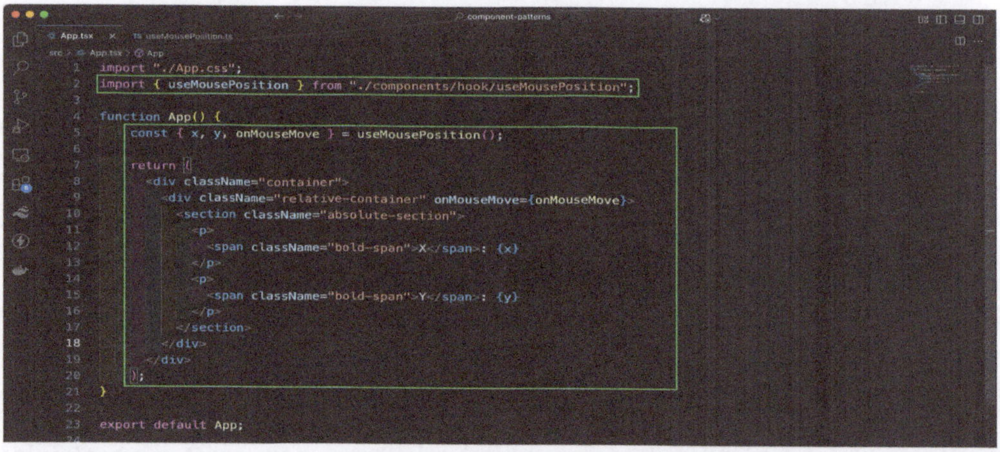

Figure 21.15: *App.tsx File*

Back in http://localhost:3000/, our app will work as earlier.

Figure 21.16: *Localhost*

Limiting Prop Composition

Now, we will learn about limiting the **prop** composition. Here, we have created a new project, and in the **App.tsx** file, we are rendering a **Button** component. Here, we are also passing a **prop** of type.

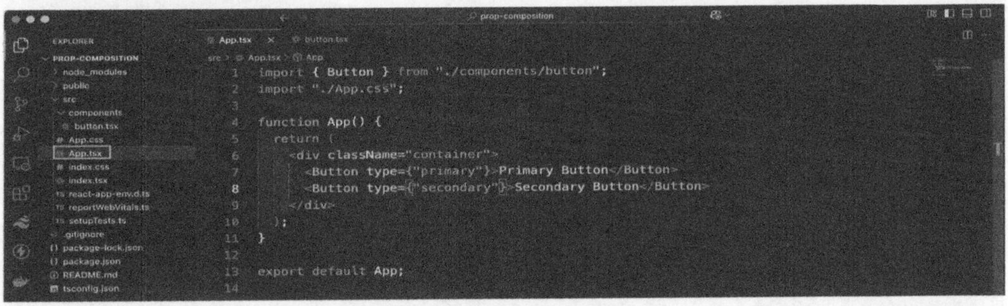

Figure 21.17: *App.tsx File*

Next, we have a **button.tsx** file inside the **components** folder. Here, we are creating a button, and passing the type as the **className**.

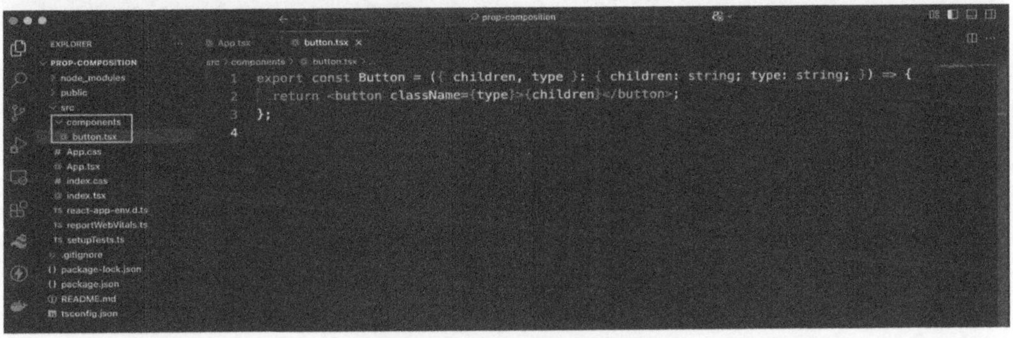

Figure 21.18: *Button.tsx File*

In the **App.css** file, we have the styles for the project. The complete styles can be taken from the project file in this chapter.

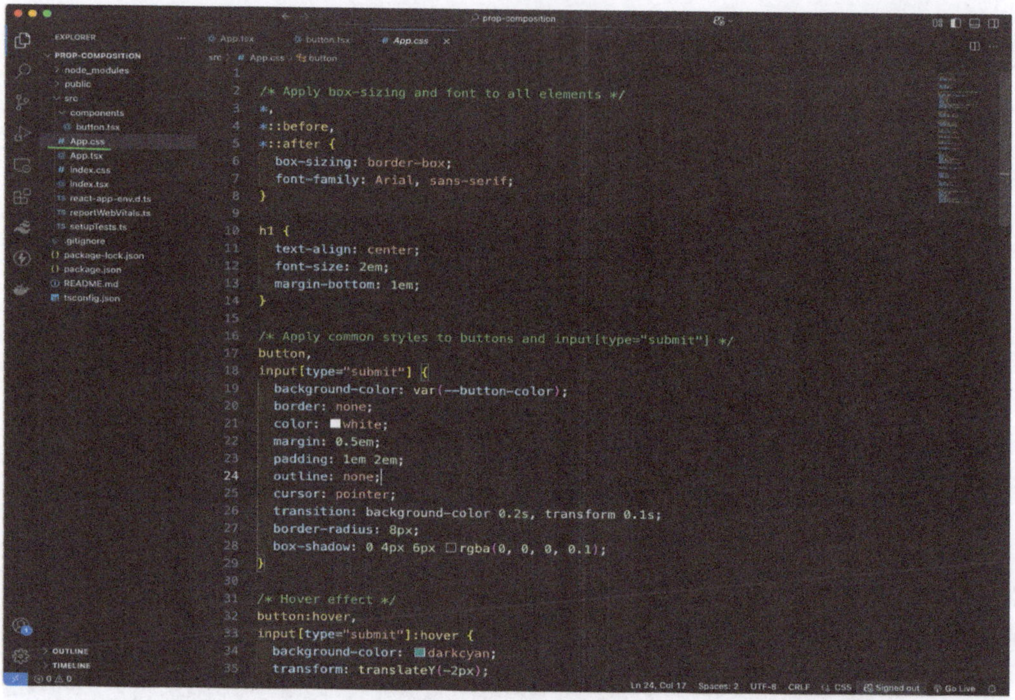

Figure 21.19: App.css File

On running the app in http://localhost:3000/, we can see the two buttons.

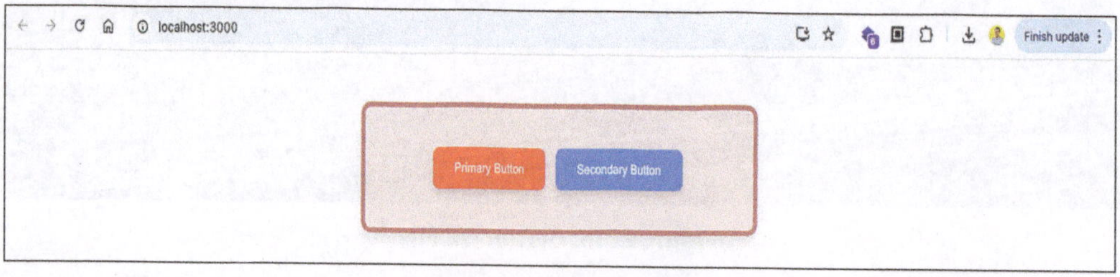

Figure 21.20: Localhost

Now, to convert it into **`Prop`** composition, we will update the **`button.tsx`** file. Here, we have created three types of props such as **`ButtonProps`**, **`PrimaryButtonProps`** and **`SecondaryButtonProps`**.

Next, we have a **`const`** of **`buildClassNames`** which adds the classes, based on the classes passed. For example, we can pass both primary and secondary, or one of them.

After this inside the **`Button`** function, we are passing the children, primary and secondary props. We are also using the type of **`ButtonProps`**, **`PrimaryButtonProps`** and **`SecondaryButtonProps`**, here. Next, in the **`classNames`** variable, we are calling the **`buildClassNames`**, and passing both the primary and secondary.

Finally, we are returning the button with the **className**.

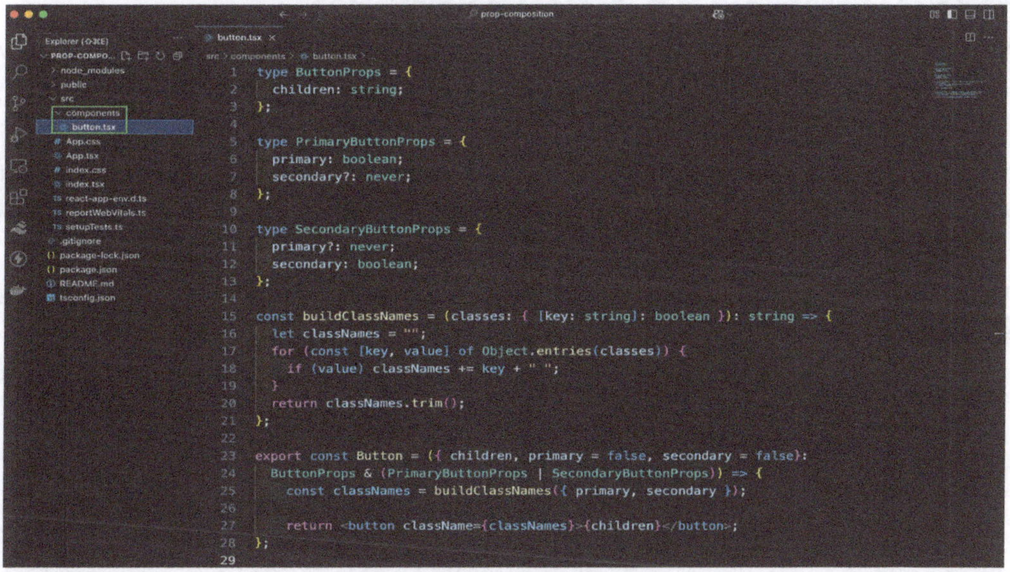

Figure 21.21: *Button.tsx File*

Now, in the **App.tsx**, the difference is the way we are passing the props.

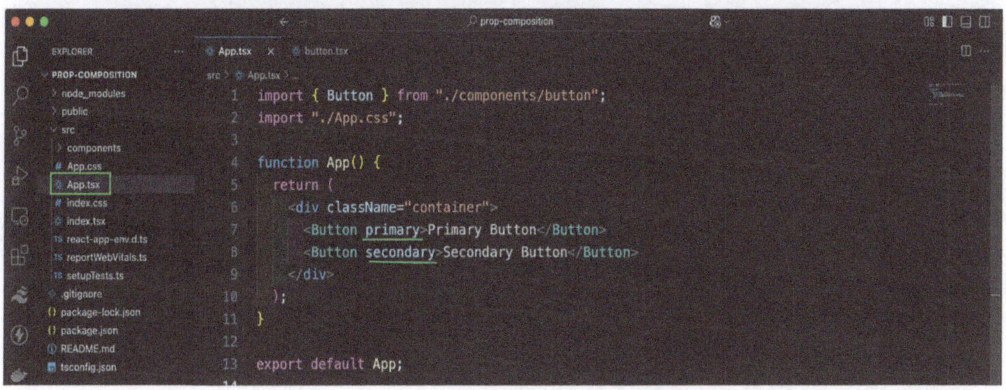

Figure 21.22: *Props Change in App.tsx File*

On running the app in http://localhost:3000/, we can see the same two buttons.

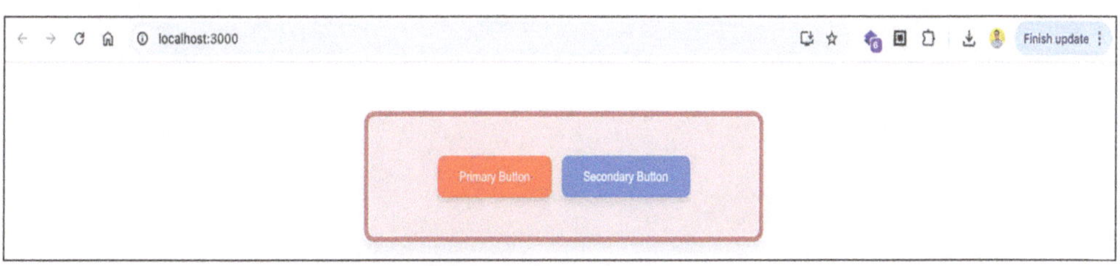

Figure 21.23: *Localhost*

Requiring Prop Composition

Now, we will look into another **Prop Composition** example. We have created a new project for the same. In the **App.tsx** file, we have expanded the state. After this, we have a **dummyText** variable, containing a long lorem ipsum text.

Next, inside the **return** statement, we are first rendering a **TextPan** component, and then passing short and expanded props. We are also passing the **dummyText** as a children prop.

Then we have a button, which on clicking, changes the expanded from primary to secondary.

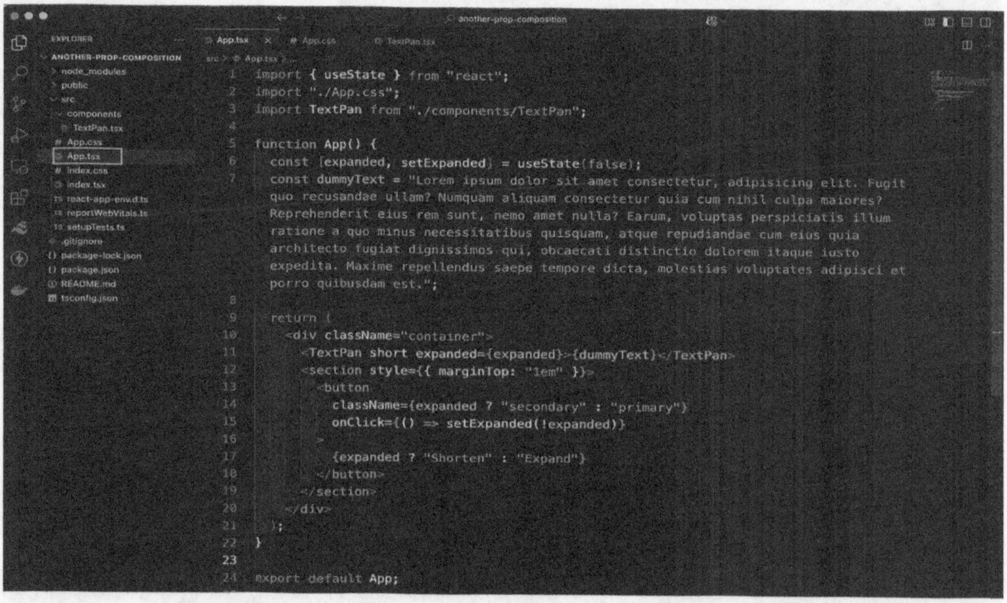

Figure 21.24: *App.tsx File*

In the **App.css** file, we have the styles for the project. The complete styles can be taken from the project file in this chapter.

Figure 21.25: *App.css File*

In the **components** folder, we have a **TextPan.tsx** file. Here, we have a type of **TextPanProps**, and also a variable of **shortString**.

Inside the **TextPan** function, we are passing the children, short and expanded props. The **shouldTruncate** variable is equal to short, and opposite of the expanded props. Inside the **return** statement, on the basis of **shouldTruncate**, we are then calling the **shortString** with children, or we are showing the complete children.

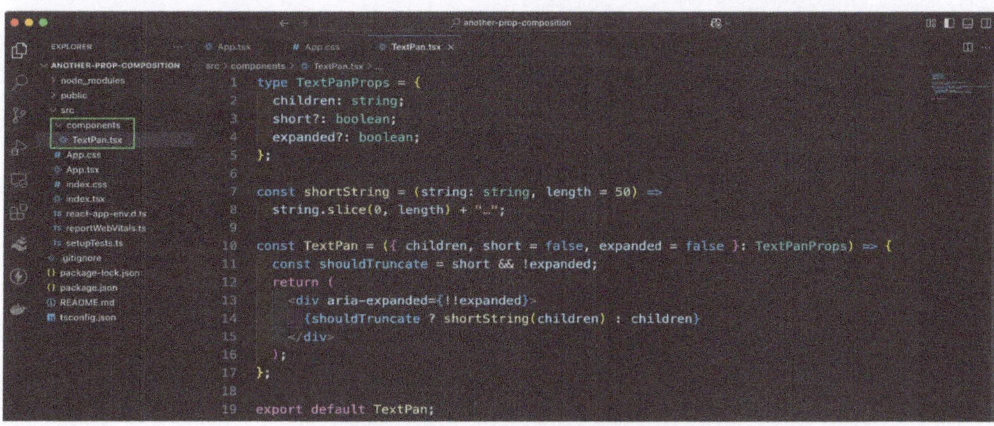

Figure 21.26: *TextPan.tsx File*

Now, in http://localhost:3000/, we can see the minimal text with the **expand** button.

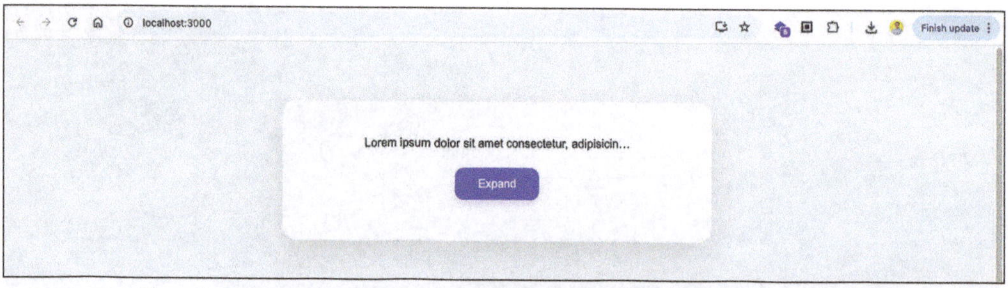

Figure 21.27: *Localhost with Expand Button*

After clicking on the **Expand** button, we get the whole text, and also the **Shorten** button.

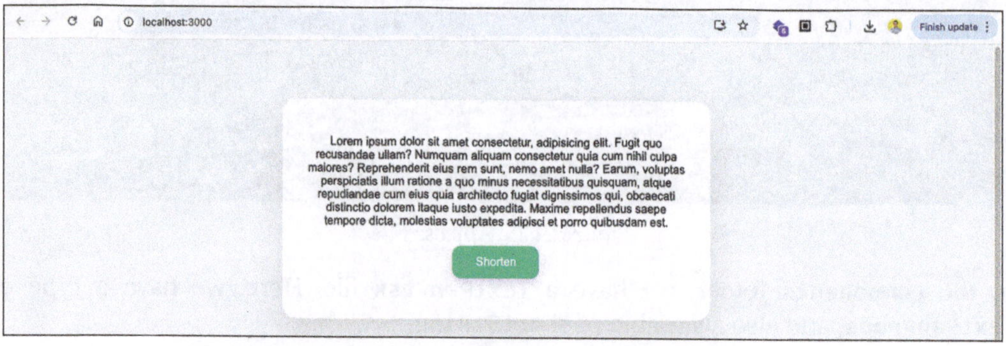

Figure 21.28: *Localhost with Shorten Button*

Now, we will change the project to have **Prop** composition. So, in the **TextPan.tsx** file, we have updated the type first. Next, we have two new types of **NotShortTextProps** and **ShortTextProps**.

Also, we have created two new functions of **TextPan** for **NotShortTextProps** and **ShortTextProps**. Next, we have updated the original **TextPan** in which the short and expanded are optional.

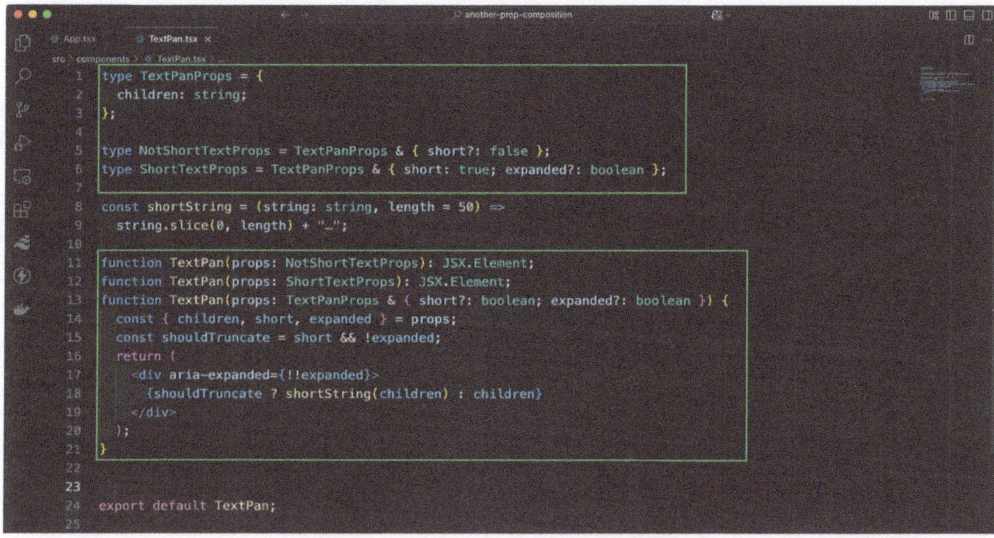

Figure 21.29: *Updated TextPan.tsx File*

Back in **`App.tsx`**, if we remove the short, we are getting the correct error.

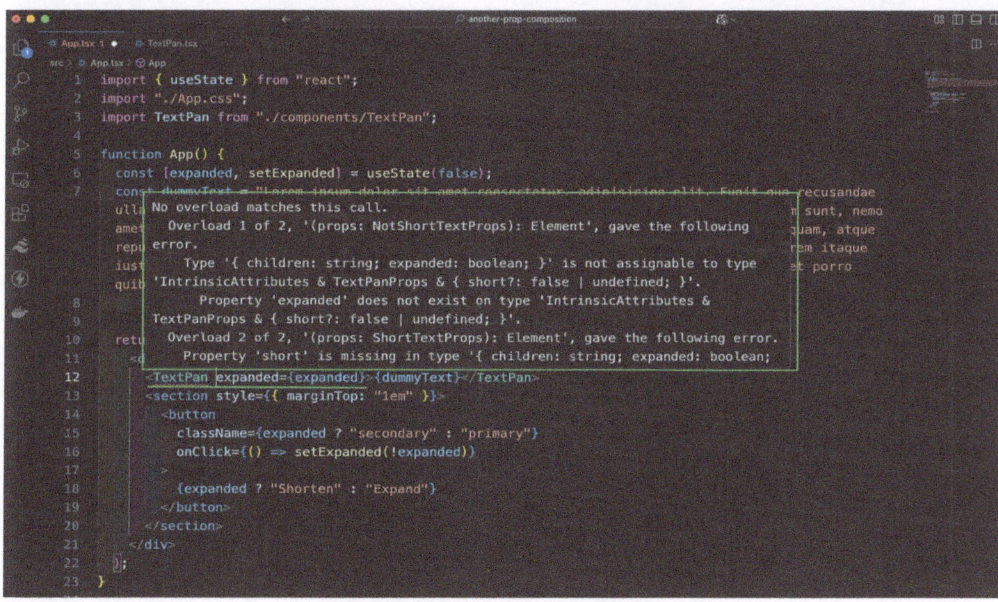

Figure 21.30: *Error in App.tsx File*

Conclusion

In this chapter, we are continuing with the Advanced TypeScript concept of Component Patterns. Here, we first learned about Higher Order Components. Next, we learnt about Render Props.

Then, we learnt about Custom Hooks. After this, we learned about two types of Prop Composition.

Points to Remember

- Higher Order Components
- Render Props
- Custom Hooks
- Limiting Prop Composition
- Requiring Prop Composition

Index

M

N

O

P

R

S

T

U